"Amazing UFO Encounters of the South"

A State by State Gazetteer over two hundred years from 1800 to 1999.

Alabama, Arizona, Arkansas, Colorado, Gulf of Mexico, Kansas, Kentucky, Louisiana, Mississippi, Missouri, Nevada, New Mexico, Oklahoma, Tennessee, Texas and Utah.

George Mitrovic

Contents

"Amazing UFO Encounters of the South" 1
Alabama 3
Arizona 12
Arkansas 44
Colorado 55
Gulf of Mexico 72
Kansas 72
Kentucky 84
Louisiana 95
Mississippi 102
Missouri 107
Nevada 138
New Mexico 148
Oklahoma 179
Tennessee 188
Texas 201
Bibliography 243

    These are encounter cases with UFOs and their occupants as well as unusual UFO sightings. Not the normal sightings of a light scooting through the sky. This means that there are a lot less reported sightings than the hundreds of thousands of UFO sightings reported every year. But they are the strangest and all from North America. This is Southern North America. There are three other books as well.

    We have reports of humanoids, and non-humanoids, coming out of these UFOs as well and interacting with people in strange and unusual ways. North America is so rich with these bizarre reports that it has taken me four volumes to record them all from 1800 to 1999.

    What is a weird, woolly world? It is a world of indefinite strange recorded events that belong outside known science and knowledge and yet are part of our accepted folklore in many cases and also our common knowledge. How common are they? You will be surprised. Are they indicative of something greater, possibly a new science? You be the judge. This is an atlas of the insane. A dialogue with the demonic and delusional. But all reported by ordinary people amongst others across the North America.

    You might notice that some of your favorites might be missing. I know that your Grandma saw something in the sky or nearby but she never did mention when and sometimes even where so Grandma's sighting will not be included. This also applies to plenty of other sightings. No dates, no entry. Even a year is enough and the name of the locality. Neither of these is a no show. But there are thousands more so find out about what might have had might still be lurking above your neighborhood. This is not your normal road map but happy travelling. You will be amazed as to what you will find in your state or even your neighborhood!

    Not all states start at 1800 either but I will try and start with datable and generally findable events.

    Enjoy this journey of exploration into what I have labeled the South which includes Alabama, Arizona, Arkansas, Colorado, Gulf of Mexico, Kansas, Kentucky, Louisiana, Mississippi, Missouri, Nevada, New Mexico, Oklahoma, Tennessee, Texas and Utah.

Alabama

1910

It is 9.00 am on 12th January 1910. Thousands of people see a one hundred foot long cigar in the sky above Chattanooga in Hamilton County, Tennessee, for one hour. The object was silvery white and glistening. There were no wings or any visible means of propulsion though a distinct chugging sound was heard. The craft was five hundred feet up and travelling at twenty miles per hour travelling North and taking ten minutes to cross the city eventually getting lost in the fog along the Tennessee River. Into the fog the airship and its occupant went and came out again a quarter hour of an hour later at Huntsville, about eighty miles away. No balloon was this fast though. This was the first year that the Zeppelin was flown commercially. And this was in Germany. Who or what was flying here?

At 9.15 am 12th January 1910 a one hundred foot long cigar was seen in the sky over Huntsville in Madison County, Alabama. This was the same craft as seen in Chattanooga fifteen minutes before. Namely a silvery-white glistening cigar travelling at five hundred feet. The craft must have been travelling at 320 miles per hour then if it traversed the distance from Chattanooga to Huntsville in fifteen minutes. No craft in this period could do this sort of speed.

At 11.00 am on 13th January 1910 the following day, the chugging silver cigar was back in Chattanooga again. This time it had come from the south, obviously on its way back from Huntsville but this time a man was seen in it.

And on 14th January 1910 the silver airship was back in Huntsville again.

By 7.00 pm 14th January 1910 the airship was in Knoxville in Knox County in Tennessee where it went South rapidly. The clear outline of the craft was seen and the sound of a motor was heard coming from it.

At noon, 14th January 1910, the one hundred foot long silvery glistening chugging cigar was back in the sky over Chattanooga. This time it was heading from the North to the southeast and it was the third day that it had been seen above the city. The airship eventually vanished over Missionary Ridge.

The following day 15th January 1910 the strange airship was back over Chattanooga at noon. The craft came from the North and went southeast finally vanishing over Missionary Ridge.

Also on 15th January 1910 a large white airship was seen over Paragould in Greene County in Arkansas. There were three to four Hominoids on board and the craft was brilliantly illuminated with a powerful searchlight. The craft went north, then South at an altitude of one thousand feet. Greene County had been visited by Hairy Humanoids early that century.

On 20th January 1910 at 8.00 am a number of witnesses saw an airship traveling East and then southwest very fast and very high up over Memphis in Shelby County in Tennessee. The craft crossed the Mississippi River into Arkansas and then turned South vanishing rapidly. And that was the end of it. Now they are here and then they are just as suddenly gone! Was it one of ours, which incidentally were not supposed to exist then, or was it someone elses?

1939

At an undisclosed location in rural Alabama in July 1939 during daytime a retired FBI agent said that while investigating unusual reports concerning a fortune-teller and military secrets, he was sent to an Alabama location to investigate the facts. Upon arriving at the residence, the agents found a woman sitting on the front porch. The agents approached the bottom steps and identified themselves. They told her that they were going to ask her several questions. She smiled and said yes but told them she was not a fortune-teller and she could read their minds. She said she had been "reading minds" for a very long time. When asked where she was from, she replied, "Another world." She was asked what she was doing on Earth and replied that she was guarding something that did not concern humans. The agents decided to take her in for questioning but she told them she had no intentions of going with them. The head agent ordered one of the men to escort her to the car but as he was walking up the steps of the porch he suddenly began trembling and fell to the ground. She remained sitting and told the agents that if they made any further attempts none of them would leave from there alive. They agreed and the agent on the ground got up unhurt. Before leaving, the agents asked for proof that she was indeed from another world. She agreed and told them to have their superiors pick an area of 100 square miles and to put markers around it and to make sure no airplanes flew over the area. The agents left and reported the strange encounter to their superiors. They strangely agreed to do exactly what she told them to. Later an internal excursion into the deserted area that was picked for the "proof" revealed that it had been completely devoid of life, including birds, plants, etc.. The agents were told to forget the whole thing and to never attempt to contact the strange woman again.

What sort of weird planet is this?

1947

Around 4.00 pm on 18th June 1947 an aerial disc was seen in the sky over Birmingham in Alabama. The object was seen by three female witnesses for over fifteen minutes.

There was a flying saucer sighting over Maxwell Air Force Base in Montgomery, Montgomery County, Alabama on 28th June 1947. The bright light zigzagged at high speed and made a sharp right angle turn before disappearing. The sighting was between 9.20 pm to 9.45 pm and made by four AAF officers including two pilots and two intelligence officers. Captain W. H. Kayko, Captain J. H. Cantrell, Captain Redman and 1st Lt. T Dewey saw a bright light just above the southwest horizon. The craft travelled towards them in a zigzag with bursts of high speed. When it was directly overhead it made a sharp ninety degree turn and was lost to view in the South. This was during a major UFO flap in North America. Wait until you read about New Mexico and Washington State in this same period. Birmingham and Maxwell are only eighty-five miles apart.

On 7th July 1947 in Decatur in Morgan and Limestone Counties around 6:00 pm Lucille Hullet and Kenneth Patterson witnessed a UFO from their front yard in Danville. The UFO was about ¼ mile South of their location and at 1,000 to 1,500 off the ground. The saucer was so bright, it hurt the observers eyes. The UFO was moving at 100 to 150 mph and heading West to East. The sighting lasted several minutes. Decatur is around eighty miles from Brimingham and all three places are almost in a North South straight line.

On July 7th 1947 in Montgomery in Montgomery County, Alabama. Tommy Bates (15) of Lanier Section observed seven silvery metallic objects flying rapidly in formation at the height of the treetops. They were the apparent size of saucers.

1948

On April 9th 1948 in Montgomery in Montgomery County in Alabama. 3:10 p.m. Lt. Col. Hughes, Air Tactical School instructor, Tyndall AFB, Panama City, Florida, while flying a P-51H fighter at 16,000 feet and just before completing a 180° left turn spotted a silver parachute-shaped 8 foot disc with a 5 foot long cable or shroud underneath suspending a silver canister or ball, at his 10 o'clock position (to the SE) off his left wing headed NW, about 300-500 feet away and 200-300 feet below him. He banked sharp left to try to follow the object, at 310 mph IAS, but it disappeared in 5 seconds without dropping in altitude. This was Montgomery's second UFO sighting in less than one year.

At 2.45 am on 24th July 1948 an Eastern Airlines DC-3 piloted by Charles Chiles and John Whitted encountered a B-29 fuselage shaped aerial object with a deep blue glow underneath and two rows of bright windows. The object left a fifty foot trail of orange-red flame. The aerial visitor had appeared suddenly, much faster than a jet. Chiles pulled the plane into a tight left turn and the object swooped past at a distance of seven hundred feet. As the DC-10 hit extreme turbulence Whitted saw the object pull up into a steep climb. This was above Montgomery in Montgomery County in Alabama. At that same time of 2.45 am on 24th July 1948 a crew chief at Robbins Air Force Base near Macon in Houston County in Georgia, reported a very bright light flying overhead. Captain Edward J. Ruppelt: "On the evening of July 24 (Ridge: Actually the 23rd), 1948, an Eastern Airlines DC-3 took off from Houston, Texas. It was on a scheduled trip to Atlanta, with intermediate stops in between. The pilots were Clarence S. Chiles and John B. Whitted. At about 2:45 A.M., (now the 24th) when the flight was 20 miles southwest of Montgomery, the captain, Chiles, saw a light dead ahead and closing fast. His first reaction, he later reported to an ATIC investigation team, was that it was a jet, but in an instant he realized that even a jet couldn't close as fast as this light was closing. Chiles said he reached over, gave Whitted, the other pilot, a quick tap on the arm, and pointed. The UFO was now almost on top of them. Chiles racked the DC-3 into a tight left turn. Just as the UFO flashed by about 700 feet to the right, the DC-3 hit turbulent air. Whitted looked back just as the UFO pulled up in a steep climb." Mongomery again. Is this all just coincidence?

In Fall in the Morning in Lineville in Clay County in Alabama the witness (a woman who wishes to remain anonymous) was drawing water from a well when an object, a round luminous ball, landed in an adjacent cornfield. Two longhaired, bearded men got out, wearing long robes with a sash around the middle, and one of them came up and spoke to her in accented English. He told her not to be frightened, and assured her she would not be harmed if she cooperated and answered some simple questions. After about half an hour's conversation, she fled into the house, where the second UFOnaut was standing in the doorway. They left and she saw the UFO ascend. In the cornfield was a flattened and scorched area. The witness only spoke of the incident when forced to do so.

Sometime in 1948 five boys saw an eleven foot tall Bigfoot in a swamp near Mobile in Mobile County in Alabama.

1956

On April 5th 1956 in Birmingham in Jefferson County, Alabama. A silvery winged figure was seen flying over a steelworks.

1957

On November 6th 1957 near Pell City in St Clair County in Alabama at 4:30 a.m. While delivering milk seven miles East of Pell City, the driver noticed the sky was lit up in one direction. He decided to investigate and drove eight miles on a dirt road, at which point his vehicle stalled. He got out and walked another mile and saw a 600-foot-long object about 200 feet in the air. He reported that the ground was slightly scorched under it. Even though his truck had a new battery, he was forced to hitch a ride home because it could not be started. Or this version? A milkman, James Moore, (34), of Pell City was delivering milk about 11km east of there, when his attention was caught by an illumination in the sky. He decided to investigate and had gone about 13km north on a dirt road, at which point his car stalled, although the batteries were new. He walked on about a further 1.5km where he encountered an object 200m long, 50 wide hovering about 60m above the ground. The ground in the area was scorched. He left and scene and after walking for several kilometres managed to hitch a lift with a friend.

1960

One morning in June 1960 in Mobile in Mobile County, Alabama. A couple were sat in their dining room when their attention was caught by a brilliant red flash in the kitchen, and they saw an elongated light come through the fan blades and rush into the dining room, where it crawled along the wall, turned pink and disappeared. It was 75cm across at the thickest.

1962

On Summer 1962 at 1800hrs in Clay in Jefferson County, Alabama. Dean Self was walking home along the Clay-Palmerdale Road, after visiting friends, when he heard a sound like a wind in pine trees, though there were no such trees in the area, followed by an unnatural silence, like being in a vacuum. Looking up he was terrified to see an object 30m above him. It was 12m long, with a cabin about 2m thick at the front. The thing had a smooth white surface, multi-coloured lights on its underside, which pulsated in rhythm to a muted throbbing sound, which seemed to affect Dean's whole body. The object suddenly vanished, the wind was heard again and then the natural sounds returned.

1964

At midnight on November 14th 1964 near Oneonta in Alabama. Riley Martin, a boxer, decided to stay in the boxing camp after a long match and recuperate. It was after midnight when he saw lights come flying silently from a northeasterly direction. They passed directly over him, close enough to brightly illuminate the surrounding area and to cause the hair of his head to crackle with static and the bushes to tremble. The craft set down in the weeds off to his right. He went to investigate and saw the ship standing nearly immobile just above the ground in a clearing. The hum of the engines was barely audible but he could feel its vibrations. He could feet static electricity all over his body and saw the leaves trembling and moving about on the ground all about him. The ship was thirty feet in diameter, flattened on the bottom and domed on top. A line of blue light circled the perimeter and a blue, red and yellow light shone from the undercarriage. The body was dull metal that glowed with a varying blue-white intensity. The dome cleared and he could see two small beings standing and looking out. Then he distinctly heard a voice saying "Come forth Martin for we must leave in haste." He literally ran beneath the ship and looked up to see a spiral door open, a dazzling white light and he was in a tube shaped chamber which nearly touched his shoulders. It was lined with thousands of tiny lights of many colors that he could feel were playing all over his body like a ripple of warm water. He then smelt a strong perfume like odor. A door in the chamber whisked open and he was blinking in the soft light of the command deck. An entity called Tan greeted him and he greeted him back. This time he was not subjected to the intensive physical examination of his childhood but was led directly to the translucent recliner type chair. The material that the chair was made of cleaved to the curvatures of his own body. It was cool but pleasant. The interior of the ship was also cool. Once again the aliens he knew as Tan and Nela started their hands-on exam of his nude body. Where his clothes had gone he could not say. He looked out and saw the lights of a city off to his right, perhaps it was Birmingham. Then he saw four dimensional video projections of two jet planes approaching at high speed. They quickly left the area and within seconds Riley could clearly see the outline of Florida and the eastern cost of South America. During the trip Martin learned that the aliens hailed from a planet called Biaveh which is 4.6 travel years from Earth.

1965

Around 7.15 pm on 6th March 1965 Mrs. B. S. Critchfield was on her front steps in Mobile in Alabama when she saw a basketball shaped object come from the southwest. It looked like it was going to crash into the street. It was encircled in the middle by windows through one of which she was able to see an entirely human appearing occupant dressed in a silver garment. She was able to see a second figure as the object rotated through another window as he stood in front of an instrument panel. The closest she came to it was one hundred and fifty feet and the lowest altitude was sixty to seventy feet and the sighting lasted about two minutes when the object disappeared to the West. The witness reported subsequent sightings.

1966

On 7th January 1966 three miles southwest of Georgetown in Mobile County in Alabama at 3.17 pm a man had to stop his car when he found a round object landed on the road ahead of him blocking his way. It was a round silver colored object that was ten to twelve feet in diameter with an eight inch to ten inch wide ring or hoop at the equator. There was a five foot hatch on the bottom and it hovered on the ground twenty feet away. It gradually climbed to the northeast with the engine whirring noise increasing. It disappeared in a few seconds.

The witness's watch had stopped and the car had to be restarted. There was a sulphur or rotten egg smell. Here is another version. At 1525hrs at Wilmer 18 year old student Barry Finch, the son of a minister, was driving his old car in a rural area SW of Georgetown on a rutted clay section of Hw 63, when, rounding a curve, he saw over the road ahead, a globe shaped object, he first thought was a helicopter, but then saw was a round object about 3-3.5m in diameter, silvery in colour and with a green blinking light on top. It also had a ring about 20-25cm out from the equator and a 1.5m hatch on the bottom. Barry brought his car to a halt about 6m from the object, which had descended to within 1.5m of the ground. The object, which gave the impression of being of glass rather than metal, emitted a whirring sound which irritated his ears. Becoming frightened, Barry tried to back away in order to circle the strange thing but was unable to start his engine. The object now began to ascend gradually to the NE. As it did so the whirring increased in pitch and volume. It then accelerated away rapidly and was gone in seconds. Barry could now start his car. He later found his watch had stopped at the time of the incident, and investigators found a chocolate brown substance, that smelled of sulphur, at the site.

On April 5th 1966 at Heflin in Cleburne County in Alabama at 4:00 p.m. CST an object emitting a humming sound was observed, and reportedly caused "anti-gravitational effects," finally disappearing in the clouds.

On September 23rd 1966 at 1900hrs in Decatur in Morgan County, Alabama. Dennis Billings had taken out the garbage into his back yard, when he heard sounds from one of his neighbour's houses sounding as if they were coming from close by. As his wife joined him, they both saw a fiery sphere, about 8m diameter, above the house. The thing seemed to be composed of a vast number of tiny particles in a state of agitation. Within seconds the agitation calmed and then thing more resembled a solid beam. This then dimmed and formed into a rocket shape, which took off and moved up into the sky in a spiral motion. While Dennis and his wife were pondering on this, they again heard distant sounds much magnified. Looking up they saw another luminous object that came down to 30-50m. It was a hemispherical object, with a flat base and blinking multi-coloured lights. In the centre of the otherwise flat underside was a sort of plastic looking, translucent cupola, in which some sort of activity could be seen. Mrs Billings became afraid and went back inside but Dennis moved to directly under the thing. After 15 minutes the thing took off and hovered for a time, manoeuvred and hovered again, before being joined by a similar object, at which they disappeared below the horizon.

1968

On March 2nd 1968 at 0755hrs in Prichard in Mobile County, Alabama a small object was seen at ground level.

On June 20th 1968 at 0200hrs in Roswell in Blount County, Alabama. Larry Ferney of Mobile and his wife were driving near Roswell when they saw an object descend from 100m. The thing had three lights, which resembled aircraft landing lights. Making a 90 degree turn the object headed down towads their car, looking as if it were going to crash into them before it levelled out 15m away. It paced the car for 10 minutes before racing upwards and out of sight. Mrs Ferney was greatly shaken by the incident.

1969

On October 28th 1969 at 2215hrs in Mobile in Mobile County, Alabama. Two Baptist College freshmen, Cedric Sutherland and Gerry Talbert (both 18) were driving along Raines Drive in the Wildwood section, near their Mobile College campus when they saw bright white lights in the sky, which they thought were on a plane. They then realised that the object was descending rapidly at 45 degrees and that flashing red lights had come on. The object then began to decelerate rapidly and began to descend into a vacant lot 15-30m from the road, flattening grass and bending trees as it did so. The lads then saw that it was a dark grey object, with luminous white panels circling the exterior, with two rings of red flashing lights, one on the top, the other on the bottom. The whole thing was 10-15m diameter and about 4.5m high. The duo braked but the object became lost to sight behind the trees. The boys called the police and Patrolman G. Pressnell inspected the area, finding evidence of flattened grass and two small pine trees had been broken. Several other people called radio and TV stations to report unidentified objects.

1971

On night in Summer 1971 near Huntsville in Alabama numerous cattle had been reported missing and disc-shaped objects were seen landing on several hills. A sheriff posse out in a stake out for the supposed cattle rustlers caught sight of several agile short squat figures that appeared to have no problem in vaulting fences no matter how high. One night several of the guards saw the creatures attacking some cattle and shot at them apparently with no visible effect. The beings were only four feet tall but appeared to weigh four hundred pounds. They were very strong and their bodies were covered in hair. The beings fled into some caves and were followed by Sheriff's deputies and guard dogs though the dogs did not venture into the caves after the creatures. The men shone their flashlights into the caves and could see shiny eyes staring back at them. Numerous cattle carcasses littered the ground inside the cave and the stench was unbearable. The creatures left behind unusual footprints.

Were these reports of Bigfoots with imaginings of bright lights around the same time? I will present you with the sightings. It is up to you as to what you will do with them. Or was it Chewbacca and his friends? Chewbacca did not appear until Star Wars in 1977.

1973

On February 14th 1973 at 2355hrs in Lexington in Lauderdale County, Alabama. Raleigh and Phil Nix saw a luminous orange oval object fly low about 300m from their home. The thing was very brilliant and larger than the large cars of the period. The object came down to less than a metre above the ground in a nearby field before moving off and then suddenly disappearing.

Three days later on February 17th 1973 still in Lexington, Alabama. A family observed an object, giving off a light so bright that it hurt their eyes to look at it, land 300m from their home.

On March 4th 1973 in Bear Creek in Marion County, Alabama. A police chief saw an oval object 15-23m long, with amber lights on the side and blue and red lights on the rear, It manoeuvred near a property for 30 minutes, descending close to the ground several times and emitting a high pitched whine.

On September 8th 1973 at 0400hrs in Lanett in Chambers County, Alabama. Wayne Meadows and another witness watched a lighted object, twice the size of a car, pass over at very low altitude.

On October 11th 1973 in the evening in Tanner Williams in Mobile County, Alabama. A 3 year old boy told his mother that he had been playing with "some old monster" in the backyard. It was grey with wrinkled skin and pointed ears.

On September 15th 1973 at 0530hrs in Letohatchee in Lowndes County, Alabama. Jerry Sanders saw a fast moving light pass low over a pond south of here.

On October 16th 1973 at 0930hrs in Tanner Williams in Mobile County, Alabama. Ira Lundy and Frank Pierce (both18) were out hunting birds when an object came from the east and passed over their heads at treetop level. It was a blue grey oval, with a saucer shaped bottom and a central rim, on which were red and white flashing lights, and a flattened top. The object appeared to three times the size of a car, 3-3.5m tall. On the top was something like an antenna. The thing came down to ground level on or over a soya bean field about 60m away. Am opening appeared and closed rapidly. At this point Lundy shot at the object with his 12 bore shotgun, and the two ran back to his home. As they did so, they looked back and saw the object wobble from side to side and take off with a sound like air going through a hose. The thing was on the ground for 3-4 minutes and they watched it take off for another 7 minutes. Diane Sweetman found 4 imprints and depressed grass at the site.

In Falkville in Morgan County, Alabama, on 17th October 1973 at 10.00 p.m. Police Chief Jeff Greenhaw was in his patrol car responding to a woman in a house who had telephoned him to come and look at a Spaceship with flashing lights that had landed in a field West of the city. Jeff took a camera. A landed UFO with an attendant was reported in the backyard of the woman's house. Jeff had seen the UFO on his way to investigate. The UFO was on the side of the road and the hominoid was like the metal Mercury. The light reflected off different angles as it walked and it looked like it was made of tinfoil type stuff. The witness photographed the hominoid four times and turned on the blue flashing light on the roof of the patrol car. The hominoid then dashed off, walking stiffly like a robot and moving very fast. Later Jeff's house burnt down and his car blew up. A photograph of the hominoid had been taken.

Near Loxley in Baldwin County in Alabama also on 17th October 1973 Clarence Paterson claimed that his pickup truck was sucked into a huge cigar-shaped UFO and he was jerked free by several creatures resembling robots. Clarence blacked out and when he recovered he was back on the highway driving at ninety miles per hour. A sulphury smell was noted and the witness believed that he had been on board for thirty minutes. The report was not taken seriously but which ones are serious and which ones aren't? In these cases I will include all reports and you can work out if they fit in or not. Or this. At 11.45 pm Clarence Ray Patterson of Pensacola, Florida, an electrician and businessman, was returning home from Mobile in his truck, on Interstate 10, when, near the Loxley exit. a huge cigar shaped object, with a green ,light on top, hovered over his truck, which was sucked into the strange craft. Once on board, he was pulled out of his truck by six short beings with claw like arms, like robots. They examined him and seemed to be able to read his mind. He was kept on board the object fro almost 30 minutes., during which time he noticed a sulphury smell. The next thing that he remembered was that he was back in his truck, doing 145 kph on Highway 297. Police Sergeant Lucien Mitchell, who interviewed Patterson confirmed that he was very frightened.

Also on October 17th 1973 in Parrish in Walker County, Alabama. Mrs Blanton and her family saw an object, changing colour, white-green-blood red, descend into a field near their home in a rural area of Walker County near Parrish. Several members of the family horridly drove to the spot, but as they got close the thing took off at high speed.

On October 17th 1973 at 2355hrs in Dawes in Mobile County, Alabama. A close encounter with an unidentified object forced a vehicle off the road.

On October 18th 1973 at 2030hr still in Dawes, Alabama. A light was seen descending into a field and possible traces were found.

Near Gardendale in Jefferson County in Alabama the main witness was going back home with her mother after a dance when they spotted a round object bright green in color with a yellow ring around it hovering above the highway. The object then followed their vehicle and began to descend in front of their vehicle. At this point the car stalled as did other cars around them. The witness then felt heavy as a light shone inside their car. Her next conscious memory was of seeing her mother trying to start the car. Later under hypnosis she recalled seeing a tall thin being approaching her vehicle apparently having a calming effect on the other motorists as it walked past their vehicles. As the being neared her vehicle her mother blacked out and then three small white colored Humanoids appeared and opened her car doors. She was then floated onboard the object and placed on a table. She could see another girl at a different table. The small beings walked around the witness's table and apparently placed a needle in her navel. She was later placed in a transparent globe and floated back into her vehicle. This was late at night in October 1973.

In October 1973 at 2355hrs in Dawes in Mobile County, Alabama. A 27-year old hospital manager saw a metallic looking domed disk with a sort of mesh like underside for 6 seconds. His new car suffered a total electrical failure.

On November 17th 1973 (Approximate Date) at 0200hrs in Mobile in Mobile County, Alabama. A 61 year old security guard observed a very bright yellow translucent object 15-30m out over Mobile Bay, and 90m from his own location. It was just 15cm above the water and was silent. The yellow area, which may have been the luminous portion of a larger, dark object, was about 1.5m square. The light jerked back and forth in a movement which reminded him of a hummingbird. He observed four silhouetted figures, 1.35-1.5m tall, who also jerked about in a corridor inside the object. A week earlier the witness had seen a blue light, and he observed an object every night for two weeks. In December 1973. he developed physical problems and died 18 months later.

In November 1973 at 0200hrs in Mobile Bay in Alabama. A cylindrical object, with entities, was seen at close quarters on the west shore.

1974

On February 12th 1974 at 2300hrs in Hackneyville in Tallapoosa County, Alabama. Kenny Sherrer (18) was driving home near Hackneyville along a road he had frequently used before, when he suddenly noticed what appeared to be car headlights among some trees to the left hand side of the highway. As he passed the entrance to an old deserted house, fiery object, resembling a mass of burning ashes and having a dull glow emerged from the driveway and began to follow him. At first the thing remained above and behind Kenny's car, but soon came alongside, travelling along the road and then rose towards the front of the car. At times it circled the car clockwise, alternately rising and falling as it sped alongside Kenny for 8km, never rising above the height of the power lines and keeping pace even at a speed of 160kph. Kenny developed a numbness on the right side of his body, which the doctor attributed to nerves but there were no other effects or traces, Investigators considered Kenny reliable.

Around 10.30 pm on 24th August 1974 a couple and their ten year old daughter were driving near Lexington in Lauderdale County in Alabama when they were driving down a long grade and their lights went out suddenly and their motor stalled. The husband braked the car to a stop and the lights came back on. At the same time immediately to the right along the road between the front door and the front of the hood they saw a figure standing by the side of the road. It was the size of a man and to the wife it didn't look like a man as it was just something blue! They both experienced a tingling sensation all over like being shocked by an electric motor or something. They drove on but the husband wanted to go back but his wife demurred.

1975

On March 20th 1975 at 1950hrs in Tilmans Corner in Mobile County, Alabama. A driving facing west/south-west in a car exiting 1-10E on Hw 90E, at the intersection of Hw 90 and Tillman's Corner saw a disc with red lights on top and two white lights rotating clockwise around the rim opposite one another at treetop level, about 200m away. The witness observed the thing for between ten and fifteen minutes as it travelled west-north west at 40koph.

Near Ryan Mountain near Jemison in Chilton County in Alabama. One evening in April 1975 a three foot wide ball of fire dropped onto the road several feet in front of the car of John Womack. He followed it until it rolled into a meadow when he stopped and got out. The ball of fire then rose and disappeared and a huge silvery object like a disc with shallow upper and lower domes appeared instead. This disc was one hundred and fifty feet in diameter and fifty feet high and was surrounded by a yellowish-blue glow. A beam of light came from it and moved slowly towards the ground, spreading out on reaching it, and the craft began to descend. As Womack retreated a beam of red light struck him in the face and he next found himself aboard the UFO and sitting in a padded chair with a metal helmet on his head. In the room were intricate devices and three sorts of beings. There were two leaders with noseless faces and mouths like porpoises, three giants at least eight foot tall with hairy torsos and brutal looking faces and six to eight creatures that were five foot tall with flipper feet, six crab like arms, two antennae and beards whose bodies were covered with greenish warty lumps and whose faces wore a grinning expression. A large TV screen filled one wall and one of the leaders using a translating machine told John that he would not be harmed and shook his hand. He was then told that demons were responsible for all evil and suffering and the ufonauts used a pill to expel them. Their planet is forty years distant and they live on food pellets. There ships are propelled by solar energy and they have been studying the earth for thousands of years. John was taken on a tour of the ship and then given a view of the alien's solar system. This was near Ryan Mountain near Jemison in Chilton County in Alabama. Or this version. John Womack was driving along the foot of Ryan Mountain, down a wooded country road, when a fireball about 1m diameter dropped onto the road in front of him and began rolling down the gravel road. he drove along slowly behind it, while it made a sharp turn to the right and went along a small creek bridge. About 30m beyond this it left the road and rolled into the meadow by the creek bank. As Womack got out of his car, the ball took off over the hill, with a sound like a blow torch. As Womack stood dazed, he heard a humming sound and saw, over the tree above which the ball had disappeared, a huge silvery disc, at least 45m diameter, 15 thick, was approaching. The object 90-120m above a meadow 30m away, emitting a low hum like a turbine. A yellow blue glow extended several metres beyond the disc. From the underside of the machine a beam of light 3m thick appeared and began moving slowly along the ground. As, unnerved, he began to retreat towards his car, there was a high pitched whistle as the light seemed to descend towards the ground, and spread out until it reached the road like some kind of fog. As the object began descending, Womack made a dive for his car but a red beam of light hit him in the face and he passed out. When he recovered his senses he was driving along only 3km from his home, 40km from the scene of the incident and it was about 0045hrs.. He suffered from anxiety, sleeplessness, feeling of unreality and he became convinced he had been taken on board the craft. After a series of dreams, aided by a visit to the site, where traces of scorched earth could be seen, the memory of such an abduction returned. He now recalled that after the red beam had hit him he had woken up in a padded chair, with a metallic helmet on his head, connected to some complex machinery by a cord. he was in a large room packed with intricate devices and equipment. There were several beings, two of whom that appeared to be leaders catching his attention. They were humanoids with egg shaped heads and mouths, like those of a porpoise, There were also three giant creatures about 2.5m tall, and 6-8 little creatures about 1.5m tall, with flippers, six thin arms with crab like hands, their bodies covered with green warts, and they had large heads. They appeared "harmless almost comical". One of the leaders, whose language was "like the croaking of a tree frog" spoke into a translating machine and told Womack that he was their guest and gave him a sedative pill. Alleged details of the construction of the ship, means of getting him on board were given as were claims they were from a planet 40 light years away. They also talked of "demons" which caused all troubles, and which the pill had expelled, other metaphysical issues and warnings about the hydrogen bomb etc. There was also a tour of the two floored ship, with rooms 15x 15x 3.5m filled with complex devices, including a sort of super X ray. The interior of the ship was illuminated brightly but the source could not be discerned. A metal cone was then put on his head, which gave him a sort of mystical experience. He woke up sitting under a tree on the creek bank watching the object take off.

At 1.00 am on 26th October 1975 near Cahaba Heights in Jefferson County in Alabama Mrs. L. E. Dison and her daughter were on a dark side road when they saw two beings that were eight foot tall wearing silvery shoes and tight fitting clothing of a dull silver color. The daughter saw that they were wearing helmets whose fronts were either luminous or light reflecting. The one nearest to the road had his arm up pointing at the sky. The second was only looking at the sky. Or this. Mrs Peggy D and her 17 year old daughter were driving back to their suburban home from visiting Mr D in hospital, down a dark street adjacent to the Coosa river, where they observed two enormous figures, 2.1-2.4m tall, standing on the right hand side of the road. They wore dull, silver, close fitting suits, with darker pants, ankle high silvery boots, fitting tightly on the top, round helmets that obscured facial details, and from which antennae stuck from either side, and face plates which either reflected the headlights or were self luminous. The figure standing closest to the road faced the street, one arm held up pointing to the sky. The second, slightly smaller, figure was looking up to the sky in another direction. Unnerved, the D's drove away. The daughter's boyfriend, following in his won car, did not see the figures, though he did see the car swerve to the opposite lane, then drive on.

On October 28th 1975 at 0230hrs in Campbell County, Kentucky. A police patrolman out on patrol drove between two soundless objects, which were at very close range.

1976

On February 18th 1976 near Okatchee, Alabama at 8:00 p.m. EST. Two women driving in a rural area reported that lights high in the sky paced their car for 13-14 miles from Chatchee to Lincoln, Alabama. Near Okatchee, Alabama they saw a large orange object in the woods near the ground to their left. Their CB radio stopped working, making no static, no sound at all. Two objects then followed them until they reached Lincoln, Alabama, where the UFOs approached to within 300-400 feet. The women saw five objects at this point. After passing through Lincoln, the objects stopped pacing the car and the CB radio suddenly started working. The two objects that had paced the car were egg-shaped and glowing with a fluorescent light.

1980

In Alabama one night in 1980. The witness had just gotten into bed when a strange squatting Humanoid appeared at the end of the bed. The being was about three-foot tall, dark skinned and leathery in appearance. It communicated by using telepathy telling the pregnant witness that her child was going to be a special boy. The witness screamed and hid under the covers the being then vanished.

1983

On February 3rd 1983 near Mobile, Alabama at 1:10 AM. a 28-year-old woman observed a very large metallic, cylindrical flying object with structural detail up close while driving on a highway near Mobile. She could see 20-30 occupants inside through the windows. They appeared to pay no attention to her, although she feels a sense of euphoria during the event. She had earlier had dreams of a UFO abduction encounter including a physical exam. Were these memories of actual encounters? Or this. Ms Pat Norris (28) was driving home when she heard a sound like an explosion and her car began to vibrate and then halted. She then saw a brilliant object, emitting a high pitched noise. The thing was a sort of elongated disc, with an upper window, through which she could see about 20-30 slender human like beings, about 1,75m tall, with large chests and heads, which were bald and earless. They had pale skins and wore white suits. They seemed to take no notice of Pat, and about 5 minutes later the object turned and flew off. After this experience Pat had dreams in which she was on a table in a room with many lights and a strange tree made of gold and silver. She was surrounded by beings, one of which seemed to be very old. When she felt cold one of the beings lay its hands on her and she felt warm. They touched various parts of her body with metal rods and questioned her, by telepathy, about her emotional problems. After these dreams, her lifelong back problems and her headaches were cured.

During May 1983 in Grove Hill in Clarke County in Alabama sometime between 7 PM and 8:30 PM, a couple driving saw an object and entities sitting and standing behind windows. The object moved at walking speed, hovered, crossed the road, then moved out of view. This was a close encounter with a an unidentified craft and its occupants. It was an oval object, about 80 feet across, about fifty feet away, and was observed in clear weather by two witnesses, typical age 62, on a farm for six seconds. No sound was heard.

At 8.50 pm on August 9th 1983 in Selma in Dallas County in Alabama there was a close encounter with two witnesses for 11 minutes. An unusual object was sighted that had unconventional appearance and performance. One metallic domed disc, about 80 feet across, was observed by one witness on a highway for ten minutes. No sound was heard.

1984

In June 1985 (Approximate date) at 0130hrs in Valley in Chambers County, Alabama. A 26 year old artist and her husband were staying at her mother's home when she was awakened by a brilliant light which lit up the whole room. She was levitated towards the light, the shirt journey across the room taking 15 minutes. Inside the light she encountered a 2m tall being with long arms brown skin that looked burnt or wrinkled. They appeared hairless and sexless and just had black hollows for eyes. The woman passed out and when she recovered she was being returned to her bed. It was now 0500hrs. Her husband had experienced nothing.

One night in December 1984 in Geraldine in DeKalb County in Alabama the witness was asleep and awoke to see their room very bright as if lights were turned on. She saw a luminous object and watched it for about one minute before the object either disappeared or turned off its lights. It was described as a gold oval object, about 20 feet across, about fifty feet away, and was observed in clear weather by the female 75-year-old witness on a farm. No sound was heard.

1985

At 1.30 am on June 15th 1985 in Valley in Chambers County in Alabama the witness was sleeping with her husband when she awoke to see a huge bright white light in the bedroom. Sitting up the 26-year old woman got out of bed and was then "paralyzed" while standing up. Simultaneously, she was levitated to about 6 inches off the floor. Slowly, and while standing, she was then taken into the huge light, which was at the other end of the bedroom. She could not move or yell at her husband. She felt somewhat relaxed while being taken into the ball of light. After she reached the brightest part of the light, she saw a six and a half to seven foot tall entity. The entity was apparently unclothed, its skin had a rough "burnt" or wrinkled texture and was brownish gray in color and had no hair. It had oval-shaped eyes with no eyeballs. Moments later she blacked out. Sometime later she found herself being levitated out of the ball of light and again traveling very slowly towards her bed. Upon lying down in her bed she immediately sprang up and found herself in a cold sweat. She could not account for at least 2 ½ hours of time. Her husband was still sleeping next to her. Since her encounter she has had depression and suicidal thoughts and her artwork has changed radically.

1989

At 8.30 pm in February 1989 in DeKalb County in Alabama multiple witnesses observed a banana-shaped object. The aerial object was observed by many people including the law. There was no sound and the sighting lasted one hour.

In Arab in Marshall and Cullman Counties in Alabama during October 1989 during a localized UFO wave, Barbara Demers and her nephew were riding a van along Ruth Road when they saw a large creature with a pair of large glowing red eyes stooping by some scattered garbage on the side of the road. It was apparently startled by the headlights, then stood up and crossed the road with one giant step disappearing into some woods.

In Wadley in Randolph County in Alabama on the late afternoon of December 4th 1989 the witness had returned from deer hunting, and while standing in the woods saw three gray Humanoids huddling together only 80 feet away. The middle gray being was taller than the others. After staring at the beings for about 20-30 seconds, he was told telepathically to leave and to "keep his mouth shut." He was under the impression that if he would have notified the other hunter with him, harm would had come to him. He was then told telepathically that their real target was his hunting partner, not him. Without saying a word him and his partner left the area. The beings were described as having big black almond-shaped eyes and were about 4-feet tall. Their skin texture was rough gray. The witness's friend was apparently abducted on a later date.

1991

In Alabama, exact location not stated, on March 31st 1991 late at night. The witness was on her computer when suddenly her power cut off. Soon after that, her phone rang. She answered it and heard heavy breathing. An eerie feeling then swept over her and feeling tired she went to bed. The next day she recalled that while lying in bed some type of powerful force like a magnet had pulled her out of bed and sped her through the air. She then found herself inside an object that was apparently whirling around. When the object stopped whirling she found herself in a room that was elaborately decorated with antiques. A large eyed chalked-colored creature entered the room and led her into another room making her lie down. Her vision became fuzzy as several other creatures performed gynecological-type procedures on her. At one point the pain became excruciating causing her to yell out. She soon lost consciousness and the next thing she knew she was back home. We have barely started and already various themes are appearing. Why? Shouldn't imagination be unlimited? Why is imagination, if that is what these sightings are believed to be, so limited in scope and description?

On the night of November 9th 1991 in Daviston in Tallapoosa County in Alabama the witness was riding around some back roads when he saw a bright light in the trees about 150 yards away. Next he saw the light come out of the trees and then noticed a round but flattened "cloud" that emerged behind the light. The cloud followed the bright light and flew over the witness and his vehicle. The light and cloud lit up the road around the witness. The vehicle's engine then went completely dead. The next thing he remembers was traveling further down the same road and noticing behind him the white ball and two clouds this time. Upon reaching home his family noticed that he smelled like "burnt cinnamon." He also found reddish purple stains on his hands that he could not explain. His vehicle had two 4-5 inches long, and wide, splotches on the front driver's side. He developed health problems weeks after the incident. The witness also noted a time loss. Later under hypnosis, he recalled that the bright light had been really a saucer-shaped vehicle. He had attempted to grab a shotgun, but was prevented by a four-foot tall gray Humanoid that took him on board the object. On board the craft his eyes were examined and apparently an implant was taken out from behind one of them. The being that performed the surgery was smaller and brown in color. Later he was taken to an upper floor inside the craft, and there he encountered humans in military style coveralls. One was apparently a flag rank officer. There he passed out while being examined again. On waking up he found himself being helped by a young soldier, athletic appearing with short cropped hair. The next thing he remembers was being escorted back to his vehicle by the "gray" type alien.

I am not judging or making opinions on this and other reports. They were all made in good faith and I am accepting them in that faith.

1992

In Alabama, exact location not given, late at night on October 8th 1992. Leah Haley remembered standing outside her house looking at what appeared to be two "full moons" in the sky. She realized that one of the moons was an object and then a beam of light that engulfed her and transported her onboard hit her. She found herself in a "contemporary" looking room, with tables adorned with crystal figurines. She also saw slips of paper underneath the figurines with the names of other people to come onboard that night. A female human-looking alien then came into the room. She had short brown hair and wore a blouse, red and gold in color with black trimming with some type of printed design, brown, beige, tan, in color. She spoke to the witness and among other things told her "her people were trapped in a time dimension and needed our help to get out." Apparently the beings then performed some painful procedures on her that she was made to forget.

1994

Around noon on November 11th 1994 in St Florian in Lauderdale County in Alabama an anonymous witness reported seeing a disc-shaped object that emitted a loud noise land on a cotton field, half a mile from his house. Two minutes later two figures disembarked from the craft and took what appeared to be cotton samples. No visible traces were left behind at the landing site.

1995

In Wedowee, Alabama at 7.00 pm one night in 1995. While riding in a van to join another group for a bingo game several church members were passing by a local poultry plant when they noticed a light on top of the building. They soon realized it was some type of flying vehicle as it began flying in their direction. The object described as resembling a "light bulb" followed their van as low as 12 feet over the road, sometimes moving within 50 feet. Two of the witnesses were able to make out a shadowy Humanoid shape in the middle of the object, moving inside. As they drove under an overpass they found that the light was still with them. Some frightened passengers tried to duck and hide. Just before reaching the intersection of I-20, the object took up into the sky at a steep angle, trailing a trail or streak. The next day two of the witnesses complained of hurting, teary eyes, and dark circles down to their cheeks. The main witness claims her eyes were both brown before the incident, but she now has one blue and one green. Conjunctivitis is not a rare side effect of UFO phenomena.

1996

At Huntsville International Airport in Alabama on the afternoon of May 25th 1996 it was reported that numerous witnesses spotted an unusual aircraft swoop down and land on the runway without tower permission and taxied over to the privately owned airplane parking area. The craft was described as a triangle-shaped object. The tower called the pilot but received no response. Three small occupants emerged from the object and began walking among the parked airplanes. Airport security then chased the beings across the runway right in front of a landing Delta airliner. Delta passengers described the beings as child-like in appearance, wearing metallic suits and white helmets. The three Humanoids ducked into the terminal and through the baggage area still being chased by airport security. Police were called in but when they apparently cornered the trio near a yogurt stand, they ran into what seemed to be an invisible barrier and could not get close to them. The Humanoids then ran out through the baggage area. At the same time that Army personnel were arriving on Humvees, the delta-winged UFO began to move. Witnesses saw the three occupants in the cockpit window. The object then rose straight up and took off at high speed.

True or false? I report them, you choose what to do with them.

1997

At 8.00 pm on March 29th 1997 in Phoenix City in Lee and Russell Counties in Alabama the witness had gone out about a mile from his house to film the Hale Bopp comet when he saw a bright square-shaped light hovering overhead. It started getting very cold and the witness noticed an odor resembling ether. He kept filming the object. Soon he went home and was told that he had been gone for 4 hours. He thought he had been away for only 45 minutes. He was also told that an unknown bright craft had flown at low altitude over the house. Later when he checked the video he claimed that he had captured the object and strange beings on the film. There was no other information on this sighting.

Arizona

1896

During December 1896 airships were reported from Arizona. As a reminder there were no Zeppelins in North America or airplanes at this time. The Wright Brothers had not taken off at Kittyhawk yet and the Zeppelins had not left Germany.

1897

On 24th January 1897, there was a great explosion heard over the town of Tombstone in Cochise County in Arizona. There was an explosion as something came rollicking down out of the sky and a fragment of a meteor fell at Saint David also in Cochise County, nearby. Our first meteorite for the year 1897.

At noon on 12th September 1897 there was an aerial explosion over Yarnell in Yavapai County in Arizona. A deep thundering noise was heard. The noise seemed to proceed from the Granite Range on the Yarnell side of Prescott. A large meteor had been seen in the sky and appeared to have struck the Earth at this time by all accounts. The luminous object was seen by a male witness at Mount Walloth. There were noises from the sky during the period. Meanwhile in Yarnell there were odd occurrences in the sky. Incidentally these had happened nearby before and would be quite prolific in the future. It seems that this area near Flagstaff meteorite crater is a magnet for other meteorites in greater numbers than the normal average. This is our original theme. Why are some areas more prone to phenomenal attack than others? Why in some respects are some times as well?

1898

On 12th September 1898 at Yarnell in Yavapai County in Arizona, there was an aerial explosion over the town and a deep thundering noise was heard. The noise seemed to proceed from the Granite Range on the Yarnell side of Prescott. A large meteor had been seen in the sky and appeared to have struck the Earth at this time by all accounts. Another meteor hitting the Earth near Yarnell? It sure is! The second of even more to come and only a small time period to repeat in as the previous aerial occurrence in this area was only in 1897.

Groups of meteors cannot take over one year to finish a single fall in one small area. Was this a different sighting exactly one year apart or was it sloppy note-taking?

1899

On 7th March 1899 a luminous disc was seen in the sky over Tonto in Gila County in Arizona. Was this the same disc that was seen in the sky over El Paso, Texas, only five days before? Now it's disc number sixteen followed by number seventeen.

On 8th March 1899, Doctor Warren E. day reported seeing a luminous disc travelling with the Moon all day over Prescott in Yavapai County in Arizona. At its earliest it had been very near the Moon. On 12th September 1898, the previous year, a meteor had been reported to have crashed into the Granite Range between Prescott and Yarnell, also in Yavapai County. It is this incidentallity of place that is really confusing as there had also been an even earlier meteorite fall in the same area in 1897 as well. This is indeed too much for coincidence.

1904

On 15th January 1904, two of Mr. Barringer's employees heard a loud hissing noise and saw a meteor falling North of the then-named Barringer meteor crater near Flagstaff in Coconino County in Arizona. The particular meteorite was found on 24th June 1905. If everything is random and the Earth is hurtling through Space, never actually occupying the same area of Space twice relative to itself, then how and why is the area around the Flagstaff-Barringer meteor crater in Arizona so popular for meteor falls of indeed all sizes. Is it as if there is a homing beacon there near the enormous crater produced twelve thousand years ago or is it just a magnetic attraction or merely coincidence. Coincidence might have to be ruled out though as the odds of astronomical objects repeatedly hurtling through Space and colliding with the one lone pocket handkerchief sized window area on Earth is beyond any probability. There had been meteor and stonefalls around here before. Once in 1897, once in 1898 and twice again in 1899. Well above any probability. You cannot have a continuous meteor shower for six years or can you?

1909

In Phoenix in Maricopa County in Arizona on July 5th 1909. It was early morning. "To be awakened from a sound sleep, to see a silent, weird, floating body directly over one's head, dipping, circling and bobbing here and there is not an event that will be forgotten very soon. That was what happened night before last to Mr. Turnbull, the picture man, who sleeps on the tin roof of his home during these hot July nights. Mr. Turnbull attended the celebration and coming home very tired, withdrew for the night to his cot on the roof. How long he had been asleep he could not tell, but during the black, still hours of the morning, when the ghosts walk, he was awakened by a strange hum and subdued clicking of machinery. For several moments Mr. Turnbull could not locate the noise and was commencing to think that perhaps someone was ransacking the house, until the point of an anchor caught the corner of the bed clothes and jerked them off the bed up into the blackness of the night. And yet he could not locate the queer noise exactly, though by this time he knew that it must be directly over his head. At this moment the moon peeped from out the clouds and Mr. Westburg could see a huge black, oblong object away up, perhaps a mile in the night an object that circled around and around, then shot ahead for some distance, then circled and returned. By this time Mr. Turnbull had collected his senses so that he could call, and waving a pillow in circular swoops, called to the black oval bag overhead what was wanted. No reply reached him, but the occupants of the airship dropped a miniature parachute, decorated with a hundred lights that before burning out told him the object overhead was the imperial airship from Hong Kong that is taking a world trip and intends to circumnavigate the Earth before the exposition at Japan next year. So precisely did the Mongolians of the upper world figure the downward course of the parachute that after circling for a diameter of over a mile, the weird object dropped in the very middle of the tin porch on which Mr. Turnbull slept. Though from time to time reports have been received regarding this imperial airship, no one has paid particularly attention to them, but since the event of last night Mr. Turnbull has left no wire unturned to gather information regarding it, and there is no doubt that before tomorrow evening, the greatest advancement in aerial navigation will have been recorded. Why the airship has not dropped any word before reaching Phoenix is not understood, but the ways of the Chinese are not to be reasoned with and besides they probably are not thoroughly versed as to the cartography of the western coast. When asked as to what he considered the rate the airship was traveling last night, Turnbull said he thought about 150 miles an hour. Why it will take this airy monster a year to go around the globe is another item that cannot be explained, but more than likely they will make side trips somewhere. The message that was dropped can be seen in the studio of Mr. Turnbull." Arizona Republican, Phoenix, Arizona, July 7, 1909. As I always say. I report them, you decide on them but even though some are extremely out there do not give up on them yet.

1912

On 19th July 1912 there was a loud detonation like a cannon in the sky over Holbrook in Navajoh County in Arizona. Then fourteen thousand stones of different sizes fell from the sky. A building was struck by them and a man was missed by only a few meters. These were L-chondrite or low iron meteorites. There was an earthquake in the same area one month later on 18th August. Falling stones in Arizona? This was the sixth time.

It is a very popular place for stones to fall. If all places on Earth are theoretically equal as far as the receiving of falling astronomical phenomena goes then there should be equal distribution of meteor crashes all over the face of the Earth. Why is there not then? At Irkutsk in the early Nineteenth Century there were stonefalls associated with earthquakes as well. Incidentally there was a report that a man was missed being hit by only a few meters.

1938

In the Arizona Desert in 1938. During the afternoon Steve Brodie and a friend were searching for precious stones on an isolated Mesa, when Brodie heard his companion give a sharp shout of surprise. As he looked up from his work, he saw a black-cowled figure at the base of the mesa. Another man in black immediately joined this strange figure. The first intruder pointed a rod at Brodie and the young man found himself unable to move. He then heard his friend begin to run. The other cowled figure then pointed a similar rod at Brodie's companion and Steve heard him scream. At once the air was filled with the acrid odor of burnt human flesh. Brodie then watched helplessly as a third figure approached him with what appeared to be a set of small earphones. When the black-cowled, shadowy-faced figure went behind him, Brodie felt something beneath his ears, and then he blacked out. All Brodie could remember about his captivity was three or four brief periods of consciousness. During these times he found himself penned with other humans in cage-like enclosures. On each occasion, just as Brodie's head would begin to clear, a black-cowled figure would approach him, freeze him into immobility with the rod, and adjust the headset. One day he found himself walking near Times Square, not remembering how he got there. Can you believe it? We are sometimes not on the planet that we take for granted.

1943

North of Prescott in Yavapai County in Arizona in Summer 1943. During the afternoon Pierre Perry, president of Arizona's Copper Mountain Mining Corporation was on his way to inspect a certain mineral deposit. Journeying with Perry were an anonymous prospector and Isidro Montoya a Mexican miner. While fording the Agua Fria River on horseback, Montoya who was in the lead shouted, "El Diablo, El Diablo!" (The Devil). "Overhead," states Perry in his affidavit, "a most terrific drama was unfolding that lasted only a few minutes. A military plane was in sight and so were two large unidentified flying objects that looked like balloons without baskets. They were luminous and bright as the sun. The UFOs stood still as if watching for the plane to approach, and then pounced towards it. At the same time, they projected a violent luminous ray that could be compared with the large beam of a lighthouse. The coherent energy beam hit its target and brought it down. The three onlookers saw the pilots eject from the plane, but another beam from the unknown craft caused the parachutes to catch fire and the men plummeted to their deaths. The two bodies were later found," added Perry. While unnerved and muttering, Isidro Montoya was by no means a stranger to such visions. After crossing himself he reportedly told Perry that he had seen "El Diablo" many times before. The affidavit goes on to indicate that a third spherical intruder joined the two existing UFOs and the trio vanished South toward Mexico at breathtaking speed.

1946

A witness under hypnosis stated that on 19th January 1946 his car had stopped in front of a "Mexican Hat" shaped object. He believed that he was abducted by three beings that glided and had no feet and a radiant glow. The witness reported that ten hours had disappeared and he had communicated telepathically with them. This was near Flagstaff in Coconino County in Arizona.

Near Yuma in Yuma County in Arizona during Summer 1946. There was a reported crash of a disc-shaped craft in western Arizona, Apparently the craft was stored for some time at Yuma Base in Arizona and after that moved to Wright Patterson AFB the same year. Three dead aliens of small height were also recovered.

1947

In the Papago Indian Reservation in northwestern Arizona in January 1947. Around 5:00 p.m. two friends; W. H. (on Navy leave) and C. C. (just out of the Army), were on a jeep-scouting trip looking for desert property. It was growing dusk and while traveling on a dirt trail they encountered Air Force personnel armed with carbines. Challenged by a Second Lt. they were asked for identification and their reasons for being in the area. While parked during the interrogation, WH could see other military personnel about a quarter of a mile away grouped around an object that appeared to be partially sunk into the sand. It was disk-shaped with a glassy dome on top, about 30 feet in diameter and with three landing legs. On its outer edge were two rings, which seemed to have windows in between them. The military appeared to have just arrived at the site. There was no evidence of an encampment or of any heavy equipment, at least from their point of view on the trail. The military personnel had probably just arrived at the crash site from an air base near Phoenix. Other data indicates that the disk was dragged for a long distance and finally moved to Muroc (later Edwards) AFB where it was placed inside hangar #27. Transportation of the disk was not too difficult as a result of its size and of its light-weight nature. Another piece of data comes from revelations of a top scientist using the pseudonym of "Dr. Epigoni" who was interviewed by Ron Madeley. "Epigoni" used to work in Edwards AFB, starting in the late 60ties until 1971 or 1972, and the disk from the Arizona crash site was apparently still being kept in

Edwards, at the time inside a large hangar on the surface and apparently it was still unopened. The recovery and subsequent study of the disc was done under a covert operation named "Blue Haven." The dome on top of the disk appeared to be made out of a glass-like material and using flashlight instruments; and four seats were visible through the dome. The disk was totally seamless. Another witness; an air force sergeant told Reilly Crabb (president of the Borderland Science Research Foundation in Vista California) that in 1967, he had seen a disk-shaped craft stored in a surface hangar in Edwards AFB, sitting on high landing gear with sharp edges and sloping up to a domed cockpit area in the center, and was probably 25-30 feet in diameter, with air force personnel in blue coveralls milling all around it. According to Epigoni, four alien creatures were found lying down on the ground outside the disk, but the disk itself was tightly closed, with no visible entryway. The aliens were about 5 feet tall, with light brown skin, dressed in silvery looking coveralls, real bright in color. Their eyes were like that of a dog, black in color, apparently covered with black lenses. They had small ears, noses and mouths with teeth. Blood samples indicated that their blood was black and very thick, like oil. The bodies were also x-rayed. They had six-fingered extremities. The bodies were kept in a special highly secured and isolated biomedical facility in Edwards AFB beyond several decontamination rooms. Research scientists came to the conclusion that since there was no deterioration of the bodies and they were apparently not dead, they would leave the bodies intact and would not perform autopsies, since another spacecraft might come into the area, as they presumed, and rejuvenate or reactivate them and at such time they may open the disk and allow the scientists in. Apparently these aliens have been in a state of suspended animation for many years and research personnel had attempted to enter the disk, but without any results. Presumably, as a result of at least 25-30 years of futile attempts to open the disk, the spacecraft was moved to a special underground chamber in Edwards and kept totally frozen in liquid nitrogen in a state of conservation until the day when it could be opened by a more powerful tool that would not destroy or substantially damage it. A man who allegedly saw the disk reportedly disappeared.

Around 1.20 pm on 29th April 1947 two women, Mrs. Olavick and Mrs. Down of Tucson in Pima County in Arizona watched nine white discs and another object behind a steamy cloud in a completely clear sky. They were arranged in a V formation and moved up and down in an erratic manner and in and out of the unnatural cloud for five to six minutes.

And suddenly the 1947 UFO Flap occurred.

On Tuesday 10th June 1947 at 11.00 pm Mrs. Coral Lorenzen watched a light rise across the Mexican border, assume a spherical shape and then disappear amongst the stars. The sighting lasted ten seconds and was seen from Douglas in Cochise County in Arizona. This was during the great 1947 UFO flap.

Around Tuesday, 17th June 1947 Louis Cefola, a Nogales watchmaker, thought he saw discs over the Washington Camp Mountain Range, about twelve miles East of Nogales, Santa Cruz County, Arizona. The number of objects that appeared to be one foot in diameter were unrecorded and resembled a reflection against the sky.

Mrs Leon Oetinger was visiting the Grand Canyon in Coconino County, Arizona on Thursday 26th June 1947 when she spotted a large silver ball that was falling too swiftly for an airplane in her sight for almost one minute. Two other witnesses were her son Dr. Leon Oetinger Jr and Miss Carol Street.

The following day on 27th June 1947, and above Tintown, near Bisbee in Coshise County in southern Arizona, at 10.30 am. Mr. John A Petsche, an electrician at Phelps-Dodge Corp as well as one other witness independently reported a disc-shaped object overhead that came to earth near Tintown around 10.30 am. Electrical worker, John A Petsche and five other people independently saw a shiny disc shaped object that appeared to land near Tintown. Among the other witnesses were John C Rylance, I W Maxwell, and Milton Luna who were at Cole Hill, about 2.5km from Petsche.

During the afternoon of 29th June 1947 Luis Bazurto and Armando Macias were sitting with their families in their front yard when they saw six discs fly in at speed from the West and disappear to the northeast. The objects were the size and shape of a large dinner plate and flew in circles, first in one direction and then in another. The noise of neighborhood youths had attracted his attention to the objects. This was at Camp Little in Santa Cruz County, Arizona, just northwest of Nogales.

Still on the 29th June 1947 and over Tucson, in Pima County, Arizona, Charles O. Weaver and his wife reported seeing nine or ten very shiny metallic objects moving in a southwesterly direction. Two of them were faster than the others and they were out of sight within a few minutes. This was at 1.20 pm.

Around 9.10 am on 30th June 1947 Navy Lt, William G. McGinty was flying a P-80 from Williams AAF at 30,000 feet when he saw two gray circular objects about eight to ten feet in diameter each diving at an inconceivable speed from an altitude of 25,000 feet. They appeared to land twenty-five miles South of the Grand Canyon.

At 9.00 pm on 1st July 1947 Mr. and Mrs. Frank Munn witnessed an aerial object moving East at great speed over Phoenix in Maricopa County, Arizona. It was moving too fast for an airplane and too slow for a falling star. It was larger than a star and appeared yellow in the moonlight. There was no smoke or vapor trail.

At the same time 1st July 1947 and still over Phoenix Mrs. Earl Tutt had her attention called to an aerial object by her son, Harold Nice, fourteen. It was a bright object streaking earthward without wavering. When close to the Earth the object suddenly stopped, paused for a second in the air and then took off eastwards at incredible speed. Both sightings appeared to be of the same object. This is not meteoric behavior.

On the Pima Indian Reservation, just South of Chandler in Pinal County, Arizona. At 9.30 am on the morning of Tuesday 1st July 1947 Mr. Robert E. Johnson, Juvenile Probation Officer of Chandler County, reported a lone silver colored discus-shaped object traveling at a good rate of speed heading North. It was visible for two to three minutes at an altitude of 5,000 to 10,000 feet.

On Saturday 5th July 1947 at 7.45 pm Mr. And Mrs. Bert Trice and Mrs. Randy Recardo saw an object moving from East to West across the sky at an altitude of seven thousand feet. The disc was clearly visible and as bright as the Sun, paused for a moment, gained momentum and then disappeared from sight. This was over Phoenix in Maricopa County in Arizona.

Later the next morning 6th July 1947 at 10.00 am Miles Casteel, head football coach at the University of Arizona saw something that was wavering in the sky and flying South at high speed. The object was too fast to be a plane. This was above Tucson in Pima County, Arizona.

At that same time that same day 6th July 1947 above Tucson Mr. W. D. Magness, an employee of the Air Material Command at Davis-Monthan Airfield, and Miss Faye Edwards, saw an object North of the sun which was at first stationary, then moved northwards and then wobbled like a kite. The object was visible for eight minutes and vanished North.

Also on 6th July 1947 there were two more sightings over Tucson in Pima County in Arizona. At 4.30 pm Walter Laos saw two round white aluminum colored objects about five to six feet in diameter that were flying at two hundred miles per hour and were heading towards Sabino Canyon. At 5.00 pm Joseph Hendren, a retired lawyer, and his wife were on their front porch when they saw three objects that at first looked like kites. They were silvery like the sun reflected off aluminum and were coming from the direction of Davis-Montham Field to the East and they were heading North. They were very high up and a later arriving two-some were smaller than the first UFO seen and they gravitated backwards and forwards in and out from the larger one. The larger one traveled on a straight and steady course whilst the two smaller ones moved up and down and in and out.

About 1.00 pm on Sunday 6th July 1947 Frances Howell saw a circular object about two feet in diameter float like a kite to the ground near his home. When he, his wife and several neighbors approached the spot the object rose slowly into the air and then took off at high speed towards Phoenix to the northwest. The object was described as flat and thin and made of a transparent aluminum like material. This was at Tempe, just outside of Phoenix in Maricopa County, Arizona. Here is another version. Mr and Mrs Francis Howell who were in their yard with another couple noticed a circular object north east of the house. It was descending with a "kite like" motion. The object, which appeared to be about 60cm in diameter, was flat, thin and appeared to be made of an aluminium like but transparent substance. The disc descended behind a row of trees, and was the witnesses approached to within 600m of the site, rose up at 45 degrees then moved away rapidly to the north west.

On July 7th 1947 still in Phoenix, Arizona at 4:00 p.m. local time Mr. William Albert Rhodes observed an elliptical-shaped object that spiralled down from 5000 feet to 2000 feet and then ascended at a 45 degree angle. Two photos were taken of the object. The speed of the object was estimated at 400-600 mph. The size was 20-30 feet with a visible canopy. The color was grey and it made a noise like a jet on approach - no sound was heard though while in view. Analysis based on camera data indicated a diagonal size of about 40-50 feet.

On Monday 7th July 1947 at 4.50 pm three patients at the veterans hospital said that they saw an oval shaped flying saucer about twenty-five feet in diameter and of a light metallic grey in color and wobbly in flight at an altitude of 4000 feet. This was in Tucson, Pima County, Arizona.

At dusk on Monday 7th July 1947 William H. Rhodes took two or three photos of a heel-shaped object with a concave trailing edge that was circling and banking North of his home in Phoenix in Maricopa County, Arizona. In the photos there is a white spot near the center of the object. The object originally approached from the West and made a whooshing sound and made three clockwise circlings above him before speeding of to the southwest at phenomenal speed but with no noise. There were twin vapor trails caused by two points at the tip of the trailing edge of the craft.

At 10.00 pm that night of the 7th July 1947 Charles (Bill) Ely and flying instructor Frank Markel, or Marbel, were approaching the airport at Kingman in Mohave County, Arizona, when two bright lights approached them from the East at an altitude of six hundred feet which they were on at the time. Ely blinked his landing lights twice to indicate that he was about to land but received no response from the other craft. Soon the lights were only 500 to 600 feet away and still approaching and Ely banked his plane to get out of the way. The lights then separated and continued going on their westward flight. The lights were unusual in that they were bright but cast no beam and were about twenty feet apart.

There were two sightings over Nogales, in Santa Cruz County in Arizona on the morning of 8th July 1947. In the first sighting at 8.15 am John W. Phillips and his assistant William Barker reported seeing a disc flying high and fast in a southwesterly direction as if heading for the Gulf of Lower California. In the second sighting at 9.45 am 8th July 1947 multiple independent witnesses saw a disc flying high over the city. Sam Marcus and Guy Fuller saw a disc soaring high over in the middle of the sky and a few minutes later Arthur Doan reported seeing the same object that later was still visible in the northeast sky. This same object was also seen by police Desk Sgt.. Pete Mincheff. Doan and Marcus referred to them as flying tortillas. A tortilla is a type of Mexican pancake.

Also on 8th July 1947 Mr. William Holland, William Harman and Lewis Zesper, a former Airforce pilot, observed an oval metallic, grey object at an altitude of four thousand feet above the mountains East of Tucson in Arizona. The object was twenty-five feet in diameter and wobbled as it flew in a North to South direction.

Back in Nogales in Santa Cruz County, Arizona that afternoon at 5.30 pm 8th July 1947 Mr. and Mrs. E. A. Lamier and their son Freddie saw seven very shiny discs flying in an easterly direction over the northern horizon. Freddie had attracted his parent's attention to them and the discs were visible for about five minutes before they faded out. A few minutes after this they group of witnesses then saw a solitary disc heading west, the opposite direction to the original passage.

Over Yuma in Yuma County in Arizona at 8.15 am on 8th July 1947 Henry Varela, R. N Villa and Henry Hodges of the Arizona State Highway Department saw two silver colored disc-shaped objects streaking silently, one behind the other, in a straight line in a northeasterly direction. They were shaped like saucers and were very high up in the sky.

At noon 9th July 1947 a crowd of thirty neighbors including Mr. L. C. Van Camp, an instructor in electricity at Phoenix Technical School, saw three flying saucers darting in and out of clouds over the northeast section of Phoenix in Maricopa County, Arizona. The three objects were moving East to West against the wind and entering and leaving cloud formations. Through binoculars the discs appeared to be made of glass and were spinning around. Eventually they flew away. The weather bureau at the airport said that they were not weather balloons.

The last UFO report for Wednesday 9th July 1947 was from Douglas, Cochise County, Arizona, when Mrs. C. D. Kline and her neighbors saw a silver object slow down as it passed over the city as if it was looking it over.

On Wednesday 9th July 1947 at 6.22 am in Tucson in Pima County, Arizona, Mrs. Adella Williams was waiting for a bus when she saw a flying disc due South of her. The object was the size of an airplane and traveling fast. At first the object appeared round but lengthened to an ellipse as it moved further away. Originally it was traveling East but banked and changed course to the southeast towards the Rincon Mountains.

The last UFO report for Wednesday 9th July 1947 was from Douglas, Cochise County, Arizona, when Mrs. C. D. Kline and her neighbors saw a silver object slow down as it passed over the city as if it was looking it over.

At 11.45 am on 10th July 1947 Mrs. L. B. Ogle of Douglas in Cochise County in Arizona saw a small bright object which quivered and appeared to hover immediately outside a downstairs window. It appeared to be seven inches in diameter and the window was five feet from the ground.

It is 2.30 am on Friday 11th July 1947 and Mrs. Anna Potts of Yuma in Yuma County, Arizona, is woken by her dog barking and she goes outside. She saw something swooping down over the housetops and the telephone wires and at first she thought it was a bird. She soon noticed that this was not bird but a round, spinning, flat white-colored object that was moving at high speed but making no noise. She followed it for five seconds before it disappeared over the housetops.

On 11th July 1947 Mrs. W. P. Hopkins of Douglas in Cochise County in Arizona watched a disc-shaped object that was reflecting headlights in the Fifteenth Street Park.

At Grave Creek in Paradise Valley in Maricopa County, North of Phoenix in Maricopa County, Arizona in October 1947. Early in the month a crashed UFO was reported to have been seen that was 36 feet in diameter and had two Hominoids in it. One was sitting and the other was halfway out of the hatch. Another reported UFO crash? More dead Aliens? Only 470 kilometers from the last reported crash at Socorro in New Mexico only a few months before. Each crash was West of the previous one. Is there a pattern here? There had previously been a luminous disc seen in the sky here in 1899. The witnesses were Selman Graves, 22, and his brother-in-law Bob Melody, 16.

On October 14th 1947 eleven miles northnortheast of Cave Creek in Maricopa County in Arizona. At 12 noon Ex-AAF fighter pilot J. L. Clark, civilian pilot Anderson and a third man saw 3-foot "flying wing," black against the white clouds and red against the blue sky, flying straight at an estimated 380 m.p.h., at 8,000-10,000 feet, from NW to SE in about 45-60 seconds.

1948

One night in September 1948 near Prescott in Arizona Kathryn Brown was in her car when she suddenly got the feeling that something was about to happen. She felt great power and gentleness around her. She was not afraid, even though she could not hear the car radio and engine. Then she saw the familiar lights ahead of her car and fell into what she thought was a deep sleep. She woke two hours later feeling hungry and having lost two hours. Later she recalled being on board an object and meeting a tall, human-like figure with long brown hair, blue eyes and who spoke English. He seemed to be the leader. The rest of the crew were shorter than the witness with greyish white skin and wearing what appeared to be space travel suits. They used telepathy to communicate with her. After entering a small passage way she was taken to what appeared to be a command center. There she was shown a window that had been invisible from the outside. She also saw what were apparently dials and abstract drawings. The tall man and one of the others showed her how to operate the dials. The floor was very shiny and made her feel light. Her next memory was of being back in her car. The same witness was involved in other encounters.

1949

On March 7th 1949 at Window Rock, Navajo Nation, Arizona at 6:10 p.m. There was a sighting of a round object that was fire red in the center shading to blue at the edges. It was 3 feet in diameter [?], traveling at an estimated 200-300 mph, in the North at elevation 40°-45° disintegrating at the end. There was no sound.

On April 28th 1949 in Tucson in Pima County in Arizona at 5:45 p.m. Howard Hann [Hamm?], Mr. Hubert [Huber?] and Tex Keahey saw a a very large bright, sausage-shaped object, with no fins, wings or protuberances, travel from NE to SW, over a period of 12 minutes or so. The object was shiny metallic and reflected the sun, and appeared to be revolving as it moved like the "slow roll of an airplane." There was no noise, nor was there an exhaust or a vapor trail. There were no wings or engines or "protuberances of any sort." It appeared to be traveling at 300-600 mph.

On May 8th 1949 and also in Tucson, Arizona at 9:30 a.m. Four witnesses reported a motionless, metallic, circular object at 4,000 feet that started moving West then turned to the North. The object was moving horizontal, then made a rapid climb at a 45-degree angle to 20,000 feet until it was out of sight after 10-20 minutes.

On May 9th 1949 and still over Tucson, Arizona. At 2:30 p.m. a silvery object, 25 feet' in diameter and moving at 750-1000 mph in a SW-NE direction for 6-10 seconds was seen.

On June 24th 1949in Mesa in Maricopa County in Arizona at 3:45 p.m. Five objects were observed by two witnesses. One object moved vertically and was described as steel grey and at least one was a disc with two flanges. They appeared to be travelling at 400 mph.

1950

On 20th May 1950 between 12.15 pm and 12.20 pm Dr. Seymour L. Hess, a meteorologist and astronomer and an expert on planetary atmospheres was at the Lowell Observatory in Flagstaff in Coconino County in Arizona when he saw a bright spherical light from the observatory grounds. The luminous object which he described as dark when it passed in front of a cloud and was observed through binoculars would have been three to five feet wide and moving at one hundred miles per hour. There was no sound of an engine though. Flagstaff is in Coconino County.

1951

On 2nd November 1951a gigantic green fireball was seen blazing over Arizona to the astonishment of 165 witnesses at least. Several of the witnesses stated that it travelled parallel to the ground before it exploded. There was no sound and the green fireball seemed to just disintegrate. Was this the same green fireball that scared the passengers and crew of a plane flying over Abilene in Texas around the same time? Also on 2nd November 1951 over Abilene in Taylor County, Texas the Passengers and crew of an American Airlines DC-4 saw a bright green UFO like projectile that paced them. They were in an American Airlines DC-4 above Abilene. The UFO left a white trail and was holding the same course as the plane when it suddenly exploded hurling red balls of fire in every direction. It was like a Roman candle and fortunately none hit the plane. This is not our first pacing of an aircraft either. Or exploding UFO.

Near Phoenix in Maricopa County, Arizona during 1951. A couple driving at night towards the city saw on the side of an isolated road a landed disc-shaped object surrounded by light. Numerous short figures were seen walking around the object. They were too frightened to stop and kept on driving.

1952

Near Catalina near Tucson in Arizona around 17th June 1952 the female witness was walking along a desert trail looking for interesting rocks when she noticed a ball of fire in the sky that descended behind a mountain ridge. The witness walked towards the direction where it had gone and then stopped to pick up a sparkling rock when she noticed a small gray man walking towards her saying "Do not be afraid" apparently by telepathy. She then fell asleep and woke up later lying on an examination table in a small room illuminated by a fuzzy light. Four little gray humanoids with large bald heads and huge bulging black eyes were examining her with instruments. They pulled down an apparatus with a light from the ceiling and ran it up and down her body.

A small device was apparently planted in her ear and another in her abdomen. She was also shown a book with strange symbols and a scene with three stars in a large three-dimensional viewing screen.

On August 4th 1952 near Stanton in Martin County, Texas. Near Stanton a ranch woman, Mrs Flora Rogers, saw an object descend at 16-24 kph and pass across the pasture road close to her, at 6m altitude. She stopped the car, leaned out of the window and observed that the object was wobbling in mid air, was shaped like two turtle shells stuck together. From a crack in the rim came three oar like projections that moved slowly back and forth. The object was 3m long, 5m wide, 1m thick, green-grey army camouflage colour and emitted a blue flame from a spout at the rear. Suddenly the object ascended at terrific speed, making the witness so shaken she could not stand.

On August 31st 1952 at 1245hrs in Matador in Motley County, Texas. The wife of an air force officer and her daughter, driving out from Matador, encountered a pear shaped object about 40m above the ground, just off the side of the road, about 150m away, moving slowly towards the east. The ladies drove on another 50m, stopped and got out of their car. They now estimated that the object was larger than a B 29 plane. It was silent and featureless save for a single porthole in the side. The object then speeded and rose rapidly in a sort of spiral motion. The thing was travelling against the wind.

1953

On January 30th 1953 at 1925hrs in Yuma in Yuma County, Arizona. Wells Alan Webb, Felix Gebler and Grove Kihorny, passengers in a car driving by Spain Air Field, observed a flickering and dancing light above one of the planes parked there. When they first saw it, it was at an altitude of 12m, but it rose, slowly at first, then ever faster to lose itself among the stars at an angle of 60 degrees.

On 5th May 1953 a scientist near Yuma Air Force Base in Yuma County saw a silvery disc encircled by dark bands though the bands could only be seen through polaroid glasses.

At Kingman in Mohave County, Arizona on 21st May 1953. An object constructed of an unfamiliar metal that resembled aluminum was seen on the ground. It had apparently impacted twenty inches into the sand. There was no sign of structural damage. It was an oval thirty feet in diameter with an entranceway hatch that vertically lowered and opened that was 3.5 feet high by 1.5 feet wide. There were two swivel seats inside an oval cabin and there were lots of instruments and displays. Near the craft in a tent was a lone occupant that was four feet tall with a dark brown complexion, having two eyes, two nostrils, two ears with no earlobes and a small round mouth. The little hominoid was clothed in a silvery metallic suit with a skullcap of the same material. The hominoid was very slender with disproportionally long arms. Only two sightings in this area's entire history and this one has to be a doozey! Mind you we are in Arizona. Mythology or actual event? Who will know when we are dealing here with events that are all regarded as mythology or non-truth of some sort. Whose tent was it? The Humanoids or someone else's? Fritz A. Werner, then an Air Force project engineer on an atomic test explosion in Nevada, was taken with 15 other specialists in a blacked-out bus to (he thinks) a spot near Kingman, Arizona and there escorted by military police to a crashed UFO surrounded by guards. The object was oval and looked like 2 deep saucers, one inverted on the other; it was about 30 feet in diameter, the convex surfaces 20 feet in diameter. It had impacted 20 inches into the sand without any sign of structural damage. It was made of a metal resembling brushed aluminum. An entrance hatch 1.5 feet wide x 3.5 feet high was open; another member of the team looked inside & saw 2 swivel seats, an oval cabin, & "a lot of instruments & displays." In a tent pitched nearby W. saw the dead body of a human-like creature 4 feet tall, wearing a silvery metallic suit & skullcap of the same material; it had a small round mouth. The skin of its face was dark brown; "this may have been caused by exposure to our atmosphere." Werner & the others were made to take an oath that they would not reveal what they had seen. Werner also said that he had been in contact with a professor in Germany working on anti-gravity—"using the earth's magnetic fields as a form of propulsion" — for the USAF, and that this project produced a working, but impracticable machine. Raymond Fowler verified that the atomic test mentioned by Werner did exist, and that his diary for May 21, 1953 contains a reference to "a job I can't write or talk about." Werner holds a master's degree in engineering and has published several technical papers.

On May 21st 1953 in Prescott in Yavapai County in Arizona. Eight disc-like objects were observed maneuvering in the sky for an hour or so beginning at around 10 AM. There were three observers, Bill Beers, a pilot, Ray Temple, and O. Ed Olson. Two of the discs were stationary, while the other six discs participated in maneuvers not unlike a dog-fight. They said the six swooped around in formation, "peeled off ", and shot directly up and down in a maneuver that could not be duplicated by a plane. When they moved, they varied from very slow to speeds faster that a jet plane, the observers said.

1956

On January 19th 1956 at 1430hrs in Peach Springs in Mohave County, Arizona. A group of people driving east along Hw66 near Peach Springs saw a sudden flash of light and realised that it came from an "odd" shaped, bright metallic object, which came down very low, as if to land. It then emitted a cloud of smoke and began to dart about and turn around, just a metre or so from the ground. It rose up into the sky, performed complex manoeuvres and circled the road, before coming low again, and then rising once more, all in silence. The smoke seemed to come from the centre of its underside.

In the Santa Catalina Mountains, northeast of Tucson, Pima County, Arizona. At 8.00 pm on the night of 7th February 1955 residents of Tucson watched a huge fire burning in the mountains with flames estimated to be thirty feet high. The following morning a search party went to look at the devastation at a height of 3,700 feet up on a ridge covering an area of 800 yards. Large rocks had been scorched black but there were no bare patches of ashes and no charred large objects. The fire had even jumped over giant rocks and areas of dry grass yet other areas had been scorched to a depth of four inches. The amount of tinder should not have burnt for more than a few minutes yet the fire lasted for several hours.

On March 30th 1955 at 0315hrs still in Tucson, Arizona. Musician Andy Florio was driving on Hw 80 between Tucson and El Paso when he encountered a bronze coloured discoid machine 30m diameter, 7.5m thick with circular openings around its rim, from which amber coloured lights protruded. From its roof came blue-green lights and it made a sound like a modulated electrical hum. It manoeuvred and then tipped on its side, projecting a brilliant beam of white light, burning Andy's arm and blistering the paint on his car. The radio stopped and his lights and motor lost power as he felt a tingling sensation. The battery was found to be drained of half of its acid and the radio was burned out. Andy suffered from nausea for some time afterwards.

1956

At Peach Springs in Mohave County, Arizona on 19th January 1956 at 2.30 pm. People in a car on a Highway travelling East saw a flash of lightning then an odd-shaped small object with a bright metallic glare dropped close to the ground as if it were about to land. Suddenly a great cloud of smoke came out of the object and it began to dart here and there turning over and over again. It moved along only a few feet from the ground for a short time and then gained altitude until it reached the side of some hills to the North. It made strange patterns in the sky and then came near the ground again and circled the highway area. There was no noise and smoke came out of the bottom. The sighting lasted twenty minutes. Odd behavior for an allegedly controlled craft?

1959

Near Phoenix in Maricopa County, in Arizona on October 12th 1959. That evening 16-year old Brian Scott (to be involved in future humanoid encounters) was in the desert coming home from a birthday party when he saw a ball of light hovering over his dog, which was running in circles and jumping at the object. The ball was oval-shaped, Scott recalls; "semi-solid with it becoming more solid toward the center. It was six to eight inches in diameter and reddish-orange. The ball of light came right at my head until it was just a few inches from my face and then it went straight up." As it did so, strange thoughts and pictures apparently communicated from the ball flashed into Scott's mind.

1960

In Tucson, Arizona in May 1960. One night Charlie Green was apparently abducted from his bedroom by two short, thin beings with dark eyes and large heads. A second witness saw the abduction from outside. He saw Charlie coming out of the window between two beings and rising up into a hovering 30 feet diameter object. No other details were remembered.

In June 1960 at 0730hrs in Pearce I cochise County, Arizona. Mr and Mrs Prude were riding their horses along a dry wash trail on their ranch near Pearce when they saw two gun metal grey discs, about 5m diameter and lacking surface features approaching down the centre of the wash at an altitude of 15m. Mrs Prude ducked automatically. The things were completely silent and the Prude's horses did not react to them.

On June 10th 1960 at 12.15 am in Globe in Gila County, Arizona. A lady known to Coral Lorenzen but who wished to remain anonymous was driving her sleeping husband and two children about 25km east of Globe at 105kph. As she pulled round a right hand turn and straightened out, her headlight caught a small figure, 90m ahead on the right of the road. As she slowed, the figure turned towards her and she saw that it was 90cm tall with broad shoulders, long arms, and dark skin and with a pumpkin shaped head in which there were eyes that appeared to be projecting light. The body seemed covered by a kind of fur. She accelerated away and woke her husband who wanted to go back and investigate, but she and the children refused.

1961

In Granite Dells around ten kilometers northeast of Prescott in Yavapai County in Arizona during November 1961. The mother of the witness in a previous incident, woke up one night to see a tall, rather thin, humanoid figure standing at the foot of her bed. He wore a one-piece silvery-white jumpsuit and identified himself as 'Itan.' "Itan" communicated with the witness by using telepathy. She was told that he came from a planet that existed in another dimension.

1962

On August 7th 1962 in Oracle in Pinal County, Arizona. A night crew at an IBM site was outside smoking when they saw a brilliant light overhead, apparently descending over the site. They went in and called their Commanding Offcier. Two planes were sent up from Davis-Monthan AFB to the south, and as they approached the object shot straight up. When the planes had passed the thing descended again, hovered and then sped away.

1963

In May 1963 or following month at 2045hrs in Phoenix in Maricopa County, Arizona. A woman walking with her two children saw. In a side yard no more than 6m away and about 5m above the ground, a round object with three concentric circular rings decreasing in size from the edge towards the centre. The thing was slightly larger than a compact car and possessed an indescribably beautiful whiteness and brilliance. It had sharp lines except for a rim like halo and an area of even more intense brilliance. The top was white and bottom dark and metallic. The object hung silently, just quivering slightly from time to time.

On the left of the lawn, not far from the mass was a middle aged man with a hose, who appeared to be paying no attention to the object. The woman tried to speak but was unable to do so. It seemed as though she and the children were "frozen in time" and she could not even hear the usual sounds of crickets, dogs, cats etc. She then felt very afraid and forced herself and the children to walk away. As she did so she felt a sense of euphoria. When she arrived home it seemed to be later than expected. She pondered going back but felt that the object would be gone. She now felt sad and depressed. The street lights were not affected.

1964

On June 3rd 1964 at 2200hrs on Black Canyon Highway in near Golden Valley in Mohave County, Arizona. An importer from Tucson was returning from a trip to Wyoming along Black Canyon Highway when, near the Verde Road crossing in Golden Valley he spotted a dirigible shaped object hovering above the ground in a canyon to his right. The object, which was clearly silhouetted against the hills, was surrounded by a cold blue glow. As the importer approached, it turning a curve to his right, he caught the thing in his headlights. It then rose vertically and disappeared to the south west. The observation lasted 15 minutes.

1965

During July or August 1965 around 6.00 pm Mrs. V. T. and her daughter observed a triangular shaped object fly overhead low and slowly in Phoenix in Arizona. The mother counted thirteen windows around the perimeter of the object and in one window she saw a figure who walked into view with his arm raised as though touching something on the inside wall. He then dropped his arm, turned to the window, and looked directly at the witness who felt that he was looking at us. The daughter did not see the man but only the craft. It had a red light in the forwards point of the triangle and two blue lights in the rear. The figure was slim, human-shaped, and wore tight fitting clothing. He appeared to be of average height although she only saw him from the waist up. The object passed over treetop level and the witness started waving at it. She then ran inside to get her camera but when she returned it was gone.

On August 9th 1965 at 1245hrs in Mesa in Maricopa County, Arizona. Mrs Biggs and two other witnesses observed an object the size of a Goodyear Blimp, glowing like white hot metal, hovering close to the ground. It moved up and down and sideways, tracing out a square

1967

On Feb. 16th 1967 at Kingman in Mohave County in Arizona. At 11:45 p.m. a soldier and his wife saw an oval object with red and green body lights approach their car at low altitude late on a cloudy night. The ground was illuminated by a moving light beam emitted from its bottom center. A few minutes later the object reappeared about a mile away followed by two white lights flying in step formation, one of which landed or nearly landed. The remaining light merged with the large object. Or this. Soldier, Max Recod and his wife were driving near Kingman when they saw an oval object with one green and three red lights approaching below the 100m cloud ceiling . As the thing passed over, it illuminated the ground with a beam of light. The object then went behind a hill only to reappear followed by two white lights, one of which landed. The main object then ascended into a star like point, which seemed to absorb (or be absorbed by) it, and then went up out of sight.

On April 12th 1967 in Phoenix Arizona at 8:59 p.m. A bell-shaped object buzzed a car which experienced electromagnetic effects on its engine, banked, turned and flew away. Three people out driving saw, to their left, a luminous red-orange bell shaped object that emitted yellow pulses. The thing hovered over a streetlight and then dived towards the car, at which the car engine stopped. The thing then banked first to the east, then to the west before taking off. As the trio continued their journey they saw the same thing eight more times and also a strange white object. During this time the car engine worked normally.

On April 21st 1967 at 2155hrs in Tucson in Pima County, Arizona. While out driving a female architectural designer, had her attention drawn by her mother to a yellow object with a dome on top and a flat underside which descended at a 30 degree angle with a swaying motion, as if to land. It emitted a beam of light pointing upwards and apparently landed in the Rillito River area. No traces were found.

In Western Pima County in Arizona on June 30th to July 1st 1967. On around the above date, a disk-shaped object about nine meters in diameter with a dome on top, crashed for some unknown reason in the desert near the Organ Pipe National Monument; a reservation in the western part of Pima County. The disabled craft was detected and found by the military. The retrieval team was then sent to the crash site. A pre-fabricated hangar was then built around the debris and equipment was brought to the crash site by helicopters and trucks.

On July 2nd, R. T, a Marine with the rank of PFC a trainer in the Canine Corps at Camp Pendleton, San Diego with an Alpha Red (Top Secret) Crypto Clearance, and other marines, were flown in a light cargo transport aircraft to the site, landing on a makeshift strip carved out of the desert. The windows of the aircraft had been blacked out. At the site, among the cactus and tumbleweed, were tents, a small Quonset hut and what appeared to be a small pre-fab hangar. Busy around the structures were men in military fatigues without insignia. Told nothing about the status of the operation he was assigned to a post for guard duty, given orders and told to use only one designated path to the mess hall and latrine. Curious, R. T. decided on the fourth day to see what was so hush-hush and took a different route to the mess tent near the hangar. When the guard there had his back turned, he peeked inside the hangar and to his shock saw a metallic disk or saucer, about 30 feet in diameter. On top was a dome. Around the craft were men at work and tables on which were technical instruments. He also saw a large walk-in refrigerator unit on skids and several empty body bags. If there were bodies, they had already been shipped out or maybe they were in the freezer. R. T's one good glance into the hangar was also his undoing. The guard nearby nabbed him and he was escorted to the headquarters' tent where he faced the officer in command, a Colonel "P" from the USAF medical corps. Reminded of his security oath he was confined to quarters and sent back to Pendleton for punishment. He told his story 13 years later. In 1980 R. T. was visited by a man dressed in black that lasted for 45 minutes. During the meeting, his dog, a shepherd, behaved uneasily. At one point the stranger in black asked for a glass of water, but when he was approached, he uttered, "Don't touch me!". R. T. also noticed that during their conversation about UFOs, the visitor always spoke in third person, using "we" or "they." According to R. T. the visitor, while describing a UFO incident, suddenly produced from his briefcase a half dozen color photographs. Each showed small cadavers or parts, not human, in what appeared to be a hospital operating room. The bodies were about 4 feet tall. One photo was a close-up of a hand with four fingers, long and slim, with no opposable thumb. Another showed the top of a humanoid head, the flesh cut open and drilled into. Still another showed the upper torso of a chalky white complexion with an incision into its chest, and another showed a body burnt in its suit. But there was one photo that really convinced R.T.; it showed three doctors in the process of dissecting a body on top of a slab with a gutter around its edge. Later R. T. refused to discuss the subject, because of "threats." The disk from the crash site was later transported to the Yuma Marine Corps Base and hidden in a hangar there. Sometime later a military convoy removed the disk in the middle of the night to a more secured and highly secret underground compound on the territory of the Fort Huachuca Military Reservation in Arizona. Most probably no less than three short humanoid bodies were extracted from the crashed disk and also taken to the underground facility.

On October 9th 1967 at 1740hrs in Tucson in Pima County, Arizona. In a residential area east of the city limits the 13 year old son of a prominent local businessman was cycling home and had just negotiated a detour onto the slope when he noticed, on the ground 13m away, a cylinder that was stood on end and was supported by two legs angling out from the bottom, ending on pads and joined by a curved bar just above these pads. The object was 2.5m tall, 50-75cn wide and was [partially obscured by a tree. The boy cycled to within 10m of the thing, at which the aluminium coloured object rose into the air with a slight rocking motion, and disappeared from sight in 12 seconds, going straight up. As it did so, the object made a deep low pitched hum. Though the object reflected the sunlight, it did not reflect the surroundings. The boy, who was considered very reliable, found two marks on the hard surface at the bottom of the wash, 105cm apart, diameter 335mm.

On December 24th 1967 in the evening in Tucson in Pima County, Arizona. A couple driving near Tucson saw an amorphous red light, which approached their car. The car engine and headlights both failed. The thing went over their car and left to the south, at which the engine and lights came back on.

1968
Near Flagstaff in Coconino County in Arizona during Summer 1968. In the evening the witness and her daughter were driving across the Mojave Desert, about two hours outside of Flagstaff. The daughter began to shout that she saw a spaceship in the sky. The sky was unusually cloudy, and she looked to where her daughter was pointing and saw first two and then three lights moving rapidly in the sky, turning at ninety degree angles, pulsating and disappearing, etc.. She decided to pull off the road onto a dirt trail she saw on the right, leading into the desert. They were away from the road lights, but she thought she could still see them at a distance. They watched the sky together, when suddenly in the front of the car there appeared a huge, dark and glowing object with a partial row of lights in the middle. The next thing she remembers was her breath being knocked out of her as she somehow went through the windshield of the car. She remembers looking back for an instant and the car was completely empty of herself and her daughter, and she was stepping into an opening in a vehicle. She couldn't see her daughter and she asked in terror about her. "She's going to be all right," was what she heard in the center of her mind, and she was strangely soothed and unusually happy. The beings were tall, about six and a half feet, and seemed to be robed in a fabric that emitted a type of light periodically, during movement. Their skin was silvery and their eyes were round and a violet-blue that sometimes streamed out on her with a feeling of love or long lost family; it was almost like a homecoming. Their eyes were closer to the surface of their faces than humans,' and the nose wasn't well defined. Their mouths were fascinating. Sometimes it seemed that they weren't dressed at all, and the body definition wasn't sexually differentiated.

She was standing with two of them and noticing that they had no hair, but there was something like fabric that was crumpled and folded behind their backs. They seemed to be smiling, without moving their mouths. As soon as she thought "hair," one of them seemed to produce beautiful reddish gold hair all over its head. This frightened her. The room she was looking into was about twenty five feet wide and semicircular. It was rather dark, and filled with TV screens running the full wall area, stacked upon one another three and sometimes four rows high. All sorts of pictures appeared on the screens, and strange symbols, and terrains she'd never seen. Under the screens was a type of built-in-desk, curving all along the wall. In the middle of the room was a long table with three or four chairs that were movable. There were three beings in the chairs, two of them facing the screens and moving around, while another one at the desk area stood from time to time, moving things around. They did not look up. They seemed to be of the same slender body type as the two that stood with her, but were not quite so tall. Those two seemed to be laughing all the time and sometimes there was a sound like wind. They kept saying, "Welcome, welcome!" in her mind, and laughing. They then told her some strange things about human origins and alien intervention on the planet Earth at various times in the past and future. Then they started speaking to her about her individual history. There was a whole generation of beings that came to Earth in the far past and took up Earth life. They were from the family of "Ranm." That root family was their name root also, but either that planet wasn't in existence anymore, or it was now inaccessible. They said that was why the old god names were as they were on Earth; Rama, Brahma, Ra in Egypt and Abraham, etc.. in order that humans might remember. But so much confusion set in that the names became designations for gods, heroes, and that wasn't the point at all. Rather it indicated the name form of the origin of them and some of us, being from other star systems. Then they began telling her, her name in their tongue, 'Shalisha Li Ekimu Ranm,' and kept saying it in her head until she got it right. They said those words meant much more, and could be found in Earth literature. There was such love flowing through them, as they helped her with the name and the earth lineages that went back to the stars. This communication wasn't exactly like 'words' but were rather images or sound pictures that moved between them. Then they took her through a gray, curved corridor to the right of the entrance where she'd come in. She can remember not being able to walk, and then walking with ease. They came to a room at the end and to the left of the corridor. This room contained the ship's driving mechanism. In front of her was a huge crystal, perhaps three feet across in the middle. It looked like two pyramids placed base to base, although at times it seemed multifaceted and totally brilliant and jewel-like. The crystal seemed suspended in the air, and around it was a matrix of wires or tubes connected into a solid type of material concealing the ends of the tubes in a dark smooth mass, so that the entire thing rose about four feet from the floor. They told her to put her mind into the crystal, and as she did she'd be able to learn how to fly the ship. (!) One of them telepathically told her how to do it, she tried and failed, but they kept coaxing her and she could hear them smiling, "Go on, you can do it!" Finally she got it right and they began to move out, first above the Earth and then through the angular pattern of space that was also time. She asked why she had to do this, and they only said, "So that you can remember flying and piloting when necessary," and then there was laughter. After the initial information was placed in the crystal and wire matrix, nothing more was necessary, but they stood there anyway until they said, "Time to return to Earth." Frantically, she panicked and asked about her daughter and was soothed again by them saying she was okay. Then they said they were sorry, but didn't say why, and then there was great love. As they moved to the exit place, they said her name again several times, and something about "soul lineage." She was reluctant to go, but the next thing she knew she had gone through the car windshield again, and found herself hanging out of the window gasping for air; she began to cry and was covered with sweat. Her daughter was in the backseat crying. Her daughter told her never to touch her again, and that she knew who she was and she hated her. She tried to calm her and asked what had happened to her, and she shouted, "I'll never tell you! Leave me alone!" After the incident, the witness hair began to fall out and her mouth started bleeding, and she was exhausted.

On August 26th 1968 at 1950hrs in Gleeson in Cochise County, Arizona. Teacher and pioneer rancher Mrs Pearl Christianson had just arrived at her ranch and had stopped to open the gate when she saw a large silver disc, traling sparks, sat on the south side of Brown's peak. She sat in her car, observing this object for 5 minutes. As she went through her gate she saw a second, very shiny, gold object. She watched the objects, which were mostly stationary but occasionaly moved simultaneously, through field glasses, allthought the brightness hurt her eyes, until they disappeared about midnight. Mrs Millard Mayfield, operator of the Gleeson Museum, also saw a light on the peak that night. When the two ladies investigated the saddle between Brown Peak and Torquise Mountain they found the rocks were too hot to touch and a strange acid odour Other investigators found cactus burnt at the base but not at the top, others were totally carbonised. Burnt spots 10-20cm diameter were also found.

Around 3.00 am on 15th October 1968 near Kingman in Arizona Michael Watts and a hitch hiking passenger saw a falling star that stopped and then shot back up again. They got out of the car and walked towards a distant light source at ground level. At the site they heard a sound like digging and dimly saw two shadowy forms that were four feet tall. They were fifteen feet away. The figures had large heads and abnormally long arms. When the hitch hiker suggested they go back for a gun the figures vanished. Other maneuvering lights were observed. The light on the ground proved to be four lights one of which took off into the air. Then something sounded like a train passing by at a distance. It had a string of lighted windows in which silhouettes of passengers could be seen. After this a dark lens-shaped object having a flat dome on top and a row of pulsating multi-colored lights around the edge approached the witnesses quite closely. As dawn came the ground light could be seen to be on a pale cigar-shaped object. Cloven foot prints were found where the beings had been seen. Watts believed that he had a memory lapse.

1969

On December 5th 1969 in the early evening in Liberty in Maricopa County, Arizona. Cliff Patterson of Buckeye was driving :from Avondale on Hw60 when he saw a bright light in the sky, north of Liberty. At first it looked as though a spotlight was being directed down from the dark sky to the ground., but gradually the glow spread out in an oval shape near the top of the beam.. From the underside of this shape, red yellow and blue lights appeared. The thing seemed to keep moving away as Cliff's pickup truck approached but it stayed close to the earth for a time, before the main beam of light went out. :Then the other colours disappeared and only the blue light remained as the object appeared to head off into the west. A patrol car and several other vehicles also stopped. The light was also seen by Mrs Jones as she passed through the area. The light was last seen moving towards Tonopah.

1970

On August 7th 1970 at 2230hrs in Prescott in Yavapai County, Arizona. Mr Vell, a photographer with the Evening Courier was with Will May and his wife when they observed a group of 5 objects that zigzagged, made formations, and appeared to land in an area between Prescott and the airport. Vell took two photographs showing zigzag lines and a glow obscured by the mountains.

On the evening of 10th August 1970 Mr. Titus Lamson saw a rainbow colored UFO moving over the village of Hotaville. Old records mention a Hotaville, also called Hotevilla-Bacavi on the mesa near Oraibi in Navajo County in Arizona. It had a dome, a round thing and an aerial on top. It lighted up and became translucent so that he could see a man inside the dome wearing a gray uniform. The object then disappeared over a ridge. There are historical records for Titus Lamson in Hotevilla in Arizona. Several sources state that this happened in New Mexico.

1971

During the night of 14th March 1971 near Apache Junction in Maricopa and Pinal Counties two young men, Brian Scott and Nick Corbin, were in the Superstition Mountains to gather snakes. They saw a light coming over the mountains and it approached them. The next thing that they knew was that they were hastily leaving their campsite. Five years later under hypnosis Scott remembered the object emitting a purplish light from underneath approached and hovered over them. He felt a pulsating pulling feeling and the two men were lifted up into the craft. Inside they were separated and Scott was led by a seven foot tall entity down a corridor to a door which upon approaching shattered. Inside in a small room filled with mist he encountered four or five similar creatures. They were seven feet tall, with grayish skin similar to that of a crocodile and three fingered hands. Scott was stripped and placed against a wall panel that was very brilliantly lighted. The room was cold and mist emerged from vents in the floor. A machine directly in front of him appeared to scan him and a new entity, nine feet tall, communicated telepathically with him and asked why he was afraid. The beings that examined him had huge ears, no hair and slit-like mouths. Their feet were elephant-like with three broad toes. When the examination was completed Scott was reunited with his friend and returned to the ground with no conscious memory of what had occurred. However both felt an unspecified terror of such a degree that they packed their gear and returned to town. Brian Scott was told that the aliens had a method of displacing their ships through space by using a series of hops. They were guided in their trajectories by a number of space navigation beacons placed strategically throughout the galaxy. Here is another version. At 9.00 pm Brian Scott (24) and a companion were camping in the Arizona desert when they found themselves levitates into a 60m diameter saucer shaped object. They found themselves paralysed in a small room. Several 2.1m tall ugly beings with sloping shoulders, crocodile scaled skin, elephant like feet and hands with three fingers and a recessed thumb, emerged and undressed them. The two men were taken away in opposite directions. Scott, supported by two beings seemed to glide rather than walk through a heavily fogged area, stopping at a door with an insignia and flashing lights at the top and sides. When one of the beings touched it, the door seemed to explode and they entered a brilliantly lit room. Scott found himself, unable to move, placed against a sloping wall. Two of the beings stood beside some sort of consoles, a third by a pole on which there was a sort of mobile box with many small coloured blinking lights and two intense large ones, one of which seemed to hold his gaze, while the other probed his body. He felt a series of uncomfortable though painless sensations, including bleeding, urinating and feeling that his chest had been opened and his heart taken out for a brief moment. He then felt a pull on his head and the lights went out, followed by the lights on the box. He then detected an unpleasant odour and out of the fog came a being similar to the others but 2.7m tall. This being communicated with Scott by means of telepathy and suggested that the beings were clones of a central computer, which could also assume humanoid form, and were hatched in a laboratory on the second floor of the craft. The being also claimed they were "checking the original biological plantation on planet Earth", this interspersed with vague comments on philosophy, the beings purpose and a promise to return. Scott then went on a "telepathic trip" though time, seeing the destruction of Earth in an atomic war, and a visit to the beings home planet, a harsh purple hued world, surrounded by a dome, and with two suns, which planet he sensed was a happy place. Scott was then taken from the wall and returned to the small room, where he met his friend who looked grey and drawn. They dressed and were floated to the ground. They could remember nothing of the incident, which came to light when Scott was given hypnotic regression in 1975. The friend, though located, showed such anxiety during regression that further details could not be obtained. Scott's behaviour caused suspicion and he had been in jail, but the investigators felt that not all of his story could be discounted.

Near Globe in Gila County in Arizona in 1971. One evening a teenage boy working on a large ranch doing a roundup was somehow lost from the rest of the crew and wandered about the area for several days without either water or food. He passed into a semi-conscious twilight between consciousness and unconsciousness. During the time he was in this state he was aware of several little men around him giving him continued help and directions. They were able to lead him out of the range where he finally made it to Globe, a distance of about 50 miles from where he was lost. They did not give him either food or water, but somehow he had strength. He could plainly make the people out and thus he was not sure whether they were "ghosts" or real things. But he did manage to say a few words to them and they responded in turn to him.

1972

In Summer 1972 in daytime in Phoenix (Maricopa), Arizona. While D.G. was working in his leather shop, a man entered; he was of medium height, and his eyes were very strange—a solid yellow with no pupils. He had prominent cheekbones and no hair under his hat, nor eyebrows or lashes. His skin was a milky white, almost translucent. His mouth was wide with thin lips that never moved. He seemed to bring into the shop an icy coldness. He communicated with D.G, telepathically, saying, "Observe and reflect. We will gather. He touched D.G.'s cheek with a long index finger, saying, "The mark will tell." His yellow eyes seemed to emit rays of light that moved over D.G.'s body. D.G. was unable to move, or to reply. The man turned and left the shop and D.G. has the distinct impression that he will return. He does, on Dec. 4, 1975. There is no UFO involvement in this series-of "contacts."

Between Phoenix and Tucson, Arizona one night in October 1972. A man named Ed Foley was driving between Phoenix and Tucson when he encountered a circular UFO and a robot like "figure or object" that emerged from it and hit him with a beam of light. At that point Foley experienced "an alteration of consciousness" as though he had left his physical body. He "mentally" entered the object, and was able to communicate telepathically with the beings on board (not described). The thrust of the information gleaned from these occupants was that they needed "artificial replenishment" of an "essence of life" for their survival. These "juices" they obtained from the simpler forms of life as well as from living animals, excluding man. "They take blood and vital fluids from some glands of various animals… They are not concerned about the flesh and leave it intact," avoiding humans as much as possible in their harvesting of fluid substances. Or this version. At 11.45 pm Ed Foley from Mesa was driving along US10 near Casa Grande when he stopped to relieve himself, shutting off his car lights and engine but leaving the radio on. He heard a high pitched sound on the radio and saw a light in the sky, approaching. As it got closer Ed saw that it was a golden-yellow disc, surmounted by a shallow dome. From the thing's underside came two beams of light, from which emerged things that looked like squat cylinders, a smaller on top of a larger, with antennae from their sides and four legs. As these things descended the noise on the radio increased in pitch and debris under them swirled around. One of the cylinders flashed a beam at Ed and he got a vision of the interior of the disc where humanoid beings were working, and received "information" about their world. The beam then went out and the strange double cylinders disappeared as the disc took off.

1973

On March 21st 1973 at night in Apache Junction in Maricopa and Pinal Counties in Arizona. When Brian Scott returned to the site of his 1971 abduction he reportedly had the impression of having again experienced being taken aboard a UFO by the same 9-foot entities as earlier; this time he also encountered a short, squat being known as "The Host." However, the experience seemed to be "projected" rather than "solid," and the voices of the entities "didn't seem to come from their mouths." He said that on this occasion he found the pair of boots that he'd lost on the earlier encounter.

Around midnight on 23rd June 1973 Roberta T. in Phoenix in Arizona observed what appeared to be a star-like object that descended until it came to a spot just above the trees beyond her patio at which time it appeared to be a large, illuminated spherical object. As it hovered there a square opening appeared on the side facing her like garage doors opening. Illuminated brightly from within she observed a human-like figure approach the opening from one side cross over and then bend down to do something. When she uttered an exclamation to herself he abruptly looked up and out at the witness peering directly at her by leaning out of the opening. He was visible from the knees up and seemed to be wearing a tight garment. He dropped his head down as he looked at her and she could see he was tall with a large head and with hands that appeared to be busy working on instruments. At that point she heard a humming sound and looking off to her left saw a second, smaller object approaching in the same direction. It went past a post and then disappeared. She then looked back toward the first object and found that it had gone. She then fell asleep and when she woke later found herself lying in a different position. Under hypnotic regression she remembered seeing the same figure appear on the patio. She was told not to be afraid and then taken somewhere by being floated upwards. She recalled seeing a dog that had been constantly barking also floating in the air. She was in some dark enclosed space where she couldn't see and an instrument was placed on her head which made her uncomfortable. There were others around her but she felt them rather than seeing them. She had an impression they were talking to each other in a language that she could not understand. When she awoke on the patio it was some four or five hours later.

In late July 1973 at 1.30 am near Wickenburg (Maricopa) in Arizona. Sharon F, recently divorced, was moving from Phoenix to California. Driving West on Route 60 with a trailer, she observed a bright light in the dessert close to the ground that paced her car for about 20 miles in the vicinity of Wickenburg. She grew increasingly uneasy at its presence and, finally, terrified she pulled with much relief into a truck stop where she knew she would find others. The time, as she later recalled under hypnosis, was 3.27 AM. She could not account for a period of 90 minutes. About August 4th 1973 at 11.00 pm near Indio (Riverside County). California. A week or ten days later, she had to return to Phoenix for more things and she asked her brother to go along with her for company. While driving up a hill somewhere in the vicinity of Indio, she began to receive pictures in her mind and had a sense of a presence. These "images" came in greys and browns; she would counter them by thinking of bright colors. She could sense a kind of puzzlement regarding her color images. She found the "gray" images unpleasant, and had the sense of an interior, with gray-green walls, which had three vague "forms" in it. Feeling that she was daydreaming and tired, she forced her concentration back to her driving and noticed colors by reflecting on the dashboard and asked her brother if there was something in the sky. She and her brother both observed briefly a light over the highway changing colors from blue, to green, to red, to yellow, then to a brilliant white. Then it vanished, in view less than a minute. Her brother was very excited. The trip continued, apparently uneventfully. In hypnotic session with the investigators in February 1977, Sharon is asked to examine her image of the gray interior more closely. She describes the gray-green walls, with at least one black line, or slot, on the back wall. She is with three vague shapes or "shadows." It's not a pleasant place; she feels there's another experience at another time. She is asked to go back to that experience (an abduction on her drive from Phoenix, possibly?) and she finds herself in another room with a window looking out on an orange sky. There is a white bench in the room. The room is very sterile. Then she finds herself in a huge place with a domed ceiling; she is standing beside a 20-foot high crystal, set at an angle so that it points toward the sky. It's green on the bottom half, and it turns. There are other similar crystals in this place; about five in all: they are hooked to a large piece of machinery. It's similar to a generator. The crystal is connected to the machine by a rod. The whole room hums. There are two other people with her: one, dressed in grey, looks older, with grayish hair. The younger man, in black, is taller. They point out a formula to her, which is on the wall: it is composed of script letters. She is brought out of the trance and is given the post hypnotic suggestion that she will recall the formula and be able to reproduce it on a piece of drawing paper, which she does.

On October 18th 1973 at night in Yuma Test Center in Yuma County, Arizona. Sgt Thomas Spilde was on patrol just west of HW 95 and north of the Matinez lake road. He was driving up a hill for security check on three trailers when he saw an object approaching from the east. He lost visual contact momentarily but stopped his vehicle and located the object again. The thing was stopped about 450m to the north at eye level. It was oval shaped, much larger than a fighter and was surrounded by bright blue strobe type lights and emitted a swishing sound similar to that made by a rope being twirled through the air. During the three minutes that the thing hovered Thomas was able to hold his radio mike out of the jeep so that the dispatcher could confirm the sound. The object then moved towards a chemical testing area, hovered for a couple of seconds and then headed north and up at high speed. There was a second witness, civilian Saied Joseph.

On October 22nd 1973 in Sun City in Maricopa County, Arizona. Two people saw a blue object hovering over an abandoned house, which caught fire.

Near Mesa in Maricopa County in Arizona during October 1973. One night Ernest Chesser was camping with his family near this city when he reportedly was abducted by tall blond, Nordic-type humanoids. He was given a physical examination and telepathically communicated with a female alien and had sexual relations with her. There were also tall gray-type creatures onboard the craft which seemed to cooperate with the Nordics. No other information.

During December 1973 two men camped on the Reavis Ranch in the Superstition Mountains in Arizona observed a UFO landing and taking off from the Circle-Stone site. They saw green colored individuals disembark. These creatures then got back on board and took off in a giant flash of light. Circle-Stone is near Apache Junction in Maricopa and Pinal Counties. The ruins are not a circular space of standing stones but were possibly used to track astronomical events.

1974

On March 27th 1974 at night in Kingman in Mohave County, Arizona. Two couples driving back to Phoenix from Las Vegas were changing drivers when their attention was caught by a huge silvery platter shaped object, the size of an American football field, with three huge spotlights beaming down, approached, stopped and hovered over their car for 5 minutes. One of the couples was so afraid they started praying. The object had a fiery trail behind it while moving and left a steel-blue haze where it hovered.

1975

On January 13th 1975 at 2025hrs in Childs in Pima County, Arizona. Mrs Kathy Soulages (26) was visiting the home of Mr and Mrs Clarence Hale and went outside to view the sky, whereupon she almost immediately observed a large oblong object, with red white and green lights, rotating clockwise above the mountains to the west, about 1.6km away. She got the Hales, who confirmed the sighting. After 5 minutes, a round red object appeared to emerge from the bottom of the cylinder and began descending towards the mountain, as the cylinder moved out of sight. The disc hovered over a powerline. Then another object emerged from this disc and began to follow the powerlines until it was at ground level on a small island in the middle of the Verde River. The object dimmed and brightened as it came down the mountain, sometimes dimming for minutes at a time. When it reached the island, it emitted two brilliant flashes that lit up the area, and was seen no more. The Hales now went back into their house and Kathy went home. At 2200hrs Kathy went outside to look once more at the mountain, where she observed the red disc take off and hover. She called her husband out and they both observed the thing through binoculars. Kathy then called Mrs Hale, who also saw it. Kathy saw the cylinder again at 0040hrs. She compared the cylinder to a Boeing 747 and a Pullman car; the disc was orange and humped and the third object was a pale orange glow.

On February 26th 1975 at 0200hrs at San Carlos Reservoir in Pinal,Gila and Graham Counties, Arizona. Mr G (45) a cement mixer from Phoenix was sleeping on top of a camper parked on the bank of the reservoir, two companions being asleep inside. He woke up for no apparent reason, to see a strange structure consisting of a number of uprights and cross members, from 10-15cm in width, covering an area about15m wide, 10m high, hovering about 3m from the camper, 1.2m above the ground. The further edge of the thing as at about the edge of the reservoir and the whole thing was moving northward at about 1.5kph. As G got his glasses for a better look, the object started moving eastwards and then north again, so he banged on the camper to arouse his companions. The other men did not see the black object. During the experience G noted that some fibreglass fishing poles were tapping against the fishing boat, which was parked a short distance from the camper, and fish were jumping out of the water in an area from 30m north to 30m south of their location and within 15m of the shore. After 15 minutes G went back to sleep, only to be awoken again at 0305 by a bright light and prickling sensation like an electric shock. The light came from an object 12-15m diameter at 0200 elevation, titled to a 20-30 degree angle. This light was coming from a slit, which opened and closed, on the upper portion of a curved dark structure of a dark object, which was clearly silhouetted against the night sky. G tried to wake his companions but the object had moved away into the distance before he did so. As it left, it came directly overhead and G could see a number of holes with lighted circumferences around the outer edge. The fish were jumping and the poles vibrating again. Or this report. n February 26th at San Carlos Reservoir in Arizona at 2 a.m. Mr. G, 45, a cement mason from Phoenix Arizona, was asleep on top of a camper which was parked on the bank of the San Carlos Reservoir, which is located on the Indian reservation of the same name in southeastern Arizona. Mr. G's two companions were asleep inside of the camper and he was bedded down with a sleeping bag and electric blanket on top of the camper because there was an alcohol-burning heater in the camper which aggravated his respiratory trouble. The temperature was approximately 26 degrees, the sky was clear and there was a full moon. For no apparent reason, at 2 a.m., Mr. G. woke up. He immediately saw a strange structured object hovering about 10 feet away from the camper, four feet off the ground. It consisted of a number of uprights and cross members from 4 to 6 inches in width and the whole thing covered an area of about 50 feet wide and possibly 35 feet high. The further edge of the thing was at about the edge of the reservoir and the whole thing was moving away toward the North at about one mile per hour. Mr. G. reached for and put on his glasses for a better look. The object was still moving but had begun moving in an easterly direction. The object made no noise but Mr. G. has a 35% loss of hearing in both high and low frequencies so there may have been sound which he was unable to detect. Mr. G. banged on the top of the camper to alert his companions, who took some time in getting out. The object continued moving, but headed North again instead of East and was out over the reservoir and headed toward a marshy area where another camper was parked about ¾ mile away. It was almost at the location of the camper when the other men came out but they didn't see it, probably because their eyes had not adjusted, whereas Mr. G. had had it in sight continually. Also, the object, which was black, did not reflect the moon's light and was not very visible by [to] them. During the presence of the object, Mr. G noted that some fiberglass fishing poles were tapping against their fishing boat which was beached a short distance from the camper. Also, fish were jumping out of the water in an area 100 feet North and 100 feet South of their location, and within 50 feet of the shore. The men checked the lines on the poles but there were no fish on them and they could not account for the vibration which caused the tapping. Mr. G. later theorized that it may have been a combination of the sound made by the jumping fish and the vibrating poles which woke him initially. G. finally went back to sleep. The episode had lasted approximately 15 minutes. He woke up again at 3:05 with a bright light full on his face, shining through the blanket which he had pulled up over his face to block out the moonlight and keep him warm. He grabbed his watch, put on his glasses, and checked the time. He felt a prickly, tingly feeling and was shocked at first. Uncovering his head, he located the source of the light. Off to his right "at about 2 o'clock" was an object approximately 40-50 feet in diameter and tilted at a 20-30 degree angle. It had a curved upper structure and the light was coming from a top portion. The light source was a sort of slit which closed, then opened, became dim, and then went out. The object itself was dark and plainly seen against the night sky. At this time, G. was rapping on the camper again to wake his companions. The object began moving, and when directly overhead he could see a number of holes with lighted circumferences arranged around the outer edge. He didn't count them, and kept beating on the camper to awake the others. Before the others gained access to the outside, the object had disappeared into the distance. However, the fish had been jumping and the poles were vibrating all during this sighting also.

On March 9th 1975 at 1945hrs in Alamo Lake in La Paz County, Arizona. Stuart Hill, a young Prescott man was fishing from a remote campsite on the north shore of Alamo Lake when he observed a light rapidly descending towards the lake at a 60-70 degree angle from the southwest. It decelerated and hovered about 9-12m above the water, about 150-200m away. Hill immediately put out his lantern. The object appeared to be at least as long as an American football pitch, and was of a flattened American football shape, surmounted by a dome that emitted very bright white light. At first Hill could only see the lights. Under the white dome were three red rectangular lights, arranged horizontally, which glowed individually in sequence, left to right. Then all three lights came on simultaneously, increasing in intensity. The lights then repeated the sequence, each sequence lasting one second. During the sighting Hill heard a whine like a jet, which increased in intensity and when the object was hovering, Hill heard a humming sound. The dome light went off, the noise stopped, the whole structure glowed an intense orange, which illuminated the ground brighter than daylight for four or five seconds. This then went out, the three red rectangles reappeared and the object shot off into the clouds at 45 degrees. His dog was afraid and ran into the tent.

On March 11th 1975 at 2330hrs in Hell Canyon in Yavapai and Maricopa Counties, Arizona. A 46 year old professional pilot was driving south along US 89 from Ash Fork to Prescott. While crossing the bridge over Hell's Canyon, about 30km south of Ash Fork he noticed red glow and several smaller lights in the canyon to his right. He first thought that it was a railway station but realised that it wasn't and so turned back. Arriving back and looking down he saw three or four dim red lights in the 150m wide, 60m deep canyon. Somewhat unnerved he drove on again towards Prescott. Suddenly a white light emerged from the side tributary canyon, 30m behind and slightly to his right, at a low altitude. . It swept a bright red light back and forth across his car, as he accelerated up to 200kph. The thing followed him for 3km, crossed over to his left and continued to follow him as he passed another car. About 37km from the bridge he slowed to turn right and as he turned, noticed a white light, with a pulsating red light on the front, which followed him down the road for several kilometres until he lost sight of it in a built up area on the northern outskirts of Prescott.

On March 28th 1975 at 2000hrs back in Hell Canyon, Arizona. Miss D M, a young school teacher, was approaching the Hell Canyon Bridge when she 0bserved what she first thought was a fire truck, with very bright red and blue lights, travelling towards her from the right. She then realised that there was no side road. The lights appeared to go under the bridge, reappearing on the left going very fast. They then stopped just east of the bridge, maintaining an inverted L configuration, without changing colour or intensity. There was a vehicle parked in a lot next to the bridge. The witness was frightened and drove rapidly on towards Prescott.

On June 10th 1975 in Arizona. At an unspecified location two brothers were out smashing tin cans for recycling when a circular object with dull dark surface descended and hovered a metre or so away, emitting a humming sound. The boys tried to throw rocks at things, which seemed always to avoid them as it moved back and forth. After about 15 minutes the thing took off over the desert. It returned and took off again three times before it finally departed. Two months later one of the boys was cycling home when this, or similar, object came down close to him and paced him about 30cm from his face. By the time he reached the driveway the object had left.

On August 17th 1975 at 2225hrs in Keams Canyon in Navajo County, Arizona. A 33 year old police officer saw a strange bright light, surrounded by red and green rotating ones. He lost sight of the thing, but after about 3-4 minutes, his car engine, headlights and radio all failed for no apparent reason for 30 seconds.

This next report is a classic UFO case. Near Heber which is eleven miles South of Snowflake in the Sitgreaves National Forest in Navajo County in Arizona on 5th November 1975 Travis Walton and a woodcutting crew were out in the forest. Mike Rogers, 28, the driver, Dwayne Smith, Alan Davis, or Allen Dalis, Kenneth Paterson and John Goulette as well as Dwayne Smith, Kenneth Peterson and Steve Pierce all saw a large luminous object like a hovering luminous disc over the trees. It was a glowing golden light with a milky yellow glow. There was also the whine of machinery. The craft was solid with windows and was fifteen to twenty feet across and shaped like two pie pans placed together with a smaller bowl shape on top. Suddenly

Travis Walton jumped up from the wagon and ran close to the object that was now only one hundred feet away. Walton was bathed in the golden light from the craft. Then a blue ray of light flashed from it and Walton fell to the ground before being thrown back several feet as if having an electric shock and flew back ten feet and hit the rocky ground on his right shoulder. Then Travis vanished. Unknown to the others he was lifted off the ground, his body arched backwards, arms and legs outstretched. The other witnesses fled in the cart back to town and returned with the Police. Travis Walton was gone and there were no signs of him. Five days later Walton appeared ragged and unshaved in a telephone box near Snowflake and claimed that he was abducted by Humanoids from the UFO. They were shorter than five feet tall and had very large bald domed heads with enormous eyes that were almost all brown with barely any white. The mouth and ears were small. They had five fingers and looked frail. The Humanoids had white marshmallow-colored skin on their bodies. They wore loose orange-tannish-brown coveralls with no zippers or buttons. There was also a man dressed in blue coveralls who wore a bubble helmet and was six feet two inches tall. Long hair covered his ears and he weighed 200 pounds. Under hypnosis Walton had found himself after the shock lying on a metal table with severe pains in his head and chest. There were three Humanoids bending over him. They had narrow faces and their hands had five fingers without nails. When Walton was found he also had marks of strange injections in his arms. Here is the larger version. At 6.15 pm Michael Rogers (28) and his six man wood cutting crew (Travis Walton (22), Ken Peterson, John Goulette, Steve Pierce, Allen Dalis (21) and Dwayne Smith) were driving back to Snowflake from their work in the Sitgreaves National Forest about 19km south of Heber, when, as they drove through the trees, Walton and Dalis, who were passengers in the front cab driven by Rogers, noticed a glow among the trees and drew the attention of the men who were smoking in the back to hit. As they reached a small clearing in the wood their attention was drawn to a glowing object hovering about 5-6m above a pile of freshly cut wood, about 30m away. It was an oval object 4.5-6m diameter and 3.5-3m deep. It was a dim amber colour with opaque dividers. It was encircled by a narrow rim, giving it the appearance of two shallow dishes placed rim to rim and was surmounted by a milky white dome. Walton jumped down from the truck and ran towards the machine. At close quarters it resembled a sort of giant light bulb with no surface features, and which was emitting beeping sound. As Walton watched, the object began to wobble on its axis, emitting sounds like those from a generator. The object was observed to project a blue-green light at Walton, hitting him the upper chest, blinding and stunning him, and, according to Peterson, flinging him to the ground stiffly. This panicked the crew into driving out of the area at breakneck speed. As they drove away they saw a light take off at speed to the north-east. They then decided to return to see what had happened to Walton. On arriving at the site they saw some heel marks in the ground but no sign of the man. Searches carried out on the 6th through to 9th found no trace of him and he did not resurface until between 2330 and 2355 on the night of the 11th. Walton could recall awakening in pain and with a metallic taste in his mouth, lying on his back as if on a table, with a luminous rectangle which gave off a soft white glow. He was aroused from his daze by the sight of three creatures, less than 1,5m tall, standing near him. They had huge domed bald heads, with no eyebrows or eyelashes, which gave Walton the feeling that they were huge foetuses. They had large brown eyes and were dressed in loose fitting brown coveralls with caps and facemasks similar to those of surgeons. They appeared to be carrying out some sort of medical examination (Walton in his daze had thought he was in hospital until he saw these creatures clearly). Walton jerked off the table, knocking off a plastic strap and pushed one of the creatures, which seemed oddly soft to the touch and which fell back on one of its fellows. When Walton grabbed a piece of tubing and threatened them with it, the beings backed out of the room. Walton was now able to see that the room was irregular (c. 2m high, with three walls 3.5m long) and of dull, featureless, metallic consistency. The hot, claustrophobic atmosphere forced him into the corridor. He looked in the next room that just had a chair in it and which appeared to darken as he stepped further in. He could see stars all around, either through, or projected on, the walls. As he sat in the chair, playing with some buttons, a dark tanned man about 1.8m tall, dressed in blue overalls with a transparent helmet on his head, entered. This man just smiled at Walton's questions and led him into a bright airy hanger in which there were a number of oval craft. He left him a room, in which there were two men and a woman who "looked like they were from the same family". They had "dirty blond" hair, bright hazel eyes, and wore coveralls but no helmets. They too refused to answer Walton's questions and they led him to a table, where he became hysterical again. They put a mask over his face and he lost consciousness. When he recovered he was on the highway outside of Heber, with the circular craft hovering about 1.2m above the highway. A white light on the underside went out and the object seemed to disappear on the spot.

On December 4th 1975 near Phoenix, Arizona. During the morning, a man in a light blue suit came into the witness's leather shop, wanted merely to know how the witness felt. At 5 P.M., the same man accompanied by a woman entered Doyle Goats' shop. He was "gone over thoroughly with a small object (something like a small hand massager). Then there was contact between the woman and I, sexually. The next set of contacts occurred at some unspecified subsequent time, again first in the morning, with just the man in a blue suit, and again with both man and woman at 3.00 p.m., with sexual contact again with the woman. He was tested with equipment that opened like a briefcase, unfolding three sections, one of which was similar to a "scope" or screen. At one point he felt he was completely "dissected" by this machine. They conversed with him not telepathically, but by "mind linkage." (What's the diff?). He has already been hypnotized, by someone in Phoenix and someone in LA. A magazine article was prepared but he withheld publication because they would not include a solicitation for others to submit their stories. And on and on. They can be quite weird at times but remember that we are dealing with the quite weird to begin with.

1976

At Williams Air Force Base in Mesa in Maricopa County in Arizona. In January 1976 late at night a security guard finishing his rounds encountered a huge brilliant red light hovering above some trees near a construction site. As he approached the site to investigate, he was able to see a large hovering saucer-shaped object with a hump on its center bottom section. It was surrounded by red light. As the witness moved closer to the object, he heard a low whirring sound and it descended and landed on tripod like gear. A stairway-like protrusion descended towards the ground. Then a figure appeared and began to climb down to the ground. The humanoid was described as eight-foot tall, with long dangling arms, a huge torso and two stump-like legs. His face was long and oval shaped and it had two large tear shaped eyes. The witness felt paralyzed as the creature began moving towards him using high loping steps. The witness felt a strong humming inside his skull and smelled an odor resembling rotten eggs. Moments later, on the road behind him a car went by. This apparently caused the creature to walk back and board the object which then lifted off at high speed and disappeared.

At Tucson in Pima County, Arizona, on February 4th 1976. Late at night the witness again woke up to find herself on a now familiar examining table. The room was silvery colored and hazy, illuminated by a white light. The table was in the center of the room, which had two flat walls and one curved wall. One of the walls was completely covered with control consoles and instruments. There were also recessed three-dimensional viewing screens. The beings with her were described as short Grays, with large heads and huge black eyes.

On a late afternoon in April 1976 Frank Ramsey was returning back to the ranch after taking some pictures of the sunset when he felt compelled to walk down the road and past the ranch. Reaching a crossroads he saw a bright white sphere hovering over the area near Loy Butte in Yavapai County in Arizona. The sphere seemed to flash back and forth from different locations at the blink of an eye. It then dimmed and then flew behind a nearby hill. The witness then walked towards the hill and noticed a figure standing on the side of it and waving a light at him. The witness yelled out at the figure and it began walking towards him and the witness then realized that the sphere was on the ground behind the figure. The figure was human-shaped and appeared to be made out of light. The witness attempted to run but apparently blacked out. He woke up later standing on a rock and disoriented. He later had vague memories of being inside the sphere and looking through a port hole at the stars. He also remembered several beings with oversized heads and large almond-shaped eyes. Or this. Frank Ramsey was at a ranch near Loy Butte in the dark after taking photographs of the sunset scene when the surroundings became illuminated. Looking up Frank saw a sphere of light about 9-12m above the ground. The object seemed to blink out and then reappear kilometres away, only to flash and return again, this happened several times. Frank ran back to the ranch but as he did so he saw someone on a hillside flashing a light at him. Thinking it was friends, Frank ran towards the figure but when he got within 30m he realised that his friends were driving back to the ranch in the distance and that the figure was stood next to a sphere in which there was an opening, though which he could see a soft light. The figure was also glowing. Now afraid Frank began to run away but found himself paralysed. Suddenly the object was gone and Frank found himself 2. 5km away with the camera in his hand. As he walked back he had flashes of memory of being inside the sphere and looking out through a window, with short beings with large bald heads with almond shaped eyes and no visible ears.

On June 26th 1976 in Phoenix Arizona. This was D.G.'s third contact (see Summer 1972 and Dec. 4th 1975) and as in the previous experience, there were two visits on the same day.

a.) Sometime during the morning, the same man involved in the Dec 1975 experience returned. The visit was brief and D.G. had the impression that the man wanted to know how he was, and that it was important.

b.) At 1530 the man returned accompanied by the same woman as earlier. D.G. was again led into the back room of the shop. There he was stripped and given a physical examination, at which time his whole body seemed to have been taken apart molecule, by molecule and reassembled in "lines" on a screen like device that looked similar to a brief case when folded up. He also had another sexual contact with the woman, and experienced an "intermingling" of the minds of the aliens, in which all minds are one, etc.. etc.. He felt the same coldness as before. He passed out and when he came to his visitors were gone. It was ten minutes to five.

On July 10th 1976 during the day in Phoenix in Maricopa County, Arizona. A woman sat in the right had rear seat of her parents' car saw a silvery disc hovering about 60m above a vacant lot. The metallic looking thing covered the whole area of the lot. When she drew her family's attention to the thing they thought she was referring to a small plane passing over and when she looked again the object had gone.

In Summer 1976 in Prescott National Forest in Yavapai County, Arizona. A student and his two younger siblings were playing around a campsite when they saw a large metallic looking cigar shaped object hovering 60 feet overhead. The youngsters fled to their mother but when they returned to the spot with her the object had gone.

At Childs in Pima County in Arizona during September 1976. Two witnesses watched a huge cigar-shaped object with gleaming lights inside, descend slowly over the river. A hatch opened and a small disc-shaped object emerged and landed by the river. Several figures were seen to emerge from the object and began to collect rocks and other items from the river. They moved like androids or robots. There was no other information.

Near Kelvin in Pinal County in Arizona around noon in October 1976. Four men digging a turquoise vein in a desert area suddenly noticed what appeared to be the desert floor moving across the sky. It came out of the western sky, and it was silent. The apparently camouflaged object then stopped at about a football field away from the witnesses. It then descended and landed. A ramp came down and two men dressed in normal leisure clothing, (shorts and t-shirts) walked down the ramp, next two women and then three children. The men went back to the object and brought out something resembling a barbeque. The women took out something resembling a cooler, while the men brought out a table and some chairs that appeared metallic. The children brought out some toys while the women appeared to be bringing out some food. One of the men walked over to the witnesses and asked what they were doing. The witness explained that they were searching for turquoise, and the man answered by saying that he would never understand human fascination with rocks, and then he walked away. Soon the group of "visitors" picked everything up, waved at the witnesses and left. Why not? Why not indeed after apparently travelling across the universe. Might as well stop for a snack before you go back.

1977

At 7.30 pm on 10th February 1977 Ms. Lois Stovall saw from her window a luminous object approaching her house from the North. She and her grandmother, Mrs. Alice Buckner, went to the yard for a better view and saw it hovering over some trees less than fifty feet away. It was capsule shaped with the cylindrical axis vertical and transparent on the side facing them with dark vertical bars. Through this could be seen a flame-like light and a human shaped figure all over grey in color that looked puffed up like a balloon with ridges or rings running round the appendages. She could not see any hands or feet. This figure in an inflated suit about four feet tall was standing in a space only barely large enough for him and was in a crouched position. The light was between his feet. Mrs. Buckner walked directly under the object and tried to touch it but it was two feet too high. She could see that there was a window in the head-part of the suit and could barely make out there was some sort of face behind the window. Then the object began to ascend and passed out of sight to the South. Ms. Stovall saw three helicopters with glowing red cabin lights flying very low over the adjacent school grounds. Mrs. Dessie Turner, a neighbor, also saw the object while it hovered and estimated that it was six and a half feet tall and two and a half feet in width. She thought that she could see a shadowy figure inside it. She also saw the helicopters….or were they? This was in Tucson in Arizona. Or this. Lois Stovell sat in her living room couch, when through the window, looking towards the Cavett Elementary School, she saw a light rising to the left of the school, like a plane coming over the horizon. She felt unable to take her eyes off the light, which she found strangely beautiful. It rose and came round the Southwest corner of the school, passing behind two trees to the south, then curved towards her house at below treetop height, descended to just above a bare patch on the school lawn, hovered for a moment, then continued to move again. She then told her grandmother, Mrs Alice Bruckner, who was in the same room, and they both went to the door to get a better look. It came over the school fence and hovered over a small tree in their yard. They approached to within 15m, and the object seemed to come even closer. It was a cylinder with blunt, rounded ends, the top rather more so than the bottom. The side facing them was transparent, and in its lower part was a light like a flame with streamers of red and blue, with a white, but not brilliant mass. This transparent area was divided by dark vertical bars from top to bottom. When right under the craft, Alice raised her arm, but the object was about 60cm out of reach. As she raised her hand, the object rose slightly, changed course . As the object rose, she saw crouched behind the bars, a grey, human shaped figure, about the size of a 6 year old boy, which appeared puffed up like a balloon. Its suit had ridges on its arms and around the waist. No hands, feet or facial features were visible. The figure was crouched with the arms extended as if holding non existent controls. The object was independently observed by her neighbour Mrs Dessie Turner, who had been attracted by a light through her bathroom window. Mrs Turner went to the front door, saw the object, which she estimated to be 1.95m high, 75cm diameter, and the figure. The two women stood watching as the object crossed over the Turner house and disappeared to the south. All three women saw at least three helicopters over the school ground and five or six in the distance while the "capsule" was in sight. No one would admit responsibility for the helicopters.

On February 21st 1977 at 1930hrs in Tucson in Pima County, Arizona. Dorothy Sanders and Trudy Clayton were driving North West of the High School when their attention was drawn to a peculiar silvery airplane moving in a strange jerky fashion, easily visible in the dark sky. It was completely smooth with neither markings nor lights, was cross shaped with wings that were as cylindrical as the fuselage. It kept changing direction, descending from aircraft height to about twice that of the telephone poles, flying backwards and forwards across them. Despite its low altitude it presented only the apparent size of a small plane. When the women rolled down the window and cut the engine, they could hear a faint hum. The women drove on for 15 minutes, but when they returned the thing was still there. They drove off again after 2-3 minutes. When they reached the Sanders house, they saw the same or a similar object at higher altitude. It was also seen by Dorothy's niece, Carolyn Howard and another relative, David Howard. Carolyn stayed out when the others went in. At one point the object suddenly dived earthwards, its wings no longer visible, and appeared larger than the nose of a 747. Carolyn was sure that it would crash, tried to scream but found that she couldn't, and the thing curved up at the last minute. At this pointy she fled inside.

On March 12th 1977 at 1915hrs still in Tucson, Arizona. In charge of her two sisters and brother while her parents were out, Madeline Kerlin (15) went to call her brother Eric (11), who was playing with a neighbour, Tammy Fannin. She noticed a bright light in the North East drew the two boys' attention to it but went indoors after a short while. Eric and Tammy saw the object descending in the west and ran towards it. As they approached, they saw that it was a circular object with bright yellow lights rotating round the rim in a slow anti-clockwise motion (about 2 revs per minute). As the thing moved along, it performed peculiar scooping motions. Twice it tilted at an angle, revealing a small dome, which was the same colour as the rest of the object, on its top. At one point it stopped over the Diversion Channel and the boys tried to reach it but were stopped by the Tucson Motel perimeter fence. They followed it to where the Diversion Channel went under the Benson Highway. The object was now very large and low. Eric kept falling over in the gravel as Tammy walked towards the thing, arms outstretched, but it rose up to 75m, dimming its lights as it crossed the highway and then putting them on again. As it reached aircraft height the lights went out. They had been observing the object for 30 minutes. The children then went inside to watch TV but then heard a sound like a pulsating jet and ran out, with Eric's sister Andrea watching from the door. They now saw an object that reminded Andrea of the top third of a sphere with completely smooth outlines. It was dark grey in colour with reddish orange lights rotating around its underside at about 1 rev per second. It was flying at a 20-30 degree angle, just above the treetops. It was only half the size of the previous object, but much closer. It moved from the east to the North-West and then turned west, passing over the house, just above treetop height at helicopter speed, leaving a short double trail. The first object was estimated to be 7.5-9m in diameter, the second 3.5-6m.

On April 4th 1977 and still in Tucson at 1:30 AM. A 52-year-old woman was watching jackrabbits by moonlight on the Veterans Administration Hospital grounds when she heard a whirring noise and looked up to see a luminous white UFO coming down for a landing. It was ellipsoidal in shape with fuzzy contours, and landed approximately 30 to 40 feet away. The top of the object was a soft luminous pink, and something like a horizontal periscope or boom protruded from the right side. The object was about 40 to 50 feet in diameter and about 20 feet high. The whirring ceased when it landed, but she saw no landing gear. Then a human-like figure, well over six-foot tall with very broad shoulders, walked toward her from the UFO. She had not seen him emerge through a door in the craft. He wore a silvery one-piece uniform that was tight-fitting, like a frogman's wetsuit, and he had on mitten-like gloves. He spoke to her, saying "I am Onleel. I want to talk with you, come with me." She saw only his eyes and no other facial features. The eyes were large and dark. The voice was probably telepathic and it seemed to come from his eyes. She felt compelled to obey. The next thing she remembers she is inside the ship, with no recollection of how she got onboard. Or this. Witness K. O. C, a retired female military officer was out walking when she encountered a landed object and a being about 1.05m tall, which came within 2m, and said its name was "Oneel" and invited her on board to talk. Her next memory was being inside a room with panels, where there were four smaller beings, one of which was at the controls, whom she took to be females. She was then led into a smaller room where he was offered a drink that he declined. The experience lasted an hour. The beings asked her various intimate questions. The next thing she remembered was walking home.

At 3.30 pm on 12th April 1977 in Tucson in Arizona two young girls walking under a highway overpass by a canal were following a path up a hill when they suddenly saw an object hovering over some brush nearby. The craft was dark gray and apparently metallic and shaped like a drum. It had four to six long spider-like legs hanging from its bottom. It then rose slowly and disappeared to the southeast following a curved path. Suddenly from out of the bushes under where the object had been hovering, a thin human-like figure emerged. It had long brown hair and was wearing a blue top and dark pants along with strange looking boots. Behind the thin figure were five similar but shorter beings. The group then walked briskly in single file towards the desert and disappeared from sight in the distance. Or this report. Andrea K (13) and Bridgitt O were walking east up the Tucson Diversion Channel towards the junction with Julian Wash. They were coming up the sloping access road from the bottom to the south side of the wash, when Bridgitt saw, three blocks east, just above the confluence point, a dark grey drum shaped object with 4-6 legs hanging down from its outside edge. It resembled a huge grey spider. It was rising from bushes a 100m or so east of the point. It rose up to 9m then shot off towards the Southeast, in a swift curve, out of sight. The girls described the object's legs as being thin and joined in the middle. The drum was a sort of squaring oval divided by 5-6 vertical divisions. There were no windows or openings of any kind. When it tilted away from them, they noticed a sort of crosshatch pattern on the underside. The legs terminated in roundish pads. Before they could really take in what had happened, they saw, in the clump, a strangely dressed tall thin humanoid figure with long dark brown hair, which gave the impression of being a woman and was dressed in a blue jacket with brown trousers and footgear. Following this person were five identically dressed but smaller figures, who only came up to the shoulders of the first one, who was of normal height. The figures moved quickly out of sight in the direction of Ajo Way and the water detention reservoir. The "woman" stopped and looked back at the smaller figures who caught up with her, The next day the two girls found three sunburst marks in a regular triangular pattern in the soil at the site.

1978

On February 2nd 1978 at 2000hrs in Phoenix in Maricopa County, Arizona. CCM (sex not given) and his/her son Bruce were leaving the house of M's mother, Kay Burlingham, when M saw, about 9-12m from and above 12th Street what looked like two lighted cylindrical bird cages made of thin silver coloured wires, drawn together top and bottom to make fat sausage shapes with rounded ends. The two cages moved around one another as if swinging on a common pole, always the same distance apart from each other and above the ground. At the bottom of each basket was a bright light, which did not light up the surroundings, though it created a glow at the bottom of its cage. Each basket was 3-4.5m high and 1.5-1.8m in diameter, the wires about 13-25mm thick and about 10-15cm apart. The things emitted a soft humming sound. CCM ran back to his/her mother's house, aroused Kay and pointed out the objects, then 45-60m away and rising. The contraption went south out of sight. CCM then re-joined Bruce and they followed the objects south until they went out of sight. Kay had seen a silvery connecting bar linking the two baskets.

On March 6th 1978 at 0400hrs in Florence in Pinal County, Arizona. Elementary school teacher Jerry Ysaaguerre was lining his music students to go into class when one of the children drew his attention to a dark metallic grey flat circular object hovering over some trees a distance away in the southeast. It was titled at 10 degrees towards them, revealing five equally spaced round markings and two lighter straight lines on the underside. The object moved suddenly sideward, stopping again a short distance to its left, where it hovered for five seconds before it moved straight away in a 90 degree change of direction, towards a small dark cloud, where it stopped and hovered again. In a few seconds it started to move again, once more moving smoothly to the left, stopping again for a few more seconds. It then moved straight away and ascended out of sight.

In the middle of March 1978 in Mesa in Maricopa County in Arizona around 2.00 am James Minton was up late reading when he heard a loud humming sound coming from outside. Going out to investigate he was stunned to see a large hovering disc encased in a purple haze hovering very close to the ground. As his fear became curiosity he approached the object. Suddenly close to the object a Humanoid figure began to materialize. It became a man-like figure wearing a brilliant greenish outfit, a wide belt and a pair of tightfitting boots. It stood there and stared at James and appeared to have some type of emblem on its chest and what appeared to be luminous tentacle-like appendages emanating from the top of its head. The Humanoid carried some type of instrument in his hands. After performing several tasks around the object and completely ignoring the witness the strange being disappeared into the purplish haze that surrounded the object seemingly blended into it. The object then rose up and disappeared from sight.

On July 22nd 1978 at 1800hrs in Phoenix in Maricopa County, Arizona. Two men sat out one of their homes heard a sound like thunder and saw a brilliant flash of light. When they looked up they saw two rotating silvery objects that became transformed into dark triangles, one of which lifted a cactus out of the ground and then smoothed over the earth to remove any trace of its presence. Both objects then took off in a flash of light.

Near Phoenix in Maricopa County, in Arizona one afternoon in November 1978 two women traveling back home on a lonely stretch of highway in the desert, noticed a tall hitchhiker standing on the side of the road. They stopped to pick him up. He was described as clean-shaven with long blond hair and brilliant blue eyes and dressed casually. The man greeted them warmly and told them that "they" had been waiting. The witnesses next recalled the vehicle being floated up into an object that was hovering over the desert. Inside, both women were separated and the main witness was suddenly surrounded by several short, large headed humanoids with huge staring eyes and slit like mouths. They spoke to her by using telepathy and told her to lie on a table where she was examined and several samples were taken from her. She was then taken into a large room where there was a prominent window. Then an elderly bearded man wearing a robe entered the room. She conducted a short conversation with the man and next recalled waking up in her car on a lonely desert road with her friend.

Near Scottsdale in Maricopa County in Arizona in 1978. At 7:30 p.m. the witness was driving in a remote area when he suddenly lost control of his vehicle. His car continued on until he came up to the top of a hill and was commanded to stop. He left the car and found himself walking in a valley that was filled with light. He was then ordered to climb a nearby mountain; it took him five hours to reach the top. He did not recall much after that and had one hour of missing time. Later under hypnosis, he recalled that as he was walking in the valley a bright beam of light shone on him. He then saw ten beings dressed in white standing in a circle. The beings were five-foot five inches tall, wearing skintight outfits that covered their faces. Their heads were elongated and they had a large round black lens over the eye area. Their mouths were slit-like and the noses were holes. They had small chests and thin arms. He was then taken onboard an object where he was examined and some robot-like beings cut inside his nose. When the witness was released he saw two hovering objects one larger than the other.

1980

On March 6th 1980 in Warren in Cochise County in Arizona at 1.00 pm a disc hovered over mine tailings in Warren and then flew along the ridge of a mountain. It turned on its edge and flew off to the South. The entire sighting lasted eight minutes.

In the White Tank Mountains in Maricopa County in Arizona at 11.30 pm on June 28th 1980 three witnesses had driven to an isolated mountain area when they all apparently drifted off to sleep. The main witness later awoke in a trance to see three small men wearing helmets and diving suits surrounding their vehicle. All three witnesses then exited the car and were floated over a nearby canal and towards a silvery dome-shaped craft on the ground. As they neared the craft they could see another little man standing on a rim that protruded around the bottom of the object. The little man pointed something resembling a flashlight at the main witness, then a rectangular opening became visible and all three witnesses entered the object. Inside there was a room that appeared to be the main control room filled with buttons and display screens. Five little men staffed this area. The main witness was then taken into another room filled with bright blue lights. Inside this room she met a very tall man whose face was covered with a veil with symbols on it. She was then directed to sit on an L-shaped device after removing her clothing. The tall man communicated with her and apparently performed several tests and examinations on her. The little men later returned her and the other two witnesses to the car.

In Paradise Valley in Maricopa County in Arizona on August 25th 1980. A young man named Russell was driving West on Bell Road the night of the full moon. Russell then saw an orange ball of light coming from the southwest. When it got closer, he could see a domed flying saucer that had three hemispherical appendages on the bottom side of the craft. Russell then lost a short period of time. Later he recalled seeing several humanoid beings that brought him inside the craft; where he sat at a table with a metallic plate positioned in front of him. The aliens used this touch-plate to control the craft; it was evidently their interface to propulsion and navigation, a kind of mental avionics. Only when the alien was in contact with the touch plate would the ship's systems be activated. At one point the domed ceiling darkened, and Russell could see stars projected against the inky ceiling. It appeared that lines connected one star to another, indicating a route traveled by these visitors.

1981

Late at night on May 8th 1981 in Glendale in Maricopa County in Arizona the witness was lying in bed attempting to fall asleep when he noticed three 4-foot tall figures appear at his bedroom door. He was unable to move but noticed that all three entities wore helmets. One of the beings took off his helmet and the witness now realized that they had very pale skins and luminous wrap around eyes. The being communicated with the witness and told him that they were from the "Pleiades" star cluster. The witness suddenly heard a loud buzzing sound in his head, jumped up and noticed that the three beings were gone.

1982

On February 15th 1982 at 2330hrs in Yuma in Yuma county, Arizona. Two military police officers were on patrol on the Cibola Range of the Yuma testing ground when they saw an orange sphere approach from the north and land on top of the radio tower in the centre of Cibola, about 500m away. They stopped for a better look, at which the sphere descended the tower and came towards them. They turned and drove away and as they did so, the sphere, which seemed to be about 30 m diameter, passed overhead and headed off to the middle mountains at speed.

One night in April 1982 in Sedona in Coconino and Yavapai Counties in Arizona Nancy and her daughter were in a camping tent in Fey Canyon. Her baby granddaughter was also with her. That night she saw a lighted disk and a small entity entered the tent and grabbed her arm. All three were abducted. She recalled that the entity spoke "inside her head" and that they were rearranging her molecular structure for the purpose of facilitating communication and travel. She does not recall what happened between the time she left the tent and returned. She has been involved in previous encounters.

In June 1982 at night in Arizona. A young man was following his parents' car on his motorcycle though the Arizona desert when a circular object surrounded by bright white lights began to manoeuvre about 20m above him. He parked up for a better look as the thing moved around making a humming sound. It then just shot off. He continued on his journey at up to 150kph but found he was really late when he met his parents at the next town.

In mid-August 1982 at 0145hrs in Lukachukai in Apache County, Arizona. Two men and the son of one, were travelling to the Rodeo when about 15km out of town they saw a point source of light come out the sky and approach within 30m, at which point it flared and disappeared leaving a circle of haze. 8km down the road they saw a glow in canyon to their left. They were unable to see what it was so they lifted the boy up and he saw that the light came from sort of unusual object on the canyon floor. They were afraid to investigate and after a few minutes drove off.

At 11.15 pm on November 1st 1982 in Phoenix in Maricopa County, Arizona the witness recalled lying naked on a table made out of something resembling leather. He was in a dimly lit room, with a door that opened with a swooshing sound. He saw a four-foot six-inch tall creature, slender, with long thin arms, with six fingers on each hand. It had a large bulbous head with slightly bulging eyes. With other similar beings the witness was apparently examined. The witness could not remember any additional details.

In 1982 in the late afternoon in Maricopa County, Arizona. Don Warwick was walking back from a camping trip along a narrow dirt road and, having gone over a rise, saw a light ahead. He first thought that it was a truck coming towards him, but then realised that it was static. Getting closer he saw that it was an unusual object, around which were dwarfs 1-1.2m tall, with large eyes. Don raised his gun at the creatures, at which they ran back into the object. Don got down from the bank on which he was standing and ran off. The strange object followed him and hovered overhead for 15 seconds before it accelerated away vertically.

1983

At 11.00 pm on June 12th 1983 near Sierra Vista in Cochise County in Arizona during a moving trip, the witness' girlfriend reported seeing a large Humanoid standing by the roadside somewhere West of Texas Canyon on I-10. Shortly after a bright star-like light paced their vehicle. Minutes later the vehicle seemed to "drive itself" with no control by the driver. After turning into Route 90 the witness saw a bright flash of light in the sky to his right. Still later down the road the witness found himself in the driver's seat and his girlfriend in the passenger seat. They then turned off onto a gravel trail to the left in preparation for turning around when he then saw a large disc-shaped craft in front of the vehicle with eight to nine short Humanoids milling around it. Three of them started to approach the vehicle, and the witness remembered nothing else until they appeared to be traveling on the proper highway again. There was a substantial amount of missing time reported.

On September 12th 1983 at night in Phoenix in Maricopa County, Arizona. A trucker and two teenagers saw a luminous sphere descend from the sky, hover and then split into two, which portions girated around each other. They were joined by another truck driver, who also saw the spectacle before the objects took off.

1984

During September 1984 driving South on Hwy 89 a few miles South of Kayenta in Navajo County in Arizona at approx. 60 mph I saw a person dressed in total white that appeared in the middle of the road forty feet in front of me. I skidded to a stop, but not in time to avoid hitting the white person. I checked the area and the vehicle and found nothing. There was bright moon lite so I had a good view of a large area. There was no sound of impact as if I had hit something and left the area. Half a mile later the engine dies and the headlites failed. Interior lites, brake lites, emergency flashers and radio are all dead. I checked the battery with VOM and a flashlite and registered 0 volts. I escorted my family into a safe area off the highway and returned to my vehicle for blankets. The interior lite came on. I checked the battery again and it registered 12 volts, so we continued on. I checked the engine voltage at the next lighted stop and found 14 volts with the engine running. Upon return to Denver I checked the battery, cables, generator, other wiring and found nothing unusual. I considered a main fuse breaking, then in some way shorting itself to regain electrical power but the fuses showed nothing including burn marks, etc.. I had the vehicle for many years after the event and nothing similar happened.

At 9.00 pm on September 4th 1984 at Alamo Lake in La Paz County in Arizona a UFO traveled from land to water chasing and stopping our fishing boat. My brother and I were moonless night fishing. At 9 pm we noticed what looked like a vehicle approaching which immediately got our attention for there wasn't a road on that location on the North side of the lake. We had stopped fishing and had no lights on yet this vehicle was coming straight at us. We see low brush in front of its lights indicating to us it was about three feet off the ground. When it reached the bank opposite the bay we were parked at, it kept right on coming at us. The speed was slow up to this point. We had a great fear come over us and threw our poles, seat cushions and everything we had taken out of our boat to bank fish and started the boat. I was driving at full speed with no lights on and the craft was keeping parallel with me. I thought my brother said something and I slowed, then the motor died. It had never before done this. My brother screamed "What are you doing?" I said it died. Frantically we tried to start the motor while the craft just sat motionless. Its lights did not indicate a wake from our boat had hit it nor did our boat receive a wake from it. We both pulled the lanyard on the motor until we were wore out and out of desperation my brother stood up and with his arm waved it and yelled quit f****** with us. Immediately their lights went out and I pulled the motor and it started. I sped to the opposite shore. We got out and with great fear watched the lake till morning. The lights never reappeared. My greatest regret was when their lights went out. I didn't shine my flashlight at it to see what it was for on a moonless night it's pitch black and when you see lights you can't see what is behind them. My brother and I both agree we believe some outside force put the great amount of fear in us, unlike we ever had before or since. One other aspect we noticed was not time loss, rather just the opposite. We sat watching the lake with lights off for hours, believing the sun should be coming up only to wait hours more. The closest it got to us was approximately 20 yards while on the water.

On October 8th 1984 at 2325hrs in Yarnell in Yavapai County, Arizona. A man was driving his 2 year old son home from a funeral and they had pulled over for a break and were talking about time travel when they saw a small object descend down to 15m. There were two people in the thing, who waved at the witnesses, who waved back. The object then took off out of sight.

1986

On March 7th 1986 in Arizona. At an unspecified location on Hw8, about 110km out of Yuma two navy men saw what they first thought was a radio tower with flashing red lights in the south-east. They then realised that the thing was much closer and smaller than that and was a black cylinder with flashing red lights on either end. The object crossed the road about 6m away and they saw it was 6m tall and 1m diameter. It travelled across the road at 3m altitude and then went down to about 1m. From the black featureless thing there then shone out a sharp beam of light, about 10cm diameter then swept the road. The object moved out over the desert and was lost to sight. If you follow Hwy 8 east for around 110 kilometers you end up near Aztec in Yuma County. If you had gone west you would be in California.

At 11.30 pm in June 1986 in Tucson in Arizona on different occasions the witness awoke with the feeling that some type of evil presence was just outside her bedroom window. It seemed to have complete control over her and the witness was completely unable to move and helpless. She was able to see its shadow on the moonlight against the curtain over the window. It appeared to have a very large cranium, small pointed chin, and skinny neck, thin shoulders and a skinny upper torso.

Near Sedona in Coconino and Yavapai Counties in Arizona on an evening during November 1986 a couple that lived in an isolated area was watching television when they noticed a flashing blue light falling to earth in their property. They thought it was a plane crash and they both rushed to the site. As they neared the place, they came upon a large disc-shaped object on the desert ground. Around the object several small figures with large heads seemed to be collecting ground samples. One of the witnesses uttered a cry that attracted the attention of the little men. The couple then ran as fast as they could and as they attempted to climb above a low hill they were struck in the back by something that knocked them down causing extreme pain. They both lost consciousness. They later came to and found themselves eight miles from where they had originally been before, with no further memory.

Near Mingus Mountain in Yavapai County in Arizona some time in 1986. A motorist passing by the summit of the mountain noticed some bright flashes of light on a side canyon. He stopped and left the car and proceeded to investigate. There he came upon a landed disc-shaped object on the side of the canyon. Three humanoids were walking around the craft. One of the humanoids raised his hand in a gesture of greeting. At this point, the witness ran back to his vehicle and sped away. The disc then followed him briefly, positioning itself in front of him, and then it departed at high speed. Or this? A pilot driving long Hw89a from Sedona to Prescott had his attention caught by flashes in a canyon. On investigating he came across a disc shaped object on the ground. Around it were three humanoid beings who were walking around. They seemed to notice and pilot and one raised his arm in greeting but the pilot raced back to his car and fled the scene. As he drove away the object came down in front of his vehicle several times, as if trying to stop him, before it flew off.

1987

Late at night in Spring 1987 in Sedona in Arizona a man and his wife had gone to visit a local channeler known to be in contact with possible "space entities" but due to some miscommunication the night they went no one was home and the house was totally dark. They then noticed a light at the rear of the house and saw someone moving around. Thinking that everyone was on the patio they decided to walk around the back. As they made their way around to the rear of the house they were stunned to see a line of luminous beings that were apparently descending from the sky in stairway-like fashion. The beings gave off a bright light that illuminated the whole area. The couple ran to their vehicle and left the area.

In the Santa Catalina Mountains in Pima and Pinal Counties in Arizona during July 1987 in the afternoon. Christa Tilton experienced a three-hour missing time period in which later under hypnosis she recalled being dragged into a craft by two small aliens after they had rendered her unconscious. The next thing she remembered was waking up on a table inside some type of small craft. A guide greeted her and gave her something to drink. She believes that it was a stimulant of some kind because she was not sleepy after she drank the substance. The witness was then taken out of the craft and when she looked around she noticed she was standing on top of a hill. It was dark, but she saw a light near a cavern. She walked up to this area and it was then that she saw a man, dressed in a red military type jump suit. Her guide seemed to know this man; he greeted him as they came closer. Tilton also noticed that he wore some type of patch and was carrying an automatic weapon. When they walked into the tunnel, she realized they were going right into the side of a large hill or mountain. There they met with another guard in red and she saw a computerized checkpoint with two cameras on each side. To her left was a large groove where a small transit vehicle which carried people further inside. To her right she saw a long hallway where there were many offices. They took the transit car and went for what seemed to be a very long time to another secure area. She was then told to step onto some type of scale-like device that faced a computer screen. She saw lights flashing and numbers computing and then a card was issued with holes punched into it. It appeared to be some type of ID card. Her guide did not speak much but did tell her that they had just entered Level One of the facility. She was eventually transported to a lower level. There she saw additional armed guards. She was then taken down another hall and there she noticed a horrid smell. She then saw huge tanks with computerized gauges hooked to them and a huge arm-like device that extended from the top of some tubing down into the tanks. In a large laboratory like room she saw a small gray being with his back turned doing something at a computer. She was told to sit on a table in the middle of the room. About this time a human man dressed like a doctor, entered the room. He wore a white lab coat with a badge. The temperature in the room seemed awfully cold. At this point Tilton began to cry and to tremble. She then felt a stabbing pain. She screamed and the human doctor stood next to her and rubbed something over her stomach. The pain immediately subsided. Soon she became drowsy and was apparently returned to the point of the original encounter.

1988

At 1.30 pm on August 14th 1988 in Ruby in Santa Cruz County in Arizona a man by the name of Sam had driven to an isolated area near this location, which is an old abandoned mining town and was engaged in taking pictures of ancient ruins when he suddenly heard a loud swishing sound followed by what resembled a sonic boom. Looking up he saw nothing, thinking it had been a low flying jet. He walked down a dry wash and as he rounded a rock outcropping he saw a short "man" standing a short distance away at the edge of the wash. The figure looked directly at him and the witness quickly snapped a picture of the man, then the figure turned and ran quickly up the brush-covered hill. The witness gave chase but the little man quickly disappeared over the summit. The figure was described as short with light gray skin, large bulging eyes, a small thin mouth, and a rather large hairless head. It had small nostrils and a very long and broad chin. It had a slender build and his fingers appeared slightly longer than average. The skin was very light-grey. The fingers had two joints and there were no fingernails. The clothing looked metallic and was a light lead grey color. It wore a dark metallic loose fitting garment. The witness described the expression on the Humanoid's face as "pleasant."

At 4.00 pm in August 1988 in Cottonwood in Yavapai County in Arizona the witness was sitting outside her home on a metal fold up chair smoking a cigarette when she heard a low thrumming sound that seemed to vibrate above her and inside of her. And then she saw three ships moving towards her in a V formation. As the ships came over her she could see that they were metallic, black and segmented. As the ships hovered directly over her some sort of energy beam was sent down and enveloped her and immobilized her. She then saw two little blue beings beam down. One was on her right and the other on her left. They were very short, blue and she could vaguely see through them. The little beings did not communicate and just stood there looking at the witness who felt total love and compassion coming from them. After about 30 seconds the little blue beings vanished and she felt a distinct change of vibration. The energy around her then disappeared and she was able to move again. She thought of the experience as totally positive.

1989

Also in Sedona Arizona at 3.00 pm on August 10th 1989 the witness was alone at home and was taking a nap when a loud cracking sound suddenly woke her. She felt paralyzed and a strong tingling sensation came over her entire body. She then noticed a small being standing by the head of the bed. The being was 3 ½ feet tall, whitish grey in color and was wearing a tight fitting jumpsuit. It had a large head and large dark eyes. The being then communicated with an unseen entity using a strange almost digital musical sound. It seemed to be relaying information about the witness's well being. The being suddenly was gone and the witness was able to move again. Her muscles were sore and she felt nauseated afterwards.

In Oak Creek Canyon, near Sedona, Arizona in September 1989. One afternoon four women had hiked up to Steamboat Rock to enjoy the beautiful scenic view of the area and as they were trekking down from the summit, two of the women became separated from the other two as they lagged behind. They reached an area of sparse stunted pine growth and noticed a shimmering form beginning to take shape near some trees. As both watched, the finely outlined features of a beautiful young woman with black hair and angelic features came into full view. She made a friendly gesture towards them, smiled warmly, and then vanished.

1990

During March 1990 in Coconino County we were on our way back from Las Vegas Nevada going around 89A over the mountain road of Jacob Lake and the North rim of the Grand Canyon. My aunt thought it would be fun to play in the snow so we pulled over. We were in a type of gorge where the road cuts through the mountains. As we were playing I thought I could hear someone yelling. It was loud because I heard this sound over my cousins' snow fight. I guess my aunt heard the same thing because she had a weird look on her face and as we were ready to leave the area we all heard the second howl. This time it was loud and clear and deep so we high tailed it out of there. My aunt did not want to know what made that noise. I believe the howl I heard was not from the local wildlife. On another occasion there was no noise, but me and my cousin were fishing down Oak Creek Canyon North of Sedona in Arizona when we stumbled across tracks and a nest.

At 3.00 am in July 1990 in Long Canyon near Sedona in Arizona two men camping in the area were returning back to camp when they saw bright blue flashes of light over their vehicle. Moments later a glowing white object with six portholes flew by at high speed. Later one of the men left the camp, going off to sleep alone. He was in his sleeping bag when he heard the sound of a rushing wind that suddenly stopped. He now began hearing footsteps outside his tent. The tent flaps suddenly opened and a strange being looked in at him. The being was described as reptilian in appearance with two huge round piercing eyes. The witness does not remember what happened next and only woke up when his friends arrived at his location. Sedona is one unusual place.

Late one night in October 1990 near Prescott in Yavapai County in Arizona driving through an isolated dirt road a husband and wife experienced trouble with their truck as the radiator apparently overheated. Grabbing a flashlight, the husband stepped outside to inspect the damage. Soon he was surprised to see his wife staring wide eyed, mouth agape, out at the direction of the driver's side window. She was white as a ghost. He asked his wife what was wrong, but she just kept staring. Walking back to the driver's door he looked towards the moonlit meadow. He saw a line of trees and what appeared to be an old brick wall and standing in front of the wall a small translucent white stocky Humanoid form, about 3 feet tall, with tiny round eyes that appeared to be black as the night from the distance. The figure slowly took a step or two towards the couple, its short stubby arms on its side. In a panic state the husband screamed and lost the batteries of his flashlight. At the same time he looked over the moonlit field again just in time to see the short figure scamper around the side of the wall, out of view. He quickly poured some water into the radiator and switched on the truck's ignition, as his wife slammed the hood shut. They stared over the wall again and saw the small, white head of the ghostly entity peering over the top of it. Terrified, they watched the entity's tiny hands grip the top of the wall and hoist himself clean over it, landing on its feet it then began running towards them. At this point the engine of the truck stalled several times before starting. As they drove away the small white Humanoid was only a few feet from the edge of the road—the edge of the other side of the road, thankfully, but close enough that he could see dark empty holes where the eyes would have been, its mouth open in a wide leering grin, revealing a row of small pointed teeth. Its skin seemed to be rolling as it ran towards the truck. As they headed down the road he looked at his rear view mirror and saw the figure, quite a bit back now, turning away from them, walking alongside of the road in the opposite direction. They drove on for about 20 minutes before stopping again.

At Mesa in Maricopa County in Arizona late night in 1990 a 21-year old woman awoke in the night to discover she had half an ear missing. Rising from her blood soaked sheets, she saw what she called a flying reptile with large red oval shaped eyes, winging its way across her lawn. Local police could not find any logical explanation. The previous sightings in this area were of UFOs and Humanoids.

1991

At 2.00 am on February 16th 1991 near Tucson in Arizona the witness suddenly awoke and went outside her home to see a huge metallic cylinder-shaped craft hovering over the area. It had a pink pulsating light on its front and a blue light at the rear. She could also see a large door. She suddenly found herself inside the object where she saw different types of equipment illuminated by a brilliant blue glow. Inside the craft she encountered three types of Humanoids, one was human-like that appeared to be in charge, several small grey Humanoids with pear-shaped heads and huge black oval-shaped eyes, and a third type of being described as tall and reptilian in appearance, with green scaly skin and huge golden-colored eyes.

At 2.00 am in June 1991 near Yuma in Arizona two 18-year old men were driving in an isolated road outside of Yuma when they saw in the desert about a half a mile away a UFO with changing colored lights that moved very quickly around the craft. They pulled over to watch for about 3-5 minutes and started to leave keeping the object in view at all times. Suddenly their next memory was of driving in the exact same place, but at 8.00 am. They were both in a very calm state and did not even talk about what they had seen.

At noon in September 1991 in Sedona in Arizona the witness was alone at home when she suddenly felt very tired and had to lie down in her bed. Moments later she saw a man standing at the end of her bed and the bedroom walls then seemed to dissolve. The man was described as of average height, with slightly slanted eyes and wearing an unusual type of three-piece suit. The witness felt that the being was friendly and felt no fear. Suddenly numerous little beings then appeared all around the taller being. The witness then felt a severe pain on both sides of her groin. She attempted to gain control and asked the taller entity if they were from the "light" side? She received no answer. After much mental struggle the witness was able to command the entities to leave.

One afternoon in September 1991 near Sedona in Arizona a man named Victor was hiking in an isolated canyon when he stumbled upon some white trucks and men in white suits. One flat-bed truck carried a wingless craft on its bed. Victor felt that he was being observed. He had his video camera at the ready and scanned the scene below his position when he thought he heard a noise in the bushes behind him. When he turned to look, he saw a creature peering back at him and then duck out of sight. This creature looked like a typical gray alien. On another hiking expedition into the canyons, he had become lost. He was walking in one place in daylight, then he found himself in an unknown location and it was suddenly night.

In September 1991 in Maricopa County between Baseline Road and South Mountain Park, at the intersection of 16th Street and the canal. My uncles sighting took place at the intersection of the canal and 20th Street. The incidents were about one week apart. One night while driving near a canal, down a road near South Mountain Park in Phoenix, my friend and I saw a large black creature with a burly body walking on all fours or dragging its front limbs like an ape cross the road in front of us. It looked at us with a face similar to a Sasquatch or orangutan and then was lost in the darkness. I was driving a Volkswagen bug and it was as large as my car. I found out through my Grandfather that my Uncle saw something similar to what I saw (At this point I hadn't told anyone what I had seen). I contacted my uncle about his sightings. My uncle is a construction worker who goes to work real early and on two occasions he observed a creature like the one I saw as he drove down a road close to the road that I was on. The creature crossed to the same canal that I was near. The second time my uncle saw the creature he stopped his truck and grabbed his pistol and a light and tried to follow the creature through the orchards that line the roads. He said he couldn't catch up to it but he saw lots of displaced grass where it had passed. My uncle turned back after following it for about 100 yards as it was dark and he was alone.

Between 1991 and 1992 in Maricopa County outside the Metro Phoenix area near Goodyear my best friend and I were big night hiking fanatics, and decided to go to one of our usual hiking locations just outside of the Phoenix area. We picked up two of our friends for company, and away we went. We arrived at our destination somewhere between 9.00 pm to 2:.00 am. We parked our truck near the main road, but far enough into our recreational area where it could not be seen from the road, so no one would think the truck was abandoned. Close to where we parked and bordering the North side of this riparian area is a CAP canal, and bordering the South 3/4 of a mile is a major road. That night we would be hiking through the northern half of it, and cover 2 to 3 miles to the East. We all walked down the canal road and left it after a while, to hike through small trails with sections of dense vegetation. On our way back we returned on the canal road, following it back to the truck. As we were walking, my three friends became very boisterous, reminiscing about old times, and even singing songs. The strange thing about this was that I usually take part in this rowdiness. I instead was walking just behind my friends and was not interacting with them at all. As we were about 3/4 of the way back, I heard a tremendous guttural growl coming from our left (south) from across a field of dry grass. This jolted my senses! I could not believe my ears! I immediately stopped in my tracks, and knew the closest thing to this sound would be an African Lion, and yet we were not in the Serengeti. I jerked my head left, and at the same time slowed down the cadence of my steps. What I saw sent shivers up and down my spine! There were trees and heavy foliage at the opposite side of the field. In the middle of this grove stood the tallest and fullest of all the trees. It was this tree that was being violently shaken, all the while hearing this lion type growl. Now my senses were telling me this was something bigger than a bear, but as strong as a rhino. I completely stopped walking, turned to face the direction of the tree, and reached down my leg to undo the safety catch on my bowie knife sheath. I became fixated on the tree until it stopped shaking. I immediately crouched down on the hard packed dirt road and began surveying the whole area. After what could only be a minute or two, two short dark bi-pedal creatures ran from under the tree's low hanging branches towards me. They were 3 ½ to 4 feet tall, husky build, with long hanging arms, and had a dark furry-looking outline. They ran straight toward me crossing the dry grassy field, and crouched down about half way across. They ran extremely fast and seemed to almost float across the grass, with no apparent head bob. Incredibly, there was little or no noise coming from them tromping down on dry grass. Since I regularly tracked rabbit and javelina at night, I was able to see and hear with extraordinary skill. At this point I had tunnel sight and hearing. I blocked out all of my friends noisy antics. I spent thirty seconds to one minute watching the creatures staring back at me. I was getting very paranoid, so slowly I got up and made a number of steps to my right, while keeping my head and eyes pointed toward them. I then felt comfortable enough to turn my whole body toward the direction of my friends and start walking. I had to keep my eyes on the creatures. They stood very still. So I started jogging away, looking over my shoulder frequently. At this point I noticed how far ahead my friends were, and totally oblivious to what had just happened. When I caught up to them, I stopped them and told them what had happened. They thought I was joking, which I was not. As I was trying to convince them, I kept looking over my shoulder to see if there was any more activity. My friends finally took my pleas to heart seeing I was afraid, and asked what we should do. I told them that we should slowly jog to the truck and leave. We stopped occasionally to look back, but did not see anything. After this night my friends always believed that this was a story cooked up by me to make the hike more interesting. I had stayed away from hiking in this area for a few months, then decided to go back a couple of times, only never to return again. My feelings are the same as they were then, that to go back would certainly put me and anyone else with me at a high risk of danger. There were a few brush fires in the surrounding areas the last couple years, which may have caused the creatures to. If they are totally gone, they would have left through the Indian Reservation, and on to parts of Southern Arizona. It was at night in the spring or fall season. The temperatures were mild, not hot or cold. The moon was in a phase where we could see the terrain enough, where flashlights did not need to be used very often. This is a riparian area with plenty of food and water. There is constant water run-off from the Central Arizona Canal that feeds the dry Gila River

Creek Bed. There are also a few water retention areas close by. There are dense sections of tree growth, due to the large amounts of water in the area; making good cover for these desert inhabitants. There are plenty of snakes, rabbits, owls, hawks, coyotes, and javalina to feed upon as well.

1992

At 11.00 pm in April 1992 in East Tucson in Arizona Byron T Weeks and his ex-wife were watching television when his wife noticed some lights in the window. Weeks walked over to the window and pulled aside the lace curtain for a better look. There were lights at the top of the window looking down and through the window, focused on the pair. The lights were arranged on an arc, with two yellow lights centrally and then a red and a blue light on each side, like a tilted half circle. Seconds later the lights righted to a horizontal alignment and went straight up without a sound. A couple of days later they both saw a saucer-shaped craft about 40 feet in diameter at dusk. It reflected like a mirror and had antenna like pipes sticking out of the pillbox thing on the top. It flew silently down their street a few feet off the ground. A few days after that Mr. Weeks had gone to bed in an upstairs bedroom and was fast asleep. Sometime during the night he was awakened. It felt like coming out of general anesthesia. He was lying on his back in a room filled with a bright moonlight level of illumination. He was able to breathe normally but otherwise seemed to be paralyzed. Standing around the "bed" were seven faintly luminescent beings. They seemed to all be dressed in white caftan-like robes. They were about 5-½ feet tall, and were stocky in build. He could see no hair on their heads, and the eyes were large and dark, and perfectly round. The foreheads were prominent and bulbous. The head in general was large and the face was broad with a square chin. He could see no whites to the eyes. No ears were visible, but a small mouth and nose were discernible. They seemed somehow "Buddha" like. They made no sound, but it seemed that they were reading his mind. Weeks had the distinct impression that he was being rapidly fed telepathic information. After what seemed to be a few minutes, his consciousness just "winked out." He awoke normally the next morning. For some reason the witness felt that the beings were from some Galactic Federation, to which Planet Earth does not yet belong.

Late at night in July 1992 in Sedona in Arizona the witness, a well-known local psychic, professional artist, and channel was suddenly awakened by voices talking in her bedroom. Looking up she saw several beautiful man-like figures wearing white sparkling uniforms standing at the foot of her bed. The figures had blue upside-down triangle insignias on the breast area of their uniforms. Another figure with flowing blond hair and wearing a two-piece uniform with gold braided epaulets and a large gold triangular emblem on his chest appeared to be the leader. A sort of spotlight shone on him and he smiled at the witness. He reassured her and a peaceful feeling came over her. The next day she was also visited by numerous entities including a blond young woman wearing a shiny white uniform with a golden upside-down triangular insignia on her breast area.

In Scottsdale Arizona late one night in Summer 1992. A woman was checking on her husband in the bedroom when she saw two to three short grey skinned humanoids with large heads and black oval-shaped eyes that were apparently injecting or extracting some type of fluid from her husband's head. He appeared to be sleeping. The woman was unable to move as the beings then entered her seven-year old son's bedroom and repeated the same procedure apparently using a long needle-like instrument. Are these illusions or dreams or visions of another reality?

During August 1992 in Maricopa County North of a farm on the North side of Watermelon Road, that ended where the river bed starts near Gila Bend, my sister and her friend had gone horseback riding down to the river bottom just North of the farm we lived on. I decided to ride out and meet them, so I took out one of our real gentle horses that never got excited and jumped on him bareback. My parents' two dogs (rottweilers) were with me. When I got to the North end of the farm I had to turn West and ride parallel with the Gila River. There was a barbed wire fence between me and the river bottom. The other side of the fence was overgrown with salt cedar trees. There was a cement ditch on the other side of the road which led to a big sump full of farm runoff water. When we got close to an opening in the fence, the two dogs started sniffing the air and acted a little excited and the horse was getting real antsy. I thought they could smell the other horses and I was close to them. All of a sudden the horse just stopped and started trying to rear up and when I looked around the dogs were gone. They had started running through the field back toward my parents' house. I heard something and looked at the trees and standing behind a tree looking straight at me was what I thought was a gorilla. Then it stepped from behind the tree in full view. It was very tall because the fence didn't even reach the top of its leg, and it was covered from head to toe in long brown hair that was all matted and had salt cedar branches tangled in it. It just stood there looking at me with a curious look on its face. I held the horse as long as I could hold him and just stared back trying to comprehend what I was seeing. I was riding bareback and knew I couldn't stay on much longer if I didn't get away. I let the horse take off running to get to the road leading back to the house. We had to run about a quarter of mile along the river and this horse was in a full out run, yet this thing seemed to be staying with us through the salt cedars. It was running on two legs along the fence just inside the trees with us. When I turned on the road toward the house I looked back and it was just standing there. I ran all the way home and told my dad and brother who laughed at me and told me I was just seeing things. They did however drive down to the river bottom looking for my sister and her friend. They didn't see or find anything as far as what I had seen. My sister and her friend said when they were coming out of the river their horses were acting scared but they didn't see anything. A few years later, my dad and my uncle had found a strange set of large bare foot tracks with what appeared to have claws in the mud near the same location. My dad and uncle found strange tracks which appeared to be large primate type with claws a few years later. I was told a few years later that two kids went to the river and went back to town scared and told their parents that a gorilla had chased them in the river bottom. I didn't know them and I had never told anyone other than my family about what I had seen because they laughed at me and I never wanted to be teased about it. I still prefer to stay anonymous. It was late afternoon, or early evening before sun set. What has this to do with UFOs? Who knows but this is one weird area.

1993

Near Casa Grande in Pinal County in Arizona one night in November 1993. The witness encountered some strange beings under an obscure overpass along state Road I-19. At one point a yellowish skinned short entity quivered with an expression of surprise or irritation. The being had a large pear-shaped head and huge dark oval shaped eyes.

1994

One night in May 1994 in Sedona in Arizona a local man reported being taken on board a spacecraft. He remembered seeing several Humanoids with large black almond-shaped eyes and large heads. Something was apparently done to his knees and temples, possibly implants.

Late at night in May 1994 near Flagstaff in Coconino County in Arizona a couple was camping in an isolated pine forest. During the very chilly night they built a campfire but for some unknown reason the fire kept failing. The woman felt uneasy and scared for no apparent reason. As the temperature dropped they sat in the car. Shortly thereafter the woman saw a bright star-like object above the tree line. The light moved from side to side and up and down. After about 20 minutes they looked to the West and saw five more similar lights above the tree line. These appeared to be balls of light that danced around very quickly. As they watched the balls of light the original light descended down behind the tree line. While observing the lights a multi-colored craft came out of the distant northwest sky. It flew at incredible speed and quickly out of sight. Increasingly scared both witnesses prayed. Soon the lights from the sky were gone but an oblong bright white light illuminated the forest floor. Both then took a shotgun and a pistol and settled in the tent. Soon they heard what seemed to be persons walking outside. They sat and listened to what sounded like six to ten people walking around in every direction with an occasional tap or prod to the tent. After an hour a sound came over the tent while simultaneously the ground under the tent floor moved like waves of energy. The wife then looked up through the screened roof and saw a bright ball of white blue light in the sky, just about the tree line. From this light came a large white colored beam of light shining into the tent. The number of "persons" or creatures outside the tent increased, sounding like 30 to 40 of them. Occasionally they heard a sound like whipping wind, along with what sounded like a yipping barking noise that gave them the creeps. At one point a pulsating orange white blue light glowed right next to the tent on the forest floor. It grew larger in size then just disappeared. At daybreak both left the tent and found strange footprints in the dirt and handprints on the dust of the car. The footprints "were toed cloven hoofs" and larger three toed feet. The four-fingered handprints had a skeletal, very long thin look. Frightened they left the area. Their families did not believe their story and they were told that they were "possessed".

In Yuma in Yuma County in Arizona at 1.00 am on September 20th 1994 a young man suddenly woke up to a bright light shining in his face and several figures standing around his bed. He then found himself in a large round, cold, seamless metallic grey room with a reddish tint. He was sitting on a bench next to a blond woman and a man with tattoos that appeared incoherent. He saw tables and cows in the room and beings that seemed to be removing things from the cows. He saw two types of beings. Large ones who seemed to be in charge, these were described as lizard-like, very muscular, with almond-shaped black eyes with yellow slits in them. They also had several smile-shaped parallel ridges on their faces. The smaller beings, who were the ones working with the cows wore some type of helmet. Moments later he found himself on one of the tables. The next moment he was back in bed sweating.

1995

In Arizona, exact location not given late at night in 1995. A humanoid female being leaning over the bed awakened Elizabeth London at night. It was apparently giving her an injection on her left arm. When she asked the humanoid what she was doing, she was told telepathically that when she had come to visit them last time she had brought germs indigenous to Earth. Soon she was rendered unconscious, and then she found herself in a medical facility with a contraption on her head that resembled a beekeepers hat. It was metallic on top with a very lightweight metallic mesh covering her face and neck. Somewhere in another room, she was being monitored as to the chemical analysis of oxygen as it was exhaled from her lungs through the metallic mesh of the "hat". She attempted to remove the hat but the female being came through the door of the room, and told her she must keep the hat on until her lungs were regulated.

Meanwhile back in Sedona, Arizona. During 1995 late at night a middle-aged couple, William and Rose Shelhart were driving outside of Sedona when they spotted a bright light in the sky following them. It soon became apparent that the light was playing a game of cat and mouse with them as it chased them down the road and eventually landed in a field next to them. That was the last thing they consciously remembered. Their next memory was arriving at a hotel in Sedona, several hours too late. Realizing they had missing time, they later sought out a hypnotist and recalled an incredible onboard UFO experience. They recalled being taken on board the craft and examined by nearly human looking uniformed extraterrestrials. While William's recall was negligible, Rose was able to recall most of what happened, including an actual conversation that she had with the aliens. According to Rose, they were invited onboard and treated with kindness and respect. "They were just saying that they were here to help us. They told me that William was in another room receiving additional messages." Rose asked where they came from. The aliens gave a typically enigmatic and evasive answer, replying, "We are from a place you don't know about yet." When asked about their purpose for coming here, their response was decidedly positive. "They said they are helping certain people here because they will help humanity." Rose was unable to obtain any further useful information. She and her husband continue to have sightings and encounters, and William reports that he was healed of carpal tunnel syndrome as a result of his interaction with the aliens.

1996

In Chandler in Maricopa County in Arizona late in the night of January 28th 1996. A woman reported a visitation by undescribed "aliens" into her bedroom, which apparently examined her. The next morning she awoke with bizarre scars & other anomalies on her body. Are these illusions?

In Tonto Hills near Cave Creek in Maricopa County in Arizona on April 16th 1996. A couple that had observed a large diamond shaped craft land in the same area back in February, observed a large craft landing nearby. It was white, diamond shaped, and had green and red lights around it. Three entities (not described) walked around it as if searching for something. The sighting lasted for 15 minutes.

At 3.30 am on May 1st 1996 in Tucson in Pima County in Arizona hours after hearing strange noises coming from outside the window, a 7-year old body was sleeping when a creature jumped into his bedroom through the open window and climbed on top of his chest. He described the creature as having large reddish eyes, a wrinkled face, and large pointy ears.

At 10.30 pm on June 4th 1996. in rural Apache County several people were staying at a rural home near Concho and were sitting around the kitchen table when one of the men looked out the kitchen table and saw along with another woman a bright UFO streak by, apparently crashing. The witnesses said that the object left a wake of fire. They jumped into a jeep and raced off in search for the crashed object. They crossed State Highway 61 and drove along an old cattle trail and soon came upon an elderly couple that had parked their white van on the side of the road and both of them were outside staring into the fields. They asked the witnesses if they had seen a UFO crash and they told them they were going to try to find them. The elderly couple had been driving westerly along Highway 61 toward Show Low in Navajo County when they saw the object streak by and appear to crash. The witnesses then drove to the area where the object had apparently crashed. This area had few trees, some scattered cedar and junipers and a lot of rock and canyons. After about an hour of driving they arrived at a very deep canyon and could drive no further. Deep in this canyon was the crashed UFO. It was an oblong, egg shaped object. The color was strange—it was the color of Caucasian skin with a fading tan and it faintly glowed. The glow was sufficiently enough to illuminate the bottom of the canyon. There were two "pillars" (for lack of a better word) at the front of the object. These pillars may have been posted on either side of a door—although a doorway was not visible. It was about the size of a barn. Oddly the witnesses also saw a helicopter on the scene and a black pick up. They were baffled as to how the truck could have gotten down the remote canyon so quickly, unless there was some road that they did know about. They watched the scene for a while then left. Apparently none of the witnesses ever returned to the site of the alleged crash.

Near Kingman in Arizona late at night in July 1996 John Wright was asleep in his second story bedroom when he heard a number of loud crashing sounds from a lot across the street. Because coyotes and the local youth both liked to enter the unfinished houses at night, John assumed it to be common trouble of one type or another. He immediately grabbed his mag light and narrowed a beam over at the location. As he panned over the front of the houses, a pair of red glowing eyes looking directly at him startled him. Assuming it was a coyote John threw his clothes on and armed himself with a 30-06 deer rifle and proceeded to investigate. As he approached the house, he heard a strange mechanical whirling sound, almost like a servomechanism of some kind, only much louder than he had ever heard before. He approached the house and leveled his rifle at the house when a large mechanical robot of some kind came barreling out. The thing was roughly human in size and proportion, but had a large, domed head and flailing mechanical arms, the joints of which appeared to be servomechanisms. Startled, John fired his gun at the machination but didn't think he hit it. He did not wait around to find out either. He ran to his house and locked the door. John reloaded his rifle, broke out his shotgun and pistol, and barricaded himself in his study. Ten minutes later he heard a car drive up. It was the local sheriff, who came to investigate the shot John had fired. John explained the encounter to a shocked sheriff who then went with John over to the house. Something had indeed rummaged through the empty house. Construction material was strewn about everywhere and someone or something had drilled many equally sized holes in the wooded planks used to construct the roof.

At 3.00 am in November 1996 in Tucson in Arizona for a month the witness, Elizabeth Wall, had been seeing dancing lights just outside her home. She would be compelled to look outside and also had the feeling of being watched. The night in question she was suddenly wide awake and was unable to move. The whole room was filled with a whitish-bluish light and she saw a tall hooded figure walk across the window in her room. At first she was frightened but then felt calm and she then apparently went to sleep. Her roommate saw a similar figure hovering over his bed that same night.

1997

At 1.10 am on March 14th 1997 about 18 miles southwest of Tucson in Arizona I was a 42 year old electronics engineer who operated a small home business, doing contract jobs for various clients. I had lived in Tucson for some time, and felt that the city was too noisy for me to concentrate on my work. I wanted to live in a quiet rural area where I would not be disturbed, and in 1996 I purchased a house in a sparsely populated area southwest of town. I had a neighbor across the road from me and there was an unoccupied house further to the North. My property extended about 100 feet from the front of the house, and then there was a barbed wire fence. It had 5 wires, the top one being about 4 feet high. It was usually quite dark at night out there, however I had installed some floodlights on the front of the house, which I could turn on if needed. I went to bed around 10 PM, March 13th and was sleeping soundly when the event began. I was awakened around 1:10 AM on March 14th by the sound of someone attempting to open the bedroom window, about 6 feet away from me. The sound was like nails on a blackboard. The window was on the front of the house and consisted of double-pane glass with track-locks on it, and a set of blinds which were closed. Although I could not see who was trying to get in, I had a profound feeling of being in mortal danger. It was as if whoever was outside meant to do something terrible to me. I've always had a good sensitivity to the feelings of people and animals and I was confident that what I felt was genuine. As quickly as I could, I rolled out of bed, away from the direction of the window, and grabbed a 12 gauge shotgun from the closet. At this time my emotions changed from fear to intense anger and a strong determination to kill the attempted intruder if he got in. I pumped a shell into the chamber, which made an audible noise, then ran to the living room window, which was only about 10 feet from the bedroom window, also on the front of the house. That was where the switch for the floodlights was located. I hit the switch, and was totally shocked when I saw this thing, which was now moving away from the house towards the fence. I got a pretty good look at the back of it, for about 5 seconds. It was definitely not human. It was about 6-7 feet tall and had a large head, similar in shape to a football helmet. It was very thin and the arms were quite long. It wasn't exactly running, but it was moving smoothly and very quickly. It reached the fence in just a few seconds, and then, without slowing down, it jumped right over the fence like a hurdle jumper in the Olympics, and kept on going. It continued down to the wooded area where the unoccupied house was, and within about 30 seconds I saw a disc-shaped object rise up from there, and move off towards the South. It was about 40 feet in diameter and passed by the front of my house at a distance of about 130 feet, about 60 feet above the ground. It had steady yellow-reddish lights on the bottom of it and made no sound that I could hear. My state of mind collapsed into total shock and an overwhelming feeling of fear. All I could think of was what might happen if it came back. I spent the rest of the night virtually paralyzed with fear, hiding behind a couch in the living room, clutching the shotgun. When the sun began to come up, I started to regain some of my senses. I carefully went outside and looked around. Everything seemed normal, except that by my bedroom window I found some footprints. There hadn't been much rain and the ground was rather hard, but a few of the impressions were fairly clear. The prints were about 10-11 inches in length, very thin, and with 3 large toes. I should have photographed them, but at the time my only concern was my own safety, and I decided to go to a hardware store and get some bolt locks to secure the doors. This I did, and on the way back I stopped at a small cafe a few miles from my house, to pick up some coffee and breakfast. I entered the cafe, ordered some food, and then noticed that a casual friend of mine was there. He lived in a trailer a few miles to the South of me. When I saw him I simply said "Man, something really weird happened last night" and he replied "you're not kidding… a UFO came up the canyon". I was startled to hear that, and asked him "What time?" and he replied "About a quarter past 1.00". When he said that I panicked and left the cafe without even taking my coffee or food. (Some months later I actually tried to find him, to ask him for some details, but I was told he had left the area back in March) Anyway, I returned to the house and installed the locks on the doors. The following day I went into town and purchased a bunch of heavy plywood and boarded up every window in the house. I didn't have a television and didn't happen to catch any reports about the so-called "Phoenix lights" until several years later. As to reporting the incident I considered it but was doing some military contract jobs and was afraid that I might be typed as a lunatic or a security risk and lose my clearance. In addition I simply had no desire to talk about it. The whole thing was just too disturbing. Eventually I moved away from that area, and although it's been a number of years since it happened, I'm only recently feeling able to talk about it.

In a desert location in Arizona during November, 1997. 22-year old Duane Berger and a friend Mark were camping in an isolated area, and as daylight faded, they had built a campfire and were sitting around eating. Soon they began to hear "terrible screams" that seemed to be coming from an old mine nearby. After a few moments of nervous discussions and assessment of the very eerie situation, the two young men decided to investigate the matter. Armed with a tire iron the two friends entered the mineshaft. They had walked a dozen yards when they saw a greenish glow ahead of them. As they got closer they could make out the dark figures of two men in hooded robes. It was clear that they intended to block their progress farther into the mine. But as the two young men drew nearer to the light, they noticed that the two figures were barely five feet in height. They then boldly demanded that the hooded figures release the women or whoever they were hurting. Then a deep, mechanical voice boomed out of the hooded figures in unison and told them, "The women are beyond your help! Leave at once or perish! Leave at once, or you shall join them in the caves." The robed figures then produced some type of wand-like instruments and directed a yellow light at the two young men that held them both immobile. Next, they aimed a greenish beam against a wall of the mineshaft. The wall of solid rock seemed to melt away, allowing them to walk into the wall and disappear. Within seconds, the wall was once again nothing but hard rock. After a few moments the two men were able to move again and fled the area quickly, knowing that there was nothing they could do to help whoever was being detained in the caves. This is not our only rock wall door reported in North America either.

At 6.30 am in December 1997 in Tempe in Maricopa County in Arizona the witness, who had been sleeping in her car waiting for her school to open suddenly woke up and looked out to see something resembling a black car but she thought nothing of it and went back to sleep. A few minutes later she woke up again and glanced towards the driver window. There she saw a 4 to 5 foot tall dark figure. She attempted to reach for a hidden knife but was unable to move. Her body felt numb but she was not afraid. A few minutes later she was able to move but the figure was gone. She has also reported encounters with a cloud like silvery being that turns into billions of white shiny particles and dissipates into nothing upon being seen.

1999

Late in the evening of October 13th 1999 near Phoenix in Arizona a father and son were hunting grouse in an abandoned field when they saw a bizarre looking craft hovering nearby. It was shaped like a barrel with bright red and green lights that flashed in a rapid circular pattern. It never touched the ground but it hovered about a foot over it. A door opened and a being dressed in bright yellow proceeded to use some kind of device that emitted several flashes of light towards the witnesses. Both could see a strange marking on the craft that resembled that of a rooster or a type of bird. The son wanted to shoot at the craft but the father convinced him otherwise. They watched the craft and Humanoid for almost an hour when finally the door closed. Soon they heard a loud noise similar to a vacuum cleaner and the craft lifted up approximately 150 feet into the air. It then flew straight ahead and disappeared over the horizon.

Arkansas

1847

Around mid-afternoon on 8th December 1847, at Forest Hill, Hempstead County, Arkansas, the sky suddenly clouded over as black as night. The black clouds were lit from above by a red flare. Suddenly a loud explosion shook houses and rang the bell in the church tower as a barrel-sized flaming body crashed to Earth just outside of the town. The impact made a hole eight feet deep by two feet in diameter and the bottom of the hole smelt of sulphur and was hot enough to boil water thrown in on it. Within twenty minutes the sky was clear again. It seemed that it was only sulphur in the bottom of the cylindrical hole. Sulphur, especially in commercial quantities, does not do low flying orbits of the Earth. Nor does it explode before it hits the ground! Nor do clouds gather during meteor showers even if they were made of sulphurous compounds. Maybe the sulphur came from somewhere else and required a Hell of a lot of heat to accomplish this? Otherwise it would have burnt up completely in entry through our atmosphere. If the large mass was all that was left after conventional entry then the sulphur mass must have been several tons in weight before it entered our atmosphere. And that is even more improbable. But it is not the first time that sulphur has been recorded to fall. Sulphur had already fallen in the Orkneys in 1818 and Allport, England, in 1827. So few reports and yet we have precedents emanating from them. Sulphur was always associated with Hell. Or the entrance to Hell. Is Hell a lot closer than we think?

1886

At 3.17pm on 27th March 1886 a farmwife was cooking the noon meal at Cabin Creek in Johnson County in Arkansas when she heard an overwhelming roaring noise in the air above her. The house shook. The witness ran outside in time to see the tops of several pine trees flying through the air as if they had just been lopped off. In fact they had been shorn off by a 107 pound iron meteor that had just landed in a field. The trajectory though was unusually low for a normal meteor which is usually vertical. This one had come in sideways. A lot of our phenomena tend to come in sideways at times. This particular meteorite was seen and heard by people in Crawford, Franklin, Johnson, Pope, Logan and Yell Counties on both sides of the Arkansas River.

1897
At 1.00 am on 21st April 1897, ex-Senator Harris of Harrisburg, Poinsett County, Arkansas, heard a strange noise. On going outside to investigate he saw an airship landing on his property and was met by the airship's occupants who were taking on a supply of fresh water. There were two young men, a woman and an elderly man on board. The elderly man talked of an invention developed by an uncle who died 26 years before and that the group had a Hotchkiss Gun on board and planned to go to Cuba. They offered Mr. Harris a ride but he declined. The elderly one also mentioned other technical things as well. The third of our travellings to Cuba in 1897 in the United States or a giant red herring. We never received reports of airships over Cuba though. Maybe they got lost. We certainly were getting prominent witnesses lately but were they actually reliable?

At 6.00 pm on 22nd April 1897 Captain James Hooton was the railroad conductor on the "Iron Mountain Railroad" near Homan near Texarkana in Miller County in Arkansas. Mr. Hooton was out hunting when he heard a sound like a locomotive when there should have been none nearby. He saw an airship land in a clearing. There was a medium-size man on board. The man was wearing sunglasses and tinkering. The witness was dumbfounded as the hominoid spoke to him saying "Good day, Sir. Good day". Hooton replied "Is this the Airship?" The hominoid replied "Yes, Sir". Three or four other hominoids then appeared out of the keel and Hooton saw that the keel was in two parts. The front was like a knife-edge and the side of the ship bulged towards the middle. Three large wheels were along each side. They became concave as they moved forwards and to Hooton sounded like Westinghouse airbrakes. Hooton was told that the craft was propelled by the use of condensed air and airplanes as the craft's party vanished below. A two inch tube began to spurt air and the three large wheels commenced revolving. The ship rose with a hissing sound and the airplanes suddenly sprang forwards turning the sharp end of the craft skywards. The ship veered from side to side and the sidewheels revolved so fast that one could barely see the blades. The craft rose into the sky and vanished out of sight. If we tried to build a craft on these specifications it would not fly. It is as if the phenomena are trying to appear as normal as possible but are strangely subject to misinterpretation in the design stage as they are never quite right or correct for their period. Remember that this is 1897. There are no airships around let alone monsters the size of those reported. There is obviously another origin. Even if it is to explain the variety of craft around. The first possible explanation is that the craft are not from very far away at all as there would be too high a cost in sending a myriad of varied craft across the far reaches, or even the near reaches of Space. Any fuel and construction costs would be high irrespective of what type of economic system was in existence. It is cheaper to send one or two craft possibly with the purported ability to disguise themselves. If this is the case then it would not matter what the craft were described as it would be all camouflage, the real shape of the craft, if they are craft, always hidden as would be the real appearance of the pilots, possibly even all of our phenomena. It is all smoke and mirrors? Or is it? We have different groups of pilots all indicating different origins. Why was the Earth then, if we allow for the Interstellar theory to exist, so popular in 1896-1897? There was a massive airship flap that started on the West Coast in late 1896 and ended in late 1897.

On 22nd April 1897, Judge Lawrence A. Byrne of McKinney Bayou, Homan, near Texarkana in Miller County, Arkansas, saw a landed airship. There were three hominoids near it that appeared Japanese. They were hospitable and showed him around the ship that was anchored to the ground. The machinery was made of aluminum and the gas to raise and lower the monster was pumped into and out of an aluminum tank. Different types of pilots and crews. Differing technologies acknowledged in the conversations with the pilots. All attempting to appear normal though in an abnormal context. You may not be aware that there were no airships in the world yet capable of the manouverings reported. In fact there were no airships. It is as if the technology being reported was what technology could be reported as in the future but was not yet possible. Have the fairy folk changed their appearance and technology? Or is it too early for this sort of discussion? I am just throwing observations at you. Like the reports, do what you want with them.

On May 4th 1897 at 7.30 pm an airship passed over Jenny Lind in Sebastian County in Arkansas. An airship passed over Jenny Lind and three men on bicycles pursued it until it landed by a mountainside spring. Its pilots who gave their names as George Austerlitz and Joseph Eddleman, talked with the three bicyclists for a while, saying they subsisted on birds which they overtook in flight. They offered any of the men a free ride and took James Davis to Huntington, fifteen miles away.

On 6th May 1897, Deputy Sheriff John McLemore and Constable John J. Sumpter, were out around midnight near Sugarloaf Mountain not far from Hot Springs, Garland County, Arkansas, when suddenly their horses stopped and then would not approach a brilliant light that was ahead of them in the sky. They lost the light and then found it again before it vanished behind a hill. On investigation the horses stopped again and one hundred yards away the two men saw two hominoids with lights. The men loaded their Winchesters and approached the hominoids. They questioned one who had male and female companions. This one was heavily bearded with a lantern and told the two men that the hominoids were travelling through the country in an airship whose sixty foot outline was visible behind them. A younger hominoid was filling a sack with water twenty yards away and the female was kept in the dark holding an umbrella. The lawmen were asked if they wanted to come along for a ride and they declined though both of them were wet as it had been raining. The lawmen asked the bearded one why the big light was being turned on and off all of the time and was told that it was to conserve energy and light consumed great amounts of it. The craft then vanished quietly into the night sky. Both witnesses did not recollect hearing or seeing it depart. Were they blanked out? More bearded hominoids along with a woman and another technological but possibly impossible explanation.

1909

On 12th December 1909 at 10.00 pm much of the town of Mabelvale in Pulaski County in Arkansas which is near Little Rock, saw a strange light that resembled a searchlight travelling South at a rapid rate of speed. The object was also going up and down like a bird in flight. The sighting only lasted a few moments and Mr. Morris initially saw the airship above his house. The sky was cloudy at the time and the craft flew underneath the cloud cover.

Back to Arkansas and in Little Rock in Pulaski County a cylindrical shaft of light was seen in the sky by several witnesses on 19th December 1909. The light stretched across the southeast sky. Sometimes they yawn across the horizon like the portal to another sky. Like a split in the Heavens. Who is to say that they are not?

On 20th December 1909, and back in Little Rock, Arkansas, where at 12.00 am a powerful beam of light appeared over the town. The light probed across the sky seeming to come from a cylindrical flying shaft. The searchlight stretched from East to West. Are they looking around?

1910

It is 9.00 am on 12th January 1910. Thousands of people see a one hundred foot long cigar in the sky above Chattanooga in Hamilton County, Tennessee, for one hour. The object was silvery white and glistening. There were no wings or any visible means of propulsion though a distinct chugging sound was heard. The craft was five hundred feet up and travelling at twenty miles per hour travelling North and taking ten minutes to cross the city eventually getting lost in the fog along the Tennessee River. Into the fog the airship and its occupant went and came out again a quarter hour of an hour later at Huntsville, about eighty miles away.

At 9.15 am 12th January 1910 a one hundred foot long cigar was seen in the sky over Huntsville in Madison County, Alabama. This was the same craft as seen in Chattanooga fifteen minutes before. Namely a silvery-white glistening cigar travelling at five hundred feet. The craft must have been travelling at 320 miles per hour then if it traversed the distance from Chattanooga to Huntsville in fifteen minutes. No craft in this period could do this sort of speed.

At 11.00 am on 13th January 1910 the following day, the chugging silver cigar was back in Chattanooga again. This time it had come from the south, obviously on it way back from Huntsville but this time a man was seen in it.

And on 14th January 1910 the silver airship was back in Huntsville again.

By 7.00 pm 14th January 1910 the airship was in Knoxville in Knox County in Tennessee where it went South rapidly. The clear outline of the craft was seen and the sound of a motor was heard coming from it.

At noon, 14th January 1910, the one hundred foot long silvery glistening chugging cigar was back in the sky over Chattanooga. This time it was heading from the North to the southeast and it was the third day that it had been seen above the city. The airship eventually vanished over Missionary Ridge.

The following day 15th January 1910 the strange airship was back over Chattanooga at noon. The craft came from the North and went southeast finally vanishing over Missionary Ridge.

Also on 15th January 1910 a large white airship was seen over Paragould in Greene County in Arkansas. There were three to four Hominoids on board and the craft was brilliantly illuminated with a powerful searchlight. The craft went north, then South at an altitude of one thousand feet. Greene County had been visited by Hairy Humanoids early the previous century.

On 20th January 1910 at 8.00 am a number of witnesses saw an airship traveling East and then southwest very fast and very high up over Memphis in Shelby County in Tennessee. The craft crossed the Mississippi River into Arkansas and then turned South vanishing rapidly.

In 1910 in Fulton County (Arkansas. A young brother and sister, Jack and Myrtle (7) Lee saw a "zeppelin" shaped object hovering just above the trees 50m away. It was bright and silvery and no openings nor anything hanging from the underside. The youngsters stood rooted to the spot as the object began moving then just disappeared. They had a feeling that they were being watched.

1920

One night in July 1920 in Hot Springs in Garland County, Arkansas. An aerial object was seen moving from south west to north east. Either in or under the thing, people could see a human like figure.

1948

Around 8.00 pm in July 1948 three blue-green balls were observed by seven witnesses in a yard for thirty minutes in Rogers in Benton County in Arkansas. The bouncing balls moved vertically, veered off horizontally and regained their bobbing motion. There was no vapor trail, exhaust or noise.

In Hot Springs in Garland County, Arkansas, on 8th April 1948 all of the town were witnesses to one inch in diameter doughnut shaped hail that fell. Ice forms around a dust nucleus we are led to believe. What sort of nucleus is a hole? Previously near here in 1847 darkness filled the sky and a flaming sulphurous body crashed to Earth. In 1897 two lawmen saw a light in the sky, followed it and are reported to have met people from an airship here.

1951

In March 1951 at 2230 in Pine Bluff in Jefferson County in Arkansas. Clifford W. Bowman, 48, was driving with his wife over Union Bridge when he saw an object with multicolored lights-pink, yellow, and white-in the air 50 feet away. It was round, about 30 feet in diameter and 7.5 feet high, and had lights in window-shaped blocks." It made a sound like an electric motor. His car's headlights went out : then , as the object approached within 40 feet, his motor cut out. The UFO stopped and landed in a field, its lights no longer revolving. He stopped and started to walk toward it. Then he saw "something" run around the UFO and get in, after which it immediately took off. The entire encounter lasted 10 minutes or less.

1952

On July 24th 1952 at 2300hrs in Fayetteville in Washington County, Arkansas. Mrs Margaret Rebensky and her mother Mrs Julia Lindsey were driving on West Genesee Street, when Julia drew Margaret's attention to six bright lights in the sky. At that moment one of the lights came down right at them, flew over the car bonnet and shot back to join the formation. It was an intense white crescent shaped object, the apparent size of a "honeydew melon" (ie about 15-22cm).

1953

On the St. Francis River in Northeastern Arkansas during November, 1953 late at night seven-year old Riley Martin first saw strange lights above the river near his home. At the time his family lived near the western bank of the Saint Francis River, which is one of the tributaries that feed into the Mississippi. The lights appeared above the river for three nights straight at around the same time in the late night or early morning. They were coming closer with each successive visitation. On the third night the brilliant lights were close enough to his house to cast the glow of their presence onto the walls of his bedroom. It was on the third night that Riley decided to go out and investigate. Strangely his two brothers, who shared the room with him, never awakened to witness the lights, even when he tried to wake them. He was never successful. Perhaps this was by design, because ordinarily, he would not have been awake at that hour of the morning. There were four of the lights, and he had watched them, fascinated by their acrobatic displays. They would shoot across the river from the West and come to an immediate standstill above the river. Then slowly they would circle in a follow-the-leader manner. Or the fourth one would remain stationary while the smaller three circled it. After a time, the fourth light would disengage itself from its companions and descend, glowing ever larger, toward the treetops near the river. He could not detect any sound. The lights would often change in color and intensity from yellow to white, to red, green and shades of blue. On the third night the lights were very close, and it seemed to land behind the trees less than a quarter mile from his home. He put on his jacket and went out. He was accompanied by his faithful and fearless mixed breed dog, Brown Boy. They soon approached the spot where the ship had landed. Peeking through the bushes, he saw a saucer. It stood in a clearing suspended about twelve feet above the ground, and though it was moored by three flexible legs, it slowly danced about, like a cork bobbing on water. Shortly the ship pulsed pinkish, and Riley found himself focused in a light beam emanating from the ship. Out of the light strode two little people. They were dressed in shiny blue jump suits and wore bubble type helmets. He was only seven but they were hardly as tall as he. His faithful dog, Brown Boy, didn't make a sound of protest as the two beings took him by the arms and led him toward the ship. When he stepped directly beneath the saucer, there was a blinding white light, and the next thing he knew they were aboard. He found himself lying nude on some kind of table similar to an operating table. When the little people first approached him on the river he was momentarily terrified. After they entered the craft, the two small aliens had removed their helmets and he could now see them clearly from the waist up. The male was about four feet tall and the female was a few inches shorter. In actual appearance, male and female differed just slightly in features. The heads were noticeably larger than normal in proportion to the body. The eyes were large, unblinking ovals. The male's eyes were a light to deep gold color, while the female's eyes were blue. The shades of their eyes tended to change depths, depending upon the light and perhaps the emotion. Their arms were long, the fingertips reaching almost to their knees. Their feet looked flat and kind of splayed. Their hands were long and delicate and had only three fingers and a thumb. The forefinger was longer than the middle finger. They had no outward earflaps, but tiny holes where the ears should be. The nose had no cartilage and was almost flat against the profile. The mouth was thin-lipped and looked like a slit on the face. The teeth were tiny and uniform, like baby teeth. The chins were sharp and receding and gave the face an egg-like shape. The female's skin tone was gray white, and the male's complexion was yellowish brown or golden. The skin colors also changed at times, not in basic color but in subtle tones. They did not articulate with their mouths but communicated via telepathy. Riley reported that the actual examination was left to a group of entities he called "Stagyians." He could see and feel their long spindly hands. Their touch was cold and clinical. He could not move his body, but he could move his eyes and head with effort. The Stagyians were very ugly creatures indeed. They stood nearly six feet tall and have dark red leather skin draped loosely over their skeletal like frames. Their heads were long and prune-like and the eyes tiny black and close set. Even onboard the craft they both wore some kind of breathing device over their mouths and at times he could hear their rapid shallow breathing. He was later to learn that the Stagyians in spite of their physical appearance were considered to be the Pacifists even among the aliens because of their ability to store and retain vast amounts of data and recall and disseminate the same. The Stagyians hold many scientific and other brainy positions among the Biaviians Federation, with whom they are affiliated. The Stagyians also communicated via telepathy. However, Riley could never comprehend any of what they were saying. During his physical examination he was touched from head to foot and scanned with some kind of light probe that resembled a giant eye. Riley was eventually returned to the banks of the river by his home, after a long trip onboard the Biaviians ship.

1954

On April 22nd 1954 near Hot Springs in Arkansas. At 11:00 p.m. a ten-foot diameter sphere chased men on foot and in their car. It dodged a beam of light that was directed at it. Six workmen who had gathered to ride to work initially watched a gleaming ball hovering over the house for twenty minutes. On one occasion the ball dived towards Les Heatherford who ducked to avoid it. The ball of light was ten feet in diameter, circled the house slowly, stopping for a moment at irregular intervals. The ball followed the men when they left in a station wagon and drove towards Pearcy. They worked at Reynolds Metals Company aluminum plant. They tried to put a spotlight on it but each time they did it would dodge the beam. The ball suddenly disappeared as they reached Pearcy. Or this? A ball of light 3m in diameter chased some men on foot and in their car. When a spotlight was directed at it, it moved away. It circled a house, stopping several times, dived at a man working in the yard . There were six witnesses altogether (Les Reatherford, Fred and Harley Skeets, John Vaughn and Tom and Dayton Henderson), all employees of Reynolds Metal Co and the observation lasted 20 minutes.

On November 11th 1954 in Fouke in Miller County, Arkansas. A woman walking in a wooded area came across two very tall (c 1.9m) tall women dressed in silvery one piece suits. They smiled at the witness before walking off into the woods.

1958

Near Black Rock in Lawrence County in Arkansas. One night in Summer 1958 Trucker D. Smallridge was driving near Black Rock Arkansas after leaving an all-night diner when he suddenly blacked out. Soon, without any recollection how, he found himself parked on the side of the road about 60 miles away. Soon after that he abandoned the truck trade and became a preacher. One night as he slept, the room was suddenly surrounded by a "limpid" blue light. Soon after this he appeared to float "down" and immediately found himself in a large room where a group of Humanoids or beings wearing bright white robes sat around a huge "table." The Humanoids appeared to be discussing him and spoke among them in an unknown language. The Humanoids spoke to him also and strangely he was able to understand them. According to Smallridge, the Humanoids predicted the assassination of Martin Luther King and Senator Robert Kennedy. He claims to have spent 2 hours with the Humanoids. Suddenly he was brought back at very high speed to his bedroom in California.

1965

During August 1965 in the Ozarks in Arkansas in a very isolated area a man and his son encountered a large, round orange object which seemed to glow but did not emit heat. It hovered about a foot from the ground just below the trees. The man was in front of it and spoke to it and the object seemed to come towards him. He blacked out and lost about an hour and his son does not remember anything.

1966

Over Malvern in Geneva County in Arkansas on Tuesday 16th August 1966 UFOs were seen in the area and six days later there were five different sightings of a Humanoid. Amazing how often now we have sightings of odd creatures or Humanoids in an area after an alleged UFO sighting. The report did not say whether it was a hairy Humanoid or not.

Around Malvern in Geneva County in Arkansas on Monday 22nd August 1966 there were five separate individual witnesses who saw an eight foot tall walking luminous orange and yellow creature. UFOs were seen in the area six days before. They've landed and they're heading out!

In Blowing Cave in Cushman in Independence County in Arkansas during 1966. Late one afternoon several spelunkers, among them George D. Wight, were exploring the cave when they spotted a light at the end of the tunnel. As they approached it, Wight noticed a narrow crevice, just big enough for him to squeeze inside it. Then he found artificial steps. He called to the others and they climbed through the opening. The tunnel expanded and they suddenly came into a large corridor, 20 by 20. The walls and the floors were smooth and the ceiling had a curved dome shape. Soon they encountered blue skinned but otherwise human-like individuals.

The strangers communicated with the witnesses, telling them that they had instruments that could measure people's emotions. They learned that the tunnels went on for miles. They were led to underground cities populated by entities that included serpent-like creatures and large hairy bipeds. Later, using an elevator-like device this incident, Wight apparently returned to the cave and was never seen again. As I said, I report them.

1967

On February 28th 1967 in Piggott in Clay County in Arkansas. A 21-year-old man reported that an unidentified object glided parallel to his car about 300 yards away. The object then abruptly headed for the car, swerved away, and left at terrific speed. In another sighting three men saw six red whirling masses, two over a factory. These departed and two more appeared. In a third sighting a woman and her daughter saw a hovering flat oval with reddish lights, which then slowly moved away. A dog barked excitedly during the sighting.

On March 2nd 1967 still in Piggott, Arkansas at 11:30 p.m. CST. About 130 miles north-northwest of Memphis, Tenn., a junior high school science teacher and coach saw four lights that hovered at treetop level, then joined by more lights. The lights maneuvered around in different directions, sometimes hovering, then moving on.

On 10th March 1967 near Piggott in Clay County two men were motoring in a remote area when their truck's engine failed. Before they got out of the vehicle to investigate they saw a fifty foot wide saucer descend to the ground in front of them. Two bizarre looking aliens emerged from the object and walked over to the truck. The Humanoids were of average height with large heads, flat on the back, gray in color. They had normal eyes, mouths and noses. They wore tightfitting gray diver's suits. The two men reported that they felt like they were being bombarded with vibrations and had the uncanny feeling the aliens knew what they were thinking. Rolling the truck windows down the men spoke to one of the aliens who told him that they meant no harm and they could continue their journey if they promised to keep the meeting a secret. They obviously did not do this.

On March 12th 1967 in Paragould in Greene County, Arkanas. On the Braden property at the south edge of Paragould, Mrs J Braden Hackmanm her two daughters, and one of their boyfriends saw a saucer shaped object floating 50m away, between 6-15m in the air. From it came white lights, which searched the grounds. When Mrs Hackman ran towards it these lights went out and were replaced by red lights that shot out from all sides, like Roman Candles. The witnesses felt a vibration and heard an alternating beeping sound. As the thing came closer it stopped and then left in a few seconds.

On March 21st 1967 at 1930hrs in Homer Township in Benton County, Arkansas. A luminous orange object, with a row of square windows and a red light on one side hovered, emitting a whirring sound and then disappeared behind trees. Cows in the area behaved oddly.

In Conway in Faulkner County in Arkansas in November 1967. A stainless steel sphere fell from the sky. Not our first one either. Previously there had been the fall at a very low angle of a meteor at Cabin Creek, Arkansas, and in 1909 a strange light that was going up and down like a bird was seen over Mabelvale.

1969

In Texarkana in Miller County in Arkansas in March 1969. One afternoon the witness (involved in other encounters) was at the local library researching a school project for her daughter and was sitting at a rectangular long table reading. After reading for more than an hour she heard a gasp in the room and looked up to see one of the most striking, beautiful women she had ever seen in her life. She was very tall, close to six feet. She had on heels and an upswept hairdo that made her look even taller. She was absolutely regal looking; she seemed to have perfect skin and wore a flawless tailored suit. The strange woman came and sat down on the other end of the rectangular table. The witness was watching her closely, along with most of the other women and a few other men in there. She then noticed that the stranger was gazing at her. She did not stare but calmly watched the witness without let up. The witness felt unkempt and ill at ease under the stranger's stare. After several minutes of the uncomfortable gazing the stranger asked the witness if she would come up and talk to her. Without hesitation the witness got up and went, at the same time wondering why she did, she felt some type of "force" guiding her actions. The stranger said something to the effect, "We are going to talk about you" and then added, "Your name starts with an R, does it not?" The witness said, "Yes, my name is R." In a matter of fact way the stranger guessed that the witness had four red headed children and that one of her children had been born with black hair which had turned red later, which was an absolute fact. The witness was dumbfounded and amazed at the same time. The stranger predicted that the witness would divorce in 1980 and marry another man (something that did come to pass). Most bizarrely the stranger told the witness that she had a "mission," something to do with "reptilians." To her knowledge it was the first time the witness had heard the word reptilian as in a being or entity. She then asked the witness if she knew what a "coven" was. The witness said no and the strange women explained to her that it was part of the "Wicca" religion, she added, "It is the study and love of Earth and how to work with Earth energies." The witness was confused, and was not even vaguely familiar with the terms being used by the stranger. The woman then told the witness that the number 13 would be "very powerful for her." After additional information regarding other "Wicca" matters the witness was told to go home and draw a pentagram in her den and then make an offering (a cake) and at the same time chant certain words. Later the witness sat on a chair and did exactly what she was told and when she opened her eyes she saw standing before her, in her den, what she was only able to described as an "upright alligator," about 4.5 to 5 feet tall, with greenish scaly skin and red glowing eyes with vertical pupils. At that same time her youngest daughter came down to the den and also saw the strange entity. Terrified they both went to their rooms and had trouble sleeping that night. The witness would see the strange tall woman in the library on other occasions, but was afraid to talk to her.

1970

On April 21st 1970 at 2100hrs in Burdette in Mississippi County, Arkansas. Two women who wished to remain anonymous had just exited from Hw 55 at the Burdette Interchange when they saw an extremely bright light hovering about 20m over a field. Pulling over, one of the women lowered her window for a better look. The object began to descend, hovered and then began to rotate, exposing two very bright white lights, with two small blue ones between them, on a rotating part. Smaller white lights outlined the shape of a saucer surmounted by a pole with a small yellow light on top. There was no sound. After about 3 minutes the thing made a whistling sound and moved off towards Blytheville at terrific speed.

Above Fayetteville in Washington County in Arkansas in October 1970 there was a spectacular aerial flashing and booming display which attracted general public notice one evening. A silver disc was visible over the town before orange colored flashes occurred. Calls to Police came from as far away as Cassville, Missouri.

1973

In Spring 1973 at night in Berryville in Carroll County, Arkansas. A woman looking for her dog in a rural area outside Berryville saw what she thought was a silver coloured helicopter on the ground in a neighbouring golf course. As she reached a clearing she encountered a group of human-like figures dressed in white coats, and two humanoids, gathered around a horse which appeared to be in pain. The beings spotted the woman, who fled from the scene back to the golf course, where the strange machine had now left. She was struck by something which burned her and made her ill.

Around midnight during June 1973 in Bentonville in Benton County in Arkansas the five year old witness was awakened suddenly and saw what appeared to be a square shaped object with several different colored lights on the outside hovering in his room. His next memory was of being face to face with an undescribed Humanoid. He remembers "doing things" with the Humanoid. His next memory was of being back in bed. He suffered from ear aches after the incident and also had strange dreams. Were these dreams though? What were the things that were being done?

On October 2nd 1972 in the early hours in Paragould in Greene County, Arkansas. Mrs Cozart was awakened in the night by a clicking noise and coloured lights flashing through the bedroom windows. When the noise and lights creased she went back to sleep. The next day a flattened area 3m by 6m was found on the neighbouring Harrison Branch Farm soybean field. At 2200hrs. the previous night her fifteen year old daughter and a friend had seen an object hovering 60m above the farm. It was a silvery object with red and green lights. Both the Cozarts and their neighbours saw the object leave.

On December 29th 1973 at 1800hrs in Flippin in Marion County, Arkansas. High school student Steve was driving home with his friend John through a heavily wooded area, about 3km northwest of Flippin. About 100m from an intersection they saw a white light, which they first thought was a reflection. The thing rose to just above the treetops and came towards them, descending to less than 5m above them,. It was a spherical light 2.5-3m diameter, the outer fringes had a translucent appearance, while the centre was a much brighter white light, which gave the impression of being solid. Both Steve and John became frightened and John, who was driving accelerated, upon which the object went straight up. There were no unusual effects on the car.

1974

One night in 1974 in Snowflake in Navajo County, Arizona. Steve Paulson and his girlfriend were out camping and watching the stars after a meal. The woman had fallen asleep when Steve saw a point source of light descend from the sky to within 1.2m of him, taking on the appearance of a luminous sphere. The thing hovered for abo0ut 2 minutes and then took off slowly and dissipated, just as the girlfriend was waking up.

1976

On September 10th 1976 at 1500 in Cabot in Lonoke County in Arkansas Mrs. Wm. H. Doyal was sitting in the driveway of Cabot High School, waiting for her daughter, when she saw something "like an airplane seen head on, surrounded by mist" over the high school building. On its underside was a rotating blade. She then felt paralyzed and heard a voice telling her not to be afraid. She wouldn't be harmed. She was going on a journey. Then another voice said they must hurry, the Air Force was getting too close." She felt as if she was lying down and vaguely recalled seeing a vertical row of 6 lights. She felt a sense of unease for the rest of the day and awoke the next day with a severe sick headache.

About September, 1976 in the daytime Nr Fayetteville in Washington County in Arkansas. The source of this story is a retired businessman who moved to New Mexico and opened a small business there. In 1977 he became friendly with Mrs. L, a middle-aged lady, who with her husband, had recently resettled in New Mexico Her story (Part I) follows. One day in 1976 while she was picking apples some distance from her home (thereby dating the incident somewhere around September—tb), she fell from her ladder seriously injuring one of her legs. As she lay there, too weak to rise or call for help, she saw two figures approaching. One was tall and thin, the other was much shorter. As they neared, Mrs., L, saw that while they were Humanoid in appearance, they were not humans, They had an unknown device with which they began to treat Mrs. L.'s badly bleeding leg. In 15 minutes all bleeding and pain subsided, leaving no trace of a scar. The beings then presented Mrs. L, with a metal plaque with some carving or drawings on it. She thanked them and asked if they would like to go to her house for something to eat. One being replied that they did not eat, but consumed only "juice," When she offered fruit juice, they said they did not drink the same kind of juice that humans drank. They were arresting in appearance and, according to Mrs. L. when they spoke, their voices seemed to emanate from their midsections. The taller one had the voice of a mature woman; the shorter that of a child. The beings walked away and Mrs. L returned home with the plaque in her possession. She even showed her New Mexican businessman friend the artifact, who had knowledge of engraving; he was unable to identify either the markings nor the metal. The images included pyramids and 6-pointed stars.

In late November. 1976 in daytime near Fayetteville in Washington County. One day about six weeks after her first encounter Mrs. L.'s dog was missing, and she set out on foot in search of it. She crossed a golf course near her property and entered a wooded area. At the edge of a clearing she discovered a bizarre scene. Two men in white coats were apparently in the process of mutilating a horse that lay on the ground; two more men dressed in what seemed to be "Air Force" uniforms stood by watching, while two "AF" helicopters were seen on the. Ground: also in attendance were what seemed to be the same two Humanoids that Mrs. L. had encountered earlier. Frightened by what she saw, she turned and began to run away but she was apparently discovered, as she heard someone running after her for a brief while. Then she heard a helicopter, which quickly overtook her and began descending. A blue beam of light was directed upon her producing serious burns in the area of her right breast and burning part of her clothing. For whatever reasons, the helicopter departed, and Mrs. L. sought help for her burns, and eventual hospitalization. While in the hospital, Mrs. L. made a mistake: she told everyone just what had happened to her. Shortly, "strange people" began to question her. She believed they were FBI agents, although no credentials were ever shown. After her release, the county sheriff took her to a psychiatric clinic for evaluation . She was given numerous tests and went through "pure hell" until the doctors finally released her with a "clean bill of health." But the sheriff still branded her as "crazy," placing the blame for the mutilation of the horse on her, which apparently did occur as she reported. In addition, the same "strange people" continued to visit L.'s home, asking the same questions repeatedly, and becoming such a harassment to the couple that they were finally forced to sell their home and move to New Mexico, Things went fine in New Mexico for a few months, but then the same "strange people" sought them out and the questions and harassment began all over. She finally told her New Mexican friend that she and her husband would be moving again, this time to Texas.

1977

At 11.15 pm in the middle of August 1977 a man who had stepped outside his house to secure his car windows observed an object with flashing lights hovering about a nearby tree. Under the tree stood two tall men like figures totally dressed in black who stared coldly at the witnesses. Suddenly the witness was unable to move and felt a powerful vibration penetrate his head and body. At the same time both figures turned simultaneously and disappeared into the woods. As soon as he was able to move the witness ran panic stricken into his house. This was in Flaxton in Arkansas.

1981

On June 6th 1981 at night in Little Rock in Pulaski County, Arkansas. Two teenagers saw a 1.2m long rectangular object and a smaller disc shaped thing manoeuvring over a shed and garage in one of their back yards. A tree at the site was found withered.

On June 21st 1981 at 0300hrs in Hot Springs in Garland County, Arkansas. While out driving Mrs Eason noted that her headlights kept fading and brightening, while the area was illuminated by alight on the top of a nearby hill. She woke her husband Bob and pulled up. He got out of the car and noted that the whole area was illuminated and felt his hair stand on end. As he moved to get back in the car the headlights came back on again.

1982

On August 27th 1982 in Conway in Faulkner County, Arkansas. A group of people in a housing complex including Ottie Maltibia, Margaret Abrams, Gwen Crenshaw, Margaret Abrams and 7 children were sitting outside when they saw two circles about 1.5m diameter hovering about 1m above the ground. Each of these circles had a double row of lights along the perimeter, orange on top, yellow on the bottom and seemed to be vibrating. The lights disappeared with an ever increasing sound.

1984

At 7.00 pm on May 1st 1984 in Glen Rose (Malvern) in Hot Spring County in Arkansas the witness had taken their dog outside. It was already dark. I noticed what I thought was a star. The longer I looked, I thought this was a very bright star, A star, but too close to the ground. I do not know how long I was outside looking at the light. I went into the house, where my two teenage daughters and a boyfriend was and told them to come look at what I had been watching. Again, I don't know how long we were outside. All of a sudden the light started toward us, (going east). It took some time, and then I thought it was a helicopter. There was no sound though. It was triangular in shape, and had 2 or 3 different colored lights besides the white light in the center and dark in color. It went over a neighbor's house. My daughters are teenagers approximately 14 and 16 and the boyfriend 16, and myself saw this. I have on my left thigh, a hole, sorta pitted. I wrote an author of a book years ago and he seemed to think I had a encounter of some kind, and said I could go to a hypnotist, but he warned this could be traumatic.

Yes, I am leaving the original writers punctuation and emphasis. I like it.

1986

In late August 1986 at 2050hrs in Lockesburg in Sevier County, Arkansas. A couple driving 3-7km south of Lockesburg, turned a corner to see two huge blue-white lights descend ahead of them and head towards their car, their brilliance forcing the couple to stop in the middle of the road. The lights levelled off about 800m ahead and continued towards the car only 5-6m above the road, at over 160kph. The lights appeared to be about 1.5-2m diameter and the distance between them was wider than that of the two lane road. The thing then suddenly stopped 15-18m away, the lights dimmed down. They now saw two rows of lights, blinking on and off in random for about 10 seconds, after which the lights dimmed. They could now see that the lights were on a rectangular object at least 30m long. The bottom row of lights was about 2.5-3m above the base and the upper lights about 2m below the top. The thing's general surface was battleship grey in colour. After only seconds the object began to rise vertically to about 60m, at which the lights went out and they were unable to see it any more. They heard no sound from it during the incident.

1989

On November 19th in northwestern Arkansas. Dale, as we shall call him here, is concerned that the public he serves might read his story and thereafter have serious doubts about his integrity and perhaps even about his sanity. "If I had just seen some strange lights or something crossing the sky, it would be a different story," he says. "I would have gotten a little good-natured ribbing from the guys and laughed it off and went on." But what did happen to Dale was much more than that. The incident can only be classified as a close encounter. A very close encounter. As Dale drove his patrol car down that remote gravel road in the wee hours of Sunday morning, November 19, 1989, he had no inkling that he was about to have such a once in a lifetime experience. He only knew that the shift, which had begun the previous evening, was developing into a long night of inactivity. "There was absolutely nothing going on," he remembers, "so shortly after midnight I decided to try checking some of the back roads. We have the same problem as they do everywhere else with the local teenagers wanting to slip off somewhere and have a few beers. I know they're just looking for something to do, but I know a few of their favorite spots and I decided to go check them out. Not to write tickets, you know—we usually just make them pour the beer out and send them on their way." At approximately 1:35 A.M., the deputy came around a sharp right angle corner on a narrow gravel road and got a very unpleasant surprise. "The corner there is not only sharp, it has brush growing out where it keeps you from seeing around it until you actually make the turn. When I got around it far enough to see down the next stretch there sat an old Chevy right out in the middle of the road without a sign of a light on it anywhere. It was out where there was no room to get around it and it was just around the corner. I almost hit it. If I would have been going a little bit faster I probably would have. As it was I had to slide to a stop on the gravel to keep from it. The patrol car's nose ended up not a bit more than ten or twelve feet from the rear end of the other car." Dale admits readily that his first reaction was one of anger. "I looked up and there were four teenagers standing alongside of the old Chevy, with all four doors open. Two boys on the driver's side and a couple of girls on the passenger side. They were just standing there, and the first thing that ran through my mind was that they had picked the dumbest place in the world to stop and listen to the radio—you know how kids will do, standing there with the door open and the radio on. But then I noticed something really weird. I had slid to a stop that close behind them, making a lot of noise on the gravel, and none of them even turned around and looked at me. They were just staring at something on down the road in front of them. I figured it had to be something mighty interesting, so I put the car in park and opened the door so I could stand up and get a better look. My car had turned just a little bit when I skidded on the gravel, so my headlights weren't pointing straight down the road, but there was enough light that I could just barely make out a dark bulk of some sort that looked like it was kind of across the road a ways ahead of the other car. The first thing that ran through my mind was that a farm truck had lost control and rolled over on its side, crossways in the road. I immediately reached down and turned my spotlight on and turned it around to shine down in that direction." Instead of the serious accident that he had expected to see, the beam of the spotlight revealed what Dale referred to as "a scene right out of the twilight zone." As he began to describe what he saw, his years of experience took over and he chose his words carefully, as if testifying in court. "The thing looked like it was made out of some sort of metal, but it wasn't shiny like chrome or anything like that. It was dark gray and dull-looking, sort of like galvanized tin or something on that order. The shape was—well, I hate to say it, but it was just exactly like you would expect a flying saucer to look. Two saucers, really, with one of them upside down on top of the other. I remember noticing that I couldn't see any joint where the edge was, which 'really struck me as being odd because it looked like two halves joined together, but it was just smooth, with no line." Dale's emotion as he continued with his description of the object was obvious. "What really got to me, though, wasn't the looks of the thing. It was what it was doing. It just sat there in the air, not touching anything. It was absolutely motionless, except for a sort of wobbling motion, and not much of that. The bottom of it couldn't have been more than three or maybe four feet above the road, if that much." In response to a couple of direct questions, Dale gave a little more detail concerning the UFO's appearance. He estimated it to be about thirty feet across, stating he was fairly certain of that dimension due to the fact that it was right down over the road, giving him something of known width for comparison. He also said that the entire surface of the object was smooth, with no dome or windows. As strange as this sight was, it did nothing to prepare the deputy for what happened next. About two or three seconds after he shined his spotlight on the object, the light died abruptly. Not only that, but the rest of his patrol car's electrical system went with it. The head-lights, radios, and engine all cut off as though some master switch had been thrown, plunging the entire scene into total darkness. "I'm not a bit ashamed to tell you I was scared," Dale said. "Then I heard one of the girls standing up by the other car sort of sobbing and she said, 'Oh, my God, it got him, too.' That didn't help matters any." (Later, after talking to the four teenagers after the incident was over, he would understand the significance of that remark. About three minutes before he came around the corner, the other vehicle had rounded it and the driver had noticed something which appeared to be on the road just beyond his headlight beams. He had said something to the others and at the same time flipped his lights up on high beam. They had seen the same thing as Dale would be looking at in his spotlight beam minutes later, and had also gotten only a few seconds to look at it before their car had gone dark and silent. They had gotten out of the car and just stood there, wondering what to do and staring at the dark bulk, until the patrol car had arrived on the scene.) In the absence of noise from his vehicle's engine, Dale was instantly struck by the absolute silence. "I expected to be hearing whatever it was that was holding the thing up, a jet or an engine or something, but there just wasn't any sound at all. Nothing. Not even the normal sounds you get here out in the country at night. One thing, though. You know that ringing you get after you fire a gun or there's some other loud noise? You don't really hear it, like it's coming from anywhere or anything, it's more like it's just there in your head. It was like that, my ears were ringing. But there hadn't been any bang or anything to be the cause of it. The ringing wasn't loud, just enough so it was noticeable when it got so quiet." (He also said that he thought maybe the "ringing" was just because of his fear and excitement, but it remained unchanged throughout the UFO's presence, then faded out when the object departed. He has since decided that something from the object was the direct cause of the ringing in his ears.) The abrupt change from the scene being brightly lit by the spotlight to the total darkness which followed its failure left the officer unable to see anything at all for a few moments, but as his eyes slowly adjusted to the change he could see the vague bulk of the object still hanging close above the road. He walked slowly up to join the four youths standing beside the other automobile. From this position he first noticed that the darkness in the vicinity of the UFO was not total — there was a soft bluish green glow on the gravel of the road directly underneath the object apparently emanating from the bottom of the thing. It wasn't very bright, just enough to produce an indistinct round spot where the individual stones could be made out and the color was distinguishable. Dale said that the five of them found themselves talking in whispers. "There was this overpowering feeling that we were being watched, even though we couldn't see anybody and there were no windows on the thing for us to be looked at through," he remembers. "We just stood there like we were waiting for something to happen, but we didn't know what. I tell you, a lot of weird things went through my mind. 1 was scared, but not because it had really done anything to be threatening. When I got to thinking about it, I guess when two different cars came around that corner and shined bright lights on it while it was just minding its own business, whatever that was, maybe whoever or whatever was in that thing might have felt like they were the ones being threatened. After a little while, I was almost wishing, something would go ahead and happen. I guess the waiting was starting to get to me." Finally, about a minute and a half after Dale joined the teenagers at their car, something did begin to happen. "The first thing I noticed was that the glow on the ground was slowly getting bigger, like it was spreading out. Then I realized it was because the saucer was beginning to go straight up, real slow. There still wasn't any sound, though, except that ringing in my ears, and when the thing got to maybe twenty five feet or so in the air, even that began to fade out." It was also at about that point that the five witnesses got their first look at the source of the glow that they had seen on the ground under the UFO. Dale describes what they saw: "On the bottom of the saucer there was a sort of ring of light, about the color of one of those yard lights. It wasn't made up of little lights, the whole ring was glowing. It looked sort of like a neon, but it wasn't like a tube, it was flat, even with the bottom of the saucer." When he was asked to estimate the size of this glowing circular band, Dale said it was "probably about ten feet across, and the ring itself was about a foot wide." The UFO's slow vertical ascent continued until it was approximately a hundred feet or so above the roadway by the deputy's estimate. "It was like it just wanted to be sure it was high enough to clear the trees," he speculated. The glowing ring was the most noticeable feature now, centered on a vague round shape silhouetted against the slightly lighter sky. After seeming to pause and hover for a couple of seconds, the object suddenly shot off in apparently horizontal flight. As Dale put it, "One second it was just sitting there, and the next all you could see of it was a bluish-green streak tearing across the sky toward the northwest." The already shook witnesses had one more shock coming, however. At the exact same moment as the UFO took off from its hovering position above them, the lights and radios on both vehicles came back to life as suddenly as they had died a few minutes before. Dale laughed about the result. "When the thing had knocked out the kids' car, they had the radio on a rock and roll station with the volume all the way up. I don't have to tell you what happened when it came back on full blast all of a sudden like that. We all jumped like we had been shot at." Both vehicles, when the drivers tried to start them a few moments later, started normally. The deputy spent several minutes talking to the four young people after the incident was over. All of them were in agreement that they would not report the encounter for fear of being thought crazy. It was only after thinking about it for several days that the officer mentioned seeing a UFO to a member of another department, who knows AUN's editor and assured Dale that he could tell his story without fear of being laughed at or having his name used without permission. He made a phone call and was interviewed in Springfield, Missouri less than three weeks after the sighting. Dale was obviously shook by his experience. He said that he went back to the scene of the encounter later that same day, hoping that daylight would reveal some evidence of the UFO. All he found was the skid marks in the gravel where he had made his panic stop to avoid running into the old Chevy. He admitted that he had not driven that road after dark since the incident, and indicated that he probably wouldn't for "at least a while yet." His relief at telling someone about what had happened was obvious, but he seemed to be disappointed that the interviewer couldn't give him a firm answer as to what he had seen. He did seem to be reassured by the knowledge that others have had similar experiences in the past, almost as if he doubted his own perception. Dale paused for almost half a minute when he was asked what he thought about his encounter, gathering his thoughts carefully before answering. Finally, he said, "I was always one who took all these flying saucer stories with a big grain of salt, but I know what I saw, and if others have seen the same thing and had the same thing happen to them it just makes me more sure. What I saw was as real and solid as an airplane, and I looked at it in the spotlight for a little bit from no more than a hundred feet away, at the most. If it would have been a car I could tell you the license plate number. It wasn't just a glimpse of something off in the distance, is what I'm getting at, so it would be awfully hard to convince me it wasn't some kind of plane. As far as where it was from, I don't know. If anyone would have told me before this happened that they believed these things were from another planet I would have laughed at them, but I'm not laughing any more. It would almost be easier to believe that then it would be to think we've got anything like that, that can do things it did without making any noise." One thing the deputy was completely without hesitation in saying. "Whatever caused the cars to die like that, the saucer or whoever it was on it did it. It was like the lights from the first car bothered them when they shined on the thing, so they got it first. Then when I showed up and shined the spotlight on them, it was like they just cranked the power up on whatever they used to get the kids' car and reached out a little farther and killed mine. There's no doubt in my mind at all that it was done deliberately. I don't claim to know why, but you know how you just get a feeling about something? Well, I got the feeling that they didn't intend to hurt anybody. They just got disturbed while they were doing whatever it was they were up to." Dale smiled as he added a thought that struck him as funny. "Hey, I couldn't figure out what would be back on a lonely road like that in the middle of nowhere to interest a flying saucer, but maybe they were just but parking like our kids do. Wouldn't that be something?" Before ending the interview, Dale was asked how he would feel if he ever got the chance to see another UFO. His answer expressed the feelings shared by several people who have had close encounters of the type he experienced. "I guess I'd have to say I'd like to see another one some time, but on my own terms. If I would have driven up on that thing the way I did and it wouldn't have killed my patrol car, I might have even tried to walk up closer. But I couldn't leave because my car was dead. I felt trapped. If I'm going to watch something like that again, I want it to be my decision." As you read on you will find reports of courting couples attracting Bigfoot. You will also find reports of the same activity attracting UFOs. Remember, I only report them but they do start getting more commonplace. Unless you believe that thousands of people got together to compare notes and make sure they were all the same.

1996

In Fayetteville in Washington County in Arkansas at 7.35 pm on July 4th 1996 the witnesses had just finished firing off fireworks and had entered a patch of woods away from the pasture to enjoy the warm night for a few minutes. In the woods they noticed a light about 100 yards away. Thinking that it was somebody shooting fireworks in the woods, they walked towards it. As they approached, they saw in a clearing, three triangular shaped objects hovering just above the ground. Lights were pointing down off each point of the triangles. Three strange beings, stood around speaking among themselves in gruff voices. The beings were described as tall and covered with very thick hair that covered their bodies completely. As the witnesses approached, the beings seem to sniff the air and glared in their direction. The beings then quickly ran into their ships, which shot away into the sky emitting a bright burst of light, knocking the witnesses to the ground. The crafts seem to elongate as they accelerated. Are these Bigfoot or what?

You can judge. I only report them. Yes, I know. You are sick of this comment.

1999

In Northern Arkansas at midnight on September 3rd 1999. A 35-year old man, Mike, and his friend Henry were using their computer at home, when Henry looked up and saw a Humanoid standing outside the window. The figure appeared white grayish, with large black eyes and was about 4 to 5-feet tall. It just stood at the window staring at Henry. Henry turned his head briefly looked back and the figure was gone.

Later in Northern Arkansas at night in the middle of September 1999. Henry heard a loud humming sound in his living room; his friend Mike who was in the living room also heard it. At this point Henry saw a short gray Humanoid with large black eyes behind the couch in the living room, Mike did not see it. Both now saw a white ball floating outside the bedroom window, moving in a jerky up and down motion. Both went outside and saw an object with flashing colored lights hovering over the area. The craft appeared to be triangular in shape. At one point the object briefly approached the witnesses, then left. Apparently the Humanoid had disappeared at that point.

Colorado

Every now and again I would be looking at the data for each state. Some did not seem to have enough. This is the problem with not having dates for sightings or not having locations. I have read so many books with wonderful stories in them but no places or no dates or neither. For the purposes of this book these wonderful episodes cannot be included. But there certainly are hundreds more.

1897

This was the year of the Great 1897 Airship Flap.

On 30th March 1897, a bright light was seen sailing to the northwest over Denver in Denver County in Colorado. It was too slow for a meteor. In fact several of the bright lights sailed to the northwest. This was during the 1897 Airship Flap.

The Leviathans kept on moving and sometimes hovering. Over Cripple Creek in Teller County in Colorado on 19th April 1897 all of the town saw an airship at an altitude of one mile. The craft was large and cone-shaped and was visible for six hours.

1924

On 6th July 1924 a meteorite missed a man by only one meter in Johnstown in Weld County in Colorado. During a funeral procession there was a remarkable fall of stones. The largest was 23.5 kilograms but the others were considerably smaller. It was a diogenite which had been pummeled and structurally weakened by four eons of intermittent brecciation. Usually only a small number of these stones hit the ground.

1929

In April 1929 in Ward in Boulder County in Colorado. A photo was taken by Edward Pline, at the sawmill in Ward where they lived at the time. He thinks it was 1929 and somehow the month of April was mentioned in the original post. He was about six years old then. His father was there to photograph the saw mill for some reason or another, and, allegedly, as he was taking the photo, he described a "terrible thunderous bellow," and "a large round thing as big as a very large boulder that moved through the air above them" which he photographed.

1931

Near Holyoke in Phillips Coungty, Colorado in Winter 1931. At 2:00 p.m. after a snowstorm, the 17-year old witness was riding his horse, checking on stray cattle. As he was going over a small hill and down to a draw that was about 25-30ft deep, he had reached the area around the middle of the draw when he looked up towards the west and noticed an elongated oval-shaped "machine" in the air. The object was aluminum in color and a door that was transparent like glass opened. It looked like a doorway and a man appeared in it. The man looked human but was not as tall as a normal human. He looked down at the witness. He appeared to be wearing a uniform darker than he was. The witness momentarily looked back down since he was on a horse that stumbled quite a bit. When he looked back up again, the object was already gone.

1932

At Mt. Cameron in Park County, Colorado in June 1932. One afternoon Mr. William Lamb (involved in other encounters) had climbed Mt. Cameron when he ran across giant tracks 17 inches long and 4 to 6 inches wide. He later saw a fireball drop out of the sky, and a transformation took place. The fireball vanished into thin air and there stood a creature; 8 feet tall and looking much like the description of the "Abominable Snowman." The creature took off after Lamb, who after several narrow escapes, managed to get away by jumping off a cliff into a pine tree. That is how Lamb managed to escape his pursuer. Lamb believes this creature to be of the same breed as the Abominable Snowman of the Himalayas. This is not the first Hairy Humanoid and UFO combination sighting either.

1935

On 8th August 1935 a man was missed by being hit by a falling meteorite by only one meter in Briggsdale in Weld County in Colorado. It was reported that a farmhand was working in a field when it whizzed past his head, narrowly missing him. When he heard a thud the farmhand found a molten mass in the ground that was so hot that he could not touch it. It weighed about half a pound and was the size of a turkey egg. Incidentally it was reported that another meteorite had fallen near Briggsdale in the late 1940s. Is this a strange coincidence? Incidentally there had been a similar meteorite near-miss in Johnstown also in Colorado only fifty-nine kilometers to the southwest of Briggsdale on 6th July 1924.

1940

Somewhere in Colorado in 1940. A Venusian "scout ship" reportedly landed on Buck Nelson's family property. Members of the crew offered to fly the whole family to their home planet for a visit. Only Buck, then 4 years old, wanted to go. The Venusians agreed to return one day when he was old enough to make a mature decision on the matter. The Venusians reportedly returned in 1953, 1954 and 1955, this time contacting Nelson, now living in the Ozark Mountains of Missouri.

1947

Around 9.00 pm during March 1947 an unidentified object was sighted that had an unusual appearance or performance. The object was observed in clear weather by two male witnesses around sixteen years old for twelve seconds over Alamosa in Alamosa County in Colorado.

On July 6th 1947 in Buckley NAS in Arapahoe and Adams Counties in Colorado during the day both LeRoy Krieger, Aerologist, Second Class; James Cavalieri, hospital apprentice, reported a bright round silvery object shooting up and down noiselessly for several minutes. It then left at high speed.

1948

On July 4th 1948 near Longmont in Boulder and Weld Counties in Colorado witnesses saw a revolving silver circular object that soared upward at "terrific speed."

One night in summer 1948 in the San Luis Valley in Colorado, Sister Wolf, five years old, was playing in the front room next to a window facing East. Suddenly she noticed a bright silver object over the corner of the field. A man in a silver suit was standing on the ground with a rod, checking the land. Suddenly the man turned around and faced the witness and a bright light like lightning went straight towards her face. The man then put the rod into the ground and vanished into the object which then took off and left. Later her grandfather found a burned circle at the site. Nothing ever grew there again. The silver rod was still there. As he just lifted the rod lightning went out of it in a straight line and hit her right in the center of the forehead and it shocked it. It was like an electric shock and she just took off running. Within a week of the encounter she reported enhanced psychic abilities and could see the dead walk among the living. Her grandmother had told her that she had seen a Star Person and that she had been blessed. Her grandfather called it a Thunder Being.

1949

On April 15th 1949 at Peterson AFB, Colorado Springs in El Paso County in Colorado. At 3:30 PM flying objects the color of unlighted, frosted electric light bulbs hurtled over the base. The Intelligence Division of the Fifteenth Air Force investigated: "Objects followed straight course. When first seen, the object on the left was an apparent distance of five feet behind the first, and with an increase of speed overtook the first object in about two seconds and flew in close formation with the first object. This fact seems to preclude the possibility that these objects were meteors. Object was first sighted by T/Sgt. Morbeck, who was watching a B-25 pass over the field, and observed the objects passing above the B-25, going in the opposite direction, and called them to the attention of Major Bullock and M/Sgt. Fink, who were standing near y and remarked: 'Are those airplanes? Boy! They are sure fast.'"

1950

On 29th January 1950 Mr. Quintana of Denver saw a silvery-green ovoid object hovering about fifteen meters above a slope and landing slowly in a ravine on South Table Mountain in Jefferson County. It shot upwards at high speed and had a diameter of twenty meters with a revolving middle band. A greenish light flashed upon it and the Mr. Quintana felt a rush of air and a pungent smell.

During 1950 at 10.00 pm between Castle Rock & Franktown both in Douglas County in Colorado. Marc Damerst, driving without lights by the light of the full moon, came over a hill and saw an elliptical object 500 feet off the road, hovering 75 feet above the ground. He stopped the car and got out to watch. Lights came from a row of windows that encircled the objects, "like portholes around the body of the craft. There were blue exhaust flames coming straight down from it." No noise like an engine, but a quiet hum. He could see shadows of figures moving past the windows, "but I was too far away to distinguish form or shape." He watched for 5 minutes then reached for a cigarette; the moment he flicked his lighter, the object suddenly streaked off, disappearing in ten seconds. Damerst had numerous subsequent sightings, but none as close or detailed.

1955

On 16th April 1955 in Colorado around 4.30 pm a five year old boy was in a field bringing the cows home for his father to milk as his brothers and grandfather fed the rest of the livestock. Suddenly a very large white colored oval shaped object landed in the road ahead of him. He could feel warmth coming from it. He did not feel any fear and approached the object and touched it. It felt cool to touch despite the heat. His next memory was of seeing two people come towards him and stand in front of him. One of the figures who was wearing a blue shirt and white pants extended his hand out to the boy and then led him to a doorway on the side of the landed object. His next memory was of standing in the road with his cowboy boots in his hands and his grandfather running to him asking where he had been. It was already 1.30 am or nine hours later than he was last seen. He tried to tell his grandfather what had happened and his grandfather told him not to talk about it. Later his grandfather told him that whilst searching for him he had seen a flash and then saw a bright object lift up and take off at high speed. When he ran to the location he found the boy standing on the road with his boots in his hands.

Near Greeley in Weld County in Colorado one afternoon in August 1955. The main witness and his grandfather were walking down a dirt road when a strong gust of wind suddenly struck them. When they looked up they could now see an object sitting in the middle of the road. His grandfather picked him up and told him not to be afraid, that no one was going to hurt them. As they stood there, three "people" came towards them. One went straight to his grandfather and said that the young child did not understand. His grandfather then told him that they were going inside the object to "look around." Strangely the witness felt no fear as they went inside. One of the men walked over to a small shelf and took out a ring with red and blue lights on it and placed it on the child's head. After that he was then able to understand everything that was said. He could feel that the craft was moving but it was barely noticeable. He asked the man if they were in fact moving and he said; "for quite some time," and asked the witness if he wanted to look around with him. That's when the child noticed that his grandfather was not with him and when he asked where he was, he was told; "with friends," and that he would soon be with them. The boy then told the alien guide that he wanted to be a pilot and was taken to a large room where he heard a loud humming noise and was told that this noise was made by a "pulse magnetic engine" in the craft. He then asked the aliens where they were from, but the only answer he received was that they, "were good people" and that someday he would understand, but not now. They then walked down a long hall into another room; there the boy asked for something to drink and was given a liquid that "was different and tasted very good." He was then asked to touch the glass to see what happened, and when he did that it suddenly turned very cold. He was then taken to his grandfather in a field with numerous persons walking around next to a huge craft as big as a football field. The aliens were all human-like in appearance. His grandfather then picked him up again and removed the apparatus from the boy's head and returned it to one of the male aliens. The boy's next conscious memory was of feeling a bump and both him and his grandfather walking down the same dirt road but it was now very dark. His grandfather turned to him and told him never to tell anyone about it.

In 1955 in Lakewood (Jefferson), Colorado, Lloyd Arnold (then 49), was in his home in Lakewood when he had an out of-body experience in which he was taken aboard a UFO and examined by five occupants of normal height and appearance, although they had darker than normal skin (but not Negroid). One spoke English, the other a tongue he has never heard. He recalls acceleration "like a jet, but more severe," when he was flown to a place where other humanoids were gathered. "Call it a dream or hallucination, if you will. It was vivid and real. I was fully conscious and knew that I could stop it if I chose, but I have an immunity to fear." His first UFO sighting was in 1913, and he has had many 'other sightings and experiences.

1958

At Adequate Springs in Colorado (location unknown) in 1958. At 1: 00 a.m. a mine operator locked the operation up for the night and began driving home. The next thing he remembers was being on the street of the town four to five miles away with no recollection of driving the intervening distance, covering very dangerous road. Under hypnosis, the following story unfolded: he saw a light around the bend of the mountain road. When he rounded the curve, two bars of intense light straddled the road with a single bright round light above. His car died and the headlights went out. He sat there in the dead vehicle watching the lights, and three entities emerged and came toward him. Needless to say he was petrified. The individuals came to the car and stood on the left and right sides and in front. He had a feeling of impending death. When the hypnotist (Dr. James Harder) tried to push further, the witness developed a pain above his left ear and was not able to remember anything else. Subsequently, the witness believes that he and his family have had several other UFO experiences, plus other odd happenings involving psychic phenomena.

1959

On Blanca Peak at the southern end of the Sangre de Cristo Range in the Rocky Mountains in Colorado. In August 1959 at night a newsreel cameraman Bud Cooper was on a dirt road when he encountered a large transparent cylindrical object. He encountered three beings, one of whom gave him a tour of the craft and explained its electromagnetic propulsion system. Blanca Peak is at the tripoint of Alamosa, Costilla and Huerfano Counties.

Near Fort Garland in Costilla County in August 1959. One night the witness was driving in the desert with a friend when the car ahead of them suddenly disappeared. Later around sunset, he went alone to take photographs and was sitting in the car when he apparently experienced a time lapse. He remembers standing in a transparent cylinder inside a large room; there he saw several humanoids wearing armor like outfits. They communicated with the witness by using telepathy and told him they were in a hovering space station above the earth. He was taken to a room where he was shown an anti-gravity device. He was also told that they had taken the vehicle and driver that he had seen to disappear earlier.

1960

In Left Hand Canyon in Boulder County in Colorado Ray Hawks whilst driving a tractor with a shovel loader attachment heard a detonation in the sky and looking up saw a disc in the sky. The electrics of the tractor suddenly died and the UFO dropped vertically out of the cloud. The craft hovered 650 feet from the witness and 200 feet up and wobbled as it stabilized itself. The craft looked like two concave discs joined at the rim and it was one fifth deep as it was wide. It was a dull aluminum color and the surface appeared velvety. There were a series of shiny metal plates with caps around the perimeter and one of these was giving off dark blue smoke around the edges. There was an intermittent hum like an electric motor phasing and idling and the smoking plate began to tilt from within. This was replaced by another one that clicked as it locked into place. The hum became high-pitched and the disc became surrounded by a shimmering field, elevated itself and vanished. The tractor then worked again. The disc was 200 feet in diameter by twenty feet thick in the middle and was seen two miles South of Buckingham Park and seven miles North and two miles West of Boulder. Quite a standard sighting actually. This occurred at 3.10 pm on Thursday 11th August 1960.

On Saturday 24th December 1960 in Durango in La Plata County in Colorado a dozen witnesses including Mr. Polson, also called Folsom, and his neighbors saw a huge intensely lit object landing on a peak. The craft had a dome in the middle and revolving lights on it. The next day the Polson's pet dog ran into the house and died at their feet. At the area where the UFO landed there were many overhanging tree limbs that were broken as well as many strange footprints. Some were human but they were fifteen inches long. There were other tracks and they were only five inches long. The tracks went to a deserted cabin and circled it and then went back to the landing site. The Polsons neighbor's dog which had disappeared on the night of the landing was never seen again. They like dogs. As pets or lunch I'm not sure though.

1962

The night of 18th April 1962 General Laurence S. Kuter, NORAD, took off and was climbing through 10,000 feet when he saw a meteor come out of orbit. The object was cherry red, clear green, with a long white and red tail and he estimated it as being near Colorado Springs in El Paso County, Colorado. At the same time reports of the same object came in from Idaho, Utah and Arizona by OCD Regions Navy aircraft, B-52 crews and DC-8 pilots. All the reports were alike in shape, color, and general direction of travel from South to North.

Fifty minutes after the Colorado Springs sighting, shortly after midnight, early on 19th April 1962, there were numerous reports to the FAA and AFLC command post of a luminous aerial object that was observed over Los Angeles in Teller County, Colorado, near Colorado Springs, Montana, Kansas and Utah. Captain Shields of the 733 Troop Carrier Squadron, Ogden, Utah, reported to the AFLC that the object appeared around 0300Z and was bright like burning magnesium that was traveling from the southwest to the northeast. This was the same time as the Eureka, Utah, sighting.

At Estes Park in Larimer County in Colorado in June 1962. An 18-year old shipping clerk was getting ready to go to bed when he noticed a white-blue flash from his balcony and saw a blue globe which landed about 400 meters from his location. The witness was then unable to move. A second UFO (light) approached within 60cm of the witness and a strange musical voice told him to go inside the sphere. Inside was like a blue void, or a glass ball. He was then transported into a larger, dark UFO where he encountered several humanoid beings about 1.60m in height, wearing black overalls, with disk-shaped shoulder straps and a snake-like embroidered pattern on the pockets. They introduced him to a beautiful female alien who communicated with him telepathically, "putting pictures in his mind." He was told that they came from a faraway remote galaxy. Another version? A 19 year old semi-literate shipping clerk was about to go to bed when his attention was caught by a blue white flash and from his balcony he saw a blue globe come to rest on a mountain top 400m away. As the youth stood paralysed, the light bobbed towards him, stopping only 50cm away. A strange "musical" voice told him to enter the sphere, which he found to be an empty blue glassy bubble. In this device he was taken to a large black craft, where he encountered several beings in black uniforms with disc shaped shoulder pieces and serpent motif on their pockets. These beings included a beautiful girl 1.6m tall with copper coloured skin, blond hair and blue eyes; and also a "leader", 2.2m tall, who conversed with the witness "by putting pictures in my mind". The beings claimed to be representatives of "far galaxies".

On October 24th 1962 at 1200hrs in Fort Collins in Larimer County, Colorado. Railway employee Lester Sadler saw a grey-white circular object descend to the ground west of the city. Another witness saw a large orange object land at the foot of the Dixon Canyon Dam on Horsetooth Reservoir. Both reported the matter to the sheriff's department but searches were fruitless.

Also in October 24th 1962 at 1240hrs in Cedaredge in Delta County, Colorado. Mrs Rex Allen saw two parachute like objects landing on the northwest edge of the Grand Mesa. Searches were fruitless.

As well on October 24th 1962 at 1520hrs in Eckert in Delta County, Colorado. Mrs S Shoup saw a disc shaped object, shaped rather like a parachute, apparently coming out of an aircraft and landing. It was also seen by Mr and Mrs Gib Williams, but they were unable to make out a shape.

At 6.15 am on the morning of 26th October 1962 a luminous UFO hovered over the Horsetooth Reservoir near Masonville in Larimer County in Colorado. This was the third UFO visitation to a reservoir since 19th August when a UFO was seen over the Sheffield Reservoir system in England followed by the Oradell Reservoir sighting of September 15th that same year in New Jersey.

1963

In 1963 in Arkansas at an undisclosed location in the north of the state a woman reported that an object landed near her property and that occupants were seen. When the object had left she found burnt trees and damaged plant life at the site. The geologist from the University of Maryland who reported this did not investigate.

1964

On May 1st 1964 at 1730hrs in Walsenburg in Huerfano County, Colorado. As Russ Quintana, custodian Lonzini Meter Company was sitting in his car at the main street railway crossing, waiting for a train to pass, he observed to his north, a huge, white, very shiny object, with what looked like a hook on the bottom, descending from the west, as if to land on the hill facing Hill School. He then lost track of the thing as trees obscured his view. The next day he found a V shaped hole in the ground.

1965

One evening in September 1965 a witness in the Gunnison River Valley in Colorado saw a black triangle from the highway that was heading towards the mountains in the northeast. It flew about forty miles per hour and was no more than three hundred feet above the ground. It made no sound and had no outside lights. If the moon had not been full he would have never noticed the object. He got out of the car and watched it gliding almost overhead. On its left side nearest to the witness there were a number of port hole shaped windows. A yellowish light was coming from within and he could see the outlines of a number of small Humanoid creatures with large heads coming to the windows to peer down at him. It continued on and out of sight in a few minutes. The object was very large and very black.

1966

On 23rd March 1966 at 5.00 pm several witnesses including a postman Mr. Louis di Paolo and Mrs. Eula Mae Hoch, Assistant Editor of the Trinidad, Colorado, "Chronicle News" saw two UFOs hovering near Trinidad in Las Animas County in Colorado. The craft were clearly visible between the witnesses and the mountains in the background and had metallic surfaces, flat bottoms and dome shaped tops. They were estimated to be within half a mile of the witnesses and Mrs. Hock compared their apparent size to a six inch plate held at arms-length which would make them huge. Mrs Eulah Mae Hoch, the assistant editor of the local "Chronicle News" was in her kitchen when her 10 year old son Dean called out that there were flying saucers outside. She was not too impressed and suggested that he call her if they returned. When he did so a few minutes later she went out with him. Over a ridge, about 800m to the south, two domed disks were manoeuvring, one of the objects just clearing the trees. The other tilted and reflected the sunlight. The objects manoeuvred soundlessly for minutes. A total of 7 children and 5 adults independently reported the incident.

On April 7th 1966 at Littleton in Arapahoe, Douglas and Jefferson Counties in Colorado. Time not reported. A group of people on a picnic saw white, blue, and red lights in a wooded area, and heard a weird buzzing sound. EM effects occurred on their car when a white object followed them as they left the area.

At 11.30 pm on 7th April 1966 six seventeen year old boys and girls in a park shelter in Daniels Park in Douglas County in Colorado heard footsteps on the shelter roof. Two boys went to investigate and heard a buzzing noise that seemed to surround them. In a field they saw two red lights that were one foot in diameter. Meanwhile those left in the shelter saw a very tall man dressed in black standing outside. They left and started back to their car when the buzzing started again. They then saw two blue lights low in the sky which were then joined by a very bright light. Watching from the car they continued to hear the sound and saw four things like footballs with domes on them. They drove away with difficulty for the engine kept stalling and were followed by a huge light which did not reflect in the rearview mirror. This is another report. At 1845hrs 6 teenagers (Alan Scrivner (17), Donald Otis (17), Michael Simington (17), Patricia Retherford, Kaye Hurley and Mari Zola) were on a picnic in Daniels Park, parked about 10mm from an old dugout shelter house, where they built their fire. After eating their lunch they heard a sound outside so Donald and Mari went to investigate. From the shelter Patricia and Kaye saw a figure standing next to Mari, who heard a sound, turned her flashlight toward the figure, but saw nothing herself. They said nothing to Donald and Mari when they returned. At 2130 they heard the sound of someone walking on the roof of the shelter and Donald went out to investigate again, this time with Michael. The girls in the shelter again saw a figure 1.85-1.90m tall, wearing a long dark coat like a raincoat. Outside the two boys saw no figure but noticed an unusual quiet, then a buzzing sound, followed by a rustling. In a nearby field they saw something resembling a car with large circular rear lights which moved around. When they got back the others told them about the figure and they decided to leave. As they walked to their car, they were again aware of a pervasive buzz, then a brilliant white light shot out, along with two, dimmer, blue ones and a brighter one below them. Four of the witnesses stood on the hood of the car to get a better look and saw four oval objects with domes on top. Three of the objects were off to the right, the fourth came round from the left, changing to red as it approached, emitting red rays from the bottom. Their 1954 Ford car kept misfiring and the radio was filled with static. When they eventually got the car going, all except Michael, who was driving, saw a road 9m diameter on the road behind them. It came close but retreated when they left the park area. The engine and radio then functioned normally. Michael was quite unable to see the object in his rear view mirror. The incident was reported to the police who seemed impressed by the youngsters. (This account is a reconstruction based on various versions which gave somewhat different details)

In Denver in Denver County in Colorado during April 1966 a UFO was seen to land and Humanoids emerged from it. Even if we have to allow for a few extra Humanoids they are getting pretty normal too.

One afternoon in 1967 in Colorado. Col. Harvey G Rolfe was driving when he observed a circular object 5km away. It landed over a slight rise briefly and then took off vertically, ascending at high speed. At the site Rolfe saw a scorched area about 1.2m square and around it four imprints over a space of about 3.6m square.

1967

On March 26th 1967 (Approx. date) at Mount Blanca in Costilla County, Colorado there was a landing report.

In March 1967 in Dry Creek Basin in Arapahoe County in Colorado at 11:00 p.m. A luminous inverted-bowl shaped object moved slowly, then accelerated. The witness's car engine, radio, and lights experienced EM effects.

On April 6th 1967 at night in Redvale in Montrose County, Colorado. Someone out driving (sex not given) out driving crested a hill and saw a 30m diameter orange object. The car lights died and engine backfired though did not go out. The interior of the car seemed to get much hotter so the witness turned round but the thing paced the car and hovered over a roadside store. Part of this event was seen by another witness.

On May 14th 1967 at 2315hrs in Alamosa in Alamosa County, Colorado. The two rear tyres of a car burst when a cigar shaped object, with a throbbing red glow, came within 100m of the car. The thing then shot off.

At Chimney Rock in Archuleta County in Colorado in Mid-June 1967. A month after seeing a strange crescent shaped light over the Great Sand Dunes National Monument and painting a picture of the light, the witness Mrs. Blundell was visited by a strange character at the Pine Cove Inn. The man was deathly pale, had very dark hair, and wore a dark suit. He told Mrs. Blundell that he was not from our universe and could not read but could name the contents of any book in any library. He expressed interest in obtaining the picture of the light, but said he had no money and would return on a later date. The strange visitor then departed in a vehicle with Arizona license plates. He was not seen again. This was during the afternoon.

On 11th July 1967 a falling meteorite struck a building in Denver in Denver County in Colorado. The meteorite weighed 230 grams and was discovered in the roof of a warehouse in the northeast of Denver.

On August 27th 1967 at Texas Creek in Fremont County in Colorado. At 10.00 pm college student Kenneth Flack was driving between Salinas and Canon city, when about 1km west of Texas Creek he pulled ahead to overtake a car and camper-trailer, when his engine suddenly failed. Both he and the drivers of the other two vehicles pulled to the side. Flack now noticed in a field to his left 300-400m away a silver grey oval object with a flat base and three stilt like legs. He crossed the road, climbed the fence and walked towards the thing, which he now saw was about the size of a house. As he approached the oval section swivelled round to face him. He now began to walk away from it, but as he did so a bright light hit him, He felt as though was being hit by icicles, put his hands up to ward it off and then passed out. The other people went to his aid and told him that when the beam struck him he had been enveloped in a bluish white glow, which held him for 5 minutes. It then took off, its kegs folding under it and headed off towards Denver. As the light went out Flack fell to the ground. The people in the camper got his address and took him back to the dormitory. He failed to get the addess of these and the person in the other car. He claimed to have received a letter from the woman in the camper saying she had sent a photograph of him surrounded by the light to the Condon Committee, but this was never verified.

Around 2.00 am during August 1967 near Ovid in Sedgwick County a woman was up late working in her kitchen cleaning and polishing her cupboards when suddenly there was a bright light that filled the entire room. It seemed to come from the yard. The light was blue white in color and came from an undetermined source in the yard. She became frightened and locked all of the doors. She then woke up at 7.00 am. Later under hypnosis she recalled floating through a tunnel of light that appeared to be semisolid. She then found herself on an examination table with her head inside an oven like contraption. Two men stood by the witness. One of them held a small black book. Another figure stood above her. Two other men approached the witness carrying hoses with round ball metal ends. Later she recalled looking outside the window of the spaceship and seeing the countryside.

Near Alamosa in Alamosa County in Colorado on Wednesday 13th September 1967 "Snippy" the horse was found with the flesh completely stripped from its head and neck and the vital organs were also missing. There were also fifteen circular exhaust marks found on the ground covering an area of one hundred by fifty yards. The Chico bush was flattened and near it were six identical holes two inches wide by four inches deep. Individual witnesses had seen a strange object in the sky at rooftop level on the day the horse had disappeared and later there was a high radiation count in the area where the horse was found. Looks like the menu was getting exotic now. When were they going to add long pig to the menu? Or had they already? Quite a varied menu it seems. If you are not sure what Long Pig is just look in the mirror and view this formerly Polynesian delicacy. Other sources state that Snippy was actually called Lady.

At Lakewood in Jefferson County in Colorado on October 10th 1967. At 12: 45 a.m. Norman C, driving home, was flagged down by a man with a forked goatee, well over 6-feet tall wearing a jacket with four gold bars on each shoulder. The man talked to the witness without moving his mouth, presumably by telepathy. He asked where the North Star was, and what the date was; in response to the answer, he replied, "In your primitive time." He asked what the witness had in his mouth; on being told it was a cigarette, he replied, "Oh, one of your… vices." He asked about the car and called it; "your primitive mode of transportation." When the witness asked who he was and where he was from, the man replied, "I cannot tell you now, but my colleagues and I will return." Then the man walked about four feet away and vanished. Norman then heard a noise, looked up and saw hovering overhead a red object the size of a football field. With a whining noise it went straight up, joined two more objects, and disappeared at tremendous speed.

On October 28th 1967 at 1930hrs in Naturita in Montrose County, Colorado. David Barnard (30), his two sons (10, 8), along with his brother in law Jack Kerns (41) along with his 15 year old son were returning home from a hunting trip, southeast of Maturita, travelling along a mountain road. Near Lone Cone Mountain they observed a fiery orange ball moving above the treetops in the distance. It then seemed to come down the ridge towards them and the party stopped to watch it. . The two men observed the object from 300m range in their rifle scopes. It appeared round, with a dome on top, from which protruded an antenna and had coloured lights, which appeared to be square windows, around the bottom. Around its base were a group of 7 or 8 flickering, apparently revolving, blue lights. The object appeared to pace them to State Route 80, where it disappeared from sight.

At NORAD in Cheyenne Mountain in Colorado Springs in El Paso County in Colorado during 1967. According to researcher William F. Hamilton III he met a certain M.J. in California who had been a captain with the office of Naval Intelligence. M.J. said he held a C-4 clearance. It, along with P-4 and S-4 was a specialty clearance. "S" stands for scientific. In 1967, his superior reportedly sent him to an underground facility (8 levels down) in the vicinity of NORAD headquarters at Cheyenne Mountain to check on the recovery and examination of discs that had crash-landed in the southwest. He had entered a corridor or tunnel to a larger area where he saw two discs through a large window. One craft had a large opaque dome sitting on a ring atop a disc with a flat metal finish. This particular craft had a symbol on its flange. He was amazed to see ladders and scaffolding all over the discs and men crawling on these, making various studies and measurements. Nearby were two alien-looking bodies encased in glass. The bodies were no more than 4.5feet tall, had slits for eyes, and normal proportioned heads (unlike the enlarged cranium humanoids). They were dressed in flight suits and appeared to be preserved cadavers. The entrance to the examined craft was out of his view. Suddenly while absorbed in looking through the glass a sergeant major and a member of security challenged him for being in a restricted area. A lieutenant, observing this, also came over and asked to see M.J.' s credentials and his authorization for being in the area. M.J. showed his ID and authorization but he was still asked to leave the area. He stated that this incident sparked his further interest in the subject and when he had returned to his post, he often kept an eye out for any documents referring to aliens. One document he saw described an incident in which a live human-like alien was picked up in Death Valley, California (date unknown, probably in or after 1967). M.J. believes that Naval Intelligence has some authority in the secret UFO program.

1969

At Uravan inMontrose County, Colorado one morning in June, 1969. The young witness was living in the West end of Montrose County and early one morning he was awakened by the barking of the family dog named 'Tippi,' outside his bedroom. Tippi never really barked unless someone or something was in a yard that wasn't supposed to be. He remembers waking up and hearing Tippi's constant barking and wondering why his older brother sleeping in a bunk bed above him and his parents, were not waking up to tell Tippi to be quiet. Finally he had enough and decided to turn over in his bed and look out the window himself. What he saw he couldn't believe. He saw a small circular "ship" with its landing gear down and hatch with stairs folded down to the ground. Next to the ship were several green colored lizard-like aliens. Their eyes were bright yellow and they seemed to have webbed hands. Their bodies were thin and scaly and their feet were V-shaped. The witness thought that they 'were searching for something.' Suddenly another alien came out of the ship. 'He' was much bigger than the others and seemed to be giving orders. Tippi again began her barking and the alien came closer to the house and appeared to be upset about the barking and began walking towards Tippi, looking her over.

The witness then jumped out of bed and ran into his parent's room to wake them up. He remembered how hard it was to wake his mother up since she acted as if she was drugged or something. Finally she woke up and he told her that something was going on outside and it was going to hurt Tippi. Sluggishly his mother followed him to bed, and she said she couldn't see anything outside; all she wanted to do was sleep. The last thing the witness remembered was seeing a dark figure trying to look into the window and then going to sleep.

Near Denver in Colorado on July 15th 1969 at Midnight. A group of four men driving from Denver saw a slow moving 'meteor' and followed it up a road toward a hill. When they got there they saw a UFO land. One man got out of the vehicle and tried to shoot at it but the gun misfired, so he ran off into the dark. The car stalled and two more men got out and went towards the UFO. It was a disk with a dome and two revolving plates going in different directions. It was black and silver with a tail with a red light on it. It had orange and yellow lights that glowed. They then saw two very large "men" exit the UFO, both about ten feet tall with very long arms that reached to their shins. One entity picked up a rock half the size of a VW Bug and carried it into the UFO. The other entity pulled a giant bush out of the ground and dragged it into the UFO. The UFO hummed like "burnt wiring" but had no smell. The yellow and orange lights then became brighter and the UFO lifted off the ground and went straight up. They attempted to locate the man who had run off into the dark but decided to go back down the narrow road. Yellow lights followed them and then they were stopped by a road block. They couldn't turn around so they stopped. Five men wearing black shiny helmets that went to their shoulders and wearing one-piece 'braided' uniforms and strange boots with individual toes would not let them pass and came up to the car windows on both sides. It seemed to the witnesses that they were there most of the night. The next thing they remember was being back in their building with their car parked in the lot. They had no memory how they got home. The man who ran off into the desert showed up in Denver two and a half days later with no memory of how he got home. All four men remember the same thing and thought of reporting the incident at the time, but didn't know to whom.

1970

On October 13th 1970 at 2030hrs in Dove Creek in Dolores County, Colorado. Dale Kell (17) and his girlfriend Diane Bard (18) were motorcycling north when they heard a whooshing sound to their left and saw an object, the shape of a jelly bean, and rise into the air from the sagebrush. The thing had three lights close together on its top. One was large and bright, the others were smaller, orange and white respectively. The thing lit up the area like day and emitted a sound like dull thunder. The object was 6-9m long and remained at ground level, hovering immediately overhead at one time. The couple drove along with the object in pursuit. As they approached a house, the lights on the object went out. They went to Dale's house and brought his family back to the spot. Six people watched as the couple drove down the unpaved road and again the object rose out of the sage brush and followed them. A Dove Creek farmer and his wife, the Whyte family of Towacc and another couple saw a bright object flying near Ute Mountain at 2030.

1971

On May 24th 1971 at 0300hrs in Mount Blanca in Costilla County, Colorado. A group of campers at a cabin at the foot of Mt Blanca were awakened by loud noises outside, and saw a flash of light and shadowy figures. Unusual footprints were found at the site.

On September 4th 1971 at 2230hrs on Big Danger Mountain in Johnson County, Arkansas. MRS Tessie Lamley and Mrs Mary Rommel, both of Little Rock, were visiting the Arthur Henderson farm, south of the Big Danger Mountain, when both saw unusual objects Mary saw two objects in a meadow, 400m east of the farmhouse; one was hovering, with many pulsating lights, the other was manoeuvring, with a massive bunch of white pulsating lights all over it. Tessie saw red pulsating lights, which glided in silently from the southwest over Dardanelle Reservoir. She lost sight of the lights when they went behind trees. Both women estimated that their sightings lasted two or three minutes.

In 1971 in Loveland Park in Larimer County, Colorado. Two young men saw a car in a canyon some 15m below the road. The car was undamaged but a couple in it were semi-conscious. The woman told the highway patrol that they had seen a light before the incident but did not know how they had come off the road. 15m from the car was a 20m diameter stained circle.

1972

On September 13th 1972 in Burlington in Kit Carson County in Colorado. A rural family, who police say are responsible people, reported that a UFO "as big as a house" flew parallel to their car as they were driving down a country road at night. One witness said the object landed and took off twice in a nearby field. The object, according to the witness, was round and big, and "rays" appeared to be coming out of it. Or this version. Ronald and Geraldine Ludwig and their 12 year old daughter were out driving when Geraldine saw a white glowing object, the size of a house, giving off a dull light. The thing paced the car, turned the corner with them and then veered over the car. It landed briefly in a field of tall corn, shot up back into the sky, flaring up, and then descended again, lighting up the field. They saw that it was large, round and appeared to have rays coming from it. The family were unnerved and drove home, where they reported the matter to the sheriff, but his investigations found no traces.

1973

On 27th October 1973 a building was hit by a falling meteorite in Canon City in Fremont County in Colorado. Had invisible meteorites or some such been causing the skyquakes? On 27th October 1973 the state of Florida was shaken by a skyquake that shook buildings in four counties. This was three days after skyquakes had struck Pennsylvania, Maryland, West Virginia, Ohio and Indiana on 24th October at 9.00 pm when windows were rattled over a wide area. Earthquakes are rare in Florida due to its limestone foundation that cushions shocks. The meteorite was a stony H6 chondrite which punctured the roof of a garage.

1975

At 8.00 am during May 1975 near La Junta in Otero County in Colorado a couple driving to Lamar suddenly noticed a hovering elongated doughnut shaped object about the size of half of a football field hovering at a height of three hundred and fifty feet. It had a highly polished metallic look. They pulled off to the side of the road but could not get close to the object because of a barbed wire fence. They watched it for a while when suddenly three or four little white clouds popped in from the East followed by a huge cloud that moved in front and covered the metallic object. When the cloud moved on the object had vanished. Both witnesses felt calm and peaceful. Under hypnotic regression the wife remembered trying to run towards the object but her husband told her to stay in the car. Suddenly she found herself inside the object where two beings, one male and one female, greeted her. They were very tall and thin and beautiful. Their hair was long and blonde and so were their eyelashes. The male entity wore a silver belt. She did not want to leave the craft but suddenly found herself back in the car. There had been sightings of similar blonde haired aliens in California that same month. Tourists?

In Summer 1975 at 0800hrs in La Junta in Otero County, Colorado. A couple driving from Boulder to Lamar on a deserted road on this bright morning saw a metallic elongated object with a central hole, about half the length of an American football field, at about 100m altitude. The couple watched the object for 30-45 minutes, from the other side of a barbed wire fence. The woman sent it a mental message, at which 3-4 small white clouds appeared travelling east to west, followed by a large cloud that covered the metallic thing. When it had passed the object had gone, so they continued their journey. Years later under hypnotic regression the woman recalled wanted to run towards the object, but being restrained by her husband. Nevertheless she found herself inside the object, where she encountered two beings, male and female, 1.9m tall, thin, with long blond hair and eyelashes and white skin, dressed in blue jumpsuits. They gave her a message of peace and told her to return.

In Summer 1975 in Franktown in Douglas County, Colorado. A solid looking army green thing, looking like a helicopter, landed about 100m from a house near Franktown. A female witness was terrified by the incident.

At 10.00 pm on 21st August 1975 in Logan County in Colorado Sheriff Graves and his Deputies went out to investigate an unknown helicopter coming in from the East. Seventeen ground units were involved and the Sheriff was in a plane with two Deputies. There were cattle mutilations in the area. The night was clear and there was no cloud. The chase ended at 4.00 am in Northern Nebraska over a missile silo. By this time the mystery craft had turned off its lights.

During August 1975 in Washington County in Colorado the body of a mutilated heifer was found. It appeared to have been dropped from a height of several feet. There was nothing there though that it could have been dropped from. Or had there been? Had it been what the Sheriff and his Deputies had been chasing?

In Summer 1975 at 0800hrs in La Junta, Colorado. A couple driving from Boulder to Lamar on a deserted road on this bright morning saw a metallic elongated object with a central hole, about half the length of an American football field, at about 100m altitude. The couple watched the object for 30-45 minutes, from the other side of a barbed wire fence. The woman sent it a mental message, at which 3-4 small white clouds appeared travelling east to west, followed by a large cloud that covered the metallic thing. When it had passed the object had gone, so they continued their journey. Years later under hypnotic regression the woman recalled wanted to run towards the object, but being restrained by her husband. Nevertheless she found herself inside the object, where she encountered two beings, male and female, 1.9m tall, thin, with long blond hair and eyelashes and white skin, dressed in blue jumpsuits. They gave her a message of peace and told her to return.

In the Rocky Mountains in Colorado one evening in October 1975. A U.S. Air Force security officer Jim Carter was hiking in the mountains when he saw a light on the hill and went up to investigate and saw two individuals standing there. They called him by name and said, "How nice of you to come." as if they were waiting for him. Down the hill Jim could see a lighted disk on the ground. He said he must have been there for about five minutes. Jim studied the two beings closely. "They seemed young and very thin." He said. "They were about 5 feet 6 inches tall, I would say. Their tight fitting clothing was like a flight suit. I noticed it changed color from brown to silver." Jim said they were very fair, with large eyes. "They looked perfectly normal and relaxed. They had blond hair with something over the head, but I could see some hair." Their facial features were fine and the thing that impressed him the most was their eyes which were very large and striking. Jim added, "They seemed completely sure of themselves. They handled the situation very well. Nothing happened that was phenomenal. They didn't give me any earth shattering information. I guess I had some illusion that they might give me a cure for cancer or something like that because they seemed very intelligent." The beings said they would come back and talk again someday. Jim didn't say goodbye, he just knew it was time to go. The visitors had spoken in ordinary English and didn't seem to use telepathy, which is often reported in similar cases. They didn't tell Jim where they came from but he felt they were from a distant world and came in peace. Both visitors went back into the craft that was resting on the ground. There may have been someone else waiting for them within the vehicle. The lighted disk rose from the ground and shot up into the night sky leaving Jim alone with his thoughts. He tried to tell his family and others what happened but most everybody didn't believe him.

In early September 1975 in Huerfano County, Colorado. Two telephone company operatives working on a mountain top saw a sort of helicopter land in the valley below. An occupant got out for a short time and then re-entered the thing, which took off.

On September 22nd 1975 at night in Crowley County, Colorado. The driver of a pickup truck was almost forced off the road by something resembling a helicopter. He used his CB to call for help and when police arrivrd they found in a frantic state. One officer shot at the thing and heard a ricochet. Personnel from several agencies chased the thing, which made a sort of whistling sound, first to the west and then to the north, where it went out of sight.

On October 9th 1975 (approx. date) in Carr in Weld County, Colorado. Something like a small blue and white helicopter circled and landed on several ranches, including that of the Sidwell family

In October 1975 at 0400hrs in Sterling in Logan County, Colorado. Some kilometres south-west of Sterling, two cattle men were sat out watching out for feared cattle mutilators, when they saw three human like figures which seemed to glide over the feed lot fence. The sheriff's department was called and though officers reached the spot in minutes, so sign of the intruders could be found and there were no footprints in the muddy field.

Also in October 1975 in Sterling, Colorado. Two young women reported that they had shot at a hairy humanoid that had entered their lot. The thing then ran off. Broken branches were found at the site. Is there a connection between some Hairy Humanoid sightings and UFOs? Do they come from the same dimension or dimensions?

In Fall 1975 in Washington County, Colorado. A rancher' daughter was in the house alone when she saw something resembling a helicopter fly over a field about 100m away, going down below the height of a building on the property. It came within 30m of the house, and she heard a sort of muffled sound.

On November 2nd 1975 (or 9th) at 2030hrs in Otis in Washington County, Colorado. Reporter Bill Jackson was driving his wife Cheryl and young child home to Sterling when 30km north of Otis their attention was caught by a red light approaching in the overcast sky. They first thought that it was an aircraft and were concerned that it was flying dangerously low. They stopped and Bill got out, at which he noted that the thing made no sound. The object then passed over at less than 30m altitude, so low that Bill thought he could have hit it with a stone. It was an elongated object with at least 12 rows of multi-coloured lights and with indentations on its underside and was travelling at no more than 65kph. After about 4 to 5 minutes the Jacksons drove off at speed.

1976

In Hall Valley in Clear Creek County in Colorado. On May 23rd 1976 around noon. Three mountain climbers were near the summit of a mountain in a very isolated area and had found some peculiar tracks on the snow when they spotted four figures approaching them; two men, and two women. Despite the inhospitable location, all four were wearing light clothing and each had a peculiar strap across their chests and backs. One of the men, apparently their leader, was tall and husky, with a crew cut and deep set blue piercing eyes, his female companion was tall and very attractive. The second couple seemed normal but was considerably older. After a brief conversation in which the odd foursome gave conflicting answers and called motorcycles "two wheeled vehicles," the four left quickly, walking up the steep mountainside at impossible speed, apparently without leaving tracks and quickly disappeared from sight.

On June 9th 1976 at 10.00 pm near Echo Lake, (Arapahoe) Colorado. Michael R, Lusignan, a patent examiner, was hiking near Echo Lake when he became lost. About 10 P.M. he saw 2 rectangular objects "float" down and land by a creek. Thinking they might be rescuers looking for him, he went to them, but found 15 to 20 men, women & children "dressed in Indian or gypsy clothing", who talked in low whispers. He could not understand anything they said. They set up camp and made him move to another campsite for the night. The next morning they were gone. Lusignan was found by rescuers 4 days later.

About August 5th 1976 at 4.00 am near Sterling (Logan), Colo. After 3 successive nights in which cattle were mysteriously killed and mutilated in a feed lot, 2 cowhands were on the watch at 4 A.M. when they saw 3 human-like figures" go over the feedlot fence. The figures didn't move like humans, but seemed to glide. They called police, who arrived within 6 minutes, but the figures were not to be found. Although the ground was muddy, no foot prints were found near the fence, and no mud upon it.

1977

It was reported that near Clearwater, Colorado about January, 1977. The main witness and his wife had bought a ranch in an isolated area in 1975, and for more than a year they had been experiencing strange sounds, UFO manifestations and Bigfoot sightings on the property. There were some cattle mutilations as well. One night the witness and his eldest son went up to the top of a hill to examine a burned spot from the previous year. As they sat in the car, a beam of yellow light shone on them from nearby woods. Walking towards the trees, they discovered a buzzing black box, clearly seen in the light of the full moon. As they approached, it changed tone, now sounding like a swarm of angry bees. The two retreated to the safety of the car. The witness told the young man to stay by the car and went back to the spot where the black box had been; it was now gone. He saw a light in the trees and, walking toward the light, came upon two individuals standing near the light source. As he approached, they spoke to him, saying "How nice of you to come." Some distance away, down a slope, was a disk, illuminated, about 50 or 60 feet away. The two beings apologized for the trouble they had caused, promising a more equitable arrangement. They told him several things he was not to repeat, but which had no special meaning for him at the time. They regretted damage done to several of the cars, but they did not acknowledge responsibility for any of the local cattle mutilations. They told him he was wise to have backed off from the black box, which was nearby. They pointed in a particular direction and the tone on the box changed; as it did, a Bigfoot type creature got up off the ground and walked toward the box. The tone changed and the creature dropped. The meeting lasted five minutes. In appearance, the beings were similar; human looking about 5'6" in height, and wearing a tight-fitting outfit like a flight uniform. The suits changed colors from brown to silver. Their complexions were fair and they had blond hair, not long. The most notable features were the eyes, which were very large but otherwise normal looking. They were different in subtle ways but could pass as humans in ordinary situations. Before the witness walked away from the scene he was told by the beings that he would see them again. Or this. At an undisclosed location a man walking to the top of a hill saw a light amid the trees below him and felt drawn to the site, where he became surrounded by a glow and his legs immobilised. Two almost human male beings, 1.65m tall, with large eyes short blonde hair approached. Their tight fitting suits turned from brown to silver as they did so. They stood by a dimly lit disc. The beings seemed to expect him, apologised and shown him a black box, which knocked over a hairy humanoid. He could not remember what the beings said him and he felt it was irrelevant. Nonetheless he felt that they were friends. Before the incident he had a number of anomalous experiences including poltergeist effects, appearances of hairy humanoids, cattle being mutilated and strange lights and objects seen around the place. Afterwards he was woken in the night to see a 2m tall, bald headed being with large eyes and long thin arms and legs and large eyes. The thing, which wore a helmet and had a box on its chest, gave the witness the impression that it was old and helpless.

In February 1977 at 2.00 am at Clearwater in Colorado. On a weekend not long after his encounter in the woods, Jim was at the ranch sleeping on the couch. It was a weekend, as John was out from Denver, About 2 a.m., Jim was suddenly fully awake, and found he was unable to move. He was looking toward the French Windows. He saw, standing there before the window, a being seven feet tall, unlike the two he'd seen earlier. He was very thin, and had a box-like device on its chest, pointed, with three hose like extensions on either side, and wore what appeared to be a "space helmet over its head with a plastic covering (visor?). "It was more or less pathetic in appearance—almost helplessly pathetic. It was just looking at me in the same way that you would look at a patient on the table, not cruelly or indifferent—just looking." Jim kept making noises trying to call out to John and Barbara, and suddenly it just vanished. He was able to then call out, and when Barbara and John came in the room there was nothing to be seen Following the earlier encounter, the nuisances at the ranch house had let up—the disasters, the pounding on the house, and the noises. Then, following this appearance, the hostilities started up once more. ,After an accident with paint resulting in a fire on the porch, they decided it was time to leave the ranch.

1978

At 10.20 pm on 14th October 1978 in Denver in Colorado Peggy Otis was traveling by car with her young daughter when she saw a massive dome shaped object descend overhead emitting sparks from underneath. The adult witness jumped out of the car and now was able to see a figure moving within the object. She received a telepathic message telling her not to be afraid and not to forget. The craft then flew out of sight emitting a humming sound. Later under hypnosis the witness was able to recall what the figure inside the dome looked like. The Humanoid was described as having a white head, no ears, large slanted eyes and was only four-foot tall. It appeared to be holding something resembling a steering wheel.

1979

In April 1979 at 0200hrs in Colorado. At an unspecified location a woman and her young son were wakened by orange light pulsing into the room from outside. The woman thought it may have been police cars and got up to see what was happening. She saw not an orange light, but a blue one, pulsing, on the underside of a domed disc which seemed really close. She felt transfixed by the thing and unable to decide what to do. After a minute she just went back to bed.

On August 11th 1979 at 2300hrs in Wheat Ridge in Jefferson County, Colorado. An 18 year old college student and his girlfriend, an 18 year old telephone company employee, were sat in a car looking at the houses at the foot of a mountain off Soda Creek Road, a sparsely populated region, when they noticed a white light two thirds of the way up the mountain. They wondered how a house could be built that far up, where there were no roads. The terrain was too wooded, rocky and steep for a helicopter also. This light then seemed to increase in size, becoming four times as bright as the houses at the base. From the distance of 1.5-2km it then seemed to consist of a cluster of four lights, with a dark space in the middle. After about three minutes the light source silently rose over the mountain top, hovered there for 3 seconds and then dropped down behind it, a glow remaining over the mountain. There was no radio reception in the valley that night.

1980

In Spring 1980 a horse that was penned in a corral with four other horses was found dead from an unknown cause. The corpse was mutilated by clean incision around the anus and one eye was clouded over with a grey film. This was in Cripple Creek in Colorado.

At 11.45 pm on November 18/19 1980 near Longmont in Boulder and Weld Counties in Colorado a couple was returning home one night when an intense blue beam of light shone on their vehicle. They heard a swishing sound and the car lights dimmed. At the same time they felt the car being lifted off the road. The next conscious memory was one hour later. The woman found odd marks on her lower abdomen. Later under hypnosis the husband described the car being lifted into a hovering domed object apparently suspended above a heavy mist. A strong odor pervaded the area. Inside a five-foot gray skinned being wearing a shiny gold colored outfit led them into a brightly lighted area where they were examined nude on a table. The beings were described as having elongated bald heads with narrow chins and four elongated fingers. They communicated with the witness by using telepathy. Or this. A couple were driving home to Longmont when their car was struck by a blue light beam and they heard a swishing sound as loud as a jet taking off. Their car lights dimmed and the radio developed static then faded out. They then felt the rear of the car lift up from the road. The light and sound then disappeared and they continued their journey at 80kph. Looking at their watches they discovered an hour unaccounted for. On reaching a petrol station, the man, getting out of the car was disorientated. The following day he found a rectangular mark on his abdomen. Under hypnotic regression the male witness recalled that the car was transported into the vicinity of a large domed object. The car was surrounded by a red mist with a strong odour. A door opened in the domed object, they were drawn in, greeted by a grey skinned being with a "long" head and long thumbless hands, which seemed to be able to read his mind. The man was then placed on a table, which seemed to have materialised out of gas. There he was scanned by a floating light, felt that the entity was "in tune with his mind", spots on his skin were burning. Both he and his wife were naked, and she was screaming. He also felt that his memory was taken out of him, then returned with additional information. After the examination the couple were allowed to leave the craft and return to their car, still suspended in space. The blue light then surrounded the car again and it was returned to the road. The man claimed they had given him extra strength and knowledge but he did not want this. The wife refused hypnotic regression and the couple later left without leaving a forwarding address.

1981

At 10.00 pm in late Fall 1981 in Denver in Denver County in Colorado the witness who lived in the outskirts surrounded by several acres of open ground was in her kitchen cooking when she felt compelled to go look out the front window. Her dog did the same. She was startled to see what she thought was a group of children standing at the edge of the lawn near a street light. She then realized the figures were not human, but short beings with oversized bald heads with thin bodies and long arms. Their color was a dark shade of brown. Their movements were jerky, irregular and quick, almost insect like. The witness became frightened and her dog hid under the bed until the next morning. The beings then apparently left.

On Interstate-70, Rocky Mountains, Colorado on November 29th 1981. That night truck driver David, accompanied by his girlfriend Lia, was heading back to New York from a vacation in California. It was a clear, chilly night, and the moon was full as they drove through Colorado, thirty miles from the entrance to the Rockies (Eisenhower Tunnel). There was going to be a total lunar eclipse that night, so both wanted to be up in the mountains to see it better. There were driving on a flat, straight road when David looked up and saw a bright red star slowly move across the sky. He thought at first it was a satellite, but then it stopped and shot straight down below the horizon. He thought that was strange, and wondered what it was because no satellite or aircraft could possibly do what he saw the red light do. After about five minutes, both noticed another ball of light, but this one shot up from the horizon and then moved slowly overhead. As it reached the point directly above the couple, it began to move at the same speed as the car, making it appear motionless. David described the object as resembling a red ball of light and added that it was impossible to tell how high the UFO was, but he guessed it was two thousand feet or so above the ground. No matter how much he tried speeding up or slowing down, the object stayed directly over the car. Lia added that it looked like it was spying on them and that she felt some kind of telepathic communication with the object; she suddenly yelled out "they want to capture us!" while David tried to make an escape. Both say they became frightened. There was no one else on the road. The UFO followed them for another ten miles and then suddenly streaked backward. They lost sight of it. David, still shaken, continued driving and turned on the radio, hoping the music would take their minds off of what just happened. After listening to the music for half an hour, the radio reception became static-filled and distorted. David's first thought was that perhaps the mountains were blocking the signal. He looked in the rearview mirror and saw a distant light on the road approach very quickly. It was getting brighter and brighter and then all of a sudden, flash! It was right behind them, about ten feet off the ground. David described the object as being some type of disc that glowed white in the center and red around its edges. The object was about three times the size of their car and moved completely silently. David described the lights as being a sort of fluorescent white and red and they couldn't see any windows. David floored the gas pedal and was now going ninety miles per hour, yet the strange object kept the same distance from the car with seemingly no effort at all. The object maintained its distance, about ten feet behind the car, regardless of whether David slowed down or sped up again. Lia panicked and screamed that the object was a UFO, and that the aliens onboard wanted to take them. David thought that perhaps the two of them were going to be kidnapped and put in a zoo on another planet. As he watched the UFO in the rearview mirror, a figure appeared at the very front of the ship. David said, "It was strange, it was as if this being was always there but was hidden behind the light. When it came very close to the front, I could see the figure's outline very clearly." He described the "alien" as being very slim with a large head and large, slanted eyes that seemed to glow yellow despite the creature hiding behind the ship's lights. David then head a voice in his head say, "You will not be harmed. We are interested in studying you and the female." He said that when he heard the voice there was also a loud buzzing sound inside his head. David yelled out, "I don't care who or what you are! If you want to communicate with the human race, then why pick us?! Get away, we don't know anything!" The car was now traveling very fast, and they were approaching the entrance to the Rockies. The eclipse was over and the moon was setting in the West. David was shocked to see a sign in front of them, "Denver." The couple, along with the car, seemed to have been transported through the Rocky Mountains! They continued to drive, hardly speaking to each other, and stopped at the nearest motel. They both took showers, feeling unclean and extremely tired. They stayed at the motel overnight and left for New York in the morning. The rest of the trip was uneventful. It seems David and Lia experienced at least four hours of missing time. The mileage of the car only showed an eighteen-mile difference between the time of the close encounter with the UFO and when the couple found themselves on the East side of the Rocky Mountains, but in actuality, this is a distance of over a hundred and fifty miles, they also still had almost three quarters of a tank of gas left.

1982

On February 18th 1982 at 0130hrs in La Junta in Otero County, Colorado. While driving home through small town Colorado with his wife Marilyn, Terry Wejs began to feel an intense thirst which required him to take some stops for coke. About 30km east of La Junta Terry saw a light in the sky which he first through was beaming down from a cliff and then realised came from two columns of light on an object at about 600m altitude and roused his half asleep wife to watch it,, but the light had now disappeared. Shortly after this the thing or something similar reappeared, with two columns of light on its underside, beamed at their car. The red and blue flashing lights came on and the thing plunged from about 600m altitude to about 5m above the road, and passed over their car as another car approached to the right. They were able to see that the thing was a rectangle, about 18m long and as thick as a car. The passing car accelerated away and the object went into the southwest. About 5 minutes later it reappeared from the southwest and swept low over the road ahead of them. This was repeated a number of times, the object retreating when they entered towns. Eventually they spent the rest of the night in one such town to escape the thing.

In Colorado in February, 1982 a forest ranger stationed at a remote and desolate mountain area was out conducting a search in his snowmobile after witnesses reported flashing lights in the mountains. As he headed back to his cabin after failing to locate anything, he spotted some peculiar footprints in the snow, which led to the wooded area. He dismounted from the snowmobile and walked towards the woods. As he was about to enter the brush, a small five-foot tall man with a very large head and huge eyes stepped out with his hand raised and palm open. He wore a tight-fitting greenish coverall. Next a beautiful blond haired woman with brilliant blue eyes also stepped out of the woods. She wore a light colored, thin gown and was barefooted. As the witness walked back to the snowmobile he heard a strange crackling sound and when he looked back the short entity had disappeared. The witness eventually took the blond woman to his cabin. There he was compelled to have sexual relations with her, and when he woke up the next morning she was gone. The witness claims that about 18 months later he saw the same blond woman standing in front of his house holding a small golden haired child.

On May 9th 1982 at 0900hrs in Laporte in Larimer County, Colorado. Eddie and Dorothy Robinson saw a silvery object on the ground in a meadow about 800m away. The thing's underside was "pod shaped" and about 1.2-1.5m long. The thing took off with a sound like that of a propeller plane. Police investigated but no traces were found.

On August 13th 1982 at 1855hrs in Jefferson in Park County, Colorado. Ed Stonor and his wife Denise were driving to a camp site, with their 14 year old daughter and their dog both asleep. 6.5km south of Jefferson n Denise saw two yellow-white lights that came down low over the car. The next thing they remembered was that it was dark and they were 65km further along, the time now being nearly 2300hrs. Under hypnotic regression the usual abduction story emerged as did multiple other episodes.

On August 30th 1982 at 0200hrs in El Paso County, Colorado. Elizabeth Conway was awakened by a sort of ticking sound and saw a red glow coming through her screen door. Thios came from a large orange sphere that descended at an angle towards a pond about 100m away. The object, which was at a lower angle than the moon, touched down on the pond for about a minute, still emmitng a sound, which resembled the sparks from an electric motor. The thing then took off at a 45 degree angle and the ticking sound ceased. The next day Elizabeth discovered she had a rash on her arms which had not been there before. This had almost gone the next day. During the observation her horses acted up, and neighbouring dogs also acted up. Later an oval area of depressed grass about 9m diameter was found at the site.

1983

On October 23rd 1983 near Gardner in Huerfano County in Colorado a cow was mutilated. There was a reported encounter with monstrous beings.

On October 25th 1983 in Wet Mountain Valley in Custer County in Colorado a cow was mutilated. There were UFO sightings near Greenhorn Peak as well as a reported encounter with monstrous beings.

The following day on October 26th 1983 in Huerfano County in Colorado a cow was mutilated and bright spotlights were seen. There was a reported encounter with monstrous beings. One object was observed.

1984

On April 13th 1985 (or following week) at 2330hrs in Northglenn in Adams and Weld Counties, Colorado. A couple were dropping off a female friend at the car park of the AT and T building in the outskirts of Denver, and as they approached the building their attention was caught by red and white lights shining down on the roof. When they stopped they saw that the lights were hovering 6m above the roof, about 20-30m from their location. They seemed to be an oval formation about 9m long, 6m wide and to be attached to the bottom of a dark object. When they opened the door they heard a faint hum but were not sure where it came from. When they slammed shut the door again, the object rose about 15m then stopped. The thing then began moving away, the couple tried to follow it, but it was lost to sight. The couple forgot about the incident for 4 years and only recalled it when reading a magazine article about UFOs.

1985

At 7.30 pm March 16th 1985 in Dotsero in Eagle County in Colorado ranchers saw a hovering disc 2000 meters away. It shot up and hovered again. It was an intense white light with red, green, and blue lights. There was an electromagnetic effect as the car stalled as the rancher drove to a neighbor's ranch. It was observed by more than three witnesses at a ranch for 45 minutes.

1987

On August 8th 1987 near Denver, Colorado a security guard sighted a large circle of light over a pasture near Denver, Colorado. Two cows were found dead and mutilated the next day.

At 3.20 am on October 25th 1987 in Fort Collins in Colorado during a heavy snowfall witnesses saw a flashing 20 foot in diameter object on the roadside. The craft then followed the vehicle for a mile. A figure was briefly seen inside the object.

1989

At 2.30 am in August 1989 in Wheat Ridge in Jefferson County in Colorado the 11 year old witness was laying on his bed in the basement of his grandparent's house when suddenly he woke up lying in a most peculiar position. He was lying on his back with the covers pulled up to his chest and his arms lying over them. He then heard his parents breathing (sleeping in the next room) deepen dramatically. For some reason he began to stare at the only window in the room. Just then an alien-type figure appeared to float through the wall and its head went through the window. After it levitated through the wall it began floating in jerking motions towards the right hand side of the bed. When it stopped next to the witness an uncontrolled fear enveloped him and he attempted to scream but was unable to. Then the alien touched the middle of his forehead. It only had 3 fingers and a thumb. The witness felt completely paralyzed and the alien began controlling his breathing in attempt to prevent the witness from screaming and from suffocating. The Humanoid was a "typical" gray, with smooth gray skin, huge black eyes, about 4 feet tall, with a large head. The witness eventually calmed down and at this point the alien removed his hand from the forehead and floated back out the same way he came in. He does not remember anything else of the encounter but feels that there was some missing time involved. A week later he found a scar on the back of his leg.

At 10.00 am on September 6th 1989 in Rock Creek Canyon in El Paso County in Colorado bow hunter Juan Maestas was quietly stalking a herd of young elks uphill in a wooded area when he heard a twig snapping to his left. He froze in his tracks. He turned his eyes to look at the source of the noise and was stunned to see "a fat ugly little guy, about 3-feet tall," who turned at the same instant and stared at him. The little man was about 50 feet away next to a tall pine tree. As they locked eyes, Maestas was able to discern the little man's wrinkled forehead, clean-shaven face, and pink hued skin. He was wearing what appeared to be green overalls with suspenders and a flat-topped floppy hat. His hair was reddish and was sticking out from underneath the cap. He had little eyes that seemed red and bloodshot. The little man sort of gave Maestas a smile and suddenly darted behind a tree. Maestas quickly ran to the spot but the little man had totally disappeared. Two weeks earlier, very close to this same location, a family of five on a picnic had witnessed the same or very similar entity that was also dressed in green overalls and hat. Was this a local with a few recessive genes or an alien hominoid?

1993

On Feb. 24th 1993 between Mosca and Hooper, both in Alamosa County in Colorado at 10:30 AM. a silent bell-shaped object, the color of brushed aluminum, buzzed a car being driven by two women on Highway 17 in the San Luis Valley. It headed off toward the sound flying at 100 feet above the highway.

At 1.00 am on August 19th 1993 in Baca Chalets in the San Luis Valley in Colorado the witness who had been having difficulty in sleeping was watching late night television and turning off the light when she heard noises coming from the kitchen. She called out but got no response. Puzzled she climbed back into bed, and shut off the light. Seconds later just as her eyes were getting accustomed to the dark, "through the wall, ten or twelve creatures, about three and a half to four-feet tall" glided into the room in a "tight group", less than three feet from where she lay. She sat up in amazement, looking at them. When they originally came in she could see right through them but as they got into the room they became solid. The beings clustered around the foot of her bed looking at her. She felt the entities, were 'cold, and completely indifferent, maybe a little curious." They were small and slight and had huge almond-shaped eyes. Sleeping next to her was her five-year old son. She suddenly thought of the boy and became afraid, thinking, 'They are here because of him!" She then forcefully told them to leave "If you're not of the light, leave and do not come back" the witness said. The beings then silently glided out the wall, the way they came in. The same night the source of this account reported feeling a presence and seeing peculiar shadows in his bedroom, about two hours before.

During August 1993 a former U. S. Marshall named Leslie D. Weisenhorn was irrigating fields on his ranch one afternoon when he saw a large silver dome squatting on the ground in a pasture. He estimated its size to be fifty feet wide by ten feet high. Leslie went to get his guns in case it was rustlers but when he returned it had gone. There were no tracks or marks in the field but there was the carcass of a three hundred and fifty to four hundred pound calf that appeared to have been spun around in the same spot. The dead calf had precise and bloodless incisions on it. Another dead calf was found in August, again, but in 1995. This was near Holly in Prowers County in Colorado.

In Huerfano County, Colorado in September 1993. An elderly hermit living in a remote ranch land on the eastern slopes of the Sangre de Cristo Mountains reported seeing a "ship" land near his cabin. Two bearded human-looking beings came out of the craft and floated towards his cabin, shining a very bright spotlight at it. The hermit claimed that when they pointed the light at the cabin it went right through the wall. Holding a gun he was blinded and paralysed as the light illuminated the inside of his cabin.

Late one night in September 1993 near Loveland in Larimer County in Colorado Judy Mickelson (involved in other incidents) remembers being beamed up into a pewter-colored space ship and let into a bright white room. From there, a shower like thing came over her and another thing like a dryer blew over her, and then she was ushered by little creatures about 4 feet tall with big eyes into a room that was colored in earth tones. A tall, slender human shaped being had his back turned to her and told her to sit in something that looked like a dentist chair, which formed around her and perfectly supported her body. When the alien turned around, she got a good look at him: He stood about 7 feet tall, had big shoulders, blond hair and blue eyes. His clothing, she said consisted of a one-piece satiny blue suit with a little cape and a belt with some kind of strange emblem on it. He told her his name was Sanada, and he told her they were far from Earth—that they were on the dark side of the moon. He told her that he and his race live in underground housing on the moon where they work as miners. He also told her that there had been a lot of interaction between his race and the U.S. government. Figure that one out.

In Baca, San Luis Valley, in Baca County in Colorado in October 1993 at 2145. On numerous occasions a local couple had seen a two to three foot long creature darting around their yard. It appeared to be partially translucent and tapered at both ends while opaque in the middle. It moves quickly leaving no tracks, the couple's dog apparently responded to it, and it seemed to disappear into thin air. One evening it was seen entering the living room through the closed stereo cabinet doors, scampering silently across the floor to the other side of the room, and out a spot in the wall six to eight inches above the floor, within inches of the couple's feet.

At 1.00 am on November 18th 1993 in Baca Chalets in the San Luis Valley in Baca County in Colorado Kimmy Martin awoke with a start. She looked into the gloomy night outside her window and felt somebody was watching her, and then something moved on the porch outside. A large group of gray-type creatures then peered in the window at her. She was not sure if they were physically in manifest or just on the other side in "etheric" form. Not frightened by their presence she watched them for almost an hour, while they watched her. Finally the witness told the beings to go away and let her sleep and the 20 to 25 visitors then trooped away obediently.

At 11.00 pm on November 29th 1993 near Eisenhower Tunnel in Clear Creek County in Colorado the two witnesses were driving on a flat straight road when they suddenly noticed a bright red star-like light moving slowly across the sky. The light then stopped and shot straight down below the horizon. Moments later the same or similar object approached their vehicle and then began pacing them, positioning itself directly overhead. The object followed the car for about 10 miles and then shot away out of sight. A short time later they began hearing static on their radio and as they looked behind they saw a fast approaching bright red-white light. The object was suddenly behind their vehicle and now appeared to be a glowing white disc-shaped craft. The driver accelerated to 90 mph but the object easily kept pace. As the driver watched the object in the rear view mirror, a figure appeared at the very front of the object. The figure was very slim and had a large head with huge slanted eyes. The being's body was dark but its eyes were a bright yellow color. At this point the driver heard a voice in his head telling him that he would not be harmed, that "they" were only interested in studying him and his female companion. A period of "missing time" was soon reported afterwards.

1994

Near Crestone in Saguache County in Colorado in 1994. A man driving on an isolated road saw something zip out in front of his car. He slammed on the brakes, but he was sure he had plowed right into it. He screeched to a stop and looked in his rearview mirror and was stunned to see a group of 15 to 20 undulating, transparent three-foot long creatures. "They were not all there, it's like they were only partially visible." He quickly drove away. (Source calls the creatures "Prairie Dragons.")

On the night of September 2nd 1994 in the Greenhorn Mountains in Huerfano County in Colorado a local hunter was at his campsite when a large group of "aliens dressed in camo appeared" and before he could react, he was gassed, captured, and tied up. They never spoke to him and never fed him. He claims he survived by eating grasshoppers. The camo-clad, human looking entities appeared to be conducting "some sort of maneuvers." The group then began boarding a small silver object and the witness was astonished when the object "expanded" to accommodate them all. The object then took off, morphed into the shape of a bear, then morphed into "a three headed wolf," then turned into a cloud! Later law enforcement personnel searched the area and found the witness's truck trashed, the remains of the campfire and "his half-burnt clothes" scattered around the area. At the same time a second hunter was reported missing in the same area, when he finally showed up, he "raced away in his truck without saying a word."

1995

At night on August 15th 1995 in Northern Sangre de Cristo Mountains in Colorado a local Vietnam vet claims to having seen a large boomerang-shaped object appear from the North and hover over his high-mountain property. He claims to be missing "40 minutes" of time and that his trailer and truck were moved "6 inches" (based on the altered location of the building and truck tracks) during the alleged experience. He claims he had a 4-inch rectal welt after regaining consciousness. He further asserts that he has lost 20 lbs in two weeks and that his "pet black bear" is now missing. The man claims that strange sightings have been occurring since the middle of June 1995, and that he has discovered "piles of carcasses" up slope from his 9,000-foot elevation land. He claims the carcasses have been in various stages of decay, and that they are comprised of mostly cattle, but also horse, fox, raccoon and "every type of animal" found in the area. He also said that two weeks before, he found "tiny 4-toed human tracks" around the perimeter of the area his trailer sits. He has noted attendant military activity as well. Often, after sightings, he notices unusually heavy military aerial activity, and is convinced the government is involved. After one sighting episode where he was able to photograph the craft, the next day while he was gone, somebody ransacked his trailer, and took all his film and camera equipment.

One night in October 1995 in Crestone in Saguache County in Colorado the witness, Michael, suddenly woke up on board a flying saucer. He was in the forward section of the ship and looking down through a large window. To the right was a panel of raised buttons. They were shaped like diamonds and squares and they were in primary colors. He kept looking around and saw three alien beings standing toward the back. They had dome-shaped heads and slanted eyes. They were wearing white robes and they were of different heights. The witness received the distinct impression that the aliens did not want him to look at them. He then decided to look at the controls. "As I looked over to my right at the bank of controls, it was almost as though, hidden to my left behind the wall, there was a plastic covering in the shape of the control panel. It went around (covering the control panel) just slightly faster than my eyes, so, I was looking at a shiny white, curved panel. I imagine they covered the controls as a containment procedure. I thought boy, this is interesting, they're either handling my mind, or this is really a real phenomenon. So what am I going to do now?" As he looked at the window and thought if the window was able to do anything, there was a flash and the window was suddenly covered in not only letters and numbers but also hieroglyphics in orange color. The witness had the impression that the machinery and the object reacted to his thoughts and somehow he was able to control some of the movements and maneuvers. At about three thousand feet up he was looking down at an angle at some mountains. He sees a ray of light going down, and it lights up this huge gold aura at the base of the ray. The witness suspects that he is being shown the location of a long lost wagonload of gold lost hundreds of years ago. "The ship was interacting with my mind. I asked the beings, 'so are there any more locations of lost gold? And suddenly another six to eight miles North he was being shown another one'. He remembered being over a particular hill and the object tilting over at an extreme angle and him looking down at this rather large amount of 'something' in the ground that emanated a golden aura. The witness then asked the beings about the major canyon treasures (gold) in this area. Very quickly he was suddenly looking down at a mountain full of gold, he noted where it came up close to the surface, where a crevice might be located for a person to find something. The aura around this gold was about a quarter mile out. The aura seemed relative to the amount of gold he was seeing. Suddenly he heard a kind of voice or thought that seemed to come from the back of the ship, which was kind of gravelly, kind of commanding. It said, "That's enough". The witness said thank you and woke up in his bed.

1996

At 2.00 am on August 24th 1996 in Poudre Canyon in Larimer County in Colorado while on a camping trip the witnesses spotted several lights flying over the area. Later more lights appeared overhead then they all heard a whooshing sound. The two men in the group were retrieving water when the lights appeared and as they returned to the camp the lights landed nearby, behind some trees. The smaller lights began "whirling" behind the trees. Soon two 3-foot tall beings approached the campsite. They approached and backed off several times. All through the night the beings kept walking back and forth from the lights to the campsite. A box-like structure was also seen above the nearby trees at one point. The beings and the lights finally departed at about 6.00 am.

1997

Near Red Wing in Colorado on August 22nd or 23rd 1997. Witnesses reported a C-131 transport plane dropping a "huge box" just North of the Atlantic Richfield CO2 plant in Huerfano County. Several locals set off to investigate. Several of them then saw two men wearing "jet-packs" on their backs flying up and down, around and between Sheep and Little Sheep Mountain, apparently looking for something. Other witnesses saw a craft that had the appearance of a large clear bubble. From the bottom of the bubble sparks were being emitted with a "clattering sound." A witness evidently fired a gun at the strange object as it passed overhead, and later that evening he was confronted and then accosted by three men (not described). The men wrestled him to the ground and one of them grabbed his neck and he was immediately rendered unconscious.

At night in Mesita in Costilla County in Colorado on August 22nd 1997. After watching a huge golden colored light hovering over the area, witness Thomas Peay claimed to have then experienced three concurrent nights of lucid dreams featuring "aliens" and being taken out through the window and into a small object then taken into a larger object. The aliens are not described. Mesita is almost a ghost town and the area is dead flat so any light in the sky would have been extremely obvious.

On September 2nd 1997 one mile West of Sedalia on Highway 67 a quarter mile southwest of County Highway 105 in Douglas County. At 5:30 A.M. I was traveling East on Highway 67, after I stopped to pick up my newspaper from our box on Hwy. 67. I was traveling at a slow rate of speed since I just started up after stopping for my newspaper when I observed in my headlights a large, black object run from the North side of Highway 67, across in front of my vehicle, and went up an incline on the South side of Highway 67. In my opinion, it was not a bear, elk, deer, cow or any other four legged animal as it was running on two legs with arms about two feet from the ground. It ran at a very rapid rate of speed and when it crossed in front of me it peered over its right shoulder which was curved and humped over. It continued its stride while keeping eye contact. I know I never saw anything like this and I lived in this area for twenty-nine years and never saw anything like this. I was very frightened and do not know what this creature was. There is a creek just 500 yards from where I observed this creature. There are many scrub oaks and undeveloped land in this area. The terrain varies as the Highway is level but to the south, the direction it headed, has an incline with scattered scrub oaks and some open valley space.

In Saguache County in Colorado at 3.00 am on December 14th 1997 a witness reported seeing a large triangular shaped craft hovering over a field. It moved slowly over the house then over some grain silos. It then came back over the house and shone a beam of white blue light out of its middle and something like a small figure was taken up into the beam. Lights around its edge flashed in rhythm when it left.

At Lakewood in Jefferson County in Colorado on December 24th 1997 around midnight the witness had gotten up to obtain a glass of milk and was sitting in bed looking out the window. The moonlight illuminated the whole area. He then saw the figure of man walking directly to his window from the neighbor's yard. As the man got closer, the witness could see that he was wearing a purple shirt, blue jeans, tennis shoes and had shoulder length blond hair and carried what appeared to be a red book. The witness was stunned as the man appeared to walk straight through the fence and he then noticed that the man had large black slanted eyes. Afraid, the witness ran to the living room and did not see the strange figure depart. A bad dream?

Gulf of Mexico.

In the Gulf of Mexico on 1st April 1952 the Captain and crew of the "S.S. Esso Bermuda" saw a UFO dive into the sea 200 miles South of Lake Charles City, Louisiana. The object was obviously an aircraft yet none were reported missing. It was not a meteor or a meteorite. There was no sound so is this still related to the exploding invisibles of earlier that same year?

In the Gulf of Mexico on 27th March 1968 at. 2.10 am. The crews of the tanker "Alfa Mex 11" and the Mexican Warship "Guanajuato" saw two or three objects in the center of a bright ball of fire during an earthquake. The waters of the Gulf were churned up into fountains of spray as the object passed over. At the same time twenty-five miles from the ships at Vera Cruz in Mexico there was a deafening rumbling noise and a bright light seen in the sky. It got closer and the noise kept on. The strange meteor that the ships had seen loomed over the scene. It dipped towards the ground and then shot up and off again heading back in the direction that it came. This was no meteor. Aquatic UFOs? Technically USOs or Unidentified Submarine Objects.

Also that day at Vera Cruz Llave in Vera Cruz in Mexico, on the Gulf of Mexico, on 27th March 1968 at 2.10 am. The population of the city heard a deafening rumbling noise that got louder as a strange light appeared from the direction of the Gulf of Mexico. The noise got louder and the earthquake which was happening at the time got more active. The strange light in the sky then dipped down and then ascended before virtually doing a U-turn and heading back over the Gulf. This was not a meteor. It seemed that the earthquake came and went with it. Was this the same light seen by the crews of the two ships? The same thing had apparently happened here on 27th March 1958. Was this a misprint?

Kansas

1873

In Kansas on the morning of 5th July 1873 at Fort Riley in Geary County, the assembled troops on the parade ground saw a huge silvery serpent that repeatedly swooped down out of the sky onto the parade ground causing such chaos that the parade had to be abandoned. This was approximately one hour after the strange happening at Bonham that caused one death. Whatever was the silver serpent agitated about, or was it braking very hard as it reversed its thrust or its dive? How would you feel if you suddenly came crashing down out of one dimension and towards another reality? I would put on the anchors myself. Just because we have not mastered the art of interdimensional travel does not mean that others haven't! That is if interdimensional travel indeed exists or is possible. And others might not have mastered it yet either. They were still trying. But there has to be an origin or starting off point for many of the phenomena and it usually does not appear to be where they are first sighted. Maybe it was a learner driver? All levels of culture would also have all levels of experience. This was the same morning as Fort Scott, also in Kansas, and Bonham in Texas.

That same morning 5th July 1873 at Fort Scott in Bourbon County, Kansas, all of the inhabitants of the fort-township saw a huge silver serpent flying through the sky about halfway above the horizon. The shape of the aerial object was that of an apparently perfect huge serpent. Was this the same flying serpent that had terrorised Bonham, Texas, that same morning? And then flown to Fort Scott? Followed later by Fort Riley?

On 5th July 1873, a man living about five miles from Bonham in Fannin County, Texas, saw something like an enormous serpent floating over his farm. Had the Ratibor and Rybnik red object then flown over North America to release the serpent of Hell itself? Later that same morning 5th July 1873 as the man witnessing the enormous aerial serpent, workers in a cotton field near Bonham were terrified by a shiny serpentine object that swooped down out of the sky again and again. This scared the horses so much that one team threw their driver and he was crushed under the careening wagon wheels. Had the Bonham aerial serpent arrived from near Mars or only a spot that seemed near to the patch of the sky that Mars was occupying at the time? This was the same time as Fort Scott in Kansas that day as well as Fort Riley.

1878

On 30th July 1878 the section men on the K.P. Railroad seeing a storm coming up very fast got their hand-car onto the railroad track and started full speed towards Edwardsville in Wyandotte County in Kansas. They had gone only a short distance when they saw coming around the curve at Edwardsville what appeared to be a locomotive at full speed. The men jumped off the car and got it off the tracks as fast as possible and then saw that it was not a locomotive. The luminous object came down the track giving off a volume of dense smoke with occasional flashes resembling a head light in the center of the smoke. It came three quarters of a mile from where they first saw it and then it turned off the track at a pile of cordwood, went round it once, then went off in a southwesterly direction through a thick wood.

1881

Around 10.30 pm during November 1881 nine aerial objects were seen over St Joseph in Buchanan County by seven witnesses for half an hour.

1890

In 1890 a farmer in Kansas was asleep under a wagon in a hayfield when he was awakened by a brilliant flash and a crash like thunder. Dirt was thrown all around him and sitting only sixty feet from where he lay was a meteor 188 pounds in weight. Good thing that he parked the wagon where he did.

1891

In August 1891 at night in El Dorado in Butler County, Kansas. Journalist William Allen White was awoken by the sound of music and looking out of the window he saw a group of small humanoids only 7.5-9cm tall dancing. He looked away and back again and they were still there. He went back to bed but later looked out again. The beings were still there, but as William looked, the things faded away.

1897

Now for the 1897 Airship Flap.

On 27th March 1897, the good citizens of Topeka, Shawnee County, Kansas, were disturbed at 9.30pm by a large object described as a blood red light that appeared in the sky West of the city and was observed for more than three quarters of an hour travelling to the northeast. The aerial object also disappeared and reappeared a number of times. Many of the citizens took to their cyclone cellars when they saw it. The light passed the State Capitol where it was seen by several hundred people as well as Governor Leedy who stated "I hope that it may yet solve the railroad problem".

On 28th March 1897, an airship was seen at Concordia, Cloud County, near Atcheson in Kansas, 22 miles South of Belleville. This one or these ones were different. They headed South.

The same day 28th March 1897 an airship was seen over Belleville in Republic County, Kansas, fifty miles North of Salina. Strange lights had been seen in the sky and had been seen travelling over Nebraska and Kansas. This was a blindingly bright light that seemed to be drifting aimlessly overhead. But you normally don't get meteors aimlessly drifting overhead though. It's usually more like wham, bam, thank you m'am and we don't care if you did not enjoy it they are so fast.

On 1st April 1897, one hour after Kansas City, Missouri, an airship was seen in the sky over Everest in Brown County, Kansas. This was sixty minutes after the sighting sixty miles away in Kansas City. This aerial object was described as an elongated balloon with a boat-shaped gondola beneath it as well as two wings and a bright light which dimmed slightly when the craft moved but increased in brilliance when the craft was stationary. Citizens of this town observed the airship for about 80 minutes, for a period of which the object descended below the clouds, which were illuminated by its powerful green-blue lights. The object was canoe shaped, 7.5-9m long. From the car four light wings were extended, two on either side, with triangular ends. Above the car, a large dark bulk was visible. When the object rose the lights dimmed and when it descended close to the earth, it became as bright as a locomotive. It flew swiftly to the horizon, swooped rapidly towards the earth and then swept away to the south.

Airships kept returning. Many of these commonly observed movements and situations were observed that year but are literally impossible for astronomic phenomena to duplicate. On 3rd April 1897 an airship was seen over Topeka in Shawnee County in Kansas, that for a short period would reappear on consecutive evenings.

On 4th April 1897 there was still one hovering over Topeka, Kansas. They were always similar but quite often not the same. Does one suspect that there is too much variation in the sightings?

On 5th April 1897 the Topeka airship or whatever was still there. Realistically speaking one could not have a plethora of airship styles. It must have been just a few but interpreted differently by the observers The only constant was Time and Space.

On April 15th 1897 at Highland Station in Doniphan County, Kansas. A airship crashed and an injured pilot was taken out of the wreckage. He said he was Pedro Sanchez from Cuba. The next day he had recovered enough to take the wreckage away.

On April 19th 1897 at 2230hrs in Yates Center in Woodson County, Kansas. Farmer Alexander Hamilton and his family and staff were awakened by a disturbance among the cattle. Thinking his dog was worrying them, Hamilton went to investigate and saw an aerial object slowly descending over his cow lot about 200m away With is son Wall and tenant Mr Heslip, they came within 50m of the object which was hovering about 10m above the ground. The thing consisted of a cigar shaped object about 100m long, under which a transparent carriage was made of some glassy material, alternating with solid red strips. The interior was brilliantly lit, and there were three external lights, a brilliant headlight, which rotated around, and two smaller ones, one red, the other green. Inside were six strange beings, two men, a woman and three children, who spoke amongst each other in an unknown language. The beings seemed startled by some noise and turned the beam on the witnesses, and a wheel, about 10m diameter, below the craft began to rotate making a humming sound. The thing rose to about 100m and hovered over a heifer, putting a red rope around it. Despite Hamilton and Heslip's efforts the thing took off, taking the heifer with it, heading to the North West. The next day the hide, head and legs of the beast were found in a field about 5km away.

Is this the same report? At 10.30 pm on 20th April 1897 Mr. Alexander Hamilton, ex-House of Representatives, as well as his family were woken by a commotion amongst the cattle on his property at Le Roy in Coffey County in Kansas. Mr. Hamilton went outside where he saw an airship descending by his barn. Mr. Hamilton roused his son and a tenant and the three of them went to the corral with axes. They were within fifty feet of the craft which was hovering thirty feet above the ground. The craft was three hundred feet long hovering over a heifer that had stuck itself in a fence. The craft had a glasslike illuminated carriage underneath it in which there were six hideous beings jabbering in an unknown language. The rest of the ship was a reddish color. A searchlight then hit the witnesses as the great turbine under the ship was activated and it rose to three hundred feet. There was a red cable around the heifer's neck that was half an inch thick and tied with a slip knot which the witnesses could not get off or loosen. Unable to release the animal from the fence the men cut the wire. The heifer then was lifted up by the craft and then disappeared along with the craft to the northwest. The next day the hide, the head and the legs were found in a field by a neighbour. Anyone for rare beef? Yates Center and Le Roy are only fifteen miles apart.

Also during April 1897, an airship was reported to have dropped a half peeled potato onto Atchison in Atchison County in Kansas. Were they going to Greece to get more potatoes?

1905

In Summer, 1905 (approximate date) at night in Liberal in Seward County, Kansas. William Bathlot was returning to his home in Beaver County Oklahoma, from Liberal, when he observed a luminous sphere, larger than a human head, on the road, about 3m ahead of his team. When he got closer, William could see the road through the thing. It then took off and landed again a short distance from the road, in wild plum brush. He went to the site but could not see anything, though he had an unpleasant sensation of being watched.

In Autumn 1905 (Approximate date) in the evening in Beaver County, Oklahoma. William Bathlot (qv) and his hired hand were out looking for a lost cow when a luminous sphere appeared in front of them. They tried to walk round it, but it moved to block them, and would advance and retreat with them. They got within 4m of the light, which was about 45cm above the ground, silent, transparent and with no sign of it being attached to anything. When William fired his shotgun at it, the light just disappeared. There were no traces.

1909

In Chanute in Neosho County, Kansas on March 9th to March 10th 1911. Balloons have formed the habit of night prowling, according to the story told by the occupant of a flat on West Main Street. Being aroused at 2 o'clock yesterday morning, he chanced to glance out of the window and saw a large balloon floating away toward the North and West. It was flying low and by the light which it carried, he could distinguish the forms of its occupants. He thinks there were three of them. Lawrence Daily Journal-World (Lawrence, Kansas) Friday, March 10, 1911.

1919

On 8th October 1919, a large fireball as big as a washtub struck a building in Salina in Saline County in Kansas. Bricks were ripped out and a second floor window was demolished. After this the ball exploded, showering balls of fire around which eventually floated away in all directions. The balls of fire were the size of baseballs and they travelled along trolleycar and electric light wires. They floated in a snaky manner. Incidentally an electric switch box across the street was ripped open and a transformer destroyed leaving the East side of town in darkness. The balls of fire just floated away? This area of Kansas has and will have a history of strange phenomena.From icefalls to giant Kangaroos, from UFOs to Hairy Humanoids. Some places are just lucky I guess.

1926

Around 1.00 pm over Wichita in Kansas six flying manhole covers circled the plane of Bert Acosta, a stunt pilot. They were three to four feet in diameter and approached to within ten feet of the plane. This was in January 1926. Bert was flying from Wichita in Kansas to Colorado Springs in Colorado.

1946

On September 11th 1946 at 0500HRS in Ulysses in Grant County, Kansas. Mrs Karen Campbell driving home to Pona City (Okl) from a trip to Denver, had just reached the west edge of Ulysses when she coming towards her at high speed, about 1m above the road, a dull, copper coloured, circular object, as wide as the road and about 1.2m high, surmounted by a sort of oval cupola. The object banked and took rapidly, making a sound like a rushing wind as it did so, and revealing some sort of structure on its underside. Karen drove away at speed and was greatly shaken by the experience.

1947

On 6th July 1947 in Clay Center in Clay County in Kansas. 1:45 p.m. AAF pilot Major A. B. Browning and crew flying B-25 E to Kansas City saw a silvery circular object 30-50 feet diameter pacing the aircraft at a little lower altitude then shot off at high speed heading E at 11,000 feet at 210 mph.

Also on July 6th 1947 during the day in Kansas City in Jackson County, Kansas. While playing basketball in a field near US24, Miss Barbara Mehner saw a dark grey object, 13cm in diameter, circle above for sever; times at 60cm altitude.

At 2.00 am on October 29th 1947 Walter Blackwell, 67, just North of Yoder Ridge near Hutchinson in Kansas had gone out to pick pears in his orchard and was unable to get to get back to his house for 24 hours. He claimed to have seen Haley's Comet streak out of the northeast followed by a snow-like cloud inhiabited by people and animals.

On November 15th 1947 in Wichita in Sedgwick County in Kansas at 2 a.m. USAF Maj. R. L. Wallander, Capt. Belleman, A/3c Phipps saw an orange object (a blue streak?) varied in shape, as it made jerky upward sweeps with 10-15 sec pauses. 3-5 minutes.

1948

At 4.56 pm on February 18th 1948 a farmer in Stockton in Rooks County in Kansas saw a four foot wide disc that approached to within six feet of him and appeared to aim some type of tube or pipe at him. The object then wobbled and emitted some flames and shot away flying towards the northwest. At 5.05 pm a Mr. Wray took a photo of an irregular shaped UFO North of Norton in Norton County in Kansas. Another version? A farmer, about 23km west of Stockton, was at his hog pen 30m from the house when he heard a disturbance amongst the poultry. Looking around he observed an object hovering above his house. It settled to the ground north of the house, and he saw it was a funnel shaped object 1.3m long, at head height less than 2m away. A sort of pipe was pointing at the witness. It was surrounded by "fire", which increased in intensity as it took off towards the north west, emitting sparks and rising rapidly. A few minutes later a tremendous explosion shook the area.

1950

On June 30th 1950 at 0005hrs in Cunningham in Kingman County, Kansas. Reverend Ross Vermillion (26) was driving with his wife along the flat Hw 54 about 14-15km west of Kingman, heading towards Cunningham when he observed first a red and then a white light. He slowed down and woke his wife. They were then joined by another car, driven by Dwayne Mulnix, a pharmacist. After observing the thing, which seemed to be hovering over two tractors in a lot, for a time, they drove closer to it. Ross described it as like two saucers, rim to rim, about 80m diameter, 4.5m thick, made of a metal like Alcoa, surmounted by a sort of canopy 3-4.5m diameter. The outer 3-4.5m of the disc was rotating. Ross thought of shinning his headlights on it, but his wife persuaded him against this. Mulnix did keep his lights on and when they approached the thing took off, going out of sight in 6 seconds.

At Anthony in Harper County, Kansas in 1950. At 2: 10 a.m. husband and wife farmers were awakened by a bright light shining outside the window. They went out to see what it was and observed a large triangular-shaped glowing object hovering above the barn. A smaller object then detached itself from the larger craft and landed behind the barn. The husband walked towards the barn to investigate and the wife stayed behind. She was suddenly started to see, standing ten feet from her, a humanoid being composed of pure light. She was not able to move or speak. The entity told her not to be afraid; that he was a messenger sent to reveal certain knowledge to humanity. He made several predictions.

1952

On August 24th 1952 in Frontenac in Crawford County, Kansas. At 6:00 am a man driving through a woods encountred a strange object and stopped to observe it. It looked like two turtle shells glued together, about 25 m long, with a humanoid creature in what ap peared to be a control cabin in front. Windows lighted by an intense blue light and a throbbing sound were also reported. The object was oscillating and suddenly flew straight up with a strong humming noise. The middle section supported what looked like propellers. The object hovered 3 m above ground.

The following day on August 25th 1952 in Frontenac-Pittsburg in Crawford County, Kansas. At 5:35 a.m. radio station musician William Squyres saw 70-75 feet inverted platter-shaped dull aluminum color object to right side of road about 40° elevation and 750 feet away with a "man" inside visible in a window. He stopped the car and got out to look from 300 feet away, object had "rocking motion" and deep throbbing sound, series of 6-7-inch "propellers" then after 1/2 min rose vertically at high speed from 10 feet height and disappeared in a gap of broken clouds but not behind clouds. Later found 60 feet circle of grass matted down in the field. 1/2 min. Or this version? William V Squyers, 36, a musician at Station KOAM Pittsburg) was driving along Vale Road in a wooded area, about 400m from US 160, on his way to an early morning performance, when he encountered a strange object on the right side of the road 225m away and stopped to observe it. He walked to within 30m of this object. It looked like two turtle shells glued together, and was 22.5m long, 12m wide, and 4.m thick. It was hovering at an altitude of 3m. In a "control cabin" at the front, the head and shoulders of a humanoid creature were visible. There was a diagonal row of windows , lighted by an intense blue light, through which moving shapes could be seen; a throbbing sound was also noticed. The middle section supported a row of propellers 15cm in diameter. The craft was oscillating and suddenly it flew straight up, "like a light cord when you release it", with a strong humming noise. The only possible trace was an 18m circle of broken weeds.

Two days later in Pittsburg in Crawford County in Kansas at dawn on 27th August 1952 a musician named Squires was driving into town when he saw a UFO hovering above an open field. The craft was composed of two huge discs, one above the other and between them was a round cabin with three or four curved windows that gave off a bluish light. The craft was 75 feet in diameter and was hovering ten feet above ground. Along the crafts outer edges were a series of propellers about six to eight inches in diameter that were spaced closely together. The witness got out of his car and approached the craft. As he approached the craft he dimly saw movement inside that appeared shadowy and human-like. There was an odd machinery noise as well and the ship suddenly lifted vertically and vanished. UFO or misidentified luminous Phenomena? Shadows inside? Light-effects or Humanoids? A misidentified Meteor? Can the human brain misidentify when under stress? We know that stress can affect memory and concentration. Can it in fact affect perception? How we actually sense things? Can stress or sudden shock and the stress from it cause misidentification of Phenomena? Is the actual witness translating the event into parameters that they can make sense of? Is there a common symbolistic language that we can call on subconsciously to make right or to normalise these stressful situations? Previously there had been a sighting of a wild Hairy Man near the Osage River near here in 1869.

1954

On May 5th 1954 in Goodland in Sherman County, Kansas. A farmer working the fields went over a rise and saw a silvery disc shaped object, standing on legs. As he looked the legs retracted and the thing took off with a loud whistle, rose to 30m, hovered, rocking slightly and the tilted and shot off to the east.

In Coldwater in Comanche County in Kansas during September 1954 at 8.00 pm John J. Swain, 12, the son of a farmer, was returning from the fields on a tractor when he spotted a tiny man twenty feet away behind a terrace. The odd man had a very long nose and ears and seemed to fly whilst moving and flew over a small hill to a saucer-shaped object on the ground. The UFO then rose five feet above ground, a panel in it opened up and the Humanoid, no bigger than a five year old child, popped inside it. The craft then lit up and vanished at considerable speed. John returned with his parents as well as the Sheriff the next day. Wedge shaped tracks were found in the soft dirt that were not human. The Humanoid was 3.5 to four feet tall. The small men would reappear quite often as well. Are we looking at different genera and species even of phenomenal creatures and possibly some of their craft? Or this? John Jacob Swain (12), the son of a farmer near Coldwater, was coming in from the fields on his father's tractor, when he saw a small figure about 120m away, who disappeared behind a terrace in the field. He drove up to the terrace and saw, no more than 6m away, behind the terrace, a small figure crouching down. As it jumped up, John saw that it was the size of a 5 year old child (c 1.05-1.2m tall), with very long pointy ears and nose. It was dark, wore shiny clothing and had two cylinders on its back. The figure looked at John then floated or flew over a small hill toward a disk shaped object hovering 1.5m above the ground. An opening appeared through which the little creature entered. The object then lit up and took off at high speed. The sheriff investigated and next day went with John and his parents to the site, where they found wedge shaped marks in the soft dirt. Some accounts say these marks were footprints 12cm long, 5cm wide, with extremely narrow heels. There were about 100 of them in a circle.

1958

On November 11th 1958 at 0135hrs in Topeka Shawnee County in Kansas. Mrs Kinney, a colonel in the Civil Air Patrol, had gone to bed alone, her doctor husband being away, when her room was filled with a deep amber light and her dogs became agitated. Looking out she saw an 8m diameter sphere about 10m away in her yard. She went to investigate but as she opened her porch door, the thing took off vertically. A neighbour had seen the thing heading towards the house and had feared a fire. Her dogs also acted up. The tower personnel at Topeka airport had also seen the light. Wiring in the Kinney house had burnt out and Mrs Kinney developed sensitivity to light. The two dogs which had faced the thing developed cataracts.

1961

On August 12th 1961 at 2100hrs in Kansas City in Wyandotte County, Kansas. Two 21 year old students in their final year at Drake University, Tom Phipps and James M Furkenhoff, were driving in their convertible with the top down, when they observed a large object in the sky, about three city blocks away. They first thought that it was an aircraft about to crash, but as they approached closer they saw that it was an oval object, shaped roughly like a sledge, with running boards, just less than half the size of an American football field. The running boards seemed to have lights that caused it to glow a pale yellow. Two high vertical tails ran from the rear edge to the centre of the metallic contraption, which was hovering at 15m altitude. After staying right beneath the object for about 4 minutes, they drove away, suddenly afraid. As they did so, the object veered away to the east, disappearing in 5 seconds.

1964

On September 11th 1964 at 0500hrs in Ulysses in Grant County, Kansas. Karen Campbell was driving home to Penca City (Okl) when, 7 hours from home, she was frightened by a round object, with an oval dome 1.2m high, the width of the road and of a dull copper colour, travelling towards her at about 1m altitude at high speed. It climbed rapidly, avoiding a collision and floated over the car with a rushing sound.

On December 12th 1964 in Fort Riley in Kansas a large lenticular disc-shaped craft with a fish like fin in the rear section and about 35 to 48 feet in diameter and about 12-18 feet high crashed at the military reservation. It had a smooth, aluminium like surface and a black band of squares around its rim. Nine dead aliens were apparently found on board. The bodies and craft were moved to Wright Patterson AFB.

1965

On August 1st 1965 (Approx. date) in Wichita in Sedgwick County, Kansas. Witnesses at the weather bureau and the McConnell Air Force Base saw an egg shaped object 90m long hover on or slightly above the ground for a short time. It displayed red, yellow-white and green-blue colours. **Xxx 24.05.20 continue from here**

On August 2nd 1965 at 0340hrs in Caldwell in Sumner County, Kansas. Two young police officers, Dave Lowe and Eddie Roberts, were on patrol when they heard a police radio report about two objects moving in a southerly direction toward Wellington, South Haven and Caldwell. They headed towards the airport on the eastern edge of town where they saw two vague objects in the sky, which objects quickly disappeared. Soon afterwards another report came in of an object north of Caldwell. At first the pair could see nothing but then Dave saw a light like headlights behind a rise in the ground about 30m away. He jumped onto the dashboard for a better look. He saw a brilliant egg shaped light 90m long, with white, red and blue-green lights, which merged and blended. When the officers regained their composure they pursued the object, pulling east on Highway 81, where the thing went behind a hedgerow and disappeared. When they revisited the spot in the morning no traces were visible. The observation had lasted 3 minutes. Shortly before this Dave had heard an engine sound like an aircraft but no aircraft was seen.

In Abilene in Dickinson County in Kansas at 1.30 am on 4th August 1965 Mr. Don Tennopir, a truckdriver, was on Highway 15 about twenty-five miles South of Abilene enroute to Lincoln, Nebraska carrying a full load of peanuts when suddenly the lights on the truck went out. Then they went back on, then went out etc.. Then Don saw a saucer thing that went over the truck with a sizzling or windlike noise and almost touched the cab. The object was twenty feet up hovering only one hundred feet in front of the witness who hit the brakes. The craft then took off to the West and then the South and the sighting lasted for twenty seconds. The luminous object appeared to be fourteen to fifteen feet in diameter by two feet thick and had a hump in the middle about four feet high. There was a distinct spot in the hump or dome which could have been a window. The object was orange colored and shot off reddish rays in spurts. Ho-hum. Here is another version. While driving along Hw 15 about 35km south of Abilene, en route to Lincoln (Neb) with a cargo of peanuts, truck driver Don Ten(n)opir of Beatrice (Neb) was surprised when his truck lights went out, came on again, and then went out again. He braked hard as an aerial object swooped down to within 6m (or 60cm) of the road, not more than 30m ahead of him., after passing over his truck with a sizzling sound. As Don's truck stopped the object rose up a bit, slowly took off to the west and then headed south. It was in view for more than 20 seconds and despite his fright Don was able to see that it was circular, about 4-4.5m diameter, orange coloured, like the reflector jackets worn by highway repair men, 60cm thick, with a hump, 1.2m thick at the centre, on which was a dark spot resembling a window. The whole thing gave the impression of a saucer with a cup in the middle. From the object, flashing red rays were emitted. A car coming in the opposite direction had swerved around the object and the driver began to speak to Don. Before he could say much the object emitted blue sparks from its underside and took off making a sound like the wind rustling the trees. Don and the other driver drove away at high speed. Doe was so afraid that he was pale and his hands were trembling when he was interviewed by a reporter. He had reported the matter to the police but nothing came of that.

On November 17th 1965 at night in Agra in Phillips County, Kansas. Rita Gorake and Mill Miller, who had earlier seen a bright object moving up and down in the sky, returned to the site with Van Bradley and Carol Herbel. After a wait of five minutes, the object returned, coming from behind and lighting up the whole car. They started the car and the object followed them back to town. It was a bright light, low above the ground, quite large, with an indistinct outline and three windows.

1966

On March 26th 1966 in Wichita in Sedgwick County, Kansas. Johnny S (11) saw two disc shaped objects, which made a humming sound, land in the driveway of a neighbour, who found a piece of concrete that had been moved and that sand had been swivelled into the driveway.

In Wichita in Sedgwick County in Kansas in March 1966 a landed UFO was seen. Something normal. Previously there had been a fall of fish also at Wichita, Kansas, in 1899 and in 1956 there was the spontaneous combustion of Mrs. Olga Godfrey also in here in Wichita.

In Liberty in Montgomery County in Kansas in April 1966 a UFO was seen to land and Humanoids emerged from it. Normality at last.

1967
  Around 1.30 am on 13th January 1967 nine year old Freddie Amos woke up to see a round object hovering motionless low over an adjoining field. It was 25 feet in diameter, had a dome on top, short wing-like protrusions and three wheels on the underside. There were red lights on the end of the wings and a blue light on top of the dome. A man stood looking out with another man sitting at a desk behind him. He was wearing a crinkly green uniform that covered him all over. The face was in shadows and the features were not seen. This terrible man frightened the boy. He got back into bed and watched the object which circled the house and hovered again for five minutes at its original position before flying off. In the morning some of the cows were found to have broken through the fence of the pasture so violently that one broke her leg. A pond in the pasture continued to remain unfrozen although the temperatures were well below freezing. This was near Isola in Kansas. Unfortunately Isola does not appear anywhere on the internet or in my collection of atlases.
  On February 8th 1967 in Rossville in Shawnee County, Kansas. That night three teenaged boys saw what looked like two car lights that came down to within 20 feet of the ground. The object shone a light beam on the witnesses after they had pointed a spotlight at it (light reaction).
  On February 11th 1967 in Madison in Greenwood County, Kansas. A landing report.
  Also on February 11th 1967 in Kansas City in Jackson, Clay, Platte and Cass Counties, Missouri. Two people saw an unidentified object at low level.
  On February 27th 1967 at 1905hrs in Topeka in Shawnee County, Kansas. Television interference was noted when a top shaped object with red and blue lights on its surface hovered over trees.
  At Towanda in Butler County, Kansas on 1st March 1967. At 9.00 pm four young men and Marshall Virgil Osborne saw a flying craft with revolving red, white and blue lights which had landed and then rose 300 feet before heading southwest. Or this. Along a road northwest of Towanda, several young men saw revolving red, white and blue lights in the vicinity of the water well. City Marshall Virgil Osborne returned to the area with two of the boys, and as the patrol car turned into the roads leading to the wells, they saw the lights rise from ground level to 100m and take off in a south-westerly direction. The lights appeared to be some object of indeterminate shape, and they illuminated the trees by the river as the thing passed at speed.
  On March 21st 1967 in Hillsboro in Marion County, Kansas an "Upside-down cup on a saucer" hovered over a car, which rocked violently. That Evening three people saw a flash of light, then an object that appeared flat and like an upside down saucer. The object turned red and approached the car, which began to rock violently. As the object neared the engine quit. Or this. About 1,5km west of Hillsboro, Miss Mary Beth Neufeld of Lehigh and several friends had their attention caught by a brilliant light that seemed out of place in the cloudy starless night. They drove towards the thing, whereupon it flashed and came towards them. It was a flat object, surrounded by an inverted cupola. When the object came overhead the car rocked violently from side to side and engine stalled. When the object left suddenly a few moments later the engine restarted itself. The girls then drove to Hillsboro and reported the matter to the authorities.
  In Spring 1967 near Medicine Lodge in Barber County in Kansas. A witness observed a landed object near Highway #160, around which small figures were moving; footprints were left at the site. Small humanoids were seen who disembarked and circled around the craft. Footprints of the humanoids reportedly were photographed.
  In Kansas City in Wyandotte County, Kansas in June 1967. The main witness along with several others were in a sparsely populated area late at night when he observed what he described as a World War II airplane with no lights, suspended in midair. He was driving his 1967 Chevrolet and there were five occupants in the car and all he remembers was the airplane first to the right and then to the left of his car, which emitted a yellowish beam from its rear. He then drove to an area where there were caves used for storage, near the meeting point of two rivers. Driving along a gravel road he observed an individual facing the road in a green panel van wearing dark black sunglasses. He remembers telling the others how strange this was when a red light came from behind him and a county Sheriff's patrol car and two deputies got out and all the occupants of the witness vehicle got out and were questioned as to why they were out in this area at this time and he told the deputies they were looking out for UFO's and they told him to go home after checking their ID's. The witness thought it was kind of strange that the deputies did not question their story or laugh. A week later while in his rooming house, the witness went to take a shower on the third floor when a young man with long blond hair and wearing a white outfit and dark sunglasses walked into the restroom and came straight to the shower. As the witness opened the door the stranger grabbed him by his groin, turned and then left. Immediately he got dressed and ran to the lobby to report this to the desk clerk and asked him if he had seen a young man with blond hair wearing dark sunglasses come down and he said no. At this point another man came downstairs and reported that a similar looking young man had entered the shower but had not touched him. After all this the main witness was examined by doctors and an X-ray clearly showed that an object which the doctors could not identify was lodged near his femur bone. As of two years ago this object is still at the same place according to the witness.

On September 14th 1967 at 2000hrs in Wichita in Sedgwick County, Kansas. Mike F (11) and friends observed a disc shaped object with windows around its circumference land in a field near some trees. The boys ran home and did not return. The thing was first seen as a bright light descending to the ground. At ground level the lads saw lights rotating behind the windows and noted that the thing was surmounted by a cupola. One of the boys' mother went to the site and saw the lights, but would not let the boys return to the site.

1968

On September 4th 1968 at 2030hrs in Valencia in Shawnee County, Kansas. Mrs Oberhleman and her family were driving on Valencia Road, south of I-70 when they saw two white lights hovering over an alfalfa field at a crossing. These lights resembled car headlights but were higher than the treetops. The family could not see any solid object behind these lights, which they watched for about 1.5km before they turned south again. When they arrived home, they saw four lights over the field, in a double decker formation. As the family turned, the two top lights went out. Then the other two lights accelerated towards them, passing by their right on the other side of the fence at treetop height. Mrs O got a good look at one of these lights and saw it was an object the size of a small plane but of unconventional design. It accelerated towards I-70 and then suddenly darted back, past them, to the south again.

1969

On April 14th 1969 at 2330hrs in Hill City in Graham County, Kansas. Edwin H Bohl Jnr of Logan was driving, with his family on US24 east of Hill City when they saw an object with multi-coloured lights come down to within 25m of the highway at 45 degree angle from his car. The car engine died and they sat there for three minutes as the object hung in silence and then moved away slowly and soundlessly to the east, following the highway towards Stockton.

On April 19th 1969 in the evening and still in Hill City, Kansas. Two people saw a multi-coloured at a location 8km east of here. As the thing came within 30m of their car, the vehicle's engine failed. The thing hovered at 25m altitude for three minutes and then moved slowly away, after which the car started without trouble.

In 1969 at 0200hrs in Topeka in Shawnee County, Kansas. A 17 year old youth was driving home when he saw an object on the road ahead. He drove to a nearby farm and returned to the site with another witness and both saw the object. They left to get more witnesses but when they returned the object had gone. Three imprints 375mm by 100mm, with a toe like extension were found, arranged in a triangle of sides 2.1-2.4m.

1970

In Pratt in Pratt County, Kansas in September 1970. About seventy miles west of Wichita chunks of white hot metal weighing hundreds of pounds crashed to the Earth. Just recently in August 1970 metal had fallen onto Adrian in Texas.

In November 23rd 1970 in 0545hrs in Franklin in Crawford County, Kansas. An object paced a vehicle travelling from Franklin to Smith for 2 hours 35 minutes.

At Humboldt Hill in Allen County, Kansas, near Iola in 1970. Several individual witnesses saw strange lights in the area as well as unusual catlike creatures. Car engines stalled during these sightings and the tracks of big cats were found as well.

1971

In Peabody in Marion County in Kansas shortly before dawn in January 1971 Stewart and Lyle Leppke were doing their early morning farm chores when they observed a a lighted object in a cattle lot. When they flashed their light on it they saw a diminutive figure only two feet tall moving about near the object which had small windows on it. They immediately went to the house to nitify their mother who called the Sheriff. The object had departed by the time that he had arrived. The boys said that the object hovered a few feet off the ground and when it departed it tipped to one side and then sped rapidly away. Or this version. Wilbur Leppke's two sons, Stewart and Lyle, were doing their morning farm chores when they spotted a lighted object in a cattle lot. When they flashes the tractor lights on the object, its light diminished and they saw small figures less than 60cm tall, moving outside it. The brothers also noticed small windows on the object. They ran in to tell their mother, who saw something in the field and called the sheriff. The object then rose a couple of metres above the ground, hovered, tipped on one side then sped away. The sheriff did not arrive until the object had left. The boys' teachers said their stories remained consistent.

On June 13th 1971 at 2215hrs in Larned in Pawnee County, Kansas. A motorist driving near Larned found that his engine misfired as he saw a an object with a double cone shape, flashing red and green lights, hovering near the road. He drove on and did not seen what happened to the object.

On July 29th 1971 at 0330hrs in Smolan in Saline County, Kansas. Mrs Evelyn Meyers was awakened by a thunderstorm and went into her kitchen. Through her window she saw a large blue light about 400m away, which started to move towards her house. It went up and down and threw off sparks. It lit up the highway, almost hit the house and then backed up and disappeared into the trees. Evelyn saw the light perform the same manoeuvres three times.

At Delphos in Ottawa County, Kansas on 2nd November 1971. Tuesday. Sundown. Darrell Johnson and his wife Irma Johnson were inside their house. Ronald Johnson, sixteen, their son, was in a sheep pen behind the family home when he heard a rumbling sound and then saw blue, red and orange lights flash in a nearby grove of trees. The lights illuminated an object like a giant button mushroom that was nine feet in diameter and hovering two feet off the ground. The glow grew so intense that it hurt Ronald's eyes. The animals went crazy probably thinking that the Intergalactic Butcher had arrived. The family dog went berserk, the sheep began to bellow and the UFO took off with a whine like a jet engine. Robert's parents arrived in time to see a small blue light fading away on the horizon shortly afterwards. The Johnsons photographed the spot and it revealed a flourescent glow in the shape of the object that had landed. The UFO left a shiny doughnut ring on the ground. The ring would not absorb water and was found to have a layer of Silicone formed on it. The landing site was also irradiated and radioactive. An odd feature though was that when the witnesses touched the ring their fingers went numb permanently. Here is another version. Ronald Johnson (16) was tending the sheep in their pen with his dog, on his father's farm 800m north and east of Delphos. He looked up when his mother called, then heard a rumbling sound as an object suddenly became illuminated. This object was slightly domed at the top and base, with a slight bulge at the centre, illuminated by multi-coloured light that covered its entire surface. The thing was hovering 60cm above the ground, and there was a bright glow between the base and the ground. This light contained steady blue, red and orange elements, and was so bright that it hurt Ronald's eyes to look at it. The object was about 3m high, 2.7m diameter, and was rather less than 25m away. The dog was quiet but the sheep were bellowing. The object continued to make a sound like the vibration of an old washing machine. Then , after a few minutes, the light at the base grew brighter and expanded, and the thing ascend at considerable speed at an angle, the sound changing to a high pitched whine as it did so. It cleared a nearby shed by over a metre. As the sound changed Ronald suddenly became blinded. When he regained his sight after a few minutes, Ronald saw the object in the sky and ran home. His father, Durrel Johnson (52) was sceptical at first but went out and saw a light, like an arc lamp, , half the apparent diameter of the moon , moving away in the sky. When they walked to the landing site they found that the soil was glowing, as were parts of nearby trees. The surface felt strange and Mrs Erma Johnson (49) found that it seemed to numb her fingers. A branch was broken off a tree and there was a ring of dried soil, 2.5m diameter, 20-30cm thick. Various analyses of the soil samples came to differing conclusions. The object was said to have returned on 27 April 1974, Ronald developed psychic powers, and encountered a mysterious wild girl.

At Weida, near Manhattan in Riley County, Kansas on 4th November 1971. A retired Army dentist, Dr. Dean H. Stewart, reported seeing a cigar-shaped object with an orange nose cone and a white body as he was duck-hunting on a lake.

During November 1971 near Hillsboro in Marion County in Kansas Luke was driving when he saw a silver saucer-shaped object descend and hover twelve feet over a nearby field. Going closer to investigate he saw a hatch open and a ramp descend to the ground. Two beings that were about four and a half feet tall with large bald heads and wearing white robes came down the ramp and communicated telepathically with the Luke. They gave him a feeling of calm and security. Luke asked if he could see the interior of the ship and the two entities escorted him aboard. Inside the ceiling was brightly lit and the floor had an acrylic finish while banks of computer like instruments lined one wall. A master control panel contained five rows of four buttons each. Two high back chairs on invisible swivels faced the control panel. After his tour Luke was escorted back down the ramp and the ship soared out of sight. He claimed to have contacted the occupants on other occasions through astral projection.

1972

On February 25th 1972 (or following day) at 2100hrs in Larned in Pawnee County, Kansas. High school junior John B was leaving Larned for home when a large white light appeared before his car. The object lowered itself down in front of the vehicle and kept about 100m ahead, keeping in front as John speeded up and slowed down. The thing circled the car and then followed it into his parents' farm, where it hovered over the coral. John ran inside and closed the curtains. The next morning the bottom two wires of the coral looked as though they had been cut and twisted, and were found in a pile in the coral. Several of the cattle had burnt patches ranging from the size of a man's fist upwards on their hides where the hair was scorched. His parents, had seen no sign of the object when they arrived home 30 minutes after John.

On March 22nd 1972 at night in Wyandotte County, Kansas. Several teenagers observed a long object with red lights all round, moving in a stop start motion in the sky. The thing landed briefly in a field before taking off in a north-westerly direction.

On July 27th 1972 at 0130hrs in Garden City in Finney County, Kansas. Henry Guerrero was sat in his car with his workmate Bob Apsley, near to their workplace (Master Feeders II) 50km south of Garden City when they noticed a strange bright amber light travelling at 80-95kph close to the ground about 1.5km away. It was much larger and brighter than a truck clearance light and there were no roads in the area where it was visible.

In Central Kansas in Summer 1972. Late at night the witness was driving on an isolated road when he saw bright lights in a field. Thinking that it was a farmer with a tractor he drove to the source of the lights. He parked his car and walked toward the lights. Soon he came upon a humanoid figure, described as having four arms, tall, well-built and wearing a tight fitting black coverall and a black skullcap. He also wore white gloves and a white belt. His facial features were not quite human; his eyes were large and round. The humanoid spoke English and told the witness that he was fourth in command of the nearby vehicle, which the witness was unable to see due to the glare. The four-armed humanoid said that he was making minor repairs to the object and that he himself was a miscreation on his own planet. He appeared able to use his four arms efficiently. The witness conversed with the humanoid and persuaded him to let him onboard the craft. Inside the craft, he entered a room and soon went into a trance-like state and does not remember the trip. After arriving to what appeared to have been a "space station," he saw many different types of humanoids. During his stay there he was given a translator device and was shown many locations including libraries and large glass like buildings. After what seemed to have been two weeks, he was returned to the same spot where he was taken from. He saw the luminous craft leave without making a sound.

On August 19th 1972 at 0200hrs in Gem in Thomas County, Kansas. John I Calkins (23), assistant manager of a Nickersons farm restaurant, was wakened by the howling of his dog. Looking out, he saw three lighted objects over his house, which objects rose up and disappeared. He then heard strange high pitched whistles and sounds like a vacuum cleaner, so he called the police. Looking out again he saw objects in the sky, changing colours and lighting up the area, so that he could see that his dog had its paws over its ears. One object 7.5-10.5m diameter, 4.5-6m high, with a domed top and bottom and points at each end, emitting a brilliant light and a beeping sound, land on the Quonset Building, 45m from his caravan. John became cold with fear and had to go back inside. A call had already been received by Thomas County sheriff's office at Colby, from another witness and patrolman Paul Carter (22) was dispatched to the scene. As he turned off Main Street at 1-70 and headed south, he saw an object moving northeast to southwest, which settled in a pasture north east of his position. The thing was large, very bright changing from red and green flashing lights to a steady white light that was too brilliant to look at. The thing was an oval 9-10.5m wide, 6-7.5m high and resembled an inverted bowl. It was hovering 3-5m above the field, which it illuminated. Paul called in for help at 0207 and his patrol partner, Dennis Brown (22) rushed to the area in his own car, arriving in time to see the object take off from the field and head away to the southeast. Taking the patrol car they followed the thing and contacted Oakley Police, 30km to the southeast, who watched the object. As the object shot away over the field, Dennis took three Polaroid photographs but nothing came out. They then appeared to have received the call from Gem and drove to that scene. As they approached they saw several red and green lights either hovering or moving swiftly in the sky. The pair went out as far as Rexford but then returned to Gem, where John Calkin confirmed that the two officers were very pale and shaken. No traces were found at either the Gem or Colby landing sites. Up to about 30 other residents saw lights in the sky until about dawn at 0620.

On August 22nd 1972 at 2100hrs in Salina in Saline County, Kansas. Mrs Patty Herman (23) of Russell was driving eastwards on Hw1=70, about 40km west of Salina, when she saw a very bright white light, rimmed with red lights. Which lit up the whole highway, rise up from behind a hill to the south. It passed north over her car at very high speed. The thing was large but Patty was unable to make out its exact shape. About 15-20 minutes later, when about 15km west of Salina Patty saw two other, similar objects together perform an identical manoeuvre.

At 1.00 am on 1st October 1972 a seven year old boy was sleeping in his room in Potwin in Butler County in Kansas when he heard footsteps. He looked at the bedroom door and saw two short gray figures staring at him. He yelled for his Dad who came in and searched the room but found nothing. Apparently the Humanoids came back into the room and took the boy into a room with a table where there three Humanoids in the room. One looked like a doctor and was apparently in charge. He was taller than the other two who appeared to be assistants. The boy was hysterical at this time and began yelling for his Dad. Then a person resembling his father came into the room and the boy calmed down. The Humanoids rolled the boy to his side and performed some kind of procedure behind his left ear. The witness believed that it was an implant. The alien resembling his Dad, or so the boy believed, then told the boy not to touch the back of his ear until the morning. The boy then found himself back in bed.

1973

On June 19th 1973 at 0040hrs near Peabody in Marion County, Kansas. At least four people watched three very low moving round objects pace a lorry some 5km west of Peabody.

On November 16th 1973 at 2045hrs in Coffeyville in Montgomery County, Kansas. Four teenagers double dating in a car in a country parking spot noted some 6m behind them a white sphere, about the size of or just a bit bigger than a basketball, low above the ground. It emitted a soft glow that did not illuminate the surroundings and had a slight bobbing motion. The four got out to investigate, and as they approached the light moved slowly away, increasing in speed as one youth tried to outflank it, and wove its way through the trees till it was out of sight. They stood around talking about the incident for a couple of minutes, until the cold drove them back to the car. They were about to get back in, when they suddenly saw an object slowly descending through the overcast. It resembled one plate inverted over another, with flashing red, yellow and blue lights around the centre and a bright light shining up from the top, lighting up the clouds. They estimated the object was about 1.5km away and about 30m in diameter and that it was hovering about 200-300m below the cloud cover. The top light then went out and after about 30 seconds the object began to move slowly towards the group. When it had halved the distance it stopped again for about 10-12 seconds and then a white sphere dropped out of the bottom and sped away to the northwest, after a while descending at an angle before flattening out and speeding away. About 10 seconds later another sphere dropped out of the object, followed about a minute later by a third sphere, red this time, which descended to about 60m and sped overhead. The large object then slowly rose into the cloud cover. The whole episode occurred in complete silence. No effects were noticed on electrical equipment etc.

1975

Around 7.00 pm near New Cambria in Saline County in Kansas during March 1975 a young teenage couple were driving to the country and right after crossing a cement bridge that spanned a river they pulled into a farmer's access road and parked at the edge of a field alongside a bend in the river with the car facing East. They soon noticed a strange light that suddenly approached their location in a kind of a blur or warp speed mode. Suddenly at tree top level was a dark rectangular object with one red and one green running light positioned together on its underside at its center. They stared in amazement and after about five minutes they noticed that it had moved to the right. It seemed to be moving in very slow motion towards the other side of the river. After another five minutes they decided to drive away from the area and as they turned onto the cement bridge they saw that the craft had returned to its original position above tehm and slightly back from the bridge. They stopped their car and got out to have a look at it. It was twenty to twenty-five feet wide and had what seemed to be a large rectangular window running across the middle third of its front. Standing inside to the left side looking down at the witnesses were two beings which the witnesses could only see from the waist up. They were four feet tall with abnormally large upper heads and large black eyes that appeared devoid of emotion. The skin was pure white like the moon with the texture resembling that of an albino salamander. The eyes ran almost North South with the heads. The craft hovered silently the whole time. After about a minute of eye contact with the Humanoids the witnesses re-entered their vehicle and rapidly drove away from the area. They could still see the craft hovering where they had left it.

At Russell in Russell County in Kansas on 4th July 1975 a dazzling low flying metallic funnel paced an auto nearly blinding the two women inside it.

In White City in Morris County in Kansas on 19th July 1975 on an early Saturday evening Jan Maddox and Richard Gustafson saw four metallic spheres land in a field. The pasture suddenly blazed up and three burning rings in a triangular pattern were found. Photos were taken. Or this. Farmer Richard Gustafson and his girlfriend, reporter January Maddox, were driving to Junction City when, as they drove past Skiddy Cemetery, they saw a large shiny object in the sky. On it were four cylinders, three in parallel and one below the middle one. The thing descended rapidly, taking 3-5 seconds to reach the ground. The couple first thought that it was a plane crash and rushed to the site. When they got over a rise, they found the field on fire, but no trace of any plane. There were three rings of fire, about 1.5m diameter, burning in the grass, about 4.5-6m, apart in a triangle shape. Two men arrived with sacks to put the fire out. January took some Polaroid photographs of the site.

In July 1975 (or following month) at 2100hrs in Pittsburg in Crawford County, Kansas. A married couple out driving saw what they thought was a meteor. This however stopped and then approached them on level flight. The thing, which was discoid or cylindrical, with a row of luminous panels, seemed to cover the road. They pursued the object, noting a dead silence in the environment, and the thing seemed to respond to the woman's comments. It then accelerated somewhat and then just disappeared. The couple noticed an unusually large number of animals running around.

1976

On the night of 20th June 1976 near Colby in Thomas County in Kansas a young couple with a baby were driving when they observed three UFOs then a group of four and then a single low flying one. Thereafter they could not account for ninety minutes of driving nor for the time elapsed. Under hypnosis the couple recalled being abducted and physically examined. The UFO was one hundred and forty to one hundred and sixty feet high. Then three helmeted Humanoids of medium height were seen who controlled the witnesses by telepathic commands. After the experience they had needle marks on their arms, strap marks across their wrists and ankles and rashes and sores on their backs which healed quickly. The creatures looked like skinny versions of the Michelin Man. Another version. Near Goodland in Sherman County, a teenager couple (19, 18)and their baby were driving from Ohio to Colorado, when on the western border of Kansas they saw three, then four, then a single unidentified object pass overhead and later found that they could not remember 90 miles of driving and experienced missing time. Under hypnosis they recalled an object like two deep plates rim to rim, 12m high, 40-50m across. Below the thing's rim were two clockwise rotating rings. They were taken on board by three 1. 65m tall, helmeted beings who moved the couple from room to room in a courteous manner. They later had unusual marks on their bodies and paranormal experiences.

In Summer 1976 in Ottawa (Franklin), Kansas. A man and his family saw a glowing sphere descend to the ground; a small humanoid occupant was seen to leave the craft & walk about the area before returning to the UFO. Small footprints were found. 2 other sightings of a similar object were reported the same day.

1978

In mid-February 1978 a hole six feet in diameter was found in the lake ice on Wyandotte County Lake. There was also a hole in the ice on a nearby farm pond.

In mid-March 1978 a UFO was seen to crash into Wyandotte County Lake in Wyandotte County Lake in Kansas.

1979

In early March 1979 two boys found a dead alligator or caiman in a creek in southeast Johnson County.

On August 2nd 1979 at 2230hrs in Herndon in Rawlins County, Kansas. A mother and daughter out cycling observed a strange light hovering to the south. The girl returned home for binoculars and they were joined by the rest of the family. The object was triangular, metallic, 15mlong and low to the ground, with red lights at each tip of the triangle and one in the centre. It also had additional red and white lights. Mrs Wurm, driving home with her teenage son and daughter, also observed the thing low to the ground, hovering over the farm feeder. The thing made an odd humming sound. There were other witnesses across the area. Some estimated its altitude as 60-100m

1980

Late at night in Summer 1980 at Topeka in Shawnee County in Kansas in a dream like state the witness remembers waking up and finding himself in a small room, paralyzed, lying on top of a bunk bed. Using his peripheral vision he saw a Humanoid sitting cross-legged on the floor. He described the Humanoid as having long arms, a big head, with a pointed chin, a slit for a mouth, two holes for a nose and large eyes shaped like tear drops that wrapped around the head. It had a thin neck that looked too small to hold the weight of his head. He then hears someone trying to scream and sees the Humanoid now bent over the person on the bottom bunk. Realizing this other person is his brother he breaks the paralysis and jumps down from the top and pushes the Humanoid. It flies across the room. He wakes his brother and both began to run down a hallway into a very large room. The room has a wall covered with lights and buttons, resembling a control panel. The room is also full of tables with people on them. They attempt to run out some huge double oak doors, but these are shut closed. The whole place reminded them of a "castle." Suddenly he wakes up back on his bed with his brother sleeping besides him.

At 2.13 am in November 1980 near Salina in Saline County in Kansas on a cold clear night Donna Butts, her mother in law and two children were en route to Kansas City and had been following a semi tractor-trailer for miles. As they approached a hill and curve they noticed a bright light beyond the hill and the whole area lit up. The truck and the witness vehicle suddenly slowed down as they both saw a huge brightly lit object hovering above them. Both the trucker and Butts panicked and accelerated their vehicles. The object was huge and consisted of three triangular sections. It had green and glowing peach colored lights and at the bottom it had a huge white light and was emitting a loud vibrant hum. As the witness was about to pass the truck the object shot down a beam of light that hit the highway directly behind her car. The beam followed the car and hit the truck. It then suddenly disappeared, and so did the truck. At the same time several small aircraft and helicopters appeared to circle the object and the area. The small aircraft seemed cubical in shape and appeared to be playing tag with the helicopters. She also noticed army trucks in the area. Later under hypnosis they learned that they had been taken onboard the object where the main witness had a conversation with certain entities. No other information.

1981

At 3.00 am in September 1981 in Solomon in Dickinsons and Saline Counties in Kansas the five-year old witness woke up in the middle of the night to find a short gray figure standing by his bed. It appeared to be doing something to his abdominal area. He felt a slight discomfort and a slight pressure on his upper legs. The terrified witness closed his eyes until the gray being left.

1989

At 12.40 am on November 7th 1989 near Goodland in Sherman County in Kansas two women driving in a remote rural road began to notice a bright object with multicolored flashing lights maneuvering slowly over the area. They stopped the vehicle several times to get a better look. One time a ball of light descended near their vehicle and hovered above a nearby field. They then saw a cone of soft multicolored light shine towards the ground from under the object. They also noticed strange "black waves" resembling heat waves approach their vehicle. They finally drove away experiencing several types of emotions and feelings. Upon reaching their destination they realized that they had lost 2 hours of their time. Later under hypnosis one of the witnesses recalled floating silently upwards towards a bright object overhead. She found herself in a circular room encircled by windows and panels and lit up by a diffuse pinkish white light. She encountered several 5 ½ foot tall slender Humanoids with large hairless heads and tiny pointed chins. They have huge slanted dark eyes and white skin. The beings communicated with the witness using telepathy and seem to glide across the floor gracefully. The witness sees no apparent clothing. She feels calm as one of the beings touches her forehead, she then watches her friend go through some type of examination on a nearby table. The other witness is also regressed and recalls similar details. One of the witnesses reported experiencing a series of nose bleeds after the incident.

1996

At 1.30 am on August 24th 1996 in Osborne in Osborne County in Kansas the 17-year old witness was sleeping in the basement of his grandparent's home when some flashing lights awakened him. Terrified he was unable to move. As he woke up the blinking lights stopped, he kept his eyes opened for a few minutes and then the blinking lights started again. Every time the lights blinked he could see creatures around the bed looking at him, as the lights blinked faster and faster the creatures began to move toward him and one of them put its three fingered hand on his forehead while the others (there were four) started tugging at his covers. The creatures were gray colored with shiny silvery clothing and large heads, with really big black pearly eyes. One of the creatures touched his forehead and a paralyzing fear came over him. Two of the beings then grabbed his left leg and poked his calf on his left leg. They held a strange metallic object with buttons or switches on it, they jabbed his leg and pulled it out. When that was done one of them touched his forehead, looked at him and he perceived a mental message that said: "If you tell no one we will return to visit you." Then the blinking lights stopped and it became very dark. He then heard a loud humming noise that gradually diminished in volume. His grandmother reported hearing strange noises in the house.

Kentucky

1875

In 1875 (approx date) in the evening in Greenville in Muhlenberg County, Kentucky. A young girl sat on the porch of her rural property near Greenville saw a large luminous sphere take off slowly from the cemetery and come down the dirt road. When it reached their house, the front gate opened of its own accord and passed by the girl, who became paralysed. The thing then went up the house stairs and disappeared.

1879

In November 1879 in Owingsville in Bath County, Kentucky. At a spot some 10km east of Owningsville, Mrs Goodpater took her washing outside and saw a man hovering some 6m above the trees. The figure moved its arms and legs and assumed various poses before taking off out of sight. She and her children observed the thing for 25 minutes. A neighbouring farmer James Nealus saw something like a balloon but no-one in it.

1880

On 28th July 1880 the same day as Louisville, at Madisonville in Hopkins County, Kentucky, something strange was seen in the sky that had something like a ball at each end. The object sometimes appeared in circular form and then changed to an oval before passing out of sight. Madisonville was in the same period as St Louis in Missouri as well as Louisville in Kentucky.

On the same day 28th July 1880 as the sighting over Saint Louis, at Louisville in Jefferson County, Kentucky, between 6.00 pm and 7.00 pm, a being like a man was seen in the sky surrounded by strange machinery that the Humanoid was working with its hands and feet. The craft appeared to be ascending and descending under intelligent control. The craft vanished with the cover of darkness. The object had been moving in many directions as well as ascending and descending at low altitude. The Humanoid also had small wings or fans on his back that he was flapping busily to stay aloft. This one was nothing like a balloon. An amazing observation with this research is how the technology tends to mirror how the observers would have created the observed technology if they were capable at all of fantasizing or creating it. These seem to be blueprints of illusions and dreams come to life. How much of this is true? Are these observations a form of our planet or its inhabitants dreaming?

Still in Louisville and late July 1880 where there are several reports of a strange Humanoid wandering around that was as agile as a monkey. The Humanoid had a long nose, pointed ears and long fingers and wore a uniform of shiny material including a long cape and a metallic helmet. Under the cape was a large very bright light with which he would scare people, particularly women. The Humanoid even got so familiar as to pull off their clothing while they were stunned. His favourite method of escape was to spring smoothly over high objects like haystacks or wagons and then vanish on the other side to the bewilderment of those brave enough to pursue him. This is like Springheeled Jack in England. The Humanoid confronted the victim, usually an attractive young female, opened his cape and flashed his light at which time a blue ball of flame usually hit the victim's face. There was no apparent victory other than shock though. In the ensuing confusion he would leap away. A very Springheeled Jack type of figure. Was he the strange figure seen pedalling through the sky on 28th July also over Louisville? Is the stunning bright light or flame the origin of the word "Flasher" for an exhibitionist? The same day strange things were seen over Madisonville in Kentucky.

1886

On February 12th 1866 at night in Bracken County, Kentucky. Nathanial Squires and his family were awoken by a commotion among their African-American workers and by a blue light illuminating their room. They saw by the fence separating the workers compound from the house yard a huge creature like a horned ape with long arms terminating in paws, hoof like feet and a long tail, which it swished around. It was belching out fire.The thing seemed to disappear into a fire, which suddenly went out, leaving no trace of the creature. The thing was seen by other neighbours on this and the following night

1887

Near Hawesville in Hancock County in Kentucky on December 10th 1887. During the afternoon an immense balloon was observed sailing over this city on Saturday afternoon at a great height and was in view for a long while, when it began rapidly descending. Yesterday it was found in an old swamp about ten miles South of Hawesville. There was also discovered the emaciated remains of a man who had evidently been emptied from the basket several yards from where the airship had fallen. It is the theory that the aeronaut was already dead before the balloon reached the earth as no serious bruises were found upon his body. No papers or evidence has been found to indicate who the unfortunate man can be. Kansas City Times (Kansas City Missouri) December 14, 1887.

1893

On 26th August 1893 in the morning a few minutes after sunrise the sun took on a peculiar color over Leslie County in Kentucky. Thirty minutes after sunrise the sky became filled with thousands of discs the size of wagon wheels. They were all in motion and changed shape into triangles, squares and odd forms. There were various colors including red, green and black. The sighting lasted sixty minutes.

1897

Now for the 1897 Airship Flap.

Near Louisville in Jefferson County in Kentucky before daybreak on April 12th 1897. Augustus Rodgers, a local farmer encountered a brilliantly lighted huge oblong shaped craft traveling low over the area. He called his wife and they both watched as it disappeared towards the southeast at high speed. Before it left, both witnesses were able to see a human-like form standing in the front of the ship as if it was directing its course. This was during the Great Airship Flap of 1897.

Near Lexington in Fayette County in Kentucky. On the evening of April 17th 1897 three men reported seeing an airship on the ground and a man about 40 years old disembark from the craft and fill a bucket with water from a stream. The witnesses attempted to engage the man in conversation, but he refused to reply to their questions and promptly flew off.

Back in Louisville, Kentucky, on April 24th 1897. That evening a man heard a buzzing noise and looked up to see a cigar-shaped craft about 200 feet in the air. Before the airship flew off to the south, the witness was able to make out the form of a man standing at the stern of the object: "He looked at me, and I waved my hat. Two other men were sitting at the helm." Thomas J Casey was behind his home when he heard a buzzing sound and saw a cigar shaped object at about 60m altitude. At the rear of the object a man was standing and two others were sitting in the helm. The man at the rear looked at the witness, who responded by waving his hat.

At 7.00 pm on April 27th 1897 near Elkton in Todd County in Kentucky. A family living South of town was sitting at the supper table when the furious barking of the ever-faithful watchdog suddenly startled them, and as is usual with children, they all rushed out to see what had caused the excitement of the canine. The family described seeing a large, cigar shaped affair with immense white wings. It was not very high, and the guy ropes and rods could be seen plainly. Three men were visible, and they frantically waved their hands as they passed. The machine had a zigzag course and seemed to be out of working order.

1907

On April 16th 1907 at 2000hrs in Breckenridge, Kentucky. Three people, H Keenan, Emily Keenan and J B Bates, were near Mrs T A Keenan property when they saw a conical light near a deserted cabin about 2.5km away. The thing moved like a boat on water towards Mrs Keenan's house, where it hovered for about 15 minutes. It then approached the witnesses. Inside the light a dark shape was seen moving around. The thing then retreated to a hollow, emitting flashes of light as it did so

1927

During the summer 1927 a witness saw an airship that resembled a perfectly shaped huge fish with big fins that were extended outwards near the front and small ones near the rear that sailed over Wolfe County in Kentucky.

1942

In April 1942 three Kentucky trainmen, R. M. Danner the engineer, Bill Iversole the fireman and Charles Furnash, the conductor, were waiting for the signal to start the train from Springlake in Kenton County, Kentucky, when they noticed a powerful searchlight that was originating from above. The light pointed down a hillside to the West about 300 feet higher than the train which was down in the Licking River Valley. The luminous object then moved North with no sound. "I was the engineer on the second shift that shoved trans [sic] over the Northbound Hump. While we were waiting for the signal to start shoving the train from Spring Lake (south end of the yard), my attention was called by the fireman to a powerful search light that was originating from above. The light pointed down alongside a hillside to the West about 300 feet higher than us. We were down in the Licking River Valley. The hill ran all the way to the Ohio River, South of Covington, Kentucky. Where the light was originating, we could not make out the [?] shape of any object. Strange thing about it was that it was stationary at times (the UFO?), except the beam of light. Then it would begin to move North with the light. There was no sound.

1947

On July 7th 1947 at 2040hrs in Louisville in Jefferson County, Kentucky. W B Robinson and W P Meecham and, independently, Mrs J P saw a fiery disc descend vertically with a whirling motion. The glow was visible for two seconds after landing.

1948

Around 1.15 pm on 7th January 1948 the control tower at Godman AFB was contacted by the Kentucky State Highway Patrol inquiring about a curious craft reported by inhabitants of Maysville which is a village eighty miles from Louisville in Mason County. Godman AFB had no information and called Wright-Patterson AFB but they had nothing to contribute either. The Police called in with new reports less than thirty minutes later. Owensboro and Irvington to the West were giving accounts of a circular craft 250 to 300 feet in diameter travelling in a general Louisville direction at a pretty good clip.

That same day at Godman Air Force Base near Franklin in Simpson County in Kentucky, adjacent to Fort Knox, Wednesday 7th January 1948, Captain Thomas Mantell, 25, and thousands of other witnesses saw an unusual object in the sky around 7.20 pm to 7.55 pm. Five P-51 fighters were alerted and took off to investigate. Four of the fighters did not possess oxygen cylinders and had to drop out of the chase at 14,000 foot altitude which was the official limit for their aircraft. Captain Mantell's P-51 fighter chased the unknown round white object until at an altitude of 9,000 feet Mantell's plane went into a fatal dive for no known reason. Mantell radioed "It looks metallic and its tremendous in size and it was moving at half Mantell's speed. Now its starting to climb.1'm going on up to 20,000 feet. If I'm no closer I'll abandon chase". No more was heard and the wreck was found ninety miles away. Mantell's watch showed 3.18 pm when it stopped. The plane started to fall from 20,000 feet and exploded half way down. And how many crashes or collisions have there been so far? The Airforce originally stated that it was the planet Venus, which they should have been used to by now and not prone to sending up aircraft every time that the planet Venus appeared. Then they stated that it was a weather balloon. Why send up five planes for one of these either as airfields send up numerous weather balloons and scientific test balloons each day. They also know what they are. The five fighters were sent up after something that the Airforce did not know!

One night in 1949 in Sebree in Webster County in Kentucky two witnesses were entering a parked truck in front of a house when one of them noticed a bright light approaching them from the direction of the railroad tracks. Moments later, as one of the witnesses was attempting to start the truck, the light got closer. It floated towards the front of the truck and both witnesses could now see the outline of a human-like figure directly underneath the light. Both witnesses were frightened and scrambled out of the truck. One of them momentarily froze and could not move. Finally while they went inside to get other witnesses the floating man and light vanished.

1950

On 20th September 1950 several buildings in Murray in Calloway County in Kentucky were struck by falling meteorites after a brilliant fireball was seen over Illinois. The meteoroid exploded in the sky and several pieces hit the ground fifteen kilometers East of Murray. The meteorites were carbonaceous chondrites. The largest fragment was 3.4 kilograms.

1952

In Summer 1952 (or previous year) at 2200hrs in Lexington in Fayette County, Kentucky. A 12 year old boy, who later became a member of the American Astronomical Society was cycling home from a boy scout meeting on this warm night. As he turned right onto a C road he suddenly noticed a blue green hazy disc 80 degrees above and ahead of him, travelling along the path immediately to his left. It seemed to descend behind a house. The observation only lasted about 5 seconds but the boy was terrified. The disc was 30m away at 15m altitude when he first saw it. It was about 10m in diameter and appeared to be more gaseous than solid. It descended steadily behind the roofline of a two story house 35-40m away to about 10 mts and banked 20-30 degrees to the right.

1953

On August 20th 1953 (Approx. date) late at night in Louisville in Jefferson County, Kentucky. A young boy asleep in his grandparent's trailer, awoke to see a very thin being with an oval head and large dark eyes. When the thing realised that the boy was awake it stood straight up and walked out of the room and down the corridor in a jerky fashion, 1 like something viewed through a strobe light. The figure then just vanished on the spot.

1955

In Kelly in Christian County in Kentucky, near Hopkinsville, on Sunday 21st August 1955 at 7.00 pm eleven witnesses, three children and eight adults incorporating the Sutton family had a most terrifying encounter. Teenager Billy Ray Sutton went to the well to have a drink of water and came back and stated that he'd seen a flying object land behind the farmhouse. All eleven thought it was a shooting star. An hour later a creature was seen. Firstly as a glow. It was a little man with its arms raised as it approached the witnesses. When twenty feet away it was shot at by two of the men. It somersaulted and vanished into the dark and the men went back into the house. The Humanoid then appeared at a window as the men fired guns through the screen. The Humanoid appeared to be hit and vanished. The men went outside again and saw another creature on the roof, shot at it and knocked it off. Another Humanoid was in a tree at some distance and they also shot at it. The Humanoid floated to the ground and the witnesses realized that their bullets had little effect. They could hear bullets striking the Humanoids and then hear them ricocheting off them. The Humanoids tumbled to the ground and then got up again. By 11.00 pm the people decided that they were no match for the dwarfs. They abandoned the house and drove to Hopkinsville Police Station. One man alone had used four boxes of .22 shells. The Suttons were all sober and visibly frightened. All said roughly the same story and were not a drinking family. One Policeman saw several strange meteors from the direction of the Sutton farm as he went to investigate and several strange indentations were found in the ground around the house. The Humanoids apparently had large eyes which were probably very sensitive as the Humanoids always approached the house from the darkest corner. They did not appear to have any pupil in the eye or an eyelid and they did not like going near houselights or near doors. When approaching they had their hands up in the air and they floated when they fell down. They were 3.5 to four feet tall and had huge hands, large pointed ears and their arms were almost hanging to the ground. As for clothing it appeared to be made of nickel-plate. The eyes seemed to be set on the sides of the head. A busy night in Kelly. Or this report? Billy Ray Taylor (21), a lodger at the Sutton farm, went out to the well in the back yard, from where he observed a silvery object with a multi-coloured exhaust come silently from the south west at about 10m altitude, and then drop into a gully. He informed members of the family of the incident but was laughed at. At about 2000hrs. the dogs began barking and Taylor went outside, with the head of the family, Elmer Sutton (25). The dog fled under the house and the two men saw a sort of glow approaching the house. Outlined in this glow was a dwarf about 1m tall, with an oversized round head, arms that seemed to stretch to the ground and huge eyes that gave off a yellow glow. The creature seemed to be made of luminous, silvery metal. It walked towards them with its hands above its head. The men grabbed their guns and when the creature got within 6m they fired, at which it summersaulted backwards, scrambled upright and hurried off into the darkness. The men then rushed back into the houseThe occupants of the house were Elmer's wife Vera (29), his widowed mother Glennie Lankford, the farm operator John G Sutton (21), his wife Alene (27) and brother in law O. P. Baker (35), and Mrs Lankford's children by her second marriage, Lonnie (12), Charlton (10) and Mary (7) Lankford, and Taylor's wife June (18). Inside the party saw the creature at a window and fired at it through a screen, and as Taylor ran out to see what was happening, a claw like hand grabbed his hair. Alene dragged him back into the house and Elmer came out and shot the creature off the overhand, and another, on a tree branch, which floated to the ground after it had been shot. Another creature then appeared around the northwest corner of the house. These creatures move very rapidly. When they were fired at directly, the bullets made a metallic sound when they hit them. Their large eyes had neither lids nor pupils. They had large floppy, triangular ears with a wrinkled leathery skin. When approaching they came slowly, with arms raised, but retreated on all fours, their arms seeming to provide the main propulsion. Their legs appeared inflexible. On one occasion a creature was shot from the roof and floated to a fence 12m away. They kept returning despite being shot at repeatedly and at 2300hrs. the whole party climbed into two cars and rove into Hopkinsville. There were investigations by police and state troopers. One officer at the Shady Oaks Restaurant, 3-5km out of Hopkinsville saw several "meteors" pass overhead on a slightly descending path, making a whining noise. Investigations that night failed to find any trace of the creatures, but after the police left Glennie saw a creature by the window frame and Elmer again shot at it. No traces were found.

1959

On 30th January 1959 at Covington in Kenton County in Kentucky a woman reported seeing a strange creature that was grayish in color with a lopsided chest, ugly tentacles and rolls of fat running horizontally over a bald head. Two hours before just across the border near New Richmond in Clermont County in Ohio a truck driver on US. Route 52 saw a bizarre gray ugly creature with tentacles crossing the road ahead of his truck. These were two separate reports of the same unusual creature.

Also at Covington just across the Ohio River from Cincinnati sometime in February 1959 a motorist saw a large two legged creature on a bridge. Similar creatures were being seen around Hamilton County in Ohio at the same time.

On September 7th 1959 in the morning in Wallingford in fleming County, Kentucky. Mail carrier, Walter Ogden observed an elliptical object hovering low over the ground. The object rose vertically, emitting a blast of flame and then sped away horizontally. A stained ring 30cm wide, enclosing a circle 4m diameter was found.

1960

On November 17th 1960 in Lexington in Fayette County in Kentucky. Three UFOs were seen to follow two jet aircraft. One object closed in on the jets, then stopped, repeating this several times. Witnesses described it as round, rotating, color changing from gray to silver as it turned.

1961

In August 1961at 1.30 am in Rogers in Wolfe County in Kentucky. Mrs. Quinn suddenly woke to find a "terrible-looking creature" standing beside her bed: "a big blob with a small round head with no neck, looking like a roly-poly." Around its big eyes were wrinkles that glowed. It moved across the room to the bed where her daughters, Brenda and Judy (14) were sleeping. Judy awoke to see something "like a huge tar baby with enormous eyes. I knew it wanted me to go somewhere. I found myself slipping off the bed. Suddenly, the thing released its strange force & it was gone." Another version. A woman visiting her in-laws was sleeping in her room with her baby and two daughters. She was awakened by a feeling of a powerful force pulling her out of bed, and saw, beside her bed, a black creature with a small round head, no neck, big "mean but sad" eyes, around the top of which were wrinkles that glowed. It moved over to where the girls were sleeping, and the 14 year old, also had a sensation of being awoken by this force. Its eyes seemed to ripple and it seemed to communicate that it wanted her to go with it. When she screamed it vanished. The bay refused to suckle after the incident.

1963

On July 18th 1963 at 1400 near Fern Creek in Jefferson County in Kentucky. Four boys 8 or 9 years old were playing in a field when they noticed something like snow falling that disappeared after reaching the ground. Looking up, they saw a cigar-shaped object like a small blimp, from which came a disc-shaped object that disappeared behind the woods. A few minutes later they noticed a small being, 3.5-4 feet tall, standing at the edge of the woods. It wore tight-fitting white clothes and had a large helmeted head, with goggles; 2 tubes ran from the helmet. The boys approached, throwing clods of dirt, and the entity pointed a black cylindrical object at them, hitting two. They ran to the house. The wounds were 6-inch circles of "sunburn" that took a couple of weeks to heal. Small, deep footprints different from the boys and three impressions 15 feet apart, were found in the field next day, as well as a 30-foot circular area in the woods where the vegetation was crushed.

1964

On May 22nd 1964 at 0900hrs in Hopkinsville in Christian County, Kentucky. High school cafeteria employees observed the landing and take off of a round object emitting four beams of light. Grass was found flattened at the spot.

1966

On a summer day in 1966 near Fort Knox in Bullitt, Hardin and Meade Counties in Kentucky the witness was alone sitting in a wooded area when a man wearing a peculiar outfit suddenly confronted him. The man wore a one-piece outfit closed at the neck, long sleeves and pants that seemed to go right into the boots. The beige outfit had a single metallic belt with a silver box attached on the front. A small blue light flickered occasionally on the box. The man had very fine blond hair and friendly pale eyes and communicated with the witness telling him that he was from another world a great distance from earth and that his name was Zo. Eventually the being left, leaving behind a low buzzing sound that lasted a few minutes. The witness claimed several additional contacts.

In Rockcastle County in Kentucky on Saturday 17th September 1966 several groups and individual witnesses Joe McFarland, 17, and Edward Alcorn, 17, began to feel weak and woozy in the woods. Suddenly a strange light appeared above and around them. It became real bright. They could also see a bright circle of light above them that was thirty feet across. This lasted a few seconds then died down. There was no noise. The boys went and got Alcorn's brother, sister and a friend. All of them saw the strange light in the sky plus a smaller light between the trees. It would blink once and then three times. It repeated this several times. There were also individual witness sightings of UFOs in the area at the same time. Could wooziness be mistaken for giddiness? If it is giddiness then there are already correlations with hearing related problems in association with phenomenal activities before primarily UFOs. Giddiness is generally associated with problems within the inner ear which is responsible for balance. So we are not just interacting with phenomena on a visual level but in many cases on an auditory and even extra-auditory level as well. The problem could be caused by a pressure field event as well?

On October 18th 1966 at 0555hrs in Cynthiana in Harrison County, Kentucky. Walter Stone (20) od Carlisle was driving to work at the Kawneer Steel Plant in Cynthiana when on Highway 30,a bout 3km east of that town his car lights picked up an object, which flew over his car at terrific speed. The thing was top shaped, with a white light or flames on the underside, and a ring of red light or flames around its outer edge. The thing emitted a whine that hurt Stone's ears and a sort of force seemed to hold him down on his seat as it passed over. The experience left him scared and shaken.

In Stephensport in Breckinridge County in Kentucky during Autumn 1966. Joe, a 9-year old boy at the time, woke up to a loud thrashing noise outside of his bedroom window at approximately 1.30 a.m. He went to his window to peak outside, but there was nothing in view. Naturally, Joe went to his living room to investigate the sound that continued to bang against his house. When he came to the living room, he pulled back the curtains of the front door window. To his surprise, he was staring at a 5'6" to 6" tall man of amphibious characteristics, with dark brown scales covering its entire body. The creature had webbed feet and hands and little dark eyes. Joe recollects that the brief moment he seen the creature's face, it appeared to have huge rows of gills that flared out on both sides of its face, resembling that of a lizard. Joe doesn't remember the creature having a nose, lips, muscles, or genitals, but there was a ridge-like feature starting from its forehead and running back over the top of its head. After a brief moment Joe peered at the creature through the window, it quickly ran for the creek next to Joe's house. Joe, shocked, ran to an adjacent window to catch a glimpse of it as it ran away on two legs toward a creek about 75 yards from his house.

1967

In Shelbyville in Shelby County in Kentucky at 9.00 pm on 15th January 1967 a male teenager saw an erratically moving bright light southeast of town. The light was elongated, almost cylindrical and was soon joined by another one. Both hovered over the one spot and then vanished. Fifty minutes later a power failure threw most of the city into darkness. Just before the blackout a soft blue light was seen over the substation. Several residents claimed to have seen the unusual craft over their houses. What else is new?

During January 1967 Lola Dills was driving in Frankfort in Franklin County when she saw a black object with long spindly legs or stems at the bottom and sides. The side stems were weaving and gesturing and appeared to end in pincers. The creature moved by placing the lower stems one in front of the other. The head consisted of a round part eight inches in diameter that protruded from the top. The sides had a shaggy look and the front was white with two eyes. A bump with two small holes lower than the head may have been a nose. The mouth was a slit below the nose. From it issued a shrill sound heard just as Lola was passing. Then Lola saw another and another with slight variations. Weird? Giant slaters? I am only presenting this catalogue of the absurd, not judging them.

1973

On September 29th 1973 in Obiob County in Kentucky during the evening. A couple saw a bright-red light swoop down close enough to the earth to light up 1-1/2 acres of land, nearly causing a 7-car pile-up on SR 78 near Reelfoot Lake.

On October 11th 1973 at 2000hrs in Madisonville in Hopkins County, Kentucky. A woman, her daughter and 13 year old grandson were driving west of their home in Madisonville when they observed an egg shaped object 1.5-1.8m long, giving off white and then red, pink and blue lights, which illuminated the road. The object, which was at between 6-8m altitude, began to follow them . The daughter, who was driving, was so scared that she carried on driving at 110kph, the silent object pacing them to the left.

On October 19th 1973 in Campbellsville in Kentucky. 9:30 p.m. Two men followed an object that looked about the size of a B-52, then lost sight of it behind a cluster of trees. "I do a lot of flying myself," one commented, "and when I first sighted this object I thought it was going to land at the airport."

The following night on October 20th 1973 in Campbellsville in Taylor County in Kentucky. A family had an early morning encounter with a "triangular-shaped object about the size of two cars" hovering about tree-top high not more than 100 yards" from their home. "Early Saturday morning about 2a.m. a dog awoke our little boy," said Richerson. "My wife went to calm him down and while she was bent over to pick him up she looked out the window and saw this glowing object across the road. She came in and woke me up and we stood there for about 15 minutes watching it hover in a field across the road. I wish now that I had gone out but it startled me."

On October 23rd 1973 in Russell Springs in Russell County in Kentucky A woman saw two 3-ft tall beings in her carport who walked around the side of the house, entered a craft "shaped like a washing tub" sitting on the ground, which then rose over the house and disappeared. The men were reddish and walked like they were on tip toes. The ground was disturbed where the craft had been sitting. Campbellsville is only 24 miles from Russell Springs. Or this version. A woman in Russell County, near Russell Spring, went out to feed her dogs and encountered, on her carport, two dwarfs 90cm tall, red in colour, who walked as though they were on tiptoe. After observing the woman for a few moments, the beings walked round the side of the house and entered a bight object, shaped like a washing tub, which took off and flew directly over the house and disappeared. Sheriff Wendell Wilson who investigated noted that the grass and ground was disturbed at the site and that the woman was genuinely frightened.

In November 1973 at 0200hrs in Florence in Boone County, Kentucky. A woman was awoken by a loud humming sound and went to the back door to look outside. Hovering over her patio, which extended 3m beyond her door, was a large sphere with flashing red and green lights in its centre. The thing was wobbling and moving from left to right. The woman ran upstairs, screaming, to her teenage children. When they went to investigate the thing had gone. The witness was so shaken she had to take sedatives.

1974

Late one evening in 1974 in Mayfield in Graves County, Kentucky. Donna Mitchell was playing with some friends were playing in her living room on this dark, wet evening when, looking through the window, they saw a dark male human figure looking through the window. This unnerved the children and they turned away. When they looked back a short time later, the man was no longer there.

1975

In 1975 in Spottsville in Henderson County, Kentucky. Two men out hunting racoons saw a large luminous disc emerge from underwater in the Green River and fly off at terrific speed. Their dogs bolted in panic.

On May 10th 1975 at 2130hrs in Florence in Boone County, Kentucky. Chuck D (15), a boy of high academic and sporting ability, went out to fetch in his horse, which was at the other end of the 3 acre (1.2 hectare) field/ As he did so he heard a sound like a buzzing of bees and turned round to see an object shaped like a mantra ray, 6m long, 3m wide wing tip to wing tip, hovering 6m above a neighbour's vegetable garden 25m away, The thing was bobbing up and down like a cork on water and Chuck could feel the ground vibrate. On this object there were two light sources; a luminous green rectangular section on its underside, resembling a green traffic light, about 2.4m long, 1.2m wide, faced with a row of circular lenses; the other, a red light on the object's tail. On the top of the object was an unlit, featureless raised dome. The porch light was reflected on the body of the thing, giving it a metallic green cast. While Chuck stood transfixed an olive green beam appeared, which did not widen and which appeared to probe the neighbour's garden. Chuck noticed dust in the beam was swirling and the branches on a nearby tree were swaying. . The beam proceeded to make wider probes of the gardens and yard and when the beam illuminated the swimming pool Chuck noticed that a blue glow surrounded the electricity wires. The beam then hit Chuck, who found himself; paralysed but still conscious. He seemed to see mathematical symbols and equations, which didn't make sense to him, in his mind's eye, followed by various other scenes, such as standing on a cliff looking out a red sea, and floating in space. During this time chuck felt very cold. When the beam went out Chuck fell on his face and no longer felt cold. The object was still in view. After Chuck got to his feet, the buzzing got louder, and he could also hear a metallic drumming sound. The object then moved into a vertical orientation, the tail increased in brilliance and then became a blur. This was followed by a purple flash, followed, 3-4 seconds later by a loud thunderclap. The object was now just a red light in the sky, which went straight up, curved, levelled off and then gave off a white flash. Chuck's parents noted his flushed appearance when they got home. His head cold vanished overnight.

On October 22nd 1975 at night in Covington in Kenton County, Kentucky. An engineer on the 14th floor of the Municipal Building, observed, through binoculars, a disc shaped object with a "catwalk" around which lights were rotating, and with peculiar wings. It went around the building, close and at low altitude. It moved away before the witness could take a photograph.

1976

In Hustonville near Liberty in Lincoln County in Kentucky at 1.30 am on 6th January 1976 Mary Louise Smith, Mona Stafford, 36, and Elaine Thomas were returning home on Highway 78 at night after a birthday dinner celebration when they saw an intense red glow in the eastern sky. The glow grew and hovered at treetop level near their car. All three witnesses saw a domed disc plunging towards them. It flashed three shafts of light onto the highway. The massive object then stopped short and paced the car which became filled with blue light and a suffocating heat. The lights on the craft went out. Then Smith realized that they were racing down the road. Smith could not slow down the car as they were heading towards a gateway in a stone wall. They felt as if the car was being pulled. They got home. Smith, the driver, stopped the car and got out. Stafford pulled her back. Everything was silent. Smith, with tears down her face felt the onset of terrific headaches and the others felt the same. They were missing a period of one hour and twenty minutes of time. Strange red marks were found on their necks and backs and cold water burned their skin. The following day they found that small areas of paint had bubbled away on the car as well. Under hypnosis they alleged that Stafford was taken from the car and found herself lying down in a hot dark room. White light forced her back as an eyelike device examined her. Several small creatures stood around wearing surgical masks and gowns. Thomas was in a chamber with a window. Four foot tall Humanoids with dark eyes set in grey skins stood around her. A cocoon was placed around her neck and she choked when she tried to speak. A bullet shaped object was placed above her left breast. Smith remembered being pulled backwards. She was surrounded by intense heat that burned her.

The Humanoid had large dark slanted eyes with pupils. The witnesses suffered sun-burn and skin and eye irritation after the event. Under regressive hypnotism all of the women, who were in their mid-thirties, indicated some type of medical examination had taken place. The witnesses had encountered the landed UFO on the highway. One of the witnesses had ended her menstrual period six days before but on the day following her menstrual bleeding began again as well as the usual menstrual cramps. Here is another version. At 2330hrs near Stanford Mona Stafford (35 or 26), owner of an arts and crafts shop, was returning from a restaurant with a friend of hers Elaine Thomas (48) and a friend of Elaine's, Mrs Louise Smith, to whom she had recently been introduced. They were driving down Rt 78 about 1. 6km south of Stanford, when Mona and Louise saw an intense red glow in the eastern sky, rapidly descending. Mona thought it was a plane about to crash and asked Louise to hurry to the spot, so they could help. The object then stopped at treetop height about 100m away. They now observed it was a huge disc shaped object, at least the size of two houses (c 30m diameter), surmounted by a brilliant blue white dome, the light from which was reflected on the metallic disc. Below the disc was a row of round windows, through which a red light was rotating counter clockwise; below these there was a row of yellow lights. The object rocked gently from side to side, then circled the car to behind. They had gone another 400m when the car was lit from behind by a brilliant blue light. The women appeared to have stopped for an instant, seen that the light was a beam from the disc, and quickly got back in the car. As they drove on they noticed a complete silence, including absence of wind, their skin began to tingle and they developed headaches and severe eye pains. They realised their car was doing 135kph but Louise, who was driving was unable to stop. The car was pulled to the left, then seemed as though it was being dragged backwards over humps in the road. Looking out they saw what appeared to be a strange wide road stretching far ahead of them, though there was no road like it in the area. A red light on the dashboard indicated that their car had stalled, though they still had the sensation of moving forwards. Then suddenly they were in Hustonville, 13km beyond the point where they had first seen the disc. When they arrived at the Smith home they found it was 0125, though the journey should have only taken 50 minutes. .Louse's watch hands were whizzing round and she had searing pains on her hands and face when she went to wash and her pet parakeet panicked when she reached out to touch it. All three women were experiencing great pains in their eyes and had curious weals on the backs of their necks. Louse's car developed engine trouble. These troubles led top the matter being reported to the press and thence to hypnotic regression by Dr Leo Sprinkle. These revealed vague memories of terror in being dragged into a wall of blackness, lying on a table with a huge eye over head, medical examinations by five short humanoids wearing surgical garments. There were recollections of another woman on the table and at looking though at the sky through a long tunnel. Elaine recalled the entities as being 1. 2m tall, with one large blue and one black eye. Mona later felt impelled to return to the site.

On July 18th 1976 at 2345hrs in Mitchellsburg in Boyle County, Kentucky. Charles Gilpin, his wife, 8 year old son and baby were driving home in their pickup truck when their attention was drawn to something hovering above the road. They stopped the truck and were unnerved to see that the thing was a disc shaped object about 25m in diameter. As they watched the object approached until it was hovering less than 10m above the truck. Frightened, they now tried to back away, but the truck began swaying all over the road. Finally Charles managed to turn it around and began to drive away. Though the speedometer read 135kph, judging by the slow passage of the scenery (and by a subsequent test drive over the spot), he was sure that he was going no more than 25kph, and they felt that the object was pulling them back in some way. After they had gone 400m the object overtook the truck, Charles's arms were sore from holding onto the steering wheel. They had now reached the drive of their farmhouse and the object seemed to let go of the truck, which leapt forward. Mrs Gilpin and the children ran into the farmhouse, where the object moved over the rooftop, so close that they could hear a humming sound and feel a breeze coming off it. Meanwhile Charles felt frozen into his truck and unable to join his family. When the object moved away, the family restarted their journey. Nearing gravel Switch they saw 18 people standing outdoors and watching the object as it moved across the farmlands at low level and disappeared into the distance.

1977

On January 26th 1977 at 2230hrs in Anchorage in Jefferson County, Kentucky. Neil (10) and William (8) B were in bed, while their mother Louise (40) watched TV in an adjacent bedroom and their elder brother Kelly (12) watched it downstairs. Suddenly the boys' room became brilliantly illuminate from the outside and, going to their window, they saw a large, yellow object, so bright that it was difficult to look at, in the air just beyond nearby trees. It was twice as large as a house, with reddish and greenish lateral edges and perhaps a red light on top. The thing had a flattened underside and a domed top and was either hovering or moving very slowly. Neil stood, transfixed, at the window, while William screamed for his mother to come. Louise saw that the object was just above the treeline, about 25-30m altitude, and about 100m from their house. It appeared to be a yellow glow, the size of a large airliner. It moved away slowly, hovering at treeline 300m to the south, where it suddenly disappeared. The dogs were barking throughout. Kelly noticed no effects on the TV at the time, but some were noticed later.

In Prospect in Jefferson County in Kentucky at 1.00 am on 27th January 1977 Lee Parrish, 19, was driving home from his girlfriend's house when he saw a large shape that approached from above the trees. The craft flew 100 feet to the side of the road. It was rectangular and glowed like the setting Sun and drew Lee's frightened gaze. The car radio then failed as Lee lost control over the vehicle. Lee was virtually under the craft. It then took off at tremendous speed. When Lee got home his mother commented on his bloodshot and painful eyes. The seven minute drive had taken 45 minutes. Under hypnosis everything went black. The UFO was hovering directly overhead and turned black, then white, and the witness was blind until he found himself in a white circular room twenty foot high by twenty feet across. To the witness's left was a black slab-shaped object as high as the ceiling with a rounded bulge at the top. An articulated rod-like arm reached out from its side. To the witnesses right was an object the size and shape of a Coca-Cola vending machine which had a single unarticulated arm or probe. Ahead of the witness was a white rectangular object six feet high with a square sloping protuberance on top. It glowed. Lee was sure that the objects were alive and aware of him. The arm on the black object reached out and touched the witness on the left side and back. It hurt. The red object touched the witnesses right shoulder and just above his right ear. There was a sudden pain like a needle. Then the red object merged with the white one. There was a rhythmic noise like sandpaper scraping together and the white object then merged with the black one and vanished. The witness was left alone in the empty room. Then he remembered being back in his car. Or this. Lee Parish (19) a driver and general worker at the family firm, was driving home from his girlfriend Kathy Johnson in his jeepster, west on Highway 329, when, about 6.5km before the intersection with Highway 42, he saw an object hovering above the treelike about 30-65m from the road and at an altitude of 30-45m It was about 12m long, 3m high, perfectly rectangular and emitting a brilliant light. Lee felt compelled to look at this light, though it was much too bright. he wanted to leave the area but was unable to act and no longer felt that he was in control of his car. After about 15 seconds the radio failed. When he was directly under the object, it sped away faster than a jet. When he got home his mother drew his attention to his painful bloodshot eyes. he realised that the 7 minute trip had taken 45 minutes. Under hypnotic regression he said that when he had got under the object it went black then white, then he lost his sight. When he recovered from the dazzle he was not in his jeep but in a circular all white room 6m diameter, 6m high. Inside the room were three "sentient machines"; a black one, as high as the ceiling, on his left, jug shaped with a small "head" and a handless single joined rough skinned "arm". the rest of its body being patchy rough and smooth. It touched Lee on the side and back, hurting him. To the right was a red think like a coke machine, also with a single "arm" that gave Lee the feeling that it was scared, but which "reluctantly" touched him on the right, and gave him a prick.. The third "entity" was white, Lee's height, (1.8m) stood facing him; it was solid, bulky with a square "head" sloping at 45 degrees to the body. It was featureless and glowing, its arms remained stationary, and Lee got the impression that this was "the leader". The whole craft seemed to rock back and forth. The red object then behind or merged with the white one, which made a rhythmic scraping sound, then merged with the black one, which then disappeared leaving Lee alone. He was then back in the jeep, which was suspended above the ground, as it had been when he left it. The jeeps electrical system failed the next day.

On 31st January 1977 three buildings and a car were struck in a meteorite fall in Louisville in Jefferson County in Kentucky. There was a bright fireball accompanied by sonic booms and four fragments fell where the Jewish Parking Garage is now. It was an ordinary chondrite.

On July 15th 1977 in Bellevue in Campbell County in Kentucky at 10:45 PM. Mrs. Fern Frey (name changed) was lying in bed with her 11-year-old daughter who was asleep. She was shocked to see her bed light up with a bright green glow. Thinking her home was being burglarized, Mrs. Frey jumped out of bed. (There was a lot of this "jumping out bed" this summer). The glow was coming through one of the two windows in the bedroom. She cautiously peeked through the curtain and watched in bewilderment as the green light retreated, "just like a liquid being drawn up through a straw." In a matter of seconds the light was "siphoned" up into a low hovering object that was shaped like an inverted saucer a couple of hundred feet away. She guessed it was about 30' in diameter and was metallic. The moon's glow reflected on it and she could determine that its visible surface was clearly divided into equal-sized squares. The bottom was in darkness, appearing flat, and it was into this section that the recoiling beam of light was drawn. The object then gracefully lifted and disappeared into a wooded area. The previous month there had been a large black cat seen in this area.

On December 20th 1977 (approximate date) at 0110hrs in Fort Mitchell in Kenton County, Kentucky. Rick and Judy G were watching the late show on TV when the living room was illuminated by a green glow through the curtains. Going to the window, they observed a green, glowing, egg shaped object on or just above the ground 15-30m away. It was 3-4.5m diameter, its centre encircled by a solid row of green flickering lights. After about three minutes it slowly rose vertically and then levelled off and disappeared into the wooded area beyond the house.

1978

At night on 28th January 1978 a man running his hunting dogs in a field just South of Pine Knot in McCreary County in Kentucky saw a brightly lit disc-shaped craft land on a nearby clearing. It was only one hundred yards from the witness. Apparently two eight foot tall Humanoids emerged from it. They had yellow browned complexions and gave off a very putrid smell.

At 9.30 pm on November 29th 1978 at Richmond in Madison County in Kentucky three witnesses in a car had been chased down a rural road by a flashing UFO. At one time it shot a blue flame out of the front and the car stalled and the lights went out. After the car chase the object was seen to circle a house and surrounding fields at 100 to 300 feet off the ground. It was cigar-shaped and about the size of the Goodyear Blimp. Vickie Allen and Lise Leger were driving down Log Cabin Road, when they were chased by a large object, flashing blue and white lights, which hovered over their car, causing it to stall.

1979

In Independence in Kenton County in Kentucky in July 1979. Late one night Warren O. Stone, 28, was awakened by an electrical, scratchy buzzing sound in his ears. He sat upright on his bed. The sound got louder and louder. White flashes of light, too bright to imagine were flashing in his head with his eyes closed. The sounds and light centralized within his brain, brighter and louder and then there was an explosion of light with a boom, and a feeling as if a stick of dynamite exploded within his head. He looked down to see his wife sleeping as if nothing had happened. He had a severe headache immediately, but managed to fall asleep sometime later. The next thing he knew he was in his front yard; he had just build a house in the center of four acres, several hundred feet from the road. He then saw a round craft with a highly polished metallic outer skin and what appeared to be a honeycomb area on the bottom hovering nearby. A hatch opened that formed a ramp down to the ground. An alien, described as a male human, with long blond hair and very mild mannered, that called himself either 'Alan' or 'Adam,' the witness could not remember. There was also a female with dark hair, but he didn't talk to her. He asked the witness if he would like to go for a ride, and Warren agreed. He could remember seeing his house from above and then all the houses in the area, and then the blackness of space. Before he knew it they had returned. He felt strange to know how things looked from above because at that time he had never flown. The alien explained the propulsion system to the witness and showed him two engines. They looked something like snails on their sides; they were about eight feet in diameter and three feet tall. Each outward spiral was narrower than the preceding one. In the center was a generator, which the witness believes was an "ion" generator. The flow of released energy spun outward and was compressed by the spirals where speed and pressure was increased. At the end of the spiral network the outlet manifold turned upward and rearward and connected to a propulsion plate. The plates were about 4' tall and 9' wide. These plates attracted the matter stream, collected energy, and in the center the polarity changed and created outward thrust. The witness next remembers awakening and having the propulsion system clearly outlined in his mind. He reportedly made sketches and diagrams of the alien propulsion system.

On September 26th 1979 at 2030hrs in Three Forks in Warren County, Kentucky. Houston Smith (69) was awakened by a sound similar to sound escaping from a tyre. Getting out of bed and looking out of his window, he saw a large fiery ball, emitting a red light 9-12m in the air, which disappeared after a few minutes. A number of other residents also saw the light.

1980

On February 12th 1980 at 2145hrs in Jackson in Breathitt County, Kentucky. Five employees of the Citizens Bank (Shirley Chandler, Margie Clemons, Paul Weaver, Ray E Fitts and Bertha A Charles) were driving along State Highway 205 when they observed two unusual lights, which they first thought came from an approaching vehicle. The red, green and blue lights came on and the object moved from the hillside to their right, passed over the highway and suddenly disappeared. It was an oval with steady white, red, blue and green lights, and which made no sound.

On March 9th 1980 at 2100hrs in New Castle in Henry County, Kentucky. Mrs Anna Ricketts was disturbed by barking dogs and looked out of her window to see a strange, very bright, object, hovering about 6m above her yard, 15m from the house. Because of its brightness she could only make out that the thing resembled a wingless piper cub, with three antennae projecting out towards the ground from the underside. She awoke her husband Wilson, and they went out onto the porch, but the object had moved North-West towards Sulphur Road, where it shot up and down and side to side before it disappeared from sight. As they watched they saw a much smaller object with multi-coloured lights close to the ground on Sulphur Road. They called the police but the objects had gone before they arrived.

At 11.30 pm in March 1980 in Big Bone in Boone County in Kentucky Jackie Jones, Dave, and son Jason were ready to retire for the night when they suddenly heard an unusual sound coming from the boat dock. The noise sounded like a combination of a lion and elephant roar. Jackie turned on the outside light, which connected to the boat dock when they saw the outline of something moving in the weeds. The creature was estimated to have been 2-3 feet wide, around 300 pounds, 5 feet in height and seemed to have a flat face. However, no eyes, ears, or snout could be seen, possibly due to the darkness. The witnesses said the creature tried to jerk their trailer home around, as if trying to push it over. Dave then decided to go out and investigate.

When the creature advanced toward him, he became frightened and shot at the creature with his shotgun. The creature then appeared to jump back into the river and quietly swim towards the East. (Apparently the shotgun did not have any effect on the creature, since it was seen again the next day.)

On September 20th 1980 at 0410hrs in Hartford in Ohio County, Kentucky. Lisa Birge (12) was awakened by a sound like a motor. She went to the window and saw what she thought was a shooting star and excitedly went and woke her mother Laura. Laura saw a light just above the trees in front of the house, which dimmed when it moved and brightened when it stopped. She woke her husband Thomas, who came to the window in time to see the 1.8-2.3m wide light move from the trees to directly over the front yard. It hovered and moved fast in all directions without a sound. Just before daybreak Laura and Lisa went to see if the light was attached to anything. At that the light went straight up, hovered just below the clouds and disappeared.

1982

At 10.40 pm on March 18th 1982 in Flatwoods in Greenup County in Kentucky Mr. J. Duty, an Army reservist, watched a domed disc-shaped UFO hover off to the left side of a highway. The disc had red, green, blue, and white lights around its base which blinked in rotation. It made a humming noise, circled the witness's car, then flew away. Or this. A baker, cook and army reservist driving home saw a domed disc to his left and stopped to observe it. At the base of the dome red, green, blue and white lights rotated and the thing gave off a low humming sound. He observed the thing for about 15 minutes after which it took off and departed on a circular trajectory.

At 4.00 pm on October 16th 1982 in Boyd County in Kentucky a cube-shaped object tumbled across the sky while being pursued by two military jets. Any sound was masked by the jets.

In 1982 at 2230hrs in Mount Sterling in Montgomery County, Kentucky. A man returning from a late night visit to a grocery store saw an oval light about 60cm long gliding along 30-35cm above the ground. The thing came from a house porch , down the path and on to the road in front of the witness, forcing him to brake. The thing continued onto the grass on the other side of the road.

1983

At 8.00 pm during February 1983 in Barber County in Kentucky a petroleum geologist was at an isolated area performing preliminary exploration and was sleeping in his tent when he suddenly woke up with a feeling that he was being watched. Crawling out of the tent he noticed a strange pulsating orange glow through the fog. He could also hear a low frequency hum. The witness grabbed a gun and a camera and walked towards the direction of the light. As he reached the edge of a gully he came upon a huge round object with pulsating orange lights. The humming sound increased as the witness prepared to take a picture of the object. Suddenly two short faintly glowing bluish figures appeared by the object. The witness apparently snapped a picture and suddenly fell into the ravine hitting his head and knocking himself out. When he came to the beings and the object were gone.

1985

At 3.00 am in Winter 1985 in Riverview in McCracken County in Kentucky the witness was suddenly woken by a low humming sound. A brilliant light flooded the room. The witness became angry and began screaming. Three beings now appeared and began walking in unison towards the witness. The beings were short Humanoids with the tallest one in the middle. They all had huge heads, large dark eyes, and long thin arms. Their skin was grayish green in color. The witness jumped out of bed and grabbed the tallest of the Humanoids by the neck and squeezed. The being's neck instantly snapped like a twig and his head fell backwards. The two shorter beings then proceeded to back away robot-like apparently holding the taller being. Then all three stepped backwards into the light and disappeared.

1987

In Western Kentucky in March 1987. This is a first-hand report from a retired medical doctor who alleges he accidentally found the skeletal remains of two Humanoids, possibly of alien origin, on his farm in western Kentucky in March 1987. The source was eventually able to reach the doctor through his friend, Bill Boshears, who first aired it on his radio talk show in Cincinnati. Since the show, having been warned to "shut up" in no uncertain terms, the doctor, nonetheless, entrusted the source with his name but would not reveal the location of his farm or give him, or anyone else, his unlisted phone number. He also advised that some of the details he shared about the investigation by the Air Force should be kept confidential. The doctor, when he talked with the source on his friend's phone, was cordial, but brief. He said that it was during a routine evening stroll on his farm property of 400 acres that he discovered the extraordinary evidence. Next to a burned out circle, about 4feet in diameter, in an open grassy field, he found the skeletons of two Humanoids entities about four feet apart. Without a trace of clothing, some of the bones, he said, showed residual ligament, with evidence that predators had been at work. As a doctor, he was certain that the bones were not of animal origin and on closer examination, he was shocked, he said, to find that the structure was bipedal, about 4feet tall, with a large skull and cat-like jaw, a barrel like rib cage with long arms and three fingers. For sure they were not human. The doctor's next move was to call the sheriff, who without hesitation, called the Air Force. The next morning at sunrise, said the doctor, he was surprised to see three helicopters land in a clearing and many people, some in uniform, some not, being deployed over a wide area. Greeting him was a Colonel (name known to the source) who cordially introduced himself and stated his mission; remove the bones and tinder-soil, test and remove the burned circular soil and comb the area for any other evidence. Later in the day, fresh soil was filled in the excavated areas, and the doctor was told that the soil in the circle had been baked at 3,000 degrees. When asked about the time factor of body decomposition (allowing for predators) he estimated, according to cursory examination, that the aliens had been exposed for less than a hundred days. Reminding the source that "they put the fear of God in me" after his trip to a military base for further interrogation and where he was shown photos of other alien corpses, he expressed interest in the source's research and source suggested that they have lunch together soon. He agreed, but never called.

On August 22nd 1987 in Hawesville in Hancock County in Kentucky at11:00 PM. A lady observed an object for about 3-5 minutes. The locale was described as rural with fields and hills. The sky was clear. The object was observed in the NW near the ground, estimated at 15-20'. The object was stationary, but was closest to her as she drove by it. With the help of her husband they estimated the distance as 50 yards. There as a possible abduction attempt (stalking). "I was traveling West on U.S. 60 about 11:00 PM. I had left my parent's home in Hawesville and was headed (West) to Lewisport, alone. I first noticed some bright red and blue lights to my right (North). I thought it was an airplane or lights from an industrial plant. As I approached the object I noticed brilliant gold, blue and red lights on what seemed to be on the sides of the object. It gave off a white glow beneath the object, which lit up the ground below and surrounding trees. The object hovered over the same location. As I approached this, I became very shaky. My knees were so weak (that) I could not apply pressure to the gas pedal. I watched the object for a few minutes. I finally got my legs to move and left as fast as I could. I had a terrible feeling of being alone and lost."

1989

At 11.30 pm on June 13th 1989 in Frankfort in Franklin County in Kentucky Miss Somerby, a 36-year old woman, saw a massive rectangular-shaped flying object while driving in her car late at night. The UFO had a pipe structure clearly visible on the bottom. The witness experienced an episode of missing time. No other information.

1993

On March 4th 1993 East of Lynnview in Jefferson County in Kentucky. At 11:45 AM. a large ball-of-light buzzed a police helicopter and released three smaller fireballs.

Between 10.00 pm and 11.00 pm on September 7th 1993 in Bardstown in Nelson County in Kentucky Rick was night fishing in Deatsville. On the horizon miles away three separate white lights ascended. One went to the left and two to the right. They were hovering over the far off ridge line. Suddenly the one on the left shot over to the two others at a none man-made speed! It stopped on a dime! I'd say it covered a mile or two in a fraction of a second! They stayed grouped up and then, this is what gets me…they didn't just fly away or off. It was in a direction I've never seen anything go! Away and up at a 75degree angle and again at a speed that was not human-like! I saw another white light in Boston also in Nelson County in Kentucky a few years later. Hovering above the tree line up in the woods. Just one this time. I was like…I've seen this before. My brother and I have also seen the same red football sized orbs in the woods. I told him "I'm seeing red orbs everywhere". He said "like that one?" He was seeing them and not saying anything too!

At Fort Knox in Bullitt, Hardin and Meade Counties Kentucky one night during 1993. The witness was lying in bed when he realized the bathroom light that was usually on was off. He tried to get up, but could not move. He also tried to scream but nothing came out. He then found himself in a different place, surrounded by several short pale figures with huge dark eyes. They seemed to be examining him. Then one pressed his finger against the witness forehead right between the eyebrows; suddenly he was back on his bed. He found a small scar where he was touched.

1995

Near Lexington in Fayette County in Kentucky during Summer 1995. One afternoon in a farm area, a man looked outside to see his young kids playing on a field and standing near them, two short man-like figures that appeared to be wearing white smocks. Startled he yelled at his children who apparently had not seen the intruders. The two little men then ran up a hill and behind some farm buildings and were lost from sight. A search failed to find anything.

1998

On Lynch Mountain, also called Black Mountain, in Harlan County in Kentucky at 6.20 am on June 9th 1998. Several witnesses in a vehicle watched a tall glowing figure, without a neck and a large head, large on top and small at the bottom. It glided through a guardrail towards the vehicle. As it passed by, the vehicle shook very hard.

Louisiana

1800
A is for airships and in this period there were only hot-air balloons and these hot-air balloons were very rare unlike aircraft today. The locals reckoned that an aerial object, a strange type of airship, that was sighted hovering above Baton Rouge in East Baton Rouge County in Louisiana on 5th April 1800 was no star or meteor. The luminous object just hung there motionless in the near sky and this is something that stars and meteors cannot do. No one in this period flew balloons at night either so one of these has to be ruled out as well. All we have is a hovering light. The locals also described it as having a degree of brightness little short of the effect of sun-beams. A considerable degree of heat was coming from it and a few seconds after a tremendous crash similar to that of the largest piece of ordinance caused what was described as a very sensible earthquake. Where the light fell there was scorched vegetation and the surface of the earth was broken up. But it had hovered beforehand. Meteors and asteroids do not hover.

Everything in the Universe moves including the Universe itself. Nothing traveling can stay in the same place at the same time unless it is doing so under its own power. This light hovered for a considerable period. Only Hummingbirds and various insects can hover. This was not a gigantic luminous Hummingbird or a huge insect. Incidentally balloons never flew at night as this was regarded as too dangerous to do so safely. Was this a UFO or a meteor? After all meteors cannot hover and do not stay around long enough to have the effects of heat to be recorded as coming from them for a considerable period.

1860
Sometime during 1860 at Shreveport in Caddo County in Louisiana the witness's attention was drawn to a strange light in the heavens. It appeared to the naked eye to be three hundred yards in length extending from North to West appearing just above the tallest trees. The color was that of a red hot stove and from the center beautiful rays representing the sun drawing water would ascend to a considerable height. It was watched for one hour with no change perceived in it.

1897
On April 19th 1897 at 1200hrs in Lake Charles in Calcasieu Parish, Louisiana. A man out driving in his buggy saw an aerial object that approached rapidly. When it got within 800m it emiited a powerful whistle that terrified the horses, which bolted, throwing the witness to the ground. When he got to his feet he saw an aerial object coming to ground 30m away. Two men descended on a rope ladder and came to the witness's aid and invited him on board, where he was taken to a 4m by 2.5m cabin in which there were reclining chairs. They told him about their propulsion system and gave their names as Warren and Wilson.

1946
On September 6th 1946 in New Orleans, Louisiana. A red ball of light was seen moving very low and very slow over New Orleans.

1947
Seven miles North of Shreveport in Caddo County in Louisiana on the morning of 7th July 1947 military aircraft pilot Harston saw a bright silver object about the angular size of the moon. We had had another UFO above Shreveport previously in 1860.

1948
On September 18th 1948 in SE Shreveport in Caddo Parish in Louisiana at 5:00 p.m. A draftsman at home using high-powered binoculars to watch an L-6 aircraft at 10,000 feet altitude at 60° elevation to the SE traveling 100 mph, for Air Force Day, saw a bright white aluminum half-spherical object traveling the opposite direction in level flight at about 20,000 feet altitude 21/2 miles away ground distance at 100-150 mph heading South. There was no trail and he lost it when he tried to view it without binoculars. The object appeared to be 1/3 size of the L-6 (35.5 feet) but 2x the distance, or about 24 feet

1949
On May 20th 1949 at Pontchartrain Beach in New Orleans, Louisiana at 4:25 p.m. Tulane University Associate Professor of Political Science (USAFR Lt Col) John E. Kieffer of 12th AF, Kelly AFB, San Antonio, Texas, was lying on his back at the beach when he sighted a bright, shiny silver flat spherical object in the ENE headed WSW [towards him] joined by 5 smaller similar objects grouped around the larger object which made a large circle over New Orleans Airport, then the main object made a rotation around its horizontal axis and disappeared. It was at 45 degrees to 50 degrees elevation initially. There was no sound and no visible means of propulsion.

On December 4th 1949 between Covington in St.Tammany Parish and Hammond in Tangipahoa Parish in Louisiana at 4:35-4:38 p.m. A USAF pilot of a C-47 transport Flight AF 5566, Maj. F. E. Whitaker, Base Legal Officer of Walker AFB, Roswell, New Mexico, copilot 1st Lt. P. H. McDavid and crew chief engineer Staff Sgt.. C. Thomas also from Walker AFB, while flying from Carswell AFB, Dallas, to Keesler AFB, Miss., at 180 mph at 5,500 feet heading 90° (E), saw a bright silver sphere about the size of a jet fighter [50 feet?]

come towards their aircraft heading about 300° or about W nearly head on at 1 o'clock position [from about 120° ENE] at about the same altitude, 5,500 feet, at high speed in excess of 600 mph or faster than a jet then after about 30 seconds the object turned abruptly to the south, then stopped and bobbed up and down. The object made several accelerations and decelerations and sharp direction and altitude changes during the sighting. It was very maneuverable in all directions with Whitaker describing it as appearing to "bounce all over the sky." The object disappeared by a sudden burst of speed crossing the field of vision in about one second. There was no vapor trail, exhaust, distinguishing features, or sound noticeable above the C-47's noise. It was the apparent size of a half-dollar on a windshield.

1951

On January 1st 1951 at 0700hrs in Oak Grove in West Carroll Parish, Louisiana. About a dozen members of the Sewell family observed an object shaped like two saucers placed rim to rim. It travelled west to east above a line of trees 400m away. Between the two halves of the object, which was 10-15m diameter, was a row of windows. The object was of metallic appearance resembling brass. It moved silently at high speed. After maneuvering for 15 to 20 minutes the object rose vertically, disappearing from sight in a couple of seconds

1953

During summer 1953 near Camp Polk in Vernon Parish in Louisiana. Army personnel reported seeing an ovoid or eggshaped object about nine to ten meters in diameter with a kind of collared structure on top crash land into soft, sandy soil. The craft also had a revolving horizontal fin-like protrusion on the equator that was still rotating. Some of the army personnel were ordered to guard the craft until ambulances arrived. A door that opened formed a ramp. The ground around the crashed craft burnt into a powdery substance and became extremely hot. Three aliens were reported to have walked away from the site with one of them carrying a stretcher. The beings were described as four foot tall with large helmeted heads. They legs were stiff when they walked and they were wearing tightfitting dull metallic greenish suits. They also wore mittens and seemed to speak in an unknown language. As I have said before, I report them, you work out what you are doing with them.

1957

In Spring 1957 at 2355hrs in Krotz Springs in St. Landry Parish, Louisiana. Mr Heitman and his passenger Beard were driving between Krotz Springs and Lebeau, the straight stretch of road tempting him into speeding at up to 130kph. Heitman then saw a red light behind them on the empty road, and fearing that it was a police officer out to get him for speeding, slowed to 80kph. The red light quickly closed to within 15m of their car, only 3m above the road. They could now see that this was not a police car light, but a disc, 1.2-1.5m diameter, 45-60cm thick, giving off a red glow. Heitman accelerated up to 160kph to shake the thing off, but it kept pace. When they got within 400m of Lebeau, the thing rose to 30m. As they passed through the town, the disc increased its speed, turned to the left, rose up to 100m and then sped off in the direction of Lafayette.

In New Orleans in Louisiana on 1st June 1957. A UFO that looked like a blue streak fell into the Mississippi River. I said that they love water.

On June 3rd 1957 in Shreveport in Caddo County in Louisiana between 8:30 [9:35?] -9:30? p.m. Shortly after takeoff from Shreveport Airport, heading for Lake Charles, Louisiana , and climbing, Capt. Lynn Kern and FO Abbey Zimmerman flying Trans-Texas Airlines Flight 103 were told by the control tower that a small light was visible nearby. They saw the star-like blue-green pulsating [?] object hovering (approaching?) at their 10 [2?] o'clock position at about 400 feet then climbing rapidly to 1,000 feet paralleling the airliner then at 110 knots speed (130 mph later 165 mph) but at higher altitude and 1/2 mile away. Kern flashed the landing lights and the object responded with a beam [?] of light. Then a second blue-green pulsating object joined the first on the opposite side of the airliner (then at 9,000 feet) and the air crew confirmed from the tower that it had both objects on radar and visually through binoculars. The objects headed S at 170° climbing to about 10,000 feet and followed the airliner to Converse, Louisiana , (about 45 miles S of Shreveport) where the pilot queried ADC radar site, England AFS, in Alexandria, Louisiana, which confirmed the 2 targets in the airliner's vicinity at 9,700 feet. The objects disappeared from sight in a cloud deck to the SW.

On October 7th 1957 at night in New Orleans, Louisiana a man called the New Orleans police to report that a flying saucer landed in his driveway, and its crew of little green men came into his house and stole his wallet, his shoes, and his dog. The police did not investigate. We have had stranger reports.

On November 7th 1957 at Lake Charles in Calcasieu Parish in Louisiana. While driving alone, a woman's car engine began to sputter and then stop completely. She glanced up and saw a silvery disc about 200 feet overhead. It was approximately 15 feet in diameter. After a few seconds, the disc moved North at high speed. Her car could then be restarted.

In November 1957 at 2300hrs in Provencal in Natchitoches County, Louisiana. Welder, Haskell Raper Jnr, was in the last couple of kilometres of his drive to Provencal from his work in Shroveport, and despite the rain and wet road, he was driving at 130kph, when, over the crest of a hill, he saw an object from which a light beamed, about 300m ahead on the road. Fearing that he was about to collide with a truck, he braked. He was still speeding though, when the beam swung round on to him; as it did so a strong pressure decelerated the car rapidly, halting it 4.5m from the object, which despite the dazzling light, Raper could see was oval, 4.5m long, 2.7m high, with a fringe of drab, "army green" colour. On the machine he could see the letters UN following some numbers. Suddenly a sort of heat wave struck his car, and he dived out in panic as the engine caught fire. The machine then rose, with a sound like a large diesel engine, soon vanishing into low cloud. As Raper ran from the scene, his petrol tank exploded, Raper ran home, reported the incident. On investigation his 1956 Ford was found to be completely destroyed.

On 11th December 1957 Mary Louise Tobin, a school teacher, was driving on State Highway One when she saw an object that she compared to the rising sun in the vicinity of a smoking car. The driver, an elderly lady, came out with a child who seemed to have suffered burns. The unknown light went away and the disabled car did not catch on fire. This was near Chestnut in Natchitoches Parish. Two belligerent UFOs within a month of each other in the same area?

1960

At Lacamp in Vernon Parish in Louisiana on Monday 18th April 1960 Mr. Monroe Arnold, a physical scientist, saw a round fiery UFO come charging in from the South at high speed. It touched the ground 300 meters from the witness with flames and a loud explosion and continued bouncing in a westward direction for 300 meters before finally rising up into the sky again and turning West and vanishing. The ground was scarred in nine places where the object had impacted with the Earth. There were also traces of an unknown type of metallic paint. Wasn't there a learners permit displayed on the craft? It is reassuring to know that higher civilisations, if we allow for them, drive as badly as we do. They might be Human-like after all. Previously there had been a fall of fish at Marksville in 1947 and a cloudless point rainfall at Alexandria in 1958. Here is another version. At 7.00 pm a farmer, Mr Arnold saw a fiery red object about 3.5 by 2.5m descend from the south at high speed, emitting a loud rumbling noise. The object ploughed through the trees, striking the ground 300m away, then bounced like a stone on water, hitting the ground in nine places making loud explosions which were heard by other residents, who also saw flames. The object then ascended to the west. The whole incident lasted just 3 seconds. Furrows and scorched grass were found at the site where the tree had been decapitated. A substance like metallic paint was found. Arnold was thought very reliable.

1961

In New Orleans in Louisiana in 1961. Around 8.00 p.m. the main witness and her fiancé Joe were in the parking lot of a local restaurant and were in an area that faced a cemetery separated by a chain link fence. This was in the very back of the parking lot and was favored by young people who wanted to "neck." They were talking when the main witness noticed something moving in the cemetery between the tombs. It seemed especially odd since the people moving seemed to be small, maybe 3½ to 4 feet in height. This cemetery was bound by a railroad track, an interstate, Main Street, two restaurants and vacant land. There was no residential property bordering or close to the cemetery. The activity was brisk. She could see shadows between the graves moving back and forth that were busy at some sort of task. She also noticed that they seemed to go toward the right. She then saw small lights with some of the movement. Her fiancé noted the activity and asked her if she was seeing what he was seeing. He described the same details. Both witnesses entertained the thoughts that the figures were "children" playing for some uncanny reason in a cemetery. As they sat in disbelief, just watching all the activity, they also noted that they were the only ones parked who weren't necking and probably the only ones noticing the activity. They watched for at least ten more minutes fascinated. Then all the movement seemed to move to the right and was no longer back-lighted so they could no longer see them. The witnesses shrugged and continued their conversation. Within several minutes they then saw on the right, lights coming on in a large circle. These were not any kind of lights that the witnesses had ever seen. Although they were illuminated they did not give off light as is usual. Rather they were pure, the opposite of pitch black. Both stared fixedly as a large object lifted from the ground. Their windows were open and they could not hear any sound. They were about 60-80 feet from the object. It lifted straight up slowly and then it stopped where they could clearly see that it was round and had a rounded top and a flat bottom. Then the white lights went off and a triangle of lights appeared underneath the craft, one red, one green and one white. Then it took off toward the West at an amazing rate of speed. The day after the sighting the witnesses gathered several of their closest friends and visited the site where the craft had been. There they found a perfect circular area of flattened grass that was not burned or otherwise damaged.

1966

In Haynesville in Claiborne County in Louisiana on Friday 30th December 1966 at 8.15 pm an American nuclear physicist was driving South with his family. It was overcast and raining when he saw a stationary light in a forest near ground level. It was a pulsating dome of light. It alternated between dim red and bright orange. At one point the luminosity became greater than a car's headlights which woke two children in the back seat. The Professor was so impressed with the amount of light that he returned next day with a scintillometer. The light had been one mile from the car. The next day there was no bird, animal or insect life in the area at all. Large numbers of cattle had disappeared that night as well. Had the Intergalactic Butcher Shop arrived again? Life had left? Or this? North of Haynesville, a nuclear physicist and his family were driving north on Hwy 79, through heavy overcast and drizzle. In the vicinity of a wooded area the wife called her husband's attention to a red-orange glow through and above the trees to the left. The light, appearing as a luminous hemisphere, seemed to emanate from a source at ground level in the woods. This light pulsated from red to orange and, at the closest point, became a brilliant white, swamping out the car headlights. After about 4 seconds the light subsided to the pulsing red-orange. Having stopped to get his bearings, the physicist continued on his way. Investigations suggested that the light source, about 1-1.5km away at nearest approach was giving off about 500 megawatts, that game in the area had declined sharply since 1966, that farmers had detected similar lights and reported losses of cattle, and that several slightly radioactive burnt out oil slicks were found. These were associated with oil wells in the areas.

1969

On August 23rd 1967 in Hamilton County, Louisiana there was a landing report.

Near Bogalusa in Washington County in Louisiana on September 26th 1969. During the night the main witness was on his way to visit his aunt and uncle, along with a friend who was sleeping in the passenger seat. Both men were enlisted in the Navy at the time. He was driving on a split 4 lane highway and it was a very dark and calm night and he had his window down. Listening to his radio, which was turned down, he noticed that they were running into some low overhanging fog which was about 20 or 30 feet above the highway and seemed to travel with the car and pulsate like a wave action above the car. That's when he saw about five bright lights shining at the car from behind. He first thought it was some kind of truck or bus until it passed him off to the left and crossed the low median and positioned itself on the driver's side traveling the same speed the witness was. It was a long cigar-shaped craft with clear windows on its side just above the center of the craft. He could see beings onboard due to the background light inside it. They were not human (not described). He had to keep watching the road ahead while driving but watched the object as much as he could. The craft was about 60 feet long and he could only see about 15 feet of it protruding below the pulsating fog. His was the only car on the road at the time. There was no sound and his friend never woke up during the incident. The witness does not recall any details. His next memory was of arriving at his uncle's house and having breakfast.

1973

On October 6th 1973 (Approximate Date) in Winnfield in Winn County, Louisiana. Three people watched a brilliantly lit object pass at very low altitude over an area near Beech Creek Bridge, between Winnfield and Sikes.

In Avery Estates in Saint Tammany Parish in New Orleans in Louisiana on 10th October 1973 several witnesses saw a UFO hovering over a housing estate. Radio, television and citizen band radio were effected. Jimmy Fisher saw a big silvery hamburger-shaped UFO hovering 400 to 500 feet above his house. Fifteen or more witnesses were watching the craft including a Police unit including Lieutenant Robert Lonardo and Captain Huey Farrell. Lonardo had a tape-recorder and switched it on when the UFO made a noise like a generator hum that was rising in pitch and intense energy. The noise was a cross between tires at high speed and the noise inside a tornado. There were several sightings over the next few days.

Near Pine in Washington Parish in Saint Landry County in Louisiana on 15th October 1973 Sheriffs Deputies chased five red orange objects through a twelve mile stretch of woods. When one of the Deputies turned on his patrol lights the object appeared to descend and approach the Police cruiser. The UFO swooped and scared the Officer who put out his lights after which the UFO then took off. When he switched the lights off again, the objects disappeared as into a cloud. The things descended below the treetops several times. There were other witnesses.

On October 16th 1973 in Baton Rouge in East Baton Rouge County, Louisiana there was a landing report.

Also on October 16th 1973 in Hancock County, Louisiana an object landed and an occupant was seen.

On October 17th 1973 near Crowley in Acadia Parish in Louisiana An offshore oil platform crew saw an oblong object with several colored lights hovering about 1,000 feet overhead emitting a whining sound. As the object descended to within 100 feet, the platform's electric power system failed.

Also on October 17th 1973 at Powhatan in Natchitoches Parish in Louisiana There were at least 10 reports from central Louisiana. A pulsating luminous object changing colors was seen near the woods, illuminating the terrain. A luminous object was seen hovering and gliding along above ground in a field an on another occasion a luminous object with window-like markings was seen hovering overhead.

At Spring Hill in Webster County in Louisiana on 18th October 1973 Angel Hair fell from a clear sky. Glistening fibers were festooning trees and power lines during a UFO flap. Spring Hill is 65 kilometers northeast of Shreveport and 92 kilometers northwest of Ruston.

At Shreveport in Caddo County in Louisiana that same day 18th October 1973 Angel hair fell from a clear sky. Glistening fibers were festooning trees and power lines during a UFO flap.

At Ruston in Lincoln County in Louisiana still that same day 18th October 1973 Angel hair fell from a clear sky. Glistening fibres were festooning trees and power lines during a UFO flap. Shreveport is 104 kilometers from Ruston. They were both manifesting the same phenomenon.

On November 4th 1973 at 2330hrs in Pine Grove in St. Helena Parish, Louisiana. Brian Hoffman and his wife along with two friends who did not want their names given out, were hunting deer, parked by a dirt lane north of Pine Grove. They had not been parked long when an intensely bright light suddenly appeared and hovered about "three tractor trail lengths" from their car. The other man turned his spotlight on the thing, which seemed to reflect the light back at them like a mirror. They horridly left the area.

Between Winnfield in Winn Parish and Sikes also in Winn Parish in Louisiana a woman driving home on a foggy night encountered a three foot tall Humanoid at the Beech Creek Bridge. The Humanoid had a large oval head with deep red eyes that seemed to attract her. The body was silvery with arms that seemed to split below the elbows. This was on the night of 7th November 1973.

On November 14th 1973 (Approximate Date) still in Winnfield, Louisiana there was a landing report.

1974

At 5.30 pm on 21st November 1974 fourteen year old Lance Edwards was walking at dusk when he saw two brightly luminous objects flying low over some nearby houses. He pursued them running down a nearby farm road and came upon one of them resting on the ground at the edge of the woods. Its brightness dazzled him so that he had to cover his eyes. Then feeling like someone was watching him he turned and saw a strange figure just behind him. He started to run but ran right into the figure and was knocked to the ground. He picked himself up and took off frightened. The figure was small, reaching only to Lance's chest but it was stockily built. It had no neck and had a pushed in nose similar to a Pekinese dog. The color was bluish like a bruise. The youngster reported the encounter to his father who took him to the Sheriff's office in Plattenville in Assumption Parish in Louisiana.

1975

On the night of 11th November 1975 a woman was sitting outside when she saw a large disc over the house in New Orleans in Louisiana. Suddenly she found herself apparently inside the object where she was confronted by several tall human-like beings with long blond hair that communicated with her by telepathy. She saw shown around the craft and then returned to her home. Later that night her and her husband watched two disc flying over the house. A large flattened circle of grass was found near the house the next day which turned brown and remained the same color for a few years.

1976

In Bossier City in Bossier Parish in Louisiana on January 26th 1976. A woman reported what she thought was a "bizarre dream" of seeing a saucer-shaped object landing in the nearby schoolyard. Two Humanoid figures came out of the ship and approached the house carrying a metallic rounded case. The woman in a panic, attempted to awaken her husband who was asleep on the couch, but he would not wake up. The beings came to the door and asked her to come with them in exchange for money. (!) They said she would only be gone for a few minutes but it would seem to her to be years. Later she drew a picture of an insignia the Humanoids had on their belts (not reproduced in the brief report). She additional described the Humanoids as having dark gray skin and wearing similarly colored jumpsuits. Her daughter found a burned circle of grass in the schoolyard across the street where she said the craft had landed. Allegedly grass would not grow there for a couple of years. As of 2014, the witness is still alive and now lives in a nursing home.

1977

On January 21st 1977 in St. Bernard Parish in Louisiana. Two adult males were doing some [mildly] illegal poaching along the Dike Canal, one guy in a boat and the other moving parallel on the shore. They were not in close approximation when the man in the boat saw a bright red light in the sky. Suddenly the light seemed right around him as the boat was engulfed in the glow which extended to the surrounding landscape. It was too bright to see through to make out any shape behind it, and the only thought that the poacher had was that this was the game warden and he'd been busted. But there was no noise, so no helicopter, and the light flew away into the woods. His partner was already back at their camp, and saw none of this. When the boatman paddled back to camp, his story was met with derision. The two both got into the boat and began to go down the canal, this time using the outboard motor as power. The light reappeared and moved in on them. The boatman's hair was felt "standing on end" with fright. Worse, although the motor was running, the boat was not moving--seemingly held in place by whatever this was. Then the light quickly left and "the boat lurched forward with great force, as if what was holding it back released the motor's power once again. Both men were thrown but neither fell out". The light again flew at low level into the trees and continued on for some distance until they lost it. They estimated that the light was about 15-25 feet in diameter, mainly circular [though hard to see], of a "diamond texture" [by which they apparently mean that it appeared faceted with diamond shapes], and strikingly fast only when it moved toward them. Both men reported "nausea, stomach aches, and fever, for a period of two days following". They intuitively connected this with the incident but the researcher did remark that it was flu season. Neither witness was interested in UFOs and neither used the terms UFOs or flying saucers during the interviews. Normal checking revealed no balloons nor aircraft in the area at the time. Another version. At 2045hrs a coypu hunter was boating along a canal when his boat was enveloped in a brilliant light and all the ambient noises ceased, returning when an object shot way. The hunter picked a friend and continued his hunting, only for the strange light to reappear above them. The silence again descended, the hunter's hair stood on end, there was a feeling of warmth and though the boat engine kept running the vessel just stood still. The light came from a 6m diameter circular object, the surface of which was covered with a diamond pattern, hovering 20m above them. The object then moved off, at which the boat leapt forward, knocking the men down. The thing then hovered over a oil refinery and then over another spot, projecting its beam downwards. The whole affair lasted 30 minutes and the hunter felt he had lost 20 minutes.

On January 22nd 1977 at 1930hrs in Chalmette also in St. Bernard Parish, Louisiana. Mrs D. S., her daughter Connie (11), her son Terry (13) and her 36 year old brother, along with a family friend Mrs A B and her 4 year old son were driving out of the Schwegman shopping centre. They were turning into Jean Lafitte Parkway, passing a white trailer, when Terry drew their attention to a large, lighted object, hovering above and behind the auditorium. Mrs B stopped, and for 5 minutes they watched as the thing made a sort of circular motion around a static position. It was of metallic appearance, larger than a car, perhaps as large as a house, dome shaped, with extensions on either end. The dome was flanked by two bright red lights, with another, yellow-white in colour, in the lower middle. On the underside were three propellers. The whole thing appeared to be spinning. The party were within 600m of the thing, which they were sure was not a plane, helicopter or blimp. When the car behind them blew its horn, they moved on, and the object began to move slowly northwards. When it stopped again, 400m further on, they turned onto the central reservation and kept it under observation for another 10 minutes. After "bouncing around" for some time, the object appeared to lower behind the trees, across a field and rise up again. It then tilted at a severe angle and went behind the trees. The party could see the lights shining through the trees, but first the red lights and then the white one went out. No traces were found by the investigators.

On June 17th 1977 at night at Cotile Lake in Rapides Parish, Louisiana. Dale Schexnaider had spent a day fishing and swimming with a couple and their two young daughters and as he and the girls were carrying stuff back to his truck from the camp, he became aware of a low frequency vibration. Above the trees he saw a beautiful pin point of light coming from a disc shaped object 25m across, 15m high, with a bubble like top and with two steady lights and other lights which revolved and flashed. The object began to glow and illuminated the trio with a sort of floodlight. It then directed three-five intense electric blue, thin rays at them, which centred on their bodies. Dale heard crackling sounds, noticed that their bodies were glowing an eerie blue and felt trapped in a force field that mad movement slow and heavy, as if in a dream. After about 10 seconds the light and field suddenly vanished and the thing glided away with only its steady lights on, the humming fading as it did so.

1979

Near Baton Rouge in East Baton Rouge Parish in Louisiana. During October 1979 at night the main witness and a friend were driving in his 1970 Buick Electra 225, when the entire car was transported onboard a UFO. While going at about 70 miles per hour they noticed a blue light to the right of them above the trees moving with them. Suddenly the light moved over them and his car lost all electronics. As they slowed to a stop, the car began to rise up into the air and finally was inside the UFO and the bottom of it closed under them. Once inside and both terrified, some doors opened and figures began to move toward them. While being still extremely frightened, at the same time the main witness was also interested and curious about these beings and their flying craft. One figure in a gray jumpsuit approached his side of the car and two figures clad in blue suits approached his friend's side of the car. He began receiving an audible message from the one that approached him and they weren't going to harm them. He was saying "Do not be afraid, we will not harm you." At this point he began to calm down. His friend was extremely excited and was shouting and cursing at the same time and he screamed at him to shut up. He opened his door and got out and started to ask questions as to what was going on, and why do you want us, and how does your ship fly, and if he could see the rest of it, etc.. The figure that approached him, led him away from the car and toward a door. He looked back at his friend and the two figures were laying him in a propped position on the seat and he was apparently asleep. The main witness was then given a tour of the ship and talked at length with the aliens. Apparently he was onboard the ship for about four hours. At one point he remembers getting hold of a book that had different colored pages in it and asking the aliens if he could keep it. They told him he could but later took it back before releasing them. When released he was given a warning to share and give to the people of the nation. For years he had been afraid to tell its content, because of repercussions, especially since he had served 31 years in the USAF. Now he is retired and feels he could now share what he was told. The beings onboard the UFO told him that they had been watching our planet for many years. They stated, that in that time they realized that we are a war-like world and have pursued bigger and more destructive weapons of war. They further stated that they had contacted all the governments of the world and tried to warn them and persuade them of an alternate direction, but to no avail.

At that time, they also realized that ultimately the governments of the world (not all) were controlled by the people. As such, for this reason, since the governments were not listening, they were picking up people from all walks of life to give this message to in hopes that a terrible tragedy could be prevented. At this point they asked him if he knew what a quasar was. He let them know that he did and they seemed somewhat surprised when he told them it was a sort of intergalactic storm of planets being destroyed. They said that if our nations continue this war like attitude and use these ultimate weapons that we have developed, that we could destroy this planet. In doing this it would trigger a quasar which in turn would destroy their planet. They said, also that before they would let this happen, they would destroy mankind. Happy news?

1982

On December 30th 1982 at dusk in Coushatta in Red River Parish, Louisiana. A number of people saw a double circle of lights, one inside the other hovering at treetop height, emitting a sound like a fan or a helicopter. The thing just disappeared. Broken trees and an acid smell were detected at the site.

1986

On May 11th 1986 in DeRidder in Beauregard Parish in Louisiana at 9:45 PM. A three-foot diameter disc with lights buzzed a car with three witnesses traveling on Highway 26. It was at only six feet altitude. There were no electromagnetic effects noticed. The object next shot straight up into the sky and disappeared.

Mississippi

1922

On 2nd February 1922 a man missed out on being hit by a meteorite by the distance of only three meters! This was in Baldwyn in Prentiss County in Mississippi. Baldwyn and Baxter in Missouri are three hundred and six miles apart approximately. This distance for a meteorite is the same spot and only six years apart. Baxter had a meteorite fall in 1916.

1929

A man walking from Coldwater to Greenleaf saw a ball of light come down from a fence and land in the road. The plate size thing moved slowly at ground level. The man got down on all fours and touched the thing as it went past, but he felt nothing. This was near Coldwater in Tate County.

1935

In July 1935 (approx. date and year) at 2030hrs in Polkville in Smith County, Mississippi. Mrs Pennington, her three sons and daughter were walking back from her sister's about 2.5km from their home, when their attention was caught by a light ahead. As they approached they saw it was a shaft of light, about 10m wide, covering the entire width of the road. They were unable to see where it came from. Unable to get round it, they hurried through it with no ill consequence. After they had gone about 400m further on the light just went out.

1942

On August 29th 1942 in Columbus in Lowndes County, Mississippi. The control tower operator at Columbus Army Air Base saw two round reddish objects hover over the field.

1947

One evening in June 1947 in Greenville in Washington County in Misissipy . Andrew and his mother had gone outside to get some wood for the fireplace and as they walked off the porch into the front yard they observed a huge red ball of fire coming out of the sky. His mother exclaimed "Oh my God! The world is going to end." All of a sudden the fire went out and they saw a huge ship with various lights, red, yellow and possibly green. His mother yelled for his grandfather who came out onto the porch but was unable to speak and just stared. The craft lit up the area as if it was daylight. At the time they did not have electricity and used oil lamps for light. The witnesses saw people standing in the windows of the craft that were located beneath the dome. The ship landed and that is the last thing that the witnesses remembered.

1949

On January 1st 1949 in Jackson in Hinds County in Mississippi. At 5 p.m. Pilot Rush flying a private plane saw a cigar-shaped object cross the sky in front of the plane.

1954

At Greenville Air Force Base in Washington County in Mississippi on the evening of June 20th 1954. The main witness was an electronics specialist and a civilian employee at the Air Force base when one day some military authorities escorted him and several other civilian employees into a large aircraft hangar and ordered them to stay there until they were told they could come out. None of the questions about what was going on were answered. The military men closed the hangar doors and left. The men in the hangar hung around the area where the hangar came together and they discovered they could peek outside and see what was going on. A disk-shaped aircraft about 40 feet in diameter descended vertically and landed on the tarmac outside the hangar. Several men with cameras filmed the entire incident from elevated scaffolding. Other cameramen stood on the ground. A door opened on the aircraft and a child-sized alien being walked down a short ramp. The alien used a hand-held 'computer' to communicate with the military personnel. The aircraft was on tripod landing gear with wheels, and several men were ordered to push it into the hangar across the way. Once the alien aircraft was inside the hangar, the men closed its doors. Several minutes later they pushed the alien craft back outside and it soon lifted vertically and silently and quickly darted away. As soon as the alien craft was gone the civilian men were allowed to leave their hangar. These are all from reputable sources. Do you believe them or not?

1956

On 1st June 1956 in Belton in Lee County in Mississippi the witness was going out to empty the trash when he saw a six foot five inch tall well-proportioned bright blue glowing human shaped figure that was apparently looking at his neighbor's back porch light bulb. At this point the witness could hear a voice in his head telling him to be calm and not to be afraid. The witness's mother came outside at this time, distracting the witness briefly, as he pointed towards the figure and it vanished.

1957

At House, 15 miles northwest of Meridian on Mississippi State Highway 19 on Wednesday 6th November 1957 at 7.25 pm. Mr. Malvan Stephens, 48, was on his way to Memphis in Tennessee when he saw a large egg-shaped UFO drop out of the sky and land directly in front of his truck on the highway. At first he thought that it was a weather balloon though there seemed to be propellers on either end of the machine as well as on top. Malvan left the truck and was confronted by two men and a woman who were 4.5 feet tall, had pasty white faces and wore grey coveralls. They seemed friendly and they tried to communicate in a rapid fire language with Malvan. One even tried to shake his hand. They then got back into their craft after having finished their one-sided conversation and it took off into the sky. The contact lasted two minutes and the witness was visibly shaken and white as a sheet. Did Malvan see anything other than a large energy source? Did the truck stop on its own or as a result of proximity to the energy source? Knowing as we do that these energy sources can influence electric fields then could it also be possible that the very fine electromagnetic tuning and configurations in the human brain and sensory organs can be effected as well? We have seen paralysis in association with many of the phenomena which cannot be directly attributed to the energy sources physical appearance. By this I mean that Klieg Conjunctivitis and sunburn can be directly attributed to very high energy sources but not necessarily paralysis. Recent research into schizophrenia and other brain disorders indicates some malfunctioning of electrical circuiting in the brain which has a tendency to induce hallucinations both auditory and visual, and possibly tactile. Are some of our witnesses prone to disassociative disorders prior to the witnessings or does the phenomenon trigger these episodes in witnesses that have never had the problem before? Or is it both? House is in Lauderdale County just northwest of Collinsville in Mississippi.

1960

Back in Jackson in Hinds County in Mississippi in November 1960. At 9: 00 p.m. five members of a family were driving back from shopping down a country road South of Jackson, when they observed an entity about one meter tall, run from the side of the road in front of them, into a ditch that it tried to climb up. The entity had pointed ears, claw-like fingers, a balding head and human eyes. It was wearing a tight-fitting suit with a sort of backpack, from which a tube ran to its mouth. The family just drove on.

1958

Near Plain, now called Richland, in Rankin County in Mississippi during December 1958. At night a mother and her three young children (including Chris Neely) were driving along isolated Harper Road after purchasing ice cream. In those days the road was a dirt road with 6-foot high embankments on both sides. After about 1/ 8 of a mile or so they spotted what they thought was a child running in front of the car. It darted out of the darkness in front of the car; first it ran to the left side of the road, stopped, then attempted to climb the embankment and ran back towards the right side of the road. It appeared frightened or confused. The car slowed down to a crawl. As they passed they got a good look at the figure, which they described as human-like but resembling a dwarf or elf about 2-3 feet tall. Its face looked almost human, but the eyes were a little bigger than human's eyes. It was wearing what appeared to be an "astronaut suit," with a tank of some kind attached to its back. It did not have a helmet. It appeared to have hair on its head, but not much, just a few strands down the middle. It was small and thin with narrow fingers. Its face had high cheekbones and the hands were long and slender. The witnesses did not stop and continued on.

1965

At 9:40 a.m. on January 20th 1965 in Long Beach in Harrison County in Mississippi. A silver-like object was seen moving west, traveling slow and high and passed directly above the observer. The object was transparent as if made of glass or plastic. It seemed to have two people aboard. One in front and the other seemed to be sitting facing the back of the capsule holding something large like a camera. The length of observation was not reported.

1966
One evening during summer 1966 twelve year old Eve was playing in her backyard with her cousins in Gulfport in Harrison County. She began to feel a strange sensation like something or someone was calling her or watching her. She turned to look behind her and was stunned by the sight of a craft in the distance. The craft had an array of colored lights that were blinking on and off and encircled the strange craft. They seemed to be a color that she had never seen before and were very bright. The more she looked the more she wanted to look. The lights made her feel happy. She could not take her eyes off the craft. Whilst some of the other children ran inside the house Eve stayed outside. It was much closer now and she could see two beings through a window and could make out part of one of their bodies and another being seemed to be controlling the craft. They appeared to be conversing with each other. They were thin with long dangling arms. Suddenly a beam of light shot out of it and seemed to head straight for her. She ran into the bushes with the beam of light close behind her. She was now kneeling, shaking and crying to herself. The light beam was moving apparently scanning the ground close to her. The object was totally motionless. Soon the light disappeared up into the craft, not turned off, but drawn back into it in one motion. Within a moment the craft disappeared. Looking up into the sky Eve saw three similar craft that appeared to be moving in unison. Soon the objects made a type of jerking motion and in a flash they were gone.

In Scott in Bolivar County in Mississippi on Thursday 1st September 1966 several individual witnesses saw a Bigbird that resembled a white flying man. It was going up and down in an erratic manner. There are isolated reports of what I call Hombirds or Manbirds and suddenly the whole chicken coop is left open and flocks of them are suddenly seen in a variety of locations. The Devil's chicken coop has certainly been left wide open.

1972
On September 15th 1972 in the morning in Tupelo in Lee County, Mississippi. A school teacher driving along the Hw 6 near the Bissell community saw a large oval object on the road. The dull aluminium coloured object was soundless.

On November 23rd 1972 (approx. date) in the evening in Polkville in Smith County, Mississippi. Burford Jones (28) and his brother in law Clark Pennington (16) were returning frim a hunting trip when they became aware of a large dark object low over their heads, blocking out the stars. On its underside was a bright white light, which obscured the rest of the thing. Clark raised his gun towards the thing, but Burford dissuaded him from shooting. At this point the thing moved silently about 150m at about 65-80 kph. They now saw that the thing was hovering 25m-30m above the ground, and that the light came from an area 5-6m across on the underside. The top was still hidden in the gloom, but it appeared to be circular and bout 10-15m across. The two ran back home.

1973
On March 18th 1973 at 1935hrs in Polkville in Smith County, Mississippi. Timothy Pennington had just finished putting the luggage in his car boot for the trip back home from his parents' when he saw, looking south, a bright white light, about half the angular diameter of the moon, moving at treetop height at somewhere between 45-80kph. It passed behind a tree at about 10m altitude. After a few seconds he went in and got out the rest of his family (wife, brother and parents) and all saw the thing hover for a while and then seemingly retrace its path. Mrs Pennington Snr heard a faint buzzing sound.

On October 3rd 1973 in the evening in Corinth in Alcorn County, Mississippi. Arlin Mohundro, the sales manager of a local radio station, saw an object hovering 30m above the ground behind the radio station. When it got closer, Arlin could see that it was a black oval object, the size of a car, with red, white and green lights.

At Tupelo in Lee County, Mississippi on 3rd October 1973 a Deputy Sheriff and four Park Rangers saw a hovering UFO that was the size of a two-bedroom house and had red, green and yellow lights on it. Incidentally Tupelo was Elvis Presley's birthplace.

On October 7th 1973 in the evening in Petal in Forrest County, Mississippi. Constable Charles Delk was driving back after unsuccessfully investigating a UFO report when he saw, above Petal High School, a top shaped object with a short antenna on top. It was about 10m diameter, the wider portion uppermost and was surrounded by a yellow band of light. It emitted a humming sound and had four flashing lights. Delk followed it for about 50km towards the Tallahalla swamp. When he got close to the thing his motor and radio cut out and would not work for 15 minutes, after which they restarted as if nothing had happened. Delk then followed the object through the town of Ovett and past a swamp, after which the object did a double flip and disappeared.

On October 10th 1973 at Magnolia in Pike County in Mississippi a round, shiny, metallic object was seen on or near the ground. Something rectangular about the size of a small person emerged. It was a small four foot tall robot-like figure. It appeared to inspect the area and then re-entered the object and it took off.

At 6.00 pm and also in Magnolia Mr and Mrs Rumfield saw two shiny metallic circular objects hovering close to the ground. A robot like thing, 1.2m tall, emerged from an opening in one of the objects, and it inspected the ground before re-entering the object. Both objects then took off.

At Pascagoula around the Pascagoula River in Jackson County in Mississippi on Thursday 11th October 1973 there were individual sightings of hovering UFOs in the Pascagoula area.

That same night in Pascagoula, 11th October 1973, it was 9.00 pm on a Thursday and Charles Hickson, 42 or 45, and Calvin Parker, nineteen, were fishing on a pier on the West bank of the Pascagoula River. A bright blue light attracted their attention when a strange zipping noise filled the air and a luminous silvery saucer was seen to land 40 feet from the pier that the two men were on. It made a whirring noise and was blue grey and hovering one foot above the river. There was no wind or blast from it and it was eight feet across and eight and a half feet high. It had two portholes on one side and no seams or rivets and had oscillating lights. One end of the egg-shaped object opened and three Humanoids floated out of it. They were pale and fuzzy and ghostlike and were five feet tall, naked and with their skin hanging in folds like an elephant's skin. There were no eyes but a narrow slit and there were sharp pronounced noses and no lips. The Humanoids had long arms that ended in lobsterlike claws and oddly enough the legs looked fused together. The Humanoids legs stayed together and did not move. They made a buzzing sound. Two of the Humanoids approached and grabbed Hickson and took him to the ship. Parker fainted. Both men later found themselves on board the ship. They had moved whilst they were unconscious. Whilst Parker remained unconscious Hickson could only move his eyes as he was laid down in midair. An optical device like an eye came out of the wall and examined him. No pain was felt and Parker floated. The eye scanned the front of Hickson's body who was in a separate room to Parker and was examined lying face down. The Humanoids turned him over and he was moved to a 45 degree angle and the eye still examined him. When he was handled the Humanoids were very gentle. At one point he was left alone in the room. The Humanoids then returned and took him back to the original spot where they had been on the pier. He seemed to float down. Parker was returned at the same time and could hardly speak. The UFO vanished. The Humanoids hands were like pincers or claws and they seemed to act more like robots rather than sentient beings. There were also independent sightings of UFOs over Pascagoula that night as well as the rest of Jackson County. Or this account. Charles Hickson (45) and Calvin Parker (18) were fishing in the old Shaupeter Shipyard when their attention was caught by a blue light, over the bay, which circled the area and descended to within 60-90cm of the ground, over the bayou 12-40m behind them. They went towards the river, Parker becoming hysterical. The object was about 5-6m long and from an opening in the end emerged three creatures, about 1,5m tall, pale grey in colour, with wrinkled skin. Their heads seemed stuck down to their shoulders. Their arms ended in claw like appendages, with two digits, about the size of a normal hand. Their legs appeared to be fused, as if standing on a pedestal, and they seemed to float above the ground. The creatures had two small, conical, ears, slits where the eyes should have been, a small sharp nose and a hole below that. One of the creatures emitted a sound like the buzzing of a machine. The creatures grabbed the two men, Parker passing out as they did so. Hickson lost all sense of feeling when the creature touched him and found himself being floated into the craft. The two men were taken into a bare area, well lighted, but no indication of where the light came from. Their bodies were scanned by an instrument like a huge eye. They were left on their own for 15-30 minutes, before being floated out again. When Hickson tried to speak to one of the creatures, it just buzzed in reply. When they were released, the object itself emitted a buzzing sound and left. Both men were terrified by their ordeal. Hickson suffered from nightmares, stigmata on the arm, and later claimed other contacts.

The same night as the abduction of Parker and Hickson Mr. Larry Booth who ran a service station near the Pascagoula River in Pascagoula was at his home when he saw an object drifting in the air at thirty to forty miles per hour. It had lights all around it and was spinning and was so close that had it been a helicopter it would have jarred everybody in the neighborhood. There was no sound coming from it at all.

On Interstate 90, between Biloxi and Gulfport in Harrison County in Mississippi on 15th October 1973 a taxi driver reported that his car had been stalled by a blue UFO that had landed in front of him. As he sat staring at it he heard a tapping at his windshield and saw a crablike claw and two shiny spots. The Pascagoula Humanoids are back? It was only four days after the Pascagoula sightings.

On October 15th 1973 at 2130hrs in Lambert in Quitman County, Mississippi. A single witness observed an oval object at very low altitude over cotton fields near Lambert. It was huge and orange.

Also on October 15th 1973 at 2130hrs in Marks also in Quitman County, Mississippi. A single witness observed a huge orange object low over the railway tracks. Marks and Lambert are less than four miles apart north to south, Marks being north of Lambert.

On October 16th 1973 at night in Gulport in Harrison County, Mississippi. Several people saw a lighted aerial object land in a field near the old Kiln-Picayune Road in Hancock County, near Gulfport. It then took off again. Though the field was wet, the object started a fire.

On Oct. 16th 1973 in Hattiesburg in Forrest County and Lamar County in Mississippi. Motorist driving to work, object landed on top of his car, all four doors flew open, then closed and he felt weight lift off car, saw a lighted object with blue, yellow, and gold rings around it moving away to south.

On October 17th 1973 in Eupora in Webster County in Mississippi. A 50-foot wide, dome-shaped UFO hovered 2-3 feet above Highway 82 at twilight, seemingly suspended on a "beam of light." The primary witness' car lights went out and the engine died when it was 100 yards from the craft. Another car stopped just behind him. A second UFO hovered about 60 feet above the first, illuminating it with a light. Both craft were similar, like inverted cups, and had greenish blue flashing lights. A catfish-like creature came out from the top of the lower UFO, holding onto a handrail. It had gray, fish-like skin, a wide mouth, one glowing eye, flipper-like feet and webbing between the legs like a "flying squirrel." It had a feather-like object on its back which opened and closed when it moved.

On October 23rd 1973 in Hattiesburg in Forrest and Lamar Counties, Mississippi. A strange object was seen on or close to the ground

On 6th November 1973 in Pascagoula in Jackson County in Mississippi Mr. Raymond Ryan, 42, saw an unidentified underwater object following his boat in the Pascagoula River. The submarine craft had a light on it. Ryan left the river and summoned his twin brother Rayme Ryan and the two of them went back to the brackish water, found the object and poked at it with their oars. They then went to the Coast Guard Station and at 9.40 pm the Coast Guard sent a 16 foot boat to investigate. The underwater object was located in four to six feet of water and moving at a rate of six knots. There was an amber beam five feet in diameter that was attached to a large bright metal object. They could not retrieve the object as it would keep moving away and then reappear elsewhere. At 9:20 p.m. Officer Nations stated that he and Officer Crews were in the Coast Guard vessel and were approaching the Ryan brothers in their boat. "One fisherman was there beside the boat. From 50 yards I saw the light lighting up the boat. It was a dim light, moving in a straight line in a northwesterly direction at four to six knots. When we got directly over it, I could see that there was a light amber light source about four inches long which cast an oval-shaped beam straight ahead for four, five, or six feet. Beneath the four-inch light source and attached to it was a metallic rod a couple of feet long and about four inches wide." Nations and Crews tried beating the object with boat oars and hooks, but it went out and reappeared 20 yards away. "The Ryan brothers chased it around in their boat and reached it again before we did. They beat it with their oars," said Nations. Crews also described observing the light coming up from the water and onto the Ryan's boat as the Coast Guard vessel approached. "Three boats started chasing it," Crews explained. "Each boat tried to get on top of it. Then it was under all three boats. I looked down and saw a metallic object three feet long, three or four inches wide, and shiny like stainless steel. It went 20 or 30 yards, then went out. Then it lit up again on the same course and we tried to hit it with oars. The light went out and then it relocated again." At 10 p.m. they lost it. Or this version. At 8.20 pm Raymond Ryan (42), his son Earl, (16) brother Rayme (42) and nephew Larry (17) were fishing for mullet and trout in the Pascagoula river, with members of the Rice family when Rayme called the others' attention to a luminous object in less than 3m of water. When Raymond swung his oar hard into the water, the light went out. The object appeared again, even more brilliant. This went on for some time and they were able to make out that this object was almost 3m in diameter, round and of metallic appearance. It resembled the rounded top of a parachute, with rib like lines running from a dark lump in its centre to the outer rim. It glowed milky white when the light was on. They reported the matter to the coast guard who sent a boat crewed by Charles Crewe and Alan Nations. They reported that the light was oval, about 90cm by 1.2m amd when it passed under the fishing boats that had gathered they could see that it came from a metallic object. When they put oars into the beam of light, the light seemed to shine through them. The light went out and reappeared about 10m away, but dimmed when they gave chase.

1974

One day in January 1974 in Biloxi in Harrison County, Mississippi. Two female college students driving from Gulfport to Biloxi along a coastal highway saw a large ovoid object, with lights emerge out of the water and come close to their car. Despite its proximity it was soundless. They briefly came off the road and then drove off at speed.

On February 19th 1974 at night in Hattiesburg in Forrest County, Mississippi. TV engineer Harold Stanton along with a professor from the University of Southern Mississippi and several other local residents saw a series of 7 objects, which flew in formation and manoeuvred. Five of them landed a field and took off in formation, joining the other two in the air when the witnesses tried to approach. The things intensity varied from a bright glowing orange to a dull blue rotating halo, with neon like glow.

Near Pascagoula in Jackson County in Mississippi during February 1974. During the evening while squirrel hunting, Charles Hickson had knelt down beside a tree to eat a sandwich. Through the bush, he says, he could see part of a metallic craft apparently on the ground. Suddenly he heard a voice. "It was like a radio signal or something inside my head." They said; "Tell people we mean you no harm. You have endured. You have been chosen. There is no need for fear. Your world needs help. We will help before it's too late. You are not prepared to understand. We will return again soon." Hickson picked up his gun and went straight home. The same voice with the same message, came to him again a month later in his backyard.

On August 12th 1974 in Laurel in Jones County, Mississippi. An Air Force officer and his wife were chased in their car by an oval object, which bathed their car with a blue light.

1977

On May 25th 1977 at 0420hrs in Taylorsville in Smith County, Mississippi. In response from a call from a truck driver who had seen an unusual object, officer Steve Sasser was sent to the scene. He saw about 30m above the ground and to the left of the road, a rectangular object with a white luminosity. The thing was moving up and down. The truck driver said he had seen the thing as low as15m. Steve called his chief Tony Blakney, who tried to take a photograph but without success. Other people in town saw the object.

1980

At 10.30 pm on December 3rd 1980 in McLain in Greene County in Mississippi on Highway 57 Mr. and Mrs. Lowrey had the FM radio of their car quit, the car's headlights dim, and the car heater quit when a luminous, blue-white ball of light came briefly over the right side of the car's hood. They estimated the light to be about a foot in diameter and only a meter away. The seat belt alarm also came on during the encounter. Or this report. While driving north with her husband on Hw. 57, about 15km south of McLain, Janice Lowrey (19) saw in the east an illuminated ball that slowly approached the car at eye level and came briefly over the right side of the bonnet. From a distance of only 1m it appeared to be 30cm in diameter, solid, sharply outlined and self- luminous, however it was not bright enough to illuminate the bonnet. It was white, with a blue tint in the centre and soundless. It did not hit the car but turned back to the east so rapidly that Janice could not follow it in the clear sky. Her observation lasted for 10 seconds. Her husband, Robert (25), did not see the object but he noticed that the headlights dimmed, their horn ceased working, and the seat belt buzzer came on even though he was sure he had removed it when he first purchased the car. The radio lost its station and the heater quit. These effects persisted for the remainder of the 25 minutes journey but when he re-examined the car 30 minutes later it was found to be working normally.

1988

Near Natchez in Adams County in Mississippi at 5.00 pm in October 1988 the witness was riding his three-wheel ATC on a deer hunting expedition along the Mississippi River when the engine suddenly stalled. He then noticed two of his friends up ahead pointing at the sky. Looking up he saw a huge object about 400 yards away moving in a westerly direction very slow. It emitted a powerful humming sound and it had red, white, amber, green and bright blue lights. There was also a long object attached to it that tapered at the end to a u-shaped fork. This fork moved up and down and had electricity arcing from tip to tip. He also saw numerous other antennas on other protruding objects on the saucer-shaped object. On the upper middle section there seemed to be lots of windows with amber lights coming from inside. On several occasions he seemed to remember seeing a couple of sets of large eyes looking down at him. He felt as though he received a telepathic message but could not remember its contents. It disappeared out of sight towards the West behind some trees.

1989

At 7.30 am on January 18th 1989 in Glen Allan in Washington County in Mississippi an aerial object was seen. It had the shape of an airplane fuselage and possible had a stabilizer fin. It was silver and no windows were seen. There were no lights and it was the size of a Boeing 747 flying at approximately 1500 foot altitude. There was no sound and it appeared to be travelling about 300 mph. Forest animals froze as the cylinder passed overhead. It was observed in clear weather by a male 52-year-old witness in a forest for over one minute. How does a flying object avoid friction with the atmosphere? Is it really here or is there a shield of some kind that prevents friction and the subsequent noises?

1990

On January 20th 1990 in Boyle in Bolivar County in Mississippi a silvery object with two rows of lights paced just ahead of a car for two to three miles. Then the engine and lights failed until the object departed.

Missouri

1857

It is 5th October 1857, and the citizens of Saint Louis in Missouri are trembling in awe at a great meteor hovering in the sky. Actually they are probably trembling due to the massive earthquake occurring at the same time. There was also a report of a great explosion also at the same time as well as vivid flashes of light in the sky. On the eighth of October 1857, at 4.20 am, the Meteor, which had been hovering over the city for three days now, exploded and the ground shook violently. There were also lightning flashes and luminous entities in the sky as well. A meteor hangs around literally for three nights which is three nights longer than they normally hang around. There is also an aerial explosion as well as an earthquake? Must be one of those dang crazy coincidences again. Though there is still no recognizable link between earthquakes and aerial phenomena.It must all be coincidentallity.

1875

In Brownsville, now called Sweet Springs, in Saline County in Missouri in early May 1875 at 11:30 p.m. Wednesday last was a mild and summer-like day, and old weather prognosticators predicted the coming of good rain. But it is not of the rain we propose to speak, but of the sights that were seen on that night by a number of our citizens. About half past eleven or twelve o'clock, an inmate of the Central Hotel, on awakening, had his attention called to a glare of lights which he observed out of his window, near which he was lying. At first he supposed it to be in a dwelling, but there being so many, and at such a late hour, his attention was called to solve what they meant. From the peculiar nature of them, he aroused a number of the inmates to witness the strange proceedings. Balls of light from the size of an egg to that of man's head, and changing from a white to that of a reddish glare, were floating about in the air, as though they were animate objects. At first there were but a few of them, and seemed to be about twenty or thirty feet from the ground, but in a short time the number increased, and a regular carnival was held. They moved around like apples on disturbed water, then like they were engaged in a waltz and at times falling into ranks like soldiers marching to and fro. They appeared to be over an old field at the East end of the town, and numbered about half a hundred. The strangest part was in the wind up. While the witnesses were all eagerly gazing at the lights, a cloud came from the west, which was about the size of a door, and of a grayish or smoke color. It had the form of a man standing in an upright position. As it neared the lights it began to change its form and color, and finally assumed that of a black coffin. On passing to the east, it hovered over the field which, contained the balls of light, and rested at about a distance of forty or fifty feet from the ground. The lights began in procession, a march was made around the coffin with seeming funeral tread, and when a complete circle was formed a halt was made. A lid seemed to rise from the coffin, and with slow movements, the lights entered the same, were lost to view. The coffin-like object was then wafted southward, and on reaching the graveyard settled down and was seen no more. A great number of our citizens witnessed that night's phenomena which will be very memorable. Auburn Daily Bulletin (Auburn, NY) May 5, 1875.

1877

On 3rd January 1877 a meteorite crashed to earth and narrowly missed a man in Warrenton in Warren County in Missouri. It was a carbonaceous chondrite and struck a tree and broke into pieces. It was originally 45 kilograms in size originally.

1880

On 28th July 1880, an airship was reported over Saint Louis in Missouri. Another alleged airship in the pre-airplane age? These are getting to be more numerous as well. Why Saint Louis again instead of somewhere new? Always the regular haunts or so it seems. The same day strange things were also seen over Louisville in Kentucky.

In Missouri in 1880 during the daytime. A man hunting in the hills saw a round craft descend from the sky and land on top of a nearby hill. He climbed up the hill to investigate and came upon a large silvery ball-shaped object in a clearing. A hatch or opening became visible on top of the object and two short human-like figures emerged. One was a female and the other a male both described as "very handsome looking." They attempted to communicate with the witness in a strange dialect, and then retreated back into the silvery ball, which then took off into the sky and vanished.

1881

Sometime in November 1881, at 10.30 pm a most unusual and wonderful formation of stars appeared over Saint Joseph, Buchanan County, Missouri. At first a star was seen to shoot in the direction of the moon and when within two feet of the moon stopped short. This was followed by four other stars which took positions a few inches distant and in a direct line behind the first. Then directly behind an inverted triangle with the five original stars protruding in a straight line from the tip of the triangle they remained stationary in this position for half an hour. Then they broke formation as regularly as they had assembled.

1886

On 23rd November 1886 a man and his three sons were pulling corn in a field near Edina in Knox County in Missouri when suddenly there was a flash of lightning. The farmer was injured as was one son and the second son was dead. The third son had vanished into thin air. Micrometeorites? A burst of antimatter? Merely an act of lightning? Or coincidence? There was no lightning storm at the time. Are we discussing energy forms that can travel through the Earth with only slightly less difficulty than when they travel through the air? After all lightning comes up from the ground as often as it comes down from the sky.

1896

In August 1896 at night in Howell County, Missouri. Ezra and Serepta Vickers and their children Pearl May (9) and Ben were sat on their farm porch when their attention was caught by a circle of lights descending towards them. It stopped over the barn and they saw that it was a saucer shaped thing, with blinding lights which lit up the barn. The family fled indoors, from where they watched the object, Ezra praying in terror. The next day three steers were found dead at the site, their bodies drained with blood. Other cases were supposed to have happened.

Sometime in 1896 two postal clerks were in a train going North from Trenton, Grundy County, Missouri, in heavy rain when they noticed a round rose colored light rising and coming within one hundred feet of the train. The light soon rose between the horizon and the zenith and the wind became very strong from the East but the light held its course due North. The speed varied and sometimes it would outrun the train and sometimes it would fall behind. The light vanished behind the Linville Railroad depot. The size of the light was unknown as there were no parameters to base size on. Our aerial light even liked pacing trains at high speed and that is something that even the most advanced Zeppelin is incapable of. We are looking at something else. And soon we would be looking at lots of them.

1897

On 1st April 1897, at 8.00 pm there was a ninety minute sighting by approximately ten thousand people in Kansas City, Jackson County, Missouri of an object in the sky that had blue, green and white lights on it. The airship also had a searchlight. After ninety minutes the craft shot upwards into the sky and vanished. A balloon cannot do this. Whilst in view the airship travelled in a rollercoaster fashion, going up and down, and travelled at sixty miles per hour, crossing the city at 45 degrees above the horizon and turned reddish as it moved away. Some of the aerial phenomena had searchlights and brightly colored lights of different hues on them.

On April 1st 1897. (approx. date) in St Louis in Missouri, While walking along Skinner Avenue by Forest Park, Joseph Joslin encountered a landed object and a small humanoid creature. The being hypnotised Joslin into going on board its craft. He was away for three weeks but could not remember much of what happened on board or how he got back to earth.

On April 5th 1897 at 2230hrs in Bethany in Harrison County, Missouri. An aerial object passed overhead at 800m altitude and 40kph. The next morning Joh Leib and Ira Davies reported that the airship had crashed on the farm belonging to J D Sims. Two mutilated bodies were found at the site and documents suggesting the object was an airship.

On April 12th 1897 at 10.00 pm in Maysville in Missouri. The airship landed for half an hour. It came to the ground in a vacant lot North of U. S. Marshall Crenshaw's home and was soon surrounded by nearly the whole population of the little city. There was only one man on board who appeared to be Norwegian. Scandinavian oaths fairly poured from his lips as he hammered at a peculiar little contrivance in one of the long, gill-like flanges on top of the rear portion of the ship. All that could be seen about the little air vessel was an apparently Danish inscription. In thirty minutes everything seemed to be repaired and the mysterious visitor was gone. This was during the Great Airship Flap. An aerial machine, first seen as a light on the north-eastern horizon, came over the town at less than 100m altitude and descended in a vacant lot, north of US Marshall Crenshaw's house. Around it a crowd of almost the entire population of the town gathered. There was a pilot on board, who appeared to be swearing in Norwegian as he made repairs to a gill like flange in the top rear portion of the airship, but he would not speak with the witnesses. Inscriptions ion the airship appeared to be in Danish. After 30 minutes the repairs were completed and the airship and its pilot took off.

15th April 1897 was a very busy day indeed. An airship was seen over Saint Louis in Saint Louis County, Missouri, and Birmingham in Van Buren County, Iowa. St Louis is still popular.

Now we are in Springfield in Greene County, Missouri, on 16th April 1897 and a Mr. Hopkins, a well respected Gentleman in these parts, encountered a landed airship with two beautiful but naked occupants. One was a beautiful female who was picking flowers and wearing jewels in her hair. Both of them were speaking in an unknown language and the female was making apparent exclamations of delight concerning flowers. The witness asked them where they were from and they pointed to the sky saying something like Mars. The hominoids allowed the witness to examine their craft and made certain gestures concerning his clothes, watch and grey hair that indicated to Mr. Hopkins that they had little or no comprehension of ageing or time. Now we have the Nude Women's Airship and Flower Collecting Team. With no concept of time. The witness also assumed they did not know anything about ageing either. Here is another version. While walking through the hills east of Springfield, W H Hopkins, a travelling salesman from St Louis, encountered an aerial machine, by which stood a man and woman, both naked. The woman, who was picking flowers, had golden hair tied by a jewelled band. She was talking in a foreign language, her voice being like "low silvery bells". The man, who was nearer the ship, had dark shoulder length hair. Both occupants, who were of outstanding beauty, were fanning themselves with curiously shaped fans, as if suffering from the heat, though Hopkins found the weather cool enough for an overcoat. As Hopkins approached, the woman, who was of medium height, leapt back in terror and the man approached in a threatening manner. With difficulty Hopkins was able to persuade the pair of his friendly intentions and they showed him around the ship. There was a luxurious cabin, illuminated by a sphere, which gave off a soft white light when agitated. Similar spheres were attached each propeller and at various points along the sides. When struck, these began to revolve and brilliant lights of various colours were emitted by the sides of the ship. Finally the pilot struck the mechanism on the propellers and Hopkins sprung out as the craft rose up and rapidly vanished from sight. The occupants seemed baffled by Hopkins' clothes and watch. And he got the impression that the pair came from Mars. Hopkins' wife, friends and employer said he was a sober honest and churchgoing man.

A winged airship was seen over the hills in Hillsdale County in Michigan the following day 17th April 1897 as well as Ann Arbor in Washtenaw County, Michigan, Waterloo in Blackhawk County, Iowa and Saint Louis in Saint Louis County in Missouri. Again.

There were two other reports from Missouri during April 1897 that might have been the one sighting, if there was one, though both places are one hundred miles apart. At Moberly in Randolph County it was reported that an aerial craft had crashed to earth and metallic traces were found. The other report was from Bethany in Harrison County where it was reported that a farmer wrote to the local newspaper claiming that he saw an airship crash into a flagpole in town. The bodies of two occupants were found that were mangled beyond recognition. You be the judge.

1901

Sometime in 1901 a flying disc was observed by three witnesses over New Haven in Franklin County in Missouri. A noise was heard as well and the sighting was in a forest. An elderly man, his wife and hired hand observed, in some woodlands, a dome shaped object "like a turtle", with three lights like large eyes that shone like lanterns. The object was about the size of a haystack and made a buzzing sound.

1902

In 1902 in Ivy Bend in Stover in Morgan County, Missouri two people waiting for a ferry to cross the Osage River heard a sound coming from the river. A silver grey top shaped object passed in front of them at treetop height. It was spinning and travelling much faster than a boat. It disappeared out of sight down a bend in the river.

1920

Around 6.00 pm 8th June 1920 a cylindrical object was seen at an altitude of seventy-five feet by two hundred people. The craft made a ninety degree turn to the East and disappeared into a cloud. This was above Rushville in Buchanan County in Missouri. Meteorites do not do ninety degree turns.

1925

On December 23rd 1925 at 1615hrs in Springfield in Greene County, Missouri. Rev. A.J. Graves and three companions were sitting opposite the Little Creek Cemetery when they saw a luminous column about 3m high, with a luminous star on top, appear in the graveyard. It was seen three days later, and on two subsequent occasions.

1930

Near Piedmont in Wayne County in Missouri in August 1930. The main witness (now 96 at the time of writing this and still very 'sharp') lived outside Piedmont on a farm that has been in the family since the 1850's. He lived there with his mother, father, grandmother and siblings. When he was a child, whoever was the youngest had to sleep on the sleeping porch of the house. None of them wanted to sleep there because the "little people" would visit and they were all afraid of them. He remembers that his mother and grandmother told stories about the little gray people who visited the farm at night and that the stories were in the family since before the Civil War. One night in particular, when he was 10-years old, he was lying in bed on the porch when he saw a gray being with big eyes walk up to the window and look inside at him. He was frozen in fear. The entity just kept staring at him. The next thing he knew, there were three of them, all about 4 feet tall with no hair, big black eyes, a small nose and mouth, and thin, standing next to his bed, and he remembers thinking that he had no idea how they got inside. He was even more afraid and wanted to pull the covers up over his face but couldn't. He doesn't know what happened after that. The next morning he woke up and they were gone. They never appeared during the day, only at night. He never saw a craft of any type, but sometimes late at night the family would hear a humming sound coming from the low depression area around the pond about 100 feet from the house, but never went to look to see what it was. He thinks they were afraid to. They also saw small white balls of light in the yard and around the farm at dusk and after dusk but never knew what they were. The lights were about the size of a softball. The whole family was sure to be inside after dark and they just didn't play outside after dark – the older family members made sure they came inside and as he thinks back on this it must have been because of the little people who would "take them." That is the term his mother and grandmother used; they would say that the little gray people would take them at night but always brought them back before morning. It was almost like talking about fairies or something magical that was their little secret. It was not something they spoke about to other people – they kept it to themselves and still do to this day. He claims that he still sees them sometimes, only inside the house where he sleeps now. He sees them come in late at night, usually around 3:00 a.m. but for some reason he just falls asleep and doesn't remember any interaction with them. He doesn't let anyone sleep on the porch. His children and grandchildren have also seen the gray people. They are not as afraid of them anymore, just look at them as being visitors rather than something that will harm them.

1932

On 10th August 1932 a falling meteorite struck a homestead in Archie in Cass County in Missouri. The meteorite missed a person by less than one meter. This was an H chondrite meteorite. Five stones were seen to fall or heard to land near witnesses. Mr. Harry Christiansen was working on a windmill seventy feet from his house when he heard and explosion in the heavens about 3.00 pm and saw an angry cloud in the sky. He ran to the house and called his sister when he heard a whizzing sound and saw a half pound meteorite land about five feet away after passing within eighteen inches of his head. As he entered the house he heard another rock hit the corner of the house and a third hit somewhere outside. Was this meteorite from the same shower that struck Brazil six days earlier? On 4th August 1932 the fall of a meteorite unroofed a warehouse in Sao Christavao in Brazil.

1938

Near St. Louis, Missouri in 1938.. The mother in a family involved with numerous encounters, recalled seeing a flying disk type craft on the ground and numerous entities that appeared to be in a rush, around it. They then re-entered the craft, which left the area at a tremendous rate of speed. One of the entities appeared to be a little girl, fragile looking, who had large black eyes with no white parts apparent, but with more rounded eyes than a "typical gray humanoid." The girl also had a pointed chin, high forehead, and very fine thin hair. The mother noticed at least one other entity accompanying the 'hybrid' girl that looked entirely human; it was described as a 6 foot tall white woman, with brown hair and brown eyes wearing some sort of tight-fitting one-piece uniform.

1941

In Spring 1941 at Cape Girardeau in Cape Girardeau County, Missouri, Charlotte Mann, a Texas woman whose grandfather was a pastor of the Red Star Baptist Church, told Leonard Stringfield, that her grandfather was called out to give last rights to some crash victims, who were described as from a crashed object. There were three bodies all described as "not human". Reverend William Huffman had been an evangelist for many years, but had taken the resident minister reigns of the Red Star Baptist Church in early 1941. Church records corroborate his employment there during the period in question. After receiving his call to duty, he was immediately driven the 10-15 mile journey to some woods outside of town. Upon arriving at the scene of the crash, he saw policemen, fire department personnel, FBI agents, and photographers already mulling through the wreckage. He was soon asked to pray over three dead bodies. As he began to take in the activity around the area, his curiosity was first struck by the sight of the craft itself. Expecting a small plane of some type, he was shocked to see that the craft was disc-shaped, and upon looking inside he saw hieroglyphic-like symbols, indecipherable to him. He then was shown the three victims, not human as expected, but small alien bodies with large eyes, hardly a mouth or ears, and hairless. Immediately after performing his duties, he was sworn to secrecy by military personnel who had taken charge of the crash area. He witnessed these warnings being given to others at the scene also. As he arrived back at his home at 1530 Main Street, he was still in a state of mild shock, and could not keep this story from his wife Floy, and his sons. This late night family discussion would spawn the story that Charlette Mann would hear from her grandmother in 1984, as she lay dying of cancer at Charlette's home while undergoing radiation therapy. Charlette was told the story over the span of several days, and although Charlette had heard bits and pieces of this story before, she now demanded the full details. As her grandmother tolerated her last few days on this Earth, Charlette knew it was now or never to find out everything she could before this intriguing story was lost with the death of her grandmother. She also learned that one of the members of her grandfather's congregation, thought to be Garland D. Fronabarger, had given him a photograph taken on the night of the crash. This picture was of one of the dead aliens being held up by two men. Charlette Mann gave, in her own words, an account of what she knew for a television documentary. Some of that account is given here: "I saw the picture originally from my dad who had gotten it from my grandfather who was a Baptist Minister in Cape Girardeau, Missouri in the spring of 1941. I saw that picture and asked my grandmother about it at a later time when she was at my home, fatally ill with cancer, so we had a frank discussion. She said that grandfather was called out in the spring of 1941, in the evening around 21:00-21:30. That someone had been called out to a plane crash outside of town and would he be willing to go to minister to people there, which he did. Upon arrival, it was a very different situation. It was not a conventional aircraft, as we know it. He described it as a saucer that was metallic in color, no seams, did not look like anything he had seen. It had been broken open in one portion, and so he could walk up and see that. In looking in he saw a small metal chair, gauges and dials and things he had never seen. However, what impressed him most was around the inside there were inscriptions and writings, which he said he did not recognize, but were similar to Egyptian hieroglyphics. There were three entities, or non-human people, lying on the ground. Two were just outside the saucer, and a third one was further out. His understanding was that perhaps that third one was not dead on impact. There had been mention of a ball of fire, yet there was fire around the crash site, but none of the entities had been burned and so father did pray over them, giving them last rites. There were many people there, fire people, photographers, and so they lifted up one, and two men on either side stood him up and they stretched his arms out; they had him up under the armpits and out here. As I recall from the picture I saw; he was about 4 feet tall, appeared to have no bone structure, soft looking. He had a suit on, or we assume it was a suit, it could have been his skin, and what looked like crinkled, soft aluminum foil. I recall it had very long hands, very long fingers and I think there were three but I cannot swear to that. My grandfather upon arrival, said there were already several people there on the scene; two that he assumed were local photographers, fire people, and so not long after they arrived, military just showed up, surrounded the area, took them off in groups separately and spoke to each of them. Grandfather didn't know that was said to the others, but he was told 'this didn't happen, you didn't see this, this is national security, it is never to be talked about again.' My grandfather was an honorable man, being a preacher, that's all that needed to be said to him. And so he came home and told the story to my dad, who was there, and my grandmother and my uncle. Now my mother was expecting at the time, so she was off in the bedroom. My sister was born May 3, 1941, so we are assuming this was the middle to the last off April. And he never spoke of it again. But about two weeks later, one of the men who had a personal camera that he had put in his shirt pocket, approached grandfather and said, 'I think someone needs a copy of this. I have one and I would like you to keep one. So that's how it came about that grandfather had the picture to begin with. But he never spoke of it again. The other people seem to be very intimidated and very frightened and paranoid." Other living supporting witnesses include Charlette Mann's sister who confirmed her story in a notarized sworn affidavit, and the living brother of the Cape Girardeau County sheriff in 1941, Clarance R. Schade. He does remember hearing the account of the crash, yet does not have many details. He does recall hearing of a "spaceship with little people. There are also Fire Department records of the date of the crash. This information does confirm the military swearing department members to secrecy, and also the removal of all evidence from the scene by military personnel. Guy Hoffmann, Charlette's father also told the story of the crash, and had in his possession the photograph of the dead alien. He showed the picture to a photographer friend of his, Walter Wayne Fisk. He has been contacted by Stanton Friedman, but would not release any pertinent information.

On April 5th 1941 in Charleston in Mississippi County in Missouri. It was reported that a "Submarine" bobbed up in the Mississippi River and took aboard a negro (sic) farmer before disappearing.

1945

At 10.30 am one day in May 1945 in St James, Missouri. Hearing a loud humming sound the witness looked up to see hovering above his garage a ten meter diameter metallic domed disk. Inside the clear dome he could see a humanoid being looking out. The witness watched the craft for three minutes as it hovered fifty feet away before it soon left the area following the contours of the terrain.

1947

On July 8th 1947 in St Louis, Missouri. Student Oliver Obenhaus observed a fast object that swooped towards the ground.

On 11th August 1947 a veteran aviation pilot was seeing some dark specks growing in the sky going South and North over Saint Louis in Saint Louis County in Missouri. They were in vertical Vee formation with one on a point and the others stepped above and below in trail. The sighting happened in the outskirts of Saint Louis during a softball game. The objects were soon discerned as disc-shaped, nine in number, approaching at 25,000 feet and doing 1,000 miles per hour in the cloudless sky. At arm's length the discs appeared to be the size of a grape. They were dark on one side and light colored on the other and were flipping in unison every two seconds. Both baseball teams and twenty-five spectators watched with great interest. The ballplayers consisted of aircraft ground instructors and the other of pilot and aircraft mechanic students. They were all excellent witnesses.

1948

On the evening of July 9th 1948 northwest of Springfield in Greene County in Missouri, a saucer-shaped object made a landing in a farmer's field. Apparently winged beings came out of the craft and took soil samples. When it appeared that the extraterrestials realized that they had been seen they left quickly with their samples and flew away.

1949

On May 7th 1949 in South St. Louis in Saint Louis County in Missouri at 7 p.m just after sunset Vaughn saw the sun glinting off a flat reddish-brown object, "somewhat triangular" shaped, oscillating, the size of a private plane but faster. The records do not mention if this was Mr. Vaughn or first name Vaughn.

Six days later on May 13th 1949 a woman encountered a Gray-type alien humanoid on the outskirts of St Louis. The Gray approached her and touched her arm and then she ran away and did not look back at it because the humanoid had strange big eyes and was like nothing that the woman had ever seen in her life. She thought that it was a demon and she was too scared to scream even when it touched her.

1950

On 10th December 1950 a car was struck by a falling meteorite in Saint Louis in Saint Louis City in Missouri. Now for the return of the meteors but in this case it became a meteorite. This was an ordinary H4 chondrite and coincided with the yearly Geminid Meteor shower. At 11.00 pm a brilliant light had flared in the sky. John Hauser, 28, was driving in the 5000 block of West Florissant shortly after 11.00 pm when two chunks of hot metal pierced the convertible top of his automobile. The stopped the car to investigate and found two metal fragments about two and a half inches wide. They were partially composed of iron and identified as meteorites.

1953

The General Manager and Chief Engineer of a St. Louis broadcasting station, state that they were starting out to fish one morning in 1953 on the famed Lake of the Ozarks. Out some three or four hundred yards from shore, they were sitting there in the fog, listening for a passing boat which might help them, when they heard a heavy humming sound. They could see nothing until the fog parted briefly; then about a hundred feet from them, and not more than five feet above the still waters of the lake, they saw a shiny, disc-shaped thing. It was oscillating slowly, and both men noticed that directly beneath it the water was dancing in thousands of tiny sharp pointed waves. A moment later the fog closed in and my friends waited no longer for help; they began paddling back toward the dock, using their hats for paddles.

1954

In the Ozark Mountains in Missouri on July 30th 1954 at 4: 00 p.m. Buck Nelson was listening to the radio in his home, when a high-pitched noise and what appeared to be a foreign tongue cut across the program. He listened for a few minutes and then turned the volume down and tried to tune in to get the program more clearly, but the noise, mixed up with the babble of the unknown language, persisted. Meanwhile, his pony and his dog were both causing a commotion outside the house. Going outside, Buck was amazed to see a huge disc-like object, at least 50 feet in diameter, hovering over the house about 100 or 200 feet up, before it landed on the back of his 80-acre ranch, about 800 to 1,000ft from the house. He had a very clear close up view when it was directly over him at the back of his house near the kitchen door. It flew low and stood still in the air for several minutes. He rushed into the house to get his reflex camera, but when he returned it had risen up into real low clouds with two other such craft. He took several snaps with his camera. One photo shows two space ships among the clouds fairly clear.

1955

On February 1st 1955 around 12.00 at Mountain View in Howell County in Missouri. Three saucers that Buck Nelson had previously seen returned; one of them circled low over his house and spoke to him in English with a P.A. system. He asked questions by telepathy, and answered theirs by gesture. After assuring them of his friendliness, he was told they would land in the future, and would take him to their home planet, Venus. He could see the men in the craft who were big-boned and muscular.

On March 5th 1955 in Mountain View in Howell County in Missouri, the spacemen came to see Buck Nelson in his house. They arrived naked, but after shaking hands put on purplish-blue overalls with low necks & short sleeves.

On March 22nd 1955 at night in Mountain View the spacemen called on Buck Nelson briefly at night, and told him they had tried to approach earlier but had been "worried by a jet!.

1956

In 1956 in Stover in Morgan County, Missouri.A bright light was seen ascending from a wooded area. When neighbours investigated they found the ground blackened in a circle 17m in diameter, and several small trees broken and pushed out from the circle.

1957

In Lake City in Independence in Jackson County in Missouri on Saturday 9th November 1957 at 1.00 am a UFO appeared fifty feet above the ground and the motor of the car of the witness died. When the UFO vanished the car started again. The UFO was elongated. A man, Mr Boardman, driving home from work observed an elongated object, 16m long, hovering 15m above the ground. His car engine died as he neared the object's position, and it only restarted when the thing had left. Over and over the same electromagnetic effects. The previous sighting around here had been a dog-killing Hairy Humanoid at Sedalia in 1946 preceded by a fall of frogs onto Kansas City in 1873.

1958

Near Kansas City in Jackson, Clay, Plate and Cass Counties in Missouri in December 1958. Contactee George Adamski reported that he was picked up in a car from his delayed train by a spaceman that drove him a short distance to a grove of trees above which a craft was hovering. He then had the experience of being lifted up into the craft while the ship hovered. He reported feeling as if something transparent or a plastic curtain surrounded his body. Onboard he met the human-like extraterrestrial friends that later dropped him off in Davenport, Iowa at nightfall.

1959

In 1959 an object that was two feet long and one inch in diameter flew into a room with the sound of crushing glass. The object then hovered as it changed into a ball and then dissolved with the same sound of crushing glass. No glass was found though. This was in Kansas City in Jackson County.

1965

Around 11.00 pm on 16th August 1965 in Sedalia in Puttis County in Missouri a woman was driving home and was within a mile of her house when she saw a light in a field with smoke around it. In the ditch she noticed two large birds, one of which flew at her car. She arrived home at 12.15 am unable to account for the lapse of time. Under hypnotic regression she recalled that the birds were two entities wearing space suits. One carried a sack on its back into which the other was putting samples of grass and soil samples. They were bouncing up and down their arms flopping at their sides in a stiff manner suggestive of robots. One started to come from the ditch, slipped back, then emerged and stood in front of her. Its helmet began to glow brilliantly and she could now see that its head was wrapped up in tape-like a mummy with only the eyes visible. It was five feet tall. At this point a thing, a football shaped UFO, landed on the road in front of her car. Two beings with slightly pointed heads and wrap around eyes emerged from it and opened her car door. They conducted her into the object assuring her telepathically that she would not be hurt. The air inside the craft was heavy and difficult to breathe. Once she was inside they flew over a nearby field which caused its inner lights to change from white to red. One of the entities who did most of the talking appeared to be a scientist or doctor. He wore an insignia of three rings on his chest. Another had a red lightning flash symbol on his and she took him to be the pilot. The third entity was a woman. They were all five foot ten inches tall. The doctor put an object over her head and she felt as if something was going into her brain. A round black object was taken out of the wall and with it pictures were taken of her. The object glowed blue when the pictures were taken. On a screen on a wall was a pattern of seven vertical lines with markings between them which she thought was a tabular representation of her brain and body. Then two figures, about a foot shorter, made their appearance. They resembled gnomes and aroused fear in the witness. They appeared old and their foreheads were wrinkled. She was told by the Humanoids that they and the mummies came from different planets. Finally she was led to her car and the UFO ascended.

1966

On March 24th 1966 at 1000hrs in Florissant in St. Louis County, Missouri. An orange object hovered at treetop height.

At midnight on 1st April 1966 Ms. Darlene Underwood and her mother saw two luminous objects land on a nearby hill and observed them through binoculars. They were egg-shaped and the size of a large car. Presently they saw the shadows of one or two human-like beings and heard the beings shouting at each other very loudly in a foreign language. After this they heard the sound of a pig squealing. A point of green light issued from one of the objects and then they took off and flew rapidly away. This was in Liberty in Clay County in Missouri. Or this version. At 11.55 pm Darlene Underwood, who claimed to have had many UFO sightings since the previous Christmas, was driving with her mother when they saw two star- like points of light and followed them. They saw them land near a farm house, where Darlene parked so they could observe them for 2-3 hours. One of the objects landed on a nearby hill, while the other circled. During this time a train passed by and the circling object turned off its lights and hovered at the top of a nearby tree until the train passed, when it turned on its lights again. The object on the hill rose slightly and went behind the hill. After the train passed the two objects settled close together on the hill. Both the objects were too brilliant for any clear shape to be seen, though Darlene got the impression that they were oval. As she continued to watch she saw the shadow of a man or men then heard the sound of two men arguing in a foreign language. The witnesses were then frightened by sounds resembling those of a pig being butchered. At this time one of the objects blinked out and a point of green light was observed to come from it. The objects were the apparent size of cars or helicopters and cones of light 5.5-6m high came from them. Shortly after the commotion the objects took off and flew rapidly away, the witnesses giving chase for a while. While Darlene never saw the occupants directly she got the impression from the shadows that they were of human shape and size. Note traces were found at the site.

Around 12.30 am on 1st August 1966 Kathy Palmer, fourteen, looked out of the window before going to bed and saw a luminous object bearing red and green lights on the lawn of her family home in Springfield in Greene County in Missouri. It was about six foot long by four foot by four foot. It made a rattling sound. From a square hatchway two five foot tall slender occupants emerged who had large heads or were perhaps wearing helmets. They walked about apparently talking to each other and examined some bicycles. Then they returned to the craft and took off. The sighting was for thirty minutes. At the landing site the grass was matted down and there was a white substance which proved to be calcium carbonate. Or this? Three girls, including Kathy P (14), who was going to bed saw a landed object for 30 minutes. The thing made a rattling sound and hovered a few centimetres above the ground. It was oval, 1.8m long, 1.2m wide. A square opening appeared and two beings, 1.5m tall, slender, with large heads, emerged, walked about, apparently examining some bicycles and then returned to the object, which took off. Grass was found matted in a circle, with two marks in the grass, 1.2m apart, which were 2.5cm wide.

On November 22nd 1966 at 1000hrs in Roaring River State Park in Barry County, Missouri. A deer hunter saw a disc shaped object rising from a valley 100m away. A humming sound was heard, A tent was burned and the top of a nearby tree was found burning. A total of $600 of damage was caused. Two photographs were taken.

On November 28th 1966 back in El Campo, Texas. Bryan Ritz and Janis Dodungen were driving on Farm Road 1300 when they passed a red object on the road. It glowed a deeper red as they went past. Looking back they saw two red lights hovering less than 2m above the ground.

Also on November 28th 1966 at night again in El Campo, Texas. The occupants of a car at a campsite 35km south of El Campo were followed to El Campo by an object at treetop height.

On December 12th 1966, approx. date, at night in El Campo, Texas. Janis Bondugen was driving home on farm road 1300, just off Hwy 71, when she saw two bright lights coming towards her. She thought that it was another car and signalled that she was going to make a turn, a block and half away from the lights. Suddenly the lights merged into one big golden light covering the whole road. It appeared taller than the trees and narrow. Janis slowed down but as she saw the object continue to glide gracefully towards her, she turned and accelerated away.

In 1966 at 2250hrs in Denton in Pemiscot County, Missouri. Driving home from a midweek church meeting along Hw 77, Mrs Sadie Hagar was about to turn into the country lane 3km from her home, when she glimpsed some red lights just above the trees. At first she thought they were from a low flying aircraft, but when she next saw them realised that they were two red lights on an object hovering over a large tree in a field to the left ahead. It suddenly moved and hovered low over the road ahead. As she drove under the object, Sadie saw it was ovoid, the width of the road, with a slate grey underside. On each side were two upswept appendages on each side, which ended in red lights that appeared not to be reflected on the ground. During the rest of the journey home Sadie had the feeling was overhead, but her husband saw nothing when she arrived home.

1967

On January 27th 1967 in Greenfield in Dade County, Missouri. Vicky Cantrell and Linda Terrel were followed by a brilliant object that paced their car at low altitude until they reached Vicky's house. There, joined by Vicky's parents, they saw an object they hovered for a few minutes and then disappeared in the west.

Around 10.00 pm on 29th January 1967 Mrs. Enid Campbell saw from a window what at first she took to be the full moon but as it moved closer she could see that it was a spherical object that was white in color like a frosted light bulb. It had a shiny gold horizontal ring around the middle of it in which were numerous round holes. The object came to several feet from her window before stopping and through its semi-transparent material she could see a control panel with a lever on top and two occupants. One was seated at the panel and the other was standing. They wore shiny, silvery wet suits. Enid called her sons, Gene, 18, and George, 14, who arrived at the window in time to see the object as it rose and moved away. While it hovered nearby two smaller white luminous spheres approached and entered it through an opening after which the holes in the central ring jetted out red fire. Then the object ascended vertically and disappeared. The snow on the ground under where it had been was melted. Later the area over which the object approached the house failed to grow plants though they grew elsewhere. This was in Knox City in Knox County in Missouri. Here is another version. Mrs Enid Campbell (43) and her sons Gene (18) and George (14) were watching TV in the living room of their two story farm house 6.5km south west of Knox City when George called his mother and brother to look at the unusual size of the rising moon. A few minutes later after the boys had gone to bed Mrs Campbell looked again and saw this "moon" had not risen as it should. It was a spherical object the colour of a white light bulb, surrounded by a pink red glow or mist. Around the centre was a thin ring with several openings, about 10 cm diameter and 30 cm apart. This ring was shiny gold and extended below the edge of the sphere. Enid observed these details as the object crossed a field just to the east of the house, then toward the house, passing over a 1.2m high fence. It stopped, almost touching the ground, less than 1m from the house. In the lower right hand quarter of the sphere was a control panel in which two occupants could be seen. One was seated at the panel, the other was standing behind him. A sort of lever could be seen on top, but no other features could be distinguished in the yellow light of this control room. The beings could only be seen in silhouette, but they appeared to be of human shape and dressed in shiny, silvery "wet suits". After briefly hovering, the object took off for the Southeast. She called her sons, who were in time to see the object as a sphere, gaining altitude and moving away. As it hovered, two smaller, white, spheres approached from the north, and entered through an opening in the lower left quarter. The ring then gave off "fiery fountains" of a red coloured material which fell a short distance and disappeared. The object then ascended vertically and disappeared. The event lasted 30 minutes, The witnesses claimed that snow had melted where the object had hovered, and that a glass fruit jar was also partially melted. An area 200-300m long and 2m wide on the flight path became barren after the incident. Later the family saw strange lights and experienced poltergeist effects.

The following day on January 30th 1967 (Approx. date) in Jennings in St. Louis County, Missouri. Mrs Meyer of Emma Avenue saw an oval shaped wheel come out of the sky and come close to the street.

Around 7.00 am on 14th February 1967 Mr. Claude Edwards, 64, a farmer, saw a gray-green dome-shaped object about fifteen feet wide in his field. He at first thought that it was a parachute but as he neared it he could see that it was resting on a shaft about eighteen feet wide that extended downwards from its base. Around the edge of the dome were a number of bright multi-colored lights of oblong shape. Beneath the object were visible several entities less than a meter tall and gray-green in color. They were moving about rapidly with quick moving levers or arms, very wide-set eyes and no visible legs. There was a protuberance where the nose and mouth would be. Claude walked to within thirty feet of the object and threw two stones at it which seemed to bounce off an invisible wall. Walking up to fifteen feet he was able to feel the pressure of the invisible wall. The object was seamless and like gray-green silk. By this time the little creatures had gone back in to it. It rocked back and forth a few times and took off silently disappearing to the northeast within seconds. The creatures appeared like penguins, not humans, without a visible neck. The object looked like a big shell. Three months after the landing there were still ground traces at the site. The soil was extremely dehydrated compared to the ground around it. At the center there was a depression twenty millimeters deep sloping to thirty millimeters in the central area. This was in Tuscumbia in Miller County. Here is another version. A farmer was walking towards a large barn 100m east of his house when he noticed that one of his cows was looking into a field east of the barn. He then saw an object on the ground, 100m away, resting on a rise in the field. He walked to the northeast corner of the barn from where he could see that the object was not a parachute as he had first thought, but a shell or disc seen edgeways, about 4m diameter, 2m thick, sitting on a shaft 75cm high, 45cm diameter. The object was grey-green in colour, the texture of silk rather than metal. Along the bottom was a row of openings `5-20cm long, about 30cm apart, from which an extremely bright light, changing colours, was emitted. Underneath this object were several small things or beings moving about and moving their arms rapidly. They were the same colour as the object and appeared to have wide set eyes. The farmer left the bucket of feed he had been carrying and walked to a fence about 20m from the barn. At a distance of about 10m from the object he threw the first of two large rocks he had been carrying, but at a distance of 4.5m from the object, it just fell to the ground. A rock lobbed to hit from above seemed to bounce off something. He then walked on to this barrier, where a sort of pressure kept him back. The object now began to rock back and forth and then took off at high speed towards a ridge in the northeast, the shaft pulled up as it took off. The witness recalled that there were about 10-12 of the "robots", which were about 60cm tall, with a proboscis like protrusion from the top and with slim arms. No legs or feet were visible. No traces were found.

  Also on Feb.14th 1967 in Jefferson City in Cole County in Missouri at 7:00 a.m. a disc-shaped object was seen resting on a shaft in a field. Small beings were reportedly moving around rapidly beneath it. They disappeared behind the shaft, the object rocked back and forth, and then took off and sped away.

  On February 16th 1967 in the morning near St. Louis in St. Louis County in Missouri Raymond Wettling said a 180-foot, cigar-shaped UFO landed in a field beside Interstate Highway 70, and three silver-suited occupants of the craft invited him aboard for breakfast. "He spent a pleasant hour and 45 minutes chatting with the spacemen over coffee." His hosts showed him through the craft's two rooms—one lit up with bright red lights, the other decorated like a modern office. After he left the ship, he said, it took off straight up at a high rate of speed." No one else reported seeing it. As I always say. I report them. You make up your own minds on them.

  In early March 1967 at 2115hrs in California in Moniteau County, Missouri. While driving east on Hw 50, 5km east of California, as he was about to turn to the right on RtK, a motorist saw an unusual bright light approach from the North-East, crossing the railroad tracks at just above treetop height. As he drove along, the witness kept glancing at the object, which appeared trapezoid, with widows, which gave off a light like that of a mercury vapour lamp. The thing tapered somewhat towards the top. About 1.5 times above and to the right of the main structure was a red flashing light, near the front of the bottom was a green-blue light. The windows were between 0a half to two thirds of the way up the thing. When the witness rolled his window down no sound could be heard from the object. It followed the car along Rt K at 105kph, crossed the road, rose to clear electricity wires and then moved off towards the Lake of the Ozarks.

  In Brewer in Perry County in Missouri on 17th March 1967 several individual witnesses including Police Patrolman K. O. Walley saw a UFO land in a field. The craft had revolving red, white and green lights and Police Patrolman Walley took photographs of it. Four imprints were also found in the field at the landing site later. Why aren't there ever any trustworthy and reliable witnesses? You never hear of Police seeing these things! Sure Dude. Police are actually amongst the most common witnesses. Why did no one report the UFO leaving?

  On April 8th 1967 in the evening in St Louis, Missouri. 5km west of St Louis the manager of a local aerospace firm and 7 members of his family were having a back yard cook out when an object descended onto an open clay pit about 250m away. Another object stationed itself at treetop level and a third at about 600m altitude. In the remaining daylight the witnesses could see that the objects were metallic looking, disc shaped and about 15m diameter. They hovered for about 30 minutes, pulsating with a high intensity white light. The pulsation was separate for each object and they reflected off one another. Just after dark the objects rose vertically, one at a time, constantly increasing in acceleration until they were out of sight, a process which took only 2-3 seconds.

On April 17th 1967 back in Jefferson City in Cole County Missouri 9 p.m. a school principal and three teachers (Pistone, Wilson, Metz) in separate cars were driving home and saw a huge 300 foot WWI helmet-shaped object come over the cliff then over their cars bathing them in intense light. The object hovered over power lines for about 10 minutes then headed towards the airport. The principal drove over to airport and found two more witnesses who were attorneys. An Ozark Airliner crew saw two large round flat objects below the plane on final landing approach moving in various directions. Or this. A school principal was driving home from a PTA meeting, down a small county road, with some colleagues travelling with him in another car, when his attention was suddenly caught by a bright light over a cliff. He was afraid that an aircraft was going to crash land in a nearby cornfield, only for him to see that the thing was shaped like a World War One helmet, and perhaps 100m long. It hovered in front of his car for a moment, its intense white light seeming to come through the vehicle's roof and his hands, before changing direction and heading towards the airport. He went to join his companions in the other car and they all saw the object hover over power lines for about 10 minutes. They went to the airport, to find that the thing had overflown the facility and the pilot of an incoming plane saw the thing below him. It was also observed by two lawyers from Kansas City standing near the airport.

In April 1967 at Moberly in Randolph County in Missouri one evening a couple saw an object with a short cylindrical body, dome-shaped top, and flat bottom (turret shape). The top glowed blue-green, the sides white and the bottom red. The object had a semi-circle of white body lights that suddenly glowed and blinked around the upper rim. It performed various maneuvers, once apparently splitting in two and rejoining. Eventually it sped up and crossed the road in front of the car.

In May 1967 at 2330hrs in Cassville in Barry County, Missouri. A woman and a 16 year old girl were driving down Hw 76, when they observed a large greyish object sitting on the left lane of the highway. As they approached, the object was completely dark. It was egg shaped. About 5.5m long and 3=3.5m thick, straggling the whole left lane and covering 1m of the right lane and 1m of the shoulder. The girl became frightened and the driver pulled onto the right shoulder to pass the object. As they passed within 60cm of the thing, they saw a diffuse soft yellow circular light about 60 cm diameters shining through a sort of grill that extended down from the light to the lower edge. After passing the object, the witnesses looked back to see the end covering the highway was also illuminated by a yellow white glow. The woman later returned, with her husband, to the site, but no trace could be found. Several young men were found to have reported a similar object.

In Summer 1967 in Barnett in Morgan County, Missouri. Near Barnett a farmer observed a large disc as it landed near his home. The object was on the ground for several minutes and was bright. After it left, the witness and his grandson went to the landing site where there was a circular area of smashed plants.

One night in Summer 1967 in Eldon in Miller County, Missouri. Just south of Eldon Mrs Bailly was watching TV when she noticed a bright red glow through her living room window and went to investigate. She saw a discoid object, illuminated by a bright blue-white light,. approaching the field. The thing slowed, hovered for a moment at ground level and then landed. On landing, the upper section became dark and moonlight was reflected from from its metallic looking surface. After a short while, the object ascended at a shallow angle and disappeared in the distance. The next day Mr Baily and a relative went to the landing site, 45m from the back door and found eight oval areas where the vegetation was dry and dead. The marks were in pairs 90cm apart and 20cm diameter, The plants were damaged for some distance along the flight path of the object.

On July 10th 1967 at 1750hrs in Meridian in Lauderdale County, Mississippi. Philip Lanning was driving south of Meridian when his engine and lights failed. He got out to examine the car when his attention was caught by a large object passing overhead at 60-90m, making a sound like a strong wind. It was heading eastwards and appeared as though it would crash into some trees. Just before reaching them, the thing tilted upward and to the right and took off at terrific speed into the clouds. The object took like a dirty metallic grey cymbal, about the size of a house, with a blue top. It gave off no sound save the rushing wind.

On October 17th 1967 in Palmyra in Marion County, Missouri. Messes Weaver and Shane saw an unidentified object at low level.

In Winter 1967 at 2330hrs in Joplin in Jasper and Newton Counties, Missouri. Three teenage boys driving on the edge of town observed an object in front of their car. It drifted over a wooded area in which there was a narrow access road and the boys got out to investigate only to return when the object moved towards them. The boys then drove back to report the incident. They observed structural details, fins and lights.

1968

On February 9th 1968 at 0320hrs in Gower in Buchanan and Clinton Counties, Missouri. Mr R W B an executive of the Panhandle Eastern Pipe Line Company and part time farmer, was awakened by a disturbance among his cattle. Through his living room window he saw a glowing object about 90-100m away, around which cattle were grouped in a semi-circle. As his eyes accustomed to the dim light he saw the object was circular, 30m diameter, with concave sides, giving off a yellow-green glow. In the side of this object were 7 openings of indeterminate shape, 60-75cm diameter. The object was hovering 6-8m above the ground and was emitting a pulsating sound like that being made by a wire being swung around. The cattle were agitated and bawling and when one fled it developed into a minor stampede. After some minutes the object left rapidly to the south-west at a 45 degree angle. As it did so, the pulsating sound became two or three times louder and more rapid. The object had given off sufficient light to illuminate the area and allow Mr B to grope around the room. He had been suffering from thefts among the cattle and thought that the thing was a large helicopter used by the rustlers. He later suffered from hot and cold flushes and perspiration.

On June 14th 1968 at night in Rock Falls near St Louis, Missouri a strange object landed.

Above Rolla in Phelps County in Missouri on 29th June 1968 on an airliner flying from Kankakee, Illinois to Dallas, Texas, Mr. Jerrold I. Potter disappeared from the toilet during the flight. The plane had given a strange jolt over Rolla but no doors opened and if they were they could not have been closed again in flight. The jolt was like hitting an invisible obstacle. A miniature pinpoint in between Time and Space. Remember that we are dealing with multi-dimensions here so openings might not merely be sitting or moving over the Earth's surface but possibly even through it or over it.

On August 4th 1968 in 2225hrs in Webb City in Jasper County, Missouri. Two police officers west of Webb City saw a crescent shaped object, about 10-12m long, which gave off an orange-red light. They first thought it was the moon, but the thing then moved north, hovering over the airport and then disappearing. It then reappeared at about 15m altitude before apparently landing behind some trees north of the airport.

On August 20th 1968 at 2300hrs in Independence in Jackson County, Missouri. Robert Lingle (18) and Ricky Phillips (16) were driving on Hw 7 when they observed a brilliant object, with white flashing lights, come out of the trees to the east.

The following day on August 21st 1968 at night and also in Independence, Missouri. While travelling west on Missouri 7, near Ransome Road, Robert Lingle and Ricky Phillips (qv) again encountered a strange object The thing was round, surrounded by yellow flashing lights and was about 12m diameter. It followed their car to Holker Road where it disappeared suddenly.

In Autumn 1968 in the evening in Benton in Scott County, Missouri. Laura J was driving home to Benton frim Ilmo, following her husband, who was driving their pickup truck when she was astonished to see what looked the lights of a dusting plane flying very low over the field to their left. She slowed down as she realised the object was going to cross the road and almost certainly collide with the telephone. However there was no collision and, intrigued, she stopped and tried to attract her husband's attention with her car horn, but without success. Turning off her engine, she saw an oval object, ringed by blinking red lights, moving and soundlessly across the field until, it came to a halt above a grove of trees 400m away. She watched the thing hovering, its light blinking, for several minutes and then noticed that the night seemed unusually quiet. She then drove on to get to her husband, who returned with her to the area, where they watched the object for about two hours until it rose slightly and blinked out.

On November 7th 1968 at 1945hrs in Fair Grove in Greene County, Missouri two people saw an unidentified object at close quarters.

1969

One night in early January 1969 in Edina in Knox County in Missouri Mrs. Adeline Davis had been asleep when she suddenly found herself sitting up in bed looking out of the window. Outside, about six feet away, she saw a curious object shaped like two deep bowls put together rim to rim but separated in the connecting mid-section by a band of windows. The object was resting on three legs and its color was dark olive green. The window directly facing her was lit up and she saw an occupant inside it. The occupant was apparently working on something below the level of the window. Mrs. Davis pinched her arm to be sure that she was not dreaming and went to bathe her face in water. The figure looked up and apparently seeing the witness showed surprise then reached up for something and the object then began backing away slowly from the house just above the ground. From its bottom projected a bent white beam of light. The object then moved out of Mrs. Davis' view around the corner of the house. In the morning all of the electric clocks in the house were twenty minutes slow yet her neighbors had no power failures in theirs. Here is another version. Mrs Adeline Davis, who was tending her sick daughter and sleeping only fitfully, suddenly awoke and sat up looking out of the widow, though she could hear no sound, and saw an unusual looking object in which there was an occupant. He was wearing dark clothing with a cap like an army fatigue cap, a dark jacket with an opening down the front and a small upright collar with scalloped edges, and a scarf. He had slanted, wide spaced, eyes with fuzzy indefinite pupils. She tried several tests to check if she was awake, including going to bathe her face. When she returned the object and its occupant were still there, about 2m from her window, which was 2m above the ground. The being seemed to be working on something below the window, but then looked up. Apparently seeing the witness, he looked surprised and his mouth dropped open. He looked at her for a brief while then carried on with his work. After a while he looked up again and seemed to try and reach for something first with one hand then the other. He then looked at Adeline again and as he did so the craft seemed to back away from the house. As it did so Adeline could see a white beam coming from its base, projecting downwards, illuminating a small cedar tree at one point. After the object had retreated about 3-3.5m, it stopped, the white light went out and the object turned slightly to the northeast. She now had a clear picture of the object, which was army green in colour with a row of blue tinted windows on the side which had originally faced her, but with a shield, the same colour as the object itself, blocking the windows on the other side. From the top edge of the window framing a dark vertical mark was visible. Adeline again went to bathe her face, and when she returned she saw that the leg on the far side of the object was about 1m above the ground, that on the near side 1.5m. The object moved slowly to the north east at very low altitude disappearing behind the corner of the house. She now noticed that the electric furnace fan had stopped, though it re-started a couple of minutes later. The next morning she found the electric clocks were 20 minutes slow. At the time she had the impression that the occupant was friendly and would not hurt her, next day, though, she felt unusually nervous.

On January 14th 1969 at night in Springfield in Greene County, Missouri. A disc shaped object was seen near the ground by police officers.

In January 1969 at night in Canton in Lewis County, Missouri. Two witnesses saw an unidentified object near the ground.

On February 11th 1969 at night back in Springfield, Missouri a disc was seen near the ground.

In February 1969 at 2130hrs in Lutesville near Marble Hill in Bollinger County, Missouri. F X Peters, Gus Eftick and their families heard the Peters' dog beginning to bark, though they could see no reason. A short time later a huge elongated object with a white light on top and red and green lights on the ends dropped down into a field 200m away. Shortly afterwards the thing took off again, straight up, Marks as of a tripod landing gear in the form of three burnt patches, 6m apart, were found at the site.

At 6.40 am on 4th March 1969 in Elmer in Macon County a rural postal carrier was rounding a curve in his truck when he saw a large reddish object about half a mile to his right. It was travelling fifty feet above the ground. It was one hundred feet in diameter and hesitated for a moment before heading straight for his vehicle eventually taking up position in the air over the road and traveling slowly in the same direction as the truck. As he closed the distance a strong white light came from the bottom of the disc and shown on the road. The beam was the full diameter of the object at the top but narrowed to an eight foot diameter spotlight on the road. The beam was extremely hot and affected the driver. Also when the beam shot down the whole object changed colors and became bright blue with a red aura about it. There was also a yellow band around it which gave the impression of small racing lights as if the thing were turning. The extreme brightness made it difficult to see details. His radio was breaking up. When he got right to the edge of the beam the radio gave up completely and the truck's motor died. The truck then rolled slowly forwards as the object moved a small bit further along. Once away from the beam everything started again. The object gradually moved away flashing mightily as it passed over a power line. It had changed back to red and cruised along in synchronization with the contours of the ground and went out of sight. Or this version. Bill Overstreet (50) a route mail carrier and city marshall from Elmer Missouri was driving from there to Atlanta, when on route J 6.5km from Atlanta he noticed a bright light in the south, which seemed to be a northerly course, as he continued west. :However, as he came over the crest of a hill he encountered a reddish sphere about 30m in diameter, extending 3m on either side of the road, about 15-18m above the ground, giving off a light so brilliant that he pulled down his sun visor and shielded his face with his hands. As Bill approached it, the centre changed colour to a blue colour that wavered, and he noticed that the object was surrounded by a yellowish border rotating in a clockwise direction. He heard no noise as it moved along at 65kph, so he decided to drive under it. As he did so a beam of light, as wide as the object but narrowing to 2.5m diameter at the road, shot down in front of him. When the beam hit the road it was so brilliant it seemed to magnify the road features. :This beam was blue-white and gave off an intense heat, and when the front of his truck hit the beam, the vehicles lights and CB radio both failed, only to restart as the object. He attempted to follow it, but his engine kept missing when he got within 2m of the beam and stopped altogether when he came in contact with it. at this he stopped giving chase and watch the object continue at its modest pace and low altitude as veered north around the tower at Highway 53, and then south-east and out of sight towards Macon. It seemed to follow the curve of the land. He observed it for about 7 or 8 minutes.

On 6th March 1969 a light beam shone down onto the road ahead of a car. The dog reacted to it and as the witness drove under the beam of light the car motion slowed on its own. The witness later developed an eye irritation from the light. This was in Lancaster in Schuyler County in Missouri. Lancaster is only thirty nine miles North of Elmer where the same thing happened on 4th March just passed two days before. Or this? At 11.00 pm a woman was driving home when her St Bernard dog became agitated and then hid under the dashboard, whimpering At this point she saw a beam of light on the road ahead, which she then saw came from a silver disc hovering 300m above the road. The thing appeared to be metallic with a domed section on top. No other details were visible. The brilliant blue white beam came from an opening in the bottom of the object. The road beyond the beam appeared distorted as if by a heat haze. Her car was travelling at over 80kph, and as it passed through the beam, it slowed to about 15kph, even though the witness pushed her foot hard on the accelerator. After passing through the beam, the car picked up speed and began to run smoothly again. The witness felt no heat and heard no sound. Her eyes were irritated for three days following the incident.

The following night on March 7th 1969 (or following day) at 2330hrs back in Elmer, Missouri. Mrs Taylor was on her way home from work, travelling south on Hw3 when she saw a bright red object, about the size of a car, resting on the highway about 400m ahead. As she approached the object took off to the north-east, slow at first and then very fast.

On March 22nd 1969 at 0100hrs in Sedalia in Puttis County, Missouri. A woman and her daughter were watching TV when their attention was caught by a light outside their window. They went to watch and saw a bright white light moving towards their house from the north-west at treetop level. The thing made no sound nor did its brightness or colour show any alteration. At its nearest point it appeared as a sphere with bright lights underneath. As a car crested a hill nearby, the lights suddenly went off and the object was not seen again.

In Saint Louis County in Missouri in October 1969 there was a fall of material like spiderwebs that just floated down out of the sky and dissolved on touch. This material was analysed and found to be not of biological origin. It has actually become quite ordinary. UFO reports refer to this as Angelhair.

In 1969 or the following year at 2350hrs in Diehlstadt in Scott County, Missouri. High school senior Ronnie Burton was driving home to Diehlstadt on Hw 77 when he spotted, just beyond the next rise ,a large dark shape hanging above the road, covering all the lanes and part of the shoulder. He thought it might have been a van which had overturned and so slowed down and brightened his lights. He then saw that it was an object shaped like two soup plates rim to rim. He decided to reverse rather than risk squeezing past it. As he did so bright lights like magnesium flashes came from the top and bottom of this object, and seemed to spread over it, until the light was too intense for Ronnie to look at. :The thing rose silently to the height of a telephone pole, tilted and then disappeared. Ronnie' car motor was still running but at some point his radio had gone off. He drove home and woke his father. They both returned to the spot to see that the grass on road shoulder had been depressed as if by a heavy object. An elderly lady who lived nearby volunteered that she had not only seen this object on this occasion, but seen similar several times before.

In 1969 in Sedalia in Puttis County, Missouri a landed object burnt a 10m diameter ring.

On September 26th 1969 at 2230hrs in Boonville in Cooper County, Missouri. A married couple returning to Marshall from Columbia had just passed the last Boonville exit on Interstate 70 when their attention was caught by a fairly bright red light 5 degrees above the horizon. This they first thought was a tower light but then realised that it was moving towards them and was not sort of familiar aircraft. They pulled up as the object passed and saw that it was a cigar shaped thing with a blunt nose, which glowed bright red and as it passed soundlessly overhead, a bright light was visible in the rear section. This appeared to be a sort of exhaust trailing sparks and was contained within the object, the main body of which was not visible against the dark sky, but they estimated it must have been four times the apparent diameter of the moon. The glow from the rear was still visible when they left the area three minutes later.

On October 17th 1969 at 1300hrs in Palmyra in Marion County, Missouri. Wayne Beever and Mrs Schanz independently observed a bright silvery object reflecting the sunlight. The thing wobbled and moved slowly very close to the ground. It had gone by the time investigators arrived.

On October 18th 1969 at 2200hrs in Stover in Morgan County, Missouri. Drive in restaurant owner Victor Smith, his wife and a farmer-customer saw a round or spherical object about 1m diameter, with green, red and blue lights, moving in a straight line about 2m above the ground from the Reed-Blackman House, across Highway 52-135 to the ally edging their lot. It then moved rapidly west in a straight line and then suddenly disappeared, like light going out, just before it hit a tree. It was lightly raining at the time and a thunder shower followed.

The following day on October 19th 1969 at 0600hrs in Clark National Forest in Missouri. A glowing sphere was observed by three people to take off and join a similar object at low altitude. The objects moved from side to side.

On November 11th 1969 at 2300hrs in University City in St Louis, Missouri. Joseph Miller and Barbara Knehans (both 19) were driving down Price Road when they saw a star like point of light nigh in the sky. This descended to about 3m above their car and followed them along the road. It was about 10m long, bright white in colour with red and pink lights. :Both the witnesses became afraid and Barbara became hysterical. As they turned into Delmar Boulevard the thing took off in a westerly direction without a sound.

On November 16th 1969 at 2030hrs in West Ridge in Platte County, Missouri. James and Iva Hill and another person observed for 8 minutes a disc shaped object 15-20m diameter, with a dome, at treetop height, to the southwest. It came within 800m of them in an undulating motion. The object was red and green in colour with many gold lights. Through the transparent dome they could see several men of normal height looking down to the ground.

On December 12th 1969 at night in St. Louis, Missouri. Several people observed an object like an aircraft without either lights nor markings fly very low under the Gateway Arch. This was repeated on the night of the 17th.

1970

In Festus in Saint Louis County in Missouri on 26th May 1970 a small red-hot cylindrical object fell from the sky. Mrs. Elida Kent heard an explosion and saw a red-hot cylindrical object about two inches long lying in the grass outside her house. The article remained smoking hot for five minutes and then became heavily charred. She neither saw nor heard aircraft at the time. The object had a lead-like interior and was turned over to the Saint Louis Planetarium and never seen again. Keeping it safe is not the word.

On May 15th 1970 at 1030hrs in St Louis, Missouri. Four strange small people, a man, woman and two children booked into suburban motel. The people were so short they barely reached the desk, were expensively dressed but seemed to have problems with basic communication. Their mouths were very small and their eyes were large, dark and slanted. They seemed to eat by sucking in small morsels of food. They reacted against the lights in their room. They were not there the next day, though they were not seen leaving through the only entrance.

On July 25th 1970 at 2100hrs in Sedalia in Puttis County, Missouri. On his farm about 16km south of Sedalia and 5.5km west of RtU, Stanley Dillon heard his dogs barking and went outside to investigate In the distance he saw a blue-green light, near a ridge, about 800m to the east. The thing appeared to be stationary in the general area of a pond. After about a minute the light began to move towards the farm and was last seen beyond a low tree line, some 70m from the house. At 0100 the next morning all the dogs on the farm began barking again and Stanley and his sister Christene (21) went outside and again saw the blue-green light at the top of a 7.5m tall tree, some 70m northwest of the house. They called their mother, another sister, Mary (23) to watch. As they all did so the light went out, only to reappear at the base of the tree, a couple of seconds later. It then went out again, reappearing at the base of another tree 18m away. This light blinked and reappeared almost instantly at the top of the tree. It moved by similar progression back to the first and then again back to the second tree. It then moved away to the east and disappeared in the distance over a ridge. It was observed for several minutes during which tine one of the dogs growled and the ducks seemed disturbed. The witnesses described the light as a blue-green glow, about the size of a baseball at arm's length. It did not light up the surroundings and was silent. It was in an area of rough ground and its flight path was traversed by a fence.

On August 17th 1970 at 2000hrs in Columbia in Boone County, Missouri. Mrs Alice M Thompson was sat in her trailer on Wagon Trail Road, 11km north of Columbia, with W B Cook of Fennel Street, when they heard her colt acting up. Alice heard a sort of hollow popping sound and went to her back door to investigate. As Alice opened the door she saw an intense light shining through a nearby tree and illuminating the inside of her trailer. A moment later, a large fiery sphere, 10-20 times as bright as the moon, moved from behind the tree. Something like a long piece of rope hung from the object, with another small object on its end. The thing seemed to be at the altitude of a small plane, 200m away. Alice then called Cook and they both saw the thing move north at a moderate speed and then suddenly disappear. Several other people saw strange lights in the woods by the trailer area, among them Sidney Hughes (17); Mr and Mrs Robert Davis; Mrs Maria Moreau and Kurt Krehbiel (17).

On October 6th 1970 at 0430hrs in Rolla in Phelps County, Missouri. While driving on US63, 19km north of Rolla, Garth and Leuela Morris, along with Claude Willie and his wife, returning from Fort Leonard Wood, saw a phosphorescent object, like a huge moon, in the eastern sky. The thing descended at about 10mps, until it was at an altitude of 15m above 1.2km away. The underside of the object had a serrated surface and appeared to be dripping liquid of some sort. Moments later the thing took off at very high speed at a 70 degree angle, leaving a glow like a vapour trail.

In Cassville in Barry County in Missouri during October 1970 there was a spectacular aerial flashing and booming display which attracted general public notice one evening. A silver disc was visible over the town before orange colored flashes occurred. Calls to Police came as from as far away as Fayetteville in Arkansas.

On November 3rd 1970 at night in Missouri. At an undisclosed location, the teenage son of a farm family who did not want their name or location to be revealed, but in a rural area several kilometres from the nearest town, called his mother to look at a set of red, green and yellow lights flashing on and off just above the treetops. When two or three of these would go on, the others would go off. These lights seemed to be arranged in an oval pattern. The mother and son then saw a large white light, which came closer, further to the left of the blinking lights. They thought it might have been an aeroplane but they heard no sound and the thing suddenly disappeared. After a moment or two, the coloured oval, which was about 8km east of their home, also went out. Thirty minutes later they were indoors watching TV when the lights went out for a minute and then came back on again. This was repeated several times. When the mother contacted the power line man, he reported that there had been several complaints. There had been several power failures in the area in the previous few days.

1971

On February 18th 1971 at 0950 at St. Charles in St Charles County in Missouri. Dr. J. W. Mueller, D.C. Martin Thoele and Theodore Thoele observed a cone-shaped, "cage-like" object 10 feet wide by 10 feet high, tipped at an angle, approximately 400 feet above the street. The object was noiseless, and a string of lights extended down on what would correspond to three wires of the "cage" to a point mid-way between the tip of the cone and its base. The object was occupied by a single figure.

In Summer 1971 at night in St Clair in Franklin County, Missouri. Marjorie Armistead was resting in a lawn chair when she looked up towards the oak trees in her yard and saw hovering above them a large, dull grey, round object, surmounted by two small inverted cupolas. The thing moved away slowly overhead and as it did so she called out to those in the house to get her parents and friends, upon which the object vanished.

On July 27th 1971 at night in Vicksburg in Warren County, Mississipi. A young woman, Cindy Bartlett, driving home from lifeguard duty, became suddenly aware of flashing lights around her car while on Roseland Drive. Thinking it was another car she stopped but could see no other vehicle. Then she looked up and saw, just above the treetops, an oval object with pointed ends, flashing red and blue lights, with a white light in front, which seemed to be scanning the field as if the thing was preparing to land. She heard a beeping sound.

In late December 1971 at 0200 in the Brushy Creek area in Carter and Wayne Counties in Missouri. Reggie Bone and his wife, and two, other couples were driving down a deserted road early in the morning around Christmas Time when they saw a figure walking up the road toward them in a "frogman's" outfit, complete with flippers (or something similar!) and carrying something in his hands. They could not see his facial features, and the wetsuit covered his body and did not appear wet. The nearest body of water was Black River, about a quarter-mile away and not easily accessible to that part of the road. Temperatures were below freezing and the witnesses were so taken, aback by that none of them said anything for several miles; then one said "did you see that?"

1972

In Troy in Lincoln County in Missouri on 30th June 1972 a Hairy Humanoid with a hair covered face and no neck was seen. It left three toed footprints and was not a bear.

On or around 30th June 1972 in the Cuivre River near Cuivre State Park in Missouri two fishermen reported seeing a Bigfoot wading in the river and walking along the riverbank towards them. This was near Troy in Lincoln County.

Back in Louisiana in Pike County on 11th July 1972 there were several individual witnesses of "Momo". From July 11th there were sightings of a creature nicknamed "Momo" which was short for Missouri Monster. There were also red and green fireballs seen in the sky. "Momo" was a Hairy Humanoid with blazing red eyes and a smell like burning rubber or the sweat of a hundred High School football teams as one witness described it. "Momo" was six to seven feet tall with no neck and usually carrying a dead dog. "Momo" made strange screaming noises at night and many huge three toed footprints were found. These were no bear tracks. "Momo" was always black.

Still in Louisiana. Missouri, on 11th July 1972 at 3.30 pm Doris Harrison, fifteen, and two other Harrison children, Terry Harrison and Wally Harrison saw Momo. After Terry and Wally went to tend rabbits at the foot of Marzolf Hill Doris heard a scream. She looked out of the bathroom window and saw a Hairy Humanoid by a tree. Doris and Terry described it as six to seven feet tall and black and hairy. It stood like a man but did not look like one. The children started crying and ran to their mother. The creature had no neck and was carrying a dead dog flecked with blood under its arm. Harrison's own dog vomited for three hours afterwards and its eyes grew red. Terrible odors emanated from the previous sighting area and Mr. Edgar Harrison heard eerie howls as he and investigators prowled the site.

And Louisiana continued. On 14th July 1972 at 9.15 pm Edgar Harrison, the father of the Harrison children, who was the deacon of the local Pentecostal Church, forty-five minutes after the regular Friday evening Prayer meeting at his house, heard ringing noises such as could be caused by stones being thrown against the huge water reservoir on top of Marzolf Hill. After one loud ring he heard a loud growl that got louder and louder and closer and closer. At the same time his family came running from the house urging him to drive off. Edgar wanted to stay and find out what was causing the noise. Eventually he drove off down Allen Street across the Town Branch and stopped the car. His wife and family told the congregation "Here it comes" and the forty people turned and ran down the street. Police Officers Jerry Floyd and John Whitaker searched the Harrison residence and found nothing. Later that evening Edgar Harrison and several others explored Marzolf Hill and discovered a pungent, unpleasant odor emanating like rotting garbage from an old building.

The following day in Louisiana, Missouri, on 15th July 1972 at 5.00 am Pat Howard saw a dark object walking like a man cross the road near Marzolf Hill.

Also on July 15th 1972 near Louisiana in Pike County in Missouri. It was a moonlit night just about dusk a friend and I had gone to a party but it was a bust. When we got to the place out of town. I took off by myself down the road towards the East back to Route 70 to wait. I had been walking for about 25-30 minutes when the wind shifted from the South. I smelled something awful like a cross between a skunk and rotten flesh, like something died. As I was walking along the South side of the road I noticed someone walking about 300-400 feet away along the edge of the woods on the South side of a pasture. I thought it was kind of late for a farmer to be bringing his cows in as they were in a big hurry to get away from him. About that time I heard a God Awful blood curdling scream which I thought was the cattle screaming. I stopped to look across at the farmer and he also stopped and stood still looking at me, which I considered odd. As I continued East I watched as he matched my every move and would stop and stare when I did. The cows were gone by now and the stench was getting stronger as what I thought was a man angled his way closer to me. I stopped and stared right at the thing (at that point I knew it was not a man as it was only walking and I was almost running) It was coming straight for me. It stood close to eleven foot tall and was covered with thick matted reddish brown hair. I took off running as fast as I could for the next light down the road. It was a long way off, and as I looked over my shoulder it stepped over a four foot high barbed wire fence without touching the wire. I knew I was in trouble. I ran for the far away farm house as fast as I could go. My adrenalin going and was scared out of my wits. As I approached the fence to get to the house towards the south, I realized that not only was the house much farther than I thought, but I was met by a pack of farm dogs at the gate. As I jumped the gate (I don't even think my feet touched the gate) into the pack of dogs I didn't dare look back. I ran to the home of a farmer and pounded on the door but the farmer would not open the door. I looked at the farmer and I could tell he had seen the creature by the terrified and confused look on his face. I was so scared that I sat down on the porch in a ball and waited for the creature to leave. When I looked up the creature was headed towards the same pasture it had come from with the dogs chasing after it. That was the last I saw of it. I ran and hid behind a tree until my friend joined me. I did not tell my friend what had happened. I have raised three daughters now and for years I told the story of the monster while we were camping. About three years ago I was messing around on the web and came across a Bigfoot website. I decided to check in the area and found multiple sightings of the monster at the exact time and place of my mishap. It was a black top rural road with pPasture to South and hilly woods to the North.

Still in Louisiana on 20th July 1972 at 9.15 pm after an unsuccessful search for "Momo" on the 19th Edgar Harrison, Richard Crowe, a reporter, and Loren Smith went up Marzolf Hill. Near the tree where Doris had seen "Momo" was a circular spot where leaves and twigs had been stripped from branches and further along someone or something had been digging in an old garbage dump. Nearby were two disinterred dog graves with the bones scattered about. Tracks were found higher up the hill that were over ten inches long by five inches wide as well as a possible handprint five inches long. The prints were in hard soil and would take considerable weight to make them. At the abandoned building Harrison's dog ran away and the overpowering stench like stagnant water or rotten flesh assaulted them again. In the distance dogs were barking furiously. No "Momo" was seen but certainly smelt.

At New Haven in Franklin County in Missouri also on 20th July 1972 the daughter of Leonard Strubberg saw a Hairy Humanoid. She was driving in the early morning and saw a huge silver gray Bigfoot walking in a field.

Back in Louisiana in Pike County on the following day 21st July 1972 at 10.00 pm to 10.30 pm Ellis Minor who lived on River Road heard his dogs bark. Thinking it was another dog he flashed a light out in his yard and then stopped outside to observe a six foot tall creature with long black hair standing erect in his yard which then dashed past the railroad tracks and into the woods.

Also on July 21st 1972 at night still in Louisiana, Missouri. Two families living in a rural area between Bowling Green and Luisiana observed a circle of lights at or close to ground level for about 5 minutes. A young pregnant woman at Bowling Green saw two luminous spherical objects land in a nearby cow pasture She later smelt a nauseating odour and heard some animal screaming.

Also on 21st July 1972 a number of witnesses on Marzolf Hill saw an object that was stationary and blinking on and off. It appeared to have square looking windows about two feet in diameter from which a yellowish slight was visible. What is this to do with a Bigfoot?

As well on 21st July 1972 several witnesses had heard "Momo" scream from a hill shortly before two lighted objects were seen falling from the sky. They glowed and apparently went across the tops of trees. This was also in Louisiana in Missouri.

In O'Fallon in Saint Charles County, Missouri on 24th July 1972 two teenage girls saw a Hairy Humanoid walking at the edge of a wooded area near sundown.

On July 30th 1972 at 2100hrs in Louisiana, Missouri. Mrs Lois Shade saw an orange glowing object, with illuminated windows, which landed in the thicket on the top of a bluff and remained for 5 hours until it took off vertically and disappeared.

Back in Louisiana in late July 1972 mysterious three-toed tracks made by something with an oval foot appeared on the Freddie Robbins farm eight miles South of town.

And Louisiana continued. On 3rd August 1972 just before dawn broke Mr. and Mrs. Bill Suddarth on their farm northwest of the town heard a high-pitched howl in the yard, grabbed their flashlights and headed outside. In the middle of the yard they found four tracks of a three-toed creature. Mr. Suddarth quickly rang Clyd Penrod, a hunting buddy, who drove over to make a plaster cast of the prints which began and then ended twenty-five feet from anywhere, beginning and then ending nowhere. The prints were narrow, long and perfectly formed and clearly showed three toes.

On August 12th 1972 at 0100hrs st in Louisiana, Missouri. Edgar Harrison, his wife and children,. Ernie Shade and his wife and two doctors were among a number of people who saw an object on the hill. The thing was pulsating. Some witnesses saw square windows, 60cm across, on it emitting a yellow-orange light. Some saw red lights shoot from the thing.

On September 4th 1972 at 2130hrs in Canton in Lewis County, Missouri. Two little boys, Jeff V (7) and Bobby C (a 7th grader were playing outside when they heard a woman scream and saw an object the size of a house, with white, blue, green and red lights (one each), circling the field as if it was about to land. It then backed away. Neither boy saw any detail on the object and Bobby thought it was just an orange light. Jeff called his father Charles, who in turn alerted their neighbours, Mr and Mrs Hunold. The three adults saw the object move away to the northwest. Several people in the north part of Canton also saw the object.

On September 10th 1972 at 2110hrs still in Canton, Missouri. Melanie J (10) went to the back door on her way to go for some ice-cream with her mother, when she saw an object with flickering lights at treetop height above their home, looking as if it was about to land . The flashing red, white and blue lights were on the top part of the object, which had a round bottom. Trees obscured a better view. Melanie called her mother and they both went to alert her father. John, who was at the water front. From there the three saw flickering lights moving away. Several other people saw the object. At about this time a power blackout occurred in the south side of Quincy.

On September 14th 1972 at 2000 in Houston in Texas County, Missouri. Mr and Mrs S were watching their portable TV when the picture began to pulsate and roll. This stopped after about 1 minute. The couple went outside and saw a bright light in the south, 30 degrees above the horizon. Through binoculars this appeared to be a round shape with a flattened bottom. It had a blue white light and moved back and forth 6 or7 times before disappearing behind trees to the west. At 0300 the next morning the couple were awakened by the barking and howling of their three large guard and hunting dogs. Mr S took one of the dogs to go and investigate, but the normally courageous animal was reluctant to move. As S searched the area with a flashlight, there was a sudden bright flash of light on or near the ground, which sufficiently unnerved to abandon the search until the morning. That morning he noticed that an evergreen tree at the site, 90m from the house, had been discoloured on one side. Beyond this side an oval area of depressed grass, about 6m by 4,3m in the centre of which were three small imprints, each showing an extension or toe. These imprints were 60mm long and one was 40mm deep. A blackened area came was found in the centre of these imprints formed a triangle. These features were still visible when the case was investigated in November despite several cm of rain and snow.

In 1972 in Bates County, Missouri two young children saw an object hover near the ground and project a beam of light to the earth near their farm.

In 1972 in Brunswick in Charlton County, Missouri. Several people saw an object on the ground. Burnt ground and trees were found at the site.

1973

At Clearwater Reservoir in Reynolds County near Piedmont in Missouri on 21st February 1973 Reggie Bone, the coach, and five members of a basketball team were returning from a tournament in Essex one evening when a UFO swooped their car on Route 49. The luminous object illuminated the highway in front of it. The craft was first seen as a bright shaft of light in the sky near Elsinore and was next seen hovering near the intersection of Route 21 and Highway 34. The craft was hovering fifty feet up and only two hundred yards away. On the craft were four flashing lights that were red, bluish-green, amber and white and possibly coming from portholes. The sighting lasted five to ten minutes during which there was no sound from the craft which had followed the car for several miles. Or this version. At 8.30 pm Clearwater High School basketball coach, Reg Bone and 5 boys were driving along US 90 near Elsinore, returning from a basketball tournament, when they saw a shaft of light beaming down from the sky. As they pulled onto Rte 49, near Bushy Creek, one of the boys called the others attention to an unusual object and Reg stopped the car. The object appeared to be 15m above the ground, about 20m away, with four lights, red, green, amber and white, though no definite size or shape could be made out in the darkness. After 5-10 minutes the thing took off silently and disappeared over a hill.

The following day on February 22nd 1973 at 1630hrs in Piedmont in Wayne County, Missouri. Near here two people saw a very low flying oval object.

Also in Clearwater Reservoir during February 1973 strange shadowy forms were seen glowing underwater in the Clearwater Reservoir. These were the only two phenomenal sightings reported from this area and both from the same month.

On March 14th 1973 at night in Brushy Creek in Ste, Genevieve County, Missouri. Earl Turnbaught saw a cone shaped object hovering about 12m above a field near Brushy Creek. From the thing's top a rod was projecting, The object was dark and was only visible when illuminated by lightning flashes.

The following day on March 15th 1973 at 2100hrs back in Piedmont, Missouri. Wesley Howard, his wife and daughter, along with another person saw an amber coloured object, emitting rays, over the treetops from Hw 34. The thing suddenly disappeared.

On March 19th 1973 still in Piedmont, Missouri. Explorer Scouts Tom M (14) and Kevin K (160 were in a party camping on top of Bluff View when they saw a luminous circular object skim across the lake and disappear.

Also on March 21st 1973 at 2100hrs in Clearwater Lake in Reynolds and Wayne Counties, Missouri. Jean Coleman and Cathy Leach were driving across the dam when a disc shaped object with a reddish glow surfaced from the lake, rose silently and soared over a mountain top.

On March 21st 1973 (Approximate Date) at pre-dawn in Piedmont, Missouri. Five fishermen returned home rapidly after seeing several disc shaped objects hovering above the lake.

The next day on March 22nd 1973 (Approximate Date) in the evening still in Piedmont, Missouri. A family living in the outskirts of Piedmont were watching television when their house began to vibrate and the TV developed inference and died. Outside a brilliant light hovered at 25m altitude. It then moved and disappeared.

On April 3rd 1973 at 1130hrs in Ellsinore in Carter County, Missouri. On Rte 60, 6.5km west of Ellsinor, Mrs Raymond Stucker observed a triple teared object with a tripod landing gear at very low altitude over a wooded area across the road. It was circular, with a central band and surmounted by a dome with portholes. Later a triangle of three holes, 15cm deep, 60-90cm diameter was found at the site. Trees were found split and bark stripped off, and it appeared that ground vegetation was burned.

Later on April 6th 1973 in Ellsinore in Carter County in Missouri At 11:30 a.m. a domed disc-shaped object with portholes and landing gear came down and landed in the woods four miles West of town. At the landing site were found three holes in the ground arranged in a triangle pattern, and some damaged foliage.

Also on April 6th 1973 at 2000hrs in Charleston in Mississippi County, Missouri. Mrs Dorothy Thompson watched an egg shaped object at tree height for about 3 minutes. It had a red top, white bottom, did not flash and was silent, TV interference was noticed at the time.

On May 2nd 1973 in St Charles in St Charles County, Missouri. William Wright saw a yellow light moving back and forth near trees. Lava like material was found. Shades of Maury Island in 1947?

On May 25th 1973 at 1205hrs back in Piedmont, Missouri, Mrs Margorie Cundiff, manager of the Piedmont County Golf Club, was driving across the dam on this misty afternoon, looking at the water level, to see the effect of the recent rain, when she suddenly noticed a fast wake and waves as if someone was water skiing. Then a flat, square topped object came out of the water and made a sharp turn.

On June 28th 1973 in Columbia in Boone County in Missouri. The two major witnesses in this event are James Richards, 41, an animal care technician at the University of Missouri, and his daughter, Vanea, 16. After midnight, Vanea heard a loud, persistent thrashing sound outside their house trailer, and called her father. Richards moved to the window and saw two light beams about 5 feet apart from each other and 50 feet away from his window. The beams disappeared, and a glowing bright oval form appeared, lighting up the area. The thrashing sound was apparently trees moving as if blown by wind (wind was only 5 knots), and after the oval form appeared, this sound suddenly ceased. The night was clear and calm. As Richards moved from window to window, he noticed his dogs lying very still near the corner of the trailer that was nearest to the oval object. The dogs were large security animals, who would normally bark at various night animals and who were not easily frightened. Richard though it strange they were not barking at all the noise and the bright lights. The initial two light beams were tapered, about 4 feet wide at the top and about 2 feet wide at the bottom where they touched the ground, and the upper inner edges were about 5 feet apart. They were very bright and silver-white in color. The bright beams faded out rapidly, and a bright oval form appeared just above the location of the two beams. The oval was estimated to be 12-15 feet in diameter and near the ground. It was extremely bright, silver-white in color, the edges were fuzzy, and no surface details were visible. It was very bright at the center and a duller white at the edges. The trees on both sides of the oval were clearly visible, including trees as far away as 100 feet. The only sounds were the thrashing sounds of the vegetation as if being blown by strong wind, but one tree showed a different motion as it something were pulling that tree toward the ground. As indicated above, soon after the oval became visible, the sounds ceased, but the one tree continued to show an earthward tugging motion until a loud cracking sound was heard, and the tugging motion stopped (a branch broken off at 17 feet was found the next day). It was at this point that Richards made the observation of his dogs. The object moved away to 200 feet from the window and hovered, and now, with it less bright to the eye, the witnesses could see a blue band of light and an orange glow extending around the outer edge of the oval. At this point, possible EM effects (house lights dimmed, telephone line problems) were reported. The object's movement was smooth and slow and no sound was heard. The oval moved back near its original position and disappeared by growing smaller (glow faded). It did not seem to be moving away as it would have run into trees. Possible physical traces included marks on the broken limb, imprints into the ground, and leaves dying. Upon a later visit by investigator Phillips, leaves were dead and limbs were barren over the area. Or this version. At 12.30 am James G Richards (41), an animal care technician, his wife Shirley, daughter Vanea (16) and son Jamie (3) were in their mobile home in a wooded area at the end of a lane 800m out of Columbia. Vanea was putting a baby bottle in the fridge when she heard a loud thrashing noise coming through the open window above the sound of the record player in the next room. The outside noise appeared to be moving around a large tree and so frightened her that she called to her father. As James went to the window, Vanea closed all the doors. Looking out James saw two beams of light between the fence and the trees and about 15m from the window. They were 1.2m wide at the top, tapering to 60cm at the bottom, were bright, silvery white in colour and about 1.5m apart. Nothing solid could be seen behind them. These beams suddenly faded out and James and Vanea now saw a bright oval 3.5-4.5m diameter at ground level. It gave off a brilliant silvery light and its edges were fuzzy. It lit up the surrounding trees as bright as day. No other sound than the thrashing of the trees and the grass could be heard. The trees appeared to be moving back and forth as if in a strong wind and one tree appeared to be being pulled towards the ground. As they watched the thrashing sound ceased and then shortly afterwards there was a loud crack and the tugging motion on this tree stopped. The area was now very quiet and James moved from window to window. As he did so he noticed that his dogs, which normally barked at any light or noise, were lying very still between the trailer and a shed. At this point James loaded up his guns and began to consider calling for help. Just then the terrific light began moving away towards the north, passing below tree limbs through an open area 6m wide. It moved parallel to the ground until it reached the edge of the field, where it raised itself slightly and hovered 60m from the house. Its light had now dimmed and they could see that it had a silvery white centre, with a blue band, and an orange glow extending around the outer edge. Then the object, still below the line of the trees moved 10 degrees to the west and then back to its original position. James now tried to call for help. As he talked the lights dimmed twice and having been told that the exchange operator would ring him, hung up. When the exchange operator tried to ring there was no reply and no ring as though the line was dead. James worried as to why no one was calling him back also found the line dead. It came back to life on the operator's fifth attempt. The family contacted the Federal Aviation Authority and all seemed impressed by James' sobriety and genuine fear. When the object returned to its original position James felt his time was up and was almost speechless with fear. After an indeterminate time the light moved away through the trees again towards the field and then returned to its 60m distance location, where it got smaller though it did not seem to be moving away. Eventually at 0145hrs. the police arrived, but they did not seem impressed. When investigators arrived on the scene they found a tree broken 4.8 above the ground, dead leaves, numerous imprints on the ground, mostly 12-15 cm wide and 9cm deep. It appears that Shirley was away at the time.

On July 13th 1973 at 0330hrs in Emden in Shelby County, Missouri. At their farm, east of Emden, Terry and Linda Stice were awoken by the barking of their dog. Its bark seemed unusual, as of the animal was afraid of something . The couple went to the front door to see what was the matter, their normally brave dog staying in the porch area. Terry could not see anything so went back to bed, but Linda saw a light and called him down again. Terry saw a sort of egg shaped object, the size of a small car, hovering 5m above the ground in a clearing behind a tree. The thing had a peculiar orange colour, which Terry found impossible to describe exactly, and it seemed as though he could look into his brighter interior, but also gave the impression of being transparent. When Linda turned the house lights on, the thing seemed to flicker like a car headlight as a car moves off. It moved off at no more than 8kph. It rose only slightly and seemed to pursue a dead straight course through the trees. As it moved away the neighbour's dogs and some cattle on a hill kicked up a fuss. The object was observed for 10 minutes and it took 20 seconds to depart to the west. The FAA were called but showed no interest.

In mid-August 1973 in St Francois County, Missouri. Two deputies saw what looked like a helicopter hovering 7-8m above cattle on a ranch.

On September 14th 1973 at 0130hrs in Lebanon in Laclede County, Missouri. 8km out of Lebanon two military policemen from Fort Leonard Wood observed a red-orange sphere at treetop height 30m away, across the road. It paced them for about 800m before turning sharply to disappear in the distance.

On September 15th 1973 in La Monte in Pettis County, Missouri. A family near here observed a large glowing oval close to the ground. The object, which was seen for several minutes, lit up their house.

In Saint Joseph in Buchanan County in Missouri on Friday 21st September 1973 at 10.45 pm the witness was looking out of their front window when a strange flying craft approached at treetop level. The object was a brilliant red and blue bright light and passed over the garage and house and settled above the lawn about six feet from above the garage roof. There was no sound and the sighting lasted six minutes. The witness was petrified and the UFO hovered perfectly still for a minute or two and then started to rotate. Then a sort of ribbed shield came into view which extended ten inches from the side of the craft rising up and slanting inwards towards the transparent dome. The craft was circular. Or this? Before going to bed a woman looked out of her front window to check the weather and observed an object, emitting a brilliant red and blue light, which approached at treetop level, passed over the garage and house and settled to the lawn, hovering about 2m from the street at garage height for about 6 minutes. As the thing moved silently the lady became too petrified to move. After a couple of minutes the object began to slowly rotate to reveal a sort of ribbed shield extending upwards and inwards towards a translucent dome from about 25m from the side of the object. The thing had a rounded bottom and a high domed top, with blue and red lights glowing from its interior. It continued to rotate slowly and after 5-6 minutes it gradually moved back in the direction from whence it had come and drifted north. Through binoculars the witness observed the thing in the sky, where it was joined by a second object. The two began darting about and then shot out of sight.

On October 1st 1973 at 2100hrs in Sikeston in Scott County and New Madred County, Missouri. Special Officer ZT Jackson was driving north on Ingram Road to investigate a UFO report when, near the intersection with Tanner Road, a large bright red ball 15-30m diameter shot up from just above a soya bean field. About 15-30 police officers saw three objects manoeuvring in the sky that night.

On October 3rd 1973 at Malta Bend in Saline County, Missouri. A farm family observed a strange object in a field. Trees at the site were damaged and a burned area was found.

Also on October 3rd 1973 at 0620hrs in Cape Girardeau in Cape Girardeau County, Missouri. Eddie Doyle Webb (45) and his wife Velma Mae (47) were driving a tractor on Interstate 55 when Eddie noticed some lights about 1.5km away and approaching. These lights were multi-coloured and very bright. He called out to Velma, who had just woken and was dressing in the over-cab bunk, but she was unable to see anything because of the fog. The object had now almost caught up with them and a sort of spotlight was shining on the left rear trailer wheel. Eddie put his head of the window to get a better look and saw it came from a silvery object, about 10m diameter, 2-22.5m high, with a band of multi-coloured light across its centre. The top part of the thing was shaped like a turnip, and both top and bottom sections were metallic looking and spinning. The thing appeared to be ab out 1-1.5m above the road and straggled both lanes on their side. As Eddie looked the object seemed to rise somewhat and emitted a faint humming sound. At this point a yellow-red flash hit Eddie across the face and forehead, blinding him. He braked immediately and the truck motor died. Velma then took over the running of the truck and Eddie found that one lens of his glasses was missing. Velma drove to the office, where a colleague phoned for an ambulance. Eddie's eyes were extremely sore; an examination of the glasses frame suggested they had been internally heated; his face appeared red and hot. An ophthalmic examination showed his vision was only 20%, with difficulty in colour vision, however no organic eye damage was detected,

In Petal in Forest County in Missouri on 9th October 1973 Constable Charlie Delk chased a UFO for over thirty miles. The chase was interrupted when the car and its radio both went dead at the same time and then started up again. The object vanished after doing a double flip. The object had at first been seen hovering over Petal High School. It was top-shaped and had yellow lights all the way around it. Near the Jones-Forest County line it slowed down and some lights came out of its side like blowtorches. Then it went North toward Tallahalla Swamp and the car died.

On October 16th 1973 (Approximate Date) in Clay County, Missouri. Two witnesses independently reported that they had to swerve their vehicles into a ditch to avoid an elliptical object with blue and orange lights, standing on legs1.2-1.8 ,high. The next day one of these witnesses found burnt patches on the grass on either side of the road, which patches gave off an oily smell, and pad like marks in the ditch.

Near Eupora in Webster County in Mississippi on the evening of 17th October 1973 a fifty foot wide UFO was seen hovering two to three feet above Hwy 82 seemingly suspended on a beam of light. The primary witness's car lights went out and the engine died when it was one hundred yards from the craft. Another car stopped just behind him. A second UFO hovered sixty feet over the first illuminating it with a light. Both craft were similar like inverted cups and had greenish blue lights. A catfish like creature came out from the top of the lower UFO holding onto a handrail. It had gray fish-like skin, a wide mouth, one glowing eye, flipper like feet and webbing between the legs like a "Flying Squirrel". It had featherlike objects on its back which opened and closed when it moved.

On November 23rd 1973 in Matthews in New Madrid County in Missouri at 11:30 p.m. This close encounter began with the observation of five red lights in a curve, indicating something round. The witness was driving to her grandmother's house and witnessed the bright lights which were very low out of her passenger window to the East. When the lights got behind her she pulled off the road and got out of the car as they approached. Another car from the North stopped to see if she needed help, saw the lights and sped off. The object passed over with a humming noise.

On November 26th 1973 in Lincoln in Benton County, Missouri. Two racoon hunters had just released their dogs in a wooded area when they noticed a large red-orange spherical light across a field at low altitude. They were prevented from approaching further by a herd of cattle. The dogs passed the cattle and jumped into the truck, refusing to leave it. The men then drove on to Hw65, the red sphere pacing the truck along the narrow gravel road. When they reached the highway they saw another reddish sphere hovering toward the south. This second object was joined by the first and they both moved away at high speed. The younger man's father also saw the objects, which were flying near top and parallel to a high voltage wire from a distance of 800m.

On December 2nd 1973 at 2515hrs in Warrensburg in Johnson County, Missouri. Mrs Jay R Hodges looked out of her window and saw an orange glow. She called her husband and they both saw a 60-90m long, red-orange shape floating above the tree level. It was a hemisphere, with a flat top and rounded bottom, like an inverted bowl. Mt Hodges, a one-time aircraft observed the object for 7-8 minutes. It glowed as if illuminated by an internal fire. At the end of the observation it slowly moved away.

On December 7th 1973 at 2015hrs still in Warrensburg, Missouri. Several people observed a multi-coloured object at very low altitude.

1974

On January 2nd 1974 in Lamar in Barton County, Missouri. Vernon County farmers observed a large glowing object, with portholes, which manoeuvred at low altitude.

In April 1974 in Marshall in Saline County, Missouri. A bright light was seen near the ground and grass was found to be burnt.

On August 13th 1974 in Laurel in Jones County in Missouri just after midnight August 12/13 two motorists driving between Laurel and Meridian independently reported to police that they had seen UFOs. In one car an Air Force officer and his family saw two large saucer-shaped objects displaying a blinding bright blue light approach, then buzz the car three times.

In 1974 in Sedalia in Puttis County, Missouri. Two people saw a disc hovering over trees, the upper brachnes of which were found burnt and broken.

1975

On January 21st 1975 at night in Port Girardeau in Cape Girardeau, Missouri. A girl taking a short cut through the back yard of the house of a friend she had been visiting looked up and saw a flashing disc hovering at treetop height. She dashed back into the house and told her friend Sandra P what she had seen. When the two girls had plucked up courage to look outside they saw a discoid object, about 1.2m diameter, surrounded by four blue lights, with a white light in its centre. The visiting girl then decided to run for home and the disc followed her until she reached her home a block away. The girl's mother reported that the house lit up as if a car had shone its lights into the front yard. There were, however, no cars on the street at this time.

On June 10th 1975 at night in Pontotoc in Pontotoc County, Mississippi. Three young men were driving in a truck, exercising their dogs, and were parked on a ridge. From there they saw a light among the trees 600-800m away. It came down in a meandering fashion close to a local house, at which all but one of the dogs rushed back to the truck. As the thing passed over security lights, these dimmed. When they youths called in the last dog, the object moved towards them, hovered over another light and then meandered off, becoming a dim red light in the distance. This then flared up for a few seconds and then disappeared.

At Wedekind Roadside Park in Cape Girardeau County in Missouri at 6.15 am on 3rd October 1975 Mr. Eddie Webb, 35, a trucker, was driving on Interstate Highway 55 just South of the Jackson exit when he saw a bright object approach real fast in the air behind him. The object was turnip-shaped and in three sections. The top and bottom were of aluminum and spinning and the center was steady and composed of glittering red and yellow lights. The object was large enough to cover both lanes of the highway. Eddie woke his sleeping wife who was also in the cabin of the truck. She could not see anything out of the rearview mirror. Webb then stuck his head out of the window to look behind and was immediately blinded by a bright flash. His glasses fell off. It was a very hot flash. Eddie stopped the truck screaming that he had been burnt and could not see. One of the lenses of his glasses had fallen out of the plastic frame and appeared to have been heated internally. Eddie's forehead was slightly red as if he had a mild sunburn and he complained of pain afterwards that felt as if it were deep inside his forehead and eyes. Eddie had been driving at 55 to 65 miles per hour. The object was thirty feet in diameter and came up fast behind the rig. Next a searchlight appeared and the object rose higher into the air. There was a humming noise. There was no permanent damage to Eddie's eyes and it was deduced that he was blinded by fright. Eddie's wife saw a large ball of fire strike him in face and knock his glasses off and she took over the wheel and drove Eddie to Hospital. Wedekind Roadside Park no longer exists and was near the Missouri Veterans Home and the Cape County Memorial Park Cemetery.

On November 13th 1975 at 2215hrs in Otterville in Cooper County, Missouri. Mrs X observed a very bright blue white sphere, which approached her farmhouse, made a low pass below the trees and stopped for a short time just above the ground 12m away. The thing then ascended vertically and disappeared. Mrs X, who was alone, was so afraid she asked a relative come and stay with her. No traces were found. **Xxx 31.05.20**

On November 15th 1975 in Pacific in Franklin County, Missouri A red flying object approached a car driven by a Mrs. Prichard with three passengers then ejected several white balls of light. The metal of the car was magnetized after the encounter.

On November 28th 1975 at 0500hrs in Sedalia in Puttis County, Missouri. Mrs Carol K (23),a high school graduate was awakening by her husband closing the door as he went out on a hunting trip and she got up to check the door. She then suddenly heard a rumbling sound, like thunder, which turned into a buzzing sound like electricity in the wires. Both her dog and those of neighbours started barking and growling. Looking through the front window she saw a "weird looking star" surrounded by a blue-green halo. The thing seemed to be getting larger as it got closer. She then saw it as a white centre, surrounded by a dimmer green-blue circle. After two minutes the thing turned to the left and began to slowly descend. As it turned, the thing looked like a three pointed star with a tail and the halo was no longer visible. The thing then seemed to turn over and Carol could see spinning blades face on. The thing descended down between two trees 40m away, where it stopped for two to three minutes. It was now titled up so that Carol could see the street lights reflected on the metallic looking underside, The thing had both large and small red lights, had a white dome with three circles on it, and a sort of black cross on its back. After the object tilted the small red lights turned towards the ground and Carol could see that the circles on the dome were really raised surfaces like bubbles. The thing then moved toward her for a bit, the large lights illuminating the snow. Then the thing moved back from her, ascended again and went away over the house to the north-west. During the time the thing was in view, the buzzing and the howling of the dogs continued and the kitchen and street lights appeared to dim. Carol's dog was normally placed.

On December 7th 1975 at 0230hrs still in Sedalia, Missouri. While driving along 16th Street, on the east side of town, a 37 year old man observed a blue-white globe to the south. The thing appeared to pace his car, accelerating and moving ahead for a short time. The witness attempted to follow the object up to the end of 16th street, , at which point the object dropped down to about 6m above the ground , near a barn. He stopped and watched as the object moved away toward the east. When the object was hovering at ground level, the witness could see a dome, on which there were three windows, and there were rotating lights around the centre of the thing.

Near Springfield in Greene County in Missouri one night in 1975. A horse-farm owner and his son were driving home one night, and as they drove in between two large grassy pastures and into their driveway, they noticed a small gray-suited figure whose head was encased in a clear glass-like bubble, standing near the gate. The witnesses stopped the vehicle and watched as the being slowly faded away into thin air. Horse mutilations were reported on the farm that same year.

1976

On May 16th 1976 at 1600 in St. Louis (St. Louis), Missouri Mrs. Jane D. (name confidential), 49, was waiting for a bus in St. Louis when she saw a "space man" walking back & forth near her. He was about 5'4" tall and normally dressed, wearing a hat, and was carrying a zippered overnight bag & smoking a cigarette. His face was very white. According to Mrs. D.'s sketch he was wearing goggles and had a long sharp nose, a chin that ran to a sharp point, and a minute mouth. Mrs. D. observed him for 15 minutes before taking a bus. "People who saw him ran, or stared and then hurried past."

At Fort Leonard Wood in Pulaski County in Missouri during Summer 1976. On a clear warm summer night, the witness, a soldier, was with his platoon at the firing range conducting training exercises. He turned around and noticed his drill instructor, and a few others gazing into the sky. There was a triangle formation of lights slowly moving in the sky. All of a sudden they came to a halt. One left formation and came closer in their direction; it came to a halt for about 30 seconds and then returned to the formation. Suddenly the formation shot upward like a shooting star and out of sight. Later that night the witness fell sleep in the barracks listening to his 8-track player until he was awakened by three human-like beings with glowing white skin looking down at him. The beings looked like three military personnel, an officer, a sergeant and a corporal. Their faces gave off a radiant glow. He felt afraid and closed his eyes. He then opened them and they all seemed to smile at him. The "corporal" spoke in a very kind voice, and asked him to turn his music off and put it away. He then felt as though he floated from his bunk, to his locker, opened it and then floated back to his bunk. He then fell asleep for a few minutes, and woke up. Thinking it was a dream he went downstairs to see if the guard on duty had seen anyone come upstairs. When he asked the guard, the guard appeared to be in a daze with his M16 in his hands. The witness even waved his hands across the guard's face, and he didn't even blink. He shook him and the guard seemed to snap out of it and asked him, "What happened?" He asked him if anyone had come in the barracks and the guard said that three military personnel whose faces seem to glow had come in, that's all he could remember. A cold chill went through the witness at this point. All of a sudden the room seemed to get bright. They went to the door and about 150 yards out in the woods they both saw a very large, bright green, upside down spinning top shaped object lifting out of the woods. They both looked at each other and back at the object. It seemed to hover for about 20 seconds just above the trees and then slowly climbed; it came to a halt again for about 10 seconds and then took off into space.

After midnight on 15th September 1976 Dorothy Yarbrough, 41, awoke in her trailer home to find herself sitting on the couch with bright lights coming in her window. She took her shotgun and three shells and went to the back door. When she opened it she saw the sky so fiery red that she thought that the world must be ending. Without conscious volition she went back in, put the gun away, and walked out the front door barefoot with her head hanging down and walked to an excavation site twenty feet away. There she saw two forms standing beyond the excavation and seven or eight more forms further away lined up by a fence. They seemed to be in a state of confusion and were jibber-jabbering to each other. They were less than four foot tall with big heads and swollen cheeks. Above her head she could hear a sound like a helicopter which was shedding a bright bluish white light but she could not raise her head to look at it. She walked up, still without her own volition, toward the nearest form which was surrounded by mist. The last thing she remembered was seeing a white hand with something wrong about it near her. When she woke up in the morning in her bed she found dirt on her feet whose soles felt burned. For a week afterwards she felt weak and had a sore stomach as well as a persistent headache that took nearly two weeks to wear off. She found that she was no longer a worrier as she had been before and she also had a better appetite and temporarily gained about sixty pounds. Under hypnosis she remembered that the nearest form had big eyes, was dressed in dark formfitting clothing and carried a shiny metal rod. His hand had two thumbs. He told her telepathically that they meant no harm. She was led up a rope ladder into a round room, laid on a table and given a physical examination. Another person, a man, perhaps her husband was wheeled directly into the room while she was taken into a dome with blue lights revolving around it and then back down the ladder. She was told by the leader of the Humanoids that she would begin seeing things in the future.

In Fall 1976 at 1830hrs in Polkville in Smith County, Mississippi. Timothy Pennington was sat on his grandparents' porch when he saw a light moving at between 25-30m altitude above the ground in a hollow, apparently on a collision course. The light then rose up and passed over the house, about 15-20m above it.

1977

In January 1977 late at night in Pineville in McDonald County, Missouri. Carl Smith saw an orange light bobbing about above the trees and called his neighbour Edward Fletcher, 800m away. They saw the spherical object manoeuvring back and forth over trees and then descending to the ground and being lost to sight.

On February 9th 1977 at night in Flora in Madison County, Mississippi. Deputies Ken Creel and James Luke responded to a call that an unidentified object had been seen in an area 8km west of Flora. They were driving along Coxferry Road when suddenly an unidentified aerial object flew to a position 6-15m above their car. It shone a bright light and there was interference on the radio. It was seen by another officer, Herbert Roberts, and flashed twice in response to his blinking his headlights. He described the thing as a very bright round object, with portholes, which departed at great speed.

On February 14th 1977 at night back in Pineville, Missouri. Lawrence McCool was driving along Hw 90 near the Intersection with Rt K on this wet, stormy night, looking for a light which had been seen in the area for some nights. He saw the thing, a domed disc, about 3.5m diameter and 1.2=1.8m thick, giving off an orange light, hovering at 25m altitude above the trees. As he slowly moved drove his truck closer, its engine, CB and lights failed. After a few minutes the object faded from sight and the engine, CB and lights then worked perfectly.

Two days later on February 16th 1977 at 0200hrs in Sims in McDonald County, Missouri. Lawrence McCool of Pineville parked his truck on a ridge near the Sims Country Store, looking for strange lights which had been seen in the area. He saw some lights flying in formation in the distance. After a while he decided to drive home. At 0230 he began to hear strange noises on his CB and then the whole of truck's electrical system went dead. Suddenly a brilliant molten-copper red object, 5.5-6m diameter appeared at 12m altitude on the road ahead. After 1 or 2 minutes it took off into the overcast, at which the electrical system returned to life. It is actually Sims Country Store And Cafe 10289 E State Hwy 90 about twelve miles east of Pineville.

On February 26th 1977 at night still in Pineville, Missouri. Ivan Kanable, his relatives Evelyn and Virgil Hottinger and four car loads of people went up to the county high point in search of the light. As they did so they saw a glow in the woods below, a couple of hundred metres away. Tbey firest thought it was a fire then realised it was something else/ Through binoculars they saw two rectangular metallic objects, which they first took to be bridge markers, then realised that there was no bridge in that spot. Nothing could be found there the next day.

On March 5th 1977 in McNatt in McDonald County, Missouri. At 11:00 PM Lonnie Stites and his wife, Deborah, were driving their pickup truck around a bend in the road when "the whole area lit up like a football field light was turned on, and a very bright light was shined on our windshield." He saw a man of normal height or slightly smaller stature standing alongside the road. He was human looking, but dressed in green coveralls with square glasses and a tight green cap over his ears. He was "waving us down." Up on the hill was another figure carrying what appeared to be "a ball of electricity about the size of a basketball." The second figure was walking away from an object that looked like a water tank, about 10 feet across and 10 to 15 feet tall, with red lights going around it. The UFO was about 50-60 feet from them. Mrs. Stites said that she saw two people on the hillside carrying "basketball sized lights," and that the UFO at one point flew over the truck. They turned the truck around and drove away in great fear.

On March 10th 1977 in Big Sugar Creek, Missouri. Glen C Coonfield (60) an army aviation veteran with 10 years' experience in helicopters, and his wife, saw a large object, with a glowing front and emitting flames from its rear, descending into Big Sugar Creek Valley and then take off into the sky again. There were at least 6 other witnesses.

In March 1977 (approx. date) at 2205hrs still in Pineville, Missouri. Ron Cargile was driving through a wooded area when his CB became filled with static and he saw a glow to his left. This passed over to a tree ahead. It was a brilliant domed disc 1.5-3m diameter, with a metallic looking band around its centre. Its light was illuminating the ground. Ron drove away and as he did so his radio reception improved.

On December 27th 1977 at 0700HRS in Lancaster in Schuyler County, Missouri. An 18 year old walking the dog saw, hovering above trees, a small, grey, egg shaped object, which was in view for a few seconds only before it disappeared.

1978

On 27th July 1978 a woman driving on Highway 50 felt an impact to the back of her car followed by the feeling that the car rose by one foot or more. The car swayed and vibrated and she then saw a bright light which rose above the car and then disappeared. The car returned to the ground unharmed though the driver was shocked. This was in Union in Franklin County. Or this. At 12.45 am Mrs Cora Evelyn Winscher (52) was driving home to Arnold from Union east along Highway 50 when she felt a sudden impact on the rear of her car, which rose up to about 30cm and started swaying back and forth and side to side and vibrating. When Cora looked through her rear view mirror she saw no other vehicle only a bright light immediately behind her, which light rose above her car. During the incident her car windows were fogged up by a burst of heat. After a few seconds the car returned to the ground, the bumping stopped but the car continued. Cora was very shocked but managed to negotiate a bridge before stopping. She expected to see the boot severely damaged but all she found were indentations. Examined by police, these were about 25mm deep. Cora suffered from headaches and aching limbs for some days after the incident.

On September 15th 1978 at 0030hrs in Purdy in Barry County, Missouri. Mrs Smith was in her the house on her own, while her husband was away. Going to bed, she glanced through the front living room window and noticed an object on the front lawn, illuminated by the nearby street lamp. The thing was about 1.2m in diameter, 60cm high and resembled a white plastic bag. She went to her bedroom for a better look, but decided not to go outside. Next day she found a circular area, 1m in diameter, where the grass had a faded blue green appearance, and the tips were brown and devoid of chlorophyll.

On October 8th 1978 in Jenkins in Barry County, Missouri. 7:00 AM. A farming family noted an unusual object in a field to the south of their house. The object was 285 feet from the house and at that distance, difficult to see. It appeared as a white object of moderate size, but was felt to be probably a large piece of paper blown there over the previous evening. The family did not go over to inspect it at that time. The six family members [5 adults and a teenager] stole occasional glances in its direction over the next two hours but nothing moved. Then, at 9am, the farm owner left the house to do some chores. At that moment, the object rapidly rose from the ground to a height of 30 to 50 feet. Everyone else ran out of the house to watch. It began moving slowly and silently to the west, ascended rapidly, turned twice, and gradually flew away. The witnesses noted that a second larger and more distant object seemed also to be in the sky. These objects came into close approximation and moved off together. The landed object was described as an oval or egg shape appearing white on the ground but more silvery reflective once airborne. Its size was judged to be 4-5 feet in the longer dimension, and 3-4 feet in the shorter. One area of the surface was darker in tone, and allowed the witnesses to note that it was rotating at about a once per two seconds rate. The witnesses immediately called the Sheriff's department. A deputy arrived in the afternoon and went to the landing site, took pictures, as well as soil samples. There was a noticeable trace which measured 4 1/2 feet long and 3 1/2 feet wide. The character of the trace was described as depressed, not burnt nor dried. Soil moisture was normal. The force bearing down on the ground was not great as measured by penetrometer tests. No radioactive heightened readings were measured either. [We owe all these tests to the field's trace expert, Ted Phillips.] As time went on though, there was some easily noticeable deterioration of the grass, selectively within the trace. The only slightly reasonable alternate hypothesis that Phillips and CUFOS were able to come up with, was something involving a weather balloon. Some effort was made to check for such launches but the only known source was in the entirely wrong wind direction. The fast take-off speed is also against this theory among several other things one might mention. One other note, when the farmer arrived at the scene he said that the grass at the site was very noticeably swirled. This case was also reported in the MUFON Journal where there were a few discrepancies. MUFON reports the trace as a tripod of depressed spots within an area of depressed and swirled grass. At one point in the article the trace is described as "burnt" but more reading seems to indicate that "discolored" might be a better word. "Like a spot which has been over-fertilized". Testing by MUFON at a college laboratory showed no unusual chemicals or volatile organics, such as solvents. It was found by MUFON that that farmer had previously recovered one of the weather balloons from the local service and knew perfectly well what they looked like. CUFOS' and MUFON's reports agree on almost all details, and the trace as described by MUFON is probably the better detail. As an aside, the witnesses describe their cows and a "local" meandering coyote as merely staring at the object and not agitated in any way.

1979

At 8.00 pm on May 25th 1979 in Charleston in Mississippi County in Missouri a nocturnal light came down and landed behind a store in the town. A neon sign was effected and a clock in the vicinity was later found to be 18 minutes slow.

On July 21st 1979 at 2310hrs in West Plains in Howell County, Missouri. Teenager cousins Angela (17 the day before) and Connie were sat on the back porch of the latter's home, 11km out of West Plains while the two sets of parents were playing cards inside. Connie drew Angela's attention to a row of red and yellow lights travelling left to right ahead of them at a slow speed. The lights were too bright to be those of an aeroplane. The lights then seemed to bunch up into a single red light, as if the object had turned front on to them. It then began to approach and descend. Connie ran in to get the adults, and by the time they came out the thing was low and close, lighting up the yard with a red light. It approached two large cottonwood trees 25-30m away, but just before reaching them hovered about 8m above the ground, its light so brilliant as to make looking at it difficult. The thing dimmed, as if in response to Angela's wish, revealing an elongated object with a circular end. The thing then seemed to turn sideways in response to Angela's unspoken command. They could see that the capsule shaped object was about 8-20m long, diameter 2.5-3m. Along its side were 6 lights 35-35cm diameter. The lights on the end were three dimensional luminous spheres. When Angela stepped back, the lights got brighter again and the thing turned its back to them and climbed away.

On August 21st 1979 at 1930hrs in Sedalia in Puttis County, Missouri. Mrs JB (45) a high school and college art instructor, with a master's degree, was turning her car in the driveway going out to a bridge party, when she saw a large sphere about 45m away, hanging stationary above the trees. It was the size of a school bus and white. She followed it down the road as it moved slowly over the power lines right above the road, some 3m above the lines, 12m above the road. As she got onto the road the sphere reached a creel area 60m away, where it lifted straight up and disappeared. The observation lasted 80 seconds. This light was silent, pulsating at 1 second intervals, brighter than the moon, with fingers of light visible in the dim phase of the pulse. The thing was as wide as the road and the ditches on either side (8.5) at maximum, and wide as the road alone (6m) at minimum. In the dim phase it had a metallic appearance. There was no effect on the car.

1980

In Cassville in Barry County in Missouri one evening during Spring 1980 John Melton was driving with his family to their rural home after a baseball game. It was still daylight and as they headed along a gravel road his wife saw a glowing domed object sitting on a field some 100 yards away. The family (father, mother, two teenagers) watched with such interest they nearly ran over a little man, described as being the size of a small thin child and wearing a one-piece suit which was light in color, that was standing at the edge of the road. It so frightened John that he swerved and gave the car gas—as they looked back, the little man was being peppered with gravel from the spinning tires and ran toward the object. They didn't stop but went on home and didn't go back to look for traces. There were other low level encounters of UFOs in the area.

On the evening of November 18th 1980 over Kirksville in Adair County in Missouri hundreds of people in north-central Missouri, including a dozen Police Officers, saw a large, triangular object over a period of more than four hours. It moved slowly back and forth over an area of nearly one hundred miles, passing over many small communities and the cities of Kirksville and Trenton, which are about sixty miles apart. At one time the object was tracked on radar moving erratically at a speed of about forty-five miles an hour. The technician who saw this on the radar scope at a remote FAA facility North of Kirksville stepped outside and could see the lights of the object about six miles away.

1982

One night in March 1982 in Springfield in Greene County in Missouri the witness was traveling in her car when she suddenly lost control of the steering. She felt her vehicle being pulled by an unknown force towards a light that was hovering at tree top level straight ahead. She felt as if the car was floating. Soon she found herself in a clearing in a wooded area. Nearby sat a silvery metallic disc resting on three legs. A light shone on her and she sees folding steps descend from the object. She is drawn into the craft and through several rooms until she reaches a platform, made out of padded white silver chrome and lays down on it. Half a dozen men then appear. These are described as six-foot one inch tall, well built, with long blond hair, high cheekbones, and blue eyes. They wore tight-fitting brown jumpsuits with matching shoes and belts with a pale yellow stole draped over one shoulder. They also displayed a winged emblem on the chest area resembling a "hawk-eagle" head in center and wings on each side. She is then led out to the door and suddenly finds herself in her car. She then sees a craft taking off emitting a loud whistling sound.

1983

At 9.30 pm on March 10th 1983 in Naylor in Ripley County in Missouri a bright light near the southeast horizon approached a car. It was a cluster of red, green, orange lights and elongated design and was 150 feet front to back. It was first seen as a bright light near the southeastern horizon which approached the car with Mr. and Mrs. Waldemar aboard just North of Naylor, Missouri. The UFO turned and flew away.

At dawn in July 1983 in Mount Vernon in Lawrence County in Missouri a couple were puzzled by bright silver flashes coming from a pasture across the road from their farmhouse. Grabbing a pair of binoculars they were startled to see two small silver suited Humanoids that appeared to be "running" their hands over a black cow that was lying on its side, not moving. The small beings moved their hands in odd jerky movements and suddenly the cow rose straight up and floated with the beings into a silvery cone-shaped object on the ground nearby. The object's surface was like a mirror and reflected everything around it. Standing by a ramp on the object was a tall reptilian figure that had glaring eyes slit by vertical pupils resembling a snake. Standing on the other side of the craft was a taller and heavier hairy creature resembling a Bigfoot type being, that also had vertical yellow slits in round green eyes. As soon as the beings entered the object with the black cow, it disappeared. Or this. Looking across the road from their farm, Ron and Paula Watson observed brilliant silvery flashes in a pasture. Through binocular they saw two strange beings in silver suits running their hands across a prone cow. Then the cow and the beings floated up to a highly reflective conical object near some trees. By this thing were two other beings. To their left was a tall green skin, lizard like being with vertical pupils and webbed hands and feet. To the right was a large upright hairy creature with round green eyes in which were slit like pupils. Ron wanted to confront the creatures but Paula objected. Once the cow was in the object, the latter disappeared. Their neighbour reported one his cows missing. Under hypnotic regression Paula claimed she had been abducted by the beings two days before.

Around 10.00 pm on October 9th 1983 in Kimmswick in Jefferson County in Missouri. A group of silver-colored, oval-shaped objects with two protruding lights on top that alternately glowed red and green were seen. The lights zig-zagged with an up-down motion. Police confirmed that the objects were observed. They zig-zagged through the air. A group of silver oval objects was observed by 11 female witnesses, one of them an experienced observer, on a river for three hours.

1984

At 7.00 pm on January 22nd 1984 in Arnold in Jefferson County in Missouri two occupants of a car observed a circular object with three brilliant white lights and a corona of white light covering its entire surface. As the object approached the car the driver made a 180 degree evasive turn only to have the object pull alongside and pace his vehicle. After about three minutes the object pulled away and left the area. The driver estimated that the object got to within 150 feet of the car, maintained an altitude of about 150 feet and was at least 25 feet in diameter. A vertical shaft of white light was also observed coming from the top of the object. After arriving home two witnesses observed three helicopters moving about in the area where the object was seen.

At 9.30 pm on April 10th 1984 in Southwest City in McDonald County in Missouri a man with a shotgun drove his truck to the back of his property to check out two very large "floodlights" that were seven to eight feet above the ground. There was missing time of twelve minutes. The truck wouldn't start for two to three minutes. The witness reported that a period of time could not be accounted for. One light was observed by the male witness in a pasture for over 15 minutes.

At 9.38 pm on July 5th 1984 on Cape Girardeau in Cape Girardeau and Scott Counties in Missouri a disc with an orange halo hovered over a park at an estimated altitude of 1,000 feet. It winked out after fifteen seconds.

At 7.00 pm on July 31st 1984 outside of Rosebud in Gasconade County in Missouri a streaking, flaming object was seen. My husband and I had just gotten home from our vacation in Florida and went to Rosebud to take my husband's family their souvenirs that we had bought for them. We visited with them and left for home. We were traveling on Highway 50 heading East and as we were leaving the edge of Rosebud heading towards Gerald in Missouri I looked to my right, out of the passenger side window, and saw this cigar like figure that seemed to be on fire. A red, orange and yellowish flame, streaming along and traveling at the same speed that we were traveling down the highway and it was traveling above tree level. It seemed to be as long as a football field. As we traveled down the highway it seemed to be angling closer to us. Then all of a sudden, it hovered above Mr. M's house and trees, right along the highway just right in front of us, at tree top level. It hovered there. I told my husband "let's get the heck out of here"., and when I said that, it vanished in thin air.......almost like something heard me....... We had called a friend of ours that worked in the control tower at the Vichy, Missouri Airport and told him what we saw. He told us that other people had called in and saw it too. Then if I recall, on Channel 5 news they said that it was a Russian Rocket on fire re-entering earth's atmosphere…I never heard of a burning rocket hovering (????????????) in place for 30 seconds or so. After that, I asked my husband, "did you see what I saw?" and he said "yes" and then he asked me the same question and I answered "I sure did". Later that evening, I called my sister-in-law and told her what had happened. She told me, "Oh my God, My Mom and Dad just got back from Florida and the same object had followed them home to Rosebud, Missouri". I just wonder what that thing was??????? Something that was on a mission of some sort????????? You cannot get better than eye witness reports to show the effect of these events.

1985

At 7.03 pm on March 14th 1985 in Riverview in St Louis County in Missouri a lady driving her car saw three bright lights, two of which "went out". The other light turned into red and white blinking lights on a boomerang-shaped craft which passed directly over her and then pretty much stayed in one place from 7.13 pm to 8.15 pm while the other two lights/craft flew over the area from West to East. The "Mother ship" changed from white to red and started blinking while it receded into the West. Other objects followed and disappeared by 8:20 pm. The main object had come as close as 700 feet to the witness. The objects had faint engine sounds and were observed for over an hour.

1987

In Lake of the Ozarks, Missouri on December 10th 1987. That night a man went outside his house for a smoke and felt that something overwhelming told him, "Turn around." He did and saw what looked like two headlights in fog, but there was no fog. The lights in fog were coming over the top of the trees. They came closer and another set of lights appeared behind, then a third set, all following the same path. The first object stopped and the others came alongside. The first rose up a bit, and the last dropped down. The objects were more or less disks, forty feet in diameter and maybe eight feet thick. On their rear ends they had twin "pods." On each pod was a green "crystalline" area emitting light. The objects created "fog" around them as they moved, which dissipated behind. On the fronts of the vehicles were windows. He could see humanoids easily in the windows with large eyes, no ears or hair. He was scared and wanted to yell for the rest of his family, but was paralyzed. He then received a dense information exchange by telepathy, including information about nutrition. Then the craft began to move off and he could scream for his family. Eleven people scrambled out and watched the craft (now 200 feet away) as they leisurely left the scene.

Two days later at 9.00 pm on December 12th 1987 at Climax Springs in Lake of The Ozarks in Missouri moments after several huge oblong shaped objects were seen flying at a low altitude over the border at Eudora Kansas, a man that lived at the shore of the lake had stepped out to get some firewood and was looking across the lake when a cloud or mist descended over the area engulfing the top of the trees. He now could see three huge oblong shaped objects that suddenly stopped over the lake area. As the clouds thinned out he could see a row of lighted openings extending along the length of all three objects. The witness was stunned and felt unable to alert the others inside. The objects were dark green and appeared metallic. He then could see several human-like figures looking down at him from behind the windows. The figures had human shaped heads with larger than normal eyes. They stared down at the witness and appeared to be talking amongst each other. The witness was finally able to call the other witnesses and these were able to see the objects as they moved over the lake and disappeared from view.

1988

In Steelville in Crawford County in Missouri during Summer 1988. Around 11: 30 p.m. David Gowers and a friend, Danny, both in their late teens had decided to hitch-hike out to his grandma's house, a mile outside of Steelville on Highway 8. They left St. Louis early in the morning, going West on Highway 44. They had their backpacks, some food and cash. They were planning to buy beer and party with his cousins out there in the woods. They got a ride very quick. The person took them halfway to Cuba, Missouri which was their exit on Highway 19. Then they had a long slow period between rides and they just walked and talked for several hours, stopping along the woods by the highway to rest and eat. They finally reached Cuba from a second ride just around rush hour. It was about 4: 30 pm and while in Cuba they didn't get any rides so they decided to walk the 10 miles to Steelville. They stopped at a store before leaving town and bought a box of sugar smacks cereal and a big bottle of fruit punch. By this time it was already 6: 30pm. They were young so walking was enjoyable. After a few miles a Missouri State Trooper pulled just ahead of them and stopped. He waited for them to walk up and then he got out of his car. He asked what they were doing on the two lane black top road walking. He told him they were going to his grandma's so the trooper drove them to the Steelville Police Station which was on the way to David's grandma's house. They verified the story over the phone with his grandmother. The officer then gave them a ride to the end of town on Highway 8 and told them to get out since it was as far as he could go. By now it was almost dark. There was nobody on the road and David and Danny had about 15 miles to walk, or get a ride if lucky. They were thinking of walking for a while and then sleeping out in the woods and finishing the walk in the morning. They must have walked about an hour and it was pitch black out on the road. The sky was cloudy and there was no moon. At one point David stopped to retie his boot when Danny yelled out, "Did you see that?" He said, "No, what was it?" Danny said that something jumped over the black top road and ran into the woods. He told Danny that it was a deer, he said that it was not a deer since "it had jumped over the black top" which was almost 20 feet wide, impossible for a deer. They were arguing about the event for some time when they both saw a blinding orange, hot looking glow slicing through the clouds like a knife. He said it was a 'helicopter,' but it was moving very fast plus it was going up and back, making incredible turns. They were amazed. It must have been around 11: 30 pm and they may have walked 4 or 5 miles. They were in no hurry. They still had 12 miles to go. Then it happened; the orange glowing light came back around toward them, and suddenly it was over them. He knew it wasn't a helicopter and fear went through him like never before. The object was the size of a three story building and did not make a sound. It was the last thing he remembered, seeing this huge glowing craft over them. The next thing he remembers he was waking up inside a large glass cylinder. It went from the floor to the ceiling. He woke up feeling very calm and wondering where he was. By the time his eyes adjusted to the light, he realized he was in a craft. He was scared again. That's when he heard a voice in his head, "Stay calm," it said. He looked straight ahead and saw a reptile-looking being about 8 feet tall. It was wearing some kind of breast plate and ankle and shin covers. The being told him his name but David cannot remember it, it was difficult to pronounce. Then he looked next to him, to his right and saw Danny. He was in a cylinder also, but he was frozen in place, with his arms on the glass over his head and his fist looked like he was beating on the glass. The reptilian creature told him not to worry, he was not to be harmed. He looked around the craft and the ceiling was high. It must have been two storeys high but at floor level about 10 to 15 feet. The walls were gold with every color of the spectrum, and it was circular, very clean and shiny. The reptilian then asked him if he was interested in the ship. David then asked, "How does it work?" The reptilian told him that there were two magnetic fields holding back charged plasma streams which traveled around a ring at high speeds and high temperatures that gave the ship energy. Most of it he doesn't remember. It seems he understood what it was telling him but the reptilian was apparently planning on taking them somewhere. He told him he didn't want to go. The reptilian then told David that he (David) was royalty. That his blood was royalty and he would be treated like a king after they arrived. David told the reptilian to please take them back to the road. It did not argue with him. It just nodded. It then told him that he shouldn't be with this one (Danny). According to David the reptilian was not at all aggressive towards him. Its hand had five fingers and it had a very muscular body. It stood next to a control panel in the middle of a large room about 10 feet away from him. The light was bright but not blinding. He could see everything perfectly. He told David about a tragic happening on earth that was to occur, but then added, "We will come for you before it happens." He had no idea what the being was talking about. All he knew was that he wanted to go immediately. Their backpacks were still on their backs and he was ready for anything. The reptilian's face was very bony with green brown scales, tiny ones. And the breast plate went to the middle of where the waist would be just above a gold-black belt or utility belt, which was about 6 to 8 inches wide. The plate was gold and black with silver. It didn't wear any pants. David didn't notice any genitals in the crotch area. David didn't feel comfortable there talking to the creature, he just wanted to leave. His next memory was of him and Danny being in a pickup truck. An old man was driving and they were almost at his grandma's house. She was up because of the earlier call. She was waiting for them and he had no idea what time it was. They walked into the house and it was 1am in the morning. She told his grandma what happened and apparently she believed them, saying that she "has seen them now for a long time." David and Danny sat on the front porch all night, waiting to see it again, but it didn't show up. Years later, David started to remember more of this encounter. He never did find out who the old man was that dropped them off.

1989

One late night in January 1989 in St Louis in Missouri the 22 year old witness had fallen asleep when he was suddenly awakened by three individuals that said they were aliens. He asked them what they were doing in his bedroom and they told him that they had been in the attic and needed to go outside and asked if he could open the window for them. (!). In the morning he woke up and his window and screen were wide open and the attic entrance was wide open also (a ladder was needed to access the attic; however there wasn't a ladder around). Two of the "men" looked human and the third also looked human but with something alien about his overall appearance that the witness could not pinpoint. They were all about 5 foot tall. There was no other information.

On April 11th in Lebanon in Laclede County in Missouri around 10:30 PM. After watching the news the farmer drove his pickup out to check on an Angus heifer which was past due on delivery of her calf. When he got there he heard the cows bawling a lot more than usual. He found the entire herd gathered in the southeast corner and the Angus standing beside her newborn bull calf. He turned off the engine and lights because the battery wasn't very good and noticed a red glow through the trees to the North and thought it was a campfire somebody had left. When he got out of the truck he heard a crackling sound coming from that direction. Since the fire appeared to be most certainly on his property and much closer he went back to the pickup and grabbed a flashlight. When he turned around he got "about the biggest shock of my life." Above the trees was a huge red ball about 20-35 feet in diameter less than 50 yards away from him. When yellow speckles would show up on the surface the crackling sound could be heard. After hovering there, bobbing slightly up and down. After a few minutes the object started to move off and then rapidly, climbing at a steep angle to the northwest, slowly at first, then a distant dim red star in 10-12 seconds. A moment later it was gone.

1991

Near Springfield in Greene Countyin Missouri on July 21st 1991 around 2.00 am. Three young teenage girls had stayed up late to watch a TV program and had gone into the backyard to play on a trampoline when they noticed a white oval-shaped light moving rapidly from the side of the house into a corner of the backyard near a large tree. One of the girls now noticed a strange humanoid figure standing near the trampoline. It was described as completely white in color, about 4-½ feet tall with thin long arms and a huge pear-shaped head with two large black almond-shaped eyes. The girls then ran back into the house and attempted to tell an older cousin of the incident, but the cousin ignored them and went back to sleep. The girls then re-entered the den and continued watching television. Moments later their cat began acting strangely and the television screen went blank. At this point all three then saw the same humanoid looking at them through a window. The humanoid moved its head in a jerking mechanical manner. The girls then ran to the basement where they stayed for the remainder of the night.

In Missouri, exact location not given, in August 1991.The witness was in bed sleeping when she suddenly began floating out of her bedroom towards a light and through the wall. She felt being pulled by a strong force with a quick movement. She then encountered a strange reptilian being described as five-foot nine inches tall with a green body that appeared scaly and rough. He had pea-green eyes with pupils slanted like a cat, black and yellow in color. The being lacked hair, had a small mouth, thin arms, duck-like hands with brown webbing in between four long fingers with sharp nails on the ends. The witness felt electricity going through her hands apparently after the being touched her. She was then told that they needed human beings to make their race stronger because it was dying out.

1992

At 1.10 am on April 1st 1992 in Springfield in Greene County, Missouri a 35-year old local woman was awakened in her bedroom to witness a disc-shaped object with red lights around the bottom rim just outside her window. The witness felt herself being pulled toward the window by a "force'. She glanced at her bedside clock and saw that it was 1.10 am. The next recollection of the witness is that she awakened with a jolt in her bed and that the time was 3.10 am.

Later that year in Springfield, Missouri one evening in July 1992. A lone witness saw two short robed humanoids that were gray skinned that appeared to be gliding slowly across a field. No associated object or light was reported.

Witnesses related that on August 15th 1992, at 5:30 a.m., they were driving to work in Marshfield in Webster County in Missouri. They turned East onto Webster County Road EE from farm road 615 (along which both witnesses live) and observed a bright white light in the distance at just above treetop level. The light appeared to be stationary over an open field on a hillside approximately three to four miles away. The witnesses remarked that it looked too big to be a star and that the light held their attention from the time they first saw it. Shortly after the witnesses turned onto EE, they also observed what they at first took to be car headlights approaching them from the East. As the lights came closer, they were seen as two sets of two lights, one set atop the other, and were extremely bright. The witnesses noted that these lights were approaching at a speed considerably faster than was prudent for a car to be traveling along EE. The lights passed the witnesses without sound. Neither of the witnesses saw a vehicle and neither saw vehicle tail lights, although both looked for them. Both witnesses considered this event odd. The onlookers continued to watch the light ahead and soon noted that it appeared to be keeping pace with them at a uniform distance, despite several turns along the route. They turned onto Webster County Road West from EE. About 100 feet after the turn, the witnesses saw to their left (East), a bank of five white lights in a boomerang-triangular shape. The five white lights appeared to be preceded by a single white light, and followed by a red light on the formation's right, and a blue light on the formation's left. Eyewitness #2, who was driving, "slammed on the brakes" and put the car in park. Witness #1, the passenger, rolled down her window down and slid out to sit on the car door with her feet inside the car. They both could discern a craft outline as the lights moved very slow, almost a drifting fashion, from about fifty feet away directly over the car. As the lights passed over, five vertical beams of light shot down, illuminating the vehicle and its interior with brilliant white light. The car was illuminated for perhaps one to two minutes as the "craft" moved over them. Then, the vertical lights "switched off." The original bank of lights continued to move slowly out across a small field to the right (West), and disappeared over a small area of ground fog. The witnesses drove on, after the lights disappeared, to a hill a short distance away to try to find the lights, but were unsuccessful. The lights "had just disappeared." During the sighting witness #1 noted that the area was absolutely quite ~ completely without the usual early morning sounds of wildlife, insects, domestic pets, livestock, etc.., that are usually present in the rural setting. (When investigators visited the site, dogs at three nearby houses barked loudly and horses in a corral over which the "craft" passed neighed in an equally noisome fashion.) The witnesses also noted that their windshield, after the passage of the lights, was completely dry. Whereas before, Witness #1 had to use the windshield wipers to remove condensation. Additionally, the vehicle sputtered as they tried to leave and "acted like it was out of gas." The duration of the entire sighting was about 15 minutes, with the close observation lasting perhaps 10 minutes. Neither of the observers reported any physical effects, nor was the car damaged. And, there was no indication of missing time. The witnesses reported that they were not frightened by the experience itself, but did endure a moment of panic afterwards, when they met a car on the road and observed its headlights coming up over the top of a hill. As a final note, witness #1 made a report to the Webster County Sheriff's Department about the incident.

At 8.30 pm on September 20th 1992 in Sullivan in Franklin and Crawford Counties in Missouri three witnesses sighted a large metallic craft with several large lighted windows hovering low over a field. They could see behind the windows about twenty thin Humanoid figures moving back and forth and standing. No sound was reported.

At 2.00 am on September 24th 1992 back in Springfield in Missouri the witness apparently in a dream or trance-like state remembers finding herself in a large lighted room looking at a cow lying on top of a raised platform. Strobe like lights shone on the animal. She was mentally told that these lights were purifying the animal, neutralizing the bacteria and germs. The animal appeared to be convulsing violently. Next a tube was inserted into the animal's upper inside of the right leg, near the hip joint and then blood was apparently extracted. Several short gray skinned Humanoids seemed to be operating different apparatus in the room and one explaining the procedure to the witness. Next a gray being inserted what appeared to be a "light pen" inside the cow's rectum. It was activated and it began rotating quickly disappearing into the body. There was a strong nauseating burning smell. A large piece of what appeared to be rectum intestine was removed and placed in a container. The witness remembers being instructed to insert the "light pen" into the animal's jaw area. She saw teeth and tissue being cut by the object. The left eye was also apparently removed. The witness could not recall any further details.

1995

On January 31st 1995 in Columbia in Boone County in Missouri at 2.40 AM. The witness was sitting in his room reading a TIME/LIFE book on Stonehenge when he heard a beeping noise. He described the noise as similar to a computer beeping. After listening to the beeping for about ten minutes he left his room to try and find the source of the sound. The witness walked down the hall to the family room/kitchen area. The only light on in this part of the house was a small light over the sink. As he stood in the family room he thought he saw a movement outside the patio door. (The patio door is a typical double sliding door and the blinds were pulled open.) He approached the door within approximately three feet to try to see outside. The time was approximately 3:00 am. Within seconds a small figure walked up to the outside of the door and peered in. The figure was within three feet of the door on the outside. The witness called this figure "a little man." The kitchen light reflected off the figure so as to light him sufficiently for the witness to clearly see him. The witness described the figure as about 3 1/2 to 4 feet tall. He had a large bald head and what the witness referred to as "eyes like a fly." The figure was thin, with two long arms and extremely long fingers. The witness was unable to recall the number of fingers on each hand. The entity was humanoid in appearance and silver/grey in color. If the being had on clothing it was one piece and form fitting because the witness' impression was that it was naked. The entity leaned from the waist toward the door and stared at the witness. The young man said that he was frozen with fright and just stared back. The witness said he had never been so scared in his life. The hair "stood up on his arms." After several minutes the witness was able to break free of his fright and run to the kitchen to get a butcher knife. The boy then huddled in a corner of the family room, holding the knife and glancing back to the patio door. Because of his position in relation to the door he was unable to see if the "little man" was still there. At approximately 4:00 am the boy ran into his father's bedroom in a state of panic. He told his father what had happened. After checking the house his father phoned the Columbia Police. The police department referred him to the National UFO Reporting Center.

At 11.00 pm on July 9th 1995 in Versailles in Morgan County in Missouri near this location, two Air Force officers and a dozen other witnesses saw five very large UFOs—a triangular craft and four discs, each as long as a football field—hovering over an empty field. On the ground were 20 to 25 extraterrestrials moving about. Three different races were present. Some short ones with purplish skin and large ears, another type described as luminous energy beings, and a third group of tall Humanoids in jumpsuits.

In Camden County in Missouri one afternoon in Summer 1995. The witness had decided to explore a cave which was part of a fairly large system in the area. From what he could tell, this particular cave had not been explored for a long period of time. The entrance was very narrow and well hidden. After squeezing through the opening, he descended another fifty feet or so before the cave began to open up into a series of chambers. He moved through several of these chambers, taking his time to examine the area for possible artifacts and formations. He finally reached, what he thought was the end of the cave. At this point he began to hear a rustling sound that was echoing from a small opening near the top of the chamber. He assumed the sounds were bats and didn't pay much attention to it. But after a while he heard motorized sounds and talking. He stood up and listened for several minutes, wondering what was on the other side of this chamber. The opening was about ten feet above him. He maneuvered his way up to the opening which was flat and narrow but large enough for him to get a decent look into it. As he positioned himself to the front of the opening, he started to see light at the other end. The passageway was only a few feet long but it was just too narrow for him to move through. As he looked through the opening there was a very warm draft of air hitting his face. As well, the air had a very acrid vinegar like odor. There was a very large and well-lit 'room' with limestone walls. He noticed a small vehicle that looked like a golf cart but was very low to the ground and without wheels. He continued to observe until he started to hear voices that were getting louder and nearer. Something was making its way toward the vehicle. He had to rub his eyes because he didn't believe what he was looking at. This 'creature,' because it was not a man, stood about seven foot and had brown scaly skin. The face and head were shaped like a human with a flat nose but there were no ears or hair. The top of the head had a slight scaly ridge that extended down the back of the neck. From what he could see, it had lips and regular sized eyes. The arms were very long and muscular with human-like hands. It also had a massive 4-5 foot tail that tapered to a point. It was dressed in a gold metallic outfit with long pants and shoes. It also carried an oval-shaped bag attached to its back. This creature was looking at something on the vehicle. The witness had a camera which he used to obtain a few distorted images of the being. Suddenly while he was taking the photos, the creature stopped and turned, looking in his direction. It then made a terrible "hissing" sound as it continued to look in his direction. That was enough for the witness which quickly made a bee-line out of the cave. When he reached the entrance, he was shaking and hyperventilating. He finally reached his vehicle and drove home. He continued to explore caves in the area and has heard stories of people encountering strange underground beings, but he had never disclosed his experience. A few years after his experience, he went back to the cave but was unable to get near it since the area is now government property.

Late at night on September 15th 1995 in Springfield in Missouri the witness was awakened in the middle of the night by a bright light coming from her daughter's bedroom. Her right arm was paralyzed and she had to pull it with her left arm to turn over to see why the light was on. She had to struggle to roll her eyes down from the top of her eye sockets and saw then saw the same creature's profile (of one seen in 1987) with its arms extended over her daughter's bed. Angry, she sat up. The creature then turned and looked at her in a threatening manner, with the same huge blue eyes and the witness then passed out in her pillow. As she fell onto her pillow she saw the creature vanish. It turned into a vertical line of light within the bright light and it was gone.

1998

Near St. Louis Missouri one night in 1998. The witness woke up from a night's sleep to find herself on a marble-like autopsy table. The area she was in had a gray mist with non-directional lighting coming through. She thought she was in a walled enclosure and when she looked down at her feet she noticed what she took to be a very startled alien. This was a being about the size of an 8-year old child, very thin in build with long arms and legs, gray in color and lacking any sort of clothing. It had very large completely black, elongated eyes, with a pointed chin and large head. The entity had a very large forehead with a complete lack of hair over its body. The being appeared surprised that she was awake and came around up to her face and telepathically told her to fall back to sleep but before she did so she felt that there were others off to her left which were observing these proceedings.

Nevada

1925

At Flat Mesa, near Battle Mountain in Lander County in Nevada one afternoon in 1925. Don Wood Jr. and another American landed in a two-seater plane on Flat Mesa in the Nevada desert. While walking about the top they noticed something coming in to land. It was round and flat like a saucer, and about 8ft across, with a reddish underside. It skidded to a stop about 30 feet away. They walked up to it and found that it was an animal-like thing; nothing they had seen before. It had a mica-like body, but no visible eyes or legs. It was hurt, and as it breathed the top would rise and fall making a half-foot hole around it like a clam opening and closing. A hunk had been chewed out of one side of the rim, from which a metal looking froth issued. After a 20-minute rest, it started pulsating again, and grew very bright except where it was hurt. It tried to rise up, but sank back again. Suddenly the men saw a much larger animal, 30ft across, approaching. It settled on the smaller one with 4 sucker-like tongues. Then it grew too dazzling to look at and both rose straight up and shot out of sight in a second, at an estimated speed of 1000 miles an hour. They left behind an awful stench. The frothy stuff the little creature had "bled" looked like fine aluminum wire, and there was frothier, wiry stuff in a 30ft circle where the big creature had been. This material finally melted in the sun.

1947

A pilot reported a flying saucer sighting over Lake Mead in Clark County in Nevada on 28th June 1947. AAF pilot Lt. E. B. Armstrong from Brook AAF in San Antonio in Texas was flying an F-51 fighter at 6,000 feet when he saw a tight formation of five or six white circular three foot wide objects off his right wing heading 120 degrees eastsoutheast at 6,000 feet at 285 miles per hour. This was thirty miles northwest of Lake Mead. This was during the great 1947 UFO Flap.

On October 8/9 in Las Vegas Nevada. AAF reserve Capt. Moore saw an object traveling at 700 mph leave an almost white smoke/vapor trail and change direction from SE to W.

1948

On January 13th 1949 (approx date) at 0115hrs in Gardnerville in Douglas County, Nevada, On wakening, Mrs Sara Lampe, saw, through her window, a sort of fuzzy grey stain on the snow, which suddenly lit up into a bright disc about 1m in diameter. After a couple of minutes the light contracted into an orange stream of light, about 12.5-15cm wide, which flowed towards her window and burst into red and blue flames a few centimetres above the 75cm high porch wainscoting. No traces were found.

1949

On May 2nd 1949 in Elko in Elko County in Nevada at 11:40 a.m. CAA radio operator Mr. Small using field glasses saw 3 flying discs 30 feet diameter at 14,000 feet moving (heading?) SW at 300-400 mph make a left turn and depart ahead of a United airliner taking off from Elko airport.

1950

On January 10th 1950 eight miles [NE?] of Las Vegas AFB [later renamed Nellis AFB] (on Hwy 93), Nevada at 10:10 a.m. Civilian pilots, father and son, observed two F-80 jet fighters approaching for landing at an elevation angle of about 45° into the sun [in the SE at about 21° elevation 141° azimuth] and saw an object at an altitude of approximately 1500-2000 feet, about 25-30 feet in size. Object appeared "pure silver," round "like a balloon" (AFOSI found no balloons launched) and solid material like "a metal," with no external fittings, air ducts, antenna, supports, or exhaust trail, seeming no noise audible above that of an F-80. Direction of flight [heading?] was NNE with no tactical movement, or maneuver, motion was smooth, at first slow and then a very rapid acceleration in a horizontal ascent, disappearing over mountains to the East.

On May 7th 1950 at 1845hrs in Ely in White Pine County, Nevada. Mr and Mrs George Smith and their grandson were returning from a picnic when about 14km south of Ely they saw a silver white object hovering a treetop level. It moved back and forth for about 10 minutes, as if attempting to rise, then suddenly flew out of sight at high speed.

1952

On July 28th 1952 at 0400 at Mormon Mesa in Clark County in Nevada. Truman Bethurum was out in the desert looking for fossils when he encountered a flying saucer and was introduced to its friendly crew. Their leader was a beautiful, apparently young woman, named Aura Rhanes, (actually a grandmother), wearing a red and black outfit. Truman was told that the UFO came from a planet "Clarion", invisible to us as it was always behind the moon. The Space people subsequently contacted him several times, and once he was taken on a ride to Clarion. Or this version. At 5.00 am Truman Bethurum, who had been sleeping in his truck near Mormon Mesa, awoke to here unintelligible voices and found himself surrounded by 8-10 small men, 1.4-1.5m tall dressed in uniforms like those of greyhound bus drivers, with grey trousers, "cowboy" jackets and most wearing caps with black bills. The beings had sallow skin and dark eyes and hair. They held his arms tight and took him on board a disc shaped object, about 100 diameter, hovering a metre or so above the ground, where he met the female captain Auroa Rhanes who was 1.35m tall. She claimed to be from the Planet Clarion which was hidden behind the moon. She spoke in rhyming language described the utopia conditions of her planet, and claimed to have come to earth to restore traditional values. This was the first of a number of such contacts.

1953

In Summer 1953 in Fort Polk in Vernon Parish, Louisiana. A group of servicemen were training when they saw a large ovoid object with a sort of fin at its centre, crash land. Three occupants were killed but there was a survivor, a humanoid 1.2m tall, with a large head. It was said to have later died in hospital. As I say. I report them, you decide what to do with them.

1954

Near Reno in Washoe County in Nevada on April 4th 1954. Around dusk the 11-year old main witness was in the back seat, sitting listlessly as the vehicle traveled along the bumpy terrain in the Nevada desert. His mother; Florence, a gifted psychic, had not explained the purpose of the cross country journey to the witness. Suddenly the car stopped. The driver, a man from Brooklyn, her mother and the witness got out. A strange object manifested before the witness as the driver and her mother appeared to be in a state of suspended animation. She stood there and watched it, but felt no fear. It was more like the feeling one gets when an epiphany unfolds that set their course in time. The object, a ship of some kind, was diamond shaped, looking much like a star tetrahedron. The main witness was "beamed" onboard. The ship took off and she clearly remembers being in an orbit around the Earth, as she sat fixated looking out of a circular window. She saw three people, perhaps screened images. She sat on a bench in a circular room with a boy approximately age 5, who said nothing. If she experienced any fear, she was quickly calmed with the ethereal appearance of a male and a female in white robes. The male was an entity she had spoken to all her life "Zoroaster." From that point on, he would be more active in her life as what is called a spirit guide. She would meet the boy again, many years in the future, and would know him as Alexander. She was shown a future in which she would help shape the destiny of this planet. She remembers viewing two circular screens in which endless images were shown. One ran alongside the perimeter of the vehicle, which appeared to have scenes of human history, while the other came from a "liquid like core" in the center of the room, producing archetypical holographic messages that she watched with recognition on some level, but to this day do not fully understand. There was a momentary pause, as if the projections were finished. She next remembers being on the ground and "right time" resuming. This experience would never happen again.

On June 11th 1954 East of Sparks in Cherry County in Nevada. In the morning, Mr. and Mrs. Arthur Hoag saw 15 to 20 red cigar shaped objects in the skies moving to the North. The objects were also viewed through 12-power field glasses and they weren't anything recognizable as planes. Mr. Hoag, a newspaper man said he did not know what the objects were. The objects had small silver wings or fins that were seen about three minutes before the objects disappeared to the North at terrific speed.

On September 22nd 1954 at 2300hrs in Marshfield in Webster County, Missouri. Two employees of the Webster Gas Company of Marshfield were returning from making a delivery to Bracken, when 5km east of Marshfield on the Scout camp road they observed a formation of three clouds of silvery dots. They stopped to watch them, then saw a boomerang shaped object at 180m altitude, about 200m south west. One side of this boomerang was much longer than the other, appeared to be about 2m long in total and very thin. It was silent and appeared to be covered by some sort of plastic material. The entire object revolved very slowly. It was dark in colour, with two red stripes near the end of the wing, through which the sun appeared to shine. As they watched, the object appeared to climb to 450m without changing its rotation, this taking about 20 seconds. It then began to descend at a slower pace. After 150m it started to tumbled, then emitted a puff of white smoke and fell into a stretch of timber, though they were unable to see the actual impact because of the terrain. They left the truck to investigate and found two areas of pulverised earth.

1956

Near Nellis Air Force Base in Clark County, Nevada during summer 1956 an Airforce Officer driving at night bound for the Air Base had a small delay. His car engine had suddenly and mysteriously died and he got out and started to walk but found that he was bothered by an unfamiliar sand-dune nearby. He then realised that this was actually a circular, disc-shaped craft 100 feet in diameter with a dome on top. It then took off into the sky. There were three landing gears on the bottom and it flew low over the witness's head. The witness then went back to the car and it started immediately. He reported to Intelligence on return to the base and examination of the landing site showed three clearly defined concave depressions in the sand. When is a sand-dune not a sand-dune?

1957

In Orogrande in Otero County in Nevada on 4th November 1957 James Stokes and several other people were in a car. They halted the car as a huge pearly object passed over Highway 54. There were massed sightings of luminous electromagnetic objects moving around in the sky as well. These phenomena indicated that they could move down as well as up therefore indicating that they could equalize or neutralize gravity. These phenomena were normalized by the witnesses so as to make sense of them. This is a feature of the human brain that attempts to adapt the occurrence of phenomena into recognizable forms so as not to distress the observer completely. It does not work satisfactorily all of the time.

On November 23rd 1957 thirty miles West of Tonopah, Nevada. Between 6:10-6:30 a.m. 1st Lt. Joseph F. Long, a fighter pilot was in his car and the engine stalled. He heard a high-pitched whining noise and saw four landed 50-foot saucer-shaped UFO's to the right of the road at 900-1200 feet away. He approached on foot to 50 feet distance and the objects lifted off, flew North over the highway and disappeared behind hills half a mile away. There were ground impressions at the landing site. Here is another version. An airforce 1st Lt, Joseph E Long, was driving towards Las Vegas at 130kph, when 50km west of Tonopah his engine suddenly stopped. Getting out to investigate, his attention was drawn, by a steady high pitched whine, to four discs on the ground, about 300-400m west of the road. He walked for several minutes until he was within 15m of the nearest disc. The objects were identical domed discs, 15m diameter, and 3-4.5m thick. The body of each object was self-luminous; the domes were transparent and appeared to be made of a different material. Underneath was a landing gear of three darks balls, 60cm diameter. These discs were surrounded by a dark, rotating outer ring. The hum increased in pitch until it was almost painful, the discs lifted to 15m, the landing gear retracting as they did so. They then moved away at about 15kph, north across the highway, following the contours of the ground, and disappearing behind some hills. The only trace left behind was an equilateral triangle of bowl shaped depressions, 20-30cm apart. The observation lasted for 20 minutes. When it was over the 1956 Chevrolet worked perfectly.

1958

In Summer 1958 at night in Stillwater in Churchill County, Nevada. Four teenage boys (Gordon and Will Chism, Bill Rose and Ken Taber, were driving back to their cabin when they observed what they took to be the headlight of a car on the road behind them. As the light got within 100-150m of them, it rose up to 30-50m. They could see that it was an oval, 6m diameter, which alternately brightened and dimmed and appeared to have some sort of rotary motion. After about 10 minutes the thing moved 200m to the south. The youths returned to the cabin, swopped their swamp buggy for a station wagon and went in pursuit of the light. At first they were unable to see the thing but it then rose up to 6m. It was then joined buy a bright red sphere 60-90cm diameter, which rose from the ground and entered the main object. The object then moved towards the cabin, lighting the cloud cover and ground as it moved slowly. The lads followed it and went up onto the cabin roof. After 30-45minutes the thing became stationary about 800m away. Suddenly, without any perceptible movement it was right overhead. The boys leapt off the roof and when they looked back the thing had gone.

On August 12th 1958 in Las Vegas in Clark County, Nevada. 19km west of Las Vegas a round orange object, giving off a diffuse light, moved up and down and to the left at treetop height, went back to the original position, repeated the performance and then disappeared.

1961

In the Black Rock Desert in Humboldt, Pershing and Washoe Counties in Nevada during Spring 1961. One afternoon Johnny Sue; an American Indian, was looking for stray stock in northwestern Nevada. He was riding his horse along some automobile tracks in a very rugged area when he suddenly realized that the tracks were no longer there. Out of curiosity, Johnny turned his horse and rode back to find out where the tracks had turned off. He came upon them again, but they had not turned off, they had simply stopped, with no evidence that the vehicle had turned around, or retraced its own tracks in reverse. Puzzled, Johnny Sue continued on his way when suddenly a funny feeling came over him. Something compelled him to turn his horse into the mouth of a narrow canyon. As he rode on, he was overcame by a lethargic feeling and felt "sleepy." In this lethargic state he came upon a huge metallic object, resembling a grain storage tank, on the ground. Around this object were a group of persons engaged in various activities, which Johnny was unable to describe. Apparently the beings then communicated by using telepathy with the witness. Sensing that he was in the presence of some superior force, he then "asked" them, "Who is God?" In reply they drew a symbol on the ground that resembled a large letter "O" with the angle of a smaller "v" intersecting its upper right shoulder. After that the witness apparently blacked out. Before blacking out, Johnny Sue also had asked where they were from and saw a vision in his mind of a hard to describe world or place. When he woke up, the object and beings were gone.

At 2 a.m. on July 17th 1961 one mile North of Bonny Spring Ranch [Bonnie Springs?] near Las Vegas, Nevada. On U.S. Highway 91 [95?], 2 civilians in a car saw in the rear-view mirror a low-flying object that overtook their car, followed by a rush of cold air. It stopped, circled the vehicle, flew off and was lost to sight behind the mountains, where it may have landed but exhaustive military investigation found no trace.

1962

In South Nevada on Wednesday 18th April 1962 at 7.30 pm during an earthquake there was a brilliant flash of light in the sky followed by rumbles of noise. There were no clouds in the sky. In one spot we have the earthquake and a strange flash of light. This odd UFO was first seen over Oneida in New York where it was seen as a glowing red object traveling West at high altitude. It was too high for a plane, too slow for a missile and it was not a meteor as it had been tracked on radar which cannot track meteors. It then moved across the states of Kansas, Utah, Montana, New Mexico, Wyoming, Arizona and California. Then it landed in Eureka in Juab County in Utah.

Shortly before the sighting at Eureka, Sheriff Raymond Jackson of Nephi in Juab County in Utah noticed that the photoelectric cells on the streetlights were tripped by the bright object and he also heard a kind of roar as he saw a yellow-white flame going West. He then heard a series of booms and saw that all the lights went out. The lights in a doctor's office also went out at the same time as well as other lights in buildings that were not affected by photo-electric cells. There were several other witnesses who described that the light lit up the area like day.

Finally at Eureka in Juab County in Utah on Wednesday 18th April 1962 at 7.30 pm thousands of people, in fact the whole town saw a large UFO that landed near a power-station. It was unidentified and circular and there was a blackout lasting thirty minutes whilst the craft stayed near the power station. NORAD Radar had tracked it all the way from Canada and the UFO had landed during the earth-quake. Meteors cannot be tracked on radar. And in another nearby area we have a large UFO hovering over the area at the same time as the earthquake for the duration of an electricity blackout. Any connection?

Initially the object came in over Cuba, Utah, and apparently landed to the West of the town of Eureka. The object was bright enough to trip the photo-electric cell that controlled the city street lights. The meteor or UFO possibly fell into the Wasatch National Forest.

Also on 18th April 1962 there were numerous witnesses of a strange aerial phenomenon above Las Vegas in Nevada. The object was tracked by radar and there was possible physical evidence. Nellis Air Force Base had initially tracked an aerial object on radar for a few seconds around 7.20 pm. It was initially heading northeast and then disappeared instantly to the South at an altitude of 10,000 feet. To people on the ground it was visible as a brilliant explosive red flare in the sky that was seen by dozens of witnesses. It resembled a red flaming sword flashing across the sky. Other witnesses stated that there was a series of bright explosions that broke up its trail across the sky. Sheriff's Deputy Walter Butt was in charge of the departments search and rescue team and consensus agreed that the flaming object had headed East and there had been a final explosion near Mesquite in Clark County, Nevada near the Utah border. Butt investigated an area between Spring Mountain and Mesquite.

That same night of 18th April 1962 General Laurence S. Kuter, NORAD, took off and was climbing through 10,000 feet when he saw a meteor come out of orbit. The object was cherry red, clear green, with a long white and red tail and he estimated it as being near Colorado Springs in El Paso County in Colorado. At the same time reports of the same object came in from Idaho, Utah and Arizona by OCD Regions Navy aircraft, B-52 crews and DC-8 pilots. All the reports were alike in shape, color, and general direction of travel from South to North.

Fifty minutes after the Colorado Springs sighting, shortly after midnight, early on 19th April 1962, there were numerous reports to the FAA and AFLC command post of a luminous aerial object that was observed over Los Angeles in Teller County in Colorado, near Colorado Springs, Montana, Kansas and Utah. Captain Shields of the 733 Troop Carrier Squadron of Ogden in Utah, reported to the AFLC that the object appeared around 0300Z and was bright like burning magnesium and was traveling from the southwest to the northeast.

1963

On November 14th 1963 in Carson City in Nevada. A huge bluish-green disc was seen hovering in the northwest sky about 4:45 a.m. Mrs. Blanche Pritchett said she was listening to her radio when a bright light shining through her drapes caused her to look outdoors. As she watched the hovering object, her radio went off. A brilliant shaft of light from the UFO illuminated a hilltop. Suddenly the UFO blacked out and disappeared, after which the radio resumed playing. Other residents reported odd glows in the sky that morning.

1964

In Spring Valley in White Pine County in Nevada on 25th June 1964 Mr. George W. Rogers and his brother Mr. Bert Rogers were in a car when they noticed an object on the road ahead that was hovering at four feet. The craft then landed on a pedestal two feet high and resembled a pyramid-shaped top with the point tapering down to the pedestal. The top was curved and spinning rapidly. George jumped out of the car and ran up to touch it as it hummed and rose to ten feet up. The craft was now forty feet away and did this three or four times as George kept approaching it. Then it took off to the East over a ridge. The sides were shiny like plastic and there was an insignia or emblem on one side. A plastic UFO? Previously there had been a passenger train stopped by a mudfall here in 1879. Or this version. Rancher George W Rogers of Spring Valley was driving to Ely with his brother Bert when they noticed a peculiar object, which they thought was a crashed jeep, beside the road. They then realized it was the top of an object 1.2m above the road. The thing then rose and landed on the road, resting on a 60cm long slender pedestal, and the witnesses, who were within a metre or two of it, saw it was a pyramid shaped top with the point facing down to the pedestal. The top was curved and rotating rapidly. George ran out to touch the thing which, as he drew near, rose 3m with a loud humming sound, descending on the road 12m away. This performance took place three or four times. Finally, prompted by his brother's warnings, George re-entered the car and the object rose slowly and then moved rapidly away to the east, vanishing behind a ridge. George noticed that the surface of the thing was made of a shiny plastic like material, and that it had a red insignia on one face, which he could not make out because of the rapid spin.

1965

In August 1965 at 2300hrs in Missouri. A woman in her 20s driving home saw some lights in the sky. On the ground were things, which resembled large birds, in a ditch. The next day all she remembered was driving further along the road, with a severe headache. When she arrived home it was after 0100. Under hypnotic regression in 1977 she recalled that the car stopped and the lights went out. The creatures in the ditch were strange, small bipeds. An object descended and three humanoids got out of it. She was taken on board the object, where she was examined with the aid of an instrument like a large black eye, the occupants being particularly concerned with her red toe nails. Finally she was brought out the object.

1968

Around 8.00 pm on 23rd June 1968 the witness was driving from Las Vegas when he saw a round saucer-shaped object land on a dirt road not far away from the road. The witness drove up the dirt road to the craft which had landed on three leglike protrusions. Soon three bearded men, very human in appearance, disembarked from it. They approached the witness who had now got out of his car and expressed curiosity as to his long hair. The witness explained that he just wanted to wear it but was not into drugs. They seemed to appreciate this. They then told him that they came from a world where there were no cities where its inhabitants were born in the wilderness. They told him that cities were a danger to their society. They called themselves "Dodonians". The witness shook hands with the men and they boarded the craft which quickly left the area.

Late at night on 2nd July 1968 a man and his girlfriend were parked on an isolated desert road and were lying on a blanket near the car when they suddenly felt a strong heat wave hit them. The man looked up to see two men, both about five foot six inches tall standing next to him. Both were encased in a soft light. Both wore coveralls resembling divers suits and they had human-like faces and were baldheaded. They spoke to the witnesses in a strange unknown language. Behind the men hovered a circular object with several small lights around its middle. The two men raised the witnesses up by their arms and began feeling their naked bodies. The Humanoids then made the witnesses kneel and one of them cut off some of the woman's hair and put it into a container. The Humanoids then walked beneath the object and were then illuminated by a beam of light and vanished. The object then shot away at high speed. This was near Las Vegas.

On October 28th 1968 at 2320 in Las Vegas in Nevada a bright white light hovered over the desert 300-400 feet away at 10-15 feet altitude; then it was replaced by a group of smaller lights, red, white and blue which blinked in a pattern indicating 3 sides of a square. Behind this could-be seen a somewhat nebulous figure, not clearly defined. Duration.: 25 min.

At Nellis Air Force Base in Clark County in Nevada in 1968. Military personnel reported watching a large object hovering above the base for three consecutive days. Three small objects were seen departing the larger craft and one landed on the base grounds. A Colonel accompanied by an armed security detachment was sent to meet the landed craft. While waiting outside, the men watched a short stocky humanoid disembark from the craft. A green beam of light was then aimed at the Colonel from inside the object causing him to become paralyzed. Orders were then issued to fire on the object and humanoid but all weapons mysteriously jammed. The object and humanoid eventually departed into the larger hovering craft.

1969

On January 26th 1969 at 0500hrs in Fernley in Lyon County, Nevada. Keary Schade, a young man who lived on a farm just southeast of Fernley, was milking his cows when he noticed a red ball hovering near the ground 400-800m away. It had a red light in its centre, surrounded by a white misty glow. The light pulsated in intensity in one second brief flashes. The object moved slowly, stopped as the red light became dimmer, and then it moved and stopped again and the light went out. About 400m from its original position the thing reappeared, stopped and went out, reappeared and ascended in a jerking motion towards Reno in the west. The thing was observed for less than a minute. It had an angular diameter of 3 degrees, suggesting a diameter of 25m if it was at a distance of 500m.

Near Reno in Washoe County in Nevada in 1969. At 10.00 a.m. in a desert area 30 miles East of Reno the 7-year old witness and his father arrived at the location in their Volkswagen Van in order to do some rabbit hunting. The weather was clear with a blue crisp sky. The young witness said his father stayed in the van to drink beer, as he always did while he would go hunting rabbits with his 22 cal. rifle. A minute or so into the hunt, he shot a rabbit, retrieved it and continued the hunt. According to him, it was just a minute or two later that he saw another rabbit and began to take aim at it when something within his peripheral vision about 8 to 10 feet away off to his right side caught his eye. He was startled and just turned his head slightly to the right and realized he was looking at a "thing" standing there, staring at him. He described the "thing" as about his height, which was about 4 feet tall, very skinny, with long arms, large head with large dark eyes and was grayish in color. He said he was immediately frightened but had kept his rifle pointed in the direction of the rabbit. He remembers keeping the "thing" within his peripheral vision and noticed that it started turning its head slightly to its right in the direction of the rabbit the witness had intended to shoot. However the creature then turned its head back, looking at him and simultaneously began raising its right arm, held straight out. The young witness became extremely frightened and thought the creature was about to do something to hurt him, so he swung his rifle in the direction of the creature and fired one shot into the upper right side of its chest and it fell to the ground. As quickly as it happened the witness said he dropped both his rifle and the rabbit he had shot earlier and ran back to the parked van, crying and screaming for his dad. He said as he got to the van, his dad, who may have been intoxicated at the time, began scolding him wanting to know why he was crying and not hunting. He tried to explain to his dad that he had shot a "thing" and may have killed it. His dad purportedly responded by telling him he was only supposed to shoot rabbits and began asking what had he done with the rifle. He continued to plead with his dad to go back and see if they could help the "thing" he had shot. However his dad was adamant and 'drunk' and ordered him to go back to get his rifle and the rabbit he had shot and to keep hunting. He did as he was told and went back, found his rifle and the rabbit he had shot earlier, but the creature was gone. He looked in the area where it had been laying after he shot it to see if there was any blood but saw none. The very next thing he remembers is that as he was standing there where he had shot the creature he suddenly saw a craft hovering just above the ground an estimated 200 feet away. He saw he could only describe it as a cylinder or cigar-shaped object, metallic looking and as long as a football field. The next detail he remembered was being in some type of a "room" with beams like frame work and what appeared to be a lot of dust. He was frightened and crying, and the next he remembers is being in the back seat of the van, alone in the dark, crying for his dad who wasn't there. His next memory was he and his dad driving home in the dark. He asked his dad why they were going home at night since they usually left in the afternoon but his dad completely ignored the question. He never spoke to his father about the incident again. He believes both were probably abducted and he thinks he has had later experiences in his life.

1970

Near Tonopah in Nye County in Nevada one night in 1970. William Huff was working at a military installation and one night was walking to his barracks from a movie. "I look up and I see this beautiful light coming down over the mountains. This is the first time I had ever seen what I thought was a UFO." Huff stood there spellbound, watching a beautiful craft that came down over the desert. He could see the shape of it, and see portholes and other details. He then realized he was standing there alone, so he went back inside the nearest building to find some witnesses. The other men scoffed at him, claiming it was a helicopter. Huff insisted, reminding the men that they had helicopters on the base and that this object did not make any noise. So after Huff and one of the other men watched it for a couple of minutes, it wobbled and it shot off into deep space in a second. Somehow Huff knew that he had made "mental contact with the occupants." They knew he was watching them. He thought no more about it for years, until a professor at the University of Wyoming (Dr. Leo Sprinkle) convinced him to undergo hypnosis and answer questions about his sighting. Under hypnosis, Huff was able to remember the occupants of the UFO; he saw five men standing in front of him. They were all the same height and looked pretty much alike. They have an all-knowing look on their faces. They're very handsome. They have hair, it's not long, it's just full. They were wearing tight-fitting uniforms, no helmets. He was standing inside a large circular room. There is a bright light that doesn't hurt his eyes and he sees a center piece that looks like a control center. The men communicated with Huff without moving their lips, apparently using telepathy. Huff had a feeling that he would like to go with these people, wherever, they were going. "I don't feel like they're Gods or anything, I just feel like they are intelligent people from another place in the universe that's far ahead of us in technology and I want to learn." Huff predicted that the safest place in the world one day will be Brazil, because of the axial shift of the Earth. He said he felt the space beings were coming here to help us.

1972

At Papoose Lake in Lincoln County in Nevada one morning in Summer 1972. Major Steve Wilson had begun his duties at the Papoose Lake installation, not knowing what was located, thirty stories farther down. He had been well indoctrinated in Top Secret work and knew all the consequences of keeping the nation's most guarded secrets. The past six years had been slow and boring, he recalls and other than what he saw at Wright-Patterson AFB he felt that he was in a vacuum going nowhere. He was sitting in his office at S-4 mulling this over one morning when a Lieutenant Colonel Bennett came in. He asked Wilson if he was busy and said, "Let's go." Wilson followed the Lieutenant Colonel and they eventually wound up two stories down at the super-secret S-4 UFO technology area. As they came out on a landing, there Wilson saw eight different kinds of UFOs. There were intellectual looking people all over the area, who he guessed were scientists. He glanced at Bennett, who cut off his implied question with a curt "Forget it." The Colonel and the Major went into a cubicle where there were about 20 officers and civilians sitting around. Wilson was startled when a woman came in who was at least eight feet tall. There was not an ounce of excess fat on her body, he recalls. She wore a strange-looking jump suit, which had a "HI" pattern on the right side above the breast line. To this day Wilson recollects the details of this striking encounter. The woman had finely chiseled features. Her blond hair cascaded neatly past her shoulders. Her eyes were the bluest he had ever seen. Somehow she was different. Little did he know how different then. She sat a large crystal on the table and without warning her fingers began to glow as she ran them over the crystal. A 3-D hologram began to form above it. He looked around the room and everyone's mouth was hanging open, and suddenly he noticed his was too. At this moment in time his whole concept of life did a 180-degree turn. Colonel Wilson related that among the scenes, which the female extraterrestrial's crystal hologram displayed for the assembled group was the history of the Earth and of extraterrestrial involvement with it. That involvement included fashioning the consciousness of Jesus and sending him to live among earthlings to point to a better way to understand life and to live. The extraterrestrial woman also showed the officers and scientists' scenes from inhabited planets of other star systems. Wilson was transformed by this experience. "When it was over, I knew that, whatever part I was to play in all of this, my life as I knew it had ended forever."

1973

Early in the morning on 28th October 1973 a female witness in Reno in Washoe County in Nevada went to the window and saw three very large saucer-shaped objects hovering across the street. A ground crew of ten to twelve figures wearing dully glowing cube type uniforms. They were milling around as if searching for something. A very low pitched hum was heard but no barking by the witness's dog or others in the neighborhood. When two of the men approached her driveway she took alarm and returned to bed where she fell asleep immediately. Or this. Mrs Imogene Proctor was having difficulty sleeping and went to the window, to find, to her amazement, three very large saucer shaped objects hovering across the street. About 10-12 figures, wearing cube type uniforms ,were milling about the area. Their extremities were not visible, but they seemed to be illuminated by a dull glow and appeared to be systematically examining the area. When the witness opened the window to hear if there was any sound coming from the object, she noticed the absence of the usual night sounds (crickets etc.). The street light was brighter than usual. Her family dogs were absolutely silent, as if they had been drugged. She detected a low buzzing sound. Everything else was unusually silent and motionless. Two of the objects then approached and she went back to bed very frightened. She the suddenly went to sleep and awoke in the morning, There was no trace of the objects and no one else seems to have seen them.

1974

Near Las Vegas, Nevada in January 1974. In the late afternoon Contactee Dr. Frank E Stranges (allegedly involved with ongoing contacts with an extraterrestrial calling himself, "Val Thor") drove out into the desert in order to rendezvous with the extraterrestrials. The aliens claim to be from Venus (on a higher vibratory plane of that planet that bears life on what we call the middle astral plane; but these beings have the power to adjust their normal higher body frequency to that of Earth). On his way to meet Valiant Thor, Stranges was attacked along a desert road by several men in a large black car. The men physically assaulted Stranges. As he says, "I was thrown to the ground and kicked over and over again." Before long, Stranges had sustained numerous bruises and a badly crushed hand. In the midst of the assault, Valiant Thor showed up and rescued Stranges from the attackers. Stranges was taken inside a UFO where he was treated for his injuries. As Stranges says, "As I lay atop the soft white table, I was conscious of the beam of soft blue light that emitted from the cone-shaped equipment which was aimed first at my head, and then at my solar plexus. I immediately went into a deep sleep. Upon awakening, I felt good all over."

On February 14th 1974 in Ely in White Pine County in Nevada a round orange object paced and approached a truck. There were electromagnetic effects on the lights and engine and at one time the truck lifted off the road. Steering control was lost and there was the feeling of a vacuum. Or this version. At 4.15 am two brothers were driving a truck from Buhl (Idaho) to Helmet (California), one sleeping while the other was driving. 88km north of Ely the driver woke his brother to tell him that an unidentified object was following them. The sleeping brother did not take any notice till his brother woke him again, 10 minutes later. He then looked out of the left side of the cab to see a round orange object about 3m above the ground. Through the right side of the cab he could see three smaller blue objects at a higher altitude. One of these flickered on and off, while the other was constant. The driver said that the orange object had passed from the right tom the left. At this point the truck appeared to be buffeted by a sudden blast of wind, the lights flickered on and off, then engine began to misfire, the driver lost control of the steering and the transmission selector jumped from "drive" to "neutral" and the truck coasted to a halt. As the brothers sat in their cab, with the engine running, they observed a huge silver ball, surmounted by a dome and with short pointed wings hovering and pulsating above a hill to the left. They then saw, on the road ahead of them, a huge light, with a red light on top of it, making towards them from about 1.5km ahead. One of the brothers got out of the truck and shone his flashlight ion this thing, without effect and then went to inspect the truck to find that the drive shaft was turning. Very frightened he got back into the cab and watched the light get closer. They felt that they were in a vacuum, isolated from the rest of the world. Then either car or something else zoomed past them at terrific speed and suddenly the experience seemed to be over. They put reflectors on the road to avoid a collision and flagged down a car, which took them to McGill, where they got another truck and drove back to the wreck. The truck was a right-off. Investigations showed that the damage was caused by lack of proper lubrication and had no connection with the experience.

On July 1st 1974 at 2200hrs in Carson Valley in Douglas County, Nevada. A woman observed a large object, changing from yellow to brilliant green, and illuminating the area, come down out of the sky and land in the Carson Valley area. It was also seen from Reno, 50km away.

1975

On April 19th 1975 at 2145hrs in Carson City, Nevada. Two people stopped at a traffic light saw a metallic looking disc shaped object about 15m above them The thing was about 25m diameter, with an orange glow on its underside. It was surmounted by a dome, on which there were rotating lights. Their car radio began to emit a strange beeping sound at the rate of three beeps per second. After about 30 seconds the disc moved off at speed and the car radio returned to normal.

1976

In Las Vegas in Clark County in Nevada on 29th January 1976 northwest of town Johnny Sands, a country and western singer, was returning to Las Vegas from Pahrump and was fifteen miles South of town on the Blue Diamond Road when he saw a craft which then followed him for three miles. John's car engine started spluttering and stalled and he pulled over and got out of it. He then saw a UFO hovering 1,000 feet above him. It was like the Goodyear Blimp and was sixty feet long with portholes each ten feet in diameter. It was a rusty orange color with flashing red and white lights. As Johnny turned back to work on his car he saw two Humanoids approaching him from the landed UFO. They talked to him and calmed him down. They also asked a number of questions. They were five feet seven inches tall, grey skinned, had slits instead of ears and black eyes with white pupils. They spoke labored English and walked into the desert after ten minutes. After they had walked two hundred feet there was a flash of light and they were gone. What sort of questions had they asked? Here is another version. At 2200hrs Country singer Johnny Sands (30) was driving on the Blue Diamond Road when he saw an unusual aircraft. He did not pay much attention to it as it paced his car for 5km. At this point his engine began to malfunction, so he pulled off the road and got out to see what was wrong. As he was checking the car, he saw the object "like a Goodyear Blimp", 18m long, with a large circular ring mid section, hovering 300m above him. It also had circular windows about 3m diameter, 1. 5m apart. The object was rusty-red in colour, with flashing red and white lights on the end. It moved slowly over the mountain to the south, lighting up the mountains and appearing to land. Sands turned back to his car, then turned and looked up the road in the direction of his headlights and saw two figures approaching. He first feared they may be muggers, but as they got within 1 and 1. 5m respectively, he saw they were perfectly bald beings with neither eyebrows not eyelashes, who had gill like protrusions, which moved rapidly all the time they stood there, on either side of their faces. They had small, black, deep set eyes with very white pupils. Their small mouths never opened and they had flat pug noses. After 10 minutes they walked away into the desert. After they had gone 45-60m they disappeared in a flash of light. During the 10 minutes the beings were with Sands, they asked him several questions about earth life and warned him not to talk about the episode. They seemed to talk from their bodies and their voices were very deep. They wore silvery overalls with a diagonal white strap around their shoulders. They were 1. 7m or just under tall and their faces seemed extremely old. There was a positive polygraph test.

1978

At 5.30 pm on December 16th 1978 at McCarran Airport in Las Vegas in Nevada a married couple and a child saw a disc-shaped object with glowing white lights. The UFO made several falling leaf movements. An airline pilot flying in the vicinity also reported that a UFO streaked by his airliner although the UFO did not appear on radar.

1982

On June 10th 1982 in Las Vegas in Clark County in Nevada there were five of us laying on top of a shed roof looking at the stars listening to the radio and talking about how we had the whole summer to play because school was out. We were five boys. I will not use our names but B. was the youngest at about 9 years old, S. and G. were both were about 12 and R. was about 16 and K. was the oldest at about 17 years. B. woke me up and was scared pointing in the direction of the UFO and he looked frightened. I tried to calm him down in case he fell off the roof so that we would not get into trouble because he was the youngest and our parents would go ballistic and we were all in sleeping blankets on a small roof which made it hard to move around. He was just pointing behind me and saying "what is that?, What is that?, What is that light?" and I heard a voice that said in English "calm him down and tell him everything will be ok" and it was a very authority like voice in my head. While I was trying to calm him down he was pointing over my shoulder and I turned and there was the craft I have mentioned. R. who was one of the older boys was suspended in the air flat as a board still in his sleeping blanket. I just stared at it and B. was still behind me waiting for me to do something about the situation. I was just mesmerized by the black bulb where the voice seemed to telepathically emanate from because it was still telling me not to panic and everything was going to be Oklahoma No harm was going to be done to us. They were not going to kill us or take us and I felt calm and was just focused on it and not B. who was just huddled behind me. I started asking it questions with my thoughts and not my mouth on what they were and what they wanted and why did they have R. floating near them. It told me a lot of information very quickly and I cannot remember all of it, but what I could gather is that they lived a million billion zillion miles away and have been around a long time and we were not that important to them supposedly because we were like flakes of skin in that we had a purpose or function, but it was not a great importance, as the brain is, compared to flakes of skin (I hope this makes sense. Remember I was only 12 and this was 1982). I started asking lots of questions as in, because why and I do not understand and explain it to me and then I felt B. panicking and yelling again because he was frightened for me because to him I was just silently sitting there staring at the craft and as I looked across the shed I wondered why no one else was awake but us two and the voice told me to just go back to sleep and not to worry about B and that is the last thing I remember until the sun woke us up at around 5 to 6 six in the morning. We all got off the shed and headed back to the house. B. started asking everyone what happened. The older boys told him very angrily to shut up about it and when we went into the house and went back to sleep and we slept for at least 18 to 24 hours. Our parents tried to wake us because they thought we were sick or something because we should be running around, watching television and playing. We never really talked about it to anyone else as far as I remember and it was just put aside like nothing happened because we were ok so what was there to complain about. It reminded me of the old Bell H 13 helicopter from the TV show Mash but a little longer tail section mixed with the look of a small submarine like the seamagine aurora. It had a large black glass bulb in front with a metal structure as the tail with real bright white lights maybe 4 like flood lights. it just hovered about 15 to 20 feet away from us and made no noise. The black glass bulb front was real black as in a real shiny onyx stone. The metal looking tail structure where the lights were looked more like the outer structure of a small sub or helicopter because it had the lights attached there and sort of metal beams like the helicopter tail but stuck to the body of a small submarine but hard to make out because of the bright flood lights blocking my eyesight from that body and tail section. The front had no lights. Just this big black glass bulb as seen on the helicopter or small submarine and if anyone was sitting in it I would guess the bulb part could hold two people comfortably. The body or tail section once again hard to tell because of the lights but was not too big so maybe another two people. The whole craft was about the same dimensions as the Bell H 13 helicopter. The glass bulb part was black and the body was a dull gray metal.

It might not have great syntax but it conveys the mood brilliantly. That is why I prefer first person reports.

1985

On August 31st 1985 in Laughlin in Clark County in Nevada at 10:00 PM. A UFO, shape unknown, rose from the ground near US Highway 95. It directed beams of light on cars and a house, and radio interference was reported.

1986

On June 30th 1986 in Crescent Valley in Eureka County in Nevada I was working for a gold mine in the southern end of Crescent Valley, Nevada near the Eureka/Lander County line. The night in question we were hauling gravel from a pit in the valley floor. One time when I arrived at the pit to get a load of gravel the loader operator was standing on the deck of the loader and pointed a light out to me. It was obviously outside the earth's atmosphere, or at least several miles above the earth's surface. The light would travel diagonally down and to the right, then horizontally to the left, back down and to the right, then horizontally to the left, and kept repeating that pattern several times. Finally after a final movement down and to the right, it would go up and slightly left so as to arrive at the point of beginning. It seemed to pause for a second or two at each change in direction. It would then repeat the maneuver, which we watched numerous times before going back to work. The movements were smooth and at a steady speed, without either acceleration at the beginning of each directional change or deceleration at the end thereof. Considering that the object had to have been in space and the degree of movement, I believe it was covering a considerable distance in a matter of 2 or 3 seconds. It was dark outside at the time of this observation. I have often thought about and wondered what we observed that night. I have considered the possibility that it was a satellite, but it is my understanding they do not move that fast. An aircraft could not make directional changes like that, nor would it be able to make the directional changes without accelerating and decelerating.

1989

At 5.00 pm on January 30th 1989 in Battle Mountain in Lander County in Nevada three witnesses saw an oval object with red lights for fifteen minutes. There was no sound.

Near Yucca Flats, Nellis Test Range, in Clark County in Nevada in November 1989. An alien craft (shape unknown, probably disk or cylinder) with a crew of six crashed on the territory of the test range, probably after being shot down by the US military. Six bodies of the small dwarf-like type (probably gray) were found, all dead. The six alien bodies were moved to the nearest deep underground facility near Yucca Flats (laboratory section), for preliminary study at one of the levels there. This was accidentally witnessed by a team of workers (including an electrician). Inside the base, the six small bodies were moved on stretchers. There were marines armed with rifles with fixed bayonets pushing the witnesses back. Accompanying the stretchers were several government scientists who ordered the witnesses out of the room. The wreckage of the craft was hidden and then studied, most likely at the Nellis test range.

1991

Near Searchlight in Clark County in Nevada at 1.00 am during February 1991 James J Youlton was driving his mother and brother to Las Vegas. In an isolated stretch of highway, while his mother slept in the backseat, James and his brother spotted a strange man on the side of the road. As they got closer, the stranger started waving his hands around strangely. They noticed that he was wearing what appeared to be a red, plaid shirt and blue jeans. He also appeared to be wearing some sort of mask, as his entire head was white and had no discernible features. The same went for his hands, which looked like he had solid white gloves on that didn't separate fingers or thumbs. Youlton decided not to stop and kept driving. About five minutes further down the road, both his brother and him saw what looked at first glance to be a meteor falling off to the right side of the road. As they watched something strange happened. As it got close to the ground, it fell down in front of a small mountain just ahead of them and took a strange "bounce" as it hit the ground. As they passed by the mountain a minute later, a brightly glowing, blob shaped ball of pale blue light came up from the direction of the impact. It hovered in front of their car as they traveled around 65 mph. As they stared at the object, it suddenly moved very fast, back down the road where the witnesses had come from.

1992

In Las Vegas, Nevada late at night in August 1992. The witness who had been asleep suddenly found herself floating just above her bed. A strong yellow light appeared across the room through some type of "portal." A figure than appeared in the portal. The figure was described as human-like, bluish in color, of medium built, and with dark blond haircut like a bowl that fell to his ears. His eyes were round and blue. The figure looked at the witness, motioned to her to keep quiet then disappeared.

1993

At 8.31 pm on March 16th 1993 in the Tikaboo Valley in Lincoln County in Nevada two investigators parked out in a remote desert site began watching mysterious lights maneuvering over the area. One of the lights suddenly began to approach. It was a large object with bright square light panels that glowed with amber and blue light. As the object, now transformed into two or three bright orbs of light, passed over the vehicle, one of the men attempted to snap a photograph. At this point a state of confusion seemed to have overcome both of the witnesses, as both then became aware of a strange vehicle driving quickly away from the area. A period of missing time was noted. Later under hypnotic regression the main witness was able to recall that the object stopped and hovered over their vehicle. He was floated up through the bottom of the object and inside was met by a being that seemed to walk through a brightly lit interior wall in the craft. The being was gray in color and about 6 feet tall. His eyes were slanted and had what appeared to be black plastic shields on them, and his head was egg-shaped. He wore a two-tone gray suit, with a lighter V in the front and a black belt with a black tube on his right side. He also sported a triangular insignia enclosing a helical coil on the left breast of the suit. The being had long arms that ended in four long fingers. He then communicated with the witness then took him gently by the arm and escorted him inside a dome-like room that was brightly lit. The witness remembers seeing the other witness on the floor, as if frozen apparently being guarded by a short gray Humanoid. The main witness was then placed on a metal table that tilted 30 degrees to face a curving wall filled with a row of

computer like screens. The being said that this process was a mind-sharing procedure that would allow the witness to learn new things. After about 5 minutes the witness was returned to the exit and jump-floated to the ground about 20 feet below. Tikaboo Valley is near Area 51.
1996
At 7.30 pm on February 28th 1996 on Highway 375 in Nevada five witnesses driving in an isolated stretch of desert highway, watched a noiseless, silvery gray colored disc, flat on the bottom, land about 50 feet away. It was about 30 feet in diameter. Three beings, described as thin, gray in color with large heads, came out, shuffled around, and then went back inside the object, which promptly took off. Much of Highway 375 runs alongside Nellis AFB and Area 51. This road is also called the Extraterrestrial Highway in Lincoln and Nye Counties.

Near Moundhouse in Lyons County in Nevada during April 1996. At 11: 00 p.m. the 25-year old witness was driving his Dodge Rampage on Highway 50 East of Moundhouse. His window was down, the air was blowing on his face and the radio was on fairly loud. As he passed the Virginia City turn off on his left, he noticed some lights on the hills at the mouth of the Canyon there. There were four lights. They were a whitish blue and very bright. They were lighting up the sagebrush on the hillside on the West side of the Highway. They were about 50 to 100 feet off the ground. As he drove away he thought that it must have been a low flying jet or plane coming from Reno. He looked back at the lights and they were still in the same spot. They were not moving. He could see the brush on the hill bright as day. He then saw some "things" moving in the brush, little objects scurrying about very quick like some type of animal like a coyote or something. His heart began to thump, his adrenaline kicked in as he realized that it was something different from the ordinary. He slowed down so he could see more of it. He then began to think it was a UFO, and said out loud, "Haha, yeah you know I can see you." As soon as he said that, the lights began to turn. They were no longer shining on the bush. They span approximately 100 yards apart with two on top about 30 yards apart and the lower ones at the sides about 100 yards apart. They resembled the lights in a stadium; they were very big and bright. There were no other cars behind him. Frightened he no longer watched the road; the lights had his total attention. The lights turned around and began slowly hovering over the canyon towards the Highway, as the witness kept driving on. There were smaller lights below the larger ones that were blinking in succession. That's when he realized that it was a round object. He kept driving towards the lights and his radio became fuzzy and then silent. Soon he came upon an embankment on the side of the highway that separated the lights from his vision but he also knew that the object was moving down the canyon at the same speed he was. He came to the hill and as soon as the embankment receded, there he saw something that he claims he will never forget. It was on the top of the hill to his left, right there as the ground cleared away he was gazing into the middle of a set of windows, mesmerized he stared. The windows were long draping all the way across and around. He saw tiers or stories, he saw walls. Everything inside was white. On the left bottom story in the window he saw several aliens, all wearing white robes; he saw a female figure with a bracelet and a necklace on, either gold or silver with makeup on her cheeks. Her arm was on the shoulder of a younger one, a boy, and they were looking right at the witness. She nudged herself to the boy and spoke to the other younger children along the window maybe ten or so more. They were all smaller than a 5-year old. She was talking to the older boy without apparently speaking. At the same time the witness felt a joyful feeling as they gazed into his eyes and she then smiled and pointed at him as to show them that he understood them. She had three long fingers and a thumb. He then had a terrible feeling and looked up to the second tier or story. Two beings were there in the middle of the room. The being he first saw had a long draped back skull like that of the move "Alien" and large black eyes, his skin was chocolate brown and he too was wearing a white robe. His skull was maybe two feet long behind his head draping down. The one with the draped skull on the second story was standing and holding a clipboard against himself in his white robe, he seemed to notice the witness, his mouth dropped and his eyes bulged as the alien realized that the witness was looking at him, he seemed frightened that the witness had seen him. He was definitely surprised, his eyes were white with huge blue irises and pupils, the witness estimated that he was 20 feet away from this alien. He immediately turned to the other one in the room in front of him. The one in front of him was sitting. The witness saw a side view of him but only his head at the time. He had a human-like head, with wrinkles all over his head, which made him look very old, no hair whatsoever was evident. He appeared to be wearing a black suit; he then turned his head to face the witness. At this point the witness became frightened, the alien's face was wrinkled and old and his eyes beady, and pure black. As the witness stared at the alien he realized that it was a human, and that he must have been thousands of years old. The witness was petrified. The "human" alien gave him a snarling look but at the same time displaying an immense intellect. There appeared to be a large screen in front of the alien which appeared to be blinking. Then looking directly at the witness he raised his hand up with a very long finger and smiled or smirked as he hit a button on some kind of panel in front of him. Instantly the windows covered themselves with a fanlike shell that resembled a Chinese fan descending from the top. Corrugated riffles about one foot high each descended from the top to the middle. They sparkled with different colors and were sharp-looking like razor blades. The bottom sealed up and lights began to blink in succession. Then the craft began to spin, emitting a slight humming sound like the blades of a giant fan. The object tilted at about 45 degree angle and as it spun faster and faster the witness could only see the outline of it, like it was suddenly cloaked. It then shot up into the sky leaving a small white trail behind for a split second. The witness seems to have experienced a period of missing time.

Near Area 51 in Lincoln County in Nevada in July 1996.. A man reported having being stationed at the Groom Lake, facility known commonly as 'Area 51,' as a security guard with a high clearance. He said that he was once called into a room where people were dissecting Bigfoot type creatures. There were several complete corpses in vats of liquid similar to formaldehyde. There were body parts, hearts, livers, and such, scattered all over the tables. Once he got to peek into another room he was passing when the door opened after a retinal scan of another guard, there he saw more vats, only containing "little white aliens with big black eyes."

New Mexico

1880
On 26th March 1880, at Galisteo Junction in Santa Fe County, New Mexico, four men sighted a strange balloon-shaped craft in the sky. It was flying directly over them and from it could be heard an unknown language being spoken and inside of it they could see eight to ten figures moving around. Suddenly an object fell to Earth from the craft. It was a vase covered in what the four men took to be hieroglyphics. The men took the singular trophy back to town with them. Several days later a stranger appeared in town, purchased the strange vase for a lot of money and then vanished. Galisteo junction is near Lamy and is rather remote so strangers were not a common sight. A singular event this one, until we get to the period of 1897 onwards. After all these are not even our first alleged hominoids in connection with an aerial craft. Not even our first alleged meeting with similar creatures. It is not even our first alleged unidentified falling vessel or vase, but it is the first observation of alleged alien writing. The first alleged alien artifact to descend to Earth was in Amherst, Massachusetts, in 1819 on 13th August . You now ask me what all of this stuff is? It's all made up you say. Yes it is. Everything in this book is apparently made up or a delusion. I've never denied that from the beginning. Nothing in this book is true but it might also still be real. Here is another version. Soon after the arrival of the train from Santa Fe, the local operator and two or three of his friends, taking a short walk before retiring were startled by voices coming from above them. Looking up they saw a sort of large balloon coming from the west. As it came closer they heard voices shouting in an unintelligible language, as if to attract attention. The object was shaped like a fish and at one point it was so low that the witnesses could see ornate lettering on the outside of the car. The craft appeared to be fully under the control of the occupants, and to be guided by a large fan like apparatus. They heard laughter and strains of music coming from it, as if a party were in progress. Some articles were dropped from the machine, including a flower attached to which was Japanese paper, and a cup of peculiar design. The balloon appeared to be huge, with about 8-10 people in the car. After it passed the junction it sailed up to a great height and away to the east. The next day a collector of curios arrived on the scene, informed the populace that the items came from Japan and bought them at a high price.

1901
Shortly before 15th March 1901 a local physician had photographed a clear picture of the airship over Silver City in Grant County in New Mexico. This was reported by the "Silver City Enterprise" but the photo has been lost. The flying machine had the appearance of three cigar-shaped objects that seemed to be lashed together, the one hanging below the other two.

1909
At Los Tanos in Guadalupe County in New Mexico on April 4th 1909. In the early morning Vicente Labadie of Los Tanos, who is well known to all in the neighborhood (though of Navajo nationality) as an honest man who has no need to lie, was at our office on Wednesday this week and told us the following story: He says that on April 4th while grazing his sheep on the plain he suddenly felt the ground shake; almost making him fall over and he felt a sort of daze come over him, so he had to grab a hold of something in order not to fall, and at the same time he heard a voice of unknown origin that said, "Hey, look up," which he obeyed and he saw in the sky near where the sun sets, a dark round cloud full of stars that emitted a thunderous noise like that of hailstorm that came towards his location. Afraid, and not knowing what to think, he stood staring at the phenomenon until it passed overhead, traveling towards where the sun rises (east). As the strange cloud passed in front of him he heard another voice that said (this portion is unintelligible on the newspaper scan) but possibly said for him to leave the area. Bandera Americana newspaper (Albuquerque NM) May 13, 1909.

1938
At twilight in Summer 1938 four children including Ann Alley saw a gray clad man sail over them at tree top level. Alley later recalled that he seemed to be wearing a belt which was wide and had points sticking out of it. He also wore a Flash Gordon like cap and a wide cape. The flying Humanoid drifted across the sky

above the children as they all stood and stared speechless. He finally disappeared from sight into the distance. This was in Silver City in Grant County in New Mexico.

1942

During 1942 a fireball was seen over Lovington in Lea County in New Mexico at 1.00 am one night. At the same time hundreds of rocks fell onto the house of Mrs. D. T. Spears. This lasted for five to six nights and many witnesses saw the light. What was so peculiar about the area of the home of Mrs. D. T. Spears? Or was it the impact site of a very particular meteorite shower? This was only the second of many unusual aerial phenomena recorded in New Mexico. But remember that we are very close to Arizona, falling rock capital of the World. Another report stated that a strange red light was seen that appeared to be being carried at shoulder height all around the barn. For two hours it was watched and people tried to get close to it. They gave up around 1.00 am. They then heard a noise and went to the windows where they saw hundreds of rocks that were baseball size falling around the house. At the same time the red fireball was taking off across the range and twice as big as before. The rock falls lasted five or six nights and were even witnessed by the police.

1944

In March 1944 in Carlsbad in Eddy County in New Mexico an Air Force pilot saw a fast-moving UFO speed out of sight over the horizon.

1945

Near San Antonio in Socorro County in New Mexico around August 20-25th 1945. One morning two young boys, Remigio Baca 9, and Jose Padilla, 7, reportedly came upon a long wide gash in the earth, with a manufactured object lying cockeyed and partially buried at the end of it, surrounded by a large field of debris. They believed then and believe today that the object was occupied by distinctly non-human life forms which were alive and moving about on their arrival, minutes after the crash. They reported their findings to Jose's father, Faustino Padilla, on whose ranch the craft had crashed. Shortly thereafter, Faustino received a military visitor asking for permission to remove the crashed object. Early that morning both Baca and Padilla had set out on horseback to find a cow that had wandered off to calf. Soon they moved into terrain that seemed too rough for the horse's hooves, and Jose decided to tether them, minus bridles, allowing them to graze. He had spotted a mesquite thicket, a likely place for a wayward cow to give birth, and they set off across a field of jagged rocks and Cholla cactus to take a look. They took refuge under a ledge above the floodplain, protected somewhat from the lightning strikes that suddenly peppered the area. The storm quickly passed and as they again moved out, another brilliant light, accompanied by a crunching sound, shook the ground around them. It was not at all like thunder. Another experiment at White Sands? No, it seemed too close. They thought it came from the next canyon, adjacent to Walnut Creek and as they moved in that direction, they heard a cow in a clump of mesquites. Sure enough it was the missing cow, licking a white face calf. After checking the cow and the calf, both boys decided to eat lunch and as they did, Jose noticed smoke coming from a draw adjacent to Walnut Creek, a main tributary from the mountains to the Rio Grande. Ignoring their task at hand the two boys headed toward it, and what they saw as they topped the rise "stopped us dead in our tracks." There was a huge gouge in the earth as long as a football field, and a circular object at the end of it. It was barely visible, through a field of smoke. It was the color of the old pot his mother was always trying to shine up, a dull metallic color. They moved closer and found the heat from the wreckage and burning greasewood to be intense. They retreated briefly to talk things over, cool off, sip from the canteen and collect their nerves, worried there might be casualties in the wreckage. Then they headed back to the site. That's when things really got eerie. Waiting for the heat to diminish, they began examining the remnants at the periphery of a huge litter field. Remigio picked up a piece of thin, shiny material that he says reminded him of "the tin foil in the old olive green Phillip Morris cigarette packs." It was folded and lodged underneath a rock, apparently pinned there during the collision. When he freed it, it unfolded all by itself, he refolded it and it spread itself out again. Reme put it in his pocket. Finally they were able to work their way to within yards of the wreckage, fearing the worst and not quite ready for it. "I had my hand over my face, peeking through my fingers," Reme recalled. As they approached, they saw movement in the main part of the craft. Strange looking creatures were moving around inside. They looked under stress. They moved fast, as if they were able to will themselves from one position to another in an instant. They were shadowy and expressionless, but definitely living beings. Both boys felt concerned for the creatures, but did not want to approach any further. They appeared child-like and not dangerous. But both boys were scared and exhausted and it was getting late. The boys backtracked, ignoring the cow and the calf. It was a little after dusk when they climbed on their horses, and dark when they reached the Padilla home. They told Jose's father what they had found. Faustino Padilla said, "We'll check it out in a day or two." He thought it could have been something the military lost and they should not disturb it. Two days later accompanied by Eddie Apodaca, a state policeman and family friend, Faustino Padilla and the two boys went over to the crash site. As they topped the ridge they noted that the cow and calf had moved on, probably headed for home pasture, then they walked a short distance to the overlook. For a second time, Jose and Reme were dumbfounded. The wreckage was nowhere to be seen. Puzzled, the group headed down the canyon nonetheless and suddenly "as if by magic" the object reappeared. From the top of the hill it had blended into the surroundings. The sun had been at a different angle and the object had dirt and debris over it, which Reme speculated someone might have put it there after the crash. Apodaca and Faustino led the way to the crash, and then climbed inside while Jose and Reme were ordered to stay a short distance away. There was no sign of the little men. But incredibly the huge field of debris had been cleaned up. The main body of the craft, however, remained in place with odd pieces dangling everywhere. Both boys were then warned by Faustino not to tell anyone about the crash. The two men, now in their mid to late 60s, still have a piece of the craft and know where other parts were buried by the military. Here is another version. On August 16th 1945 in Walnut Creek in Grant County, New Mexico. Jose Padillo (9) and Remigio Baca (7) had been sent out on their horses to look for a missing cow. They entered difficult ground in a dry creek so dismounted and continued on foot but were caught out in storm and sheltered under a ledge. When the rain stopped they continued but were startled by a light and the ground shaking. Soon after this they found the cow, which had calved so decided to stop for lunch. Joses' attention was then caught by smoke over a rise. They went to investigate and found a gash in the ground, at the end of which was a metallic bowl shaped object. The ground was strewn with debris that flattened out of their own accord when crumpled. Inside the circular object Jose saw hairless dwarfs that moved around at terrific speed. They limbs were very thin. Baca was unnerved so the boys collected the cow and calf and returned home. They told Jose's father Faustino about the incident. A few days later the boys accompanied Faustino and his police officer friend to the site. The metallic object was still there, but appeared to have been moved, and of the beings there was no sign, and the area appeared to have been cleared up. The air force later confirmed Faustino's view that the thing was some sort of balloon.

1947

And suddenly it was time for the Great 1947 UFO Flap!

Around 2.00 pm on 15th June 1947 an unusual aerial object was seen over Las Cruces in New Mexico.

Near the Plains of San Augustin in Catron and Socorro Counties New Mexico on January 7th 1947. A Texas man reported encountering the wreckage of an egg-shaped craft in a desert area. Inside it was the bodies of three humanoid beings with oversized heads and large, black eyes. Soon a military team showed up and warned that that he should not discuss what he had seen. The witness was only 18 at the time and was a pilot. Flying over a field, (Plains of Saint Agustin?) reflections from metal scattered around caught his eye. He thought he saw some bodies and assumed he had come upon an airplane crash. He circled around and landed on a nearby field and walked towards a rancher's house and told him of the apparent crash. He, the rancher and his young son, started out for the site and he then told the father about the bodies at which point they turned around and took the son back to the ranch before returning to the site. He said material was scattered all over, although there was enough of the front end of the craft intact that he could tell it was "egg-shaped," with the pointed end of the egg facing the forward direction. There were three bodies (all dead) in what was left of the front end of the craft. The bodies were small (about 4') with oversize heads, no hair, and large black eyes, with no pupils. He said he pulled back an eyelid to see if there was white as in ours, but found that although it was lighter colored, there were no "white of the eyes." Their clothing was elastic-like, no buttons or zippers. When asked about skin color, he said that it reminded him of some American Indian coloring which has a slight blue to it. Something that impressed him profoundly about the craft was its plainness on the inside. There was no food, no toilet, only a bench seat, and no buttons, levers or instrumentation. There was, however part of the wall which jutted out like a smoothly-connected table which had a slight discoloration to it, and several simple symbols on it, and above it a slightly discolored part of the wall. Later in life when he saw touch-screen computers, he thought that perhaps that was what he was seeing, but of course he would not recognize it at the time. Although no wiring was seen, hanging from the sheared-off sections of the craft's wall were thick plastic-like threads, which again at the time were unrecognizable, but which he would now say were like optical fibers. They could not be broken by hand, but could be cut. There seemed to be a "wiring" path of these threads between the roof of the craft, down through the wall, and to a set of six coffee cup-sized, gyroscope-like devices, evenly spaced around the floor of the craft, at wall's edge, which were mounted in gimbals that could rock in all directions. On the roof of the craft there was a slight discoloration area with a row of dots, and a symbol beside each dot. He likened it to a solar panel. As far as the structure was concerned, he stated that the walls appeared to be porcelain-like material, one inch thick, with 0.020" metal foil on both the inside and outside. However the material including the "porcelain" was so light it seemed to hardly have any weight at all. At some point others showed up to take command of the situation. When he said that he wanted to go home, they told him he would have to stay around until at least the next day.

On Friday 20th June 1947 Mrs. Annabel Mobley and her daughter Luanne saw three groups of three discs moving in the sky from south to northeast over Hot Springs, San Miguel County, New Mexico. The discs seemed to be tied together by invisible cords and were turning in a wheel-like circle all at the same rate of revolution.

The famous Arnold Sighting that apparently ushered in the Flying Saucer Age occurred over the Cascade Range in Washington State on June 24th 1947. What had we been seeing beforehand?

On the Navajo Reservation north of Gallup, New Mexico, in McKinley County, Mrs. B. A. Tillery and her mother saw an object resembling a large glowing star in broad daylight that vanished to the southeast around 6.30 to 7.00 pm on Wednesday 25th June 1947.

Late on 25th June 1947 Dr. R. F. Sensenbaugher, a dentist, his wife and her sister Mrs. C. B. Munroe saw a disc-shaped object approaching from the north over Silver City, Grant County, New Mexico. The object vanished to the south and was the size of a half full moon and very bright. The sighting was at 8.00 pm.

At 9.50 am on Friday 27th June 1947 Mr. Albert J. Beevers, general yardmaster for the Santa Fe Railway in Albuquerque, Bernalillo County, New Mexico, saw a pale blue ball to the southeast. The object dropped rapidly from an angle of forty-five degrees and disappeared behind some buildings and trees.

Hollis O. Cummins' mother stated that she saw a shiny object streak through the sky over Capitan, Lincoln County, New Mexico, around 10.00 am on 27th June 1947. This object was also seen by a neighbor, Mr. Ern Dill heading in the same direction at the same time, believing it to have landed on Wilson Hill to the south west.

That same day Friday 27th June 1947 at the same time, 9.50 am, Mrs. W. B. Cummings was driving south on the main highway five miles south of San Antonio, Socorro County, New Mexico, when she saw a falling silver object that was blindingly bright and shiny fall to earth behind some trees to the east. The object left a short white trail.

At Pope Siding also in Socorro County in New Mexico that same day, 27th June 1947, three days after the Arnold sighting, at 9.50 am Mr. W. C. Dobbs saw a white glowing UFO hovering over the town about eighteen miles south of San Antonio. He reported it to the authorities. Ho hum already and UFOs had only been invented by the Press three days before hadn't they? But don't they seem just a little bit familiar to us as well? After all we had accounted for approximately 753 UFO sightings worldwide since 1800 that were actually documented in this series! Odd how these last three sightings were all at the same time in the same area? (Refer to "Wormholes through Space and Time" published by me September 2019 as well as "Gateways to the Gods, published 2012)

At St Augustine Pass, near White Sands, in Dona Ana County in New Mexico on 27th June 1947 just minutes after the Pope sighting, Captain E. B. Detchmendy saw a white glowing UFO hovering over White Sands Missile Range and reported it to his Commanding Officer. The object resembled a ball of fire and had been seen whilst the witness was driving through the pass.

On the morning of 27th June 1947 at 10.30 am George B. Wilcox, a retired Army Major, saw eight or nine discs in the sky near Warren in Lea County, New Mexico, just south of Hobbs. The objects were perfectly spaced one behind the other and traveling at terrific speed, passing over in intervals of three seconds. They were all the same size and would flash and then disappear with the speed of lightning.

Still on that same day 27th June 1947 Mrs. David Appelzoller saw a white object resembling an electric light bulb with a yellow flame streaming out of its rear coming out of the northeast and heading for White Sands Proving Ground. This was around 10.00 am in Mesilla Valley, near San Miguel in Dona Ana County in New Mexico. Was this one of ours or one of theirs?

On Saturday 28th June 1947 at 5.00 pm Mrs. Alda Sheets and Mrs. K. L. Bickel and her daughter saw two aerial objects traveling west to East at a high rate of speed soon followed by a third. The Bickel daughter at first thought that she was seeing the moon. It became confusing when there were eventually three moons. This was over Santa Fe in Santa Fe County, New Mexico.

On the night of 28th June 1947 Aubrey Gregg and some friends were driving along Border Hill near Roswell in Chaves County, New Mexico, when they say a brilliant bluish light flashing off and on at regular intervals high in the sky. The object was traveling very fast but not as fast as a falling star and was visible for five seconds before disappearing over the horizon.

It is now Sunday 29th June 1947 and late morning and it has still not let up in New Mexico. At Cliff in Grant County, New Mexico, rancher Arthur Howard saw a shiny object fall in broken country. A search by two pilots, Bud Hagen and Ed Nelson who made an aerial search of the area, saw nothing but they reported passing through a layer of stinking air. Was this a sulphurous emission?

Around 1.15 pm on the 29th June 1947 and fifteen to twenty miles from Las Cruces, on the road to White Sands Proving Ground, Dr. C. J. Zohn, Curtis C. Rockwood and John R. Kauke, all Naval rocket experts, as well as Mrs. Rockwood, based at White Sands Proving Ground, spotted a bright silver disc in the East traveling straight and north at an altitude of ten thousand feet. The witnesses believed it to be traveling faster than sound and it had no projections and was flat and elliptical in shape. One witness saw a vapor trail and then suddenly it vanished in mid-flight in a clear blue sky. This was in Dona Ana County in New Mexico.

On Monday 30th June 1947, a railroad worker named Price saw thirteen silvery disc-shaped objects traveling one over the other over Albuquerque in Bernalillo County in New Mexico. They were heading south but suddenly changed course to the East and then reversed to the west before disappearing. Price had alerted the neighborhood who had also seen the craft maneuver overhead.

Also on Monday 30th June 1947 Mrs. Helen Hardin saw a flying saucer from her front porch that was traveling East to west at high speed. The object was slightly yellowish and half the size of the full moon and she watched it for six seconds. Eventually the craft that appeared low in the sky went to ground outside of town. The object did not fall as fast as a meteor and made a whirlwind motion as it approached the ground. This sighting was at Tucumcari in Quay County in New Mexico at 11.00 pm.

Later that night, Tuesday 1st July 1947 there was a sighting from Albuquerque, Bernalillo County, by Max Hood, an executive of the Albuquerque Chamber of Commerce. There was a disc-shaped bluish object following a zigzag path in the northwestern sky. This sighting lasted for thirty seconds and the object vanished in the vicinity of Volcano Peak.

On Wednesday 2nd July 1947 at 9.50 pm Mr. and Mrs. Dan Wilmott saw a large glowing object appear quickly out of the southeast and head towards the northwest at great speed over Roswell in Chaves County, New Mexico. The entire object appeared to glow from the inside and was visible for forty to fifty seconds. The object was oval in shape like two inverted saucers or two old washbowls facing mouth to mouth. The depth was five feet and the diameter was fifteen to twenty feet at an altitude of 1500 feet. Mrs. Wilmott heard a swishing sound though Mr. Wilmott didn't. The speed of the craft was 400 to 500 miles per hour. Some reports state that the Wilmotts saw the craft actually explode.

On 3rd July 1947 it was reported that Barney Barnett apparently discovered a crashed disc in an arroyo at Magdalena in Socorro County in New Mexico.

On 4th July 1947 Mr. Harve Mokler, an El Paso City Building Inspector, and four others in the car, were driving through the Organ Mountain Pass and looked back and saw two shiny flying discs hovering over the White Sands Proving Ground. The two craft were the size of office desks and were almost stationary for one minute after which they then darted out of sight. The Organ Mountains are East of Las Cruces in Dona Ana County in New Mexico.

On the afternoon of 4th July 1947 the Moises S. Sanchez family of Santa Rosa, Guadalupe County, New Mexico, were having a family get-together and picnic when they saw an unusual aerial object going at such a speed that it was soon lost to view.

Twelve miles north of Carrizozo in Lincoln County, New Mexico, on the morning of 4th July 1947 John Martinez and his wife as well as Father John Hallihan, all of Vaughn New Mexico, saw an object in the sky below the summit of a small mountain at a distance of half a mile. The object was twenty to thirty feet across, metallic in color and shaped like a plate or saucer. The craft did not rise above the mountain nor did it stir up any dust.

At Carrizozo Airfield in Lincoln County, New Mexico, 35 miles from Roswell on 4th July 1947 five witnesses saw a UFO moving at approximately 200 to 600 miles per hour in the direction of Roswell. This was before the reported crash of an unknown type of craft at Roswell. The reports of Flying Saucers still possessed features that seemed peculiarly American and seemed in this supposedly early period to be fascinated by New Mexico where they had been first sighted only nineteen days before.

Near Tularosa in Otero County in New Mexico also on July 4th 1947. Close to the eastern border of White Sands Missile Test Range, a large lenticular disc-shaped craft, 99 feet in diameter, with a dome on top and a small rim, crashed. US radars tracked it for a long time; it was flying very slowly. Apparently the pilots died of decompression long before the disk crashed. Five short aliens, all dead, were found at the site. There was a small hole in one of the portholes. The craft was moved to Muroc AFB and later to Wright Patterson and moved to Hangar 18. The aliens were about 1.0m-1.2m in height, gray type with three webbed fingers, lizard-like skin, which was originally bluish-gray-green in color but the color was distorted since all were badly charred. Their origin was later established as star MD-5015 on top of Cassiopeia Constellation, 60 light years away. Several other craft from that same civilization have also crashed. As I keep saying. I report them. You process them. Are they real? None of this is supposed to be real so you figure it out.

At 11.00 pm on the night of 4th July 1947 two Franciscan Nuns, Mother Superior Mary Bernadette and Sister Capistrano were making astronomical observations of the sky above Roswell in Chaves County when they saw a brilliant white light plummet to earth. They recorded the unusual event in their logbook.

Between 11.15 pm and 11.30 pm on the night of Friday 4th July 1947 a very bright fireball with a long tail was seen by several witnesses as it arced across the sky and dropped below the horizon north of Roswell in Chaves County, New Mexico. William M. Woody, thirteen years old, and his father, in the south of the town saw the fireball coming out of the southwest and heading north with the color and intensity of a blow-torch flame. It was not as fast as a meteor and was visible for twenty to thirty seconds. The object the Woodys saw was a white object with a fiery red tail crossing their field of vision and heading northwest over Roswell. It was not a meteor and was too bright and hurt their eyes. It was also too slow for a shooting star and fell like a plummeting aircraft.

It was reported that around 11.30 am on the 5th July 1947 a boy named Gerald Anderson, five years old, and several other family members were out rock hunting on the Plains of San Augustin in Catron and Socorro Counties in New Mexico. They came upon a gully near a shallow arroyo and then saw an object that appeared to have impacted on a small slope. Curious, he and his cousin walked towards it and noticed that one side of it seemed to have been ripped open. There was a lot of debris scattered around. They also saw four apparent occupants of the craft with another one sitting next to it and still alive. Other witnesses soon arrived with some being college students from an eastern university followed by armed military personnel who made threats to all of them to leave the area. The beings were described as wearing two tone gray uniform like outfits and were small in stature. They had slightly larger heads then humans and huge bluish eyes. The hands were long and slender. No sound was coming from them.

Now for the most famous sighting of all. At Roswell in Chaves County in New Mexico on 5th July 1947 Mr. William "Mac" Brazel, a rancher on the Foster Ranch, reported that he had seen wreckage from an explosion scattered across part of his ranch and reported the event to the local Sheriff who in turn reported it to Roswell Army Air Base. Brazel was riding the range with a young neighbor boy William D. Proctor early on the morning of 5th July. Mr. Brazel and the Proctor boy tried to crumple the material but it uncrumpled itself. They tried to break one of the many small rods strewn over the area and could not. It would not burn either or be cut. When bent they could bend back to their original shape. Incidentally the sheep that they were driving would not move over the debris field which covered a field south of the ranch and they had to make a long detour around it to get the sheep to where they could safely leave them at a waterhole whilst they headed for the Proctor Ranch. The Proctors, to their later regret, did not want to come out to the site. There was also torn metal sheeting and large chunks of metal and the early morning sun made the whole area shine. Mr. Brazel had heard a loud crashing sound late in the evening of 4th July. Brazel went home wondering what to do and after taking Sunday afternoon off he went to report the matter to the Sheriff of Chaves County, George Wilcox, in his office, bringing with him some specimens of material. Brazel was seen by a deputy who examined the material and suggested that the military should be involved. Roswell incidentally is surrounded by military installations that provide jobs and inject money into the local economy. The closest was the Roswell Army Air Field, home of the "Enola Gay" that had dropped the atomic bomb on Hiroshima. There was the listening post at Alamogordo and there was White Sands Missile Base where Werner Von Braun had been brought to the U. S. to work on secret weapon systems. Von Braun had created the V2 rockets during the war. On the 8th of July a team led by Major Jesse Marcel collected debris and loaded it onto a B29 aircraft and had it flown to Wright Patterson Air Base on orders from Commanding Officer Colonel William Blanchard. Roswell initially issued a media statement stating that they had recovered a flying disc which they later stated was in fact a Weather Balloon. Marcel said that this was not the wreckage that he had found. What he had seen was thin and foil like but would not dent and there was also something like balsa wood that would not burn when flame was applied to it. There were also printed hieroglyphics on some debris. Dr. W. Curry Holden, Professor of History and Anthropology at Texas Tech University in Lubbock, Texas, appeared on the scene of the Roswell crash with a number of his students on the morning of 5th July shortly after it had happened. They were searching for areas of archaeological importance north of Roswell at the time. They all saw the craft as well as the bodies. The site was not far from Highway 285. Holden had seen a bright flaming light in the night sky a few hours earlier. Major Edwin Easley, Provost Marshall of the 509th Bomb Group then arrived at the crash site with Military Personnel. He ordered his men to the tops of ridges overlooking the site and then ordered the entire area to be cordoned off and held everyone back away from the craft whilst he checked for radiation and other forms of contamination. Frank Kaufman, a member of the 509th, with the original group, saw the craft stuck into the ground at an angle. The craft was heel shaped with a tear in its side that allowed him to see into the interior. Military cars and trucks had been parked around the impact site to screen it from view. A man in a radiation suit checked the area whilst the rest of the team stood 100 yards back talking and smoking. Once there was no radiation recorded photographers recorded the scene in close ups and recovery began. Several eyewitnesses stated that the craft was twenty to twenty-five feet long with the trailing edge slightly scalloped and the nose rounded. The front had been damaged by impact with the ground. Easley, another Officer and an N.C.O. interviewed the archaeologists and took them to Roswell. Thomas Gonzales, an N.C.O. assigned to the transportation unit on guard at the crash site saw the craft and stated that it looked like an airfoil and spoke of little men who had piloted it. There was one body sitting near a cliff, another at the side of the craft, and three more inside. All were removed and placed in lead-lined bags which were loaded onto Military Ambulances and sent to Roswell. They were slender, 4.5 to five feet tall with large heads and long and thin arms. The distance between the wrist and the elbow was longer than the distance between the elbow and the shoulder. They had large eyes with pupils as well as human facial features though with no hair but a skull covered with fuzz. They were not human and had grey skin. This was reported as the first reported great UFO crash! Actually by all accounts it was the twentieth! Beaten in fact by Benkelman, Nebraska, in June 1884, Pacific Grove, and Twin Peaks, both in California, in December 1896, Springfield, Illinois, Weedpatch Hill, Indiana, and Aurora, Texas, in April 1897, Webster City, Iowa, in 1919, Gem, West Virginia, in 1924, Folsom Swamp, New Jersey, in 1931, and Delaware, Illinois, in 1938. There are probably others that we have not defined as UFO crashes that may precede us as well. In total up until 1977 there would be 51 well documented alleged UFO crashes.

Were there two Roswell crashes or one hoax one alongside a very detailed real one. Had Marcel been sent to the hoax one to deflect media attention whilst the other site was emptied of all evidence and shipped away? There are too many conflicting stores of cover-ups and the switching of items. Marcel's unbreakable rods and pieces of foil were replaced by a dead weather balloon but a dead weather balloon would not explain or even hoax away what the archeological team purportedly saw. Marcel got to the site on the 8th of July yet we have the Woodys referring to the roads being blocked on the morning of 5th July. Had bits been left behind for Marcel to pick up after the area had been cleared which were then replaced with the weather balloon? Were there actually two red herrings? Incidentally Bazel was locked up for eight days by the military when he reported the crash. Numerous independent witnesses including undertakers for the military reported frenzied activity at Roswell AFB. The local radio station was told not to mention anything of the crash and to destroy its wire recording of Bazel's only interview. This interview was done before Mr. Bazel was locked away. If it were only a weather balloon why all the secrecy?

Glen Dennis the proprietor of Ballard Funeral Home in Roswell stated that the day after the crash, before Marcel went to the site for the official investigation, the military had asked him for child sized coffins that were airtight. Coincidence?

Early morning 5th July 1947 and William Woody, the young boy who had seen the falling object with his father the previous night decided to go out and look for it. They climbed into their pickup truck and drove north on Route 285. On approaching the area where they assumed the object had crashed or landed they found every exit East and west of the highway blocked by military sentries.

On July 5th 1947 in Albuquerque in Bernalillo County at 9:00 AM. five discs flew toward the East over the city; one circled back over the city. In the afternoon five witnesses saw a sphere manoeuvre in-and-out of clouds.

On Sunday 6th July 1947 at 5.00 am two boys said that they saw five mystery objects pass over Belen in Valencia County, New Mexico and then disappear over Sandias. The craft made a swishing sound. Were these the same five craft that were previously seen over Albuquerque?

On 6th July 1947 at 6.00 pm at Mora in Mora County, New Mexico, Mr. N. M. Barney, Mr. F. Cruz Jnr and Mr. Richard O. Branch stated that they saw a strange saucer shape flying the skies from north to a southerly direction.

On 7th July 1947 at Tucumcari in Quay County in New Mexico Mr. And Mrs. F. P. Lawrence saw something flat and round that looked like a reflection of a mirror that was traveling west. At first they thought that it was a plane but then a plane appeared and they could see that it was completely different.

At 12.45 am on Tuesday 8th July 1947 Mr. H. J. Rhoads of Las Cruces, Dona Ana County in New Mexico thought that he saw an awfully bright star as he was going to bed. Realizing that it was something else he woke up his wife to point it out to her as well. The star was very high, the shape was unknown, there was no sound and it was moving almost due west on a steady course at no great speed for approximately a minute and a half.

At the airport at Carrizozo in Lincoln County in New Mexico Mark Sloan, operator of the Carrizozo Flying Field, as well as Grady Warren, Flying Instructor, Nolan Lovelace, Ray Shafer and an unidentified man, all pilots, saw a flying saucer speeding almost directly over the field at 4000 to 6000 feet at a speed of 200 to 600 miles per hour. The craft oscillated like a feather and traveled from the southwest to the northeast over a period of ten seconds. This was at 10.30 am in the morning on 8th July 1947.

That same morning 8th July 1947 over Albuquerque, Bernalillo county in New Mexico Mrs. W. W. Parks saw a wobbling object heading in a northeasterly direction. She said that it flew low and was the size of three office desks. Later that same morning over Albuquerque at 11.00 am Grace Boardwine and Johnny Nacarato saw two discs that were weaving, dipping and circling over the city. There were fifteen other witnesses as well and Boardwine said that the discs looked like they were heading for El Paso in Texas.

At 3.30 pm on the afternoon of 8th July 1947 Mr. W. J. Schanz, a former Army Airforce instructor in aircraft recognition, as well as five other witnesses saw three brilliant objects streak across the sky over Roswell, Chaves County, New Mexico. Harvey Sparkman first spotted the objects. First one object followed by two others. Schanz believed that he had seen every type of plane in existence and the objects possessed no plane-like characteristics. They were not exactly round and instead of spinning they somersaulted with no definite pattern of movement. The sun's rays reflected off them made them so bright that it was difficult to look at them directly. The other witnesses were Mrs. Raymond Jennings, Ed Jennings, Lawrence Jennings and Linzy Jennings, all of the Jennings Fixture Company.

Back in Roswell, Chaves County in New Mexico at 8.25 pm that evening of the 8th July 1947 Mr. & Mrs. Joe Massey saw a brilliant object streaking across the sky to the northwest for a few seconds. The object was two to three feet across with a flaming tail about ten to fifteen feet in length. Remember that this is the size that the objects appear to be to the witnesses as in the sky there is nothing to compare to gauge measurement. If the object appeared to fill two to three feet of sky then it could have been enormous, at least certainly noticeable.

At Socorro in Socorro County in New Mexico on 8th July 1947 Mr. Grady Barnett reported finding a crash site west of the town where there was a complete but damaged saucer. There was also a dead crew that resembled humans with round heads, small eyes, no hair and oddly spaced eyes. Their clothing was one-piece and grey. The UFO was a metallic object, disc shaped and twenty-five to thirty feet across. Barnett's investigation was suddenly interrupted by Military personnel who cordoned off the area and removed the witnesses. Mr. Barnett by all accounts was a respectable and honest citizen. Now we have more reports of UFO crashes along with dead Aliens. Roswell and Socorro are only 230 kilometers apart and there was only one month between reports. The three events to follow in the same area were silently exploding unknown aerial lights in the sky later in the same year, a car stalling when it was swooped by a flying light in November 1957, and the landing of a UFO near Socorro in 1964. Other sources place this crash in the Plains of San Augustin south of the Datil Mountains and north of the Leura Mountains about fifty miles west of Socorro. This was in Catron and Socorro Counties, New Mexico. To the East are the San Mateo Mountains and to the west the Tularosa Mountains and the crash occurred apparently one week after the Roswell crash.

The last sighting for 8th July 1947 was at 9.50 pm over Las Cruces in Dona Ana County in New Mexico. Interesting. Mr. & Mrs. E. B. Farmer were with friends, Mr. & Mrs. Enoch Hughes and their daughter Lilly when they saw a large light coming from the south, from the direction of El Paso. The object was larger than a car headlight and was traveling at a high rate of speed leaving a tail similar to a comet. As it traveled between Las Cruces and the Organ Mountains to the East it burst into three pieces. Immediately searchlights went up from White Sands Proving Ground East of the Organ Mountains and searched the sky for quite a considerable period. Was this the same object seen heading towards Las Cruces over the Franklin Mountains only ten minutes before?

On the morning of 9th July 1947 over Albuquerque in Bernalillo County in New Mexico Mr. C. M. Conrady, a Public Service employee, and six others at a café saw two discs in the sky. The first arriving disc just hung in the sky till the other one arrived at great speed. The first disc then gave chase to the second disc and both disappeared to the south at great speed at an altitude of 8,000 to 10,000 feet. The discs were twelve to fifteen inches across, very bright and in view for ten to fifteen minutes.

Meanwhile in Roswell, Chaves County in New Mexico on Highway 70, fifteen miles west of town that same morning 9th July 1947 Mr. & Mrs. C. B. Brackley of Sweetwater, Texas, saw a flat, shiny round disc that fell from the sky as they were driving towards Roswell. The object rolled over and over, this somersaulting has been mentioned before, and finally fell to earth about two miles south of the highway. It was not falling as fast as a meteor though as it was in full view falling for 60 to 75 seconds. A meteor would have done this in only a few seconds.

On Thursday 10th July 1947 a very distinguished witness entered the fray. The astronomer, mathematician and meteor expert Dr. Lincoln LaPaz of the University of New Mexico, his wife and his two daughters were driving near Fort Sumner, De Baca County, New Mexico, at 4.47 pm when they saw a strange object in the sky. It was bright, self-luminating, elliptical, well-defined and at first motionless relative to the clouds but wobbling in flight before rising rapidly into the clouds. Dr. LaPaz used makeshift triangulation to figure the distance to the cloud bank and estimated that it was twenty to thirty miles away. This made the object 160 to 240 feet long and 65 to 100 feet thick. The horizontal speed was 120 to 180 miles per hour and the vertical speed was 600 to 900 miles per hour. Dr. LaPaz reported this sighting to the Airforce and he was convinced that due to the remarkably sudden ascent it was an absolutely novel airborne device and not a natural phenomenon.

That same day 10th July 1947 Mr. Albert Snow and Deputy Sheriff Mark Sloan sighted a moon-shaped object visible for several seconds that was heading towards El Paso over Carrizozo in Lincoln County, New Mexico.

At 9.30 pm on the night of 10th July 1947 two Highlands University students, Keith McKinney and Lester Ball saw a bright disc traveling westward at a fast clip passing directly over Las Vegas in San Miguel County, New Mexico at an altitude of 1200 to 2000 feet.

At 5.35 pm on the afternoon of 11th July 1947 six residents of Silver City in Grant County, New Mexico, saw an incredibly bright silver object that was moving with unbelievable speed from west to east. The object looked like a soap bubble according to the witnesses as it was almost transparent and was extremely brilliant. The witnesses were Mr. & Mrs. Dave Robertson, Mr. & Mrs. Fred Villio their neighbors and C. D. Grayless and Mike Morales. The object was fairly low at first then seemed to go up as it crossed the horizon and disappeared.

In New Mexico in the desert on August 13th 1947 six Native Americans discovered a still smoldering metallic disc-shaped object that had apparently crashed in the desert. Inside they found an alien creature (not described) that was injured, but still alive. Hearing the approach of military troops, the men decided to save the being from capture and take care of him themselves. Taking him to their home, they found the being could communicate with them through a crystal device that conveyed images. The Indians called the being the "Star Elder."

On July 20th 1947 near Raton in Colfax County, New Mexico. A family were driving near Raton when a blue, luminous object came down out of the sky and paced their car for about 65km. After 45 minutes the thing took off at high speed and disappeared.

In August 1947 late at night near Clovis in Curry County, New Mexico. A couple were driving 25km west of Clovis, en route to Santa Fe when they encountered a large object on the road about 50m ahead at low altitude. The thing seemed so tall that it towered into the sky above their eye line and took several minutes to cross the road. It resembled a huge railway carriage of metallic appearance, with both light and dark windows. The asphalt over which it had travelled was hot and steaming.

In Late August 1947 in Alamogordo, Holloman, Army Air Field, in Otero County in New Mexico. AMC Watson Labs Project MOGUL engineer Rosmovski and communications officer Lt. H. G. Markley tracked a stationary target at 200 miles altitude using a modified CPS-4 radar aimed at 70° elevation.

On November 3rd (4th ?) 1947 in Vaughn in Guadalupe County in New Mexico at 9:30 p.m. Colonel Hayes first observed an unusual aerial phenomena. The phenomena appeared approximately 400-500 feet above the ground when first observed and was descending slowly and steadily in a vertical manner toward the earth. It appeared slightly larger than a basketball, bright white in color like a miniature sun. At a point approximately 200 feet above the surface of the earth, the object appeared to explode although no noise was apparent. By this time the Colonel had stopped his automobile and had gotten out to watch the object. The explosion or disintegration appeared to be taking place some 40 to 60 yards distant and still no noise was noticed. At this time the fragments assumed a fiery red color and descended toward earth like numerous sparks being extinguished before touching the ground. At the time Col Hayes was down Highway 60, near a railroad and separated from the vicinity where the fragments were landing by a fence. He did not cross the fence or investigate further.

Here is another classic sighting. At Aztec in San Juan County in New Mexico on 25th March 1948 a flying craft had been detected by three separate radar units, one of which was reckoned to have disabled the UFO's control mechanism. The craft was found twelve miles northeast of town and was 99 feet in diameter with an exterior of superlight aluminum-like metal that incorporated large rings of metal which revolved around a central stabilized cabin. There were no rivets, seams, nuts or bolts and it was made of segments that were pinned together. There was no wiring in the machinery. Sixteen Humanoids were found who were all 36 to 42 inches tall and all dead inside the cabin. The Humanoids resembled Mongoloid Orientals with disproportionably large heads, large slant eyes and small noses and mouths. They had small and thin torsos, very thin necks and their arms were long and slender and reaching the knees. The long slender fingers had webbing between them. The witnesses had gotten in through a fracture in a side porthole. The Humanoids bodies were charred a dark brown color. The craft was dismantled and taken away by the military to Wright-Patterson Air Force Base. A book with hieroglyphs written in it was also found. The craft had crashed into a cliff just above the Animas River and appeared to have tried hard to miss the cliff but still managed to hit a corner before making a right angle turn which headed it straight north into Hart Canyon Another alleged UFO crash.1948 would be a big year for the reporting of them.

There is a report from Socorro in New Mexico that in early March 1948 a UFO came down that was like the Aztec craft according to an ex-army private. It was reported to have multiple compartments, a central shaft or pole, a conveyer walk and the outer shell of the craft was transparent from the inside of the craft. No occupants were mentioned. Were we on Earth doing something in this period that was disturbing the UFOs?

On 5th April 1948 in the afternoon personnel at Holloman AFB reported witnessing a disc that was thirty-five meters in diameter that was executing a series of violent turns and maneuvers. Afternoon. Geophysics Lab and/or AMC Watson Lab balloon observers Olsen, Johnson, Chance, saw 1 to 2 irregularly round, gray-white or golden objects, indistinct in outline like a majors insignia ... slightly concave on top, one [?] estimated 100 feet size. Both were rising straight up then one veered to the right, dropped, made a large loop, went upward again, then disappeared suddenly not due to distance. The other object arced off to the West at terrific or tremendous speed. Made 3 vertical loops or violent maneuvers then disappeared suddenly not due to fading away in the distance.

On July 17th 1948 five miles south of San Acacia Dam in Socorro County in New Mexico at 4:50 p.m. Two Kirtland AFB Sgt.s. on a fishing trip with their families saw a group of seven aluminum circular possibly spherical objects approach from the South at 20,000 feet then pass overhead at 1,500 mph if the altitude was correct (5°/sec angular velocity). At first appearing like snub-nosed jet fighters of unknown type, shifting from V formation to L formation to circular formation to no regular formation, at which point a regular pulsating flashing light appeared in the group at 30° from zenith to the North and at this oblique angle the objects did not appear circular. There was no no noise or trail.

On July 27th 1948 in Albuquerque, New Mexico at 8:35 a.m. a University of New Mexico scientist saw a flat metallic disc-shaped object that hung motionless in the sky for ten minutes.

On September 23rd 1948 at Los Alamos in Los Alamos County in New Mexico at 9:40 a.m. a group of Los Alamos Scientific Lab personnel, Angier, Fairchild and others, waiting for an aircraft at the landing strip saw a sun-reflecting glint in the sky from a flat circular metallic object high in the Northern sky appearing like a flat dime on-edge slightly tipped as if 50 feet away.

Also on September 23rd 1948 and still in Los Alamos, New Mexico AESS security guard Hanson ?? saw an oval orange luminous object, length/width ratio about 1.5:1, to the East crossing the sky in level flight from right to left, trailing flame, disappearing in a cloud bank to the NE.

On 5th December 1948 pilots flying over New Mexico reported two separate observations of a pale green light that was visible for only a few seconds that were seen twenty-two minutes apart. The pilots insisted that they were not meteors but very peculiar light flares. At 9:05 p.m. USAF pilot Capt. William Goede, copilot Major Roger Carter, and S/Sgt. flight engineer, flying a C-47 from Lowry AFB, Denver, to Williams AFB, Chandler, Ariz., at 18,000 feet saw a green fireball. A 2nd green fireball sighting East of Sandia Mountains. (10 miles E of Albuquerque) at 9:27 p.m. shot up from the ground to 500 feet height.

On December 5th 1948 NW of Las Vegas near Montezuma Mission in San Miguel County in New Mexico at 9:35 p.m. Pioneer Airlines Flight 63 pilot Ernest Van Lloyd and copilot James Smith saw a pale green (later said to be white or whitish-orange) fireball with pale green trail at 9:35 p.m. coming head on, while flying West on 272° heading at 9,000 feet in a C-47. They attempted evasive action but the object dropped close to ground level.

The following day on December 6th 1948 over the super secret atomic installation Sandia Base at Kirtland Air Force Base in Albuquerque in Bernalillo County in New Mexico a peculiar greenish flare was seen in the sky for three seconds at 10:55 p.m. AESS officer Joseph Toulouse driving West saw a green fireball almost directly overhead above Sandia Base nuclear weapons assembly site, slightly to the NW arching slightly downward from East to West, about 1/3 the size of the full moon, with a flaming tail.

On 8th December 1948 two pilot investigators during an investigation after the December 6th sighting, were in a T-7 aircraft when they saw one of the strange green flares. The flare was similar to the green flares used by the Air Force but was considerably larger as well as larger and brighter than a shooting star or meteor as it followed a trajectory that was almost flat and parallel to the earth, which other phenomena including flares do not do. Flares arc up and then come down after exploding. They do not travel parallel to the ground. Neither do meteors or shooting stars which generally just come straight down, though some of my reports might contradict this theory.

On December 8th 1948. about 20 miles East of Las Vegas, New Mexico at 6:33 p.m. Two AFOSI Special Agents, Capts. Melvin E. Neef and John J. Stahl, Jr., returning from investigation of green fireballs in a Beech T-7, heading East at 90° and 190 mph at 11,500 feet altitude and 5,000 feet above ground, saw a green fireball 30° to the left of their flight path, to the ENE at 60° azimuth, at an estimated 2,000 feet above their flight altitude of 13,500 ft., which shot past them maintaining almost level flight until the end to the WSW at 240° azimuth when it seemed to burn out and drop suddenly with reddish-range glowing fragments which lasted less than 1 sec. a later aerial search of the ground site in daylight found nothing.

On 12th December 1948 Lincoln LaPaz, a director of the University of New Mexico's Institute of Meteoritics, saw one of the mysterious green fireballs and stated that they were totally unlike any meteors that he had ever seen. This same green fireball was also seen independently by two inspectors from the Atomic Energy Security Service. From both observations Mr. LaPaz established that the flare had flown too slowly as well as too slowly for a meteor. He also observed that none of the green fireballs, had he actually seen more?, had a rain of sparks or a dust cloud which is normal behavior for meteoric fireballs especially low level penetrating meteors. There were numerous other sightings as well. Incidentally on February 16th 1949 a " Conference on Aerial Phenomena" which was attended by the military as well as scientists was told that the green fireballs were not part of some classified military training exercise. LaPaz stated that no meteoric phenemona move over long horizontal paths that reserved nearly constant angular velocities and constant linear velocities at elevations of eight to ten miles.

On December 12th 1948 at Starvation Peak near Bernal in San Miguel County in New Mexico at 9:02 p.m. ±0.5 min (MST). Dr. Lincoln LaPaz, USAF Capt. Charles L. Phillips, and CAP intelligence officer Lt. Allan B. Clark, returning from green fireball investigations while looking to the NW saw a green fireball at least stellar magnitude -4 traveling East to West low above the horizon about 3°-4° elevation in almost perfectly level flight until the last 0.1 to 0.2 sec when it slightly curved downward, disintegrating into 3-4 pieces though with no sound. Based on an independent witness, an AESS guard at Los Alamos, LaPaz triangulated the object's flight path at about 8-10 miles height along a 25-mile path at a speed of 39,000 to 43,000 mph.

On Dec. 20th 1948 West of Los Alamos, New Mexico an AESS observation post sighted a green fireball with a triangulated 7-8-mile West to East flight path calculated by LaPaz based on another independent observation at a different site.

On December 28th 1948 at Los Alamos in New Mexico at 4:31 a.m. An inspector at Los Alamos sighted a fireball. It was not falling as fast as a falling star (meteor) he continued to watch. For several seconds, at an estimated altitude of 6,000', the object disappeared with a green flash, lighting up a small cloud between itself and the witness.

In the same period in New Mexico during December 1948 many witnesses saw unknown objects in the sky that exploded silently with blinding flashes of green light. They were like some extraordinary type of missile yet there were no signs of damage anywhere. Earlier in the year we had a report of green clouds and green rain over Dayton in Montgomery County, Ohio.

There were many reports of mysterious green fireballs above Los Alamos in Los Alamos County in 1948-1949.

1949

On January 6th 1949 at Kirtland AFB (Albuquerque), New Mexico at 5:30 p.m. PFC Everitt saw a bright white diamond shaped light in horizontal flight from SE to NW about 1500-2,000 feet height faster than a jet, that appeared about two feet in size.

On January 30th 1949 in Roswell in Chaves County in New Mexico at 5:55 p.m. Approximately 200 observers saw an object moving West-East at 2000 feet. It was horizontal flight and the object was blue green and moving slowly. It disappeared in a shower of lighted fragments. It was also seen at Alamogordo and Fort Worth, Texas.

In New Mexico during January 1949 there were many witnesses of unknown objects seen in the sky that exploded silently with blinding flashes of green light. They were like some extraordinary type of missile yet there were no signs of damage anywhere.

On February 14th 1949 in Ganado in Apache County in New Mexico at 6:40 p.m. Dr. (deleted) and his wife were returning from Gallup (New Mexico). They crossed the long bridge about two miles due East of Ganado. As they came up the hill west of the bridge, where the road heads south, a brilliant white light was observed in the sky directly in front of the car, and somewhat above the horizon. The object appeared to hang stationary, then fell in a slight curve to the west. Mrs. (deleted) said that the object was a slightly greenish color. Both agreed that the object had an orange tinge as it fell, and that sparks appeared to trail off the object, both while stationary and as it fell. Dr. (deleted) said that his first reaction was that it was an airplane on fire, and that he had so reported to the Arizona State Police.

On February 17th 1949 near Grants (at 35° 7' ±2' N, 107°47' ±2' W), Sandia Base, and near Albuquerque (at 35° 5' N, 106° 35' W), New Mexico around 5:57-6:06 p.m. A Green Oil Company truck driver named Herman Wilcox, at Chief's Rancho Stop on Hwy 66, saw an oval luminous white light with a faint trail of white smoke in the SW at about 225° azimuth moving South in vertical climb then leveled off. Then making a gradual ascent before disappearing suddenly after several seconds. There were no clouds in the sky to obscure it.

On March 8th 1949 at Los Alamos in New Mexico at 6:35 p.m. a strange object was reported over the installation and details given indicate it was elliptical or similar in shape of fuselage to a German ME-109. The witness from the Kirtland AFB control tower reported a blue-white object in the NW horizon in a vertical descent and exploding before reaching the earth. No sound was reported. Another witness from the Los Alamos AEC Project was a security guard at station #106 and he reported a luminous object greenish white in color and West of SW. Its direction of flight was SE on a horizontal plane at about or below cloud cover. He observed this object for 2-4 minutes and speed slower than a meteor. Finally a third witness, a guard at station #103, said the object had a billowy white tail and was observed West of SW gliding in a 60-degree downward angle but was seen only for 2-4 seconds. This was the same date as the Camp Hood sightings in Texas.

On March 13th 1949 at Sandia Base, New Mexico a ball-shaped object with a tail of fire flying at a speed slower than a meteor on a slightly descending path was seen. The object appeared to be half the size of a full moon.

During daytime on March 16th near Farmington in New Mexico there was a report of a flat, oblong lenticular disc with a very tall and smooth dome with a rim and 36 feet in diameter crashed in the area. Two dead short aliens were said to have been found inside. The craft was apparently moved to Muroc AFB, now Edwards, in California. There was a small hole in one of the portholes.

On April 5th 1949 at Los Alamos, New Mexico at 10:00 p.m. heading South-North was a green flying object with a red afterglow, approximately 300' above the South slope of Fejarito Mountain. The object with tremendous speed disappeared behind the mountain.

On April 12th 1949 at Albuquerque in New Mexico at 7:30 p.m. A round white object 1/8th the size of the moon was seen moving very fast SE-NW,

On April 22nd 1949 in Cliff in Grant County in New Mexico at 9:05 a.m. At 20-degrees and dropping slowly an aluminum colored, round flat thin 15' diameter object was in view for 2 minutes as it travelled West-East.

At 10.30 am on 24th April 1949 a luminous object was seen over White Sands Proving Ground in New Mexico. Five qualified witnesses in observing aerial craft saw a gleaming, white, ellipsoid hovering over the area. The witnesses were all doing research for the Office of Naval Research. They observed the object with a theodolite as well as naked vision and knew that it was not a weather balloon which they had been tracking. The object was 2.5 times longer than it was wide and did not resemble any aircraft that they knew of. General Mills, the meteorologist and balloon expert Charles B. Moore and 4 Navy crew on a balloon launch crew (Akers, Davidson, Fitzsimmons, Moorman) saw a white, round ellipsoid, shadowed yellowish on one side, length/width ratio 2.5x, cross the sky from the South (azimuth 210° elevation 45°) to the East at about 5°/sec angular velocity, passing near the sun (126° azimuth 60° elevation). It was tracked by Moore viewing through 25x ML-47 theodolite after it came out of the sun. The object seemed to turn to the North, maintained constant azimuth at about 20°-25° when it suddenly climbed from 25° to 29° elevation in 10 seconds and disappeared by distance or dust obscuration. Distance unknown; by assuming 57 miles, velocity is then 5 mi/sec or 18,000 mph (earth orbital velocity, not escape velocity) but this is pure assumption.

On April 25th 1949 in Springer in Colfax County in New Mexico around 6:30 -7:30 AM. A 25-year-old man by the name of Abreu, and another friend, were fishing at Springer Lake, a body of water four miles NW of the New Mexico town of the same name. They were preparing bait when they heard a peculiar sound, similar to a high pitched whistle. They both thought it was some high flying ducks coming in for landing and they looked up in the air. What they saw was certainly not ducks. The objects were silvery white in color and looked like balls, similar to Christmas tree ornaments, that passed them at very high altitude and going very fast and out of sight in very few seconds." They observed the objects for over an hour and made a sketch that showed the objects in various formations as they zoomed overhead. The word: "zoomed" may be a good word to use since the witness remarked: " I do not believe that these objects could have been picked up or followed with field glasses, they were moving much too fast."

On May 12th 1949 at Holloman AFB in Otero County in New Mexico at 9:30 p.m. AF contract solar astronomer, Donald H. Menzel, of Harvard Observatory, was being driven by military car from Holloman AFB, on Hwy 70 just outside the base, en route to Alamogordo [headed ENE on road azimuth 66°], when shortly after leaving the base he saw a bright reddish star Antares about 6°-8° East [to the lower left] of the nearly Full Moon estimated to be 15°-18° above the ridge line [99.3% illuminated Moon at about 19° elevation 136° azimuth, Antares at about 11° elevation 132° azimuth] rising above the Sacramento Mountain ridge. Shortly afterward he noticed first one small round white light low about 3°-4° over the ridge to the lower left of the Moon and star and then another identical light to the right of the first and in horizontal line, about 3° apart [at roughly 122° to 125° azimuth, 5°-6° elevation, seemingly over Moore Ridge, summit 7,264 feet, 32°42'22" N, 105°51'11" W, 15 miles away]. Each light was white possibly slight greenish tinge, about 0 to 1st stellar magnitude, the left one slightly brighter, both increasing in brightness as if possibly rising above a haze layer, both initially "fuzzy" but apparently sharpening in edge contrast. Each light suddenly disappeared one after the other before the car could be stopped. Menzel estimated that as the car traveled 50 mph it created a 3-mile baseline over which he nevertheless noticed no perceptible change in the lights' azimuths, or perhaps no more than 1° to 2°, hence a distance he calculated at 180 miles and object "diameter" about "¾ mile" (4,000 feet) [correct figure 2,300 feet].

AMC Watson Labs Project MOGUL communications officer Lt. H. G. Markley while watching two balloons with radar reflector to the SE in 10x binoculars saw traveling at "unprecedented rate of speed" a round white object in horizontal light S to N several thousand feet over the tops of the Sacramento Mountains. [Case falsely explained by AF as false radar targets when no radar observation was involved.] the Sacramento Mountains are in Otero County with small parts in Lincoln and Chaves County.

In Fall 1949 in New Mexico at night. A UFO dropped out of nowhere into the car headlights of a couple. It was saucer-shaped and 50-60 feet in diameter. When 20 feet in distance from the car, it rose up and passed at a low altitude over the car. While this happened, the car radio had an abnormal amount of static. The couple did not see how the UFO left their vicinity. (Tulsa Tribune, Dec. 10, 1957) Music on the car radio was blanked out by static as the UFO passed over the car.

At Albuquerque in Bernalillo County, New Mexico in 1949 a UFO descended to 200 feet above ground level near the Airport when it suddenly exploded into a shower of reddish spray. There were no ill effects. This strange occurrence was repeated two more times over the next two nights in the same location and at the same time of night. As for unexplained explosions?

There were many reports of mysterious green fireballs above Los Alamos in Los Alamos County in 1948-1949.

1950

On March 16th 1950 over Farmington in San Juan County in New Mexico at 11:00 a.m. Several persons (approx. 10) observed 12 to 15 flat spheroid shaped objects maneuvering in the sky. The objects turned on their axis and maneuvered up and down, sometimes turning at very sharp angles. They were observed for a period of 3 to 5 minutes.

At 10.15 am on 17th March 1950 the sky over Farmington in San Juan County in New Mexico seemed to be invaded by UFOs. There had been lots of reports of UFOs over the Four Corners area for the previous two days. Most of the town's 3,600 population saw the aerial objects. From 10.15 am for an hour afterwards the air was full of flying saucers. Estimates were from five hundred to thousands. They were saucer-shaped, travelled at unbelievable speeds and did not seem to have any set flight paths. They would dart in and out and seem to avoid collisions by only inches.

On March 21st 1950 at Kirtland AFB in Albuquerque in New Mexico at 1:00 p.m. A Sgt.. from HQ & HQ Service Company, 8450th M.P. Group, Sandia Base, reported seeing four, round, silver to shady gray objects to the northeast. His location was the East side of the pit area. The object appeared to be more manoeuvrable than any known aircraft. The tactics used were similar to the change of positions during dog fights involving two aircraft, but there seemed to be no similarity to the manoeuvrability of a conventional plane. The objects were more manoeuvrable, made right angle turns and also appeared to reverse (back up) the direction of flight. The duration was about 30 minutes. Objects appeared to be at a great distance, approximately 40,000 to 60,000 feet. Another witness at Albuquerque reported objects in the East traveling southeast at 1:15 p.m. His position was from the Ordnance Area, Sandia Base. Two, white objects, smaller than a fist at arm's length at about one mile range were observed. One object changed direction to the East after completely circling the other object just prior to disappearing. Speed: Approximately 600-700 mph. Time in sight: Approx. 5 minutes. Another observer at 1:20 p.m. from the 1100th Special Reporting Group, Sandia Base, New Mexico was at a checkpoint 200 yards East of the Pit Area when he reported two objects, silver in color, approximately the size of a dime at arm's length, round, at a considerable distance in the East, heading southwest. The ten minute observation showed no conventional turns and the objects moved up and sideways in excess of jet speeds until both objects moved out of sight in the southwest.

On July 4th 1950 at night at White Sands in Dona Ana County in New Mexico walking at night in the desert Daniel Fry saw an oblate spheroid thirty feet in diameter settle to the ground 70 feet away. He was about to touch the hull when a voice warned him not to, as it was still hot. The voice proceeded to tell him that he had been chosen for contact because of his scientific background and his open mind. He was invited to board the saucer, and was taken for a ride to York City and back, consuming only 30 minutes. Such high accelerations are possible, he was told, because the accelerating force, like gravity, operates on the passenger's body as well as on the craft. Fry's host, the Ufonaut, identified himself as A-lan, a descendent of the inhabitants of the sunken continent of Lemuria. A-lan again contacted Fry on several subsequent occasions. Here is a larger version. At 8.00 pm Daniel Fry, a rocket technician, went out for an evening walk to cool down. He saw something dark coming down from the sky, which as it approach he saw was an oblate sphere, about 9m diameter at the widest. It landed gently about 20m away. Daniel approached the polished metallic looking thing which was about 5m thick. He touched the thing with his palm, at which a voice told him to back off and continued to give a pseudo-scientific explanation of why he should do that. The voice, which spoke in colloquial terms claimed to be a space person. An opening appeared and Daniel went inside to a rook 2.7m deep, 21m wide in which there were four seats. Daniel sat in one of these and the walls became translucent and the object took off, all with commentary from the voice which appeared to be directed straight into his brain. After a trip he was returned back to White Sands. Daniel later claimed other contacts.

1951

At Tucumcari in Quay County in New Mexico on Thursday 13th December 1951 all of the town were witnesses of a great fireball that appeared in the night sky and ploughed straight into a 750,000 gallon water tank. This collapsed the tank destroying twenty buildings and killing four people. No meteoric residue or a crater was found in the area. It seemed that the fireball had actually landed close to the tank but in its unrestrained course continued travelling until it struck the tank. The break in the tanks metal wall was as clean as if it was cut by a giant's knife. On 26th November 1951a fireball had crashed to Earth at Uniontown in Pennsylvania. Was this one related? At Uniontown it had crashed into a gas line. What would the probability be of two devastating meteoric events to occur in only a few days? Quite high one would suspect?

1952

In June 1952 (or following month) in the evening in Deming in Luna County, New Mexico. Hilda McFee and her elderly mother were driving home to Deming from Las Cruces along Interstate 10, when about 37km east of their destination they saw a blinding blue light ahead on the road. As they reached the scene, they saw some sort of brightly lit object, underneath which were two figures, 1.5m tall, dressed in bulky pale blue uniforms, including helmets, gloves, wide belts and boots. One of the beings seemed to be working on something, the other stood rigidly in the road. Neither took any notice of the women or their car. When the women looked back, the lights on the thing had gone out.

Over Dona Ana County in New Mexico in November or December 1952 at night. Radar installations from Holloman AFB tracked a UFO that disappeared in the area near the Mexican border south of Las Cruces and west of El Paso and Ciudad Juarez near the Rio Grande River. Meanwhile several civilians became witnesses of the crash, and information was leaked to reporters and local television. The people that arrived at the crash site saw a small silver-colored metallic disk that had crashed edgewise into a sand dune on the Mexican border. The disabled craft looked almost oval looking at it from the side; it was about 15-20 feet in diameter, with a small dome on top and an opening at the bottom-belly part about 2.5 feet wide and 3-4 feet high. A special military team was promptly dispatched to the crash site from Fort Bliss, Texas or from Holloman AFB. The first team consisted of only 10 to 15 military personnel, all dressed in fatigues and without identification patches. A low bow rig and a crane were brought; the disk was loaded upon a flatbed platform, covered by a tarpaulin and moved away to the closest military reservation at Fort Bliss in Texas. The recovery operation was watched by civilians and by television reporters who succeeded in making a short film and airing it. Shortly after that in conditions of extreme secrecy, at night a special convoy moved the disk on a flatbed, properly covered by tarp and camouflaged, from Fort Bliss to isolated area 29 at the White Sands Proving Grounds. Later a special underground facility was constructed to house the captured alien disk. Bodies of three occupants were found inside the disk. One was still alive, but the creature died soon after. A tent was erected near the disk and another one nearby. The bodies of the occupants appeared small by human standards, only 4.3-4.38 feet tall, with a large disproportional head, they were hairless and had four-fingered webbed hands. They looked Mongoloid, with small noses, slits for mouths and large slanted eyes that were shut. Their skin was leathery, reptile like and gray ashen in color. Each wore a tight-fitting metallic suit of a pale greenish-yellow color. The bodies were flown from Biggs Army Air Base at Fort Bliss to a major medical center in the eastern USA, and one of the bodies was autopsied there. Later the bodies ended up at Wright Patterson AFB in Ohio under building 18f (Hangar 18?) at underground level three in a special refrigeration chamber in a test laboratory. In 1967, the bodies were flown to Colorado Springs at another more secured and secret location. The disk is still at an underground chamber under the White Sands Test Range in New Mexico. The cabin inside the small disk-shaped craft consisted of three seats, a panel with a few simple levers and minimum equipment. A secret color 16-mm film showing the crashed disk and the bodies in a tent was shown to some specialists in several US military bases in 1953, as a psychological test. The results of the text were negative, so the decision was made to continue the deep cover up. Leon Crice distinctly remembers that TV-station WDEL-N in Wilmington Delaware was cut off the air when showing a newsreel about a crashed UFO. When Crice and his wife were watching the news on their TV set they saw a disc-shaped object shown stuck, slightly tilted, in a sand dune. It had a dome at the top and no window. The narrator said that it crashed on the Mexican border near the Rio Grande. As the film rolled, it clearly showed soldiers moving around the object and in the background were jeeps, a low bow rig and crane and some Mexicans watching. Crice also remembered that when the narrator mentioned bodies being recovered and that the craft had been shipped to a military base; his voice was cut off and the TV screen went black. There was no station apology and sometime later the news continued on another subject. According to another witness, Robert Oliveri, in 1952, a New York daily newspaper headlined this crash story in its "bulldog" or 2100 edition. Copies were delivered as usual to newsstands, the first load going to the Bronx. However, government agents confiscated almost all issues. The article said that three bodies were recovered; two were dead, one injured, still alive. The crash site was amid sandy terrain and desert like.

1953

At 8.30 pm on 25th October 1953 Jim Milligan, sixteen years old, was driving through a park in Santa Fe in New Mexico when he saw something fall in front of him. Jim stopped the car as the object landed in some bushes. He walked towards it and found a craft that looked like two ship hulls about three meters long by two meters wide glued together. When he tried to touch it the object flew away. Or this version. High school student Jim Milligan (16) was driving his car in a lonely road when something resembling a sheet of metal passed his windscreen. He braked rapidly, fearing a collision but the object landed in some roadside bushes. Jim cautiously approached the object, which resembled two boat hulls stuck together, 3m long, 1.5m wide, of dull, gun metal colour. As Jim attempted to touch it, the machine rose swiftly over a wooden fence and took off in a steep ascent towards Santa Fe. No odour or smoke was detected. Milligan was left pale and trembling.

In 1953 in New Mexico. A strange object crash landed and was found unoccupied with the doors open, In the vicinity were four bodies. These were humanoids, about 1m tall and hairless. The object was an ovoid 8m long 4m thick.

1954

Near Cibola National Forest in New Mexico on April 12th 1954 at Night. Mr. K. A., a cameraman for the USAF, was taken to a special assignment from Sampson AFB, New York to Roswell, New Mexico (later Walker Field Air Force Base). He was ordered to board an h-19 Sikorski helicopter and flown to the location of a UFO crash site. They headed north parallel to route 285 about 25-30 miles and then changed course to northwest continuing about 10 miles, where they cleared a small cliff. Suddenly below and ahead they saw brightly red, blue and yellow white flashing lights. As they flew overhead, they could see a round silvery object approximately 40-50 feet in diameter. The rim appeared imbedded edgewise into the sand. The disk had a stationary dome on its center, but the outer rim was still spinning counter-clockwise, and the lights on the outer edge were rotating in the same direction. Four small bodies were scattered outside the craft, and two more were inside the disk. All were dead. A small opened hatchway was on the side of the disk. The manner in which these bodies were positioned indicated that the aliens had tried to crawl out of the craft on their hands and knees, but all died presumably of oxygen intoxication. The bodies were abnormally proportioned, small dwarfs, approximately 4 to 41/2 feet tall, with extremely large heads, dressed in tight-fitting blue uniforms. They wore no helmets. They had light green, luminous skin. There was an overpowering stench emanating from the disk, resembling that of automobile battery acid that permeated the air. The disk was brought to Walker Field in Roswell and an attempt was made to house the object in hangar 46 but it was too small, so the craft was eventually stored in hangar 18. Heavy refrigeration equipment and other items were brought and installed. Later the disk and the bodies were moved to Langley AFB Virginia. This story is confirmed by other military men who heard their commander talking about a UFO crash near White Sands around the same time, recovered with an opened hatch and four aliens lying dead outside the UFO. Ukrainian remote viewer Irina Volyk reported that the crash was caused by the destruction of a cubic shaped container with very toxic liquid contents. She reported that the disk was flying from some subsurface alien base in New Mexico to outer space, but crashed on its route to an alien space station.

On May 18th 1954 in Cannon AFB in Curry County in New Mexico at 7 p.m. Two witnesses saw a house-size lens-shaped object land near railroad tracks, kicking up a small sand storm in the desert. One witness approached it but then ran away in fear. Cannon AFB was originally Army Air Base Clovis.

1955

At Lovington in Lea County in New Mexico during October 1955 a B-47 jet plane collided with the unknown. A ball of fire had suddenly appeared near it and according to the only survivor the ball struck the plane in mid-air. Another collision with a moving space? There had been another one reported in March that same year over Paris in Illinois.

1956

At White Sands Missile Range in Dona Ana County in New Mexico during March 1956. At 3:00 a.m. Air Force Sgt.. Jonathan P. Lovette and a Major Conningham were out in a field from the launch sites looking for debris from a missile test when Sgt. Lovette went over the ridge of a small sand dune and was out of sight for a time. Major Conningham then heard Sgt. Lovette scream in what was described as terror or agony. The Major thinking Lovette had been bitten by a snake or something ran over the crest of the dune and saw Sgt. Lovette being dragged into what appeared to him and was described as being a silvery disc-like object which hovered in the air approximately 15 to 20 feet away. Major Conningham described what appeared to be a long snake-like object, which was wrapped around the sergeant's legs and was dragging him to the craft. Major Conningham admittedly froze as the sergeant was dragged inside the disc and observed the disc going up into the sky very quickly. Major Conningham got on the jeep radio and reported the incident to Missile Control whereupon Missile Control confirmed a radar sighting. Search parties went into the desert looking for Lovette. Major Conningham's report was taken and he was admitted to the White Sands Base Dispensary for observation. The search for Sgt. Lovette continued for three days at the end of which his nude body was found approximately ten miles downrange. The body had been mutilated; the tongue had been removed from the lower portion of the jaw. An incision had been made just under the tip of the chin and extended all the way back to the esophagus and larynx. He had been emasculated and his eyes had been removed. Also, his anus had been removed and there were comments in the report on the apparent surgical skill of the removal of these items including the genitalia. The report commented that the anus and the genitalia had been removed, as though a plug, which in the case of the anus extended all the way to the colon. His body had also been completely drained of all blood.

At Holloman Air Force Base,12 miles from Alamogordo in Otero County in New Mexico in September 1956 at 8.00 am. A disc-shaped craft landed fifty yards from Highway 70 in plain view of dozens of commuter witnesses including two Airforce Colonels, two Sergeants and dozens of base employees. Radio and ignition systems of the nearest cars went dead and the sighting lasted ten minutes. The craft then took off with a whirring sound. Did it have an interest in Holloman Air Force Base?

In September 1956 at 0800hrs at White Sands Proving Ground in Dona Ana County, New Mexico. A large number of people saw a disc shaped object surmounted by a dome land on a road in the White Sands Proving Ground. The electrical equipment of cars in its vicinity all failed causing a long traffic jam on each side of the highway. The object was on the ground for 10=15 minutes, during which time some people got within 25m of the thing, which took off with a whirring sound. The witnesses were later sworn to secrecy by the CIA.

1957

At Socorro in Socorro County in New Mexico on Wednesday 17th July 1957 the passengers and crew of airliner flight 655 saw a UFO as big as a B-47 that came to within fifty feet of the top of the airliner over Socorro County, 100 miles northwest of El Paso, Texas. There were no other aircraft in the area and two passengers were hospitalized in El Paso with mild injuries. When was our last aerial swoop of an airliner? It was over Kent, England, on 31st May seventeen days before.

Between Clovis in Curry County and Portales in Roosevelt County in New Mexico on July 18th 1957. At a place located 48-56 km south west of Clovis, a whale-shaped alien spacecraft of a dull charcoal-gray color, about 30 feet in length, accidentally collided with a USAF fighter. Both aircraft crashed. The American military aircraft was totally destroyed while the alien craft was almost intact. But apparently all four of its occupants onboard died and were charred because of an intense fire onboard. The craft was dismantled into pieces and moved by train to Wright Patterson AFB. Later the craft was moved to S4-Papoose Lake installation near Area-51 (apparently seen by Bob Lazar). Four bodies of the very charred aliens were transported to Wright Patterson. Additional information by source indicates that the craft was in fact shot down by a surface to air missile from nearby Cannon AFB. This was apparently the first UFO shot down in the USA. The debris from the missile were found near the craft and analyzed. The crew in fact consisted of two Nordic blondes; one male and the other female; both killed on impact and were extremely mutilated. These were apparently the same two Nordics seen at Wright Patterson AFB in 1959. The craft was dismantled into pieces and moved by train to Wright Patterson AFB. Later the craft was moved to the S-4 Papoose Lake installation near Area-51 (this craft was apparently seen by Bob Lazar). Origin of the craft was established to be planet Troon in the Tiakouba double star system, 73.3 light years away. In 1989 this craft was temporarily stored in a surface hangar at NSA headquarters in Fort George Meade Maryland, where an experimental electromagnetic weapon was tested on it, which was then used to shoot down a UFO in Moriches Bay Long Island in September 1989. At present the craft is hidden in a new underground facility on the White Sands testing range in New Mexico. I only report them remember.

At Clovis in Curry County in New Mexico on Saturday 2nd November 1957 at 8.00 pm a UFO was seen in the sky. Something was about to happen in the area.

At White Sands Missile Base in Otero County in New Mexico on 3rd November 1957 at 3.00 am there was a report of the landing of two UFOs at White Sands Stallion Missile Site. Two military Police, Corporal Glenn H. Troy and Private James Wilbanks, were on patrol on the northern part of the missile base when they spotted a very bright object high up in the sky. They watched it descend until it appeared to be only fifty yards above the A-bomb bunkers. The light then went out. A few minutes later the object flared up bright as the sun and then fell at an angle to the earth and again lost its luminosity. The men described it as being seventy-five to one hundred yards in diameter. It was egg-shaped and appeared to have been only three miles from the witnesses. Even above places where normal air traffic was never allowed to go they appeared with apparent immunity. Eighteen hours later another two man military patrol at White Sands Missile Base at 8.00 pm on 3rd November 1957 saw a luminous hovering object only fifty feet above the same A-bomb bunkers. This was by Specialist Forest R. Oakes and SP/3 Barlow. Oakes stated that the light suddenly took off at a forty-five degree angle, went up into the sky and started blinking on and off and then vanished. It was not a helicopter. This was during the Levelland Texas sightings.

On November 4th 1957 about 8-10 [4?] miles SSW of Orogrande in Otero County in New Mexico at 1:10 p.m. James Stokes, electronics instrumentation technician, Rocketsonde Branch, High Altitude Test Division, AF Missile Development Center, Holloman AFB, New Mexico, a Mr. Duncan of Las Cruces and Allan Baker of Holloman AFB. Stokes was driving South down Hwy 54 when his radio faded and the car slowed [stopped?] as if the battery was failing then he noticed 6-12 cars ahead of him had stopped and drivers were out looking at the sky (looking behind him to the NE), including Duncan and Baker. Stokes stopped and got out, saw pearl-white oval or egg-shaped object about 500 feet wide with a slight purplish tinge heading South at high speed estimated 1500-2000 mph from the NE below elevation angle of Sacramento Mountains ridgeline, descending from about 5,000 feet above ground level in shallow dive to about 1,500-2,500 feet altitude as it swerved to the West to pass to the South of Stokes and the other stopped cars about 2 or 3-5 miles at closest, then circling around headed West and disappearing. The same or another object appeared in the NE (as if the object had completely circled) and performed the same rounded course but passing farther to the South of the parked cars [about 5 miles?] and disappeared in the West. Duncan took 35 mm film of the object. Stokes noticed a wave of heat from the object at closest approach, later that evening was sunburned, but it cleared up the next day.

On 4th November 1957 at 7.00 pm Mrs. Dale Van Fleet of Albuquerque in New Mexico saw an object hovering in the sky for five minutes at forty-five degrees elevation in the west. It was larger than a full moon and was gold in color.

On November 4th 1957 at Kirtland AFB in Albuquerque and Manzano Base/Site, a National Nuclear Stockpile, also in Albuquerque, New Mexico at 10:45 p.m. CAA air traffic controllers R. M. Kaser and E. G. Brink saw a highly maneuverable 15-20 foot egg-shaped object with a white light at its base circle over the West end of the base at 150-200 mph and come down in a steep 30° dive as if landing on Runway 26, to the North or NW of the tower at about 1500 feet. Radar tracked part of this maneuver. The object then crossed the flight line, runways and taxiways heading towards the tower at about 50 mph and 20-30 feet above ground, observed through 7x binoculars till it reached about 3,000 feet to the ENE near the NE corner of the floodlit restricted nuclear Weapons Storage Area / Area D/Drumhead Area (Manzano Base/Site A National Nuclear

Stockpile), and a B-58 bomber service site, where it hovered for 20 secs-1 min then headed East again, at about 200-300 feet height, then suddenly shot up at a steep climb at about 45,000 [4,500?] feet/minute. Controllers contacted RAPCON which tracked the object on CPN-18 radar traveling East then turning South, circling the Albuquerque Low Frequency Range Station then headed North [disappearing at 10 miles and reappearing 20 minutes later to circle around ?] to follow 1/2 mile behind a USAF C-46 that had just taken off to the South for 14 miles until both went off scope. The hovering radar target then appeared to the North over the outer marker for 1-1/2 minutes before fading.

At 12.15 am on 5th November 1957 two Santa Fe residents, Joe Martinez and Albert Gallegos saw an object in the sky with red and green and yellow lights and which gave out a great glow all over. The object was reported to have come down over the witnesses' car in Santa Fe in Santa Fe County in New Mexico.

Also on 5th November 1957 Erwin de Oliviera of the Tucumcari police was informed by an unnamed tourist that at 6.15 am he had seen a huge red object in the sky just outside Vaughn on Highway 54 in Guadalupe County in New Mexico.

Still on November 5th 1957 at 2300hrs near Hobbs in Lea County in New Mexico at 11:00 p.m. Two young men saw a red light north of the highway at a point 38 miles west of Hobbs. They watched for 9 to 10 minutes, thinking it was an oil-flare, when the light suddenly rose straight up. After pacing the car for a few minutes, the light turned toward the car, passed over it, and hovered over the Permian Basin Pipe Line Plant. As it passed overhead, the car engine sputtered, then died, and the lights went out. After the men coasted the car down the road, the motor restarted and they drove away. The battery was found to be dead the following morning and the dashboard clock was stopped. The Permian Basin Regional Training Center is in Carlsbad which is 68 miles west of Hobbs.

The next day on November 6th 1957 in Santa Fe in Santa Fe County in New Mexico. At 12:10 a.m. a taxicab company owner and one of his drivers saw a UFO approach them. They heard a humming sound as it came close. The object was egg-shaped and multi-colored. As it passed over their car, the engine stalled and the dashboard clock stopped. The UFO then pulled up and moved rapidly into the southeast. One witness later discovered that his wristwatch had also stopped at the time of sighting.

Also on November 6th 1957 and still in Santa Fe, New Mexico at 12:15 am. Taxicab owner Joe Martinez reported that that he and Albert Gallegos, while driving home saw an object in the sky with "red and green and yellow lights." He said it gave a "great glow all over."[Editor's note: The AF policy of ridicule has paid off in this instance. Neither man will elucidate any further regarding this sighting, although close friends have related the information that the object came down over the ear in which the men were riding. Both have said publicly that they aren't talking because they don't want to be called crazy.] Another version? At 12.10 am Taxicab owner Joe Martinez and driver Albert Gallegos saw an egg shaped object than they feared would collide with their car. It was huge, brilliant, with red, green and yellow lights, lit up the inside of the car and made a distinct humming sound as it passed over. As it did so the car engine stalled the car clock and Joe's wristwatch stopped. The thing then pulled up and shot away to the southeast.

At 9.20 am on 7th November 1957 Mr. and Mrs. Trent Lindsey and their twenty year old son Byron were driving south on Highway 54 when they noticed that the speedometer on their 1954 Mercury was weaving wildly back and forth between sixty miles per hour at which they were travelling and one hundred and ten miles per hour. Then they spotted a strange object in the sky to the southsouthwest that had sharply defined edges , no glow, no tail or visible means of propulsion and seemed to be made of highly polished metal. The object was viewed for three minutes on an arcing course in the southwest after which it vanished behind the Organ Mountains in Dona Ana County east of Las Cruces . This was in the White Sands Proving Ground area and was only twenty miles from where Mr. Stokes had his previous sighting near Orogrande also in New Mexico.

On November 7th 1957 at Walker AFB near Roswell in Chaves County in New Mexico. At 7:45 p.m. several long black flat objects with light blue tails approximately 200 to 300 yards in length were observed at Walker AFB by two military personnel in the control tower. The flight of the objects was wavering with a slight variation in altitude. The objects were seen through 7x5 power binoculars for about 20 seconds, and 30 seconds without binoculars. A second sighting took place of a long round object that looked like a large stovepipe 8 to 10 feet in diameter with a long trail 200-300 yards long and was seen for 60 to 90 seconds. The object made a complete 360 degree turn described as horseshoe-shaped. During the period 08/ 0140 - 0250Z (6:14 p.m. to 7:50 p.m.) like objects were reported from civilian air control personnel at Carlsbad and Hobbs, New Mexico, Wink, Texas, and a pilot of a Continental Airline Flight 184 near Hobbs, New Mexico. Walker AFB was closed down in 1967.

On the morning of November 7th 1957 a family driving on Route 54 near the White Sands Proving Grounds area, New Mexico, saw a large silvery cylindrical or oval shaped object traveling out of the northeast at about 10,000 feet. They watched it for approximately 3 minutes before the object disappeared over the Organ Mountains to the southwest. The object was traveling at "tremendous" speed.

At 7.20 pm on 9th November 1957 a housewife in Tularosa and several others observed a large rapidly approaching light which approached their car. As this occurred the car's lighting system failed. The incident took place near the junction of the White Oaks Road and U. S. Highway 54, near White Oaks in Lincoln County in New Mexico, twelve miles northeast of Carrizozo.

On November 9th 1957 near White Oaks ghost town in Lincoln County in New Mexico car lights failed as a UFO was observed. Was this the same sighting as the previous one?

Near Alamogordo in Otero County, New Mexico on 16th November 1957 many drivers and passengers of vehicles on Highway 24 saw a 500 foot long UFO that was hovering above it. It was an elliptical shape and was between White Sands and the missile center. The radios and ignition systems of the cars cut out and then a wave of heat hit the witnesses in the cars. One of the drivers received a severe sunburn yet the event happened at night. Any coincidence that during this energy storm or shower we had concentrations of sightings near missile testing centers?

1958

On February 17th 1958 at 2000hrs in Alcalde in Rio Arriba County, New Mexico. Two women, Mrs Evans and Mrs McIntosh, driving from Albuquerque to Santa Fe were starting by a brilliant flash of light that illuminated the surroundings. The passenger rolled down her window to see what was going on and was struck by a second flash, which temporarily blinded her and forced the driver to pull over. Between flashes and just after the second, the women had a brief sighting of a light orange object with a flat base and rounded top. Film in a camera was fogged and the passenger developed a severe headache followed by vomiting, rash and diarrhoea. A radiation reading was reported to be abnormally high. The woman was treated at the Lovelace Clinic but the results were apparently inconclusive.

At Portales in Roosevelt County in New Mexico on 11th October 1958 Angelhair fell like gossamer strands up to fifty feet long or strands of dust held together by static electricity. A pretty strange sight either way.

1959

At Roswell in Chaves County in New Mexico in July 1959 skyblasts occurred over a three day period. This was the same time as San Francisco in California and Amarillo in Texas.

In Portales in Roosevelt County in New Mexico in July 1959 a series of severe explosions rocked the area. They originated in the sky. They occurred in Amarillo, Potter County, Texas in July 1959, the same time as Roswell and San Francisco. They also hit Pampa in Gray County in Texas. Skyquakes shook the area though they were not registered on any seismograph. The blasts were so strong that they cracked the wall of one building in downtown. Pampa which is 55 miles from Amarillo. And on to Henderson in Warren County in North Carolina. This was after San Francisco. There were two unexplained detonations in a 29 hour period over Henderson in North Carolina? This rules out the incidence of the skyquakes in a straight line stretching from San Francisco in California to Pampa in Texas. We have a cuckoo in the nest. Henderson is not on a straight line though all the others are.

On August 13th 1959 between Roswell in Chaves County and Corona in Lincoln County in New Mexico. At 4:00 p.m. (1600 MT) (at 33°52' N, 105° 6' W). Jack H. Goldsberry, former USN PBY, flying a Cessna 170 from Hobbs to Albuquerque, New Mexico, at 8,000 feet, noticed halfway between Roswell and Corona, that his Magnesyn electric compass suddenly moved around a slow 360° rotation in about 4-5 secs, and his other standard magnetic compass was spinning wildly. About this time, he saw three small gray slightly fuzzy elliptical objects in close echelon formation passing in front from left to right and around his plane at a distance of about 450 to 600 feet and a speed of about 200 mph. The Magnesyn compass followed the objects position as they circled the plane, and after one full circle they disappeared to the rear, then both compasses settled back to normal. CAA controller at Albuquerque cancelled his flight plan and ordered him to land at Kirtland AFB, where he was interrogated by a USAF Major. "The FAA tower operator broke in and told him to keep radio silence. "He said for me to fly at once to Kirtland AFB. When I landed there I was hustled to an office and interrogated by an AF Major, the base UFO officer. Then he told me that being so close to those objects I might develop radiation sickness. He said if I developed any unusual illness to let the AF know and get to a government hospital right away. He warned me to keep this secret from everybody but my wife and to make sure she kept quiet, too." In a signed report secured later by a NICAP subcommittee chairman, Paul Cerny, the pilot said the possibility of serious radiation effects had kept him and his wife in a state of fear for weeks."

At Lake Bonita near Ruidoso in Lincoln County in New Mexico on August 20th 1959. At 3: 00 a.m. the witness and three young girls were sleeping in a station wagon, when they saw a bright fireball like object descend and land on the side of the nearby mountain. Several figures carrying flashlight-like objects apparently emerged and approached the witnesses' location, shining beams of light inside the vehicle, illuminating the area like daylight. The figures then left the area and the witness exited their vehicles and crawled to a nearby cabin. Apparently they did not see the object depart.

Near Mt. Capulin in Union County in New Mexico in August 1959. During the afternoon the main witness (10-years of age at the time) and her parents were traveling to Colorado Springs on a vacation when for some unknown reason, her father decided that they should stop and visit Mt. Capulin (an extinct volcano) located in the northeast corner of New Mexico. Her mother stayed in the tourist center while her father and she climbed up the side of the volcano and down into the crater. Then they returned to the center. She then felt a desperate need to go to the bathroom and as she was walking through the center she felt herself stop in mid-step. She felt her 'mind' lift out of her body and drop straight through the floor. How deep, she cannot imagine. Her "drop" ended in an arched tunnel deep underground. The tunnel was lighted with orange lights. Standing in front of her was a smallish being/ entity that she "knows now to identify as a reptilian." She estimated its height at somewhere around 4 feet tall. It was wearing a gray-color robe with long sleeves and a hood. The most that she could see of its face was "intense, oversized dark eyes." On its left hand (number of fingers unclear, but definitely a thumb) it held something that according to the witness resembled a modern day iPad or similar. On its right hand it held a kind of 'stylus.' It looked straight at the witness and communicated telepathically saying (apparently annoyed) "What are you doing here? We are not ready for you yet!" Then the witness' mind zoomed back through the ground and back into her head, where she stood in the tourist center. Immediately she double-timed it to the ladies room and "got relief" just in time. According to the witness she was to have further encounters with strange entities and UFOs.

1961

Between Datil in Catron County in New Mexico and Pietown also in Catron County, on 23rd October 1961 a brilliant ball of flame flashed across the front of a car and then veered into the sky. Later as the same witnesses approached a dark canyon the object suddenly reappeared and was travelling along in front of them. The object then broke into four smaller lights which followed alongside the car until they got to a small motel and service station. The car stopped and the objects took off. How does one bright light divide into four? If it was an energy flare it could. Is there a form of energy magnetism in which one of our strange energy flares gets attracted by another energy field such as a car and is attracted to or repulsed by it? Here is another version. On October 21st 1961 at 0200hrs while driving between Datil and Pietown on Hw 60, Richard and Rhoda Du Bois of Westminster California, encountered a brilliant ball of white light, which flashed down in front of their car, then slowed, turned and paced them, before streaking back into the sky, only to descend again as they were travelling through a canyon. Here it split into four smaller lights that paced them in formation until they reached a service station, where, as the car slowed, the lights flashed up and out of sight.

1962

In Otero County, New Mexico during 1962 a UFO was tracked on military radar across "two southwestern states." Jet interceptors were scrambled, but as the UFO crossed into New Mexican airspace, it began to lose altitude. The craft crashed on the desert sand at 90mph. Its flight pattern immediately beforehand indicated that any occupants were either dead or had lost control before the impact. The object was circular, 20 meters in diameter and 4 meters high. Two one-meter tall beings were found dead inside. They had pink gray skin, oversized heads, large eyes, tiny noses, small mouths, and holes for ears. They were wearing one-piece suits.

1963

At Tularosa in Otero County in New Mexico around Midnight in August 1963. The witness woke up to his aunt screaming in panic. The first thing he saw was a blue light flashing in the window. When he got out of bed and went to the window, he saw a saucer-shaped craft hovering about 50 feet off the ground, and about 80 yards away. It had lights around its center and several portholes. He could see the interior of the craft but with no real detail. His sister reported seeing a man standing behind one of the windows. The craft was smooth, with no visible breaks on its surface; it had no antenna, no landing gear, any intakes or exhaust ports. The only activity was in the lights around the center of the craft. After a while the craft moved off to the northwest at an about 45-degree angle. It first moved slowly but then it picked up speed and vanished into the distance.

North of Albuquerque in New Mexico in 1963. An ovoid disk about 12 meters in diameter and about 3.9 meters in height crashed to the north of Albuquerque and Kirtland AFB approximately between Sandoval and Santa Fe County. The crashed disk was moved to the nearby Sandia military reservation and hidden in a hangar there. One side of the craft was slightly damaged. A military contingent of marines guarded the craft, one which leaked data about the incident to California researcher Michael Johnston, who in turn forwarded the information to Leonard H. Stringfield. A scientific research team was attempting to penetrate the disk, at times even using a laser. They eventually were able to enter the disk. Five dead gray alien bodies were extracted. Two humans, apparently abducted by the aliens were also found onboard. (dead or alive?) There is supposedly a color film detailing how the disk's hull was breached. The craft was left at the base and was later transferred to another location. Data on this incident was also leaked to Budd Hopkins.

1964

On April 22nd 1964 at 2100hrs in Lordsburg in Hidalgo County, New Mexico. Mrs. Marie Morrow her 6 year old son and her friend Ruth Overlette were driving west, when 15-25km east of Lordsbury, when the boy alerted them to what he thought was a jet aircraft approaching from behind. Shortly afterwards, the car and the entire surroundings were illuminated by a bluish light, which lit everything up as bright as day. Marie braked and swerved to the right. She saw that the light was a large circle, as bright as a welder's torch, composed of many lenticular lights, and that it appeared to be only 3m above the car, and quite a bit wider than that. It gave off a whirring sound as it continued down the highway, veered north and disappeared out of sight. The observation lasted two or three minutes.

On April 24th 1964 at 5.00pm and in Socorro in Socorro County, New Mexico. Paul Kries and Larry Kratzer were driving back to Dubuque, Iowa, on Hw 60, when, about 1.5km SW of Socorro their attention was caught by a cloud of dust and black smoke 1-1.5km away. Paul only saw a momentary reflection of light, but Larry, who was driving, saw an oval object with a row of darker portholes along the side. It had a red "Z" marking on its right hand side. The thing climbed vertically out of the smoke, leveled off and moved off to the SW.

Later that day in Socorro in Socorro County, New Mexico on 24th April 1964 at 5.45 pm. Policeman Lonnie Zamora was in his Patrol Car on Route 85 pursuing a speedster when he saw an object emitting bright light and spewing out blue and orange flames rapidly losing altitude though hovering occasionally. The object made a roaring noise and drifted into a gully. The object was fifteen feet long and oval and a rocket-like exhaust appeared under it and left a bright blue flame on the shell of the saucer-shaped object. There was a vertical arrow with a vertical bar underneath it that resembled medieval Arabic for Venus. There were also mystery giant tracks. Suddenly loud sounds from the interior caused the witness to seek shelter. Lonnie saw two small Hominoids in silvery coveralls working underneath the craft. Sergeant Chavez arrived and the brush was burning in several places. The smoldering bushes oddly enough felt cold to touch and formed diagonals of quadrilaterals that were intersected at right angles with the intersecting point the most burnt. After the craft left a metallic material was found on the rocks that was found to be silicone. The bushes were charred. Also there were four deep marks where the metallic legs of the UFO had been. These were 3.5 inches deep and circular like landing pads. There were also traces of calcination evident. This can only be caused by extreme heat. What can we say? All of the classic elements are here as well as trace elements left over such as Silicone and ground calcination. But was it what was seen that left these elements? We might have to allow in our thinking for things that look like this to actually look like something else that we cannot comprehend that can still leave the same physical traces. 24th April 1964, and thereon was shaping up to be very big. Here is another version. Patrolman Lonnie Zamora (31) was chasing a speeding motorist down Old Rodeo Street, when his attention was caught by an "explosion of flame" or possibly just an explosion to the SE about 2.5km away. Fearing that some youths had caused an explosion in a dynamite shack, he broke off pursuit to investigate. He climbed his car up a gravel roaded hill with difficulty, looking for the shack, when he saw a shiny object 250m away to the south, which he suspected was a car overturned by children. He then saw it was vertical egg shaped metallic looking object, with two figures in white coveralls stood nearby. As Z approach one of the figures turned round. When he got within 30m Z got out to investigate, but as he did so he heard a loud noise rising in frequency, then saw flame under the object which started to rise vertically. As the object rose he noticed an insignia on the side. Fearing an explosion, he started to run, losing his glasses as he tripped over a car fender. When he next looked, the object was ascending in a slight SSW direction. When level with the car the flame shut out and the object continued with its shallow ascent, skimming the shack at 3m altitude. As the object ascended Z picked himself up from where he had ducked and returned to his patrol car to raise the alarm, while still viewing the object retreating into the distance. Sgt Samuel Chavez who came to the scene noted Z's terror, but was sceptical until he investigated where 4 impressions as of a landing gear and burned soil and vegetation were to be found. Z said that when he first saw the object he heard two bangs which could have been the occupants re-entering it.

At Canyon Ferry in Meagher County, Montana also on 24th April 1964 at 10.30 pm. After Socorro a landed UFO left imprints of landing gear the same as Socorro that same day. Several youngsters living at the lake claimed to have seen a lighted object which landed and then took off again from an area about 125 feet from the house. The Sheriff investigated the next day and found four eight inch by ten inch indentations in the ground that were four to eight inches deep that were arranged in an irregular rectangle roughly thirteen feet apart. The area also showed signs of scorching and a big cactus near the center of the arrangement was scorched as well. The ground was still warm. Was there actually a third identical sighting or a third assumed identical sighting? If the sightings are identical then we appear to have a Major quandary. We may have to allow for variations of sources for phenomena as well. We have a concept of a Multiverse of dimensions, possibly of many differing types. In many cases phenomena just appear to slip through, just a step out of time and place. In many other cases we appear to have deliberate and intentional arrivals and more than likely departures and in many cases accidents as well.

Still that same day of 24th April 1964 and on the north range of the Holloman-White Sands Missile test range the pilot of an RB-57 bomber engaged in a routine bomb test mission called mission control on his radio and informed them that he was not alone up there and that there was a UFO up there with him. The object was egg-shaped and white. Control asked if there were any markings and the pilot stated that there were and that they were the same as Socorro earlier that day. The pilot told control that he was going to make another pass and after completing his turn he saw that it was on the ground. At this point communications ceased. There were no more transmissions.

At 5.30 am on April 25th 1964 at Holloman AFB in New Mexico. Some twelve hours after the Socorro sighting, alien aircraft were spotted by Holloman radar and were warned off but apparently landed anyway. The base commander ordered an alert. Two interceptors were sent up to chase the alien ships from the area. The commander also alerted both Edwards and Wright Patterson. One disc-shaped craft landed while two hovered overhead. A sliding door opened and a ramp extended. Three aliens dressed in jumpsuits and wearing some type of head dress exited. They were tall grays with large protruding and curved noses and huge dark slanted eyes. Apparently a group of military officers were there to meet with the aliens. Communications were possible because of some type of device the aliens carried. Three separate cameras filmed the whole scene. The aliens expressed concerns of nuclear weapons and atomic tests and insisted on nuclear disarmament of the US in exchange for advanced alien technology. The conditions were rejected outright.

Around the same period as Socorro at Round Mountain, near Tularosa in Otero County, New Mexico on 25th April 1964. A motorist observed a bright object coming down from the sky.

At La Madera in Rio Arriba County in New Mexico on 26th April 1964 a white egg-shaped craft was seen to land by Senor Orlando Gallegos who was visiting his father and went outside to chase some horse out of the yard. He then noticed a bluish glow about two hundred feet from the house and as he walked towards it he noticed that it was caused by a butane-tank shaped thing as long as a telephone pole that was resting on the ground. The object was fourteen foot round and was shooting blue flames out of holes in the sides along the bottom. On the spot where it had landed there were markings that could only have been made by landing struts. The earth was also scorched unnaturally as well and was still smoking twenty hours later when the Police arrived to investigate it. The imprints left by the landing gear were the same as at Socorro that same day and there was melted glass as well. There were four eight by twelve inch indentations which were wedge-shaped at the bottom and at least one dozen circular tracks about 3.5 to four inches in diameter. An area of 35 to 40 feet had been scorched. How could it be that nearby on the same day the virtually identical craft lands at La Madera. If the La Madera craft was virtually identical to the Socorro craft then we may have to rule out inner witness symbolism creating the pseudoreal construction of the landed UFO as the odds should be near impossible for the two to match or so we should think with remote witnesses. Or are there generic symbolisms to draw on like virtually identical packets of soap powder? Do we also need to allow for how many other references there are by Authors and researchers who knowingly or unknowingly attempted to validate their own pet theories by altering descriptive data. This can be done quite easily and quite subconsciously when one only wants to see what one wants to see, a bit like the nature of the viewing of the phenomena themselves. Were the markings, undescribed, actually the same? Or was it the observation that markings were left tied in with the occurrence of the Socorro sighting?

At Albuquerque in Bernalillo County in New Mexico on 28th April 1964 Sharon Stull, 10, and her playmates saw an egg-shaped object that had appeared in the sky. The craft was smaller than a plane and a membranous material fell from it. Sharon grabbed the material and suffered inflammation of the eyes as well as first degree burns under the eyes and nose. Sharon then grew five inches in four weeks and within a month she seemed to have matured and grown up. She cooked her own meals, cleaned the house and took care of the younger children. Sharon grew from four foot eight inches tall and 80 pounds weight to five foot two inches tall and 110 pounds. She also had to wear sunglasses outside from then on as sunlight was too bright for her. Had Sharon been exposed to a massive radiation source which had upset her thyroid? And even into the following week it is still quite busy in the New Mexico area. Just ask Sharon Stull and her friends. She would never forget it.

On April 28th 1964 in the morning in Anthony in Dona Ana County, New Mexico. Numerous witnesses, including policeman Raul Artoche saw a reddish round object hover at low level (sic) and then take off very rapidly towards the west.

On April 28th 1964 at 12.05 am in Moriarty in Torrance County, New Mexico. Don Adams (22) of Edgewood was watching television when he was disturbed by the incessant barking of dogs and went out to investigate. Going towards his barn he saw a green object about 8m long hovering over a field. He then got in his truck and drove along Rte. 66 towards Moriarty. As he drove under the oblong object, which was hovering at 30m altitude, his engine stalled. He got out and fired six .22 shots at the thing with his pistol, the shot hitting with a metallic sound. He fired again as the thing descended towards him and pursued him. After about 100m the object veered away to the north and vanished. The dogs barked throughout the incident.

Near Stallion Site, San Antonio, in Socorro County, New Mexico near Holloman Air Force Base on 30th April 1964. Early in the afternoon the pilot of a B-57 saw an egg-shaped white object in the sky. The object had the same markings as the craft seen at Socorro on its sides and the object landed on the North Range. The same markings as Socorro? Too much for coincidence? Are we to look at medieval Arabic Astronomy for clues or is the symbol for Venus on the craft merely another coincidence? Does the symbol refer to Venus the planet or from Venus? Might it even refer to via Venus? Might it be nothing of the sort at all? Are the demons of the night merely updated and modernized even when they come by day? Is it the same as the route 497 bus?

In Hobbs in Lea County in New Mexico on 2nd June 1964 at 4.00 pm a grandmother, Mrs. Frank Smith, and her grandchild, Charles Keith Davis, eight years old were witness to a horrific event. Just outside the door of the Deluxe Laundry a top-shaped tan colored object appeared from the sky and hovered just above the boy's head. The object had a sooty tail and suddenly a blackish ball of fire covered the boy's head. One ear looked like a piece of meat and his hair was on fire and the ball then shot straight back into the sky. The face of the boy was so swollen that one could not see his nose and he had second degree burns to his face, hands and neck yet Charles had felt no pain at all. The boy's hair was on end and burning. The grandmother had been standing only three feet away and had witnessed the entire affair as did several other laundromat employees. New Mexico certainly was getting weird. Previously there had been falls of rocks over Lovington in 1942 and in 1955 the pilot of a B-52 collided with an unknown ball of fire also above Lovington. Scarcely 40 kilometers separates Hobbs from Lovington. What is it with the balls of fire?

1965

On August 8th 1965 at night in Tularosa in Otero County, New Mexico. A family was awoken by the alarm of an aunt and. looking out, saw a metallic looking disc shaped object hovering about 15m above the ground, about 80m away. There was a central band of lights, and a number of portholes, through which one witness thought she saw a human like figure. After a few minutes the object sped away.

Around 4.00 pm on 18th April 1965 Paul Villa was close to the bed of the Rio Grande near Albuquerque in Bernalillo County in New Mexico. Paul was in his truck and he saw a craft about one hundred and fifty feet in diameter that projected a beam of light that caused a small bush fire. Then another beam shot out and extinguished it. The craft also produced a miniature tornado causing the lower branches of some trees to appear blurred. The turbulence was so high that Paul thought that he and his truck would be blown away. Suddenly the wind ceased and the surrounding air became quite hot and there was dead silence. The ship landed on telescopic landing gear. Three occupants were seen who had light brown hair and tan skin and appeared to be about five foot eight inches tall. Paul claimed to have talked to them for two hours.

On September 25th 1965 at 2200hrs in Rodeo in Hidalgo County, New Mexico. 15-16km north of Rodeo, retired chemist, Dr George Walton, and his wife were travelling north of US80 when they saw at their 2 o'clock position, tow white lights, just above the ground. They first took lights, which ere moving towards the road at a right single, for those of another vehicle. George began to accelerate from 80-130kph to get ahead of the lights, which they now realised were at between 10-15m altitude and moving northwards in the same direction as themselves, about a city block away. The lights got close enough to illuminate the car, and after three minutes the lights went over the car, then changed colour to light blue before separating, one going south-east, and the other north-east. They quickly disappeared into the distance.

1966

On September 1st 1966 in White Sands in Otero County, New Mexico. A secretary to one of the range employees was driving on Highway 70, followed by her weekend guests in another car. At a point between Mars Site instrumentation site and the small missile range, a mushroom shaped object with a fiery trail took off suddenly from the ground near the road and disappeared in the distance, leaving the fiery trail. The secretary was unable to identify the object as anything produced on the site.

On the evening of 14th October 1966 during a terrible storm patrolman James Chelsea saw a plane trailing a massive cloud of black smoke. The plane disappeared in the cloud and then two black objects left and flew away from the cloud. At around 7.45 pm nineteen year old C. D. McClure was in his vehicle when he saw a bizarre man-like figure with a featureless white face emitting a sound like a crying baby. It had a black body and stood upright on two legs and was 1.50 meters in height. With each appearance of the creature there was interference with the car radio. This was in Albuquerque in Bernalillo County in New Mexico.

In Alamogordo in Otero County in New Mexico one night in 1966. Because of his high clearance, Air Force Sergeant Bill Holden was assigned to top-secret flights and special air missions. One trip took him to the above location on a mission as part of Project Mercury. It consisted of Air Force officers and civilian scientists. Although ordered to remain at a distance, Holden said he could see a vehicle shaped like a saucer parked on three legs. And to his surprise he said he also saw two aliens wearing silver/ gray metallic coverall uniforms. Before the mission he had to sign a 20-year non-disclosure statement and was asked if he objected to being involved in other similar projects.

1967

At noon on 6th February 1967 Ruth Ford sighted two fast-moving cigar-shaped aerial craft that each had two small propellers on them and a row of windows whilst she was driving between Deming and Las Cruces in Dona Ana County in New Mexico.

Also on February 6th 1967 there was a landing report from Deming in Luna County, New Mexico.

Near Tularosa in Otero County in New Mexico on 10th February 1967 at 4.30 am Richard Martinez of Tucumcari was driving home from Alamogordo when he saw a round bottomed metallic object with a domed top hovering beside Highway 54, twenty-five miles north of Tularosa. There were three lights attached to the outer circumference and one greenish colored light blinking on and off. He reported the sighting to the Police. This is New Mexico, home of frequent meteor falls, and occasional UFOs. Previously in this area there had been a fall of fish at Bingham in Socorro County, in 1952, near Round Mountain in Otero County, on April 25th 1964, a motorist saw a great meteor or bright object coming down during a flap, and on April 30th 1964, five days later, the pilot of a B-52 airplane was paced by a white egg-shaped craft that had the same insignia on the side as the famous craft that had landed at Socorro on 24th April, at 106 west 34 north as well as been seen in other places over the next few days such as the north range of the Stallion Missile Site near San Antonio on 30th April.

In March 1967 at dusk in Lovington in Lea County, New Mexico. A family of five were driving along an isolated road when a luminous object approached the side of the car, illuminating it. The car radio became filled with static and they felt their hair stand on end. The thing, the perimeter of which had a row of coloured lights, hovered very low over the car, and the 14 year old boy in the back seat saw a huge eye through a window in the object. The next thing remembered was that the car was almost in a ditch, and the one hour journey took much longer.

On May 26th 1967 at 2215hrs in Albuquerque in Bernalillo County, New Mexico. Three youths were driving on Artisco Avenue when they spotted a white light approaching from behind. It darted back and forth across the road and at first they thought it was a car driven by a drunk. The object then went above their car, keeping their speed. The car's engine and lights then died. The youths jumped out and as they looked up, the object flew away to the south-west at high speed. It made no sound.

In Summer 1967 in the evening still in Albuquerque, New Mexico. 12 year old Chris Brethwaite was one of a number of people who, on three successive nights, saw a nebulous, luminous sphere manoeuvre, and on the third night hover. On that third night Chris was alerted by a neighbour to an orange humanoid figure, 2m tall with an elongated heard and dark speckling on the roof of the Hoover-Aspen elementary school. After a couple of seconds it disappeared.

On October 9th 1967 at 1000hrs in Silver City in Grant County, New Mexico. Ron Vigill of Bayard was driving to Silver City on US90 when, on reaching the Central and Fort Bayard crossroad, he spotted a blue-green small torpedo shaped object, apparently skimming the ground below the utility wires, and the apparent speed of a jet aircraft. At the same time and only in short distance away on Fort Bayard golf course, Macario Borrege and a friend observed a welding torch blue object, with a central fiery ring, encircled by an outer blue ring. Macario saw the thing from as close as 10m as it travelled northward in the direction of Twin Sisters.

1970

At Hotaville near Oraibi in Navajo County in New Mexico. On the evening of August 10th 1970 Mr. Titus Lamson, a Traditionalist Hopi, saw a rainbow colored saucer shaped construction moving over the village in a westerly direction. It had "a dome, a round thing, and an aerial" on top. It became transparent as he watched it. Inside he could see the back of someone dressed in a gray "ski-outfit." The man, who had blond hair reaching to his shoulders, was facing an instrument panel. The craft descended slowly until it nearly touched the ground, and then disappeared over a ridge. Lamson set out to search for it with a flashlight but could not find it.

On November 15th 1970 at 1700hrs in Santa Fe in Santa Fe County, New Mexico a strange object was observed at ground level.

On December 21st 1970 in Santa Fe in Santa Fe County, New Mexico. A strange object was observed at low altitude until 0200.

1971

On January 1st 1971 at 0300hrs in Alamogordo in Otero County, New Mexico. A man, who did not want his name given, said that in the Big Canyon area south of town, he saw an object as bright as the moon, hanging wobbling in the sky. It appeared to be 30m diameter and shone through the clouds like the moon. From it shot bright orange objects that landed on the sides of the Sacramento Mountains.

1972

At Las Cruces in Dona Ana County in New Mexico twenty-three miles East of Deming in June 1972 /July 1972 Ms. Hilda McAfee, in her late fifties and her mother, were driving home from Las Cruces when they saw a bright blue light that was flashed on them from a short distance away. The light seemed to come from a lane on Interstate 10. It was a bright blinding light. Then Hilda saw an object ahead of her and she prepared to pull around. Both witnesses then saw two Humanoids under the object. Black rods four to five inches wide were near the Humanoids who were male, five foot six inches to six feet tall, robust in build and wearing blue quilted coveralls with gloves, belts and boots to match. The boots reached halfway up the calf and they also wore helmets with dark visors. The Humanoids appeared rigid and not interested in the witnesses and they continued working as the car passed by. After they had passed the object both women looked back but the object was gone. Afterwards both witnesses suffered burning aching chest and arm pains and both women said that their bones seemed to hurt. Ms. McAfee is landlady to Chaney Rogers, brother to Mike Rogers who was involved in the Travis Walton abduction. Here is another version. Mrs Hilda McAfee and her mother were driving home to Deeming from Laz Cruces on Interstate 10 at about 105kph, when, 37km west of Deeming, a beam of blue light shone on them from what appeared to be a short distance ahead on the same lane. The light was huge and blinding, filling the car and Hilda prepared to swerve round an object on the ground just ahead. As they swerved past, they saw two men, clad in pale blue bulky, quilted overalls and dark helmets, like those worn by motorcyclists, bathed in the brilliant blue light. Both appeared to be standing beside or below an obscure object which had some vague resemblance to a truck, which one of the men appeared to be working on. The beings had wide belts and gloves and appeared to be "rigid" and unaware of the near collision. They carried black rods 10-12cm wide. The light seemed to follow their car as they drove past. When the ladies looked back all was dark and there was no sign of the object or beings. Both later suffered burning aching pains in their chests and arms.

On November 1972 at 0140hrs in Corrales in Sandoval County, New Mexico. Restaurant busboy Charles Coulter (18) was motorcycling home from work along the Corrales road when, after about 2km, he noticed a very bright light at 25 degrees elevation, 5-10 degrees to the right of the path. It was about the size of a pea at arm's length and Charles thought it was an aircraft or helicopter landing light. He continued to the intersection about 5,2km south of the village where he turned east, the light following him. As he continued further on, the object kept pace, seeming to grow larger, At the Frontage Road on the east of the North-South Santa Fe highway, the object turned 90 degrees to the north, then another 90 degrees to the east. It continued to manoeuvre until it was hovering between the small businessmen' airport and the mountains to the east. Charles approached to within 135m of the thing at a crawl. He heard a sound like a hum and the air, on what had been a windy night, was very still and seemed charged with electricity. The object was now hovering only12m above the ground, 135m away. The motor cycle cut out and all the hair on his body stood on end. Then an extremely bright blue light came on from the object, with the front end of the beam reaching the ground. It reached the ground on one spot, retracted and then extended to another spot. Wherever it came into contact with the ground it obscured the terrain with its light. When it extended down onto Charles and his motorcycle he felt paralysed , was unable to let go of the handlebars and was so saturated by the light that he was unable to even see him own arms. The light then retracted back, changing into white-orange and went into an opening, which closed behind it. Charles was now able to see that this object was a sort of wedge shaped hexagon that resembled a pencil eraser with a bevelled surface. There were lights on panels on the underside and others around the perimeter.

1973

In January 12th 1973 in the evening in Farmington in San Juan County, New Mexico. A 40 year old woman driving a truck on Hw 44 south of Farmington saw a single intensely blue-white bright light which suddenly appeared and then paced her truck for one or two minutes. First seen about 3km away, it approached at high speed to within about 400m and then disappeared.

At 9.45 pm on 6th November 1973 an Air Policeman spotted a large glowing objcct hovcring over Plant Number 3, the nuclear weapons inspection facility at the Manzano Facility at Kirtland Air Force Base East in New Mexico. The object was described as an oblate spheroid one hundred and fifty feet in diameter which was gold in color and totally silent at an altitude of around one hundred feet. Nine other Air Policemen on duty in the area were alerted to the aerial intruder. A call was then put through to Kirtland East for assistance. It was reported that four interceptors, F-101 Voodoos of the 150th Fighter Group, New Mexico Air National Guard, were scrambled to intercept the object but as they grouped in the sky over Kirtland the aerial object began moving easterly towards the Manzano Mountains at tree top level. Kirtland is in Albuquerque in Bernalillo County.

In December 1973 near Dulce in Rio Arriba County in New Mexico a man hunting in the area saw a strange craft on the ground with three figures walking around it wearing green suits and some sort of helmet. When the witness turned his head away for a second the craft and figures were gone. The witness said that they just vanished in plain sight.

1974

On May 28th 1974 in Albuquerque in Bernalillo County, New Mexico. Two housewives observed an object 15-23m in diameter that landed on a nearby hill. It stayed on the ground for an hour but they were too afraid to approach it. It then took off, rotated on its central axis and moved rapidly away until it disappeared in the sky. Greyish material was found at the site by investigators.

Also on May 28th 1974 at 1200hrs in Sandia Mountains in Bernalillo and Sandoval Counties, New Mexico. Three young men out camping saw a silvery white disc and triangular object, with strange symbols on its side, land between Menaul and Copper. They were interrogated by intelligence agents who warned them not to talk.

On October 11th 1974 at 1610hrs in Cloudcroft in Otero County, New Mexico. The driver of a pickup truck saw a metallic looking object, surmounted by a dome, about 400m from the road. When he tried to accelerate his engine stalled but his tape deck continued as normal. The object then took off in a curved trajectory, disappearing in 8-10 seconds. The truck's engine then worked normally.

On December 23rd 1974 (Approx. date) at 2300hrs in Lordsburg in Hidalgo County, New Mexico. Six young men driving in the Animus Road area were nearing a hill when a brilliant blue white light came around the hill, shone its light on their jeep, lighting it up, and then zoomed away to the to the south-east at terrific speed.

1975

On January 6th 1975 at Lordsburg in Hidalgo County in New Mexico at 11:00 p.m. Three people listening to a CB radio in their parked car saw lights approaching them from behind. As the driver tried to move the car, the CB radio broke into static and the engine wouldn't start. A bluish light beam then shone on the car for a few seconds and the group heard a sound like the hum from high tension wires. The light then disappeared and they could start the car. As they drove away, they saw a blue glow behind a nearby hill. The battery on the car went dead a few days later. Or this. Mrs M and her father and husband were parked on the old Lady Mary Mine Road off the Animas Road, 5-6.5km south of Lordsburg for some fresh air. The father, who was driving, noticed some lights, and thinking another car was coming, prepared to drive over, only to find that the car would not start. Then a powerful blue light shone in through the driver's side, illuminating the foliage, and the CB developed static. The light seemed to manoeuvre fast, as if probing. When it had gone, the car started. The party could see no other vehicle. They heard a sound like electricity humming in the wires, but there were no such wires nearby. They pulled onto the Animas Road, then back on to the old mine road, too see a blue glow, like a halo, but not arched, behind a hill. Mrs M especially became unnerved and her face felt hot, so they moved out of the area.

On June 14th 1975 at 2345hrs still in Lordsburg, New Mexico. Two men in their early 20s; Rick Campbell and Steve Mentor were northwest about 1.5km north of Lordsburg when they observed an orange object, the apparent size of a house, falling at a slowly at a 70 degree angle in the vicinity of a sparkly populated area, 8km or more to the west of Glen Acre The thing landed without any sound and sent out shafts or orange light, which were so bright that Rick and Steve could not determine its exact shape. Thinking it was an aircraft that had crashed, , they contacted a middle aged neighbour Mr Roper, via their CB. Roper called the police and then drove up to the site, where he also observed the glow out to the west. A search party was organised,. At 0035, one of the searchers reported seeing an orange light moving towards him, swinging back and forth. The light then approached and then went out, making him very afraid. Another of the searchers, Patti Morris, noticed a strange absence of wildlife, and stillness in the area. No planes were down and nothing was found.

At Holoman Air Force Base in Alamogordo in Otero County in New Mexico on 13th August 1975 at 1.15 am Airforce Sergeant Charles L. Moody was watching the Perseid Meteor Shower. He then saw a glowing metallic disc shaped object falling towards the ground 300 feet away. The glowing object was fifty feet long and eighteen to twenty feet wide. It wobbled on its axis as it descended till hovering at fifteen to twenty feet. It then began slowly and steadily moving towards Moody who jumped in his car but could not start it. The UFO stopped seventy feet away and was making a high pitched humming sound. There was a rectangular window in the side of the craft. Shadows resembling human forms were in it. The noise stopped and Charles felt a numbness all over his body. He saw the object rising up into the sky. Moody then turned his ignition key and the car started. It was now 3.00 am. On the following day Moody felt pain in his lower back and within a few days a rash broke out over his lower body. Using self hypnosis over a few weeks he remembered that after the numbness two Humanoids approached his car. They were gliding rather than walking and were six feet tall in skin tight black clothing. Charles had a scuffle with them and was rendered unconscious. Next thing he woke on a slab in the craft. Next to him stood the Alien leader who was five feet tall and wearing a silvery suit. The leader had a large hairless head like the others, a protruding brow, roundish eyes, small ears and nose and very thin lips. His skin was whitish-grey and he had a large forehead, no eyebrows and no hair and large dark piercing eyes. He had very thin lips and the Humanoid asked Moody using telepathy if he would behave peacefully. When the witness promised to not strike out at them he was shown the engines of the craft. The Humanoid applied a rodlike device to Charle's lower back and the paralysis ceased. Moody was then taken to another part of the ship and shown a drive unit which was a large rod surrounded by three glass canopied holes containing a central crystalline object with one rod on each side of it. One rod had a spherical head whilst the other had a T-bar on it. There was a sweet stifling odor. According to the Humanoids it was an observation craft from a larger mothership 5000 miles away in Space and they were from a League of Space Races looking Earth over for possible future Membership. Moody was told that the Mothership was miles above Earth and was promised a future meeting with the Aliens. Close contact with Earthmen would not be attempted for another twenty years. The Alien told Moody that he would have no recall of the event for two weeks, placed his hands on the sides of Moody's head and rendered him unconscious. Moody lost an hour and twenty minutes. Or this version. Sergeant Charles L Moody, a decorated Vietnam War veteran, stationed at Holloman Air Force Base, had driven into an area of the desert, where the city lights were not visible, in order to view a meteor shower. He was sat on the front fender of his car, smoking, when he was shocked to see a huge metallic, faintly luminous, disc shaped object drop out of the sky about 90m away, He was puzzled by the unusual configuration of the aircraft, which appeared to be about 15m long, and 5.5-6m wide. It came to down to a height of 4.5-6m, wobbled like a top, stabilised, then came towards the car at walking pace. Realising it was something unusual, Moody got back into the car, only to find that it would not start, that the lights would not go on, and it appeared the car had no battery at all. By now the object had stopped still about 20m away. Moody heard a high pitched sound like a dental drill. He saw, on the centre right of the object, an oblong shaped window 1.5m long, 1m wide, through which he could see shadowy human forms. The humming stopped, he began to go numb, then he next remembered sitting in his car, while the object took off, going out of sight in seconds. He drove rapidly back home and was surprised to see that it was now 0300. He was pale and upset, He developed a pain in his back and a rash on the lower part of his body. It appeared that using some sort of auto-hypnosis, he obtained "recall" of the missing 90 minutes. he claimed contact with beings 1.5m tall, weight 110-130 pounds, with large hairless heads, somewhat larger than human eyes, very small ears, small nose and thin lips. They had black, skin tight, suits, save for one in a silvery suit, who spoke to Moody. The inside of the craft was as clean as an operating theatre and was lit by a light, the source of which could not be determined. Moody was touched on the back and legs with a rod, taken into a small dim room which descended to a room about 7.5m across with a huge carbon rod going through its centre. Around this were three glassy spheres, filled with crystals, with a rod at each end. This, he was told, was the drive unit. There was a large black box at the other end of the room, the purpose of which he was asked not to reveal. Further talks followed. Later he recalled that as he sat in his car it became enveloped in a glow, and two beings glided towards him. he fought the beings, lost consciousness, then came to on a table in a room, with the white suited leader, whose face was white-grey, like a mask. He also added that the two rooms he was were larger than the external dimensions of the craft. The being claimed that limited contact would be made over the next twenty years, and that several races were co-operating.

On November 10th 1975 at 0400hrs in Taos in Taos County, New Mexico. Police Officer David Rivera was cruising the Plaza area with his window down when he heard a sound like that of a helicopter. He turned off the engine and looked around could see nothing to account for it. He heard the noise again on Kit Carson road and, looking up, saw a large, bulky cigar shaped object without any lights flying at treetop height above, and slightly to the left of, his car. The thing appeared to be30-35m long and about 7m diameter. It kept pace with his car from when he was cruising at only at 8kph to a max speed of 110kph. The object verted towards the mountains in the north. As David turned back to the sheriff's office he saw a circular light on the mountain. He informed dispatcher Paul Vigil, who went outside and saw the light. Searches the next day were fruitless.

Near Gallup in McKinley County in New Mexico one night in 1975. A light followed the female witness and her daughter as they drove in the desert. The light became so bright, she was unable to see, and then her next memory was of approaching town, which had been 65 miles away. Under hypnosis, she recalled leaving her body and entering a round object. There she saw humanoids with heads slightly larger than average. They had large eyes, small noses, and mouths, and unusual ears. The beings were 6 feet tall, had gray white skin and wore close fitting clothes and also hoods, and cloaks. The cloaks included a symbol, which combined the nuclear symbol with the Star of David. These beings floated about effortlessly and communicated with her by telepathy. She sat in a chair in a warm, wedge shaped room, while her two daughters were in another. When she inquired about them, the beings took her to see that they were safe, sleeping in chairs. She returned to the first room where the beings ran tests, and at one point she felt as if they were tearing her body apart.

At White Sands Missile Range in New Mexico in 1975. Military Policemen (MP's) patrolling and checking empty warehouses late at night would hear footsteps coming towards them, but the flashlight would show nothing except an empty room. Then one night, two of the men were parked out in the desert having a cigarette when they heard something walking towards them. When they turned their lights on to see where the sound was coming from, they could see the grass and brush parting as if someone was walking towards them, but there was no one there. They got out of there after that. Finally one night one of the other MP's stopped reporting in. They discovered his jeep and it looked like he had tried to wedge himself behind the back seat and emptied his side arm through the windshield at something. They never found him.

1976

On 21st May 1976 near Alamogordo in Otero County in New Mexico. 35-year old Christina Bryant, along with her 4-year old daughter and a friend, were driving from Phoenix, Arizona to Lubbock, Texas when the trio noticed lights in the star-filled sky. To amuse her daughter, Bryant invented a game commanding the lights to turn blue and then red, which they did, for durations of about 45 seconds. They would stop, and the lights would go off. They also somehow had left the main highway, finding themselves on a two lane back road in the boonies. Rabbits and deer appeared along the roadside and darted. Around a bend they saw a police car with funny lights and a one-car-wreck, the vehicle tilted at a steep angle, its battery oddly hanging from the wrong side of the hood. The policeman carried a flashlight and a clipboard but seemed to be in parade uniform, with braids and medals, totally out of sync for a back country road. The officer reached for her hand, resting on the frame of the open window. Bryant remembers the sudden chill of his touch. It was so cold it scared her. There was no sign of any accident victim. They asked the officer about the wreck. He asked if they had passed anyone. About 45 minutes down the road they turned into a highway junction truck stop. The clock read 3: 00 a.m., an impossible time lapse. In Lubbock, Bryant related details to her mother, who produced a tabloid story with an article about a record number of UFO sightings. Bryant said, in the same area where she had been. But it was January of 1983, before Bryant decided to do something to find out about the missing time. Under hypnosis, Bryant recalled that the "policeman" had opened the door and helped her out. He was holding her hand for the whole time. He was nice, kind and very gentle, of average height, about 5'11", 170 to 180 lbs, blond with blue eyes, nice features. The police car was actually a ship shaped like a coolie hat. After climbing a ladder into the spacecraft, Bryant was motioned to a chair in front of a large window. Numbers appeared across the top of a screen, an apparent directional finder with converging lines, and the policeman became her playful pilot, pushing buttons that propelled them to fly against a rush of stars. "It was great" Bryant said, "I was fascinated. I knew he was not going to hurt me." The spaceman told her that his name was 'Oran' or 'Oron.' While the ship was in apparent "automatic pilot" he led her to a door, penetrating it with a motion of his hand. That's when she became afraid, when she stepped through the door. A man and two women stood in front of a cabinet near a very surgical table. Her daughter, snugly asleep, was nearby on another table. One of the women had placed a protective hand on the child. Random recollections were of white coats, a round faced man of average height who had no facial hair, girls with heavy lashes and pretty eyes, skintight caps covered their heads. They all had white, pasty complexions. She was examined with a "huge syringe" and a long silver cylinder, and a stethoscope like device. She was floated onto the table and skin was scraped from her arm, and she saw them staring curiously at her stomach. A needle was stuck in her back. Fluid was taken from an eye and then replaced. Still under hypnosis, Bryant was told to pay close attention to the people in the examining room. She panicked when she realized that they were not "people at all." The caps became skulls, with tight white flesh. The women became young boys with small faces, like a half-open book, the nose and mouth, the blinding large eyes like almonds. Their mouths she saw were merely holes and not functional at all.

At an undisclosed desert location in New Mexico one evening in 1976. After a bitter family dispute, the witness drove his truck to a prairie area southwest of town. He parked the vehicle and began walking around the area. He then heard a rustling sound from behind the sagebrush and then saw a tall figure approach. The figure left, then the witness heard a whistling noise and then became paralyzed. A tube suddenly came down, engulfing the witness and transporting him up into a hovering object. He floated through some kind of passage that took him into a room where he landed on a glass like table. As he lay there, four tall figures came into the room. They began to examine him using a strange scanning device. All the data picked up by the device was fed into a peculiar gray screen where the witness saw his internal organs. The beings were described as seven-foot tall, grayish in color, with 3-fingered hands. They were friendly and wore flexible armor type suits and dark opaque helmets. After a while the beings conversed among themselves and released the witness down the same glass like elevator or tube. Here is another version. At an undisclosed location, Tom Murillo was walking around his truck, listening to the radio when he was approached by a tall figure, Tom called on it to go away and went to go back into his truck, but before he could do so he was taken by a tube into an aerial object where four 2m tall grey skinned beings with three fingered hands undressed and examined him with a devise which showed his internal organs on a screen. The beings seemed intrigued by the number of his fingers and toes. He was then dressed and sent out again through the tube.

1978

On October 24th 1978 (Approximate date) at night in Las Cruces in Dona Ana County, New Mexico. Margaret Roberts was driving home from El Paso when a large bright metallic object, with two flashing green lights, one at the back, the other in front, descended on her car. The engine stalled and a portion of her front windscreen shattered. The object then rose straight up. The incident was reported to the Las Cruces police who found no further evidence. Joyce suffered from anxiety and problems in sleeping since the incident.

1979

On January 15th 1979 in the evening in Tijeras in Bernalillo County, New Mexico. A family driving back to Albuquerque along Interstate 40 on this windy day saw an object with three flashing lights circling a tall tower. The object then paced their truck, directing beams of multi-coloured light at it, before taking off.

On March 25th 1979 in Taos in Taos Country, New Mexico. A deputy sheriff and a companion saw a multi-coloured object the size of a car pass overhead and descend to the ground. A glow was detected at the presumed landing site for some time, but the place was inaccessible to their vehicle.

1980

Near Cimarron in Colfax County in New Mexico at 7.15 pm on May 6th 1980 a woman and her 8-year old son were driving along the desert when they spotted three lighted objects on a nearby field. The center object was the biggest with lighted windows that emitted an amber light. She became paralyzed and confused and a four-hour time loss resulted. Later under hypnotic regression the woman remembered walking over to the field and hearing cattle "screaming" in apparent pain. Four figures approached and carried the witness into a nearby object. She kicks and screams and feels extremely cold. The beings are greenish in color and move in a strange shuffling manner. A taller pale being with a high forehead and wearing a white outfit with cape approaches the group. He appears angry and says that she should not be here. At one point she is briefly touched by the tall Humanoid and feels a burning sensation. She is shown her son and he seems to be sleeping peacefully. She is apparently medically examined and experiences a lot of pain. She was then taken into a bright white room where she sees the beings apparently cutting up a cow into pieces apparently while the animal was still alive. Several beings wearing dark brown outfits with an orange insignia escort her to another room where the tall white garbed being waited. She then remembered landing in a desert area and met there by several tall beings wearing shiny clothing that shuffled their feet when they walked. She is then apparently taken into an underground facility where the tall beings, described as hairless with large beautiful eyes wearing long robes, examine her. At one point she briefly enters a large metallic room where she sees a huge container filled with floating animal and what appeared to be human body parts. She is eventually returned along with her son unharmed.

Near Pecos in San Miguel County in New Mexico at 10.30 am on July 16th 1980 a civil air patrol cadet observed along with several other witnesses a dull metallic circular object maneuvering over the area. The cadet went closer to the object as it landed on a nearby clearing. He then observed a human like figure dressed in a metallic suit emerge from the object and walk a few feet away. Moments later the figure returned to the object which quickly took off towards the northwest. Or this. On July 16th 1980 near Pecos in San Miguel County in New Mexico at 10:30 AM. a Civil Air Patrol cadet along with several other witnesses observed a dull metallic, circular object manoeuvring near Pecos. The cadet got closer to the object after it landed in a nearby clearing and took some photographs. He then observed a human looking figure dressed in a metallic suit emerge from the object and walk a few feet away from it. Moments later the figure returned to the object and it quickly took off and flew towards the northwest. The cadet was later approached by a mysterious man who wanted him to turn over the photographs to him.

On August 9th 1980 at 0020hrs in Albuquerque in Bernalillo County, New Mexico. A security guard observed a disc shaped object with a powerful light, on the ground. It then took off rapidly. Its landing had been observed a group of security guards 8km away.

1981

On September 3rd 1981 at 2240hrs in Roswell in Chaves County, New Mexico. Thomas Huntley was driving north on US285 when he encountered a sort of fog that covered the road to a height of 3-5m. As Thomas approached further he saw a beam of light in this fog and then as he got closer still the thing shot off into the air.

At 7.30 pm on December 8th 1981 south of Reserve in Catron County in New Mexico an enormous UFO shaped like an orange ball, and estimated to be 750 feet in length, made a number of turns in the sky and then executed a ninety-degree turn near Luna Mountain. The five witnesses said they saw a jet aircraft chase the UFO out of sight.

1983

During July 1983 an explosion was heard in a field near Vallecitos also in Rio Arriba County. Mud and grass were thrown quarter of a mile away leaving a crater eight feet deep and seventy-five feet wide. There are no records of meteoric impacts in this area.

1984

At 7.10 pm on April 24th 1984 at Chimayo in Rio Arriba and Santa Fe Counties in New Mexico there was radar and visual confirmation of a 1,000 foot long cigar-shaped object that followed a KC-135 USAF tanker aircraft through a U-turn over the mountains of Chimayo in New Mexico while separate nocturnal lights cavorted about in the sky. Radar blips were tracked at the time. A metallic football-shaped object, about 1000 feet across, was observed by eight witnesses at a mountain for 20 minutes.

Also at 7.10 pm on April 24th 1984 in Alcalde in Rio Arriba County in New Mexico independent witnesses viewed through binoculars a metallic ovoid that maneuvered away and back for 20 minutes. A light rumble was heard. There was radar and visual confirmation.

On the Isleta Reservation in Bernalillo County in New Mexico on May 1st 1984. At night while driving home to Albuquerque on I-25 North after playing a "gig" in Socorro, and shortly after passing the Los Lunas exit, the witness (involved in several encounters) noticed a faint glow originating from the canyon pass area northwest of his location, where the train normally comes from points west into Belen. At first he thought it might be the train then realized it was a very faint glow, but he saw it moving, so then thought it was a small aircraft, possibly a helicopter or plane. As he continued watching, he noticed that the object was traveling toward the southeast at an apparent high rate of speed, and seemed to be coming toward the general direction of his car. He watched the object move toward him for a minute or so, and then he became even more interested, as it appeared to move right in an intersecting path with his vehicle. There was not another vehicle on the highway in either direction at the time of this sighting. He watched it approach, and then became very perplexed as it seemed to be glowing somewhat like a fluorescent light bulb, not lighting the area around it, but glowing sort of within itself. In a second, it flew directly over his vehicle, at what was seemingly an exact 45 degree angle to his car, the witness looked upward over the steering wheel to see that the object he had the strong impression, was actually a living being, glowing white and at the last split second he looked up, it turned its head slightly and looked down directly at him. Since it was moving at what the witness estimated to be at least as fast as he was moving in the opposite direction, he could not make out much detail, except to say that he noticed that it had two huge black eyes. No wings were visible, as he immediately tried to rationalize what it was he had just seen. The flying humanoid had passed over his car at an estimated 100-200 feet in elevation. Two weeks after the initial sighting, he was heading down the mountain pass from Magdalena toward Socorro again from another gig with the band and this time, he wasn't alone, as the band was traveling in two other vehicles behind him. Something caught his eye at about 9 o'clock high outside the car, and he watched in amazement for a few short seconds as the same being was again coming toward him (at the same 45 degree angle to the road), only this time it was significantly lower, possibly only 50 feet above the car. The witness again peered upward over the steering wheel at the last split second, and again, the thing turned its head and looked at him with its big black eyes. Even though it was a lot closer overhead this time, the witness still could not make out much detail, except to say that the body seemed to be almost trapezoidal, tapering toward the head, and being about five times longer than the head, which was also huge compared to the body size, and had definite bilateral symmetry along its length. Again he saw no wings. When the witness and the other members of the band arrived at a "Circle-K" convenience store in Socorro for their usual "string cheese" party a few minutes later, he asked if anyone else had seen "something" fly over his car on the way down the mountain. "Yes" was the answer from the two riding in the car behind him, this was the rhythm guitar player and his wife. When he asked them what it was they said they didn't know that, "it was probably some kind of big bird or something." They did admit that it was moving really fast. About two weeks after this, the band was having a practice at their recording studio, which was at the house of two band members in south Belen, the main witness had his son James, then 5, and daughter Amy, then three along with him. The studio was located about 25 feet or so away from the main house on the property. There was a porch light above the side door of the house, which had an eave roof over the doorway. At one point his daughter said she had to use the bathroom, so he asked James to please take his sister into the main house. They played through a song twice say about 5-6 minutes, and he began to wonder why it was taking the kids so long to come back outside. As he was ready to leave the studio, both of the kids came running inside the studio door, screaming at the top of their lungs. His son James excitedly told him that he saw a "creature" above the door. They all immediately went outside to see if they could see anything and James then described what he saw, He said it had a pair of arms, wings and clawed feet, big dark eyes and big ears. It bent over toward them as they approached the house and put one of its hands up to its mouth, then James said it "spoke" saying, "Shhh. Be Quiet!" prompting James and May to quickly run into the house via the front porch and front door, so Amy could use the bathroom. James said he stood guard in front of the door, until Amy was done, then they both ran as fast as they could back to the studio. After this incident, the witness was sure he was being "targeted" but also began to feel angry, as now this was somehow involving his family.

In July 1984 at night in Dulce in Rio Arriba County, New Mexico. An elderly woman saw two grey beings wearing skin tight silvery suits stood at her bed foot. They fired a red light at her. Two officers from the Jicarilla Apache tribal police were called to the scene and noted the unusual silence of the birds, and that the woman's dogs and horses were shaking with fear. In the morning the officers saw three fiery orange discs take off some 50m away. They turned white as they took off towards Chama, where further police officers saw them.

In October 1985 at night in Santa Fe in Santa Fe County, New Mexico. A woman living alone in an isolated cabin outside Santa Fe when she was wakened from drowsing by the sound of music and then a brilliant, rapidly moving white light approached the cabin, came in through the window and hit her in the solar plexus and heart. She felt a curious vibration in her body.

1992

On April 12th 1992 near Deming, NM. 11:20 PM. The witness was driving on US 180 along the desert and was listening to his CB radio when the radio suddenly went silent and he vaguely noticed a patch of white light shining on a rise over the left side of the road. He then heard a voice in his head telling him to "watch out for the smoke. "Thinking it had been the CB radio he replied but there was no answer. Suddenly what looked like a huge luminous cloud of smoke began stretching across the highway ahead, it formed a solid curtain across the road. The witness drove into the grayish-white vapor for an hour. He stopped his vehicle and walked across the road and into a ditch but was still unable to see anything. He suddenly went into a state of paralysis and sensed the approach of two persons. Each person got on either side of the witness and placed a firm grip on his forearms. The beings had long bony fingers. He was then led to a shiny metallic object, shaped like a flattened arch with rounded ends. A rectangular opening appeared on the side of the craft. Next he remembers sitting back on a chair inside the object feeling dizzy and numb. He was briefly alone then two beings entered the room. One being was a male with a round oval face with two large oval black eyes. He was five-foot tall with a thin torso and limbs. The second being was a female, similar to the male being. The witness was then led to a dimly lit room and placed in a reclining position on a chair. He felt a buzzing stimulating sensation on his facial area and felt as if a small object was being introduced into his nose. He was then released and let outside and floated horizontally towards his vehicle. He resumed the drive and the vapor-like fog quickly dissipated.

At 9.40 pm in April 1992 in Tijeras Canyon in Bernallilo County in New Mexico Sue Strickland was traveling north through the canyon when she saw something resembling a "mini jet" streak into the canyon from behind her, preceded by a fireball of light about 2 feet in diameter. The ball of light streaked by following the paved road with the mini jet apparently following it. Near an outcrop the mini jet suddenly stopped and hovered silently. It then tilted 45 degrees and maneuvered over Strickland's vehicle. After hovering over the truck for a minute or two it accelerated and disappeared around the next curve. The witness drove up and saw it on the road ahead. She could see that it was a jet-like vehicle slightly larger than she thought with a curved canopy. She could see two figures, one inside the other walking towards the rear of the object. As she sat looking at the object and figures suddenly she found herself inside the object. She stood in an aisle with a short wooden bench on both sides. She attempted to walk towards the front of the object but was commanded to stop. After saying something to the pilot, a short, thin, man-like figure approached her. He was bald and was wearing a blue coverall with gold embroidered epaulets on his shoulders. Apparently the being attempted to implant a hypnotic suggestion in her mind about forgetting the incident, but it did not work. He looked surprised then the pilot told him to get rid of her. Her next memory was of sitting in her truck, and seeing a streak of light out of the corner of her eye.

1994

In Summer 1994 in Santa Fe in Santa Fe County in New Mexico at 3.32 am Shona Bear Clark suddenly woke up to see her bedroom illuminated by a bright light. She looked down at her foot and realized that a piece of flesh about one inch deep, and three inches long was missing. The inside of her foot was silver, but there was no blood. She then realized there were two men standing beside her, one on each side of the bed. They were standing right through the bed. They had blonde, shoulder length hair, blue eyes, and appeared to be about 50 years of age. Their skin was a bronze color, as though they had good tans. They wore robes. One was wearing red and white with gold roping around the collar. The other robe was blue and white with gold roping. The man in the blue went over her foot with his hand and said that she was totally healed. The other man put his hands on each side of her head without touching her and said, "We will be back when you need us." Then they disappeared. Her foot returned to normal, but the peculiar light stayed until six in the morning.

1995

At 11.30 pm in October 1995 in Santa Fe in New Mexico Shona Bear Clark (involved in other encounters) woke up to discover a man standing in her bedroom. He was wearing a white robe with gold roping around the neck area. He had shoulder length blond hair and blue eyes. He told her that they were "giving her back" her memories. He stood there all night as she slept on and off. After this event she began leaving her body on a regular basis.

1997

One day in the middle of May 1997 near Clines Corner in Torrance County in New Mexico a silvery disc shaped craft with a dome on top descended on a cattle field besides the I-40 highway. Motorists in both directions stopped and got out of their vehicles to see the craft. To their amazement, three reptilian like Humanoids emerged from the object and walked about nonchalantly, ignoring the crowd of onlookers. The creatures were about five feet tall and had light blue skin with dark hues and tones. The reptilians had three long, claw like fingers and toes and yellow eyes with a black, catlike split in the center. Supposedly some in the crowd photographed the events. A state trooper came along and ordered everyone back to their vehicles. The Humanoids went back inside their craft and left the area northwest bound, at a slow rate of speed.

At Roswell in Chaves County in New Mexico in Summer 1997. At 5: 30 a.m. the witness had gone outside with her cup of coffee to a picnic table in the backyard. Her Chihuahua, Bella, followed her. At first she thought her neighbor had bought a dog, a little Schnauzer. Taking a better look, she noticed it was not a dog but a "little man." Bella also ran to the fence to get a better look. They both then noticed a little man about 12 inches tall, stocky built with bushy eyebrows (gray) and a beard. He was wearing a gray woolen type shirt (no buttons) and gray pants with a rope for a belt. He had brown boots that looked like socks. Bella ran back into the house and under the bed and remained there most of the day. The little man had a funny walk from side to side and quickly ran into a Chinaberry tree and disappeared. She could not see a door or entrance but the little man disappeared into the tree. Yes, I said that I report all sightings.

At 6.30 am on December 10th 1997 in Taos County in New Mexico Ricardo Alfonso was driving to work to the Taos Elementary School when he saw a metallic silvery object hovering over a nearby field. He stopped his truck to investigate. As he got closer he hid behind a bush for a few minutes until the craft disappeared. As he sat there pondering what had happened a bright beam of light illuminated him. Then several "little men" appeared around him and everything then went blank. He awoke later face down in the field completely naked and with bruises on his body.

At 2.30 am on December 14th 1997 in Hart Canyon in San Juan County in New Mexico the night before the witness, Noel Chandler, had seen a round glowing UFO over his horse shed and for several nights previous there would be three loud thumps on the house and after checking all around outside, no cause was found. While in bed that night he became aware of a light in his bedroom from an outside source. It was bluish white. Then a figure appeared with no real distinguishing features—real large eyes about the size of horse eyes, a small mouth, and nostrils like small holes. The witness was unable to move or talk. He heard a voice in his mind that told him that "they" were here to collect sperm samples. Soon a tube about half an inch in diameter and six inches long with a ball at the end scanned his body. The tube was placed over his pubic hair just above the penis on the left side. A needle was then inserted. His left testicle was drawn up into his groin. There was no real discomfort or pain. The needle and tube were removed and taken into a floating sphere. Moments later another form came down the light, like floating in a horizontal position. It was a female with funny looking hair on her head. The needle and tube came out of the sphere and she inserted it into her navel. Then, telepathically, the witness was informed that their society was dying because they could not reproduce. They were becoming sterile. They said that by introducing new blood lines and clones they could possibly regenerate their society. Their gestation period is three to four months. Soon the bluish light started to "close" in at the bottom and they were gone. A strange smell lingered.

1998

On 13th June 1998 a meteorite penetrated a barn roof in Portales in Roosevelt County in New Mexico. After detonations were heard in the sky and smoky trails were seen a shower of meteorites, 53 of them recovered, with a total weight of 71.4 kilograms. A 530 gram fragment went through the roof of Gayle Newberry's barn amd embedded itself in a wall indicating a trajectory from East to West. The strewn field was elliptical and 7.7 by 2 kilometers in size. The meteorite appeared to be an H chondrite.

On July 31st 1998 in Tularosa in Otero County in New Mexico I was on my way to the store in Alamogordo. While stopped at the corner of Rattlesnake Road to enter US 54-70, I saw the ignition of the first booster of the start of a test at Holloman AFB Hi Speed Test Track. Almost at the point where the sled started to move, an object popped up from the left flank of the test, but behind slightly. The object exploded to a larger magenta like a coronal ball. This was from a distance of thirteen miles. The plume of the test sled formed a cone about the size of a pencil eraser at arm's length. The ball of the corona was proportionally as large. The ball followed the sled down the track for a couple of moments and then followed it on the side for a moment or two then as the sled second thrust came on, the ball followed in front of the sled for a few moments. By the time the sled got to what is known as the midway (data collection site) the object changed direction from paralleling the track, to a direction aiming almost directly at where my intersection was. At this point of its path it was slightly faster than the test sled, but on changing direction it also accelerated to a velocity that was faster than a bullet. I had really wanted to see what the core of the object looked like. All that was left were the heat risers off of the pavement in front of me. I equate that to a stream of water moving gently and having a stone thrown in or looking at an image in a mirror and having the glass of the mirror tapped and the image breaks up. This was late in the afternoon and I was looking to the west and the heat risers were quite pronounced. The object passed so fast that when I turned to look to the north Northeast, I saw nothing. It was almost a year later that a friend passed along a report from an investigator from Alamogordo that fit both in time and situation. He explained that a disc had been seen behind a place called Round Mountain East of Tularosa New Mexico, where people coming from the race track in Ruidoso pulled over to the side of the road to watch the disc. Suddenly a bunch of probes or drones from all over the Tularosa Basin came together and attached to the disc. At this point the disc departed. This filled in a lot of blanks for me. They were spying on the test.

1999

At 12.30 am on December 3rd 1999 in Bread Springs in McKinley County in New Mexico the witness had gone out to the outhouse when he saw a strange light come out from behind a large tree about 30 feet away from the house. Terrified he was unable to move as the light came closer and closer. He then apparently blacked out. He could only remember a bright light in front of him and small strange beings surrounding him and performing "tests" on him. This incident took place at the foothills of the Zuni Mountains.

Oklahoma

1897

On April 6th 1897 at 2300hrs in Guthrie in Logan County, Oklahoma. Mr Trumball, the landlord of the Arlington Hotel, saw a dark object moving in the sky. Shortly afterwards a bright light was seen at the front of the thing, projecting a beam which seemed to sweep the area. From the sides of the object flashes of light were emitted. The thing moved back and forth at high speed and at one point it came close to the ground north of the city before rising again at high speed.

1906

In November 1906, Ray Russell, twenty years old, and several others saw an unusual sight above Anadarko in Caddo County, Oklahoma, at dusk. Sixty feet up was a stovepipe shaped object that resembled a ball of flame that sank towards the ground and then approached the men, coming to sixteen feet from them. Then the craft suddenly blacked out after flattening out a little. Nor do stovepipe shaped flying objects hover and approach generally. Nor do they seem to swoop. Nor should they exist.

1924

On January 5th 1924 at 0110hrs in Oklahoma City in Oklahoma County, Oklahoma. At a farm outside the city two people observed an object that passed low over a field, making a hissing noise and frightening the horses.

Around 9.00 pm one day in January 1924 in the Osage Hills two riders saw a beam of light shining on the snow and coming from a large aerial oval object. The object had white dots on the side and a blue flame came from the rear. It made a slight hissing noise. The Osage Hills are primarily in Osage County as well as in parts of Mayes, Tulsa, Washington and Kay Counties.

1928

In August 1928 in Oklahoma. At a spot some 80km west of Tulsa Mr Stern and his sons Aaron were out driving when their car engine started to misfire. As Aaron looked under the bonnet the whole area was lit up by a terrific white light which seemed to pass over at 50m altitude and then fade and burst into many colours. Father and son stood stunned for between 15-30 minutes. When they turned the key the car worked perfectly. This was possibly in Payne County.

1930

On 6th May 1930, there was an enormous rain of mud from the sky onto Tulsa in Tulsa County in Oklahoma. How do you get mud to fall from the sky? You would need a lot of dust and a lot of rain. Normally one would not get them together though or one would need a very strong wind capable of lifting existing mud into the sky. This is harder to believe than dust and rain falling together but wouldn't this only give you dirty water as the mud would not have the time to settle so as to become mud?

1944

In 1944 at 1200hrs (Approximate) in Apache in Caddo County, Oklahoma. A man standing on his porch heard a sound like a rushing wind and saw, at an estimated altitude of 18m, something resembling a "streamlined passenger train" with about 9 coaches and what looked like inflated pillow like wheels. He observed this thing for about 10 minutes before it left at high speed. At one point it came within 100m of his house.

1945

In September 1945 (or following month) at 1100hrs in Boswell in Choctaw County, Oklahoma. A 9 year old girl was climbing a tree in her yard, while her mother was on the porch nursing the baby, when the girl had a blackout and felt suspended in the air before falling to the ground. When she picked herself up her mother was no longer on the porch but had gone inside. There was a period of missing time and mother sent the children to bed. Later mother and girl remembered seeing a metallic looking object that moved off to the horizon and changed into a series of dots. The grandmother and two older children were mysteriously not around that afternoon. Shortly afterwards the family left the house and moved into a hotel.

Near Delaware in Nowata County in Oklahoma one night in 1945. Two ladies; part of a skywatch program during WWII, were trained to spot enemy aircraft. On this particular night they saw a bright light which eventually got close enough for them to see that it was a silver saucer-shaped object. There were several bright lights and it was "beautiful." Both were then contacted by the occupants of the "spaceship." They were taken inside and showed an area that was very bright and full of beautiful lights. The occupants of the craft asked one of the women if she wanted to go with them; she said yes. But they replied that her "spacesuit" wasn't ready yet. Teasing demons?

1946

In August (late) 1946 in Oklahoma City in Oklahoma County in Oklahoma. A Disc-shaped craft with windows, Humanoid figures visible inside, hovered at low altitude. After about 1-1/2 minutes the object rotated, then sped away disappearing in seconds. At 5.15 pm Margaret Louise Sprankle, a civilian employee at Tinker Air Force Base, had just arrived back at her 22nd Street home, when, above an evergreen, she saw an object hovering at low altitude 90m away at an elevation of 45 degrees. I was a vertical disk about 22m in diameter, its broadside facing her. In the lower right hand quadrant of the disk were 12-14 square windows, through which light was shining, apparently sunlight coming in from similar windows on the other side of the disk. This light silhouetted the head and shoulders of an occupant in each window. They gave the impression of being large round, bald heads (or possibly helmets of some sort), pale in colour, with dark somewhat close set eyes and narrow shoulders. They seemed to be somewhat short and to be moving slightly. The machine was the colour of dull aluminium, silent and odourless. When the machine turned to leave she saw it was shaped like two saucers put together. As she called to her mother the object disappeared to the north-west in less than 5 seconds. The witnesses had a technical background and was considered competent and sincere by investigators.

In late August 1946 Miss Margaret Sprankle coming home from her work at Tinker AFB looked up and saw about one hundred yards away a metallic lense-shaped object standing on edge, the broadside facing her. The lower right quarter was filled with a grid of twelve to fourteen inch square windows in each of which was visible the silhouette of a head and shoulders seen against a dark background. The heads were quite round, either rather bald or wearing helmets. There was no noise. After about a minute and a half the object turned horizontally thorough ninety degrees and she could see that there were windows on both sides. Then it darted away silently at immense speed. The diameter was estimated at 75 feet. The witness was trained as an aircraft spotter. Tinker AFB is near Del City in Oklahoma County in Oklahoma.

1947

Near Sapulpa in Creek and Tulsa Counties in Oklahoma, on the evening of May 15th 1947 Frank Buckshot Standing Horse was reading his Bible under a Blackjack Oak Tree at a Christian camp. He happened to look up into the sky and thought he saw a plane. It was not. It was round like a tire. There was an island in the loop of the creek and it came down slowly and landed there. Frank saw a man come out and walk around as if to examine the object and then got back in. Frank got up to look and walked towards it when he was suddenly frozen in in his tracks. The object then tipped and started for the West before you could say "scat". Frank then ran to his brother's house but was not believed.

On July 7th 1947 at 2020hrs in Oklahoma City in Oklahoma County, Oklahoma. Housewife Mrs J P Gibbs saw a fiery flat object fall to the ground 80m from the house. No traces were looked for.

1948

On May 17th 1947 in Oklahoma City in Oklahoma between 8:30-9 p.m. Field Engineer Savage saw a frosty white round and flat object, with diameter/thickness ratio 10:1, the size of a B-29 [?] (140 feet) traveling North at 350° heading at 10,00018,000 feet and 3 times speed of a jet [1,800 mph] with a slight swishing sound for 30-minutes.

1949

At Tulsa in Tulsa County in Oklahoma in Autumn 1949. Mr. and Mrs. D. Bushnell, a plant supervisor, were out driving when an object suddenly dived down from the sky towards the road in front of the car and suddenly vanished. Swooping saucers? Remember that meteors cannot swoop. They either burn up in the atmosphere or they hit the dirt literally. Was the appearance of the car as startling to the UFO as was the appearance of the UFO to the car? Imagine hitting the brakes or trying to swerve to avoid an accident as you suddenly appear from another dimension occupying what might appear to be the same Space as the witnesses and their car on Earth. So many UFO and other phenomenal sightings possess a startled factor as if the phenomenon is as startled to see the witnesses as the witnesses are to see the phenomenon.They are quite often a sudden surprise to each other!

1951

In Anadarko in Caddo County in Oklahoma on 11th November 1951 a farmer found his twenty acre farm covered in a thick layer of leaf-like shreds of something like tin. The leaves varied in length from one third of an inch to four inches long. Was this a shredded spacecraft? Had we had other aluminum or tin falls before? We have had several and there would be more in the future.

1952

In Enid in Garfield County in Oklahoma on 29th July 1952 between Bison and Waukomis, Oklahoma, on U.S. Highway 81, Mr. Sid Eubanks saw an enormous Flying Saucer that was 400 feet wide which swept down and almost blew his car off the road with its colossal exhaust blast or backwash. The car ended up in a ditch. The craft was originally low flying and yellow-green which changed to yellow-brown. Sid also recalled that it was bell-shaped. Was this a swooping saucer or an exploding electrical or gravitational field? Was it a giant fish that had fallen at Enid?

1954

On May 11th 1954 in Lawton in Comanche County in Oklahoma a lone witness watched a disc-shaped object hovering ten feet above the ground during the day. Below the object stood a four-foot tall figure. The Humanoid disappeared in a flash of light after seeing the witness, and then the object shot away at high speed towards the West.

In mid-August 1954 in daytime in Dewey County, Oklahoma Gladys White Eagle, on a river bank, saw a "flying saucer" come straight down with a roar. A tall, lean man with a dark complexion & a long beard got out and told her the U.S. would be destroyed by an earthquake and bomb on October 13th. "He told me that in twisted words and then he laughed very hard. Then he said for me to come to the spot again today--September 17-'-but I'm not going back because I'm scared." —A follow-up story on 9/19 said that "the incident is typical of the woman & just another of the many stunts she has pulled in the past."

1956

On January 30th 1956 at 2130hrs in Lamar in Hughes County, Oklahoma. A low flying object, 40m in diameter, illuminated the ground and followed four people in a car for 16 minutes.

1957

Around 5.50 pm on 8th December 1957 between Woodward in Woodward County and Seiling in Dewey County in Oklahoma an employee of an aircraft company and two passengers were driving. The heater, windshield wipers and radio were on. He was nearing a hill in this wooded area when a bright light appeared ahead. It reminded the witness of the light from a mercury lamp. As a crash seemed imminent the car slowed down by itself and stopped as if the entire electrical circuit had failed. Above the vehicle was a sixteen meter in diameter disc with portholes around the periphery. It was emitting a current of hot air and a high pitched sound. It had a dome on top and bottom and rose as the car started itself. The car was a 1954 Dodge Coronet without automatic transmission. Here is another version. Between Woodward and Smiling, 12km from the latter, an employee of an aircraft company, driving with two passengers, wss nearing a hill in this wooded area, when a bright light, like that from a mercury lamp, appeared ahead. As it seemed as though their was going to be a collision the car slowed down by itself and stopped as if the whole electrical system, including the heater and the windscreen wipers, had failed. Over the vehicle, at about 60m altitude, was a disk 15m in diameter, with portholes around its periphery, which was emitting a current of hot air and a high pitched whining sound. It had a dome on its top and bottom. After a couple of minutes the whine increased in tone and the thing rose vertically out of sight. As it did so, the 1954 Doge Coronet's headlights came back on and the engine started by itself though that model did not have automatic transmission. The principle witness spent four hours with two officers from Kirtland AFB, who told him of similar observations, but the case was not reported to Blue Book.

1959

Near Sapulpa in Creek and Tulsa Counties Oklahoma on July 12th 1959 at 10: 00 p.m. Ottawa Indian Chief Frank Buckshot Standing Horse, 67 years old, had a long time interest in flying saucers and stories of men from Mars and Venus. On the above date he had been working all day preparing his Christian camp for a coming convention he had called; the First Indian Spacecraft Convention, in which invited speakers were 'Contactees' such as Truman Bethurum and Buck Nelson, who would tell of their space adventures on board flying saucers piloted by picturesque men from space and attractive women from Mars, Venus and unknown (imaginary?) planets such as Bethurum's Clarion. He stopped working at 8: 00 p.m., went into his house, sat down and read a book until the ten o'clock news. Soon after, his radio made a noise like a shotgun going off, and the lights went out. He thus went outside by the front door to the fuse box, he pulled the switch and the lights came on again. While he stood there wondering about the cause of this, he felt the presence of someone near him and then encountered three normal men who identified themselves as spacemen from other worlds. He went with them to an island northeast of the camp where a magnificent circular ship came down to the ground. He said this ship was about 250 feet in diameter and about 28 feet high. He was taken on board where he met a beautiful tall woman with long black hair and blue eyes. He went on a space trip to Mars, close to the moon, Venus, Clarion and 'Orean.' Later, on another trip, he went to Jupiter in an "Arrow Ship" which was 2 ½ miles long. On Mars, he saw some large rock-like buildings, and on planet Orean he saw large beautiful buildings and churches. In this list of the damned which reports are more credible than others. Do any of them have credibility or should none of them be regarded as being credible?

In August 1959 at 1400hrs in Skiatook in Osage and Tulsa Counties, Oklahoma. Two cars stalled near a bridge over a small creek, over which a shiny, silvery disk was hovering. The thing extended hose, 15-20cm diameter into the water for several minutes, and the water under the disc became rounded up. When the thing retracted the hose, the cars could start again

1963

In Oklahoma City in Oklahoma County, Oklahoma in August 1963 at 8.00 p.m. The witness was walking back home alone when she noticed a light traveling slowly across the sky. The craft or light changed course at a 90% angle and began to descend towards the witness. The witness suddenly felt a strong electrical charge move through her body without pain or heat. The craft hovered above the witness and then she was somehow pulled inside the craft through an entrance on the bottom. Inside the craft a short Humanoid approached the witness and rubbed her forehead, calming her. She was then led to another room that was divided into thirds by three doorways. There were two stools on each of the two walls and a screen on the third wall. Two figures sat on the stools. The short Humanoid that had comforted her earlier then appeared, carrying a beautiful, deep red teacup with a gold floral design. The witness mostly communicated by sign language with the beings and no words were ever spoken. Then one of the men that sat on one of the stools communicated by telepathy with the witness and reminded the witness that love was very important and that it is all that endures.

1964

On April 12th 1964 (approx. date) at 0615hrs in Oklahoma City in in Oklahoma County, Oklahoma. Mr. E Neal was looking through his bedroom window before dawn, when a strange fiery metallic sphere, about the size of a B59, surrounded by a bright shimmering halo, and having a nose cone on which there was a brighter patch, flew very low directly over the house. Neal could see neither wings nor surface features. As he was not dressed he was unable to go out and follow it.

In June 1964 in Oklahoma City, Oklahoma. Mr. E. Neald was standing in his driveway, looking across the park at the clouds, when he saw a mottled white brown object, the apparent size of a tennis ball, moving at about 6.5-8kph, about 2m above the rooftops over McKinley Street. It had no lights and made no sound.

1965

On June 19th 1965 at 0400hrs in Rocky in Washita County, Oklahoma. Two farm boys were stashing logs when they were surprised by the sudden close appearance of a brightly lighted, circular, wingless object. It was the thing's brightness which first impressed the boys; they thought it might have been a helicopter but Quentin AFB confirmed that no helicopters were operating. The dogs were set barking, though the boys did not notice if the cattle were affected. The boy who saw the thing first thought it was about to crash as they headed back into the barn. The object, emitting a bright white light, came down at a 45 degree angle, to the height of nearby telegraph wires, moved horizontally across the farmyard and was last seen over a small silo. The object was the apparent size of the full moon or larger. It appeared as a circular object, with numerous lights around the inside. Either the centre portion or the whole thing was rotating in an anti-clockwise direction. The incident lasted for less than three minutes.

On July 26th 1965 at 1900HRS in Hartshorne in Pittsburg County, Oklahoma. Mrs A Morgan observed for 4-5 minutes, an object resembling two shallow bowls attached at their rims, with a dark band around the centre. The upper part was silver with indentations resembling windows in the area just above this band and the lower part was red-grey. The thing hovered just above the treeline in front of a single tall tree, some 150m away. Calm at first, Mrs Morgan became afraid when she realised she was alone and began to run towards the object, calling out to neighbours. The thing then began to slowly move, its light remaining steady, before it was "whisked away" in an instant. Mrs Morgan became very excited about the incident and claimed several other UFO experiences.

On July 31st 1965 in the afternoon in Oklahoma City, Oklahoma. A young man was fishing at the municipally owned Lake Hefner in the northwest section of the city, when a large saucer shaped object, with a dome on top and a flat bottom, rose out of the lake, hovered momentarily and then flew away. The witness was so shocked he had to be hospitalised.

On August 2nd 1965 in Oklahoma City, Oklahoma. Five children saw a brilliant white round object without wings close to the ground in the 650 Block on Northwest 63.

On August 3rd 1965 in Lake Hefner in Oklahoma City in Oklahoma a young man saw an object rise from the lake area. Was this the same report as the previous one?

On August 5th 1965 at 2040hrs in Tulsa in Tulsa County, Oklahoma. Monty Howard observed a green object land in the field at the back of his house. It was on the ground for some minutes.

1966

In Temple in Cotton County in Oklahoma on 23rd March 1966 at 5.30 am Mr. Eddie Laxson, 56, an Aviation Electronics Instructor at Shephard Air Force Base in Wichita Falls, Texas, was in his car on Highway 70 when he came upon a landed UFO blocking the road. Eddie got out of the car and saw that there was a Humanoid in G.I. fatigue coveralls working under the UFO and seeming to be making repairs. The Humanoid wore what appeared to be a baseball cap and was carrying a flashlight and to the witness the Humanoid looked like any G.I. in fatigues. Mr. Laxson turned back to his car to get his camera as the Humanoid climbed a ladder into the craft and it took off vertically. Then the hair on the back of Eddie's neck and hands stood up. Eddie could not recognize the type of aircraft or the letters that resembled "TL41" on the side of the vehicle either. An independent witness, Mr. Anderson, a truck driver, saw the UFO from the opposite direction and other truckers had reported similar sightings in the area. The Humanoid was human-looking, holding a flashlight, 180 pounds in weight, five foot nine inches tall, had a light complexion and wore a mechanics cap with the bill turned up. The Humanoid appeared to be thirty to 35 years old, had stooped shoulders and what appeared to be Sergeants stripes on the coveralls. When the craft took off towards the river it made a noise like an electric drill. And even Oklahoma got in on the act with its wayward G.I. making repairs to his unusual craft. Or this? At 5.05 am William Laxton (56) was driving to work at Sheppard Air Force Base, Wichita Falls, Texas) where he had been an instrument instructor for 12 years. About 13km south of Temple he noticed a brilliant light to his right, which he thought was a truck which had stopped ahead. He stopped and turned onto US 70, but after going for a few hundred metres he saw that the road was blocked by a huge object sitting across the highway at 45 degrees. He pulled to the side of the road and halted about 80m from the craft the ran forward another 20m. He could now see that the object was 21-24m long, about 4m thick, with four brilliant lights on the side facing him, illuminating the area enough to read a newspaper. There was a porthole 60cm diameter, divided into 4 equal parts, below which was a door 1.2-11.35m high and 75cm wide. The craft was illuminated inside and had a "plastic glass" bubble, through which this light could be seen, in front. Vertical lettering TL4768 or 4168 was on the side. The tail had horizontal stabilisers 75cm high from the leading edge to the trailing edge of the fuselage. Under the object was a man kneeling on one knee, who rapidly got up and climbed into the craft at Laxton's approach. He was about 1.72m tall, fair complexioned, about 30-35 years old, wearing a mechanic's cap and either overalls or green military fatigues. When the man entered the craft Laxton heard the sound of a metallic door closing. At the same instant the craft rose to 15m with a sound like a high speed drill. Laxton felt the hair on the back of his neck stand up. The craft had gone 1.6km in 5 seconds, and Laxton estimated its speed at over 1,100 kph. Laxton continued his journey and 3km down the road he encountered a truck driver, C. W. Anderson of Snyder, who said that a bright light had followed him for about 30km, that he had stopped to get a better look and that other drivers had seen similar lights on the road. The object's general appearance was that of a conventional aircraft, but without engine or wings, and that neither rivets nor sections were visible on the unpainted craft.

On March 25th 1966 near Upper Sandusky in Wyandot County in Oklahoma at 1.00 a.m. a top-shaped object with bright body lights visible on its outer edge was seen hovering about 25 feet over woods, point downward, by a farm couple for about an hour.

Around midnight on 26th March 1966 Mrs. P. N. Beer and Mrs. E. Smith were driving back from Amarillo near Texahoma in Texas County in Oklahoma when they saw a flashing light. It was an object with a waffle like surface that was glowing an intense red. It came from the North and buzzed their car from the front. The engine and headlights suddenly died. The object then hovered quarter of a mile away. After ten minutes they could restart their car and left.

On April 1st 1966 five miles South of Tangier in Woodward County in Oklahoma at 10.40 p.m. a civilian man, 34, while driving reached a hilltop and saw a green object wider than the road flying North at very high speed, emitting a shrieking noise and a "heat wave." The car engine died.

Around 2.30 am two teenagers saw a large disc-shaped craft swinging back and forth over I35. Four men were clearly observed inside through a transparent opening. The area around the witnesses was brightly lit and there was the smell of ozone. This was near Randlett in Cotton County in Oklahoma.

Around 2.00 am on 22nd April 1966 near Thackerville in Love County Dr. Eula Page, a psychologist, was driving homewards from Texas with her two children and a friend. She noticed a luminous object as big as the moon darting back and forth across the highway. Just after she had crossed the Red River Bridge she came directly underneath it and stopped. It descended and hovered very close to the car. A luminous lense-shaped body more than twice the length of her station wagon was surrounded by a spherical framework that was revolving around it. On one side of the disc was a long window through which four human occupants could be seen. One stood regarding her whilst the others busied themselves with instruments and controls on the rear wall on which multicolored lights were flashing. They wore tightfitting silvery gray uniforms and had slanted oriental eyes. Her daughter said that one was a woman. Standing outside her car Dr. Page watched the UFO for about twenty minutes. A force field around the craft made it difficult for her to breathe and a hot wind blew from the sphere that smelt electrical. Finally another car appeared and UFO quickly moved away towards the river. How solid are our UFOs? Are they more electric or electromagnetic than physical?

On April 30th 1966 at 1830hrs in Haileyville in Pittsburg County, Oklahoma. A cigar shaped object, emitting sparks, was seen at an altitude of about 10m. The sparks came from a revolving cylinder on the thing. A loud explosion was heard. The witness was a 68 year old widow.

1967

On January 5th 1967 at 2315hrs in Greenfield in Blaine County, Oklahoma. Mrs Ralph Beard, her children and sister, Mrs Lillian White, were driving from Greenfield towards Geary when they spotted a large blue and green object travelling at high speed very close to the ground. After a brief touchdown about 800m from the highway, the object soared into the sky and headed south.

On March 3rd 1967 at 0035hrs in Edmond in Oklahoma County, Oklahoma. David Ellis and a friend were driving a few kilometres out of Edmond when they observed two triangular objects at 15m altitude, 40m apart. These objects were identical, 8m across at the base, with windows visible on the side, divided into three sections. Its left hand side emitted a soft red glow, there was a flashing red light in the centre and two red lights were on the right. After some minutes a beam of red light descended towards the witnesses. The then the things moved into a position where one was above the other, and flew slowly towards Edmond. The witnesses followed the objects into town but lost sight of them there.

At Clinton in Custer County in Oklahoma on 27th April 1967 a motorist was pursued by a pacing UFO hovering at an altitude of 200 feet. The UFO shone a bright light down on to him and followed the car for some distance. There were a number of individual witnesses as well. All is normal.

On May 20th 1968 and still in Clinton, Oklahoma. Albert H (15) was cresting a hill on his motorcycle when he nearly collided with an unidentified object coming towards him. He swerved to avoid hitting the thing and his cycle overturned throwing him nearly 35m and causing internal injuries.

Around 2.00 am during Summer 1967 the witness had gone outside in Oklahoma City in Oklahoma to lie on the grass and look at the star-filled sky. He then noticed three odd looking green lights arranged in an equilateral triangle hovering high above the area. He began concentrating his thoughts towards the lights thinking about the possibility of extraterrestrial life. Suddenly one of them shot away from the formation and came close to the witness. The object was saucer shaped with its bottom spinning. There were red lights on top and green lights on the bottom. It hovered briefly over the witness then landed behind a nearby church. Soon a Humanoid figure at least twelve feet tall appeared which was accompanied by an odd looking animal described as a cross between an ostrich and a buzzard. The Humanoid was all in black with arms and legs in proportion to a human. The head was like a large dome with no visible facial features. The being could apparently read the witness's thoughts and answered some of the witness's questions by nodding his head. He claimed to be from a planet in our galaxy and was looking for a place to raise his livestock. Soon the being and the bird-like animal re-entered the craft which then shot up to join the other two. Then all three shot out into space and vanished.

Around 10.00 pm on 21st October 1967 four teenage boys including Ivan Ritter and Jerry Bennett were driving East of Duncan in Stephens County. They were driving on Route 7 when they saw three little men in the car's headlights. When the driver turned the beam on high the three beings almost flew off the road and disappeared. They were about four foot tall with shiny blue-green skin or tight coveralls. Their faces were human but the ears were very large. There was a twenty foot drop off on the other side of the highway at the site making normal egress off the highway difficult. At the site the next day Ritter and Bennett found an unusual footprint in the mud of a creek bed one hundred yards from the road. It was only the size of a baby's, but with an oversize heel and only four toes.

1970

At Norman in Cleveland County in Oklahoma on July 4th 1970. Sequoyah Trueblood was sitting by his pool at his townhouse in Laurel Maryland, watching the children swimming and his wife sitting next to him, when without knowing why, he got up went into the house, changed his clothes, packed a small bag, drove to the airport and took a plane to Oklahoma City. A friend then drove him to Norman. He felt a little strange and wanted to lie down. In a bedroom he was lying down relaxing when he saw a kind of vortex of swirling lights "like a rainbow" into which he was sucked. Sequoyah then found himself standing in a beautiful garden surrounded by hedges. He felt wide awake and in front of him he saw a silvery saucer-shaped craft and a shimmering small, silver-looking being standing on steps that were coming down from the bottom of the craft. The being looked grayish and had a large baldhead with large eyes. The witness sensed that the being was androgynous, neither male nor female. The being communicated telepathically and told the witness that he had been sent to take him because "they" wanted to talk to him. He agreed to go and walked up the steps with the being. Once inside the craft, Sequoyah heard no sound, but through a small window he saw the moon, the sun, and "millions of stars" instantly go by. Soon the craft was hovering over a beautiful white city on what the witness felt was another planet in another realm or universe. In an instant he was down on the ground. The people in the city appeared to be male and female, wore white robes, and were fair skinned, with "hair that was glowing like the color of sunlight." The small being then took the witness down a street lined with beautiful white buildings not more than three stories in height to a clearing in the woods that seemed like a park. There were a number of people there, and a male said to him that if he would "pay attention;" he could see that people there were living in harmony without war or disease. The people also told him that they did not need food, for the air they breathed was converted into whatever was needed to sustain life. A sort of leader figure told him that he had been brought to this place to show him the potential of the human race. Soon he asked to be returned and was taken into the craft and then through the vortex and found himself back at home. Could the electromagnetic field of the UFOs actually effect the brains of observers and create lifelike hallucinations? Or are there natural electromagnetic fields in the Universe, indeed the Multiverse, that link it all together and could be the energy basis for the visions and communications?

1971

On April 2nd 1971 at 2020hrs in Crosstown in Oklahoma City. While driving at the Crosstown expressway, Morris Helflin saw a disc about 20m diameter, 3.5m high, above a bridge The ground beneath the object was dried and vegetation was reduced to ashes.

On May 8th 1971 at 0245hrs and still in Oklahoma City, Oklahoma. Morris Hefflin was drive home west on SW15th street when, as he crossed the bridge over North Canadian River he looked to his left and saw a beam of light coming from a saucer shaped object hovering just above the treetops about 30m south of the bridge. Morris stopped and got out for a closer look. He saw green lights on the underside, revealing the letters IX-1478. After about 5 minutes he became uneasy and drove away. The next morning he investigated the site with reporters Keitha Fish and her daughter Keitha Hewes. They found the ground where the light had been shining was very hard, dry and covered with ashes. Bark on the trees was scorched and dry vines were hanging down. Morris had seen the same object on April 2nd.

At Oklahoma City in Oklahoma County in Oklahoma during 1971 many people saw a large hovering disc. It was sending down a beam of light and seemed to have the wording IX-1478 on its underside. Why not?

Also in Oklahoma City, Oklahoma a witness observed a luminous object over the ground for several minutes. A dehydrated area and broken tree limbs were found.

1972

On August 15th 1972 in Enid in Garfield County, Oklahoma. An object 5.5m long, with a wingspan of 6m came low and skids on its underside caught a barbed wire fence and brought a post down. On one wing there was a pulsating red light.
1973
On February 14th 1973 at 0230 40 miles East of McAlester in Pittsburg County in Okla. As they were flying a DC-8 charter cargo plane from St. Louis, Missouri to Dallas, Texas, two anonymous pilots observed an object over southeast Oklahoma. They had just commenced a gradual descent from 21,000 feet in the vicinity of McAlester when the object appeared off to their right, approximately 5000 feet away, and moving in the same direction. It gave off a strange orange light and abruptly rose straight up like an elevator, then made a right-angle turn in the direction of the DC-8 and approached at incredible speed, taking a position about 300 yards away, slightly above them. It was disc-shaped, with a clear dome on top, and continued to pace the airliner in the new position. The pilot tried to raise its pilot by radio with no success. The moonlight reflected off the silvery sides of the object, which had two sets of raised fins along its trailing edge; it appeared to be about 75 feet long and 40 feet wide. The pilot switched on his radar and immediately picked up its echo on the scope; almost instantaneously the object began a series of complex maneuvers and took up a new position just below the leading edge of their left wing. It dropped to a position 300 feet below the aircraft and the two pilots were able to see two, perhaps three, indistinct and shadowy figures inside the dome; the object then moved out and ahead of the plane, executed several more maneuvers, and disappeared into the night. Here is another version. The pilot and co-pilot of a DC8 charter cargo jet had just started a descent from 6,300m cruising at 815kph in the vicinity of McAlester when their attention was caught by another object 1. km away below the edge of their right wing. They thought it was another commercial flight until it rose up and closed on their plane to within 300m. In the moonlight they could see it was a silvery, polished, metallic oblong with rounded edges "like a flounder lying on its side" The body of the object contained two very short stubby fins that looked as though they could be folded into its body, and on which were steady amber lights on the leading edge, with another set of amber lights located above and below the body of the craft. In the top centre of the machine was a transparent unlighted dome in which two or three figures appeared to be moving about. From the top rear of the object were two vertical fins, one on either side of what looked like an exposed jet engine pod, which emitted no glow however. The underside was flat with no protrusions, landing gear nor hatches. The whole assemblage was 23=-26m long and 12m wide. When they switched their radar on the craft appeared as a blip on the edge of the scope, but almost the moment they switched the set on, the object rose straight up and crossed sideways to a position just above the plane, passed momentarily out of sight, then reappeared to the left, dropped behind and below, then sped past at twice their speed about 100m below them, performed several up and down motions, then sped out of sight to the right. It went off the radar scope at a distance of 80km. The whole observation lasted 18 minutes.
On June 7th 1973 at the Keystone Dam near Sand Springs in Tulsa County, Oklahoma there was a landing report.
On July 12th 1973 in daytime at Stanley Draper Lake in Cleveland County, Oklahoma. Mark Willis observed and photographed a fairly low flying domed disc as it passed over the lake. As it did so, Mark saw steam rising from the lake, exactly under the object.
At Fort Sill in Lawton Oklahoma in September 1973. The witness claims he had been stationed at the above Army base and one night was visited by a "UFO intelligence" (no other details) who gave him some visions. He had a vision that he was shown the pilot's cabin of a large aircraft. Many gauges and controls were on the instruments panels. A handsome dark skinned man was flying the plane. A view out the front windows revealed the massive wall of a large low building. The plane was about to smash into the building. The "intelligence" told him the building was an important government building and because of the crash there would be a massive increase in national security, a threat to public rights. What is it with Lawton?
At Drumright in Creek County in Oklahoma on 16th October 1973 William Hatchett and his wife Donna Hatchett were travelling on the highway when they spotted a bright blue light to the South which was coming closer and began pacing the car. The light began descending and came towards them. Near the front of the truck was a blinding white light making a low pitched hum. When Donna climbed out of the truck William warned her to come back. She had begged William to stop the truck. She came back but got out twice more. When she returned William tried to escape. The UFO flew off in the opposite direction, gaining altitude but not much speed. The witnesses reported the pacing light to the Police in Drumright. The witnesses believed that the occupants of the UFO knew what they were thinking. Or this. In Mannford William and Donna Hatchett were driving down a country road when she saw bright light coming from the south. They first thought it was a security light on a pole, but then realised the thing was pacing them and descending. When the Hatchetts stopped the truck, the light stopped also, in front of the truck. As the object hovered it gave off a blinding light and penetrating low pitched hum. They had the feeling that there were occupants in the thing who knew everything they were thinking. Donna was so afraid that she twice left the truck cab and went into the back. William managed to persuade her to return and they set off, the object rose up in the opposite direction.

On November 17th 1973 at 0130hrs in Fairland in Ottawa County, Oklahoma. Janice Boyd and Willa Selsor watched a large orange object, with a platform like structure, land. The thing emitted a strange noise and their dogs were upset. Both witnesses were very confused about what they had seen.

On November 19th 1973 in Altus in Jackson County, Oklahoma a strange object was seen on or just above the ground.

Later on November 21st 1973 still in Altus, Oklahoma Hubert Young saw a ball of fire pass in front of his cart and hit the ground. A deep grove was found and the grass was burnt.

On November 29th 1973 at 1930hrs in Weatherford in Custer County, Oklahoma. Darrel Nickels (19), a carpenter, was driving on a rural road near Dead Woman's Crossing when he saw an illuminated aerial object, which eh first thought was a helicopter. The thing was hovering 9m to one side of and above the crossing. Darrel approached to within less than 10m and was able to observe that the object 5-6m wide, 2.7-3m high, with a silvery dome containing about 30 flashing red, white and blue lights. Around the bottom third of the object was a dark band, Darrel shut off his engine and watched the silent object for three minutes, until a bright light appeared from the thing's side, at which he drove off north rapidly. Up to 40 other people phoned the police about lights in the sky.

On the night of 5th December 1973 near Carnegie in Caddo County three men in a car saw a being with flashing lights on him which approached the car. It wore red pants and a welder's type mask. Another man reported seeing the same being and a glowing white light down a side road.

1974

On February 18th 1974 at Bowlin Spring near Chelsea in Craig County in Oklahoma. Clay Knight, age 42, dairyman and graduate of Oklahoma State University, was 300 yards from his barn at 5:15 am on an overcast morning with a storm approaching. His dog ran yelping to the house, appearing frightened. At this time, Knight saw an orange-red blinking light on the bottom of an object 50-75 yards over his head. Knight, also frightened, ran to his house, and the object followed him remaining directly overhead. When directly over his head, Knight could hear an eerie, high-pitched sound, and he thought his dog had run from it because the sound hurt its ears. The object was the size of a small bedroom, flat on the bottom, and rounded off or oval shaped on the top. It was twice as wide as it was high and had an orange-red blinking light on the bottom. Knight later walked out to his pond and saw the light out in a pasture, where it dropped below a small hill. An hour and a half later, it moved straight up, and it had a shiny tin color as it was departing. Cattle, described as excited, got through a barbed-wire fence when the object was nearby. Or this. Clay Knight., a dairyman and university graduate, was getting his heard ready form milking on his farm by Rt 2 near Chelsea. Clay was about 300m from his barn when he heard a high pitched sound and saw an oval object, with a flat bottom, about 150-220m above him. The thing had a metallic looking structure, with an orange-red flashing light on its bottom and was the size of a bedroom. Clay's dog panicked and ran back to the farm house and the cattle became agitated and stampeded through a barbed iron fence. As Clay returned to his farmhouse he saw the object out in a pasture to the north of the house. The thing then descended behind a small hill. It rose straight up 90 minutes later. The weather was cloudy and "ready to storm". No traces were found.

1975

At Vinita in Craig County in Oklahoma on 19th January 1975 a circular sphere with white lights paced the witness's car. Nearby there was a pair of unknown aerial objects as well.

In 1975 at 1900hrs in McAlester in Pittsburg County, Oklahoma. A military policeman at the Naval Depot was out on patrol in a pickup truck when his engine and radio failed. He then saw a flashing red light that he first thought was a tower light until it started darting about at terrific speed. There were other witness, some of whom saw beams of light projected down onto the bunkers.

1976

On July 12th 1976 at night in Savanna in Pittsburg County, Oklahoma. Three 14 year old boys from Savanna on a camping trip notice the air getting warmer and saw, hovering over the trees, three objects shaped like two white saucers placed together, with rotating blue-green lights in the mid-section, and a dazzling bright red light on top and a beam that seemed to search the woods. They made no sound except for a "whooshing when they rose up from the trees. Two of the objects flew out of sight and the third disappeared in the treetops. The next night the boys returned with a camera and attempted to take photographs when they observed two red lights coming down the side of the mountains, among the trees. They first thought that they were coon hunters with torches, until the lights rose above the treetops.

On October 31st 1976 in the evening in Krebs in Pittsburg County, Oklahoma. Mrs Rose Pritchard and her three sons were decorating the front porch for Halloween when a dark object, whose size and shape were lost in the night, appeared low and very close over their garage. The thing had red, elongated glowing windows. Rose and two of the boys stood transfixed while the eldest boy ran for his camera. Before he could take a photograph the lights went out, leaving a green glow that faded into the darkness.

1980

On September 8th 1980 at 0520hrs in Waukomis in Garfield County, Oklahoma. Robert and Gail Reed were aroused by a commotion among their poultry. Robert went to the back and saw what looked like a fire. Gail joined him and saw an extremely bright flashing white light, hovering noiselessly above the ground. A few minutes later the area was illuminated by a brilliant flash but there was still no sound. Gail stood in the open doorway and watched the light as it lifted up, moved closer, hovered again and then returned to its original position, before shooting upwards and disappearing. The observation lasted for 30 minutes.

In mid October 1980 near Fort Sill Army Base in Oklahoma a woman named Kelly and her boyfriend were driving on the Bailey Turnpike when they drove directly under a huge craft shaped like a rounded disk with a curved indentation in the front, which apparently scanned her boyfriend and her with an orange red beam of light, which Kelly said it felt as it "went through her files." It was very unusual and hard to describe. They got a good look at the bottom of the craft, which featured a "grid work of gray metal fins going in all directions." Additionally it was divided into four quadrants by a cross of even darker material, solid and smooth in appearance. As they drove away from the area they could still see the craft hovering above the roadway.

1982

At sundown in Summer 1982 in Sperry in Tulsa County in Oklahoma traveling South on Hwy 11 between Sperry and Skiatook in Oklahoma. My 2 year old was with me and he saw it first. We pulled over and watched the blueish green glowing long bullet shaped object for about a minute and a half. It was about sundown. It just kind of shot off and disappeared. When I told my husband what I saw he laughed at me and it made me start crying. I called channel 8 news and they said their phones were going crazy. The air traffic controller at Tulsa International said he could see it out the window but couldn't pick it up on radar. He said they were trying to brush it off as a meteor but it was flying parallel to the ground. Then I never heard another word but I have never forgotten that and would love to talk to someone else who saw it.

1988

At 11.00 pm on September 4th 1988 in Atoka in Atoka County in Oklahoma in a farm area a woman reported seeing a lighted circular object on the ground, which she mistook at first to be a helicopter, but it was completely silent. Several undescribed "persons" appeared to be coming in and out of the object. The Police were notified and apparently officers saw the object as well.

1989

At 9.30 pm on January 24th 1989 in Valliant in McCurtain County in Oklahoma two large diamond or triangular shaped objects accompanied by 4 to 5 smaller bright objects were seen by dozens of witnesses. The large objects had red, white and blue lights and hovered and moved at tree-top level. The smaller lights maneuvered. The two large triangular shaped objects that were accompanied by 4 to 5 smaller bright objects were seen for more than an hour. They hovered and moved slowly at tree-top level. The smaller lights maneuvered between them.

Late at night in the middle of October 1989 in Welch in Craig County in Oklahoma six witnesses driving along a rural road South of the city came upon a dark round object with two red lights blocking the road ahead. They stopped the vehicle, and then two 9-foot tall green glowing thin Humanoids appeared from behind the object. The terrified witnesses drove quickly away from the area.

1990

At midnight on July 12th 1990 in Tishomingo in Johnston County in Oklahoma two men were just below the Pennington Creek Dam, when they saw a white Humanoid blurry figure coming down through the trees from the nearby Rowe Septic Tank Co. The figure crossed the dam, entered the pump house, and then returned to the trees. Five minutes later, circular patterns of lights gleamed through the trees and rose to the top, then disappeared. One of the witnesses possibly had beneficial medical after effects.

1995

At Coweta in Wagoner County in Oklahoma on September 5th 1995. At 3.00 p.m. the witnesses heard the sound of a jet passing low above their country home. The man went outside in the rear of the house, facing the pasture opposite of where the noise went. At that time, something with an approximate wingspan of ten feet flew from East to West, twenty meters from the ground above the elm trees next to the house. It had a large head and a thin Humanoid body, wings like a moth or insect but it did not flap them. This entity landed. His wife saw it too. It was ten to twelve feet tall, with a red oily skin, and emitted ammonia like odor. The creature then spoke in a strange manner. The man demanded that it speak "English" of which it spoke in an older European accent. (!) It did not do any harm but the witnesses fled inside their home. According to the witness the entity claimed its name was "Ivan Cole." (?). Enjoy them, there will be more.

1997

At 2.15 am on October 15th 1997 in Duncan in Stephens County in Oklahoma the witness suddenly woke up in the middle of the night feeling a strange presence in the room. An odd feeling swept through his body forcing him to close his eyelids. His next memory was of being awake at 5.15 am with a strange presence still in the room. Once again he was forced to close his eyelids. He then woke up in the morning and was able to recall standing naked in an oval shaped metal room with small windows in the top right hand corner. Directly behind him there was a large door where the two oval walls met. In the middle of the room there was an odd looking operating table with two needle devices on robotic arms sticking out of the side. This was apparently the only object in the room. Afraid he began banging on the large door, demanding to be let out. He could hear voices in the background in his head. He was then told by an angry male voice in his head to either lay down on the table or someone he loves would get hurt. He did as he was told. He was asked to lay down in such a manner that his left hand lower back was exposed to the two needle like objects. One of the objects had a clear window on it and he could see some clear liquid inside. At the base of the needle there was a triangle shaped piece of metal and two rectangle designs on both sides of the objects. He was then told by a more friendly female voice that he will feel no pain but would feel his legs go numb and would feel paralyzed and unable to move. Suddenly the robotic arm moved closer to his back and suddenly plunged into his lower left hand side of his back. He felt the clear liquid being pushed into his body. He then felt paralyzed. After a minute the needle began sucking instead of injecting. It then moved back and the second needle then approached and performed the same operation. He woke up the next morning feeling some pain in his lower back with a triangular shaped imprint on it.

1999

On August 18th 1999 at Fort Gibson Lake in Wagner and Cherokee Counties in Oklahoma 40 year old Greg West was at home when suddenly he was overcome by an eerie feeling. Soon he found himself lying nude on some sort of table. A bright light shone on his eyes. He then encountered several four foot tall, metallic blue colored beings that had no ears. They had small black slits for eyes and were very thin and fragile looking. They had long arms and three fingered hands. A taller silvery being seemed to be in control of the situation and the smaller blue beings seemed to fear him. The witness later awoke back home. Later he found a scar behind his ear.

Tennessee

1843

Around 8.00 pm on the 9th April 1843 a luminous ball about two feet in diameter was seen in the southwestern sky near Greenville in Greene County in Tennessee. The ball was constantly emitting small meteors from one or the other side of it and it appeared to be brighter than the sun. When it first appeared it stayed still for one or two minutes and then suddenly rose thirty feet before pausing again and then fell to the point from where it started and then continued to do the same for the next fifteen minutes. The sighting lasted one and a quarter hours. This is a lot longer than a meteor sighting.

1897

Over Clarkesville in Montgomery County in Tennessee on 15th April 1897 hundreds of witnesses saw an airship in the sky.

On April 17th 1897 in Humboldt in Gibson and Madison Counties, Tennessee. Sam McLeary was travelling next to the Forked Deer River near Humbolt when he came across a metallic object 30m long, 9m wide, with pointed ends. The thing was partly impacted into the ground and partly hanging in the trees. It had a passenger compartment in which there was a single occupant, frozen solid, as was a water barrel on board, It was assumed that it was an airship that had flown too high.

On April 23rd 1897 in the evening near Chattanooga in Hamilton County in Tennessee several citizens said that they had come upon an airship on a spur of a mountain near the city. Two men at work on it explained that they had come to earth because the machinery was out of order. One gave his name as Professor Charles Davidson and said that the vessel had left Sacramento a month earlier. The balloon portion is in the shape of a shad minus head and tail and built of aluminum with a bamboo and aluminum passenger car nine feet long. Electric and naptha motors give the motive power.

1907

Near Dikeman Springs, near Dickson in Dickson County in Tennessee on April 20th 1907. That afternoon Mr. Walter Stephenson was out training his pair of bloodhounds and had just finished a long chase with his dogs and sat down on a log to rest, when things got weird. He espied upon the eastern horizon a speck, which he took to be a large kite. He paid little attention to the object, and shifted his gaze temporarily to other scenes. Soon his attention was attracted to a whirring noises and looking upward, he saw that the speck which he had a few moments before discovered in the eastern sky had approached almost directly over him, and that the object was in reality a huge balloon, but of a pattern and appearance he had never in his life before seen. He discovered that the floating mass was rapidly approaching the Earth. All of a sudden, the observer says, strains of music calculated to charm the spheres burst forth from the balloon, which circled around and around and finally landed at Dikeman Springs. A number of strange people emerged from the car, which was closely curtained with a substance that fairly glistened in the sunshine that temporarily burst through the obscuring clouds, and all going to the big, flowing spring, knelt by it in a supplicating attitude and so remained for a minute or more. Mr. Stephenson says that while this was going on he sat quietly within speaking distance, and when the strange visitors arose to their feet and he supposed their devotional exercises were over, he asked if he might be permitted to inquire who they were, and what their mission? He said that instantly a visor was lifted by one of the company and the benign face of a lady showed from underneath and said in German, "Haben sie Beten?" (Did you pray?) And instantly all were aboard, the airship rose, circled about for a minute or more and was gone in a westerly direction. Mr. Stephenson says that the incident left an impression upon him that he can never forget, and while he knows that it was some human invention, it looked and the music sounded more like that 'of angels than of mortals.' Evening News (Ada Oklahoma) July 1, 1907.

In Bold Springs in McEwen in Humphreys County in Tennessee on April 21st 1907 at 3:30 a.m. A Mr. W. A. Smith described as a respected farmer living four miles from the town of Bold Springs, told how he left for town that Saturday morning at around 3.30 am. He was just on his way when he heard strains of music. Shrugging it off, thinking that perhaps a wedding must be taking place, he then noticed that the music came from above. He looked up and "was amazed to see a large balloon of unusual size and strange pattern." Suspended from the balloon was a large closed car from within which the music appeared to come. The car was strung with electric lights, and a brilliant searchlight was carried at the front. No machinery or mechanism appeared in view, and the motive power could not even be surmised. The balloon directed its searchlight to a large spring, heading directly toward it. Finally the balloon descended slowly to the ground, about 30 feet (9m) from the edge of the spring. Smith left his horse tied to a tree and went for a closer look. As he came close he noted a peculiar party of queer-looking persons in strange garb kneeling beside the spring, apparently engaged in silent prayer. Smith decided not to make contact, but as the group returned to their aerial craft, one of them pointed to him uttering some words that Smith could not understand. In closing, the Nashville American remarked: "In justice to Mr. Smith it should be stated that his story was told here Saturday afternoon, nearly 16 hours before the Sunday American reached town. In Sunday's American appeared a story from Dickson, Tenn., in the adjoining county, chronicling the appearance of a similar aircraft, and crediting the strange visitors with speaking German." Nashville American.

Near Pleasant Spring, possibly Chester County where there is a Pleasant Springs, Tennessee on April 22nd 1907 in the evening. Herman Schubert, who with his family lived at the edge of town, claimed that the mystery aeronauts visited thereabouts as well. Schubert, who was German, regarded the aeronauts as "merely visitors from what he calls 'the old country.' The Schubert's occupied a large farm with a spring, a natural basin 20 feet (6m) wide, at the edge of a 40-acre wood lot. The spring is the headwater of a small stream, which, from its rise on the Schubert farm, is known as Schubert Creek. Schubert and his 15-year old son Carl were at the spring-house that Sunday evening. Finishing his work, it was now near dark. Carl sat at the edge of the basin. The old man heard his son calling in a half-frightened tone, so he rushed outside. At an elevation of several hundred feet the two saw a large airship or balloon; from their account it is impossible to decide which. Suspended from the body of the air machine was a large closed car, very similar to the body of a stage coach, except that it was probably 35 feet (10m) long, and had an entrance on either side instead of at the end. The airship landed at the edge of the spring and the Schuberts retreated inside the spring-house to witness the scene from there. Twelve to 14 people were seen walking to the spring "their attitude one of reverence, as though standing on sacred ground, or in a sacred presence." At the spring the group arranged itself along the edge and knelt, apparently in silent prayer, being thus engaged for several minutes. When the strange aeronauts returned to the carriage, the elder Schubert, addressing no one in particular, asked what they were doing and who they were. The party with one exception, continued unheeding on the way to the car. Only one of the party took note of Mr. Schubert's request. Turning toward the two this one of the travelers said, without raising the head covering, "Sie haben nicht gebeten; Rede uns nicht an," which Mr. Schubert says is the German equivalent for "Thou has not prayed; address us not." Mr. Schubert spoke to them in German, and the spokesman replied, evidently surprised at hearing the tongue; "Unsere Wohlfahrt ist noch nicht vallented; in guten Zeit wird die welt alles wissen." This, Mr. Schubert says, is German for, "Our pilgrimage is not yet completed; the world will know all in time." The spokesman then turned and followed his companions into the car, which rose rapidly and took a southerly direction. Nashville American, Tennessee, 23 April, 1907.

Near Dull in Dickerson County near Nashville in Tennessee on April 26th 1907. That morning. Mail carrier Asa Hickerson had been delivering the mail and was descending a steep hill with a little log building named Peabody School at the bottom, when his attention was drawn to "sounds resembling the chanting of some weird, funeral dirge, proceeding seemingly from the tops of the forest trees through which his route winded." His horse became restless and all his attention was needed to calm the frightened animal. Pausing briefly, Hickerson left his buggy to adjust the harness, when once more the strange sounds were heard, but now much louder; simultaneously there swooped into plain view a gigantic aircraft that gradually and with the ease of a huge bird, settled softly to the ground, some 50 yards (46m) from where Mr. Hickerson struggled with his now almost unmanageable roan mare. A group of several men exited the long car attached to the craft, and forming in single file, resumed their long chant, and proceeded slowly to the mouth of an abandoned oil well at the side of the road. There the group conducted a strange ritual. Forming a circle around the well, one of them carrying a long staff plunged it three times in the well after having made "sundry passes in the air" with it. The group then withdrew to the opposite side of the road where the staff, dripping with the oil, was stuck in the moist earth and set alight. The band then joined hands and again lifting their voices in song, slowly circled around and around the flaming rod, while a small spiral column of black smoke whirled slowly upwards. The ceremony finished, the group returned to the airship. Hickerson too wanted to know what was going on. So he asked, "What are you doing here?" The one who had carried the staff replied in sonorous tones "Betreue deine sunde und bete!" (Be healthy and pray) extending his right hand as if invoking a benediction. The huge vessel then with the poise and grace of an eagle rose slowly until well above the forest and headed in a northeasterly direction and was soon lost to view. Nashville American, Tennessee, 28 April, 1907. Did these events occur or was it a boring day in Newspaperland?

1910

It is 9.00 am on 12th January 1910. Thousands of people see a one hundred foot long cigar in the sky above Chattanooga in Hamilton County, Tennessee, for one hour. The object was silvery white and glistening. There were no wings or any visible means of propulsion though a distinct chugging sound was heard. The craft was five hundred feet up and travelling at twenty miles per hour travelling North and taking ten minutes to cross the city eventually getting lost in the fog along the Tennessee River. Into the fog the airship and its occupant went and came out again a quarter hour of an hour later at Huntsville, about eighty miles away.

At 9.15 am 12th January 1910 a one hundred foot long cigar was seen in the sky over Huntsville in Madison County, Alabama. This was the same craft as seen in Chattanooga fifteen minutes before. Namely a silvery-white glistening cigar travelling at five hundred feet. The craft must have been travelling at 320 miles per hour then if it traversed the distance from Chattanooga to Huntsville in fifteen minutes. No craft in this period could do this sort of speed.

At 11.00 am on 13th January 1910 the following day, the chugging silver cigar was back in Chattanooga again. This time it had come from the south, obviously on its way back from Huntsville but this time a man was seen in it.

And on 14th January 1910 the silver airship was back in Huntsville again.

By 7.00 pm 14th January 1910 the airship was in Knoxville in Knox County in Tennessee where it went South rapidly. The clear outline of the craft was seen and the sound of a motor was heard coming from it.

At noon, 14th January 1910, the one hundred foot long silvery glistening chugging cigar was back in the sky over Chattanooga. This time it was heading from the North to the southeast and it was the third day that it had been seen above the city. The airship eventually vanished over Missionary Ridge.

The following day 15th January 1910 the strange airship was back over Chattanooga at noon. The craft came from the North and went southeast finally vanishing over the Missionary Ridge.

Also on 15th January 1910 a large white airship was seen over Paragould in Greene County in Arkansas. There were three to four Hominoids on board and the craft was brilliantly illuminated with a powerful searchlight. The craft went north, then South at an altitude of one thousand feet. Greene County had been visited by Hairy Humanoids early that century.

Also on the evening of 15th January 1910 Myrtle B. Lee and her brother Jack who were children saw a bright object hovering just above the trees about fifty yards from them. it was silver colored and shaped like a Zeppelin but not quite as big. It had nothing hanging from the underside and there were no windows. When it took off they saw it start up and it completely vanished before their eyes. They called it a balloon.

On 20th January 1910 at 8.00 am a number of witnesses saw an airship traveling East and then southwest very fast and very high up over Memphis in Shelby County in Tennessee. The craft crossed the Mississippi River into Arkansas and then turned South vanishing rapidly.

1920

On June 9th 1920 at Wathena in Doniphan County, Kansas. A cylindrical object flying at about 25m altitude was seen by about 200 people at a point between Wathena and Rushville (Missouri). At Rushville the object made and abrupt turn to the east and vanished into a cloud 3km away.

1922

Near Sugar Tree in Decatur County a man walking home at night saw a light rising up out of nowhere which made his hair stand on end. The light was coming from a hollow tree stump but even when the man hit it with his walking stick nothing happened. This was in 1922.

1930

One night in in 1930 in Wayne County in Tennessee a man told his family of meeting several little men on Beech Creek Road. The little men had wrinkled faces and reddish complexions. The witness also saw bright lights in the woods. The little men apparently chased the witness who ran hysterically and apparently passed out. He later found himself lying down in a field. The lights and little men were gone. Here is another version. At 2100hrs a man walking down Beech Creek Road from Hw13 heard a sound like a bullet whizzing past and then saw two small lights just above the ground ahead. These merged to be become a single pan sized light. He then heard a sound like a motor slowing down and then saw a brilliant light resembling a circular table by the roadside. Around this was a group of 8-10 dwarfs with reddish wizened faces, long noses and whiskers or beards. The man through his walking stick at the small figures and ran off. At some point he lost consciousness and woke up some time later at the foot of South Branch Hill. **xxx**

1940

During June 1940, a nine year old girl was in a playground at Happy Valley in Roane County near Oak Ridge in Tennessee when she spotted a flying object hovering above the treetops five hundred feet away. She watched it for one minute before it tilted upwards, expelled a blue vapor and vanished. Is the blue a change of color due to a change of vibration or speed or an exhaust? Is it merely a fashionable color?

1944

At Oliver Springs in Anderson County in Tennessee at dusk during September 1944 Mr. Nelson, Mr. A. C. Butler and Mr. Albert Profitt were in a car when they saw an airship land fifty feet in front of them. It was at the height of a windshield and was hovering. The color was glossy white. The craft was thirty feet long by four feet wide. As the car eased up to it the object slowly moved away. Secret weapon? Alien spyship? None of the above near the top secret atomic weapons research laboratory? A misinterpretation of a glowing ball of energy? Or this version? Three civilian Oak Ridge employees, Mr Nelson, A. C. Butler and Albert Profitt, driving from Oliver Springs to Oak Ridge, were 3km out of Oliver Springs when they observed a white object, about 9m long, 1.2m wide, about 15m ahead of their car. The object responded to changes in the car's speed several times before rising over Black Oak Ridge. At one point Nelson called some people out of a nearby house, and they also saw the object.

During September 1944 a strange, metallic looking, tubelike object was spotted hovering over the road near the Oak Ridge atomic plant in Anderson and Roane Counties. The object moved away as a crowd began to gather. On the banks of the Clinch River a huge, black windowless building was constructed and in the middle of September a gaseous diffusion plant designed to prepare quantities of fissionable material for the development of the Atomic Bomb started operating.

1947

On June 30th 1947 at night in Knoxville in Knox County, Tennessee. Mr and Mrs C E Bellam saw a luminous light bulb shaped object low over a forest. It had a sort of tail and made a whistling sound.

On July 5th 1947 at pre-dusk in Fayetteville in Washington County, Arkansas. Farmer Henry Seay was driving his cattle home 3km north of Fayetteville when he noticed a kind of dust falling on him. Passing overhead was a glowing object, 3-4m in diameter. The cattle bolted to the other side of the pasture. The object descended to ground level for a few seconds, about 200m away, in front of a barn. The round, flattened object then rose to about 10m before moving off horizontally at 80kph, leaving a trail of yellow sparks. The same farmer had seen three similar objects at between 150-200m altitude the previous night.

At 2.00 pm 6th July 1947 at Chickamauga Creek in Hamilton County in Tennessee W. D. Seacrest was hunting turtles in a creek when he saw three flying disc-shaped objects over the area. He was scared at first and hid behind a tree. He then noticed one of the discs descend and hover over a nearby field. The witness had a good look at the object and saw a cockpit with two pilot-like figures inside the craft as it tilted. He also noticed a black hump behind the cockpit which he believed housed the engines. The other two discs stayed in the air whilst the lower one surveyed the field. It suddenly zoomed upwards, took a leading position in front of the others and all three took off at incredible speed.

On July 8th 1947 (Approximate date) in Nashville in Davidson County, Tennessee. A man driving by an airfield saw a disk land and from it emerge two "luminous beings all heads and arms and legs". They exchanged gestures with the witness before returning to the object, which took off in a cloud of dust.

In early July 1947 near Nashville in Davidson County in Tennessee a man reported that as he was driving along a highway a flying saucer landed on a field and two strange little men, all heads and arms and legs and glowing like fireflies, emerged from it and exchanged greetings with him by sign language. The saucer eventually took off in a cloud of dust.

In 1947 at Oak Ridge in in Anderson and Roane Counties Tennessee an aerial craft was observed and photographed. It was an airspace violation and the photos were confiscated.

1949

On April 6-7th 1949 in Memphis in Shelby County in Tennessee at 12:01 [12:30?], 2, 3:30, and 4 a.m. housewife Mrs. Mike Love Stewart and Dorthy [Dorothy?] Hall (and Helen Howell?), a husband and son, saw 6-9 climbing, diving, whirling yellow or silvery oval objects which avoided 3-4 airplanes, traveling from SW to SE about 45° elevation about 1 to 2 miles away. They were 1/4 of the moon's angular size.

On June 22nd 1949 at Oak Ridge in Anderson and Roane Counties Tennessee. Three women, one school teacher, another a biologist working at an Oak Ridge lab, and the third who was the wife of a member of the Security Division, AEC, at Oak Ridge observed a very odd trio of "flying saucers" for about 15 minutes: "It was described as consisting of two identical rectangular-shaped objects which appeared to be coordinated in movement and which moved in wave-like motion. The third object was circular in shape and appeared to be in level flight between and above the two rectangular objects. The rectangular objects appeared to be bright metal on top but dark underneath, while the color of the circular object was the same as that of frosted glass. The 'flying saucer,' when last sighted, was in level flight and was flying in a northwesterly direction. The weather was clear with high cumulus clouds. The 'flying saucer' flew at speed of from 10 to 15 mph over an area just about the center of Oak Ridge."

1950

On March 29th 1950 at 0700hrs in Lake Marrowbone in Davidson County, Tennessee. D Whiteside and H T William were out fishing when they heard a peculiar noise and two objects descended at speed through an opening in the clouds, coming down to about 75m altitude. They were travelling faster than planes and changed direction in unison, disappearing behind the ridge of hills to the west. The men rapidly rowed away from the area.

On October 15th 1950 at 1520hrs in Oak Ridge, Tennessee. Edward D Rymer, an atomic energy security patrol trooper, and John Moneymaker, a caretaker at the University of Tennessee Research Farm, were talking outside the guard house when John saw an object at 3,500-4,500m above the Control Zone and directed Edward's attention to it. The thing appeared as a sky writing plane with a trail of smoke behind it, but as it arced down at descended at 160kph Edward saw that it was a wingless bullet shaped object and that the smoke was a kind of tail. Edward went into the guard room to report the thing and when he came out he saw that the thing was down to just below 2m about 70m from them. The thing had the apparent dimensions of a 5 x 12cm card with tail appearing to be 6m long and about 3cm wide. This tail as grey in colour with a thin central black line and its last three quarters gave off an intermittent pulsating glow, gave the impression of rippling and seemed to be translucent. The thing appeared to be travelling at about 5kph and its main body was rocking from side to side. Even when Edward got within 15m of the object, it did not appear to get any larger but the thing picked up speed and passed over a 3m tall fence, dipped again and then rose over a 9m tall willow tree and, picking up speed, over the top of a ridge, changing to a pear shape as it did so. In the minutes following two similar objects were seen, one after another at about 100m and 150m respectively.

On October 16th 1950 at Oak Ridge in Anderson and Roane Counties Tennessee at 3:20 pm. While Special Agent William S. Price was present, a report came from the AEC Patrol to the radar station relating that a Trooper Isabell and four civilian employees at Oak Ridge had observed a "silver disc" hovering over the K-25 Plant in the controlled area. The radar screen was able to pick up an indistinct target about every three (3) or four (4) sweeps of the indicator. An F-82 fighter plane was sent to attempt an intercept of the object. The airborne radar of the fighter picked up a target which later proved to be a light aircraft. The ground observers reported that the F-82 passed under the "silver disc" while it was in pursuit of the light plane. The crew of the fighter observed nothing unusual. Nothing further was learned of the sightings."

Four days later on October 20th 1950 in Oak Ridge, Tennessee at 4:55 PM. Larry Riordan, the Superintendent of Security for the X-10 control zone, while driving to a residential area saw an object which he thought at first was a balloon which had lost its "basket." It was generally round, appeared to "come together at the bottom in wrinkles, was rather indistinct, and something was hanging below." It appeared to be 8 to 10 feet long and lead or gunmetal colored. It didn't seem to be moving but, since he was traveling and only saw it for a number of seconds, he couldn't be sure. He was sure it wasn't a weather balloon, although he thought it might have been a gas bag balloon launched by the nearby University of Tennessee Agricultural Research Farm.

On the same day at 3:27 PM the radar unit at the Knoxville Airport in Knox County detected radar targets near the area of Mr. Riordan's sighting and scrambled a fighter plane. The pilot searched the area for about an hour and a half, which included the time of Mr. Riordan's sighting, and found nothing.

Three days later on October 23rd 1950 also at Oak Ridge, Tennessee at 4:30 PM, Francis Miller, an Oak Ridge laboratory employee, while driving along a road in Oak Ridge saw an object that appeared to be less than half a mile away and between 1,000 and 2,000 feet up. It appeared as an "aluminum flash" that was traveling in a south-southeast direction. He only saw it for a few seconds. Subsequently it was discovered that a nuclear radiation detection station (a Geiger counter) in the vicinity of the sighting registered a burst of alpha and beta radiation. The purpose of this station was to detect any leaks of radiation from the Oak Ridge Laboratory. There was no leakage of radiation, however. An expert from the Health and Research Division analyzed the readings from the Geiger counter and pronounced them unexplained. This association between radiation detection and a UFO sighting was similar to that at Mt. Palomar in California on another occasion. Whether the reading of the Geiger counter was actually a result of nuclear radiations or whether the presence of the UFO induced a transient electrical fault in the counter or whether there was some other explanation is not known.

The following day on October 24th 1950 and still at Oak Ridge, Tennessee at 6:30 p.m. FBI documents show several visual sightings at Oak Ridge and a radar track at Knoxville. An unidentified object appeared at 6:30 PM at an altitude of approximately 5,000 feet in the same general vicinity as the object observed by Fry. The radar target disappeared at 7:20 p.m. The complete radar report to the CIC investigator says that targets appeared at 6:23 p.m. moving over the restricted flight zone and at 6:26 a fighter was scrambled to the area of the targets but failed to see anything.

1952

Around 11.00 pm in June 1952 at Little Spring Creek in Hickman County in Tennessee two saucers were seen that appeared stuck together with a central dome around which rotated very bright multicolored lights. It was a shiny aluminum color. Two witnesses were walking home from the movies when Carl Haynes heard weird music and singing which was coming from the brightest lights that you ever saw. Approaching to 75 yards he saw four or five little men dancing around a shiny aluminum object with an open door from which the music came. The little men held what appeared to be guns in their hands. Within ten minutes they stopped singing and put things in the space ship. They went back in, the door closed and the UFO took off straight up in a kind of corkscrew motion with a whistling noise. It became brighter as it took off. The whole episode lasted one hour. When Haynes revisited the site he found four impressions of balls and a deep sunk spike mark in the center. Another man, now deceased, had also seen the lights and heard the music. Or this version. A man heard strange sounds and "weird music". He then saw an aluminium coloured object with orange and blue glowing spots, some of which were dazzling to the eyes. There were rotating lights on a transparent sphere on its top. The machine stood on four legs, 1.3m high, each with a ball at the end, and a centre spike. The body of the object resembled two saucers stuck together, 2-2.5m thick. Around the machine were four or five men between 1.35-1.5m tall, dancing and singing in high pitched voices. Apparently seeing the witness, the beings reloaded the craft, then advanced towards him with gun like objects in their hands, but stopped, apparently unwilling to cross a creek. They then walked up a ramp or steps into the craft, which rose vertically with a cork screw motion, glowing brighter as it rose. Marks of the legs of the machine and small heelless footprints were found in the ground.

1957

At Dante in Knox County in Tennessee, near Knoxville, on 7th November 1957 at 6.30 am Everitt Clarke, 12, got up to let his dog "Frisky" out. He saw a strange glowing object in a field 300 feet from the house and went back to bed. He thought that he was dreaming. A few minutes later he went out again to call the dog. The object was still there as well as several of the neighborhood dogs as well as "Frisky" barking at it. Two men and two women were also there. They were trying to grab "Frisky". "Frisky" growled and backed away and the Hominoids sounded like they were talking in German. A man did catch one of the dogs but let it go after it snarled and snapped at him. Then the four Hominoids seemed to walk right through the glass wall of the oblong craft. One of the Hominoids saw Everitt watching and beckoned him over. Everett refused and was hysterical for several days after the incident. The grass in the area was flattened in an area 24 foot by five foot. The elongated impression was found in a field by a reporter. The grass had been pressed down in a 24 foot by five foot area. Everitt had called his grandmother immediately after the incident as both parents were at work. This is a compilation of Mr. Schmidt's German-speaking Aliens and Mr. Trasco's dognappers just one day after the event! How then do we hallucinate strikingly similar themes the following day, before even the media could disseminate the information, even if it bothered to? Could it be that the incoming visitors from through the Quasar Vacuum are manipulated into recognizable form by the observers? If this were the case then the visitors could not return to whence they had come from for their technology would have changed to that of the observers' expectations both culturally and symbolically. Or does it appear to change to fit the observers' cultural and symbolic expectations? Are we talking camouflage at a cerebral level where electrical stimulation from the electromagnetic field that has travelled via the Quasar Vacuum stimulates the observers' brain so as to cloak the actual event into that of what one would assume that the observer would assume to be occurring. Do we have very advanced chameleons that use our own cultural and symbolistic expectations as their own camouflage? God is always unknowable, that is why one cannot look at the face of God, for it is always changing. Maybe there is something to these old myths and legends after all? But who creates whom?

On November 20th 1957 at 2000hrs in Mcminnville in Warren County, Tennessee. A flashing red light passed low over the sheriff's car. Calling other police, he tried to give chase, but was unable to catch the object.

1960

Around 10.00 pm on 22nd July 1960 a thirteen year old girl saw a hovering disc with a rudder protruding from it over Martin in Weakley County. After it left the area large oily circles were found on the ground. Occupants were also seen in the craft which was twenty feet across.

In Late August/early September 1960 in the evening in Memphis in Shelby County, Tennessee. Rhodes McCarroll was sat with his grandfather on their upstairs rear balcony when they saw a luminous basketball sized sphere on the ground by the hedge. After a minute or so they also saw, stood behind this ball, a luminous naked humanoid figure about 1.8m tall holding a light at chest height. The figure had square shoulders and unusually long narrow legs. After about 5 minutes both globe and figure faded away.

1961

In Summer 1961 in Weston in Platte County, Missouri. Two witnesses were parked on a gravel road when they suddenly saw a ring of lights approaching. They thought that it was a plane, but the object appeared to hover and then land behind a distant tree line, about 1.5km away. After about 5 minutes the object ascended vertically and moved towards their car. They drove off at high speed, the thing pulling up near the car and following them for 11km into Weston, where it turned and left the road. No shape was visible behind the bright lights.

1966

Around 8.00 pm on 28th March 1966 a man driving at sixty miles per hour near Fayetteville in Lincoln County suddenly saw a large lighted object hovering three feet above the road on a hilltop. The object flew off as the car's headlights and engine died. The headlight bulbs had to be replaced. The oval object was twenty-five feet long, dark gray and had about thirty lights along its periphery.

On April 5th 1966 at Alto in Franklin County in Tennessee at 11:55 p.m. W. Smith and another stopped to watch an object hovering about 15 feet above a swamp, tried to follow it but it flew away. The object was 100 feet long and oval with a dark top and appearing cone-shaped when moving. It was making a high-frequency noise and flying between a high tension power line and a row of trees. There were animal reactions wherever the object flew over.

On October 11th 1966 in Jonesborough in Washington County in Tennessee at 7:10 p.m. Several people sighted a cigar-shaped object which, after about 2 minutes, lit up brightly and moved quickly to the North. A short while later two round objects appeared. Each had a "bulge" (dome?) on top and bright light shining from the bottom. The light changed color from white to red to green, as the two objects cavorted around each other. A witness called the Federal Aviation Administration (FAA) at Tri-Cities Airport, which sent an aircraft to investigate. The witnesses saw the plane approach, and as it neared, the objects "went out like a light." Meanwhile, the FAA had asked the witness to keep the phone line open, and said they would send another plane. As the second plane neared, it put on its landing lights, and again, the UFOs blinked out. A third plane re-routed by the FAA was directed to the location of the objects by telephone, and was seen to be closely approaching one of the UFOs, which now appeared egg-shaped. As the plane passed by it, the witnesses saw the object shoot out a light beam toward the plane. At that moment the pilot reported seeing what he thought was a meteor. The NICAP investigator was allowed to listen to the FAA tapes of air-to-ground communications, but none of the pilots reported seeing anything unusual.

The following day on October 12th 1966 and still at Jonesborough at noon there was a prolonged sighting (more than 5 hours) by many witnesses of numerous discs and the fall of so-called "angel's hair," which was sticky and reportedly caused physiological effects on some who touched it (burning sensation, itching, nausea). According to reports, dogs and cows in the neighborhood "acted odd." The main features of this sighting strongly resemble ballooning spiders, commonly seen during October in the United States. They and their webs sometimes reflect sunlight. To err on the side of caution, that explanation will be assumed. However, several witnesses experienced burning sensations when they handled the substance, and it evaporated overnight.

1967

On January 20th 1967 in Victoria in Marion County, Tennessee. A farmer driving along a back road, 6.5km from Victoria observed an object hovering 10m above the road. The thing was circular, the size of a house and gave off a green-blue glow. The witness felt his truck vibrate in the proximity of this object. People in other vehicles stopped to observe.

At 11.45 pm on 9th November 1967 two nurses driving home from a Waverly, Tennessee, hospital stopped at a traffic light in Erin in Houston County. Whilst they were stopped they saw a large UFO approach and land on the highway in front of them. At first they thought that it was the moon. Without the driver feeding gas the car began to move of its own accord until it stopped a mere thirty feet or so away from the semi-transparent craft. Inside the craft there were at least five small figures looking at them. The beings were dark green and four feet tall. The women felt completely unafraid and transfixed. The craft rose up and moved away and the women began eagerly to follow it. It led them to a rural road where they saw it land again. The lights on their car went out. They next recalled seeing a large light in the sky leaving them. They perceived no time lapse nor did they ever check the time. The young women, Miss Dianne Marable and Mrs. Pearl Robins, then drove home.

1968

On January 20th 1968 at 0200hrs in Roswell in Chaves County, New Mexico. Larry Fearney and his wife were driving near Roswell when they saw an object with three bright lights descend low about 300m away and approach to within 15m at which it levelled out and paced the car for 10 minutes before taking off vertically, going out of sight.

In Fall 1968 at 1900hrs in Greenville in Greene County. Tennessee. A married couple were driving along a rural dirt road when, as they approached the main highway, they saw a circular or oval object, emitting brilliant pulses of blue, green and red-pink light, hovering above the power lines. The wife felt that the pulsation of these lights was speeding up her heart rate and urged her husband to drive away.

1969

Near Pulaski in Giles County in Tennessee during December 1969. A respected businessman and his son reported seen a brilliantly lit globe-shaped object hovering overhead. Inside the globe they could plainly see a little man sitting there. He was about 2 ½ feet tall to 3 feet tall. His head looked too big for his body.

1970

One day in 1970 in Kingsport in Sullivan and Hawkins County, Tennessee. Mrs Hatch was diving with her 10 year old son from their home in Bristol and her place of work in Kingsport, when halfway there, they encountered a white object, which followed the telephone wires. It was of a fat oval shape, which spun as it approached the car and flew around it in circles until the Hatchs reached the town. As it left they could see a red ring on its inner edge.

In February 1970 at 0645hrs in Mosheim in Greene County, Tennessee. Housewife Patricia Long and her 14 year old daughter saw through their window, an object resembling two saucers rim to rim, with a spinning central zone, at ground level behind a row of trees. After 2-3 minutes the thing rose into the sky and had left the area by 0710.

1973

On July 27th 1973 at LaFollette in Campbell County, Tennessee. A strange object was seen on or close to the ground.

On September 13th 1973 at Mount Aetna in Marion County, Tennessee. Two people saw a very low flying red object.

On September 29th 1973 in the evening in Orion County, Tennessee. George and Vicki Rogers were driving home they saw to their left a bright red light, 2m diameter, in a field. The light was so bright that it lit up the field, and so dazzled the couple and that they and six other cars on the road were almost involved in accidents. The thing appeared to be at the height of the utility lines.

The next day on September 30th 1973 at 1435hrs in Shores Community, Tennessee. David Swanner was in a deer stand in a tree when he saw a spherical object that came across a nearby soya field, passed in front of him and sat down in an old dirt road bed, 15-19m away. It first hovered 30cm above the ground, then three legs unfolded from its base into a tripod. Two of the legs set down in the outside wheel track, the other extended over the other track, 45cm into a field. The thing was a white and fluorescent glowing sphere with no openings or external markings, seams etc. Suddenly an opening 90cm wide, 1.2m high appeared in the sphere, as if from nowhere. It was hinged at the bottom and lowered itself into a ramp. At the same time David heard a peculiar beeping sound, "like a high pitched crow call". He felt cold and sniffed his nose, at which the door slammed shut, the tripod retracted and the object took off at terrifying speed, leaving a fog of white vapour. When David went to the site and breathed this fog, he felt as though he was being smothered and then as though his lungs were being pumped full of air to bursting point. This sensation faded when he ran from the fog. The tripod left imprints 20mc long. This was the first of a series of UFO, Bigfoot and contact experiences.

At 8.15 pm on 1st October 1973 three teenagers in Anthony Hill in Giles County in Tennessee saw a huge hairy robot like creature that walked mechanically with its hands upraised. It had a large round head. An egg-shaped UFO was seen at the same time. This occurred during a thunderstorm and imprints were later found. Or this. Three teenagers; Becky Martin, her sister and another youngster, saw, during a thunderstorm, an egg shaped object, the top of which was illuminated by a white light. It flew over the tops of nearby trees and went out of sight behind them. They then saw a hairy robot like creature, with a large round head and its arms upraised in the air, which walked with a slow, rocking, mechanical motion.

At Bruceville in Dyer County in Tennessee on 2nd October 1973 at 10.00 pm Otis West and Doug Viar saw an object in the sky that had one red, one white and one green flashing light. The luminous object landed in a field and then would come up from behind trees. It looked like an orange ball and had strobe-like flashing.

At Berea in Giles County in Tennessee on 12th October 1973 James Cline was wakened by barking dogs. A farm family saw blinking lights and Cline saw a creature with a glowing white head cross the road fifty feet in front of him. Tracks from the Humanoid and marks from the UFO were found the next day. The landing marks were two feet long by twelve feet wide. Or this?

On October 3rd 1973 (Approximate Date) in Chester County, Tennessee. Joe (13) and Barry (9) S. hid in a chicken house when the spotted a green object, with red lights, which went overhead so low they feared it was going to attack them

On October 15th 1973 at 2100hrs in Estill Springs in Franklin County, Tennessee. Police Chief James Parks and Water Department superintendent Newman Chitwood were out patrolling when an object, the size of a trailer truck, with flashing and steady lights "like a million neon lights" hovered over the car.

On October 15th 1973 at 2225hrs in Crestwood Hills in Knox County, Tennessee. Mrs Charles Seymour observed a huge round ball, with a gold dome, and orange and red pulsating lights hover over a nearby creek for three minuites, and then rise and move away to the west. This was one of a large number of reports from Knox County that night.

Also on October 15th 1973 at 2230hrs in Berea in Giles County, Tennessee. A farm family, Earl Fralix, his wife and son, David Graves and his wife, along with James Cline, had all gone to bed when they were awoken by the barking of the dogs. They saw lights shining through a wooded area, apparently from a yellow object on the ground. Late the thing lifted up and they could see that it had an illuminated top, which cast a red glow in the sky, and was surrounded by lights. As they watched, James and perhaps others saw a humanoid figure, whose head glowed with a white light, run upright across a field 15m away. The object climbed into the sky and returned to the ground two or three times. At the site two half circles 10cm diameter and 6.6m apart were found (other sources give 6.6m long and 3.6m wide).

On October 15th 1973 at 2300hrs in Chattanooga in Hamilton County, Tennesee. Loranie and Susie Evans saw yellow and red objects flying overhead. They turned and landed in a field. There was a burned area 90cm long, 30cm wide.

On October 17th 1973 in Johnson City in Washington, Carter and Sullivan Counties in Tennessee there were several sightings of UFOs: a circular copper-colored object that descended, hovered near the ground and then took off straight up, a tall Humanoid being who accosted children and a glowing red sphere that alternately hovered and moved.

At Chattanooga in Hamilton County in Tennessee on 17th October 1973 a thirty to forty foot long by ten foot wide cigar-shaped flying object was seen by more than two dozen witnesses including the Police. Police Sergeant Lester Shell, 47, and Patrolman Harry Jarret, 35, got to within 100 yards of it as it was hovering twenty feet above the ground. It glowed a brilliant blue-white more intense than any airplane. Eventually it took off silently and slowly and straight up.

At Watauga in Washington County in Tennessee on 17th October 1973 a circular, copper-colored UFO was seen hovering just above the ground. A six foot tall creature with claw-like hands and wide blinking eyes reached out to grab two children. There were at least six other reports in the same area around that time. Or this. At 2.00pm Mrs Linda Green and her neighbour Ruth O'Quinn watched a copper coloured circular object hovering over a hillside adjacent to their homes. To Linda's horror the object landed on a lawn her son and a neighbouring boy were playing on across the street from her home. A door opened in the thing and a being, about 1.8m tall, with blinking eyes and claw like hands, stepped out and attempted to grab the two boys. They ran straight into Linda's house and the object took off straight up and disappeared. At least five people had seen similar objects the previous afternoon.

Also on October 17th 1973 at 1900hrs in Chattanooga in Hamilton County, Tennessee. Police received a call from a woman who reported, hysterically, that a large bright, cigar shaped, object had landed in a wooded area near the Charles A Bell Elementary School, in the Alton Park area. Sergeant Lester Shell and Patrolman Harry Jarret were dispatched to the scene. As they approached the wooded swampy area they encountrered a brilliant blue-white oblong shaped light, too brilliant for any shape to be discerned behind it. The light was hovering less than 5m above the swamp, within 30m of the offciers. The thing was motionless, twice the length of a patrol car and was emitting an unsual hissing sound. As Lester walked closer the object rose up to about 27m, made a sharp angular turn and shot away to the east. It then almost caught up with an eastbound aircraft, which it then seemed to be following. Lester called the control tower of Chattanooga airport, but both they and the plane reported there was nothing there. Strange lights were seen at various locations in the Chattanooga area, sometimes at low altitude, for much of the night and early morning.

On October 18th 1973 in the morning in Charleston in Bradley County, Tennessee. Near Charleston, several teenagers including Annette T, on their way to high school, saw two cigar shaped object, with hazy lights, hovering over houses and settling towards the ground before heading north. Annette became scared ran to a house. 15 minutes later, while directing school traffic, Police Sergt Charles Parker also saw the two objects.

On October 18th 1973 in Lebanon in Wilson County, Tennessee a strange object was seen on or close to the ground.

Also on October 18th 1973 at 1830hrs in Pickett County, Tennessee. Troy T (10) was driving a small motorcycle in front of his uncle's house when a strange object hovered a few metres above him. The motorcycle spluttered and Troy ran into his uncle's house. Several other people aged between 10 and 58 came out as the object left the scene. This object emitted a humming sound and an opening appeared in its bottom. Troy was so frightened that he could not sleep that night and did not go to school the next day.

On October 31st 1973 in Giles County, Tennessee. Mrs Helen X, along with her son and daughter, saw an object with a large light on its top and smaller pulsating lights around its middle, hover and then land in a field. After an hour it took off vertically and disappeared. A depressed area and tracks were found.

In the Shores Community, Tennessee on October 31st 1973 at 5: 30 a.m. During a rash of UFO sightings in the area, the witness, while driving to work, encountered three anthropoid like creatures, described as being hairy, with flat noses, large foreheads, pointed ears and leaving behind three-toed tracks. No other information.

In Tennessee in October 1973 one evening. According to the main witness, it was a common occurrence for his mother and him to observe strange objects in the air that looked like nothing they had ever seen. Triangular objects that would stop and start randomly. Objects that were circular that would move vertically as well as horizontally. It seemed as if they were 'performing' for them. It was explained, by his mother that they were "experimental" aircraft from the Air Force Base in Columbus Mississippi They looked forward to their "entertainment." One fall evening his parents were in the house and he was outside alone. He wandered several hundred yards behind their home and felt, heard, and saw simultaneously a large, cigar-shaped object. It was a dull pewter color. Then it emitted a white light down to the ground. The craft hovered just below tree level. He was drawn to the light, and had a feeling of total comfort, almost euphoria. He has no idea how he got there, but he came to in a room with no windows. There were no lights, but it was very bright. There were three male and one female, human-like people there. The men looked like 'super athletes,' close to seven feet tall with blond hair and blue eyes which were larger than normal. The clothing was plain, but skintight, and almost appeared to be painted on. The woman was a few inches shorter and very curvy. The witness was only 7-8 years old, but he immediately had a feeling of comfort and trust, and even attraction to her. As he was looking around he felt no discomfort. All he could move was his eyes and head. They touched him, had something like a wand and went all around his body with it. The entire time they 'communicated' but didn't talk. It was primarily them telling him the evils of nuclear power/ weapons and to always do all he could to stay away from and stop its use. They also told him that they would be watching after him and "mine," not to worry, that he would always be taken care of. Over the next few years, he had communication with them, but it was a less vivid memory. He would be asleep, have almost a feeling of a dream (lucid?) that he was aboard, and then wake up in a chair outside. He has always felt "great" after these visits. He found himself looking forward to them. He told his mother after the first and every other encounter he had. She told him that she believed him and it would make life hard for him. Sometime later, he noticed a 2-3cm hard object just under the skin on his left outer mid-thigh. He has asked several doctors, but they have had no explanation on what it is. He has had spontaneous pneumothorax (collapsed lung for no apparent reason) five times as a teenager. No problems since. According to the witness he is now a successful eye doctor with a wonderful healthy family.

1972

In late July 1972 at 2050hrs in Nashville in Davidson County, Tennessee. woman was waiting with her daughter to collect her son from work, when their attention was caught by an object shaped like one saucer inverted over another coming from the direction of the cemetery and memorial park at about treetop height. It appeared metallic, with a flat underside, a red light on top and a row of small windows around its centre. These were illuminated by yellow, pink and pale green lights and through them could be seen figures in green overalls walking about and working with various equipment. The thing emitted a beeping sound that seemed to come from the top light. The mother got out of the car and ran toward the thing, alarming her 30 year old daughter. The object moved off with a circular motion. Other motorists appeared not to notice it.

1973

In late January 1973 in Blue Creek in Giles County, Tennessee. Mr and Mrs K O Wilkes saw, about 800m away on a hilltop, a dull, aluminium grey coloured object, about half the size of a house trailer. The thing had red and green lights at either end and its top appeared to glow. The couple could see several beams of light extending up to 30m from its top. The object was about 7m long by 3m high. The Wilkes saw neither the arrival nor the departure of the object. At the site semi-circular imprints about 9m across were found and plaster casts were made of them.

In 1973 in Johnson City in Washington, Carter and Sullivan Counties, Tennessee. John Maddox was sitting on his back porch when he saw an oblong object land and then take off a short time later, in a field 750m away. A burnt area 9m diameter was found.

1974

Back in the Shores Community, Tennessee on January 17th 1974 at 3:00 a.m. Barry Swanner, 37, a 10 hour a day factory hand, living in an isolated area with his wife and two daughters, was apparently awoken by a high pitched buzzing and a voice in his head told him he had been monitored since the age of 14 by a race of beings from a planet behind the sun. It was perhaps on the same night that a caller to the newspaper on the 25th, claimed that he had seen Swanner drive up, in his truck, to a glowing white ball in the woods and enter it. The object then took off, returning 10 minutes later, discharging Swanner who drove away. Swanner remembered nothing of this. Or this. Barry Swanner (37) a 10 hour a day factory hand, living in an isolated area with his wife and two daughters (13, 5), was apparently awoken by a high pitched buzzing, and a voice in his head told him he hand been monitored since 14 by a race of beings from a planet behind the sun. It was perhaps on the same night that a caller to the newspaper on the 25th, claimed that he had seen Swanner drive up, in his truck, to a g lowing white ball in the woods and enter it. The object then took off, returning 10 minutes later, discharging Swanner who drove away. Swanner remembered nothing of this.

Still in the Shores Community, Tennessee on February 9th 1974. David Swanner was now invited by two "men" to ride in a UFO. In a few moments they passed over San Francisco, then the Hawaiian Islands; the round trip took 45 minutes, the purpose of their presence; to warn of possible destruction of the solar system by atomic bombs. Their appearance; 4-5 foot tall, with long, pointed chins, small eyes, ears, and nose, and with tall foreheads. Their lifespan; 125-175 years and they wore white coveralls. The witness was instructed to inform the public. He claims to possess proof, which "cannot now be revealed." Or this. At 6.00 pm Barry Swanner (q.v.) heard a buzzing sound and noticed disruption to television reception. Going outside to investigate, he saw a strange object like " a Dutch wooden shoe", emitting a soft white glow. It was hovering less than 2m above his garden. The body was about 5.5m long, 2.5m high and 2.7m wide, with a glass like translucent cockpit on top, through which he could see the shadowy head and shoulders of two human like beings moving about. The object slowly swivelled and moved away to the east. On its rear end were two red and blue lights, and at each top corner was an insignia which reassembled a tobacco pipe with a mark through the top. Or this. Barry Swanner (q.v.) claimed to have been taken on a UFO ride around San Francisco by two men, 4-5m tall, with long pointed chins, small eyes, ears and nose and high foreheads. They were wearing white, tight fitting, overalls. The beings gave a him kind of physical examination using something like an X ray machine, delivered a warning about nuclear war etc., and claimed to be from Plantoes from a planet "on the other side of the sun" and to lived for 125-175 years, to be 1,500 years ahead of us, use telepathy and etc. Swanner produced some curious pieces of metal as alleged proof of his story.

On March 1st 1974 at 1300hrs in Memphis in Shelby County, Tennessee. John and Carra Williams were sat on their farm front porch when they saw 5 small circular objects descending into a nearby pasture. They appeared to 60cm in diameter with oval tops and flat bottoms. On the ground they looked white, but looked silver when the sun shone on them in the air. One of the cows approached the objects, and when it approached one of them the thing would rise up and then settle down again. Joh ran and got his rifle but never fired it, but at this point the objects took off, one of them circling John and emitting a flash of light, as they did so. The next day the cow that approached the things was found dead. John, who had a weak heart, died a couple of weeks later.

On March 20th 1974 at 1500 in Lewisburg in Marshall County, Tennessee, Becky Ingram, 14, heard "voices" in her head several times since March 9th. On the above date, instead of taking the school bus home, she compulsively walked out onto the center of the school football field and suddenly found herself inside a brightly-lit room—she had seen nothing on the field—as a ramp/door closed behind her. She was confronted by two small Humanoid entities, shorter in height than she was. They had blond, short-cropped hair and were later identified as Alton and Tombo. Becky was instructed to lie on a hospital-like bed where she was examined by a glove-like implement that was passed over her. She was taken for an hour's trip "to Australia," and then returned, feeling, weak and sleepy. For several weeks after this incident she was extremely fatigued and suffered headaches and other physical symptoms. She had two more experiences in the next four months.

This next one sounds very similar to the previous one. On March 20th 1974 in Giles County, Tennessee. A close relative of the reporter Stanley Ingrams was contacted telepathically and went to a football field. He was two thirds of the way down the field, when he suddenly found himself in a craft he had not seen. He heard the door close and saw two little men. He claimed he was taken on a trip to Northern Australia and back by the two entities who gave their names as Alton and Tombo.

On May 5th 1974 at 1900 in Pisgah Ridge (Giles), Tennessee Becky Ingram, driving alone (at 14?) on a country road, heard her nickname called ("Tomboy") and was telepathically directed to a field where she saw a 100-foot, football-shaped UFO on the ground. In an open door, with a ramp to the ground, stood Alton and Tombo, who invited her on board. She greeted them with a handshake and entered, where she saw five or six more UFOnauts seated around a table, eating. She declined an" invitation to join them. They spoke in an incomprehensible tongue. She was given a "tour of the ship, including the engine room below (it was very hot), but she declined the invitation of another ride explaining that her family was expecting her. She noticed this time that Alton and Tombo walked without bending their knees.

On July 4th 1974 at Giles Pisgah Ridge (Giles), Tennessee Becky Ingram was again mentally directed to the site of her May 5th encounter where she was met by Alton and Tombo. They told her to warn her father (Stanley Ingram) that he and David Swanner were being shadowed by MIBs ("Chicoms") I who wanted to get information regarding the propulsion systems on Plantoes' UFOs. (Becky had had a run-in with these the preceding month, which had led to the disclosure of her previous encounters). There is no indication in the available data that Becky was on-board the object for this meeting. It appears to have been her last.

On November 11th 1974 at 1730 at Mount Cross in Campbell County in Tennessee. Billy Joe Lodnar, driving up Mt. Cross for a weekend of hunting, saw a blinking orange cigar-shaped object pass over his pick-up truck and then turn back toward him. (The UFO, or another, had previously been seen by the pilot of a Marine A-4C Skyhawk flying from Beaufort, S.C., who radioed that it was flying just off his wingtip.). Lodnar got out of his truck with his rifle in hand, and saw the object land in a clearing; he now saw that it was lens-shaped with a central dome. He inched his way toward the gully where the object had settled until he was 300 feet away and somewhat above. He saw a door open on the side and a small, stocky Humanoid with a large head and a "skeletal" body emerged, walking down a ramp. Its skin was grey and appeared scaly; the eyes were slit-like. As it walked around near the object, Lodnar trained his gun on it, but did not fire. The being re-entered the

UFO, where another one appeared in the doorway to pull it inside. Then the object took off silently. In a later investigation on site, broken branches and scorch marks were found.

1975

One night in Summer 1975 in East Nashville in Davidson County, Tennessee. Ann Haywood was lying awake in her bed, suffering discomfort from recent surgery, with her husband asleep beside her, when there was a sudden gust of wind, billowing the curtains, and the room turned cold. Looking around she saw figures that looked like a woman and two children come in through the window. The "children" stayed by the dresser, but the "woman" came up to her. She wore a garment with a cape, from which came two hands like pigs feet. She had an almond shaped face, pointed wrap round ears and "rat like" mouth. The figure seemed to speak to her, and suck the breath out of her. This figure continued to haunt her for a number of years and left marks on her body. Poltergeist effects were also noted.

1976

On November 20th 1976 at 1810hrs in Knoxville in Knox County, Tennessee. A strange object was observed at ground level for 30 minutes.

1977

Near Cookeville in Putnam County in Tennessee on January 27th 1977 at 2: 00 p.m. Donald Fender, 49, a self-employed bee farmer of Greeneville, was driving on Route 40 to Madison. He was in his pickup truck and his dog with him. In the vicinity of Cookeville, his dog began to act strangely, and Fender felt "like someone wanted to talk to me." Obeying an impulse, he turned off on a side road. He noticed a long balloon like thing that stretched along one side of the road for a distance of a mile or a mile and a half. White and silky in color and texture, he then saw another one on the other side of the road. Curious, he pulled off and stopped his car. His dog was by then quite agitated. Then suddenly, without any transition, he found himself inside a solid white colored cigar shaped room, or enclosure, approximately 50 feet long. He sensed rather than observed, five Humanoid entities gathered around him. They were small in size and they stared at him. One was to his immediate left. Then they began to question him about a number of things, most of which Fender was unable to remember. They also gave him certain information; they told him they "were emissaries of peace" and that they could enter Earth's atmosphere only at this point, or "window" along the road and that this spot would "become the future home of space travel." They also told him of dire events including major catastrophes that would come about in the near future. He "saw" or was "shown" various scenes, as though he were floating far above them; of areas of major destruction and devastation. These included scenes of green farmlands he identified as being English; these were devoid of any kind of life. After approximately 15 minutes, he suddenly found himself back in his truck, with no idea of how he got there. Along the roadside there was nothing unusual to be seen. His dog was behaving normally once more. He felt very strange and disturbed by the experience. Arriving at Madison about an hour later than he expected, he was unable to account for the lost time. There was a good deal about the experience that he was unable to remember. He was so upset about the experience that within the week he drove to Washington DC, to make the incident known officially. He went to the Department of Defense where, he said he spoke to Defense Secretary Brown himself. His story was met with little enthusiasm. There is more to the story that he is unwilling to divulge over the telephone to the investigators.

On May 17th 1977 in Memphis in Shelby County, Tennessee. Five police officers observed a huge triangular object, 50-70m wide and as long as an American football pitch, hovering over the high tension wires. It was surrounded by a white glow and had red, yellow and green lights. After hovering the thing shot away noiselessly at terrific speed.

In August 1977 at 2300hrs in Del City in Oklahoma County, Oklahoma. Judi Moudy (15) and two friends were sitting out talking in her front yard when their attention was drawn to erratically moving lights in the north. The lights then approached at speed and then hovered over the field across the street. As it did so the animal noises ceased. The thing was cigar shaped with lights on its top, bottom and centre, the latter of which gave the impression of being portholes. It moved to the far end of the field and descended. The girls ran towards it, at which it projected beams of bright blue light, which seemed to separate out into segments. When they reached the chain fence, they rose over it. The girls then became very tired and noticing the time as now 0030hrs.. There then appeared to be a period of missing time, as when the girls got in, they found themselves with dirt on their arms and legs and saw that it was 0300. When they awoke the next morning the two friends were covered in a rash and Judi had a severe headache. The next day they found a triangular area of burnt crop in the alfalfa field.

1978

On August 1st 1978 in Clarksville in Montgomery County in Tennessee at 10:00 PM. A six-month-pregnant woman had been taking a nap when she woke up to see a large craft hovering outside the upstairs window, over a nearby wood shack. Her husband saw the object too. She fainted but then heard a voice in a thick Middle Eastern accent that told her to open her eyes. When she did eyes she was confronted by a tall creature resembling an insect, thin and white in color, wearing a dark outfit. It communicated with her by using telepathy. There were several other similar creatures wearing jumpsuits standing in the room. Their heads were large and rounded. The witness conducted a mental conversation with the leader, and asked it several questions about its origin. The witness suddenly panicked and screamed and began to faint, and some of the creatures began backing away. But moments later a long needle was painfully inserted into her belly. She then passed out, and awoke later to see the taller creature talking to the others. At one point the witness claimed she saw several helicopters flying around the hovering craft.

At 2.30 am on September 15th 1978 at Delano in Polk County in Tennessee a 31-year old woman was lying in bed awake when she suddenly felt compelled to look outside. Over a nearby field she could see a vaguely outlined long shape that was red and pink in color. It was completely silent. She also saw two normal men of average height dressed in white suits standing about 100 yards from the window. They walked towards the house but then turned back. Or this. Sandra Hooper (31), living with her uncle on Route 1, was unable to sleep. She went to the kitchen to get a glass of water when something peculiar made her look outside. As she looked through the kitchen window she saw the bright moon and a long, pink vaguely outlined object somewhat less than the angular diameter of the moon. Her attention was then drawn to normal looking human forms in white and suits and with flashlights in the field behind her house. They came closer, but as she turned to wake her uncle, the men turned back, the red pink object landed at speed and the men just disappeared. The object then climbed away fast to the west.

1979

In February 1979 in the early hours in Smyrna in Rutherford County, Tennessee. An employee of a diner, clearing up after his late shift, had taken a brake, looking out over a lake, when he saw a huge oval or spherical object moving off down the lake. The witness flashed a light at the thing, which approached to within 50m. At this point he stopped flashing and thought of getting his gun to shoot at it, at which the thing seemed to jump back about 10m, turn in the air and disappear. The witness had the impression there was some missing time.

1988

In Tennessee in August 1988 at night. The witness woke up in her bedroom and was confronted by two short gray beings. She was paralyzed but felt calmed by staring at their large hypnotic eyes. She was floated through the house and outside towards a large hovering silvery disc with revolving red, green, and yellow lights. She attempted to touch the object but one of the gray beings prevented her from doing so, telling her that it would be dangerous. An opening on the craft appeared and a tall blond handsome young man came out wearing a tan jumpsuit. The witness was then somehow teleported inside the object. She was placed in a black chair where the blond man "scanned" her visually, apparently inducing a sensation of orgasm. The craft apparently began to move and through an oval shaped opening the witness saw what appeared to be stars. Four short gray beings then entered the room and gave the blond man a case. The blond man removed a glowing green sphere from the case and floated the witness to a nearby table, and then he placed the sphere on the witness stomach and moved it around in a circular fashion. She was told that she had been altered a little (genetically?) to fulfill a special purpose in the future.

1991

At 1.00 am on September 20th 1991 near Etowah in McMinn County in Tennessee the witness was traveling on Interstate 75 when she and others in the vehicle looked towards the East and saw an oval shaped transparent object fly straight up from the ground. After going up the object continued to pace their vehicle as it flew North alongside I-75. At one point, the object scripted an "L" with a smoke tail behind it. When the object was at its closest, about 100 yards away, the witnesses could see several figures inside it, moving their arms and hands very rapidly. The object changed directions at times, and turned abruptly and glowed. They lost sight of it North of Chattanooga. Two elderly witnesses in the car experienced severe health problems soon after the sighting and died within a year and a half. It is not known if there was any connection to the sighting and their health difficulties.

1993

In Tennessee, exact location not given on the night of October 2nd 1993. The witness woke up in a downstairs guest room accompanied by a young male Humanoid wearing an oversized red plaid shirt, faded jeans, and black leathery boots. The witness was alert and in control as the Humanoid asked several questions. While she spoke the witness noticed a silvery disc-shaped object hovering outside. The Humanoid suddenly embraced her and she became partially paralyzed. He then proceeded to have sexual intercourse with her on the floor. She felt faint and then passed out. Sometimes they get weirder and weirder and they don't exactly have a non-weird base to begin with.

1994

In Tennessee (exact location not given) on January 8th 1994 one late night. The witness remembers waking up on board a craft accompanied by a short gray Humanoid with large black eyes. The being used some type of device that he inserted in her ear apparently in order to locate and activate an "implant". The witness then asked the Humanoid several questions, which were answered. Moment's later four more gray Humanoids entered and led her inside a large hangar where she saw what appeared to be numerous military personnel. She was then rendered unconscious and later found herself back in her bed.

Texas

1873

On 5th July 1873, a man living about five miles from Bonham in Fannin County, Texas, saw something like an enormous serpent floating over his farm. Had the Ratibor and Rybnik, Ukraine, aerial red object then flown over North America to release the serpent of Hell itself? Later that same morning 5th July 1873 as the man witnessed the enormous aerial serpent, workers in a cotton field near Bonham were terrified by a shiny serpentine object that swooped down out of the sky again and again. This scared the horses so much that one team threw their driver and he was crushed under the careening wagon wheels. Had the Bonham aerial serpent arrived from near Mars or only a spot that seemed near to the patch of the sky that Mars was occupying at the time? This was the same time as aerial sightings in Fort Scott in Kansas that day as well as Fort Riley.

1878

On 24th January 1878, at Denison in Grayson County, Texas, Mr. John Martin saw a dark disc-shaped object high in the sky and flying at a wonderful speed. Mr. Martin said that it looked like a saucer and had started off looking the size of an orange and had grown. Mr. Martin watched the "Flying Saucer", his words, hovering in the one spot in the northern sky for several minutes before it went away. Objects can hover like Flying Saucers in the sky? Amazing how the term saucer would reappear several times before the official adoption of the term in 1947 after the Arnold sighting. To some researchers this was the first Flying Saucer sighting but as you have seen it had been beaten to the punch many times already.

1891

On 18th June 1891 in Dublin in Erath County in Texas the residents of the town were startled by a bright, oblong object in the sky only three hundred feet above them that Saturday afternoon. There was a sound like a bomb going off and they saw the object suddenly disintegrate hurling debris and metal over the town. This was near the Wasson and Miller Flour Mill and Cotton Gin. The bright light from it was dazzling. The following morning the weeds, grass, bushes and vegetation over many yards were burnt to a crisp in the area where the object apparently fell. There were also peculiar stones found there and pieces of metal that had a dull leaden color that resembled volcanic lava. It was reported that small fragments of manuscript and scrap in a foreign language were found as well. Initially the object, resembling a burning cotton bale, was seen hovering over the mill. Which parts of this report are real and which aren't? Then again none of these reports are. Or are they?

1897

In 1897 the Great Airship Flap hit Texas!

Shortly before 15th April 1897 several residents of Denton in Denton County in Texas saw a cigar-shaped airship with a light that was moving slowly at first and then accelerated at a terrific rate. There were windows reported on the sides.

Also on 15th April 1897 there was a report from Corsicana in Navarro County in Texas of a bright light a long distance from the earth and moving at a rather fast speed across the firmament.

Also on 15th April 1897 in the evening Mr. Brown, the City Marshall of Farmersville, said that when the airship passed over him at about two hundred feet, he could see in it two men and something resembling a large Newfoundland dog. He heard the occupants talk but could not understand the language.
And April 15th continued.

Near Cisco in Eastland County in Texas on the night of April 15th 1897 a man came upon a landed airship approximately 200 feet long and crewmen in the process of repairing a searchlight. The witness was told that the craft was bound for Cuba with a load of dynamite. Here is another version. Telegraph repairman Patrick C Byrnes was cycling towards Cisco when his attention was caught by a light in a deserted area some distance from the railway track at the Delmar siding. He went to investigate and found a cigar shaped aerial machine 60m long, 15m wide at the widest, with steel shells at either end. Its crew were making repairs to its searchlight and they explained to Patrick the workings of their craft, and of their intention to go and bomb the Spanish out of Cuba.

Still 15th April 1897 and in Texas cigar shaped aircraft were seen in the sky. They had flashing lights on them as well as blinding searchlights with which they swept the ground. They were often moving in an erratic fashion and seemed intelligently controlled and could travel against the wind. They still flew against the wind. They still had flashing lights on them. They still had searchlights but what were they searching for? Was it the same six individuals again as in the sighting involving repairs the day before?

Over Benton in Atascosa County in Texas a gigantic cigar shape cruised through the sky and across the face of the Moon that same night 15th April 1897. It was reported as a magnificent sight by the many witnesses and went to the southeast. From Texas to Tennessee and on to Kentucky the airships flew and even up to the Great Lakes region especially Illinois.

On April 15th 1897 at night in Garland in Dallas County, Texas. Several people including J N Floyd, agent N S Newland and Mr Cady saw an airship moving in a southerly direction at surprising velocity, passing a few kilometres west of Garland. Floyd got a good look at the machine and saw an occupant operating the machinery. Newland saw the object as cigar shaped with two sets of wings on either side and one wing at the rear. The witnesses were considered reliable.

On April 15th 1897 at night in Hillsboro in Hill County, Texas. A lawyer, J Spencer Bounds, was riding his buggy back from sealing a will when both he and his horse were starting by a brilliant flash overhead. As he looked, the light revolved around and he saw that it was a searchlight on a huge dark cigar shaped object flying at 300m altitude. The light came from something like the hull of a ship, which was attached underneath the cigar. The searchlight was then shut off, and a number of incandescent lights flashed around the lower edge of the thing, which was moving very slowly southwards. These lights went out and the object appeared to land on a hill 5km from Aquilla. About an hour later when the witness was within 1.5km of Hillsboro he saw the object take off rapidly and head towards Dallas at 160kph, sending out occasional brilliant sparks. The lawyer thought he had seen something from the devil.

On April 16th 1897 at 1440hrs near Hawkins Tank near Hawkins in Wood County, Texas. J. E. "Truthful" Scully was conductor on the Big Sandy-Hawkins train when, as they passed a clearing between Hawkins Tank and Hawkins, he obtained a brief glimpse of a landed object with wings in a clearing about 100m back from the track. Beside it was a tall thin man, who appeared to be making repairs with a hammer and chisel. The object's bow was pointed towards the track. Scully said that Leroy Task, the superintendent of the railroad, had also seen the object.

On April 16th 1897 at 2030hrs in Rhome in Wise County, Texas. Numerous people, including H A and BT Hambright, A J Jones, Nute Rivers and Elmer Helm saw an object like a small passenger coach with a white searchlight at the front and five illuminated windows on the side. It was travelling to the west at about 250kph at very low altitude.

On April 16th 1897 at 2100hrs in Farmersville in collin County, Texas. A dim light, the apparent size of a 50 cent piece of the period, was seen in the southwest. It was approaching at 100 kph or more, and some inhabitants thought that it was a cloudless tornado, others a large meteor. Soon it was hovering over the city. City Marshall Brown, who was making his rounds in the western part of the city, saw it pass over at 60m altitude. Inside he could see two men and a creature resembling a large Newfoundland dog. The men appeared to be conversing in a foreign language, which Brown thought was Spanish.

On April 16th 1897 at 2145hrs in Mansfield in Tarrant County, Texas. A number of people, including Captain J H Wright, C. P Witherspoon, and W H Howard, saw a cigar shaped object, the size of a box car, with wings on either side come over at 150m, descend to 100m and then take off at high speed to the south east. A sort of headlight came from its front, there were green lights along its sides and a red one at its rear.

On April 16th 1897 at night in Greenville in Hunt County in Texas. Mr. C. G. Williams was startled by the light of an aircraft landing nearby. There men came out, two of whom began to work on the rigging. The third, after asking him to keep it secret, told him they were inventors from a small town in in New York who were engaged in perfecting their craft. Electricity was used to get off the ground and wind power to turn the ship's large propeller. That man said that if Williams would mail some letters for him, he would come back and take him on a ride to South America. Here is another version. At 2350hrs Newspaper correspondent C G Williams was walking across a field when he was dazzled and frightened by a brilliant light. He tried to run away but his legs would not move. The lights then went out and he saw, in the moonlight, an immense cigar shaped vessel on the ground in front of him. Three men emerged from it, two to work on repairs, while the third called to Williams and asked him to post some letters. Williams began to write down what was happening, but the airman told him not to give away the secret and explained how they sailed from New York State. Williams was able to observe the object in more detail. It was cigar shaped, about 10m long, with large wings or fans on either side. On the front was a large wheel, like a steamboat paddle, made of some light material. At the rear was a huge fan like tail about 15m long. The aviator explained that the front wheel was turned by the wind to produce electricity. Williams promised not to give them away and they said that they would return and take him on a trip to South America. The men then re-entered the machine, which took off gracefully to the north, emitting a flash of light and a singing noise.

17th April 1897 and we are over Childress in Childress County in Texas where an airship was seen in the sky travelling West. Now it is boring again.

That same day 17th April 1897 over Dallas in Dallas County in Texas a cigar shaped airship was seen in the sky that had flashing lights on it as well as a blinding searchlight with which it swept the ground. The craft appeared intelligently controlled and travelled against the wind. It looked like a great cigar with wings and went to the southeast. There were from two to five lights on it. Ad nauseum. Dallas is only fifty miles from Greenville.

Also on April 17th 1897 at 0100hrs near Dallas in Texas. W. H. Patterson was looking for the airship along with John Phillips, when he observed an aerial object moving in the direction of Dallas at 120m altitude. It seemed to be piloted by a woman operating some machinery resembling a sewing machine. When the sails on the object were at a certain angle, a spotlight shone on the witnesses, who fled from the hotel where they had been observing it. Patterson believed that the object was from the devil.

Also on April 17th 1897 in Cleburne in Johnson County in Texas a man who claimed that "he had not touched a drop of anything except water during the evening saw an airship speed by just above the tops of the houses with a passenger in it. The passenger gave him the go-ahead sign that brakemen give on the railroad. As he was coming home from uptown, Mr J F Wade saw an aerial object moving along at moderate speed, just above the rooftops. It was so low the Wade could see a passenger in the thing, who gestured at him. It was independently seen by Mr G M Duncan, who saw two white lights in the front and a green light in the rear.

Also on or before April 17th 1897 two unnamed farmers near Abbott in Hill County in Texas saw a man and six boys descending from the sky. "they drifted down as gracefully as birds alighting until within a few feet off the ground, about fifty yards away. They remained stationary a few seconds and then re-ascended into the heavens. The day was perfectly clear, not a cloud in sight anywhere.

On April 17th 1897 in Waxachie in Ellis County in Texas Judge Love and Mr. Beatty found in the woods "a queer-looking machine" and 5 peculiarly dressed men. One of these, who spoke fairly good English told them that the airship came from regions in the North Pole….contrary to popular belief, there is a large body of land beyond the Polar seas. He said his people were descendants of the ten Lost Tribes of Israel who had learned English from Polar explorers. There were said to be twenty of these airships afloat, all of which were planning to show up in mid-June at the Tennessee Centennial Exposition at Nashville. It is amazing how many UFOs, and airship, reports include predictions that never come true. Here is another version. At 3.45 pm Judge Love and his friend Mr Beatty were fishing in Chambers Creek when, as they moved off for a better spot, Beatty in front, they encountered a peculiar looking machine on the ground near a ravine. By the thing were nine oddly dressed men lounging around, smoking pipes. One of them invited the pair to come over and inspect the object. He spoke fairly good English. The object was 9.5m long, 4m wide. It was cigar shaped, with three pairs of ribbed wings, which the crew explained were designed to catch the air, and was under the control of a member of the crew. They claimed to be the descendants of the lost tribes of Israel living in a region of the North Pole, and to have been taught their use of English by various polar explorers who had become lost there. They explained their use of electricity and development of airships as they had neither coal nor timber and said that they were among a party of airships which would land at the Nashville Centenary Exposition. The airship crew then shook the duo's hands and the airship took off towards Waco.

At night on April 17th 1897 near Stephenville in Erath County in Texas Mr. C. L. McIllhaney, a prominent farmer reported that the airship had alighted on his farm three miles from town and was making repairs there. He piloted a large number of prominent citizens including the mayor out to see it. It consists of a cigar-shaped body about sixty feet in length with two immense airplanes: the motive power is an immense wheel at each end which derives its power from storage batteries. The crew consisted of two men who gave their names as S. E. Tillman and A.E. Dolbear. They are making an experimental trip to comply with a contract with certain capitalists of New York who are backing them. They rapidly made the necessary repairs and bidding adieu to the astonished crowd, boarded the ship which rose gently into the air and sailed off. Is this all part of the wonderful world of illusion where the phenomena meets and slightly exceeds the cultural expectations of the witnesses?

On April 15th or 17th 1897 at 2200hrs in Beaumont in Jefferson County, Texas. Rabbi A Levy who farmed 3km from Beaumont heard that an airship had landed on a nearby farm. He went to investigate and encountered an object about 50m long, with wings 30m long on either side. The whole thing appeared to be made of some light material. He met one of the crew who had gone to a farmer's house top get water. This man told Levy that the machine ran by electricity and though he told Levy who built it and where, Levy could not remember either of these.

On April 18th 1897 at 0300hrs in Dallas in Dallas County, Texas. L G Smith the steward at the Hermitage Hospital was on the upper veranda looking south when his attention was caught by a huge shadow. This was projected by a rectangular object descending from the east. This object then seemed to rest on the spire of the Federal Building. Through windows in the craft Smith could see cabins and passengers, including women dressed in Easter costumes. Two men came out of the object, one descended to the steeple and the other appeared to be oiling the wings. Before Smith could wake his wife, the object had departed.

Also on April 18th 1897 at 1400hrs in Dallas, Texas. William Noll Jnr, B O Marshall and A Nussbaumer were hunting about 14.5km west of Dallas when they saw an airship on the ground.

On April 18th 1897 in Caldwell in Burleson County, Texas. An aerial machine landed on the Brazos River bottom near Caldwell to take on water and two of the crew kidnapped an African-American man who had been out working, allegedly as a punishment for working on Sunday.

On April 18th 1897 at 2130hrs in Lovelady in Houston County, Texas. Book keeper J H Johnson saw an object 45-60m long, with a green light pass overhead, about 75m above the trees. In a conical undersection he could see what like a man moving about.

On April 18th 1897 at night in Fort Worth in Tarrant County, Texas. L E James saw an aerial object land in the city park and a being about 2.2m talk get out, fasten some ropes to the side of the thing, and then re-enter it. The object then took off into the night.

At 2.00 am on the morning of 19th April 1897, a man in El Paso, El Paso County, Texas, saw a cigar-shaped craft with portholes along each side. Light emanated from the openings and there were searchlights on each end of the craft. Huge wings protruded from each side. Voices were heard coming from it as it approached from the East and passed overhead at five hundred feet. El Paso and Aurora are around 531 miles apart.

At 6.00 am on the morning of 19th April 1897, some sources say 17th April, a most unusual event is reported as having occurred at Aurora in Dallas County in Texas. Initially an airship was seen sailing over the town square, travelling at ten to twelve miles per hour and dropping in altitude. The craft was travelling due North and continued sailing over the public square. Above the North part of the town the airship suddenly collided with Judge Proctor's windmill and went to pieces with a terrific loud explosion that scattered debris over many acres of ground. The windmill, a water tank and the Judge's flower garden were wrecked. The disfigured remains of the pilot were found and they were regarded as being not of this World. Mr. T. J. Weems, the U. S. Signal Service Officer and an authority on astronomy gave the opinion that the pilot was an inhabitant of Mars. Papers in unknown writing were also found on the pilot's person. The fragments of the ship resembled a mixture of aluminum and silver. The pilot was buried on 20th April, the following day, in the local cemetery and the story was published in the "Fort Worth Register" and the "Dallas Times Herald". The grave of the airship pilot was visible for many years in the cemetery. The headstone was of crude rock and half the marker was broken off and missing. On the remaining half was an etched design that resembled a large V lying on its side. Inside the Vee were three small circles. It resembled one end of an airship or a Flying Saucer to some observers. Even the reported death of an alien along with a grave. This incidentally was the sixth airship crash reported in the Nineteenth Century, though the first reported fatality where a body was found.

Also on 19th April 1897 an airship was seen flying over the town of Farmersville in Collin County in Texas. Loud singing was also heard coming from it. Singing? We had already had singing reported from an airship over Sacramento, California, in 1896. The sound of Angels singing? Or Devils?

Still 19th April 1897 and Jim Nelson is a lone farmer in a field outside Atlanta in Cass County in Texas. Jim was badly frightened by an airship that hovered above him while slowly descending. The craft seemed to be watching him and his hair stood on end with fright. Anything is possible.

At 23.00 on April 19th 1897 near Beaumont in Jefferson County in Texas J. B. Ligon and his son went to investigate lights in a nearby pasture and found four men standing around a large dark object. One of them asked him for two buckets of water. Another, giving his name as Wilson, told Ligon that they had taken a trip out on the gulf and were now returning to the quiet Iowa town where the airship and four others like it had been constructed. According to Wilson, the craft was powered by electricity. It was 140 feet long with two huge wings on each side and propellers at its bow and stern. It was made of steel. Another version? J. R. Ligon, the local agent of the Magnolia Brewery in Houston and his son Charley, were unhitching their horses after driving home when they observed lights in the Johnson pasture a few hundred metres distant. They encountered four men around a large dark object. The men came to the Ligon house to take on water. One of these men claimed his name was Wilson and that the object was one of five airships built in Iowa. Ligon Snr returned to the object with the men and saw that the craft was 42m by 6m, propelled by huge wings, two on either side and steered by propellers bow and stern. The occupants declared that the object was made of steel and described its workings to Ligon.

On April 19th 1897 at 2330hrs in Belton in Bell County, Texas. A crowd of people saw an aerial object coming from the southwest at high speed, dipping so low that it narrowly missed the show tent in front of Peay's Hotel, and then rising up again. About 10 people could be seen on board and they spoke as it came close, but its speed was too great for any words to be made out. It was impossible to judge the dimensions of the thing.

On April 20th 1897 at 0400hrs in Mineral Wells in Palp Pinto and Parker Counties, Texas. A cigar shaped object 25m long, with paddle wheels on the ends and sides landed on East Mountain and several local inhabitants spoke with the crew who said they were planning to fly from New York to Liverpool but were having trouble steering their airship.

At 2200 on April 20th 1897 in Uvalde in Uvalde County in Texas. Sheriff H. W. Baylor, investigating lights and sounds behind his house, came upon a landed airship and three men, asking for water. One of the men, giving his name as Wilson, from Goshen, N. Y. inquired after C.C. Akers, a former sheriff whom Baylon knew well. Baylor was asked to keep the visit a secret: then its great wings and fans were set in motion and it sped away northward. The County clerk also saw it depart. A week later, 27th April, the Galveston Daily News, printed a letter from C. C. Akers, who confirmed that he had in fact, in 1877, had known a Wison from New York, who was working on aerial navigation. Akers also vouched for Sheriff Baylor's reliability.

At 11.00 pm on Tuesday 22nd April 1897 at Rockland in Rockland County in Texas Mr. J. Barclay, a farmer, heard his dog barking. There was also a whining noise and on investigation Mr. Barclay saw an oblong body with various side attachments and a brilliant light five yards off the ground and descending to pasture. The lights went out and the witness met an individual who told him that he could put down his gun and no harm would befall him. The individual who called himself Mr. Smith asked for various items and gave Mr. Barclay a ten dollar note whilst also warning him not to get too close to the machine. The hominoid wanted lubricating oils, bluestone and cold chisels. Mr. Barclay could not get the bluestone and offered the money back to the individual which the individual refused, again warning Mr. Barclay not to get too close to the machine. On leaving the hominoid promised to return, stating that he was going to Greece the day after tomorrow. The whirring noise started again and the airship vanished like a shot out of a gun. Now we are going to Greece. Ten days before it was Cuba. Another version? John H Barclay, who lived in the outskirts of Rockland, had just gone to bed when he heard his dog barking furiously and a whining noise. He went to the door to investigate and saw an oblong object with wings and side attachments of various shapes and sizes and carrying lights. When first seen the thing was stationary 5m from the ground. It circled a few times and gradually descended into a pasture adjacent to the house. John took his rifle and went out. When the craft touched down, the lights went out, but as John approached the night was light enough for him to see, after he had gone 30m, a man standing by the object. The stranger asked him to put his gun down. He said his name was Smith and asked for lubricating oil, chisels and some bluestones. He further said that the crew could not let the Rocklanders approach their airship, and on enquiries said they came from "anywhere", but would be in Greece the day after next. The object made a whirring sound and shot off.

At At 11.30 pm on 22nd April 1897 Mr. Frank Nichols was in a field on his farm outside of Josserand in Trinity County in Texas. Suddenly he heard a whirring sound in a cornfield and saw a thing with many flashing lights there. There were beings there who asked Mr. Nichols if they could draw water from the well. Mr. Nichols communicated with six of the eight beings and was shown complicated machinery and was told that the airships were being manufactured in Iowa and would soon be everyday items. Their motive power was condensed electricity and there were only a few technical hitches in the road. And now they all want water, incidentally one of the rarest compounds in the Universe but extremely abundant on Earth. We would meet several of the water hunters later as well. Details sometimes change but is seems that the themes do not.

On April 22-23 1897 in the early hours in Conroe in Montgomery County in Texas four men, including proprietor G. L. Witherspoon, were playing dominoes in the hotel restaurant of Conroe when three strangers walked in and said they had flown in their airship from San Francisco en route to Cuba and had landed not far away. Witherspoon and his friends declined an offer to examine the ship. About an hour later, after the visitors had left a brilliantly lighted airship passed over Conroe. Restaurant proprietor G L Witherspoon and three of his customers were playing dominoes when three strangers entered. They claimed to be the crew of an airship, which had landed not far out of town. They said the ship had come from San Francisco and was bound for Cuba, and offered to show the witnesses around their craft. The witnesses declined, suspecting a joke, but about an hour later a brilliant aerial object passed over the town.

On April 23rd 1897 in Kountze in Hardin County in Texas two responsible men observed an airship which had descended for repairs: the occupants gave their names as Wilson and Jackson. This is the third mention of Wilson in only a few days. Did Wilson exist?

Beaumont is 344 miles east of Uvalde which is 336 miles from Uvalde. The odd thing is that Kountze is only 20 miles north of Beaumont. Was Mr. Wilson taking the long way from Beaumont to Kountze?

On April 23rd 1897 at 0930hrs in Fort Worth in Tarrant County, Texas. While riding a streetcar past the city park, Woodford Brooks, the Secretary and Treasurer of the Polytechnic Street Railway saw an aerial object in the park by the river. He and the car's motorman, Mr Edwards went to investigate. The y were approached by a man who gave his name as Randall and said he was the captain of the airship, which was propelled by electricity and was heading for Mexico City.

On April 23rd 1897 at 2030hrs in Deadwood in Panola County, Texas. Farmer H C Lagrone heard his horses snorting and bucking, and, on investigating, saw a bright white light circling the nearby fields, eventually landing in one of them. He approached and came across five men, three of whom talked with him, while the other two went for water, using rubber bags. The trio said that theirs was one of five airships, which had been constructed in Illinois and had recently landed at Beaumont and were now heading for St Louis. They refused to say how it worked, as it had not yet been patented. Lagrone noticed that the crew were well supplied with food beer, champagne and a supply of classical instruments.

On April 24th 1897 at 2055hrs in La Coste in Medina County, Texas. James J Jones and many other townsfolk saw a strange object 12m long, shaped like "an acute angle", and apparently made of canvas, flashing a light. Through a telescope Jones saw two men on board.

On April 24th 1897 at night in Fort Duncan in Maverick County, Texas. Alerted by local residents, sheriff R W Dowe investigated and found an aerial machine on the ground on the banks of the Rio Grande outside Duncan. There they found the object and a crew of three, who claimed to be searching for a buffalo herd. They offered to give Dowe a ride but he declined.

If as I propose the details are all illusions or camouflage then it actually does not matter how absurd the details are. On 26th April 1897, a group of churchgoers at Merkel in Taylor County in Texas saw a most unusual sight. They noticed a heavy object being dragged along by a rope that was literally hanging from the sky. They followed the rope until it trapped itself in the railroad line and looking up saw the dim shape of an airship. Light was coming from the windows and there was one bright light in front like a locomotive. After ten minutes a man was seen descending the rope. The man was wearing a light blue sailor suit and he stopped when he saw the group of people at the end of the rope. At this moment he cut the rope below him and the airship sailed off to the northeast. The group of witnesses took the strange object which resembled an anchor to the local blacksmiths shop where it was put on exhibition. Hundreds of people saw the odd object. This is anchor number three reported in North America. There is too much mixing of technologies here from falling stones to turbines to giant flaps. It does not seem true and yet it is attested to in many eye-witness reports. Were the phenomena revealing themselves according to assumptions of the technology of the time so as to hopefully blend in or not to be ridiculed, in any way, so to be quickly forgotten or hopefully not noticed at all? Are we looking at presumptions of what a technology could be instead of perceptions of what a technology was? We have an inference instead of an observation? Or were they deliberately looking absurd so as to consistently discredit any witnesses? After all extremely minute electronic charges in the human brain can induce hallucinatory states, both auditory as well as visual, similar to schizophrenia so why not similar results from large electronic charges? Are these natural or artificially produced though? Are we looking at normal though bizarre processes that may be induced by random electronic fields, say during earthquakes or by falls of apparently invisible electromagnetic matter such as sprites or other newly discovered phenomena or are we looking at witness misinterpretations of energy forms produced at these times? Is it all of the above? Or something else again?

Also on 26th April 1897 a lawyer was surprised to see a lighted object fly over between Aquila and Hillsboro in Hill County. His horse was scared and nearly toppled over the carriage. When the main light was turned off a number of smaller lights became visible on the underside of the dark object which supported an elongated canopy. It went down towards the hill to the South five kilometers from Aquila. When the witness was on his way back one hour later he saw the same object rising. It reached the altitude of the cloud ceiling and flew to the northeast at a fantastic speed with periodic flashes of light.

On April 26th 1897 at night in Spofford in Kinney County, Texas. While sitting on the boxcar brake of a speeding train, brakesman Harry Babcock was struck on the shoulder with great force. He also heard a humming sound, and looking around saw an aerial object with white wings speeding away to the west.

About April 28th 1897 at 20.30 in Deadwood in Panola County in Texas. Hearing his horses stampeding, H. C. Lagrone went out and saw a a bright white light illuminating the area, then landing. When he went to the spot he found five men, two of whom went to fill rubber bags with water. The others informed him that the airship, one of five flying around the country, had been built in Illinois and was not yet patented. They were planning to produce them in St Louis. There were well supplied with edibles of all sorts, had a good supply of beer and champagne and also a full supply of musical instruments. As you do. Then it went quiet for nearly two months.

On 16th June 1897 in the sky above Marshall in Harrison County, Texas, a flying cigar with great wings was seen. The airship had two searchlights and was flying southeast. After a short rest the craft were suddenly back over Texas.

16th June 1897 was shaping up to be a memorable day. At Ennis in Ellis County in Texas the same flying cigar with great wings was seen in the sky as had been seen at Marshall, Texas, the same day. This too had a pair of searchlights and was travelling southeast. All over Texas they reappeared.

The same craft that had been seen in Harrison County was seen heading in the same direction over Beaumont in Jefferson County, Texas, as well as Fort Worth in Tarrant County also in Texas on 16th June 1897. Were they looking for their compadre that had met its end over Aurora? That it had taken from 19th April that year, to get a message to the rescuers and it then took them less than two months to get here. If we are even allowing for technology equivalent to ours then we are looking at a base on the back of the Moon or in a similar orbit. It takes several years to even get to Mars, our closest neighbor. These craft were suddenly all over Texas and nowhere else. They appeared to be looking for something. They had come from two months away. Not on Earth but not anywhere else that we presently know of. The route the craft took was to first visit Fort Worth, remember that it is recorded as travelling southeast, passed to the northeast of Ennis and then the southeast of

Marshall and was last seen heading for the Gulf of Mexico southwest of Beaumont. It passed between Ennis and Marshall indicating that it was not travelling too high but not too low either as these two towns are approximately 230 kilometers apart indicating that the craft or whatever it was travelling at an average middle distance from each of 115 kilometers and was still visible.

On 20th August 1897 at Longview in Gregg County in Texas a bright light the size of Venus appeared and was seen moving to the northwest. The light disappeared and then appeared again. All the while it was emitting flames of a steel color. Meteors do not return nor do they emit steel-like colored flames.

1898

On October 4th 1898 at 2110hrs in Sherman in Grayson County, Texas. E. W. Campbell and his 12 year old son George were riding 4km north of town along the "Eighty Foot Road" when the area was illuminated. A luminous fiery sphere 3m diameter came down to within about 1m of the ground hovered for a time and then took off at speed. It emitted a buzzing sound and a dazzling like, but the pair felt no heat from it.

1899

On 2nd March 1899, a luminous disc was seen in the sky over El Paso in El Paso County in Texas. The disc hovered over the town from 10.00 am to 4.00 pm! What was so fascinating about El Paso? A luminous disc seen in the sky. How unusual! This is our ninth luminous disc at least recorded out of fifteen aerial disc-shaped objects so far.

1909

On 29th May 1909 a meteorite dropped through a house in Shephard in San Jacinto County in Texas.

In Mart in Limestone and McLennan Counties in Texas on August 7th 1909. Early this morning while splitting wood, City Judge Davis saw an airship slowly passing over the city in a southwesterly direction. He describes it as being about 45 feet long and 15 feet in width, and containing two or three passengers. It is thought to be Mattry's ship from Chicago, en route to Marlin. Dallas Morning News (Texas), August 8, 1909.

1910

In July 1910, at 9.00 pm Mrs. Elizabeth Hamilton of Jewett in Leon County in Texas saw a bright red object travelling from southeast to northeast and over the horizon in fifteen minutes. There were five other witnesses as well. It was too slow for a meteor. It was now bright red aerial objects over Texas.

1913

On 8th April 1913 at Fort Worth in Tarrant County in Texas a circular object up in the sky was seen keeping stationary whilst the cloud cover kept moving relative to it. It was described as a dark speck that kept growing and getting bigger and bigger and then suddenly retreating and vanishing. The object never came below the clouds and yet it must have been a massive size to cast such a shadow onto the clouds moving beneath it. There were many witnesses and there was even a peculiar moving shadow along the ground at the same time.

1914

2.5 miles West of Farmersville in Collin County in Texas on 15th May 1914. At 10:00 a.m. Silbie J. Latham, then 13 or 14, had gone to the fields with his two older brothers Sid and Clyde. Two dogs, Bob and Fox, accompanied them. They were "chopping cotton" when they heard the two dogs start up a "deathly howl." The three boys walked about 75 feet to a fencerow where the dogs had something cornered. Clyde got there first and turned to the other two and said, "Boys, there's something in there. It must be something kinda bad." Then he said, "Boys, it's a little man!" Silbie looked and saw a little man some 18 inches high, just standing still, staring toward the North. He was green all over and either naked or with a frogman's type outfit on, green in color. There was a hat with a wide brim on the back of his head, but it was all of one piece with the rest of the body. He said nothing and did not even acknowledge the dogs, by now worked up to a frenzy. Right after the three boys arrived, the dogs finally attacked the being, killing it. They told their folks but no one believed them. They went back to the site several times that day, but after that they never returned. Mexican goblins in this day and age?

1918

In early March 1918 numerous soldiers saw a one hundred foot long cigar shaped airship one evening over Rich Field in Waco in McLennan County in Texas. It was one hundred to one hundred and fifty feet long and cigar-shaped and they saw it after leaving the mess hall. It came directly overhead and was no more than five hundred feet above them so they got an excellent view of it. It had no motors or rigging and was noiseless. It was a rose or sort of flame color. There were no windows. The sighting left the witnesses with the weirdest feeling of their lives and they sat in their tent puzzling over it for some time.

1920

In 1920 at 0300hrs in Freeport in Brazoria County, Texas. Fisherman C B Alves was in the Gulf Coast 80km north of Freeport when he saw four luminous disks, like plates rim to rim, 8m in diameter 3m thick, come within 100m of his boat.

1930

In Texas in 1930 around 10:00 a.m. A young woman was driving in an isolated hilly area, when she remembers turning a curve in the road and suddenly driving up to and under the side of a huge "thing" sitting by the road. She was within a few steps of it; almost under one side of it when she stopped the car. It was sort of a shiny gunmetal color; round and shaped like two dinner plates face to face, with a dome on the upper top side. It was about 100 feet across, about 15 feet thick. There was a small slender door, and the door chute let down to the ground with steps on the inside of it. The backside of the ship sat on the ground, but the downhill side was braced with two slender legs and round plates on the ground as feet. There was one man of normal size, about 5 feet, 10 inches to 6 feet tall and about 165 to 180lbs. This person walked out onto the road to meet the witness and forced her to stop while he talked to her. Or at least she thinks he talked, although she did not see his lips move, and he turned his face away and looked down. While she seemed to hear him speaking, several other persons came walking up behind him; she took the 8 to 10 of these "persons" to be a troop of Boy Scouts, about 8 to 10 years old. However when they got nearer, she saw that there was something strange about them; they looked a bit like Japanese or Chinese. They had very large slanted eyes, very large cheekbones and very thin lips. And they did not look like children but adults. They smiled at her but did not speak. She had to smile back because they were sort of pushing each other around playfully, like each one was trying to get in front to see better. The clothing they wore at first she took to be scout uniforms; tan in color. But when they came up close to her, she saw that there were no pockets, buttons, edges, wrinkles, or pocket flaps. Very clean, very neat, and nice. They wore little tight caps, cut like baseball caps with little narrow bills. The larger man was dressed the same way. Off-hand the whole bunch seemed like a scoutmaster and his troop of scouts. She had a small argument with the man; he said, "Lady, you'll have to leave the highway and go around as we have the road blocked here." She said, "What is that?" pointing to the saucer. He ignored the question and said, "Never mind, you'll just have to go around. We want the road left clear and open and can't let you through here. You are a wonderful driver and you can make it all right." (The man was directing her to drive off the road down into a rocky gully and then up another hillside to rejoin the road some distance away). She still argued and said, "I can't put this big car down through that creek and rocks. It'd tear my car all to pieces, and I could never get out the upper side, and besides you don't own this highway." But somehow she couldn't help herself, and dazedly drove very slowly and fearfully down into the creek and rough canyon. She realized that the man was walking right along the side of the car, at her elbow. She felt very safe and was able to make the crossing and was no longer afraid. This was about 9:30-10:00 a.m. and it was the last thing she remembered until she came to herself; walking in to her home porch at about 12 o'clock that night; about 15 miles distant. Where she was, where she went, what happened to her those many hours, she has no idea. Neighbors had driven along that area during the day, and later told her family that they saw her car parked on the hill beyond the canyon. Her dad was starting a search party when she came in.

1933

On 24th February 1933 a bright fireball, found later to be a four pounds in weight iron meteorite, burned the grass where it landed in Stratford in Sherman County in Texas. Also on 24th March 1933 it was reported from Amarillo in Potter County in Texas that a gigantic meteor lit up the sky with awesome brilliance. It was seen in five southwestern states before dawn and caused a thunderous rumble that rattled doors and windows as it disintegrated on its downward plunge. There had been numerous sightings of an enormous meteor over Texas beforehand. On March 24th 1933 there was another massive meteor seen over Texas and New Mexico.

1934

On 16th February 1934 a pilot flying over Texas had to swerve to avoid a crash with a descending fireball.

1935

On November 24th 1935 in Palestine in Anderson County in Texas a bright shaft of light was seen in the sky.

In Kenedy in Karnes County, Texas in 1937-1938. The witness, a young girl at the time, recalls being visited on numerous occasions at her parent's farmhouse by several little men. From what she can recall, there were usually 4-5 of them. The little men had no hair and their skin appeared to be dark to her (hence she called them 'negritos'). She only recalls seeing them at night while everyone slept. Their faces were unusual with very large eyes. They would usually gather at her bedroom window and motion for her to come out, when she shook her head "no" they offered her a 'lolly pop.' She said they did not speak or make any sound, not even among themselves; they would only look at each other. They wore strange outfits similar to 'robes' or tunics. Her mother never believed her story and thought she was making it up for attention. Around the same time, her uncle spoke about seeing lights in the distance that would seem to rise from the ground and into the sky.

1939

In August 1939 (approx. date) at night in Fort Worth in Tarrant County, Texas. Janice Williams was sleeping in her backyard when she was awakened by a noise like an electric fan. It came from a small object coming from the east at an altitude of 6-9m. It came up to her, descended to the level of her bed, close enough so she could have touched it. It looked like a miniature steamboat 1m diameter and 30cm high, with a deck around the bottom and veins running through it. It gave off a soft blue-green glow. It took off suddenly and disappeared.

1942

In San Antonio in Bexar, Medina and Comal Counties in Texas in 1942. One night the witness had to go to the bathroom, which was down the hall and past the kitchen. As she was returning to the bathroom, she happened to look into the kitchen. The kitchen was a large room with six single-hung windows at the back. As she looked at the windows, she saw what she thought were twelve ghosts. They were standing according to their height from tallest to the shortest. All the "ghosts" looked alike. They were very skinny with large heads and large black, slanted, almond-shaped eyes. There was a rim of skin around their eyes and their eyes didn't blink. Just a cold stare. They were grayish-white in color. As she stood there she realized that she could not move and could not say anything. She saw the middle Humanoid move through the closed window and come toward her. At this point, she became scared and began to cry. She noticed that it had no ears; its head was egg-shaped. It had only two small holes for its nose and its mouth was very small. The eyes seemed to be multi-eyed, like an insect. It reached out and grabbed her hand. It had three fingers and all were very skinny, bony and long. The three fingers were the same length. There was a thumb, it was very small and it looked like a nub. The Humanoid's hand was cool to the touch. Both of them passed through the closed window without breaking it. They seemed to float in the night sky. As they floated up, she saw a large object, which she could vaguely make out. The next thing she knew she was in a huge room. It looked to be two storeys high. The room was very bright but she could not tell where the light was coming from. The wall and ceiling seemed to glow. The room looked like a fourth of a circle. The room smelled musky. As she looked around she saw about fifteen children at the door between what she thought was an information panel and some compartments. There were children of both sexes and all races, including black, brown and white. They looked scared and were crying. All of the children were nude. Most of them seemed to be in shock. There was no movement. Some held their heads down. A little girl with blond hair was lying on a metal table and she was crying. All communication was carried out telepathically. The alien that brought her into this ship took off her clothes and cut off a piece of her pajamas and removed a button. Two more aliens came into the room. One looked like the others described earlier and the other was different. He had more of a human skull. His eyes were large, elliptical shape and straight. Both eyes seemed to wrap around his head and they had a rim around them. He had a small nose and a small mouth. There were wrinkles between the eyes and the nose of the aliens that had hair. His color was gray. He was very rough with her and ran all the tests on her and on the little blond girl. He seemed to be the leader. The witness experienced pain during the examinations. At one point, after the aliens performed some testing on the little girl, whom the witness learned her name was "Cyan," she felt herself floating, but her body was still on the table, she was being floated towards Cyan. She felt telepathic communication from the alien leader and soon she was floated back into her body. The next thing she knew an alien was putting on her clothing and she was shown a dark hole on the floor of the spaceship. Her next memory is being back in her grandmother's house. Dreams, nightmares, astral travel or alien contacts? Take your pick.

1947

At 3.30 pm on 22nd June 1947 Dr. Oliver Dickson with his daughter and a person by the name of A.W. Beck saw an object shaped like a blimp but pointed at both ends, like two pie-pans that were face to face. They were very bright and shiny like chrome and were traveling South in an absolutely straight line over Mount Hamilton near El Paso in El Paso County in Texas. The craft vanished in fifteen seconds over Mexico at 1200 miles per hour. The craft was thirty to forty feet across, five feet thick and at an altitude of three thousand feet over the mountain. The odd craft did not reflect the sun's rays though it was highly metallic.

On 29th June 1947 a couple from Smyer, in Hockley County near Lubbock in Texas, saw a disc about the size of the moon moving in a southwest direction.

Still the 29th June 1947 and in San Angelo in Tom Green County in Texas Mrs. Victor L. Salter and her thirteen year old son saw a disc-shaped slowly revolving object that was descending and was the size of a wash-tub. Suddenly it shot up at an unbelievable speed and disappeared.

Still that same day 29th June 1947 and at El Paso, El Paso County, Texas, Mr. And Mrs. R. C. Burgess saw a silver colored top-shaped object something like a balloon and blindingly bright traveling North at high speed and then seemed to melt into the sky in about ten minutes. This was around 4.00 pm. A blinding high-speed balloon?

At noon on the 4th July 1947 Mr. E. E. Polk saw a disc at an altitude of one thousand feet over El Paso, El Paso County in Texas that was traveling westward very fast. The object was the size of a pie-plate with ragged edges and was visible for fifteen seconds.

At 1.30 pm on Sunday 6th July 1947 Jim Purdy, a former air pilot with the Royal Air Force as well as the U. S. Airforce saw a silvery disc-shaped object flying above Lubbock in Lubbock County in Texas. The object did not resemble a plane at all and it gained speed much more rapidly than any plane that Jim had ever seen. The sighting lasted twenty seconds as the object flew in a direct line to the northeast.

At 5.05 pm on Sunday 6th July 1947 Mrs. Sadie Mccauley of Houston in Texas as well as several other passengers on her bus on the Alvin Highway near Texas City, in Galveston County in Texas saw seven flying saucers flying in a single line.

The next night El Paso in El Paso County in Texas had two visitors. One at 8.45 pm and the second at 9.00 pm on 7th July 1947. In the first sighting a woman reported seeing something that was grayish in color going from South to North over the city. In the second sighting four residents from different parts of the city saw flying discs in the sky. Mrs. Walter Turner and her husband first saw a bright shiny light over Mount Franklin that zipped along and vanished to the East. At the same time David Hunt and John Jordan saw four round flat saucer-shaped objects shooting across the sky West to South over Mount Franklin. They were fifteen feet in diameter and at an altitude of one thousand feet. They glowed and disappeared in less than twenty seconds.

Still in El Paso in El Paso County in Texas where there are two sightings for the night of the 8th July 1947. The first sighting is at 9.30 pm when Ottive Magill, a U. S. Reclamation employee said that a flying disc came at his car while he was in the Lower Valley. Mr. Magill ducked down with his dog as the object swooped overhead. Ottive heard a buzzing noise and said that the object glittered, was twenty feet wide but only four inches thick.

In the second sighting at 9.40 pm 8th July 1947 a flying disc was reported by three independent witnesses from two widely separated parts of the city. Miss Dorothy Gillespie and Mrs. Willy Mae Henderson who were neighbors saw a round silver object overhead that changed to a yellow color. Within a few seconds the object faded out over Franklin Mountain which is North of El Paso towards Las Cruces, New Mexico. At the same time Miss Ruth Miller saw an object shaped like a silver dollar and casting a grayish light passing overhead and then moving out of sight over the Franklin Mountains within a few seconds. This was the same craft at the same spot.

Also on July 8th 1947 at Acres Home in Texas a merchant seaman who swore he never touched a drop telephoned the Houston Post and said a big silver disc landed in front of him while he was walking in Acres Home Addition (on Rt. 149, just NNW of the Houston city line). A little man, two feet tall and with a head the size of a basketball, climbed out of the disc and shook hands with him, the seaman said, then climbed back in and whirled away into the blue. "Did he look like a man from Mars?" the reporter asked. "I dunno", the seaman replied. "I never saw a man from Mars."

Near San Antonio in Bexar, Medina and Comal Counties in Texas in Summer 1947. One night Percy Galloway reported seeing a movement in the sky. At first he thought it was a comet when it suddenly made a sharp right, directly towards the witness and hovered about a foot above the ground 200' away from him. The witness stood his ground and did not run away. He described the object as circular, about 72' in diameter, with domes on top and bottom. It had a black matte finish. It emitted a soft musical tone type sound. At the same time a fog-like mist, danced around its circumference. After a moment a brilliant light burst from the craft towards the witness, which had to cover his eyes with his elbow. When he took a peek, he saw a large square door that seemed to implode, and there before him, stood a tall, human-looking man. He had platinum silver gray hair and very deep blue eyes and was dressed in white tights and a thin gold belt. He radiated a warm, benevolent feeling of love. He said, "Percy come to me." The witness did, carefully but unafraid. As he approached to within 20' of the man, he was convinced that he was kind, gentle and a loving person. He spoke to the witness without moving his lips and before he could form a question to ask him, he said, "Percy, we speak by means of telemetric; much like what you humans call telepathy." The stranger told Percy that as long as he was in his presence, he could speak to him the same way. Every time Percy tried to speak, his thoughts were read before he could mouth his words. Inside the craft, they walked down a cool, cave like hall. There was soft, white light everywhere but Percy could not tell where it was coming from. They entered a room in which 30 men worked on instruments. They did not notice them. Percy asked if he could go on a ride in the craft. He was then taken to a control center where the man raised his hand in the air with the palm closed. The metal of the craft became as transparent as glass. The witness could see space. The man pointed to the planet Earth, which was about the size of a baseball. He told Percy that they were moving close to the speed of light and that they were going to move faster. He was taken to a special protective area of the craft due to the acceleration. He was placed in a room with a greenish blue light. He stood upright and although he could not move, he was aware of everything around him. A short time later they arrived at a mother ship, which was stationary at the edge of the solar system. The craft entered an opening in the mother ship. The crew and Percy left the small craft and were greeted by two human looking people. There were dozens of others present. As they walked down a hallway, Percy noticed three humans going the other way; a young white teenage girl, an old man, and a white male about 30-years old. They entered a room in which a ritual was about to start. Fifteen or twenty human looking men and women dressed in tight white pants and loose blouses stood in a circle. He felt that there was a leader present but he could not tell who he was. The participants stood with faces toward the ceiling, their eyes closed and palms opened outward. As Percy watched, each person's body took on a golden aura. The being then took Percy to another room. There he was offered white chips and crackers and a blue liquid to drink. Then he went to another room where he sat on high backed chair that looked like metal but was soft like cotton. A metal headset with two triangles on it was placed on his head. He was told that he would be able to read and understand what was on the viewing screens. The screen then lit up with images that moved at lightning speed. He saw medical data and formulas. It was like looking into the future. He was told that he would not remember anything; that it was a time capsule. Later he was returned to Earth and while hovering 500' above the ground he was lowered to the ground within a blue beam of light.

On November 2nd 1947 in Houston in Texas at daybreak Immigration Service [agent?] Brimberry saw an almost round or oval or saucer-shaped object with bright light [?] about 100 feet [?] diameter spinning in its descent.

In late December 1947 or early January 1948 at 1700hrs in Houston in Harris County, Texas. A woman saw a discoid object, about 6m diameter, 1.2m thick, with lights on its underside, moving slowly at 150-180m altitude. She called to her neighbours and they saw it for a short time until it shot off at terrific speed and disappeared.

Sometime during 1947 a silent twenty-five foot wide saucer flew low over a lone female witness in a car in Fort Worth in Tarrant County, Texas . The female witness slammed on the brakes and got out and waved. The saucer banked back and waved at the witness before vanishing. Another version? A young woman was driving on a highway on the outskirts of Fort Worth, when a discoid object 8m diameter flew overhead. The witness stopped her car and waved at the object, which tilted, the occupants gesturing back. The silent object then moved off. A friendly saucer?

1948

Some time during 1948 near El Paso in Texas a doctor was returning home on horseback when suddenly the horse stopped, head erect and nostrils wide open. Its body quivered and its eyes popped out as if seeing something invisible and then began to whine strangely as a beautiful, human-like being with a youthful face and golden hair appeared on the road just ahead. It wore a celestial green-colored garment and was enveloped in a soft golden aura. It had penetrating blue eyes. It did not speak as it kept pace with the horse when it started walking again. The doctor closed his eyes and thanked God for his experience and when he opened them the being was gone.

1949

On January 30th 1949 near Amarillo (at 34°50' N, 104°5' W) to near Lamesa (at 32°48' N, 102°22' W), Texas at 5:54 p.m. Thousands of witnesses over several states saw a spectacular green fireball on a North-South trajectory triangulated by Dr. Lincoln LaPaz as 12 mile altitude over Amarillo area descending slightly on nearly horizontal 143-mile path to near Lamesa disappearing about 8 miles altitude. No noise except slight hissing. 100+ witnesses interviewed.

In early March 1949 tiny white lights or flares had been seen appearing regularly over Killeen Base, a nuclear weapons storage site within Camp Hood in Central Texas. This set off the high-level alarm and could not be explained. Killeen is in Bell County in Texas.

On March 6th 1949 at Killeen Base, Camp Hood, Texas at 8:20 p.m. (AFOSI 29 & 30) Army Sgt. Hubert Vickery and PFC John Ransom on patrol at the AFSWP (Armed Forces Special Weapons Project) nuclear weapons storage site saw a blue-white oblong object about 2 feet x 1 foot in size travel South from 286° to 279° azimuth elevation 5°45'. Other sightings by Army patrols from 8:30 p.m. to 2 a.m.

Also on March 6th 1949 and also in Killeen Base/Site B [Nuclear Weapons National Stockpile], Camp Hood, Texas at 8:45 p.m. Army artillery observation patrol saw a light-colored round object with trail about 10° long travel South to North from azimuth 189° elevation 21° to azimuth 210° elevation 6°31'. No sound. Other sightings by Army patrols (see above, below).

Still on March 6th 1949 at Killeen Base/Site B [Nuclear Weapons National Stockpile], Camp Hood, Texas. [8:20?] p.m. Army artillery observation patrol saw a blue-white ball-like "fixed flash," the size of a basketball [?], in the NE at azimuth 40° elevation 59°. No sound or trail. Other sightings by Army patrols (see above, below.

After midnight that night on March 7th 1949 at Killeen Base/Site B [Nuclear Weapons National Stockpile], Camp Hood, Texas at 1:15 a.m. Army artillery observation patrol saw a brilliant blue-white flash of light like flashbulb in the NE at azimuth 40° elevation 66°15'. No sound. [Meteor?] Other sightings by Army patrols (see above, below).

Fifteen minutes later on March 7th 1949 at Killeen Base/Site B [Nuclear Weapons National Stockpile], Camp Hood, Texa at 1:30 a.m. Army artillery observation patrol saw a blue-white ball-like "fixed flash," size of basketball [?], in the NNE at azimuth 16° elevation 27°30'. No sound. [Meteor?] Other sightings by Army patrols (see above, below).

Still on March 7th 1949 at Killeen Base/Site B [Nuclear Weapons National Stockpile], Camp Hood, Texas between 1:30-2 a.m. Army artillery observation patrol saw a bluish-white ball-like flash of light like flashbulb in the WSW at azimuth 250° elevation 26°. No sound. Other sightings by Army patrols (see above, below).

And it continued. On March 7th 1949 at Camp Hood, Texas PFC. Max Eugene Manlove, 1st Provost Squadron, Camp Hood, Texas, observed a teardrop-shaped object, orange in color, drop vertically in front of him. Observation time: 2 seconds. (AFOSI 34) at 1:30 a.m. Two other sets of military witnesses. Very brief (2 secs?). (AFOSI 32, 33).

Quarter of an hour later on March 7th 1949 at Killeen Base/Site B [Nuclear Weapons National Stockpile], Camp Hood, Texas at. 1:45 a.m. Army artillery observation patrol saw an orange tear-drop shaped object, 2 x 1 feet in size [?], drop vertically to ground, in the ENE at azimuth 60°. No sound. [Meteor?] Other sightings by Army patrols (see above, below).

The following day on March 8th 1949 at Killeen Base, Camp Hood in Texas at 2 a.m. Army infantrymen in separate locations 1/2 mile apart sight different lights. One white seen by Payne. The other by Cpl. Luke Sims was of a yellowish red light in level flight crossing 60° of sky.

On March 17th 1949 at Killeen Base, Camp Hood, Texas at 7:52 p.m. Capt. Horace McCulloch, Asst. G-2 of the 2nd Armored Division at the nuclear weapons storage site, was preparing the test firing of flares in order to prove recent sightings were mistakes when he and his men themselves saw aerial phenomena. There were 7 separate sightings by trained artillery observers in different locations enabled rapid triangulation of large, green, red and white flare-like objects flying in generally straight lines.

On April 12th 1949 in El Paso, Texas a witness reported a grayish object that rose straight up leaving a smoke trail for 15 minutes duration.

On April 27th 1949 SE of Killeen Base, Camp Hood, Texas at 9:20 p.m. Two Army soldiers [Pillett and Belislandro?] on patrol saw a blinking violet object 1-1/2 inches in diameter 10-12 feet away and about 6-7 feet above ground in motion, passing through branches of a tree before disappearing. At 9:25 p.m., 2 miles away 4 Army men sighted a 4-inch bright light, with a 2-4-inch metallic cone trailing in the back, 600 feet away 6-7 feet above ground silently approaching from the NE in level flight at 60-70 mph, disappearing suddenly in the SW at 150 feet away. At 9:37 p.m. the same witnesses saw a 2-inch white light appear 100 feet away to the NNE flying in a zigzag in level flight about 6 feet above ground, disappearing suddenly. At 9:39 p.m. the same witnesses saw a 3rd light in the WSW.

On April 27th 1949 (and following day) at 2120hrs in Camp Hood in Coryell and Bell Counties, Texas. Between 2120 on the 27th and 2030hrs. on the 28th there were 12 separate reports of strange lights being seen around this area. One report was of an off and on light close to ground level passing through the fork of a tree. Another report was of a bright circular light seen 200m away at about 2m above the ground. It approached to within 50m, when it was the apparent size of basketball. Another guard saw dull violent light, the apparent size of a 50cent piece, which hovered and then came within 4m at 2m altitude. Another guard saw a light, the apparent size of a baseball, above the trees 3km away, another saw a light 30-50m altitude. There were other reports of lights at treetop and higher altitudes.

On April 28th 1949 SE of Killeen Base, Camp Hood, Texas at 8:30-10 p.m. Several Army security patrols sighted a variety of strange lights, mostly slow moving changing color from white to red to green, one with a red blinking light, one with a "coneshaped affair" trailing in the rear similar to one seen the day before.

On May 5th 1949 at Fort Bliss, TX. At 11:40 a.m. Army officers Maj. Day [May?], Maj. Olhausen, Capt. Vaughn saw 2 oblong white discs, flying at about 200-250 mph, make a shallow turn. A three-inch object passed through a field of fire on Waco #4 firing range.

On May 7th 1949 at Killeen Base, Camp Hood, Texas at 7:40 p.m. Lt. Mardell Ward, at the Army's UFO observation post, and another observation site, spotted a brilliant white diamond-shaped object at triangulated location 15,000 feet away at 1,000 feet 57 secs 2+ real-time triangulation altitude headed NW. Object was tracked for 57 seconds as it travelled 20 miles (at 1,300 mph) while changing color from white to reddish to greenish as it dropped altitude and dimmed then disappeared. No sound.

The following day at Killeen Base at Camp Hood at 10:08-10:17 p.m. Lt. Mardell Ward, at the Army's UFO observation post, and 2 other posts sighted a brilliant diamond-shaped object to the W moving NW or NE at 1,600 feet altitude slowly dropping. There was severe radio interference during the sighting and none afterward.

1950

On April 16th 1950, in Laredo in Webb County in Texas a small flying disc only about 6 feet wide allegedly crashed at the airport, after buzzing it. The pilot, not more than 2 feet tall, was extricated and revived with oxygen; he felled a National Guard sergeant with a blow, and again became unconscious. Three more times he was revived and fought, then died. He weighed 300 pounds and was carrying a ray pistol capable of stunning men. A lot of weight for a small person.

At 10.55 am on April 8th 1950 in Amarillo. Cousins David (12) and Charles (9) Lightfoot were fishing at River Road when they saw an object resembling a balloon coming from the south. It passed overhead at very low altitude and landed behind a small hill. David followed the object, which he found to be approximately the same size as a car tire, 45cm thick, with a rounded bottom and flat top. The two halves were separated by a 2cm gap and connected by a kind of screw. This gap appeared to be on fire. The top of the blue-grey machine was spinning. The bottom , to which a sort of spindle was attached, was still. No other openings were visible. As David tried to hold the machine, thr top spun faster and it gave off a spray that burnt his hands and face. The thing took off with a whistling sound at high speed.

In Amarillo in Potter County in Texas on April 29th 1950 a child witness, 12, saw a UFO the size of a car tire and of a bluish grey color hovering near him. The child touched it and the object shot out a gas or spray which made the child's arms and face bright red and raised welts. The object quite plainly did not want to be touched. The saucers are not happy this year whether small or large and these small and aggressive ones aren't particularly fond of children either as we shall see. Other sources state that there were two boys, David Lightfoot, twelve, and his brother Charles, 9. The object was described as thirty centimeters high with a rounded top that rotated. It had a pivot between the base and the top and took off to the northeast. Another version?

On May 12th 1950 (approx. date) at night and also in Amarillo, Texas. The night serviceman at Tradewinds Airport noticed something like an exhaust flame coming in from the west as 150-200m altitude. He tried to waken one of the pilots at the airport but failed on a couple of occasions as the thing came in at about300-500kph and swerved towards English Field. About 5 minutes later the witness came out of the hanger office to see the brilliant light coming in from the West-North-West. He switched on the flood lights as the thing came in and landed on a grassy area about 300m in front of the hanger. Stepping out for a better look he saw that it resembled an ellipse with a flattened underside and a section of the rear cut away. The thing was surmounted by a sort of bubble, the size and shape of an American footballer's helmet and from the object's rear protruded a sort of pipe, from which flames seemed to be issuing. The witness again tried to wake the sleeping pilot but again failed, so he wetn back to the front of the hanger again. The strange object remained on the ground for 3-5 minutes, then rose, emitting a whinning sound and the flames from the rear became white and about 1m long. The grass under the thing was starting to burn. The object rose to about 1.2m then took off to the Southeast with a terrific roar. The climb was shallow until it reached the end of the field, at which it became steeper. It then levelled and turned without banking and headed west at increasing speed. The grass where the thing had rested was still burning so the witness got the fire extinguisher and put it out, using almost all its content.

1951

At Lubbock in Lubbock County in Texas in June 1951 formations of UFOs appeared almost every night that summer. There were nightly gatherings of luminous glowing UFOs in a perfect Vee formation above the town. These lasted most of the summer and were attributed in the official Press to flights of ducks in formation reflecting motor car headlights off their bellies. I'd like to see that. As well as nocturnal ducks. And how come it occurred one summer only? If physical conditions are right then are not all experiments not replicable? We might have to cancel that hypothesis after all! These duck formations ? returned in July and August 1951. On 25th August 1951 Carl Hart photographed a formation of UFOs in a perfect V formation above the town. They glowed. These formations appeared almost every night that summer. There were nightly gatherings of luminous glowing UFOs in a perfect Vee formation above the town. These lasted most of the summer.

On August 2nd 1951 in Lubbock, Texas from 8:57 to 9:03 p.m. local. Five civilian men observed a metallic looking spherical shaped object hanging in the air. The only apparent movement was a quivering motion. The object after about six minutes moved straight East until it disappeared into a cloud bank. One witness, Mr. Gibbs, was very familiar with weather balloons and he was positive that the object was not a balloon of any type. Reese AFB was located just West of Lubbock, Texas.

On August 25th 1951 in Lubbock, Texas. The photographs by Carl Hart, Jr., show a V-formation of large circular objects. Capt. Ruppelt, head of Air Force Project Blue Book, reported that "In each photograph the individual lights in the formation shifted position according to a definite pattern." The main photograph was reproduced in True, May 1954. Skeptics have always had a field day with this one because it seemed to be only a set of photographs, taken by a young, inexperienced photographer, of geese, later explained as moths. Little did anyone know that even the Air Force, including the professors who also witnessed the overflights, did not buy the explanations. In fact, it appears some people, alerted to UFO activity, saw birds; others saw UFOs and the most damning evidence against birds. A professional photographer, with professional equipment and better film, could not capture lighted bellies of geese. And that's not all. A swept-back winged object was being seen around the country during the period and two radars confirmed an unknown. Listed as item 11 under photographic evidence in the Special Evidence section of NICAP's UFO Evidence.

At Abilene in Taylor County in Texas on 2nd November 1951 the passengers and crew of an American Airlines DC-4 saw a bright green UFO like projectile that paced them. They were above Abilene. The UFO left a white trail and was holding the same course as the plane when it suddenly exploded hurling red balls of fire in every direction. It was like a Roman Candle and fortunately none hit the plane. This is not our first pacing of an aircraft either. Or exploding UFO. Also on 2nd November 1951 a gigantic green fireball was seen blazing over Arizona to the astonishment of 165 witnesses. Several of the witnesses stated that it travelled parallel to the ground before it exploded. There was no sound and the green fireball seemed to just disintegrate. Was this the same green fireball that scared the passengers and crew of the plane flying over Abilene in Texas? There were also sightings of a green fireball over New Mexico and Oklahoma. Was it a Taurid fireball?

1953

At Kerryville in Kerr County in Texas on 11th January 1953 a huge oval glowing orange red object was seen in the sky by many witnesses. There was a peculiar interference with televisions and other types of electrical interference that was noticed as well. Was this caused by the phenomenon? Was this the only part of Texas to ever have only one reported phenomenal sighting in its' history?

On June 10th 1953 at 0230hrs in Houston in Harris County, Texas. Tool plant inspector Howard Phillips (33), Hilda Walker (23) and Judy Meyers (14) were sitting in the porch of 118 East Third Street, when they saw a huge shadow cross the lawn about 8m away. It rose up into a pecan tree, where they saw that it was the figure of a man about 1.9-2m tall, dressed in grey or black tight fitting clothes and with wings resembling those of a bat. The figure, which had black boots, was surrounded by a glow. It stayed in the tree for about 30 seconds, swaying in the branches before the glow faded and it was lost to sight. Immediately afterwards they heard a whooshing sound a saw a white flash, like a torpedo, cross a neighbouring house.

In Houston in Harris County, Texas on 18th June 1953 at 2.30 am. Mrs. Hilda Walker, Howard Philips and Judy Meyers were on the front porch of their apartment building in the Heights neighborhood on a hot night when a huge shadow was seen to go over their heads and across the lawn. It was like the shadow of a big Moth in the streetlight. Then the shadow bounced into a pecan tree. The witnesses then saw a flying hominoid swaying on a branch in the tree. The flying creature was a black batwinged man that was 6.5 feet tall and seemed to have a dim grey light around him who flew away very fast. Other reports state the he just faded away in front of them. It seemed to be encased in a halo aspect. The manbird seemed to be wearing a black Cape, skin tight pants and quarter length boots. There was a white flash of a torpedo shaped something that made a swooshing noise immediately after the sighting in the sky. There was a UFO in the area as well. Giant birds? Or bats, with human-like bodies? White torpedo shaped bodies flashing through the night sky? Is there a connection? Why not Bigbird s coming from UFOs? We already have met Hairy Humanoids in connection with them. And we will be meeting many more. Of both! And seeing that none of this exists then you can have any combination that you want to though for some strange reason only from a small number of choices. Far too small for the human imagination but recognisable genera in a way all the same. Was this the return of the Gargoyles?

1954

Near Amarillo in Potter County in Texas in May 1954. One afternoon the main witness and his mother and were flying from San Francisco to Amarillo, Texas. They left San Francisco and flew into New Mexico, ABQ (Albuquerque) airport and landed for fuel. They then left ABQ for their destination Amarillo. He was sitting in the aisle seat when his mother said, "Look out the window." He then saw a long silver cigar-shaped object just off the tip of their plane's wing. It emitted no sound, and he could see no wings, and no engines. Through some clear pothole-like apertures he saw a very nice looking woman reading a magazine or newspaper. She was facing left of the craft in her seat and a man was facing her on the right side of the aircraft. She put down whatever she was reading or looking at and looked directly at the witness and smiled. The object then passed their plane at a steady speed, almost as if "they were sightseeing" and then it was out of sight. When they landed in Amarillo, two men came aboard the plane and asked that if anyone had seen anything unusual, to stay in their seats because they would like to talk to them and if anyone had a camera to let them know. The men were dressed in very nice black suits and had very shiny shoes. His mom nudged him and said, "Don't say you saw anything or we will be here all day." Then they both walked off the plane.

1955

One night in summer 1955 a twelve year old girl looked out of her bedroom window and saw a small Humanoid about the size of a ten year old boy in a tight silvery uniform. They looked at each other for about five minutes. His eyes were slightly larger than normal and were friendly. He then walked away and out of sight. This was in Dallas in Texas.

Around midnight near Eagle Pass in Maverick County in Texas in August 1955. Dan Martin was driving North of town. He had just passed the Neuces River when he suddenly felt his legs and arms become numb. He quickly pulled off to the side of the road fearing that he was having a heart attack. He then saw a cigar-shaped object come from behind his car and stop across the road from him. It was hovering eight feet above the ground. At this point Dan felt compelled to get out of his car and walk across the field. As he came around the rear end of the object he encountered a medium-sized Humanoid female wearing a tight fitting silvery outfit. He apparently had a brief conversation with the woman and then got back into his car. He then watched the object take off at a very sharp angle and easily clearing the nearby treetops. Or this? At 12.20 am Dan Martin was driving through the night from Eagle Pass to visit his mother, when in a remote location; he felt in tingling in his body and pulled over and stopped. His attention was then caught by a rushing sound, like a wind, coming from behind him. An object came to a halt about 20cm above the ground nearby. It was a cylindrical object, 15-18m long, about 3.5-4.5m wide with a rounded front, in which one or two occupants were visible. There were no other openings or markings on the body. As Dan approached the thing, an opening appeared in the rear and a woman wearing a sort of mask got out. She eventually took this off to reveal a normal human appearance. She called him by name, claimed to be from Mercury, and gave him a usual contactee mission. After this she re-entered the object, which took off an angle over tall trees less than 100m away. Dan then continued on his journey and mentioned nothing of this to his mother.

1956

In McKinney in Collin County, Texas on 6th April 1956. A silvery object landed in a field only one hundred meters from two witnesses in a car. It then took off at high speed. Mr Mitchell and another man saw a silvery balloon shaped object, about 2m diameter, land in a field 100m away, about 8km east of McKinney. They stopped their car to investigate but the thing took off at fantastic speed, There had been six previous phenomenal sightings from around here. On July 5,1873, a strange and terrifying aerial silver serpent dashed down from the sky scaring people at and near Bonham and Fort Riley, in 1878 farmer John Martin saw an aerial disc-shaped object that he called a saucer, in 1897 an airship was seen over Farmersville, and again at Farmersville in 1913 a boy chopping cotton with his two brothers heard the dogs howling and went to investigate. He saw a little green man eighteen inches tall that his dogs then tore to pieces.

On June 11th 1956 at 2010hrs in Eagle Pass in Maverick County, Texas. Dan Martin (qv) had finished listening to a religious radio broadcast and was sat thinking on it, when there was a knock at his back door. Answering he encountered a man and woman, who exuded an indefinable air of otherness. They greeted him as "Mr Martin Dap o Day", invited him aboard a space ship. They took him, one on each arm, and they rose into the air. They were taken through a sort of tube into 2.5-3m x 3-3.5m room with rounded corners and a screen on which geometrical patterns appeared. They took a sort of lift into another room where there was a woman dressed like a nurse, who escorted him into an office where a man and woman were waiting for him. They were the master and mistress off the ship and delivered a theological message. He was then taken for a meal before being taken to a lecture about the origins of earth and the utopian conditions on Mercury, more theology and other stuff he did not reveal. He was then returned to his home.

1957

Around 1.00 am on 15th June 1956 the witness was woken by two beings approximately four feet tall in her bedroom. She was paralyzed and could not move or talk yet she was able to communicate with the two beings telepathically. They told her that she had to go with them. She then asked them if she could tell her mother who slept in the bed next to her. They told her no. The aliens had huge teardrop eyes. They said that she must go with them. The rest of the encounter is blank to the witness and she next found herself back in bed. She suffered deep emotional scars as a result of the encounter. This was in Edroy in San Patricio County in Texas.

Over the West Texas Plains in July 1957 the passengers and crew of a four-engined Transworld Constellation Airplane had to dive out of the path of a rapidly descending UFO with a red and a green light on it at 18,000 feet. They had been on a collision course. The UFO passed above the Constellation which had to make an unscheduled landing at Amarillo Airport where one badly hurt passenger had to be hospitalised. A bad month for falling near-colliding objects over Texas and New Mexico. These were documented separate sightings.

On September 26th 1957 at Sunset in Yellow Falls near Youngsport in Bell County in Texas. Three hundred people were said to have seen 3 elongated objects with portholes maneuvering near ground level. One of these, 450 feet long and 20 feet high, landed for 20 minutes. It was pearl-colored, glistening in the sunset light, and showed a series of circular marks on its surface. An occupant emerged, inspected the derricks of abandoned oil wells, and took off again. As observed through binoculars, it appeared to be a "monster" that was 3 feet tall, moving with strange jumps and picking up something from the ground.

On November 2nd 1957 at 0330hrs in Canadian in Hemphill County, Texas. A car driven a by a civil service employee, Mr Calvin, with Sergeant bomber as passenger, rounded a corner and went over a rise , at which his headlights illuminated a submarine shaped white object 10-12m long, 3m high landing a field just off the road. Just then a flash of light lit up the car and its headlights went out. They drove on another 30m before stopping. As they reversed the headlights came back on. The observation lasted three minutes. There was a sort of conning tower in its centre, and something like a white flag, either on the machine, or held by a figure near it. Or this version. Three miles West of Canadian in Hemphill County in Texas on 2nd November 1957 civil and military sources reported the landing of a submarine shaped object eight foot high and three times longer than a normal car in a field. There was a Humanoid standing near it who flashed a light in the direction of the witness and the UFO then took off into the sky. This was during the Levelland sightings. When Sgt. Alfred Calvin drove over a hill his headlights illuminated an object resembling a submarine, approximately 30 feet long & 8 feet high. A flash of light took place over the car, and his headlights went off. The object was red in the middle & white at the ends, and a white flag could be seen borne either on a mast or by a figure standing by the object. There was no sound, "when C. drove on, his lights came back on. This was during the Levelland sightings.

Also on November 2nd 1957 between Sherman in Grayson County & McKinney in Collin Texas. At 5:30 p.m. Mrs. James Adolf and two others reported a "strange light" alternately dimming and brightening.

On November 2nd 1957 in the evening in Petit in Hockley County in Texas. That evening two grain combines, each with two engines, were working in the fields. All the engines failed as a glowing UFO passed overhead.

At Midland in Midland County in Texas on 2nd November 1957 a large flying object with a blue light was seen in the sky early in the evening. An unnamed man and two kids reported a large bluish object, low, going West. This was during the Levelland sightings.

Around dinner time on 2nd November 1957 Odis Echols and parents observed a bulky object described as a streak of light like a fireball in the southeast over Clovis in Curry County in New Mexico.

On November 2nd 1957 between Seminole and Seagraves, both in Gaines County in Texas. At 8:30 p.m. a single witness saw a light on the highway ahead. His car motor and headlights failed as he drove closer. Within a few seconds, the light rose into the air and flew away.

On November 2nd 1957 at 2030hrs in Amarillo in Potter County, Texas. A driver saw an unidentified object on the road south of Amarillo. His motor failed. Later a pilot reported an unidentified object to the control tower.

At Levelland in Hockley County, Texas on 2nd November 1957 at 10.50 pm. Mr. Pedro Saucedo and Mr. Joe Salaz were in a truck four miles West of town on Route 116 when they suddenly saw a blinding radiation on a collision course with them. The object passed over the truck with a great sound like thunder and a rush of wind. The truck was rocked back and forth by the blast. The object had originally appeared from a field and was a bluish green torpedo 150 to 200 feet long that was seen flying close to the ground for two to three minutes. It changed to a red color and the headlights and motor of the witness's truck died and the interior of the truck had got very hot. Saucedo got out to investigate as the UFO passed directly over him. There was intense heat coming from it and Saucedo threw himself to the ground. Both witnesses fled from it. The UFO was doing 600 miles per hour to 800 miles per hour . This was the start to a very busy period around and above Levelland.

At Amarillo in Potter County in Texas on 2nd November 1957 at 11.20 pm Amarillo Air traffic Control Tower saw a blue UFO hovering in the sky. And it was apparently on its way to Levelland.

Still in Levelland on 2nd November 1957 at 11.50 pm Mr. Jim Wheeler was in his car four miles West of town when he almost drove into a blazing egg-shaped object that was 150 to 200 feet long on the highway! The headlights and the engine of Jim's car died and he got out of the car. At the same time the UFO ascended into the air as the glare was swiftly decreasing and then vanishing. The car headlights and the engine then came back on again. These may seem to be standard symptoms of UFO contact.

On November 2nd 1957 in Shallowater, also in Lubbock County, in Texas at 11:55 p.m. two married couples saw a flash of orange light in the Southwestern sky. The headlights and radio of their car failed for three seconds as they saw the light. The motor of the car was not affected. There were no thunder-storms in the area.

On November 2nd 1957 at Whitharral in Hockley County in Texas. At Midnight Jose Alvarez came across a 200-foot-long object sitting in the road on Route 51. His car engine stopped as he approached and the headlights went out. At that point, the object rose quickly into the air.

Back at Levelland in Hockley County in Texas on 3rd November 1957 at 12.05 am Texas Tech college student Newell H. Wright, 20, saw a blazing egg shaped object 150 to 200 feet long on the highway nine miles East of Levelland and one mile West of Smyrna. The headlights and the engine of the car died. He got out and lifted the hood to check the wiring and battery, slammed the hood down and turned around. Before him and occupying the center of the road was a one hundred foot wide vessel of a luminous greyish blue tone. The UFO looked like a greenish glowing loaf of bread on the road ahead and vanished after a few minutes. The vehicle disrupting phenomenon kept on occurring. Soon the UFO took off silently and was gone and the car started and Newell drove home. Midnight madness around Levelland.

On 3rd November 1957 at 12.15 am Jose Alvarez was driving ten miles from Levelland near Witharral when he came upon a hovering UFO which banked its radiance rising to intense brilliance and then subsiding to complete invisibility. The car headlights fluctuated to this pattern and after a while the UFO gave off a thunderous roar and the car started again.

At Smyer, near Levelland, in Hockley County, Texas on 3rd November 1957 at 12.45AM. Ronald Martin in a medium sized truck on Route 116, four miles West of town saw a large bright rust-colored object on the road before him that blocked the road. The electrical system of the truck then died. The object became bluish green on landing and changed to the original rust color when it took off. Meanwhile back in Levelland as well as Witharral all was normal.

Around 12.15 am that same morning Frank Williams was near Witharral when he encountered an object described as an egg sitting on the crossroads, on and off. The car's lights went out and the engine died.

At Levelland in Hockley County, Texas on 3rd November 1957 at 1.15AM. The witness was in a car when the car died. A blazing egg shaped object 150 to 200 feet long was seen on the Highway. The headlights and engine of the witness's car had died. The object was as bright as a Neon sign.

Still in Levelland, Hockley County, Texas on 3rd November 1957 also at 1.15AM. James Long was in a car on a secondary road North of town when he found it blocked by an ovoid UFO on the road ahead. When the UFO took off the car started again.

A quarter of an hour later in Levelland at 1.30 am Sheriff Weir Clem and Deputy Pat McCullough were in a Patrol Car on Oklahoma Flat Road four miles from town when they saw an enormous egg of light like a brilliant sunset across the highway 1,000 yards ahead of them. The light lit up the area for two seconds. The car did not stop though.

At the same time and also in Levelland at 1.30 am Fire Marshall Roy Jones was in a car which wavered but did not stop on sighting a UFO.

Around 3.00 am at the Stallion Site at White Sands in New Mexico an army patrol in a jeep saw an orange apparently controlled luminous object on the ground near the site of the first A-bomb explosion. It was first seen as a sunlike source fifty meters above the ground descending to ground level after three minutes and landing several kilometers away at the northern end of the testing grounds. This was also on 3rd November 1957. At Stallion Site, two military police, Corporal Glenn M Toy and Private James Wilbanks, on routine patrol, observed a very bright object high in the sky, descending to 45m above the A bomb bunkers, the light going out. Moments later the light reappeared, as bright as the sun, as the object fell at angle. It appeared to be egg shaped, 65-90m in diameter. The thing appeared to be about 5km away. At 2000hrs. that evening Specialist Forest R Oakes and SP/3 Barlow driving in the same area saw a bright light about 15m above the old A bomb bunker. The light took off at a 45 degree angle, blinking on and off and disappearing into the sky.

On November 3rd 1957 at Amarillo in Potter County at 11:53 p.m. A Navy Test Pilot was flying over the city reporting to Amarillo Tower. Kevin Harris and Sandy McKean, both Amarillo air controllers saw an object low on the horizon, then high going from dim to bright, moving swiftly, then slowly. The pilot was flying on a bearing of 40 degrees when he saw the object 80 degrees to his right. He was describing actions as they occurred to the tower.

At Deming in Luna County, New Mexico on 3rd November 1957. A UFO was seen over the town. This was during the Levelland sightings.

At Abilene in Taylor County in Texas on 3rd November 1957 there was a report from Dyess Air Force Base of the landing of a UFO in the area.

At Abilene in Taylor County in Texas on the following day 4th November 1957 a UFO landed at Dyess Air Force Base and was seen by Sergeant Jack Waddell. Do we have showers of electromagnetic forces or forms that continue periodically like meteor showers? Are they random if we postulate that they exist? Are they random if we postulate that they exist?

After midnight on 4th November 1957 a young couple saw a glowing object on the road while returning to Amarillo. The object was surrounded by a fog. The engine of their car died as they approached it and entered the fog. The battery also went dead. The car had to be pushed into Amarillo in Texas to have the battery replaced.

Around 3.15 am on 4th November 1957 two Policeman, Joseph Lukasek and Clifford Schau and a third man named Daniel De Giovanni while looking for the cause of a headlight failure observed a fluorescent object fifty to one hundred meters away from them. It was coming down from out of the sky. The car headlights functioned properly and they drive towards the object but were stopped by a cemetery wall. They turned off all of the lights and watched the object for two minutes. It apparently played hide and seek with them as they tried to reach its location. This was in Elmwood Park in Cook County in Illinois. The November sightings were not restricted to just Texas.

Around 1.10 pm on 4th November 1957 near Orogrande in New Mexico James W. Stokes, a high altitude research engineer saw an elliptical UFO sweep across the highway twice. The car radio and engine failed. Stokes claimed that other drivers were also on the road and their engines had also failed. Stokes felt a wave of heat and later his face appeared sunburned.

On 4th November 1957 three miles southeast of El Paso airport in El Paso County in Texas around 7.30 pm Border Patrol Inspector Burton saw an egg-shaped object with a bluish glow approaching from the southwest at thirty degrees. It made a whirring noise like an artillery shell after the car stalled and the headlights dimmed and blacked out. The object passed over the car at one hundred feet and headed West changing altitude at irregular intervals.

The following day on November 5th 1957 in El Paso in Texas at 7:30 p.m. A single witness saw an egg-shaped object, which was glowing with a blue color, approach his car. This occurred after his engine and headlights had failed. The object gave off a whirring sound and passed overhead at a 100-foot altitude. It moved off into the distance in a straight line, but changed altitude erratically. Is this the previous sighting?

On November 5th 1957 near San Antonio in Bexar, Medina and Comal Counties in Texas. That night near Lackland Air Force Base, civil service employee Lon Yarborough was driving along U.S. 81 from Devine to San Antonio when he saw an extremely bright object settle down in a ravine about 200 yards from him. He said he was a mile and a half from San Antonio at the time. The egg-shaped object was approximately 60 foot long and caused the lights and engine of his 1957 car to fail. He said his car was in perfect mechanical condition. The object, he said, rested a few minutes and finally took off in the direction of San Antonio. The sighting happened at night.(It is very curious that the newspaper article says the witnesses saw the object for a few minutes while PBB says the observation was 5 seconds. Who ya gonna believe?)

On November 5th 1957 at dusk in Hedley in Donley County, Texas. A farmer saw a pulsating bluish-green object just above the ground at the same time as neighbours' TV failed.

On November 5th 1957 at 1930hrs in El Paso in El Peso County, Texas. A border inspector (35) observed an egg shaped object, giving off a bluish glow, approach his car after he got out to investigate a sudden falling off of engine and lights. The object approached from the south west at a 35 degree angle, making a whirring sound like an artillery shell. It passed over his car at 30m altitude, moved off on a westerly heading, changing altitude at irregular intervals. The object lifted vertically when it reached Franklin Mountains. The incident happened 5km SW of the international airport.

On November 5th 1957 at 2130hrs in San Antonio, Texas. Lon Yarborough, a civilian at the Lackland Air Force Base was out driving when his car radio failed and his headlights dimmed. He then saw a glowing object in a nearby field. As he got closer his engine and headlights both failed. The light was egg shaped and about 20m in diameter. After about 10 seconds the thing rose up vertically to 15-30m, and then left to the south east, giving off a blast of air and a whistling noise as it did so. The radio and headlights came back on and Lon was able to start the cat again.

On November 6th 1957 in Boerne in Kendall County in Texas at 6 p.m. Mr McGregor saw an oval object, about 15 feet long, bright orange similar to glowing coals, hovering 12 feet above ground. He went to call his family but the object had vanished when he returned.

On November 7th 1957 at the Pantex AEC ordnance plant, 15 miles East of Amarillo, Texas at 7:46 p.m. Bright, flashing objects hovered for half an hour over the Pantex Atomic Energy Commission ordnance plant. The brilliant objects were reported to the State Highway Patrol office by plant guards at 7:46 p.m. and a patrolman dispatched to the plant arrived at 8:15 p.m. and reported that he, too, saw "a strange light." The patrolman said guards at the plant were "all shook up." Guards said three objects had been floating over the plant 50 feet above the ground "for some time." WhenI got there," the patrolman said, "the guards said one of the objects had landed on Farin Road 2373, three miles North of Highway 60. We drove to the area but nothing was there. But I'm convinced that the guards saw something land." The patrolman said guards told him they had tried to slip up on the objects by turning off their lights "but the things would just slip away from them when they got near." Guards were unable to estimate size of the objects. The Patrolman, also said the guards seem positive "they saw more than just lights that objects were in the sky."

At Kermit in Winkler County in Texas on 13th November 1957 at 12.15 am Mr. Frank Williams saw a bright egg-shaped object on the road ahead as his car died at the same time. Do we have electromagnetic energy storms that though forming spirals tend to travel contrary to the Coreolis effect?

At Amarillo in Potter County in Randall County in Texas in November 1957 an auto engine failed as something hurtled overhead.

In 1957 in Waxahachie in Ellis County, Texas. A 7 year old girl was exploring the field of wildflowers next to her uncle's house when she felt a stinging on her legs and looking down saw five tiny humanlike figures only 30cm tall staring at her with angry expressions. The little girl ran back to the house where her grandfather saw welts on her legs.

1958

Near Dalhart in Dallam and Hartley Counties in Texas during Summer 1958. At 2: 00 a.m. a man driving outside of town suddenly experienced engine trouble; it sputtered and died and the headlights flickered out. As he began to walk towards town, he heard a sudden high-pitched tone ringing in his ears. He noticed a faint glow coming from behind a nearby rise. He headed towards the glow and as he walked over the rise he spotted a large metallic disc-shaped craft sitting on the ground. He did not see anybody around, so he approached the object and banged on its side several times, yelling out at the same time. Suddenly he heard a loud metallic voice in his mind telling him to stop. The metallic voice asked several questions and went on to explain that their craft had suffered a malfunction and it was being repaired. He was invited onboard and warned not to touch anything. He then went back outside after a brief period of looking around. He stood watching the object and then a second similar object landed nearby. Six human-like figures emerged from this second object and appeared to move equipment to the disabled craft. One of the figures approached and communicated with the witness using telepathy in a friendly manner. The figure was described as man-like wearing a white silver one-piece suit, a helmet, boots, and gloves. Because of the glare from the light, the witness was unable to distinguish any facial features clearly. The figures then walked back to the objects, which lifted up silently and disappeared at high speed.

On November 2nd 1958 at 2200hrs in Happy in Randall and Swisher Counties, in Texas. Wayne Cole was driving home to his farm when he observed a blue object travelling about 30m above the road. When he drove under the object his car ampere metre jumped from charge to full charge and the car engine stalled.

Near San Antonio in Bexar, Medina and Comal Counties in Texas in 1958. At 3: 00 a.m. the witness, who had previously seen a strange saucer-shaped craft descend into a nearby canyon, woke up and looked out her bedroom window and saw five men approaching. One carried a large flashlight and all wore silvery jump suits with a type of hood covering their heads. Her dogs lay silent, unmoving, as if paralyzed. The group stood outside communicating with each other. They then circled the house; examining the grounds. One of the men carried a long black box. Occasionally he spoke into it. The witness felt sure that they were talking about her. Suddenly they were gone, fading away into the darkness. Moments later a domed, saucer-shaped object passed over the house. The witness returned to her bedroom and turning to her window, she saw a face looking at her. The face was described as somewhat human, but oval shaped, with almost no nose and a tiny mouth. The witness panicked and began looking for her gun. The Humanoid then walked away into the nearby canyon leaving a trail of luminous sparkles behind him. There appears to have been some "missing time" associated with this encounter.

1959

At Amarillo in Potter County, Texas in July 1959 Skyquakes shook the area. This was the same time as Roswell in New Mexico and San Francisco in California.

In Roswell in Chaves County, New Mexico in July 1959 Skyblasts occurred over a three day period. This was the same time as San Francisco and Amarillo.

At Portales in Roosevelt County, New Mexico in July 1959 a series of severe explosions rocked the area. They originated in the sky.

At Pampa in Gray County in Texas in July 1959 skyquakes shook the area though they were not registered on any seismograph. The blasts were so strong that they cracked the wall of one building in downtown. Pampa is 55 miles from Amarillo. The Skyblasts also occurred over a three day period in Amarillo in Potter County in Texas, Roswell in Chaves County in New Mexico, Portales in Roosevelt County in New Mexico and San Francisco in California. As well as Henderson in Warren County in North Carolina. After San Francisco there were two unexplained detonations in a 29 hour period over Henderson in North Carolina? This rules out the incidence of the Skyquakes in a straight line stretching from San Francisco in California to Pampa in Texas. We have a cuckoo in the nest. Henderson is not on a straight line though the others are.

On August 13th 1959 in Freeport in Brazoria County in Texas. Orville Shanks, his fiancée and two other women were out driving about 3km north of Freeport when they saw an object so brilliant that they could not properly make out its shape, approach at low altitude. As it did so their car engine and lights failed. Around the central object were two smaller ones that circled over the road and moved to the right over the fields, ponds and woods. The main object then followed them and all three appeared to land in the woods. The car lights and engine came back on again, and at the women's insistence, Orville drove on. When they returned along the route about 0000 the strange object was still there. Orville this time got out of the car and began to walk towards it. As he did so the object increased in brilliance, the two smaller objects reappeared and the thing emitted a low penetrating sound. Orville was now only too happy to agree with the women's insistence that they leave the scene. They reported the matter to the police and returned with them to the site. The object had gone, but another couple Randy Chandler and Leslie Ann Fowler had seen the strange thing depart.

Over Buffalo in Leon County in Texas on 29th September 1959 Major R.D. Braswell, AF, the Pilot of a C-47 plane heading for Lufkin, Texas, at 6,500 feet as well as hundreds of others saw a flying fire like an atomic cloud in the sky at an altitude of 15,000 feet. An object emerged from this cloud and there was a sudden flash of bright light. The object was a Braniff Airways Lockheed Electra Airliner with a crew of six and 28 passengers on board which disintegrated completely into thousands of pieces which made an eerie whistling sound as they plummeted to the ground. There were no indications of a fire or a bomb and the pieces showed evidence that they had been exposed to great heat. There were many witnesses of the UFO and at the instant of the explosion every dog for miles around Buffalo started howling. The crash occurred 68 miles southeast of Waco and the Pilot witness stated that it was like a small atomic bomb going off at 15,000 feet. Was the airliner shredded? The report does not say but it was disintegrated. We have had shredded planes before. Was it related to the Redmond, Oregon sighting only a few days before? Were we under electromagnetic bombardment or an unknown type of energy pulse bombardment that could well be cyclical and indeed capable of answering many of our unanswered questions?

In 1959 at 2115hrs in Weatherford in Parker County, Texas. A youth riding a motor scooter saw a light on his left hand side. He stopped and pointed his headlights at the thing, which appeared to be a translucent sphere, emitting a magenta coloured light, about 30cm diameter, hovering 60-90cm above the ground. When he stopped and pointed his headlights at the thing, he only seemed able to see a glow, but the object reappeared when he turned them away. Afraid, he drove on. The next day the tall grass at the site was found depressed and discoloured in an area about 1.8m diameter.

1960

On January 6th 1960 in Fort Worth in Tarrant County, Texas. A group of young people in Cobb Park panicked when a strange object appeared to land in a park.

On September 28th 1960 at 0425hrs in Wichita Falls in Wichita County, Texas. A glowing object struck the ground west of the city, turning from white to bright red. Searches by the Air Force found nothing

1961

On 10th January 1961 at 9.12 pm Mr. W.K. Rutledge, an Attorney, and Mr. George A. Thomas, a drilling contractor, were flying over King County in Texas. Suddenly at 1,500 feet above their altitude of 6,500 feet they saw something that was not an airplane. It was a large round luminous craft that was surrounded by a brilliant glow. The craft was stationary and as the witnesses approached it the object began to descend. Dozens of witnesses on the ground saw an orange zigzagging object in the sky. These included King County Sheriff Dub Holler in Guthrie and the wife of Knox County Sheriff Homer Melton, West of Benjamin. After six minutes the UFO landed West of the town. Rutledge radioed Wichita Falls to know if any aircraft were having trouble in the area and the answer was negative. Sheriff Melton organized a posse. Rutledge continued circling the landed craft. The glow from the craft was so bright that it cast light on the witnesses plane that was 4,000 feet above it. At 10.00 pm Rutledge had to fly to Abilene due to lack of fuel and shortly after the UFO took off quickly. There weren't that many luminous vertical take-off aircraft around in 1961. In fact there were none.

On April 16th 1961 in Laredo in Webb County, Texas. A strange object was seen on or close to the ground.

Over Marshall in Harrison County, Texas on 11th July 1961 at 10.30 pm. Mr. Troy Peterson was watching a meteor shower when he saw a blazing ball of fire streak in from the West and bury itself ten feet from him. Troy called the Sheriff and Deputy Lee Anderson came over. The object was too hot to handle even thirty minutes later. The object resembled a piece of charred petrified wood that sparkled and glinted and weighed 16 pounds yet was buried only four inches down. Troy said that it fell slowly. The meteor shower was not reported anywhere outside of the locality. Nothing quite like a localised meteor shower. Another report stated that there was a meteorite fall on May 30th 1961. This was reported to be eighteen pounds in weight and fell into a backyard. This was also called the Harleton Meteorite.

At Port Aransas in Neuces County in Texas in July 1961 the crew of the "Ruby", a 67 foot shrimp boat, hooked onto the unknown in the Gulf of Mexico. The unknown submerged moving object was metallic and ripped the vessels stern off. The crew was saved by another fishing boat nearby. No submarines were in the area at the time. Not that any submarines might be admitting it. There have been similar collisions with the metallic underwater unknown. Just ask the crew of the "Hattie D" in 1964

On 9th September 1961 a falling meteor struck the roof of a house in Bells in Grayson County in Texas. It was a carbonaceous chondrite. This was after a fireball and detonations were seen and heard over northeastern Texas. There were seven pieces found in total.

At Austin in Travis County in Texas in 1961 a radio report from an airliner stated that it had made eye contact with a UFO. The airliner then crashed. Something helped the plane to land in an unlandable space and then left no traces of itself behind. Normal aircraft do not take off and land vertically as they are not designed to do it. Hadn't this just happened near Sverdlovsk in Russia?

1963

Between Madisonville in Madisonville County and Centerville in Leon County in Texas on 19th April 1963 on Route 75 Mr. Louis B. Johnson of Houston was returning from a trip to Fort Worth when something lifted his car into the air, turned it completely around and set it back onto the highway travelling in the opposite direction where the car came down partly on the shoulder of the road. The witness put the car in low gear and eased to a stop. Several witnesses saw Johnson's car seem to sprout wings as it ascended and then landed gently and with no damage to the car. Cars being lifted up? If we hadn't seen it before we might have just as easily dismissed the car lifting.

In June 1963 in Marshall in Harrison County in Texas. Glen Brown was fishing in the Sabine River when a 6-foot man with chalky-white skin, dressed in a gray "jump suit" without buttons or insignia, came up & invited him to visit a spacecraft. He did so, & took a ride in it lasting several hours, during which they went from darkness to daylight and back again several times.

1964

At Dallas in Dallas County in Texas on 27th January 1964 a flaming blob bobbed and weaved in the sky and then fell from the sky onto the lawn of the Melvin L. Lewis house setting it on fire. It left a choking sulphurous smell. Meteors do not bob and weave in the sky.

On April 27th 1964 in the late afternoon in El Paso in El Paso County, Texas. Eightchildren, including 12 year old Kathy Roane, saw, from their school window, an egg shaped object 1.3m tall,, covered with something resembling a sheet, floating above their school ground. A search revealed nothing.

In July 1964 at 2300hrs in Greeneville in Greene County, Tennessee. On the H F Ramsey farm, 21km north of Greeneville on the Kingsport Road, Kathie M Riney and her parents saw a luminous round object hovering over a barn roof, which reflected the luminosity. After about 5 minutes the object took off straight up and vanished, the treetops swaying back and forth as it did so. The next day strands of a material 45cm long were found on the trees and bushes. These strands disappeared when touched. A light pole was down and the power was off during the event. The next day a bull calf was missing from the area where the "angel hair" had fallen. Police found no explanation for the incident.

At midnight on November 15-16 1964 near Pleasanton in Atascosa County in Texas. The witness had been hitchhiking to Kingsville. He was standing on highway 281 after dusk. He had been walking about a mile when he heard a movement in the brush off to his right. Something told him to turn and look back at Pleasanton but he dismissed the sounds as cattle moving. After another two miles of walking he suddenly looked to his right, West, and had cold chills run up his spine. Every hair on his head felt as if they were standing on end and his skin was crawling with goose bumps. He noticed three glowing red balls of light with the middle one larger which were about two hundred yards off the fence line and 150 feet off the ground. Then the headlights of a southbound car shone in the distance and the lights dimmed. As soon as it left they brightened up again and coming closer. The witness decided to head back to Pleasanton but as he looked North on the highway there were eight tall dark creatures blocking the road from fence line to fence line. He also heard more movement in the brush on the sides of the road and pulled out his pocket knife and opened the largest blade, turning so he could keep his eyes on them. They all moved with him as he moved backwards. Then another car appeared and the lights dimmed and the figures backed off. After half an hour he got a lift in a car. The driver had also seen the lights. He described the creatures on the road as eight feet tall and apelike. They did not appear to have hands or feet though. They were able to join their bodies together into twos, fours or all eight and then separate. They also had the ability to vanish and then materialize again. They were black, thickly haired with dimly luminous yellow eyes with a slightly brighter red center which would move around in the yellow eyeball center. They did not make any hostile moves towards the witness though and seemed almost child-like in their behavior.

Late at night in an undisclosed location in Texas in 1964 the ten year old witness and a friend had snuck out at night and were roaming the neighborhood when suddenly the landscape lit up around them. There was a thunder like sound. The main witness looked up to see a huge saucer-shaped craft hovering overhead. His friend remained in a paralyzed state. The witness saw a small craft landing nearby. Three figures emerged from it. Two were five foot tall and grey colored and the third was much larger and brown-colored. As the witness attempted to run he was grabbed by the brown being that then forced him into the small object, sometimes using an electric type gadget. He was eventually knocked out and taken up into the larger craft. His next recollection was of being fastened to a metallic tube. A dark green Humanoid woman sat on his chest and manipulated the witness sexually. A dark colored plate was placed on his face and then he was put in a small closet-like room. The floor of the room opened up and a multi-colored energy field engulfed him. He then dropped out of the craft and floated back to earth to his backyard.

1965

Around 11.00 pm during March 1965 in Greenville in Hunt County in Texas a woman had just helped her somnambulant or sleepwalking husband to bed and he was snoring when he hit the pillow. She crawled in beside him, kissed him goodnight and rolled over on her side. There standing in the hallway was a being that was wearing a clear-type helmet. He looked human and had on a gray space suit with zippers down the arms, zippers down the front, zippers down the legs and holding a crystal or glass ball in his hands. She had a feeling that he was not going to hurt them. It was like he was saying "I'm not going to hurt you. I'm just here observing you". She was not that reassured and kept trying to wake up her husband. When her child coughed in the other bedroom the being took his eyes from the glass ball and looked that way. That was too much for the woman and maternal instincts took over and she got up with "Don't hurt my children!" in her mind. She got as far as the door and he disappeared just like that.

Around 2.45 am on 6th June 1965 the five year old witness woke up in the middle of the night on his way to cuddle into bed with his parents which he usually did late at night. This night however he saw bright lights in the house and hid in the crawl space between the refrigerator and the wall. He then saw two dull bright figures that were maybe three feet tall with glowing eyes. This frightened him and he covered his face with his hands. However he still peeked through his fingers and realized that he was now face to face with them. He then ran to his sister's room and hid under the covers in between his two sisters. The boy claimed that the next day his home was visited by men in black who asked all kinds of questions pertaining to lights and fires near the barn area. This was near the ghost town of Calliham in McMullen County.

At Foggy Hill in Rural Shade in Navarro County in Texas in Summer 1965 at 11.15 pm Mr. William Howell was driving and two of his brother's children were asleep in the car when William noticed a bright object in the sky that was heading directly for the car. A bluish light bathed the car for a while in a blue haze and then the craft made a sharp turn to the southwest.

On 2nd August 1965 a luminous object was seen passing within one hundred feet of the Lewisville Dam near Denton in Denton County in Texas. They like large bodies of water don't they? That same night 2nd August 1965 the water seeking UFO still seemed to be around. Many residents stated that they had seen an object that appeared to have landed on Eagle Mountain Lake in Tarrant County in Texas. They like large bodies of water don't they?

On August 2nd 1965 near Justin in Tarrant County in Texas. Two Tarrant County deputy sheriffs saw an object as bright as burning magnesium land as they patrolled near Eagle Mountain Lake. Extensive investigation by police found no traces.

On August 2nd 1965 at 2145hrs in McAllen in Hidalgo County, Texas. A formation of doughnut shaped objects, the apparent size of a silver dollar at arms length, passed overhead. One object seemed to be in trouble, landed and then recovered and took off again.

On August 3rd 1965 in Justin in Denton County, Texas. In the Justin and Pender areas residents reported seeing a saucer shaped object land near a highway. Authorities investigated but no traces were found.

On August 4th 1965 at 0130hrs in Amarillo in Potter County, Texas. Harvey Burgman and his family were driving near Amarillo when they saw a disc shaped object hovering over the highway in front of them. The car stopped. Harvey and his children got out to get a better look. The object emitted a motor sound and had both a red and green light, which flared up brilliantly as the object seemed to disappear straight up. After the object had left Harvey tried to restart his car but found that it appeared to have a vapour lock and it took five minutes to start.

On August 4th 1965 in Dallas in Dallas County in Texas. At 1:30 a.m. a man in a car saw a red and blue light, thought it came from a police car, then was passed by a huge, orange object flying at ground level.

Around 1.00 am on 22nd August 1965 two brothers, Gregory, 15, and Ralph, 11, saw a luminous object passing by their bedroom window. It was cigar shaped and moving slowly at the height of trees outside the house. Shortly after the object passed out of view from the window the boys heard a thump on the roof followed by a knocking sound and footfalls. Being somewhat shaken one of the boys called out "Come in" whereupon there was a bright flash of light at the doorway of the room followed by the appearance of the silhouette of a man about the height of their father. By now badly frightened they hastened to their parent's room where they insisted on spending the remainder of the night. The family lived near Brooks AFB.

In Damon in Brazoria County, Texas on 3rd September 1965. At 12.00 am. Police Officer Goode and Chief Deputy Sheriff William McCoy were in their squad car. Goode, driving, had a sore and swollen index finger where his pet alligator had bitten him and it was bandaged but throbbing painfully. Goode was worried about infection setting in. They suddenly noticed a large purple glow to the west, moving horizontally that then turned and began moving towards them. The luminous object was fifty feet in height with a smaller blue light. Goode at the time had his sore finger hanging out of the car window, waving it in the breeze. Suddenly he felt a definite wave of heat on his arm and hand. They accelerated and left and the lights rose up and vanished. They sped back to Damon and Goode noticed that his finger was no longer throbbing or bleeding and was almost healed. Did the heat from the UFO do it? Healing from the sky or an electromagnetic function which sped up the healing process? Here is another version. Chief Deputy William E "Billy" McCoy and Patrol Deputy Robert Goode of Angleton were driving back to West Columbia after visiting a high school football match at Sweeny, through the small town of Damon when Billy drew Robert's attention to a purple light on the horizon. Robert did not pay much attention, concentrating on driving and rather preoccupied by a painful alligator bite on his left index finger, and considered them to be normal local lights. However after they saw the lights rise up, and a smaller blue light emerge from the general purple, Robert agreed to drive closer to investigate. Moments after they turned round the lights seemed to race towards them, stopping about 50m from the highway at 30m altitude. The purple and blue lights could now be seen to be on opposite sides of a vaguely cigar shaped grey object, 60m long and 12-15m thick. The purple light itself was the same thickness as the object, rectangular and pulsating with a brilliant mass of small lights, as bright as a welder's arc. The blue light was of similar shape but much less prominent. The purple light lit up the countryside and the interior of the car and Robert, who had been holding his wounded hand out of the open window, noticed distinct warmth coming from this light. This so unnerved him that he drove away at speeds up to 175kph. As he did so the object "snapped back" to the horizon and then took off at 20 degrees with a tremendous flash of light. After some time Billy persuaded him to return to the scene, but as they did so the light reappeared above the horizon and Robert drove off back to Angleton. He then realised that his finger had ceased to hurt and, taking off his plaster, saw that the swelling had gone down and could now move his finger with ease. According to some reports two strangers appeared looking for Robert and on finding him in a local restaurant described the object, which they said was a craft running on magnetic rays and that if he encountered it or its occupants again he should cooperate and remain quiet.

At El Paso in El Paso County in Texas on 2nd December 1965 over a million people were affected when a UFO was seen in the sky above El Paso. There was a massive blackout whilst the strange craft was seen in the sky. The luminous craft was also seen in Juarez, Mexico, across the Rio Grande River as well. San Pedro was the same day as a major blackout in Texas?

1966

On February 6th 1966 at Nederland in Jefferson County in Texas. At 5:45 [6:05?] a.m. Mr. and Mrs. K. R. Gulley saw a tadpole-shaped object about 14 feet long by 2 feet wide with 8 yellow and red neon-like lights at 250-500 feet altitude, casting a pulsating red glow on the lawn. House and street lights went out and high frequency sound bothered the witnesses' ears. The object blinked out when aircraft passed overhead then came on again afterwards. The object departed to West [or from W to SW] about 1-1/2 miles to the vicinity of the airport, where an aircraft's landing lights lit up theUFO which then disappeared about 20°-25° elevation in a slow climb. Or this? Awakened by their son's visit to the lavatory, a couple noticed that the light, which he had turned on, had gone off. Looking out the husband saw that local street lights were out but that the area was permeated by a pulsating red glow. Shortly afterwards his attention was drawn to yellow and red lights moving back and forth on some object that he estimated to be at 150m altitude. Both he and his wife detected some sort of very high pitched sound. The object then moved on from this location and was seen by the pilot of an aircraft raking off from Jefferson County Airport. The pilot compared the object's shape to that of a tadpole, with a spherical front about 2.5m diameter and a tail 1.8m long, 60cm wide, with conical bulges on its top and centre. As the aircraft approached this thing, the object's lights went out, only to come on again as the aircraft moved away.

On March 29th 1966 in Houston in Harris County, Texas. An object travelling low collided with and dented a car.

Also on March 30th 1966 in Dallas in Dallas County, Texas. Mr Kerpsey saw a strange object at very low altitude. It caused the water in his swimming pool to swirl and upturned garbage cans.

At Baytown in Harris County in Texas on 30th March 1966 at 8.00 pm Miss Donella Banning and the daughter of her employer were in her car when a glowing object hit the car and left two dents fifteen inches apart and five inches in diameter in the roof. Were they learner UFO pilots that year? Were they inefficient Kamikazes? Were they a different lot completely with good aim but lousy flying skills?

At Pecos in Reeves County in Texas on March 30th 1966 a UFO was seen to land and Humanoids emerged from it. An oblong object estimated to be 85-100 feet long, with lights at top and bottom landed near a highway, then took off about 5 minutes later.

On April 17th 1966 in Millersville in Concho County during the day a man in a car saw a sun-reflecting oval, car-sized object follow him, then cross the road behind him at 15 feet height. A 23 year old woman was driving from Millersville to work in San Angelo on this wet morning. She had just crossed the crossroads about 21km from San Angelo on Farm Road 765 when she saw a silvery metallic blimp shaped object, with protrusions on the back and top. It was pacing her car at a distance of about 85m at about 105kph. She slowed down to about 55-65kph at which the object crossed the road behind her at rooftop height. The woman became afraid, at accelerated up to 135kph, leaving the thing behind. The observation lasted about 11 minutes.

On April 24th 1966 at 0330hrs near the Pedernales River in Texas. Tom M Lasseter, an architect in Austin and a Lt Commander in the Navy Reserve, was camping by the Pedernales River, with his 11 year old daughter, when he was awakened by a fluttering sound that reminded him of a flock of quail. He saw a white, glowing, disc shaped object, about 6m in diameter, with a row of lights around its rim, hovering at treetop height about 50-60m away. The thing was rotating counter clockwise. The little girl thought that there was a double row of portholes around the centre, emitting white light. They watched the thing for about a minute, after which it moved away at between 130-160kph, disappearing g either behind an embankment or low cloud to the south west. He reported the matter to the Air Force.

Near Corpus Christi in Neuces County in Texas during April, 1966. At 11:15 p.m. the witness was camping near a lake with a fellow Scout. At night he was suddenly awakened by splashing noises and a strange odor. He looked out his tent door and saw a bright light gliding over the lake, sucking up the water. He was curious but frightened at the same time. He lay face down and watched the light move over the water. Worried, he tried to wake up his tent partner but could not wake him. He then moved back to the tent door but stopped quickly when he saw what he described as "two legged hairy monsters." He backed away from the door but could still see their images because the light was now closer. He doesn't remember much more except that he has unending dreams of being pulled into the lake and emerging inside a cavern under the lake. There was air but it was hard to breathe and he could see moving shadows. The inside of the cavern had some kind of light source. In his 'dream,' he pulled out his Scout flashlight with the rubber seal and pointed it toward the shadows and saw spider-like creatures, hairy with tall thin legs. His light appeared to bother them. The creatures then moved to his left and right as though they were trying to surround him. He could see their 'wet black eyes.' He held back his tears and tried to shout but couldn't hear himself. Exhausted and with little light left they stick him with their pointy legs and smother his breath. He woke up soaked with sweat or lake water; he couldn't tell which. He is scared every night to sleep because he knows they come in his dreams and he can't stop them. The witness believes he was abducted but can't prove it. He has had medical problems ever since the encounter by the lake.

On July 18th 1966 in Baytown in Harris County in Texas at 9:00 a.m. Service station personnel saw a white object shaped like two saucers face to face with a row of square windows in between. The object was hovering above a store about 100 yards distant. Then it began moving, rapidly accelerated and sped away.

Around 7.30 pm on 21st July 1966 the male witness saw a UFO land in the desert near Van Horn in Culberson County. Approaching its reddish glow he ran into three small creatures standing near a scrub tree. They spun towards him with one of them yelling something in a high-pitched childlike voice. They all ran back to the saucer which flashed away seconds later.

On August 6th 1966 at 1400 in Harlingen in Cameron County in Texas three children aged 6-9 noticed a dark object shaped like an upside-down cup. Then a square of yellow light appeared, like a door opening, a small creature 3 to 4 feet tall, wearing black clothing that reflected a gold color. After some minutes the door closed, and the object took off with a low humming sound. Or this version. At 2.00 pm the three youngest children of a family living in an isolated part of Texas suddenly saw a dark object with no colour or lights visible, shaped like an upside down cup, at a height of 4.5m near a tree about 10m from the house. A square of yellow light, like a door opening, appeared in which a small creature 90cm-1.2m tall, dressed in black clothing which reflected a yellow or gold colour. The observation lasted several minutes, then the door closed. A low humming sound became audible and the object took off towards the North East, rising sharply at moderate speed. The tree was found undamaged. On 3rd September at 14.00 the eldest daughter of this family was in the house, with a friend, watching TV, while most of the family were out. The set developed interference and then went out, at the same time the house became illuminated by an eerie red and yellow light which appeared to be circling or twirling. They looked outside and saw an object hovering in the same position was before. The shape was again that of an upside down cup with a flat disk underneath. It was covered with light and departed shortly afterward. No sign of life was apparent inside or outside the object. In the evening two days after this, the father of the house was sitting up in bed looking through his open door across the hall to his sons' bedroom, when suddenly he saw a small person 1.05-1.2m tall dressed in tight fitting clothes enter the dark bedroom. he thought it was his small daughter going to see her mother who was in the room with the boys, but 10 minutes later he saw something like a bar of light which appeared to crumble. he got up and went to the room, where his wife and sons told him they had also seen the bar of light, but there was no sign of a small figure and his wife told him the little girl had never been in the room.

On the night of 5th September 1966 Mr. Morrison, propped up in bed, saw a small person three and a half feet tall dressed in white tight fitting clothing enter his son's bedroom. About ten minutes later he saw something like a bar of light which appeared to crumble. The boys and their mother had seen no one enter the bedroom but they had seen the bar of light. This was in Harlingen in Cameron County in Texas.

On September 21st 1966 at 0330hrs in El Campo in Wharton County, Texas. Deputy Sheriff Ed Korenek was driving northbound on Hw 71, travelling at 190kph to clear his engine of soot when he saw a fiery mass on the highway north of him. Suddenly there was an object pacing his car at 190kph. This was another fiery mass. Looking to the front again, he saw the first fiery mass on the road about 800m ahead, three stories tall, its shape indistinguishable in the flames. He braked and tried to radio in, but found his radio was dead. He was able to glance to his left again to see that the second object was hovering over a field at Spot Thornton Airport. He headed straight for the object on the road and as he did so, the thing glided slowly off the highway to the east, sucking in the flame, which now appeared as a fiery tail behind it. Looking back at the airport, Ed saw that the second object had also now disappeared. His radio now worked and radio dispatcher Clarence Ribodeaux confirmed the terror in his voice, though Ed refused to give details. The police confirmed his reliability.

On November 2nd 1966 at dusk again in El Campo in Wharton County, Texas. On this rainy night Mrs Mark De Friend (32) of the wife of a dairy farmer, was paced by an object, which raced along in front of and to the side of, her car at speeds of 95kph. At times the object moved to the side and raced over the fields. As it passed in front, she saw that it was a misty green-blue mass, with right circular red lights. At one point the thing moved behind her car and hovered over the trees.

On November 17th 1966 at 0350hrs in Victoria in Victoria County, Texas. A truck driver was paced from Victoria to Stinton by a flashing light that came within 60m of the ground. Police officers who investigated saw a spherical light, the size of a softball at 15m, emitting multi-coloured lights. It was observed through binoculars for more than an hour.

In 1966 in West Texas, Texas. A man saw a machine land in the desert near his home. It sat on a ridge giving off a red glow. As the witness walked toward it, he encountered three small creatures standing by, and apparently examining, a shrub. When they saw him they turned around. One of them shouted in an incomprehensible language like a child jabbering, and they ran back to their craft.

1967

On February 12th 1967 in Wharton in Wharton County in Texas. That evening many people, including an airport manager, saw a bell-shaped object with a bright light in the dome and revolving red, green, blue, and amber lights at the bottom edge. The object flew over the witness's car just above phone wires along the road, appearing big enough to cover the highway. It was later seen at tree-top level, where it hovered, banked, and took off. Kenneth R Miller and airport manager Carl Nicholas were out driving when they encountered a domed object, with revolving red, green, blue and amber lights on its lower edge and a bright white light in its dome. It went over their car at the height of the telephone wires and covered the width of the roadway. Other people saw the thing at treetop height, where it stopped, banked and took off.

On February 15th 1967 in Denton in Denton County in Texas between 8:10-8:40 p.m. A teacher's car was followed by a flashing red light at various distances. Two of the witness's students confirmed the report.

On February 19th 1967 back in Wharton, Texas. That night a series of independent sightings was reported overnight southwest of Houston near the Gulf Coast in Wharton, Bay City, and Lane City. Witnesses included businessmen and prominent citizens. Exact times generally were not specified. (Houston Tribune, Texas, 2/23/67, copy in NICAP files and in Donald E. Keyhoe Archives files.) A school teacher in Wharton saw a pulsating red light at treetop level fly the length of a runway between rows of landing lights, stop at the end of the runway, reverse direction and shoot back where it had come from. A department store manager in Bay City-Wharton, ex-Air Force and familiar with aircraft, and his family, returning from church, saw a pulsating red light approaching fast and low. A bell-shaped object with a band of colored body lights around the lower portion and a brilliant white light in the upper portion crossed the road just above the treetops. A window or port was seen above the colored lights. A trail like fire appeared as the object climbed. Alerted by the above witness, prominent citizens in Lane City, including a newspaper publisher and an editor, and the Mayor of Wharton, saw a white light which approached them. They also saw a star-like light that maneuvered erratically. A farmer and his children West of Bay City-Wharton witnessed an object with white fire coming from it that lit up the night sky, and two more appeared to follow the first one. An explosion rocked the home. Or this version. Department store manager K R Miller (33) and his wife were driving home from church when they saw a pulsating red light closing fast and losing altitude, at which they pulled up and dived out of the car. The object crossed the pole at telephone height about 60m away. It was a circular object 15-18m diameter, with a band of red, amber, blue and green lights circling the lower portion. On top was a dome emitting a glaring white light. Two similar lights could be seen in the distance. The couple drove back to Wharton, where they called the Wharton Journal editor Frank Jones, who returned to the scene, where they were joined by Marlowe Preston, the publisher of the Journal, and mayor Melvin Weaver of Lane City. Jones saw, through binoculars, red and white lights, less than 400m away. Rice farmer Sipriano Barron saw a fireball crash with a terrific explosion. Two hours earlier Frank Jones's wife, a schoolteacher, had seen a large pulsating red light at treetop height near the Bowling Green airstrip. Numerous other people saw unusual aerial objects that night.

On February 22nd 1967 in El Paso in El Paso County, Texas. Bob Gaines was climbing south of El Paso, when, in a clearing in the woods, he encountered an object 10m diameter on the ground. The thing rose at high speed leaving three marks, 20-25cm deep, 45-50cm diameter, on the ground.

On March 24th 1967at 0530hrs in Loco in Childress County, Texas. Air Force Staff Sergeant John Ferguson, his wife and three children were on the FM road, en route from California to Tennessee when he pulled up in the vicinity of Loco to consult his road map. His attention was attracted by a red light, which he first thought was another vehicle until it came close, at which he saw that it covered the width of the road. John now drove off, the object following him at speed up to 160kph, profiling the contours of the landscape. It was gaining on the car when they reached a farmhouse, where the light split into two separated lights and disappeared.

At Wellington near Loco in Collingsworth County in Texas on 31st March 1967 at 10.30 pm Mr. Carroll Wayne Watts, a farmer, was returning home when he saw a strange light. He drove to within twenty feet of it on a dirt road. The light was one hundred feet long by eight to ten feet high. Watts walked up to it and found a door and knocked on it three or four times. A voice began speaking to him. The voice was genderless and asked if Watts could submit to a rigorous physical examination and if he passed it he could make a flight with them. No woman or child could though. The voice asked Watts to stand before a machine. Watts saw a map on a wall and the voice continued coaxing Watts to come inside. Watts left and got back into the car and turned his lights on the ship. It gave off a clear flourescent glow and began to move and then took on a reddish cast. The UFO took off and headed South as Mr. Watts drove away. There was no noise from the machine. The promises continue as does the mythology. Here is another version. Carol Wayne Watts (29), a respected local farmer was working in his barn when he saw a light on his uncle's adjacent property and went to investigate in a pickup. In his headlights he saw a dull grey cylindrical object 25-30m long, 2.5-3m high, floating about 60cm above the ground. Fearing a plane crash, Carol walked towards the thing. A door slid open and he saw inside. There was no crew, only machines and dials lit by a strange blue light. A voice, like a recording, invited him on board to take a physical examination. It seemed to know all about him. The voice said that they were stationed all over the world and that no-one could stop them. On the night of April 11th, Carol went out to check for storm damage and saw the light again. Before he reached the spot, his truck stalled as a small ovoid object landed beside him. He saw 4 men beside it. They were 1.35-1.5m tall, muscular and dressed in a white coveralls. They had wrap around eyes, superficial ears and noses and slit like smiley mouths. An electronic voice again urged him to take a physical. He entered the machine and a door closed behind him. There he was sat on a flexible chair. The lights went down and Carol felt pushed back and had other feelings of acceleration. After a couple of minutes a felt three bumps and a slight vibration. The door opened and he saw a large room. He was stripped and probed by delicate wires, while the beings stood in another room, studying something on an illuminated circle, as if studying the results. Carol saw a green cube on a table and put it in the hip pocket of his jeans, which were hanging nearby, but after he had dressed, one of the men reached into the pocket and removed the cube. Carol grabbed the being's arm and was knocked unconscious.

Still in Wellington on 11th April 1967 Carroll Wayne Watts saw a strange light on the way home. Again. The engine of his pickup truck stalled and Mr. Watts got out. There was an egg-shaped object directly behind him and a door opened. Four small men appeared that were less than five feet tall with a muscular build, elongated eyes and slit-like mouths that did not move when they spoke. The Humanoids wore white coveralls and asked the witness to again go with them. This time Carroll went with them and was flown to a much larger machine where he was examined by a machine which probed his body with wires. In the months following the witness saw the Humanoids again and photographed them eleven times. Carroll Watts again. The only other events to have happened in the area were in 1897 when an airship was seen over Childress and more recently on 31st March when Carroll first allegedly met the Aliens.

On November 3rd 1967 at 1815hrs in Wellington in Collingsworth County, Texas. Mrs Hazel McKinney, Mrs Paterson and another person were driving south along US 83 en route on work, when their attention was caught by a light, which they thought was car a headlight, in an unoccupied wheat field. The light grew larger and then turned south and travelled parallel to the car. It then suddenly turned and flew in front of the car, and then took off at an angle. It appeared to be a silent, silver grey cigar shaped machine, large enough to drive the car into and with a fluorescent glow in its rear.

On December 7th 1967 in the evening near EL Paso in El Paso County in Texas. Wm. C. Collins observed an object hovering about 200 feet up; it appeared to be occupied. It was not a plane.

1970

At Adrian in Deaf Smith County in Texas in late August 1970 forty-three miles West of Amarillo white hot chunks of metal fell onto the George Gruhlky ranch. These were believed to be parts of a Soviet satellite. In 1936 there was a fall of ordinary chondrite meteorites here that ranged from 6.3 kilograms in size. In total there were 22.6 kilograms of meteoric material found. Two falls of obkectss in the same spot? What a coincidence!

Near Amarillo in Potter County in Texas during 1970. The source's grandfather got a job at a local ranch. The owner told him he could live in a home nearby with his family of 12. It was a two-story house with an attic. The strangest thing was that the house was surrounded by sand dunes. No plant life was evident within several hundred feet of the house. There were no unusual happenings for a couples of days until the source's aunt Betsy discovered something. It was a den of wolves and their pups. The next day she brought her father (the grandfather of the source) to show him the den, but when they got there the wolves were all dead. The pups were missing. They had been butchered by something with huge claws. This left them with a sense of dread. The night after, they discovered the wolf's remains. The grandfather had a dream of a "little angel" telling him to take his family and leave now! It kept "begging" him to wake up and leave. He woke and realized it had been only a dream. Then he realized he had to go to the toilet. This meant he had to go outside to the outhouse which was at some distance from the house. When he got there and sat in the outhouse, something caught his eye. On a nearby hill, stood a human-like shape with red eyes, staring at the house. The words of the little angel echoed in his mind. Earlier that very night the source's great grandmother had a terrible feeling and sent her granduncle, Ray, with his family to check up on his brother (the grandfather). Ray was almost to the house when he stopped, to get some water from a nearby well. He didn't get very far when the figure with red eyes appeared in front of him. He ran back to the car and told his family to run to his brother's house. He grabbed his shotgun and bowie knife so he could buy his family some time to get away. Ray made sure the car was between him and the creature. The creature charged him quickly! He shot the creature nearly at point-blank range several times with no effect. He attempted to stab it but almost got slashed by its claws. Then, he ran as fast as he could to the house. The creature followed but, suddenly stopped short of the hill. By then the entire family was awake and saw it on the hill staring at them. Grandfather told all the girls to get in the bed of the truck and covered them with lots of blankets and other stuff to make a barrier in case the creature jumped into the bed. The men were in the cab of the truck staring at the hulking being. They drove past it, praying it didn't attack them. Its gaze was on the house. Suddenly it jumped off the hill and began to chase them. It stopped short of the line where the sand ended and grass began. The grandfather went to the owner and told him what happened. The next day they went back to pick up their belongings and saw a sight "straight out of a movie." The owner was there with his ranch hands, police and what appeared to be military-appearing personnel. It seemed that they had known about it for a while, "the family had been bait for it." A K-9 unit went in to investigate. The first floor was totally destroyed. The second floor was the same as well. The dogs then got a scent of something and started to bark at the attic door. The officers opened the door and let the dogs up it. Everybody heard the dogs fighting with something. Suddenly the dogs were thrown out of the attic window like rag dolls. They were both skinned alive! The two officers inside went inside the attic to see what it was. Everybody outside heard lots of gunfire and then saw one of the officers being thrown out the window. He was dead before he hit the ground. When everybody looked back up toward the window, they saw the creature clear as day. It looked like a huge bald, blue-skinned man with big red eyes and sharp claws. The high ranking military man present ordered its destruction. Everybody opened fire on it and the house. Two men threw grenades into the attic and it exploded. The house was set on fire. Grandfather and family left but later heard that the only body found was that of the other officer. Footprints were found leading away from the house. Nothing of it was ever heard from again to their knowledge.

1971

In February 1971 at 2155hrs in South Tarrant County, Texas. Robert Razelle, an employee of a large department store in Fort Worth, was returning home from night school, driving west, when he saw a blue light rising from the ground to the southeast, close to the Quartermaster's Store. It was a cigar shaped object 90m or more long, rising at an angle. Along its sides were bands which gave off occasional flashes of yellowish light, giving the impression of doors opening and closing. The object was totally smooth and emitted a faint sound. After 15 minutes the thing assumed a vertical posture, rose slightly, stopped, made a sharp right angled turn and then shoot out of sight to the northwest at a 45 degree angle, disappearing in 15-20 seconds. Two other students driving on the same road confirmed the sighting.

In Summer 1971 (or following year) at night in Commerce in Hunt County, Texas. A married couple, watching a drive-in movie, saw a bright object hovering 2.5-3m above a nearby pasture. The thing had an opening in the side, from which came an auburn light, and a beam of light came down from the object's underside. The thing moved about over the field and then slowly accelerated away.

At 4.00 am on 4th November 1971 Trudy Van Riper was awakened by her cats growling and carrying on. When she opened the door they all hid under the living room couch. When she looked out of the window she saw an elliptical moon lighting up her backyard. Going to the front door she discovered a strange little vehicle sitting on her front lawn like a Volkswagen with no fenders or doors. From the top emerged three small men dressed in dark garments one of which communicated with her telepathically asking "Are there any pigs in the field? They are hungry". Then she saw near the men two peculiar animals covered in fuzzy hair standing erect. She went back into the house and when she looked again the object was airborne and the moon was gone. Later she learned that several pigs had been lost at a nearby farm. This was near Austin in Texas.

1972

On July 27th 1972 in Tyler in Smith County, Texas. Joe Carter, Michael Chambers (qv) and three of their friends were sitting on the balcony of their apartment when they saw an object that appeared to rise from a group of trees across the street. It was oval shaped with two search lights in front and on its bottom was a triangle, comprising a mass of blinking white lights, with red, green and blue lights located at each corner. It came out of the trees, hovered for about two minutes, disappeared, reappeared, came across the road towards the apartment and then went behind a cloud, came out again and then disappeared. No sound was heard. During the performance the group rushed downstairs to the parking lot where they joined two other witnesses.

On 8th August 1972 near La Porte in Harris County in Texas a driver was in the left lane of two travelling at 55 miles per hour when he realized that his front fender was falling off. Suddenly his left front fender dropped down and bottomed out and his car was pushed perfectly sideways into the right lane. The startled driver reacted with a left turn of the steering wheel while he heard the sounds of tires screeching. He realized that he had been pushed and looked into his rear view mirror and could not understand what he was looking at. He saw a clear or transparent twenty foot orb in the median that was rippling and distorting scenery behind it. It had a four foot tall and three foot wide egg-shaped sphere inside just a few feet above the median. Inside the inner sphere there were large, bright, slow wiggling electrical bolts spaghettied together. As soon as the clear orb stopped wiggling everything was transparent or invisible.

On September 17th 1972 at night in Richardson in Dallas and Collin Counties, Texas. Billy Erwin and some friends were followed by a red glowing round object, the size of a basketball, which hovered over their car as they drove back from Sherman. The thing followed them in to Billy's yard, where it was seen by his mother, as it hovered 15m above the ground. The light was said to follow Billy quite regularly.

On November 3rd 1972 at 0400hrs in Austin in Travis County, Texas. Trudy Van Ripper was disturbed by her cats acting up and when she tried to put them out, they hid. Returning to her room and switching off the light, she saw, through the window, s golden shiny wheel with a centre hub and spokes, which was spinning rapidly and reflecting light. She felt impelled to go and open the door and saw an object like a Volkswagen without fenders or doors on her lawn. The top slid back and from it emerged three dwarfs with dark skin, hair and clothes who sat on its top. One of the dwarfs seemed to communicate by telepathy "are their any pigs in that field, they are hungry". She then saw by the dwarfs two animals covered with fuzzy hair, standing upright. She feared that these creatures were going to eat her, but the little man reassured her and told her that the incident would be like a dream. She closed the door and saw the small object move off towards Austin 13km away. The next morning she discovered that a neighbour had lost several pigs.

1973

On March 6th 1973 at 0200hrs in Waco in McLennan County, Texas. A 24 year old waitress was driving back to Waco from the diner where she worked, some 40-55km from town. She had driven for about 15 minutes on a quiet stretch of road when she began to feel light headed and nauseous and the car engine seemed muffled. She tried to continue her journey but the car became filled with a brilliant light, the car headlights and engine failed and she felt shooting pains through her body. She parked on the hard shoulder and saw pale pink dome shaped object in a field about 60m away. Two small humanoid creatures were moving towards her. She tried to leave the car but her legs became unresponsive. She was next aware of being in the passenger seat of the car as dawn was breaking. She had dreams of being taken on board the strange object and being laid out on a table and given a medical examination that included a metallic tube being inserted into her vagina, and a similar but smaller devise into her right nostril. She also had dreams of apocalyptic destruction. About three weeks after this experience she encountered a strange man who came to her door and asked questions about her security. She also had visits from military looking people who talked about aliens kidnapping people and planning to start nuclear war.

On March 19th 1973 at 2200hrs in Marfa in Presidio County, Texas. Two geologists, prospecting for uranium, were sitting in their car about 15km east of Mafra when they noticed horses in a nearby field acting up. Moments later they saw luminous sphere approaching from the south west, followed another similar one. The lights were half the apparent diameter of a basketball. They went behind some bushes and hovered for a few seconds before just vanishing.

Near Houston in Harris, Fort Bend and Montgomery Counties in Texas in May 1973. One of the few UFO encounter cases which also involved animal mutilation occurred in May, 1973, and involved four women. Judy Doraty, her daughter Cindy, Judy's mother and sister-in-law would have the most terrifying experience of their lives. After playing Bingo in Houston, the four women were returning to Judy's home town of Texas City, but first going by Alto Loma to drop off Judy's sister and brother-in-law. After dropping off the two in Alto Loma, the remaining four saw a strange light, which seemed to be hovering in the night sky. The sight was intriguing enough that the four women stopped, and got out of the car to get a clearer look at the source of the light. They watched in awe until the light disappeared. They then resumed their trip to Texas City. Eventually, Judy began to suffer from extreme headaches and anxiety. After being seen and dismissed by several doctors, she was referred to well-known Ufologist and hypnotist Dr. Leo Sprinkle. Sprinkle's previous experience with the UFO enigma led him to recommend hypnosis as a way to relieve Judy of her emotional trauma. There can be little doubt that Sprinkle suspected an abduction from the beginning. Under hypnosis, it was revealed that Judy had apparently been abducted aboard an extra-terrestrial spacecraft. Judy went on in detail, describing how a cow was taken up into the craft and methodically mutilated by two "small entities." During the hypnotic regression, Judy described the unusual sensation of being in two places at once. She said that she was still standing beside her car after they stopped to watch the strange light in the sky. However, Judy also said that at the same time, she was in a strange chamber watching the gruesome experiment unfolding before her eyes. Footage of this regression was included in Linda Moulton-Howe's award-winning documentary "Strange Harvests." In a 1989 interview on 21st Century Radio, Linda Howe divulged what had been learned from the experience of Judy Doraty: "Judy described . . . in a pale beam of yellow light, a small brown and white calf being taken up into a craft. Then, in an extraordinary way, [Judy) was inside the craft, and she watches the calf have pieces of it excised: the tongue, the sex organs, the eyes?" Some of Sprinkle's hypnosis session is included below: Sprinkle asks, "Is there anyone around you?" There was this long, almost forty-five-second pause, and then she said: "two little men." "[The two beings) were about three and a half to four feet tall; grey creatures with large egg-shaped heads." "It's like a spotlight shining down on the back of my car. And it's like it has substance to it. I can see an animal being taken up in this. I can see it squirming and trying to get free. And it's like it's being sucked up." She then went on to mention seeing her daughter Cindy on an 'operating' table. She went on: "They don't listen, they just ignore me . .go about their work as if it's nothing. They don't seem to have any emotions. They don't seem to care. They just take some samples from her." It would be a number of years later when Judy's daughter Cindy would also undergo regressive hypnosis. Her session only corroborated her mother's. Statement by Judy Doraty on February 01, 2003 at 19:48:28: First I must say there is no doubt that abductions exist. My abduction took place in 1973. There were 16 eye witnesses to the craft, though not all remember an abduction. My daughter who was 14 at the time and myself. This was first reported to Ellington Airforce base in Texas, who denied anything was on radar at the time. Our abduction was also returning from a bingo game in Houston, to our home in Texas City, first going by Alta Loma to drop off sister and brother in law. There was another sighting of three people coming from a bingo game in Houston that got burned by the effects of the sighting. Our sighting was almost a year before theirs. So much happened that night I would not attempt to go in detail, we were all changed and have never been the same since. We were first ridiculed so much by others who were not present (family mostly) I did not talk about it for a few years. Then my husband returned home from Viet Nam and we were stationed in Yuma, AZ. I somehow heard about APRO. I called them and told them about my sighting and the very next day, a Mr. Daugherty and his wife and a doctor. who had experience in hypnosis named Rose Tennant came to my house and spent the entire day going over what happened. Dr. Tenant regressed me and a few details came out or shall I say surfaced. I had been having terrible migraines, and just the amount of surfacing relieved much. I know I remembered a formula that was given to me by the small gray alien. I think that is what caused a lot of problems. I did not say anything to anyone else as I was still gun-shy and afraid of ridicule. A few years later I got a call from a lady Named Linda Howe. We talked a long time her trying to convince me I needed to be regressed again for a TV documentary she was doing called the Strange Harvest. For some reason I began to trust her as she convinced me she believed what I was saying. And as all abductees know this is one of the most important things to help one get on with their life. In my abduction I witnessed a small calf being transported in a LARGE CRAFT. At that time I somehow was teleported or astroprojected or something, as I was in the craft seeing what was going on as well as standing by my car I had gotten out of to see what the huge light was that had been pacing our car for about twenty miles or so. Anyway I allowed a DR. Leo Sprinkle from the University of Wyoming to do his regression. It was about a three hour regression, I fulfilled Mississippi Howe's agenda she got an Emma for her documentary, but I was left with all the information in my head that still needed syphoning. I asked her to help me write a book to be able to tell the amazing things that I was told and shown. She agreed and then kept putting it off. Both her and Dr. Sprinkle used my case for their own agenda and had little else to say to me. I guess I am trying to warn all of you to be careful who you trust. My main concern was I always wanted my abduction to be presented in a way that it would not be construed as a crazy woman venting her boredom. So again I pulled myself in a shell and talked to no one. I was contacted by Sightings to do a follow up and I called Linda Howe she told me it would make the story unbelievable to the average person and I should not do it, so I turned them down. Later I learned she a a rift with Mr. Wrinklier and that was the only reason she did not want me to be on the show. Then about ten years ago I was told by someone in the UFO community who was familiar with my case that Mississippi Howe had gone to Kirkland Airforce base was warned to keep my mouth shut but Mississippi Howe never told this to me. She told a ufologist who called me. In other words the government did not want me to say anything about a formula I was given. I became frightened and this is the first time I have shared anything. I hope someone reads this that will contact me and give me advice or help as the abduction is 30 years old, I am 63 and before I die I would love to know what many already know, and why they do not want my story told.thanks for listening.

Around 2.00 am in June 1973 Mr. Guadalupe Cantu, 19, glanced through the kitchen window and saw an orange luminous object moving thirty feet above nearby rooftops. As it drew closer he could see that it was a transparent disc-shaped object in which stood a hairy, ape-like creature without any clothing. The hairy entity was looking down at him. Its hand apparently rested on something. No machinery or controls could be seen and the UFO passed about a block away making no sound and then went out of sight. This was in San Benito in Cameron County in Texas.

On September 5th 1973 near Clint in El Paso County, Texas. A very bright aerial object apparently landed in Lower Valley near Clint.

In mid-September 1973 at 2330hrs in Carthage in Panola County, Texas. A young man driving home from a date noticed a dark shadow pass over. On slowing and looking round he saw it was a large boomerang shaped thing, about 5m thick over the trees. As he hurried home the thing paced him and then veered overhead. As it did so his lights, engine and cassette player all went out and only came back when the object had gone.

At Longview in Gregg County in Texas in mid-October 1973 silver strands of unknown material fell from the sky. UFOs were seen in the area as well.

On October 21st 1973 at 2100 in Mineral Wells (Palo Pinto) in Texas. A woman living southeast of Mineral Wells telephoned the police department shortly after 9 p.m. to report she had seen a "little green woman." Another resident telephoned 20 minutes later to report a UFO sighting at 503 S.E. 6th Avenue, also in the southeast sector.

On November 3rd 1973 at 2110hrs in Lewisville in Denton County, Texas. Norman Hearn was driving was driving near the Lewisville when his truck began to vibrate all over and the engine and electrical system malfunctioned as a saucer shaped object passed over at very low altitude . The effects passed off when the object moved away.

On the night of 14th November 1973 near Poteet in Atascosa County a man encountered a UFO about two miles East of town on State Road 1470. It hovered low over the road and tall, greenish Humanoid figures were visible behind a window. Though the witness did not stop some liquid dripped from the craft and damaged the paint on the hood of his car. Highway Patrol officers saw the damage and took samples of the residue of ashes. Or this. At 6.45 pm Ray Landrum (20) was driving on FM 1470 about 3km east of Poteet, when he encountered an object hovering low over the road. Behind a window on the object tall humanoid figures were visible. Though Landrum did not stop some liquid dripped from the object and damaged the paint on his car bonnet. Highway Patrol Officers saw the damage and took samples of the residue of ashes.

Also on November 14th 1973 at 0630hrs in Brownsville in Cameron County, Texas. Cameron County deputies Eddie Gonzalez and Frank Lopez were driving three prisoners to Huntsville State Penitentiary when a silent, round object, with a red light on the top and a yellow one on the bottom, descended to 15m above their cruiser. It followed them for 30km at speeds up to 130kph. The prisoners in the rear began to panic. Police units in Harlingen and San Benito were alerted and Patrolman Arnold Riveas of the San Benito police observed an orange object hovering 12m above the deputies' car. The object then changed to an intense white, turned off at an angle and took off at terrific speed. The unit at Harlingen also saw the light.

On November 18th 1973 at 2015hrs in Bremond in Robertson County, Texas. Mrs Fay Seeley, her sons Richard and Russell and Mrs Fay Hileman and her son Richard were driving on Hw 14 near Bremond when they saw a bright light, which then dimmed, low in the sky. Later the object appeared on first one side of their car and then the other, darting faster than the eye could follow. This object followed them, dimmed out, got brighter and then disappeared. At the Brazos River Bridge the thing reappeared again, at treetop height, as if to land. Mrs Seeley then turned the car around but the object kept following them, keeping pace but when another car approached the thing took off. It was round, with one point on the top and two on the bottom and was bright enough to cast shadows on the highway.

On November 21st 1973 at 1930hrs in Calvert also in Robertson County, Texas. Gracia Unger and others saw a slow moving object, shaped like a brick with its ends worn off, land in the River Brazos channel, near Farm Road 979 near Calvert. A dimly lit some was just visible on top. A second, similar, object also landed in the river channel. The lights on both of these went out and they submerged. There were numerous other UFO in the next week or so.

In November 1973 at Port Isabel in Cameron County, Texas. Two people saw a square object land in an alley between houses.

Still in November 1973 and still in Port Isabel, a woman saw a large object hovering a few metres above her 2m high fence and at the same time heard strange sounds on her roof. She called the police. She was surprised to find papays melons strewn across her yard, though there were no such trees in the area.

On December 7th 1973 early in the day in Bremond in Robertson County, Texas. Two deer hunters were camping at Steele Creek near Bremond saw a tremendous object hovering over them. One hunter fired at the object repeatedly with his rifle and could hear his bullets strike the underside with a metallic sounding noise. The object then rose up into the sky silently and swiftly.

On December 11th 1973 at 1830hrs in Calvert in Robertson County, Texas. Mrs Nita Smitherman was driving with her grandson Brent R(4) on the Old Hearne Road, north of Calvert when the boy began to insist that there was a "spaceship" in their pasture, near the calf pen. When Nita looked she saw an oval object, the outline of which was blurred by very bright flashing red lights. The oval was surmounted by a sort of tower, on top of which was an even more intense red light. At either ends of the object were antennae which seemed to gather and project the red light in a pulsating motion. The light on its west end was huge and maroon. Nita drove into the yard and called her husband. When he came outside and neared the fence, the object made a whooshing sound and took off faster than the eye could follow. It settled down again in the distance, behind some trees. An oval area of depressed grass was found, with white ash.

On December 19th 1973 still in Calvert, Texas. A truckload of workmen on the Eugene Gibson were paced buy an object at treetop height, which stopped when they stopped when they stopped ,reversed when they reversed and moved forward when they moved forward.

One night during December 1973 several witnesses watched a bright light hovering over a local bridge near Calvert in Robertson County in Texas. Later a blue white object landed on a nearby field and soon after a tall bulky hairy figure appeared on the bridge. The witnesses then fled the area.

Also in December 1973 in Calvert, Texas, Mr and Mrs D L were followed home in their car by an egg shaped object, which directed a powerful light on the as they drove through the Bazos bottomlands into Calvert.

Also in Calvert Texas that December Alfred and Helen Conitz saw a flat pie-plan shaped object moving erratically in the sky from their outskirts home It was observed for 30 minutes and appeared as though it was about to land at one point.

1974

In Spring 1974 at night in San Benito in Cameron County, Texas. Lupe Cantu woke up and went to his kitchen to get a drink when, through the window, he saw a bright object moving across the sky. In a transparent dome on the object could be seen something that resembled a gorilla.

On June 27th 1974 in Calvert in Robertson County, Texas. Housewife Alice Tibble was letting the dog out when she observed, hovering above an old oak tree, a blue-white object, at least 15m across, with a band of red light around it. After hovering for 15 minutes the thing took off vertically.

On July 20th 1972 (approx. date) at night in Tyler in Smith County, Texas. Joe Carter and Michael Chambers saw an oval object with a wedge and multi-coloured lights, including red and amber, rise slowly from the trees. The lights then went out and then reappeared a.beacon lights as the object flew in and out of the clouds.

On August 2nd 1974 in Calvert in Robertson County, Texas. A newspaper editor and his wife heard some strange metallic noises and saw a dark red object, which emitted roaring sound, pulsated, and chased their car for several; kilometres down Rte 979. When the object came close to their car, the vehicle began to shake as if were about to fall apart.

In August 1974 (or following month) at 0010hrs in Huffman in Harris County, Texas. Five people saw a disc shaped object, surmounted by a dome, the size of a small plane, emitting a faint hum, about 10m away. During the several minutes it was present they had a sensation of peace.

In November 1974 (Approx. date) in Calvert, Texas. A 36 year old businessman was hiking in the woods on his rest day, when, about 600m away, he observed a domed object 7.5m diameter, with green, blue and red-purple colours. There were two windows on the dome and the object rested on four metallic legs. The witness approached within 30m of the object, when a being 1.5m tall, dressed in a silver coverall with skin tight gloves stepped from behind some bushes. Through a transparent visor in its helmet, the witness could see its eyes were set far apart and its chin was pointed. The being came up to within 3-4.5m of the witness and lifted something taken from its right side to its face. The object flashed twice at which the witness fled.

Also in November 1974 (Approx. date) during the day in Fredericksburg in Gillespie County, Texas. A housewife was driving to Fredericksburg when a huge sausage shaped object swept out of the sky and hovered near her speeding car for several minutes before it veered away at terrific speed.

Still in November 1974 (Approx. date) during the day in Kerrville in Kerr County, Texas. A group of girls in a car were approached repeatedly by an object with portholes, through which odd faces peeped out.

On November 25th 1974 in Dallas in Dallas County, Texas. Dora Ellen Afelbaum was carefully driving her new car when her attention was caught by a light above her, which seemed to stay with her. Dora pulled over and parked. The light got closer so she rolled down the window but could not hear any sound so decided that the thing was not a helicopter. The light then moved and then hovered in front of Dora. She then saw what looked like dogs running towards the thing and got a glimpse of a humanoid form. Then the lights, dog, and form vanished. No other cars stopped, as if they had not seen anything strange.

At 2.00am on 15th December 1974 in Beaumont in Jefferson County in Texas a Police Officer on stake out duty watched a brilliant star-like object in the horizon. He took his eyes off it and resumed surveillance. A few minutes later he saw the light descend in a slight arch. He called another officer to his location and both watched as the object neared and actually came close enough to see a pilot in a lighted cockpit and instrument lights reflecting off his helmet and visor. The craft had a huge light on the front, was about twenty feet in diameter, but there was no light emitted from it. The craft was diamond shaped and the pilot was described as Humanoid and when he noticed the witness looking at him the craft shot away in an instant without any sound at all. Why the surprised aliens in a lot of cases? Didn't they know where they were?

At Wichita Falls in Wichita County in Texas one night in 1974. Just North of Fort Worth, a "cake tin" shaped UFO crash landed for unknown reasons. The craft was recovered in an almost intact state. Three live, generally gray-white skin type Humanoids that walked out of the craft were promptly captured by the US military. The craft was then moved to a nearby military base (possibly Fort Sill, Fort Worth or Fort Hood) and soon after to the S4 facility in Groom Lake Nevada. Two or three of the surviving aliens were also taken to the S4 facility, held prisoners and interrogated there. They apparently died later, one after the other while in custody in the Nevada base, possibly as a result of shock and wounds. The origin of the crashed object was established to have been a "gray-reptoid" type planet. You figure.

1975

On 14th January 1975 two nights before three witnesses saw a silent luminous disc-shaped craft hovering above the highway in China Springs in McLennan County in Texas a lone motorist spotted an astronaut like figure walking down the same highway. The figure wore a silvery suit and a helmet. Another motorist saw a similar figure around the same time.

On January 16th 1975 at 1930hrs in China Springs in McLennan County, Texas. A young woman out driving spotted an unusual cluster of lights hovering low in the sky, over a field. She arrived at a friend's house, to find this friend was also observing the object, which was smaller than an aeroplane and had rotating white lights. It passed over her car at 12m altitude and shot rapidly into the sky. The weather was clear and the observation lasted 5 minutes.

Near Henderson in Rusk County in Texas one day in Spring 1975. A farmer riding his tractor on his way to a field, watched a black unmarked helicopter fly over him at very high speed. The witness did not see anybody at the controls. Later that day, he found the remains of a mutilated cow on the ground. A few days later as he drove his pickup truck to collect some baled hay, he heard a dog barking. As he drove over a rise, he then spotted a black creature coming out of a nearby pine grove. The creature was man-shaped and had what appeared to be large wings. A black helicopter suddenly appeared overhead and the creature flew straight up into the helicopter and went inside it. Moments later the helicopter left. I report them, you……………do what you want with them. But are there consistent themes though. Our extraordinarys are starting to become very familiar and ordinary…..of sorts.

Around 9.15 pm on 3rd May 1975 Mr. Alois Olenick was driving to a nearby store in San Antonio in Bexar, Medina and Comal Counties in Texas when he saw an amber colored luminous object rise from a grove about nine hundred yards away. It then approached his pickup, losing altitude and becoming a blindingly bright cherry-red light. When it was directly over him the lights of his pickup went out and the engine died. Alois got out and saw a globular craft with two conical protrusions. The bottom was of highly polished metal. When the craft tipped at a 37 to 40 degree angle towards him he could see that the top half was transparent and contained two occupants. They were five foot tall or less with bald heads, large pointed ears, long noses and slit like eyes. Their skin appeared grayish and they seemed to be handling controls. There was no motor noise but a cyclonic shriek of wind came from below the craft. Then it took off straight up with a gust of wind that buffeted the pickup and vanished almost instantly. There was an odor like burning electrical insulation that persisted in the truck for some time. Alois's eyes were affected and he had to wear dark glasses for some time afterwards as a result. Here is another version. Alois 'Monk' Olenick (48), a sheet metal worker, was driving west on Mogford Road, south of San Antonio, in his 1959 pickup, to a nearby store, when he saw a strange amber coloured object rise rapidly upwards from a grove of trees about 800m into the pasture opposite the road. This object then approached his pickup at terrific speed, loosing altitude as it did so. As it approached, an amber primary light on the front of the object turned to an intense cherry red. When the object got directly over Alois' pickup his lights and engine went dead. At first Alois thought the object was a helicopter, but as it hovered overhead, he saw it was a roughly globular machine, with two projections on either side of the centre, these appeared to be part of a rim. The underside appeared to be made of highly polished metal, which cast a red glow, possibly reflected from the primary light. It was tilted at a 37 to 40 degree angle, revealing a transparent upper portion in which two occupants could be seen, outlined against a diffuse red light. One of the occupants appeared to have its hands on some controls, the other was looking directly at Alois. These occupants appeared to be no more than 1.5m tall, bald, with long prominent ears, long noses, slit like eyes, tight, firm, wrinkled grey skin "like sharkskin", and wiry firm build. He only got a look at their torso's, head, and part of the upper arm. On the control panel Alois could see several "T" shaped handles. They did not appear to be wearing head-dresses of any kind and he thought they wore leathery shirts. There was no sound of a motor, just a loud wind "like a cyclone". As the object took off straight up, a terrific thrust buffeted Alois' vehicle, and the object appeared to vanish almost instantaneously, like the turning off of a light bulb. Alois had also noticed a strong odour like burning copper as the object hovered over his truck that persisted in the truck for some time. Alois also suffered from slight eye damage and had to wear dark glasses for some months, and also some anxiety but there were no other effects.

At 9.20 pm on 5th May 1975 a domed disc-shaped object was seen on the ground in Pleasanton in Atascosa County in Texas. There were two figures inside the dome and the witness, who was in a truck, was hit by a blinding light and his hands went numb. The encounter lasted two minutes. Was this Alois but it is a bit far to go from San Antonio? Pleasanton is only thirty miles south of San Antonio.

At Copperas Cove in Coryell County in Texas in 1975 an orange light was seen hovering over a field. Individual witnesses saw shafts of bluish-white light passing from the UFO to the ground. A calf that had been mutilated was found at the spot and the vegetation around it was flattened into leaf shaped patterns arranged into concentric circles seemingly under the impact of blasts of air from above. Forty yards from the calf there was found to be a circle thirty feet in diameter obviously made by something that had come down from the sky and rested there.

1976

On October 31st 1976 at 1940hrs in Garland in Dallas County, Texas. As a small boy was being taken home for his 2000hrs. bedtime, he saw a line of copper coloured missiles fly 3m above a nearby house. Neither his mother nor other children out in the street appeared to see the objects.

In October 1976 at 2115hrs in Dallas in Dallas County, Texas. A woman out driving with her 6 year old daughter heard a loud noise when she stopped at a stop sign. Looking up she saw a huge dark, silvery grey sphere or disc, "half the size of a basketball court" hovering overhead, making a roaring sound. The thing had a misty outline, with a sort of multi-coloured haze on its boarders. The thing moved off and she felt an urge to follow it, gathering the impression that the object had control over her car and was speeding it up. With something of a struggle she eventually managed to stop the vehicle, and the mystery object disappeared. Though she had been a bumpy road, the journey at speeds of up to 120kph had seemed entirely smooth.

1977

In May 1977 at 0115hrs in Tyler in Smith County, Texas. Ronnie Patrick (18) heard a growling sound outside his house, and on going to investigate, saw two very tall black figures with no hands, feet nor facial features floating 20-25cm above the ground in the porch, He was shocked and scared. The police were called but found nothing. Ronnie later found what looked like the footprint of a baby with claw marks near the fence and felt impelled to cover it up.

Around midnight on 4th July 1977 the witness and his girlfriend had gone to an isolated field to watch the fireworks from the nearby town of Happy in Randall and Swisher Counties in Texas. Soon they noticed three white objects encircled in multicolored lights hovering over the area. The light now began shining blue-white laser-like lights to the ground. Frightened the witnesses attempted to crawl away from the area and back to their car. As they drove away the car stalled. Looking out and up they saw a huge object hovering directly above them. It had numerous bright white blinking lights. They both exited the car and attempted to run away from the area but then the witness stiffened and fell to the ground. His next memory was of lying naked on a table in a silver colored room. He felt like he was strapped to the table with straps on his neck and ankles. He noticed several surgical instruments near him on a table and that his girlfriend who was also naked was lying on a table surrounded by numerous silvery-garbed white colored figures. Two Humanoid figures approached the witness and apparently took skin samples from him. He felt no pain. Soon he found himself in another room with his girlfriend sitting next to him. He found a triangular shaped scar on his penis. His next memory was of waking up on a field naked along with his girlfriend. Their clothes were nowhere to be found.

Around 8.00 pm on 27th September 1977 near Houston in Texas Joe Venneman was driving with a friend when he was stopped by a man in a silver suit. Joe was taken across a field and into a landed object. Afterwards he had drying of the throat, watery eyes, a feeling of panic and amnesia.

1978

In August 1978 (or following month and year) at 2100hrs in Fort Worth in Tarrant County, Texas. A couple and then son were driving home when they saw ahead of them, a light hovering over the power lines. When they got closer and stopped they saw that it was a sphere 3-4.5m diameter, which seemed to be sucking up electricity from the lines. Over 3-4m minutes the thing grew steadily brighter and then dropped a little, rose up and then shot off.

On October 30th 1978 at 1830hrs in East Lamar in Aransas County, Texas. Macky Parson and a friend saw a triangular object, the size of a house, hovering 30m above a field between Lamar and Lesley. It shot a blue light at them, which temporarily blinded them. Police investigated but no traces were found.

Around 5.00 pm in Austin in Travis County in Texas during November 1978 a male, 29, in a rural area saw a copper disc about twenty feet across about fifty feet away. It was domed and open like a wading pool that revealed four seated Humanoids in tight suits and head covers operating controls and looking at each other and at the witness. It was cloudy weather and the sighting was for twelve minutes.

1979

On January 17th 1979 at 0415hrs in Quitman in Wood County, Texas. While working on a construction site, Ronnie Patrick (19) was awakened by a beautiful beam of light, with sparkles, which entered his room through the window and wall. He reached out and touched the beam, which penetrated his arm, with a sensation like static electricity. The next thing he could remember was sitting in a chair at 0700hrs., fully dressed and ready for work. Following this experience he lost 25lb in weight, suffered from hair loss, burning eyes, dry nose and mouth, diarrhoea abnormal perspiration, bruises on the legs and bleeding from the teeth.

Around 10.00 pm on 24th January 1979 John Scott Cates had stopped his car near Lindale in Smith County in Texas to relieve himself. Suddenly a blue beam of light from the sky struck him. It caused his hair to stand up like an electric charge. Two UFOs appeared and he experienced a six hour long memory lapse. He next remembered being back in the car where his engine had restarted when a ringing noise sounded. He was left with holes in his shirt and a diamond shaped burn on his chest. Or this. At 2215hrs Scott X (20) was driving about 6.5km north from Lindale when he got out to relieve himself, leaving the car engine running and a tape cassette playing. A green and yellow light with sparks in the sky hit him, winds whirled around the car and his hair stood up on end. Then two complex objects appeared, with a violet red light moving between them. Then Scott found himself sitting in the front of his car, unable to account for the time lapse. The car engine was no longer running, though the lights were still on. There was a loud ringing noise and the car engine returned to life. Cold and upset, he drove home. Meanwhile Ronald Patrick, who had a time lapse experience on the 17th, had seen an object in the distance, and a "telepathic voice" informed him that Scott had been abducted, and that he should wait at Scott's home for his arrival. When Scott arrived and got out of the car at 0530, he appeared to Ron to be 2.1m tall, white, toothless and boneless. Scott appealed to Ron to touch him, but Ron was too afraid. Scott then collapsed to the ground, the voice told Ron that Scott would be all right, upon which Scott regained his human form except for a diamond shaped burn mark on his chest, singed hair and bruised legs. The car clock was 5.5 hours off, and there was a 2 minute blank on each side of the tape.

In San Antonio Texas on July 15th 1979 at night a couple sighted three large glowing balls of light hovering outside their home. They watched as five strange creatures floated down from the balls of light. The beings were described as thin, with grayish skin, large heads, and large dark oval shaped eyes. The man ran to get his gun, but suddenly both him and his wife were overcome with sleepiness. The next memory they had was waking up in the morning to find the man's shotgun totally dismantled and placed on the kitchen table. Later a frightening abduction was recalled under hypnosis. If you are concerned about the grammar of these reports at times, I prefer the wording of the witnesses except when it is incomprehensible and needs tidying up.

In late September 1979 at night in Houston in Harris County, Texas. A woman was at home alone watching TV, when the set developed interference and her patio became illuminated. On investigating, she encountered a being less than 1.5m tall, with large eyes lacking pupils and eyelids, and without nose, ears or hair, white fabric like skin and three fingered palmless hands. It was dressed a metallic grey suit and gloves. The thing seemed to speak without opening its mouth and invited her to come with it. She blacked out and awoke at 0330, but then remembered that she had taken onto a domed disc, via a beam. There she was able to wander around and converse with the crew, which consisted of both males and females. On one occasion she heard a sound and saw a being emerge out of a vortex. She felt she had other communications.

1980

In early March 1980 at 2145hrs in Bulverde in Comal County, Texas. Fred Wirth Jnr (40) stepped outside and saw a huge, intensely bright, orange glow at an elevation of 45 degrees in the clear north-east sky. It appeared to be only 30m above his property. Its angular size was much greater than that of the moon, but it had no distinct shape. After hovering silently for a few seconds it shot off like a rocket further north and stopped, hovering, as a red blinking dot. His wife Pat (28) came out of their restaurant, also attracted by the orange glow. She became nauseous and vomited in the sink. Fred felt drained and began to sweat profusely. He drove off towards the light with his father but could not overtake it. Other residents saw the light from a distance. At 2400 Fred a saw a flashing multi-coloured light in the west.

Near Waco in McLennan County in Texas one afternoon in April 1980 a rancher out looking for a missing cow encountered two four-foot tall Humanoids at a clearing near his ranch. The Humanoids had egg shaped heads, and large almond-shaped eyes, had green tinted skins, and wore tight fitting green outfits. The beings were carrying a calf between them and as they noticed the witness they turned their heads in unison to look at him. The witness became frightened and left the area. Later at the same location where the Humanoids had been, the remains of a mutilated calf were found. No blood was in evidence at the scene.

On the early morning of August 22nd 1980 near Lake Fork Creek in Hunt, Rains and Wood Counties in Texas the witness was driving with her young daughter on a desolate road when her car radio became garbled and she heard a loud electrical noise. Then her headlights dimmed. She and the vehicle were suddenly lifted off the road and the car entered the flat metallic bottom of a hovering craft and into a bright circular room. A voice in her head told her to get out of the car but she did not move. A small Humanoid, his feet encased in mist, now appeared and opened the door forcing the witness and her young daughter to follow him. He was described as having a large head with huge oval eyes, no body hair, a broad flat nose, and a small slit for a mouth. Both were then clamped down on metallic tables and were probed by two Humanoids using different types of devices. Before being returned to the car and lowered to the ground the witnesses were fed various colored pills. Under hypnosis the witness recalled extensive communication with the beings including the disturbing statement that earth "was a fearful planet with a tendency for annihilation." She also recalled being shown seven characters, which represented the name of the place they came from. It sounded like "Asterisk" but the witness could not pronounce it properly. Or this version. At 12.30 am Mrs M.E., a young woman with a bachelor's degree in education, was driving, in a great hurry, home from her mother's, a distance of about 110km, still in her nightclothes, as her two year old daughter had developed a severe earache She had travelled about 50km and was near the three bridges on Lake Fork Creek when her radio started to drift from one channel to another. As she turned it off, she was assailed by a loud electrical noise that hurt her ears, her car lights dimmed and the car appeared to be lifted off the highway. She fastened the little one to the seat and looked out of the window to see the tops of pine trees below the car being blown as if by a wind. She then looked up to see the metallic bottom of an object with a double row of lights. The car was drawn in through an opening to a circular, brightly lit, room, with no apparent source of illumination. As she sat there in panic saw bright lights and smelled something like rain. A voice in her head told her to pick up the child and get out of the car. An opening appeared across the room and a sort of vapour rolled towards them. A little creature appeared and again told them to get out. When she refused the car door fell off the hinges. M.E. felt quite calm. The being walked with a peculiar fluid motion which made the little girl laugh. It was a dwarf with a large head, no ears, oval eyes without either eyebrows or lashes, and a broad nose with two apertures on the upper surface, slit mouth, thin neck, completely hairless body, four long fingers on each hand, horizontal naval and no visible genitals. She was unable to tell whether its putty like surface was its skin or a tight fitting suit. They entered a roundish room, the floor of which was covered by mist, and in which were tables, multi-coloured lights and two other figures. M. E. and her daughter were clamped onto peculiarly wet tables, as two probes with ball and socket joins came down from an upper dome. When ME protested about the probe touching the sick child she was told that the child was no longer sick. ME was naked on the table. She was then moved into a vertical position from where she could see peculiar writing on the wall and a sort of screen on which a kaleidoscope of colour was moving. Through a window she could see two stars. The clamps were realised and they went into another misty room in which there was a triangular bed and a drawer in which a sort of pill was kept as food. She ate these and slept 10 times. She was visited by the three beings, who said she could ask any three questions about the universe. Both questions and answers were banal. She was led through a corridor, put back in the car, which was set down on the ground again. She found herself driving automatically only about 5 minutes from home. She was extremely dizzy when she got there and became withdrawn, losing 14 pounds in weight. After another UFO experience three weeks later she became panic stricken and sold the car. The garage claim that the door had indeed been taken off at some point. Much of this story came out under hypnotic regression and precisely what detail was otherwise remembered is not clear. The little girl's earache and a rash on her thigh both cleared up.

On 29th December 1980 Vicki Landrum and her grandson Colby, as well as a friend Betty Cash, were driving through an oak and pine forest near Huffman which is near Houston in Texas when they noticed a bright light hovering over some trees ahead of them. All three of them watched as the light gradually changed into a diamond of fire. The object seemed to be some sort of strange aircraft made of dull aluminum and with a line of blue lights running across its belly. The craft appeared to be in some sort of trouble as it kept dipping towards the treeline then belching blue flames from its underside before it rose briefly. Occasionally it beeped. Betty Cash, who was driving, stopped the car and all three of them got out to get a closer look. They estimated that they were only forty yards from it. They could also feel a tremendous heat coming from it which eventually made the skin of their car so hot that they could not touch it. Vickie thought that it was the second coming of Christ and told Colby that it was Jesus and he will not hurt them. Colby did not believe either adult and pleaded with them to get back into the car and get away. As they drove off they saw a swarm of helicopters surround the flying diamond. They counted twenty-three helicopters. Within hours of the sighting all three witnesses began to have severe headaches, swellings and blisters on the skin and diarrhea. Colby had a sunburn like rash. Vickie's hair began to fall out. One week later Betty Cash was unable to walk and her eyelids were so badly swollen that she could not see and was hospitalized for twenty-seven days. Over the next eight years she returned to hospital twenty-five times with eyesight and blood problems and was later diagnosed with cancer. There were physical traces found in the car including Vickie's fingerprints set into the dashboard which had been partially melted. There were also other witnesses who saw the UFO as well as the helicopters. Cash and Landrum filed a twenty million dollar lawsuit against the American Government for compensation for their injuries but it was thrown out as no such object was owned, operated or in the inventory of the US armed forces. Huffman is in Harris County in Texas. Or this. Betty Cash and her friend Vicky Landrum (60's) and Vicky's 7 year old grandson, Colby, were driving from New Caney to Dayton on HW 1485, when near Huffman a fiery diamond object, the size of the city water tank, descended to treetop level over the road ahead of them. They heard a beeping noise that persisted through the experience. From the object's underside red-orange flames were periodically directed towards the road, with an audible whoosh. Betty stopped, afraid to drive under the object and they got out to watch. They were struck by the brilliant glow, strong heat and a roaring noise. Colby became terrified and he and Vicky got back into the car, while Betty remained watching. Finally the object rose away to the south west, seemingly pursued by about 20 helicopters. The previously cool car was now hot. Betty drove Vicky and Colby home, and then carried on to her home, feeling ill. Almost immediately she began to suffer from a swollen neck, head and facial blisters, swollen earlobes and eyelids, the latter so severe that she could not see for several days. Within four days she was suffering from nausea and diarrhoea so severe that she could not eat and had to be hospitalised for 15 days, where she also suffered from severe loss of hair. Even after discharge she continued to suffer from swellings, headaches and lack of appetite so that she was re-admitted after just a week. By the end of February she suffered from continuous headaches and tiredness such that she was unable to work. Vicky and Colby also suffered from stomach aches and diarrhoea. Colby suffered eyeburn and extreme anxiety, Vicky tingling in the scalp and some hair loss.

1981

On June 12th 1981 near Alice in Jim West County in Texas. At 2:10 pm Robert Gomez, a vacuum truck driver, was headed West on highway FR 665 toward Alice, Texas after finishing a job. His vehicle had about 165 gallons of water in the tank and no pressure. He saw a bright object in the sky that he first thought was an airplane. It increased in brightness and stopped in midair. The object was domed, disc-shaped, brilliant white in color and with a dark ring around the rim and another dark ring around its center. Gomez felt the truck slowing down and tried to accelerate. The truck's exhaust stacks were blowing smoke, but the truck had apparently been lifted a foot off the ground. Although his AM radio quit working, his CB radio was still working, so he reported what was happening to his dispatcher. Shortly later the UFO disappeared into the clouds. Smoke was discovered coming out of the water tank valve, which now showed 55 pounds of pressure on the gauge. He opened the valve to drain the remaining water, but only steam came out.

At 9.30 pm on November 24th 1981 at Marshall near Darco in Harrison County in Texas. Dale Spurlock saw a red pulsating domed disc at treetop level while driving near Darco. It was seen near a small lake and some power lines, and had four colored lights–a row of red, blue, green, and amber lights–at the base of the dome. It made no sound as it passed left to right just above the trees, and then hovered. The object tilted, and two headlights from the front of the UFO shone directly down on his pickup truck. The object was revolving counterclockwise, and left toward the East. The truck's electrical system (alternator and battery) was damaged. Or this. Dale Spurlock, an electrical power company worker, and his girlfriend were out driving in his 1876 pickup truck, on a back road when they saw a bright light moving at right angles and then turning and approaching. On coming closer, to within 12m it resolved into two beams projected by an object with a flat bottom, surmounted by a turret like dome, from which the beams came, and on the bottom of which were four pulsating lights, red, blue,, green amber, and with a red flashing light on its top. On the lower edge were four windows giving off a dull white lights and it had a sort of grill structure on its underside. The, soundless, 6m diameter object was very low, almost scraping the hedge tops. Dale drove off, the object following. It stopped when they did and projected its beams again. When the couple turned onto the main highway and object moved off. The following day the truck's alternator and battery were found to be ruined.

One evening during September 1981 in Bryan in Brazos County in Texas taking a short cut through a local nature trail the witnesses began to hear nearby dogs barking furiously. Feeling afraid he picked up two large rocks in order to protect himself. Suddenly, as he continued on the trail a huge hard to describe creature jumped in front of the witness on the trail. Terrified the witness began screaming and threw the rocks at it. The creature then scurried into the woods. As the witness ran from the area he looked back to see a huge bright light shoot straight up into the air and vanish.

On December 14th 1981 in the early afternoon in San Antonio in Bexar, Medina and Comal Counties, Texas. A woman hanging out her washing had her attention caught by a large shadow and looking up saw a humanoid figure moving through the air at about 6m altitude and at speed, forcing her to duck. The figure was gone from view in seconds.

1982

One evening in February 1982 in Fort Worth in Tarrant County in Texas Alvin Guerra was lying in bed attempting to get some sleep when a bright blue flash whooshed through his window into his room. Curious, Guerra went out to the patio to investigate. He was astonished to see a gigantic, stealth-like craft hovering about 75 feet directly overhead. It was dark gray in color, and the wing portions at its side turned up slightly. It had a small tail fin with three large thruster rockets underneath it. The vessel was silent as it turned in a leisurely 360-degree revolution. Then a soft feminine voice from somewhere nearby said, "Don't be afraid! Cooperate and we won't hurt you!" A few yards away out of the shadows a gorgeous Nordic-looking female emerged. She was about six feet two inches tall with incredibly luminous, blue green eyes. Her skin was very white, almost alabaster in appearance. Her hair was a soft beige blond color. She was wearing a light blue form fitting jumpsuit with a strange emblem on the left side of the chest area. It consisted of a short, narrow stripe, light blue in color, slanting above a darker blue stripe of the same proportions. A dark blue circle appeared beneath the two stripes. She had a head covering of some sort that hung towards the back. She repeated the words "Don't be afraid" and cautiously extended her hand. When his hand was firmly in hers, a thick blue mist formed around them. The next thing he knew, they were standing inside the hovering craft. As he stood there, rainbow-colored particles bathed him for 30 seconds. The woman then beckoned Guerra to follow her. The interior of the ship resembled the same smooth dark gray metal as the exterior. It was extremely cold inside. He entered a room where he saw numerous long cylindrical boxes resembling coffins. All were opened and empty. He was told that in those containers, they "rejuvenated" a few hours each day. They then entered the cockpit where he saw a larger version of the symbol on her suit etched on the floor. There were five other women in the room, all similar to each other operating some controls. They all smiled at him. As they exited the cockpit, they passed three women sitting in a hall, operating what appeared to be light-based computers. One of the women was at least six feet eight inches tall. The women had the ability to read his thoughts. They now entered a room that appeared to be a medical area. In this room there appeared to be about 20 other women, all very tall, between 6 foot six inches and six foot 8 inches in height. They all appeared to be young. Each was dressed in either a light blue or cream-colored form fitting suits. If the suit was light, the chest emblem was dark, and vice-versa. The women were conducting examinations on some small animals and birds. One of the women was holding a hand-held device resembling a laser. A dark blue light emanated from it. Alvin was made to lie down on a long table. Directly over his head on the ceiling he saw a dark green screen with colored lines. There was also a black screen on the wall beside the table. A holographic image of his body appeared on the screen. A laser like implement drew blood from him. He was then given a tour of the ship by the same original host that was apparently the captain. Soon at a lounge like compartment, Guerra and the voluptuous captain had sexual intercourse. During the intercourse Guerra blacked out and then found himself back on his bed totally naked and with his turquoise necklace missing.

On May 22nd 1982 in Cleveland in Liberty County in Texas a diamond-shaped object with body lights and bright "headlights" flew overhead and was seen clearly in a Police spotlight. There was abnormal silence.

At 9.30 pm on July 22nd 1982 in Katy in Harris, Fort Bend and Waller Counties three witnesses saw a dark boomerang-shaped (or V-shaped) object with bright orange-yellow "headlights" hovering in the sky. As they watched, they noticed a total silence in the area. The object finally began moving and as it passed by their location, they heard a deep humming sound. While parallel to them, they could see small round white lights inside of the V shape. It was clear weather with unlimited visibility.

During summer 1982 in Bay City in Matagorda County across from LeTulle Park a teenage boy saw a figure through his window. It just stood there looking in at him. It did not move or make any sound. It had been already standing there when the boy happened to walk by and noticed something standing in front of the window and appeared to be looking in. It was around 10.00 pm. The animal was huge in width and height. Its width filled the width of the window and it appeared to be stooped as it looked inside. After a few minutes of looking at it the boy retrieved a 30.06 and contemplated shooting through the window to rid himself of the creature. It was gone by then. This was near the Colorado River.

On September 14th 1982 at 2230hrs in Ennis in Ellis County, Texas. A couple saw an object the size of a house flying at rooftop level. The thing was surrounded by a ring of white lights and had a red flashing light. One of the witnesses saw the same or similar object as Night. then next day, so low that it had to rise to clear a water tower.

At 6.00 am on November 27th 1982 two hunters in a deer blind in Castroville in Medina County in Texas saw a multi-colored V-shaped object nearly over their heads, moving very slowly toward the West. It would stop, drop suddenly several thousand feet, move laterally very fast, then turn without banking. It never made a sound. It disappeared from view just at sunrise.

In Winter 1982 at 1900hrs in Jackson in Madison County, Tennessee. A 38 year old medical professional was driving home when he saw an oval object 9-12m diameter hovering, about 300m over a soya bean field, about 1.5km from his home. It was emitting intense multi-coloured lights that pulsed along its rim. He accelerated away and the thing seemed to follow and hover over his car, The next thing he could remember was being at home alone and hearing about a UFO report on the late TV news.

1983

On March 7th 1983 in San Antonio in Bexar County in Texas a passenger alerted the driver of car to an object overhead. The driver stopped and got out. The object disappeared in place. Later a female cab driver approached the witnesses and said she saw the same thing. It was a gray oval object was observed in clear weather for 30 seconds. No sound was heard.

At 6.30 am on March 9th 1983 in Stamford in Jones and Haskell Counties in Texas a silent 50 foot long flying wing with two headlights was seen at 50 feet altitude! The same was seen on 20th and 29th March. It had an appearance and performance beyond the capability of known earthly aircraft. It was a delta-shaped object about 80 feet across and was observed by one witness. No sound was heard.

On June 5th 1983 in Vidor in Orange County in Texas a star shaped object with three rounded protrusions was seen hovering for two hours. It left when aircraft arrived on the scene. A hovering object was observed which was observed by six witnesses for two hours.

At 9.30 pm on July 22nd 1983 in Houston in Harris County in Texas a huge silent, stationary, boomerang shaped UFO with two large orange lights and many smaller lights in the middle of the V was sighted hovering over the suburbs in Houston, Texas. It then moved away past many witnesses. There was a wind sound but no jet noise, and was lost from sight in the distance.

At 9.00 pm on September 8th 1983 in Wake Village in Bowie County in Texas two men were "star gazing" with binoculars at the witness's home. The other man spotted a rapidly moving light and the main witness tracked it with binoculars until it was blocked by a tree. It did not dim out but remained steady. It was a white star, several miles away, and was observed in partly cloudy weather by two male witnesses, typical age 33, in a forest. No sound was heard.

At 11.30 pm on November 12th 1983 in San Angelo in Tom Greene County in Texas five small discs orbiting a large triangular object were seen. It was 100 meters long and the discs were 20 to 30 feet wide. The Sun glanced off the objects.

1984

At 8.15 pm on January 27th 1984 at Seven Points in Henderson and Kaufman Counties in Texas flashing red lights from above forced a car to a complete stop from 55 mph. A mother and her 7 year-old son lost track of time when lights entered the car. Her next memory was of speeding down the highway at 70 mph. She was stopped for speeding. Electromagnetic and gravity effects were noted. The mother reported that a period of time could not be accounted for. The red lights were observed at a lake for over 75 minutes.

At 9.20 pm on February 1st 1984 in Plum Grove in Liberty County in Texas five witnesses on a farm saw fifteen 747-size delta shaped objects singly and in pairs in the sky. Triangular objects were observed.

At 7.20 pm on February 15th 1984 at La Vernia in Wilson County in Texas a slow silent 12 foot long orange glowing cigar went up US 87. Hogs were agitated. It was an orange cigar-shaped object about 20 feet across and was observed by three witnesses on a farm for over one minute. No sound was heard.

At 8.05 pm on April 19th 1984 in Llano in Llano County in Texas five people witnessed a huge dome-shaped UFO fly over their house at only 200 feet altitude. It made a loud humming noise and had lights on the rim. A jet aircraft was seen in pursuit of the UFO.

At 9.30 pm on May 21st 1984 in Longview in Gregg County in Texas a triangular object with no lights or sound was seen.

Approx. 1984-85 I was living in Longview in Gregg County in Texas in town in a residential area. It was a clear night and I had went outside coming out of the garage into the driveway facing East. I looked up and saw a large triangle shaped object fly directly overhead at a low altitude (500 -1000 feet?}. Its flight path was approx. south-west. There were no lights but I could clearly see the outline of the craft against the night sky. There was no engine noise at all but I could hear the craft push through the air, almost like a glider. This was no glider. It was flying under power. I had only told two people about this.

1986

At 10.05 pm in April 1986 in Brownsville in Cameron County in Texas two witnesses driving back home after dropping off a friend spotted what appeared to be a bright star approaching their vehicle. They stopped at an intersection to watch and noticed another man in a station wagon doing the same thing. As the object came closer they could make out a saucer-shaped craft. The object hovered over the vehicle about the height of a 2 storey high building. On the lower part of the UFO there was a bright light and it was surrounded by what seemed about a ten-foot section area, which all of a sudden started emitting multicolored lights. It seemed as if there was a pattern to the lights as they went in different directions. Above the area where the lights were being emitted there were what seemed to be glass windows and the witnesses could make out figures moving around inside. The figures were human shaped except that they had very long and thin arms. Frightened the witnesses drove away and the UFO followed them for what seemed to be about five to ten minutes. As they approached the city lights the object suddenly took off in the opposite direction. Looking back the witnesses spotted three military helicopters headed toward the general area where the UFO had gone.

Here is another interesting first person encounter. On December 12th 1986 in Bulverde in Comal County in Texas the witnesses as a group were moved to travel 20 miles to a remote location familiar to each of them. Why we went there? Why we went out of the way of our original destination? I feel like we were led there. As we parked on a remote road to enjoy some beer and good Bud. We saw it. A bright object hovering over a house in the distance. Occupants of the house yelling at it. It begins to move. I notice another similar object. We are being "scanned". I can feel it. As both crafts move behind us we realize. This is unusual. No sound. Low speed bright changing in intensity. Light. Like the sun. But smaller. We start the van. Missing time. Next thing I remember we are traveling down a road a mile away from original location. We are being followed. Guided. There were 4-5 objects at different distances. The light. As it passed thru the trees created a laser effect. Broad fields of light with great intensity. As we are led out of the area. The object comes closer. 35 feet away. 35 feet up. Size of two vans. A half sphere. As me and my friend observed. Windows began to open like there were layers to the craft. Like eyelids kind of. As the outer layer moved it revealed windows. One at a time. The fourth window revealed a head. Like greys. It looked at us. They were so close. It was so real. We witnessed the same thing. In disbelief we searched for reason. Helicopter? No noise. The face. At that moment another craft appeared on the horizon. Many lights I said. Oh crap. It's the mother ship. It was an airplane. 737. Southwest. As it flew over. I remember thinking. The noise. We could here it long before it passed over head. But these other objects. No noise. At all. Complete silence not even a hum. We left the area in a state of shock. Rationalizing what we had seen. They were looking for something out there. When I told my mother. She stated. Maybe they were looking for something. How did she know what I was thinking. She went on to say. Maybe they are looking for something here that we have in great abundance that to them is sacred. Then it dawned on me. Crystals. There are many limestone caves that produce enormous crystals some the size of small cars. Having done some research I know now the significance. Quartz crystal. It requires certain elements and ideal environments to produce. I had a close encounter of the third kind. I feel strongly that one of my friends was abducted. Her behavior. The fear. She crawled under the bench seat in my friends work van. In her good clothes. She crawled under the seat and would not come out till we got a safe distance away.

1987

At 4.00 am in February 1987 in San Antonio in Bexar, Medina and Comal Counties in Texas Ed Conroy suddenly woke up with a strange sensation and saw a small dark figure sitting on the edge of his bed. As he looked at it, it moved and flew over his head disappearing into the wall behind him. As the figure left the witness noticed that the apartment was very hot, much more than usual.

On May 31st 1987 in Austin in Travis County in Texas my husband and I were in our 2nd floor apartment. Our grown son had taken the dog downstairs outside the building to go potty. He came back up to tell us to come down and see something. We did not run but walked. We witnessed, along with many other people, a huge rectangular shaped dark object moving slowly overhead South to North. It was just getting dark and it reflected the street lights underneath and the lights of the area. There were flames shooting out around it. No sound at all and very slow. It took at least 10 minutes to go over. It was shocking to see. In the paper the next day it said it was a Russian satellite or space debris burning up on re-entry. It was not anything like that. It was being guided and slowly traveling. We are not crazy or so gullible to believe that story. Somewhere my son has the clipping from the Austin Statesman. I never made note of the exact date and time. We took no pictures. I think we were all rather dumbfounded.

1988

On the afternoon of 15th August 1988 twelve thousand people gathered on the grounds of a Catholic church in Lubbock in Lubbock County in Texas. It was the Feast of the Assumption and the church was the St. John Neumann Catholic Church which was a huge subterranean structure on the outskirts of town. Monsignor Joseph James, the charismatic leader, had stated that a miracle would occur here. Monsignor James had been to Medjugorje in Yugoslavia a few months earlier and predicted that the Virgin Mary would appear. Several parishioners had believed to have received messages from the Virgin Mary over the same period. Sometime during Mass a strange cloud appeared overhead followed by another and then another. Eventually they formed a portrait of Jesus Christ and then the astonished onlookers saw the holy face of the Virgin Mary riding high in the clouds. Many climbed that the sun danced in the sky whilst multicolored lights and shadows played in the clouds. Some claimed that their silver-colored rosaries turned to a golden hue. Odd things happen in Lubbock. This description is the same as one of the episodes at Fatima in Portugal in 1916 and 1917.

Late on the night of November 8th 1988 in Houston in Harris County in Texas Laura Liccketto was very tired and was lying on her waterbed on the right side of the bed. Some time had passed, though she does not know exactly how much of a time lapse occurred from the time she went to bed to the beginning of her experience. Somehow she was now on the far left side of her bed. She had no memory of how she had moved to the left side. She then saw an "alien" standing next to her bed about one yard from her eyes. The only parts of the Humanoid that she could clearly see was his thin chest, very thin upper arms, neck, and face. There was a glow of light in the bedroom, enabling her to see the alien's gray, mottled skin, and large, black, almond-shaped eyes. He was only about 37 inches tall and had no hair. She could not move and could only think of how "ugly" the alien was. The figure suddenly disappeared in plain sight. The witness has experienced other strange episodes in her home.

1989

At 4.43 pm on January 22nd 1989 in Texarkana in Bowie County in Texas a single witness saw a large, silver, cylindrical-shaped craft passed 300 feet below a Cessna flying at 6,500 feet.

At 11.05 pm in February 1989 in San Antonio in Texas a single witness saw a disc-shaped object which emitted a beam of light which extinguished a nearby street light. There was a humming sound. The sighting lasted a few minutes.

In Texas one night in Spring 1989. One night the witness suddenly and in a dream-like state felt herself floating towards the ceiling. She floated through it and through the sky up towards a hovering object. Her next memory was of being inside the object. Several small aliens about 4 feet tall with large eyes and thin lips confronted her. When they spoke to her, their lips would not move. Apparently they were using some type of telepathic communication. She was strapped to a flat hard table and one of the aliens put his thumb on her forehead telling her that she would not remember them inserting a "tracking device" in her. Later she was taken to a desert area and into a cave in Arizona and they told her things that she would be doing in the future. They claimed that in her lifetime the Earth would burn to a crisp and it would be Man's fault. They told her that at times they come down to earth to check on our progress and select certain individuals for contact. Before she knew it she was taken back home. As she floated back down into her bedroom, she noticed that it was raining and there was thunder and lighting.

At 2.00 am on May 15th 1989 in Tyler in Smith County in Texas the 4 year old witness was sleeping in her father's camper at a truck stop and had been left there alone. She suddenly woke up realizing that she was no longer in the truck. Everything around her was white. She could not see the rest of her body, and she remembered being very cold. Her right foot began to hurt on the left side. She saw figures around her that were "darker than light" and their features were not discernable. Then she was back in the truck. She climbed out of the camper and ran to the parking lot. She looked up and saw three pinkish-red lights zigzag around and hovering in a triangular shape. The lights suddenly disappeared. An implant was possibly found in her foot in the summer of 1999.

On August 11th 1989 in Rosharon in Brazoria County in Texas two women and a man in a car encountered a craft hovering over the road. They were abducted and had an hour time loss. They reportedly encountered large lizard-like beings. One of the women had a brown area on one leg after the incident. The craft left marks on the ground. There was no other information.

1992

Late at night on December 8th 1992 in Houston in Harris County in Texas the witness awoke and observed a bright flash of light (there was no sound of thunder following). The subject rolled over and noticed a small gray alien "wearing a harness/utility belt." The witness was instructed to follow the alien outside, where a blue/white light was shining on a spot on the ground. The witness was instructed to stand in the light, and an instant later, found himself in a large circular room (about the size of a high school gymnasium). The witness was instructed to disrobe and led out of the room and through a series of corridors and passageways. Part of the time they walked but mostly they were transported by a means unknown to the witness. Eventually they arrived at a small room where several other aliens were present. A quick physical examination was given and then a human appearing individual entered the room (the witness in prior abductions had never encountered a human). The human asked several questions as to how/why the abductee knew he had been abducted before. The witness was also asked how abductees knew/found out about other abductees and why were they meeting together. (!) A model of the human brain was shown to the subject and he was asked to indicate where the "subconscious mind was located." He was unable to indicate a location and received a mental image or impression that another abductee was being asked the same question. The human then left the room and the subject was moved to another room. This room appeared to be some type of meeting or conference room. It also was round, but the lighting and the furnishings were quite different. A number of different alien life forms entered the room, the last being the one with human appearance. The small gray aliens left the room but two of the taller brown aliens stayed. (The description of the other life forms is being withheld pending further investigation). The witness was again questioned as to the nature of the subconscious mind and to his knowledge of his abductions and other abductees. After each question the witness received images of other abductees. He could see them in a room together. They were all nude and seemed to be unaware of the presence of each other. Each seemed to be in a trance-like state and behaved as if acting out a part. Later the human took him into a side room where he was shown a "strange sort of chart or diagram" which he did not understand and was unlike any he'd ever seen before. He was then led by two tall brown colored beings through several other rooms to another examination room/laboratory where a nasal implant was placed in his nostril. The witness was then given his pajamas, told to dress, and returned to his home and bed.

At 5.30 am on December 9th 1992 in San Antonio in Texas the witness suddenly awoke to the faint sound of voices and music. She then heard someone walking away from her bed towards the stairs. She then saw a tall, slightly glowing man-like figure run past her window. He was very quick and vanished in moments. The witness remained in a state of panic and could not move for a while.

Late at night on December 10th 1992 in Houston in Texas sometime after a meeting of known abductees the witness went to sleep for the night. He was awakened by several aliens (not described) in his bedroom that, in a very quick procedure, removed a nasal implant from the subject and immediately left. (Later under hypnosis a number of other abductees reported similar events).

At 3.00 am on December 31st 1992 in San Antonio in Texas the witness remembers walking outside by herself and hearing a very loud buzzing sound. She looked up and saw a huge gray metallic disc-shaped craft drop straight down from the clouds. The witness sat down cross-legged and watched the craft change into a sphere with four legs, with strange markings land nearby. A moment later the craft lifted straight up and left in a curved flight path. Later under hypnosis the witness remembers sitting on the ground and seeing a group of very tall pale human-looking men standing in front of the object. They all wore white clothing and watched her very intently. She received mental communication from the men then remembers entering a very shiny room where she was examined by one of the men that had light hair.

1993

Late one night on April 5th 1993 in Houston in Texas after receiving a post hypnotic suggestion instructing her to defend herself from her alien abductors the witness was in her bedroom sleeping when she awoke and two short gray Humanoids with large black oval shaped eyes came in right through the wall. As one of the beings approached the bed the witness grabbed what seemed to be a black protective eye shield over the Humanoid's eye. His skin felt rough as she tore the eyepiece off. A moist liquid fell on the witness's arm. It was described as a mucus-like substance. The beings then retreated through the wall and left.

At 11.00 pm on August 18th 1993 near Dallas in Texas a young Hispanic woman called neighbors and asked them to come to her house immediately, due to some strange goings on in the house. One of the neighbor's Jill, grabbed her camera and headed over to the house. When Jill arrived at the house, the entire family was in a state of terror and extreme agitation. Two of the young female family members were cowering in a corner of the living room holding on to each other. The Hispanic woman sat in a chair curled in a semi-fetal position rocking back and forth. She then pointed to the backyard. Jill looked through the sliding glass door that led to the back yard and saw a being approximately 15 feet from the glass door. The being had glowing red eyes that seemed to be scanning the house from left to right and top to bottom. Jill began snapping pictures through the sliding glass door. At the same time the Hispanic woman heard a long ringing sound in her ears. Eventually the being disappeared. Other family members reported seeing similar beings going through doors, windows and walls the same day and possibly 2 days before. An anomalous image did appear on the developed film.

Near Dallas in Dallas County in Texas on November 15th 1993 at late night. In a dreamlike state the witness found herself in an unknown location with three short gray skinned Humanoids that were "talking" to her. They were about 3 to 4-feet tall and were telling her that Armageddon will not be what most people think it will be. There were several tall beings standing off to the side and they seemed to be observing everything and seemed "in charge."

1994

At 2.00 am in June 1994 in Atlanta in Cass County in Texas the two witnesses were camping in an isolated field near a pine thicket. At night one of them had fallen asleep while the other woke up to see a bright light shining outside the mosquito net. He woke his friend up and went to investigate the source of the light. Walking across a pasture he saw a large ball of light apparently sitting on the ground nearby. They shone their flashlights at it and it apparently blinked out. This frightened the witnesses who began to walk away. After walking for about 200 yards they heard some noises coming from the nearby pasture. Looking around they saw about six to eight human-like figures approaching the fence. They ran back to their tent and were unable to sleep the rest of the night, hearing strange noises outside the tent throughout the night.

1995

Near Dallas Texas on February 2nd 1995 at 3.00 am. The witness suddenly woke up and found herself staring at a short thin white being. She was lying on her right side and its face was only slightly higher than hers. It was about 3 or 4 feet tall. Next she saw movement out of the corner of her left eye, she looked and saw its hand lifting slowly off her shoulder. Its hand had three very long, white, slender fingers with rather bulbous tips on the ends. The creature was very white and frail looking. Its abdomen was sunken and hollow looking which made its chest seem to protrude all the more. The being moved slowly toward the top of her head. She suddenly felt that the being was "scanning" her mind. A cold paralysis or "electric" sensation spread throughout her body as she heard the being whisper something. Her next memory was of seeing the being standing by the hallway staring at her. She then went back to sleep.

1996

One night in Texas, exact location not given during May 1996. Sharon (involved in other encounters) woke up during the night to strange bumping sounds in her house. The mysterious bumping sounds woke her up periodically during the night. She was afraid to get up and investigate on her own. Finally she woke up again to see a strange Humanoid hovering in the hallway directly across from her bed. She described the Humanoid as a small Negroid being about three and a half feet to four feet tall. He wore a complete astronaut's suit with a helmet, dark blue gloves, and boots. The helmet had a clear visor, and she could see his face through it. She described his complexion as being a reddish or dark pink color with two vertical folds of flesh across the side of his cheeks. His lips were large and fleshy, and his nose, broad and flat. His eyes looked totally human and his expression was that of "complete boredom." He was holding a round, black device that seemed to her like an old style radar gun used by the police. He pointed the object at the window in her bedroom and floated there as though waiting for something to happen. She also observed a white glowing light around him that reminded her of an aura. After a few minutes he disappeared, and the hallway and bedroom became dark again. A minute or two later, the room and everything in it was suddenly brightly illuminated…then to her surprise everything abruptly went completely dark again. The next morning she found all the grass and tree leaves on the side of her house near the bedroom window were yellowed and clearly dehydrated.

In Houston, Texas at 2.00 am on November 24th 1996. During a very stormy night, the witness was having trouble falling sleep and was very restless. There was a window right above the bed. After a couple of minutes something started making her feel very strange as if she was in some sort of trance. It felt as if something was pulling her from inside. At the same time something appeared on the upper part of the closet door directly across from the window. It was a reddish figure and appeared to have wings, or something on either side of it that was moving up and down. She also saw a shadow pass by the window to the left of the bed. The creature then apparently disappeared. The witness husband did not see anything. A week after the incident, the witness suffered a nervous breakdown.

1997

On April 28th 1997 near Longview in Gregg County in Texas. At 10:00 PM. the witness was driving alone on a business trip when he had a flat tire. A truck driver stopped to assist him when they both became aware of a UFO about 100 yards away. There looked to be Humanoid figures dressed in white clothing moving around inside the craft. The object was circular and emitted an occasional flash of light. The truck driver walked closer to the object in order to get a better look. He suddenly ran back in fear yelling that they had to leave quick. Both men got into the truck and began speeding away. Shortly after the UFO silently passed over the truck and quickly flew out of sight.

One night in November 1997 near Dallas in Texas a large egg shaped or oval shaped craft exploded and crashed over the area. It was apparently involved in a dogfight with another UFO. The craft broke into two parts and some wreckage and debris was removed (in boxes) by convoy to Grand Prairie NAS. Later the debris was removed to possibly Wright Patterson AFB and some of it was taken to Fort Hood underground laboratory. Nothing is known about the occupants onboard the craft. Both parts of the craft were mirror-like, reflecting everything. What if these reports are real? Where then are all of these crashed space craft?

At 2.30 am on December 12th 1997 in Lubbock in Lubbock County in Texas two young witnesses had stayed up late studying and had gone to bed late. Suddenly a strange silence and bright flashing lights outside the window awakened them both. Frightened they both felt their covers gently drawn from their beds. One of the girls then saw standing at the foot of her bed a tall thin figure with large black shiny eyes. At this point her memory ends. The other girl then sees the main witness body rise from the bed and into the waiting arms of a tall thin figure. Another figure then appeared and also carried her into his arms. Unlike her friend she was conscious during this part of the incident. Soon she found herself in a different place, lying on a strange surface that was both hot and cold and surrounded by tall thin figures. She felt a sheet over her body but was unable to move, she could only move her eyes but could not see her friend anywhere. But moments later she saw several of the beings carrying her friend's body out of the room. Looking towards the ceiling she an object descend slowly and silently towards her stomach. It resembled a very large needle. At that point she fainted. She woke up in the morning lying next to her friend on the kitchen floor. They could vaguely remember the incident and found strange marks on their bodies.

1998

In Austin, Texas on June 18th 1998 at night. After a powerful storm and twister passed over the area, the two witnesses were out surveying the damage. As they drove along an isolated road they came upon a hovering saucer-shaped object. As they approached the object on foot, two Humanoids (undescribed) suddenly confronted them. The Humanoids asked them what had just happened. They wanted to know what the twisting funnel was. The witnesses explained the nature of tornados to the aliens and their next memory was of lying on the ground and seeing the object shoot away at high speed.

Late at night on June 24th 1998 in Austin in Travis County in Texas the witness suddenly woke up in the middle of the night and sat up in bed. She looked out of her window and saw a bright white light hovering amongst the trees. Frightened she hid on the floor and covered herself with a blanket. But the light grew brighter and brighter. She could not breathe and removed the blanket only to find four beings at her side. They were all pale in color, almost translucent. They were all the same size, about 4 feet or so. The witness felt spindly hands grab her and pick her up. There were two beings on either side of her. She was then levitated and was able to see her husband sleeping as if nothing was happening. The witness began to struggle and managed to hit one of the beings. She was suddenly alone, standing at the same spot where it had begun. She looked down and found a strange looking white object in her hands. Overcome with terror she went outside and threw the object in the dumpster. Her next memory was of waking up in a depressed state and afraid.

At 4.40 am on September 25th 1998 in Sunrise Beach in Llano County in Texas the witness was driving his truck along his paper route, when as he rounded a corner he saw a disc-shaped craft with green and orange lights hovering about 25 or 30 feet above the ground. He also briefly saw a four-foot eight-inch tall figure apparently standing on the object that quickly disappeared from sight. The truck started to slow down then there was a very bright flash of light, which apparently blinded the witness momentarily. When he was able to focus again the object had disappeared.

In November 1998 near Benbrook in Tarrant County in Texas at 5:00 AM. A deputy sheriff was driving to work when he noticed a glowing, pulsing light to his right. He could also see beams, like lasers, shoot upwards. A news program on his radio was asking if anyone near Benbrook could confirm lights reported in to them. He called them [all his calls were difficult to get through] and said he was in the vicinity. He mentioned that he'd also seen a small plane apparently flying towards the area and the radio man said that this was their spotter plane. Then the entire electrical system of his car cut out, and he rolled to a stop. [engine out too, obviously]. Even his cell-phone would not work, even though it was only on battery power having nothing to do with the car. He himself felt as though an "energy" had hit him on the top of his head and run right down his body. "It felt like someone had poured warm oil over my head". The feeling left in three minutes. The car was immediately restartable. His radio had lost all its programming. His cell-phone came back on and worked once he unlocked the code. He thought about telling his officer colleagues but decided against it.

1999

At midnight on February 14th 1999 in El Paso in Texas the witness saw a bright green light descending. It seemed to get brighter as it got closer. As it approached it dimmed revealing a silver disc-shaped object that was spinning. There were several lighted windows around its rim and the witness was able to see several "shadows" inside.

At 11.35 pm on March 6th 1999 in Houston in Texas Douglas Juenemann and his girlfriend had gone to bed when a few minutes before midnight he felt compelled to look out the window. There he saw a misty apparition. It was a face, of little substance, but with very large eyes. The other features were obscured, but he could see a non-human nose and no visible mouth. After seeing the figure Juenemann felt an "electric" sensation going through his body, beginning at his wrists and his waist. His body became numb. The sensation traveled through his body twice becoming somewhat painful. The sensation ended and the face disappeared.

In San Antonio Texas at 5.04 am on July 18th 1999. The main witness was staying with a known abductee and her child in order to offer some protection and company and had fallen asleep, when suddenly he felt movement behind him. Thinking it was she, he did not turn around. Then he felt a "body" next to him. He then felt a pleasant touch on his upper back and he felt a peculiar sensation as an "arm" passed over his ribcage. Concerned he tried to move but was unable to. He was finally able to turn his head when he saw a round basketball shaped object under the covers. He jolted to his feet and heard a slight giggling sound at the same time that the object under the covers appeared to deflate. He attempted to wake up the abductee but was unable to. Two nights later he saw a small white grayish figure standing just inches away from him that suddenly disappeared. Other strange occurrences were also reported.

At Canyon Lake in Comal County in Texas on the night of October 2nd 1999. After a party six young people were walking through a field when they noticed that their bodies began to glow in a light resembling that of a "black light." Soon they heard noises like people running through the grass right besides them. They then saw what appeared to be figures climbing up the trees. Afraid the witness began walking back to the truck and drove to a nearby old Indian cemetery. They parked about 20 feet away and decided to go into the cemetery. As they neared the cemetery they noticed something approaching them. It appeared to have a human shape and red eyes. They all ran back to the truck. One of them was pulled to the ground by an unknown force as he reached the truck. The also noticed a figure sitting between two trees, cross-legged as they drove away.

Bibliography

"Breakfast with a Bigfoot" David Alderton. Beaver Books London. 1986.

"Extraterrestrials Among Us" George C. Andrews. Llewellyn Publications Saint Paul. 1992.

"The UFO Phenomena: a Scientific Look at the Evidence for Extraterrestrial Contacts" Edward Ashpole. Headline Books London. 1995.

"Ancient Traces: Mysteries in Ancient and Early History" Michael Baigent. Penguin Books Harmonsworth England. 1999.

"Aliens: The Final Answer" David Barclay. Blandford Books London.1995.

"Great Mysteries of the Air" Ralph Barker. Pan Books London. 1968.

"Ultimate Encounter: the True Story of a UFO Kidnapping" Bill Barry. Corgi Books London. 1981.

"UFOs: a Report on Australian Encounters" Keith Basterfield. Reed Books Australia. 1997.

"UFos: The Image Hypothesis" Keith Basterfield. Reed Books Australia. 1981.

"Charles Berlitz's World of Strange Phenomena" Charles Berlitz. Sphere Books London.1989.

"The Dragon's Triangle" Charles Berlitz. William Collins Glasgow. 1989.

"The Philadelphia Experment" Charles Berlitz and William Moore. Panther Books London. 1979.

"The Roswell Incident" Charles Berlitz and William Moore. Granada Books London. 1980.

"Without a Trace" Charles Berlitz. Panther Books London.1977.

"Charles Berlitz's World of the Odd and Awesome". Charles Berlitz. Fawcett Crest Books. New York. 1991.

Bigfoot Field Researchers Organization. www.bfro.net/

"Flying Saucers are Watching Us" Otto O. Binder. Horwitz Publications Hong Kong. 1978.

"The Loch Ness Mystery Solved" Ronald Binns. Rigby Publishers Australia. 1983.

"Unsolved UFO Mysteries" William J. Birnes and Harold Burt. Warner Books New York. 2000.

"Beyond Earth: Man's Contact with UFOs" Ralph Blum with Judy Blum. Corgi Books London. 1974.

"The World's Greatest UFO Mysteries" Nigel Blundell and Roger Boar. Octopus Books London. 1984.

"Alien Animals" Janet and Colin Bord. Stackpole Books Harrisburg, Pa. 1981.

"Modern Mysteries of the World" Janet and Colin Bord. Grafton Books London. 1989.

"The Evidence for Bigfoot and other Manbeasts" Janet and Colin Bord. Aquarian Press Wellingborough.1984.

"The Bigfoot Casebook" Janet and Colin Bord. Granada Publishing. London. 1982.

"The Unexplained" F. L. Boschke. Pocket books New York. 1978.

"Encounter Cases from Flying Saucer Review" Charles Bowen. Signet Books New York. 1977.

"The Humanoids" Charles Bowen editor. Futura Books London. 1974.

"Weird America: A Guide to Places of Mystery in the United States" Jim Brandon. Dutton Books New York. 1978.

"Beyond the Fourth Dimension" J. H. Brennan. Futura Books London. 1975.

"Close Encounters of the Fourth Kind". C. D. B. Bryan. Orion Books. London. 1996.

"Creatures from Elsewhere" Peter Brooksmith. Orbis Publishing London. 1984.

"Harmonic 33" Captain Bruce Cathie.A. H. & A.W. Reed Wellington New Zealand. 1977.

"Harmonic 695" Captain Bruce Cathie.A. H. & A.W. Reed Wellington New Zealand. 1977.

www.cufos.org/HUMCAT/

"The Oz Files" Bill Chalker. Duffy and Snellgrove. Sydney. Australia. 1996.

"A World History of UFOs" Bill Chalker. Red Sparrow. Duffy and Snellgrove. Sydney. Australia. 1997.

"UFO: Flying Saucers over Britain?" Robert Chapman. Mayflower Books London. 1975.

"Yetis, Sasquatch and Hairy Giants". David Hatcher Childress.Adventures Unlimited Press. Kempton. Illinois. 2010.

"Unexplained-347 Strange Sightings, Incredible Occurrences, and Puzzling Physical Phenomena". Jerome Clark. Viable Ink Press. Detroit. Michigan. 1993.

"Unexplained- Strange Sightings, Incredible Occurrences, and Puzzling Physical Phenomena". Jerome Clark. Viable Ink Press. Detroit. Michigan. 2013.

"Strange and Unexplained Happenings – When Nature Breaks the Rules of Science". Vol 2. Jerome Clark and Nancy Pear. U.X.L. Gale Research. International Thompson Publishing Company. 1995.

"Creatures of the Outer Edge" Jerome Clark and Loren Coleman. Warner Books New York. 1978.

"Gateway to Oblivion" Hugh F. Cochrane. Star Books London. 1980.

"The Encyclopedia of Monsters" Daniel Cohen. Fraser Stewart Books Waltham Abbey Essex. 1991.

"The Great airship Mystery". Daniel Cohen. Dodd, Mead and Company. New York. 1981.

"Mysterious America: The Revised Edition" Loren Coleman. Paraview Press New York. 2001.

"Bigfoot! The True Story of Apes in America". Loren Coleman. Paraview Pocket Books. New York. Digital edition.

"Monsters of New Jersey". Loren Coleman and Bruce. G. Hallenbeck. Stackpole Books. Mechanicsburg, PA. 2010. Digital edition.

"Monsters of Massachusetts". Loren Coleman. Stackpole Books. Mechanicsburg, PA. 2013. Digital edition.

"Crypto-Zoology A to Z" Loren Coleman and Jerome Clark. Fireside Books New York. 1996.

"Strangely Enough" C.B. Colby. Scholastic Book Services New York. 1973.

"The Midnight Hour". John Robert Colombo. Hounslow Books. Toronto.

"Terrors of the Night". John Robert Colombo. The Dundurn Group. Toronto. 2005.

"Handbook of Unusual Natural Phenomena" William R. Corliss. Anchor Books New York. 1983.

"The monster of Loch Ness" James Cornell. Scholastic Book Services New York. 1977.

"In Search of Lake monsters" Peter Costello. Panther Books London. 1975.

"Borderlands" Mike Dash. Arrow Books London. 1997.

"The Cosmic Conspiracy" Stan Deyo. West Australian Texas Trading Morley West Australia. 1979.

"The Leviathans" Tim Dinsdale. Futura Books London. 1976.

"God Drives a Flying Saucer" R. L. Dione. Bantam Books New York. 1978.

"The World's Great Unsolved Mysteries" Martin Ebon. Signet Books New York. 1981.

"Flying Saucers: Serious Business" Frank Edwards. Bantam Books New York. 1966.

"Strange Fate" Frank Edwards. Paperback Library New York. 1965.

"Stranger Than Science" Frank Edwards. Bantam Books New York. 1973.

"Strange World" Frank Edwards. Bantam Books New York. 1973.

"UFOs: Past, Present and Future" Robert Emmeneger. Ballantine Books New York. 1978.

"Why are They Watching Us" Allen Louis Erskine. Belmont Tower Books New York. 1975.

"UFO Exist!" Paris Flammonde. Ballantine Books New York. 1977.

"Mankind-Child of the Stars" Max H. Flindt and Otto O. Binder. Coronet Books London. 1976.

"Great Southern Mysteries". E. Randall Floyd. August House/ Little Rock Publishers. Arkansas. 1989.

"Let's Hope They're Friendly" Quentin Fogarty. Angus and Robertson Australia. 1982.

"Lo!" Charles Fort. Ace Books New York. 1973. copyright 1941 by Holt, Rinehart and Winston, Inc.

"New Lands" Charles Fort. Ace Books New York. 1973.

"The Book of the Damned" Charles Fort. Abacus Books London. 1973.

"The Complete Books of Charles Fort" Charles Fort. Dover Publications. New York. 1974

"The Andreasson Affair" Raymond E. Fowler. Bantam Books London 1980.

"UFOs: Interplanetary Visitors" Raymond E. Fowler. Bantam Books London 1979.

"The Tungus Event" Rupert Furneaux. Panther Books London.1977.

Mirrored from "theaustralianyowieresearchcenter.com/ Yowies_Australian_history_1900.html

"Mysterious Lights and Fires" Vincent H. Gaddis. Dell Publishing. New York. 1967.

"Big Bird- Modern Sightings of Flying Monsters". Ken Gerhard. CFZ Press. Bideford, North Devon. England. 2007.

"Giants from the Dreamtime-The Yowie in Myth and Reality". Rex Gilroy. URU Publications. Katoomba, NSW. Australia. 2001

"This Baffling World" John Godwin. Hart Publishing New York. 1968.

"This Baffling World No 2" John Godwin. Bantam Books New York. 1973.

"This Baffling World No 3" John Godwin. Bantam Books New York. 1973.

"Above Top Secret" Timothy Good. Sidgwick and Jackson London. 1987.

"Beyond Top Secret" Timothy Good. Sidgwick and Jackson. London.1996.

"Alien Update" Timothy Good. Arrow Books London. 1993.

"Alien Base" . Timothy Good. Arrow Books. 1998.

"Need to Know". Timothy Good. Sidgwick and Jackson. London.2006.

"The Book of Miracles" Stuart Gordon. Headline Books London. 1996.

"Mythical Monsters: Fact or Fiction?" Charles Gould.Studio Editions London. 1992.

"Enigmas" Rupert T. Gould. Paperback Library New York. 1969.

"Oddities" R. T. Gould. Geoffrey Bles London. 1945.

"The Great Lakes Triangle" Jay Gourlay. Fontana Books Glasgow. 1977.

"There Are Giants in the Earth" Michael Grumley. Panther Books London. 1976.

"The Mysterious Monsters" Robert and Frances Guenette. Sun Classic Pictures Books Los Angeles. 1975.

"Flying Saucers Come From Another World" Jimmy Guieu. Hutchinson London. 1956.

"Monsters of West Virginia". Rosemary Ellen Guiley. Stackpole Books. Mechanicsburg. Pennsylvania. 2012.

"The Monster Trap and Other True Mysteries" Peter Haining. Armada Books London. 1976.

"Monsters of New York". Bruce G. Hallenbeck. Stackpole Books. Mechanicsburg. Pennsylvania. 2013.

"Fire from Heaven" Michael Harrison. Pan Books London. 1977.

"Vanishings" Michael Harrison. New English Library. 1981.

"Out of the Shadows" Tony Healy and Paul Cropper. Pan Macmillan Australia. 1994.

"UFOs Over the Southern Hemisphere". Micheal Hervey. Horwitz Publications. Sydney 1969.

"In the Wake of the Sea-Serpents" Bernard Heuvelmans. Hill and Wang. New York. 1968.

"On the Track of Unknown Animals". Bernard Heuvelmans. Paladin. Granada Publishing. 1972.

"The Entrancing Flame". John E. Heymer. Warner Books. 1997.

"UFO's from Behind the Iron Curtain" Ion Hobana and Julien Weverbergh. Souvenir Press London. 1974.

"They Sailed Into Oblivion" A. A. Hoehling. Ace Books New York. 1959.

"The Dragon and the Disc: An Investigation of the Totally Fantastic" F. W. Holiday. W. W. Norton and Co New York. 1973.

"The Goblin Universe". Ted Holiday. Llewellyns's PSI-TECH Series. Llewellyn Publications. St Paul. Minnesota. 1986.

"Flying Saucers over Australia" James Holledge. Horwitz Books Sydney. 1965.

"The Ufonauts" Professor Hans Holzer. Panther Books London. 1979.

"Atlantis: Myth or Reality?" Murry Hope. Arkana Penguin Books. London. 1991.

"Looking for the Aliens: A Psychological, Scientific and Imaginative Investigation " Peter Hough and Jenny Randles. Blandford Books London. 1991.

"The Complete Book of UFOs". Peter Hough and Jenny Randles. Judy Piatkus (Publishers). London. 1996.

"World's Best True UFO Stories" Peter Hough and Jenny Randles. Sterling Publishing New York. 1995.

"The UFO Experience: a Scientific Enquiry" J. Allen Hynek. Henry Regnery Company Chicago. 1972.

http://iraap.org/home.htm

https://intcat.blogspot.com/

"Parallel Universe" Adi-Kent Thomas Jeffrey. Warner Books New York. 1977.

"Terror Zones" Adi-Kent Thomas Jeffrey. Granada Books London. 1978.

"They Dared the Devil's Triangle" Adi-Kent Thomas Jeffrey. Star Books London. 1976.

"Triangle of Terror and other Eerie Areas" Adi-Kent Thomas Jeffrey. Warner Books New York. 1975.

"Flying Saucers: a Modern Myth of Things Seen in the Sky" Dr. C. G. Jung. Signet Books New York. 1969.

"Strange Creatures from Time and Space" John Keel. Sphere Books London. 1976.

"Our Haunted Planet" John A. Keel. Neville Spearman London. 1971.

"The Cosmic Question" John A. Keel. Panther Books London. 1978.

"UFOs: Operation Trojan Horse" John A. Keel. Abacus Books London. 1971.

"Why UFOS" John A. Keel. Manor Books New York. 1970.

"Flying Saucers From Outer Space" Donald E. Keyhoe. Tandem Books London. 1974.

"Aliens from Space" Major Donald Keyhoe. Panther Books London. 1975.

"Not of This World" Peter Kolosimo. Sphere Books London. 1975.

"The Devil's Meridian" Kevin Killey and Gary Lester. Lester-Townsend Publishing Sydney. 1980.

"In the Domain of the Lake monsters" John Kirk. Key Porter Books Toronto. 1998.

"In Search of Extraterrestrials" Alan Landsburg. Corgi Books London. 1977.

"In Search of Myths and Monsters" Alan Landsburg. Corgi Books London. 1977.

"In Search of Strange Phenomena" Alan Landsburg. Corgi Books London. 1977.

"Strange monsters and Great Searches" George Laycock. Piccolo Books London. 1976.

"Beyond the Impossible-A Twentieth Century Almanac of the Unexplained" Richard Lazarus. Warner Books. London. 1994.

"Someone Else is On Our Moon" George H. Leonard. Sphere Books London 1978.

"Rain of Iron and Ice" John. S. Lewis. Helix Books. Addison-Wesley Publishing Company. 1996.

"Mysterious Visitors" Brinsley Le Poer Trench. Pan Books London. 1975.

"Operation Earth" Brinsley Le Poer Trench. Tandem Books London. 1974.

"The Flying Saucer Story" Brinsley Le Poer Trench. Tandem Books London 1973.

"Secret of the Ages: UFOs From Inside the Earth" Brinsley Le Poer Trench. Panther Books London. 1976.

"The Sky People" Brinsley Le Poer Trench. Tandem Books London. 1971.

"Flying Saucers Have Landed" Desmond Leslie and George Adamski. Werner Laurie London. 1954.

"Mysteries of the Skies- UFOs in Perspective" Gordon I. R. Lore and Harold. H. Denault. Scientific Book Club Edition. London. 1969.

"Flying Saucers-the Startling Evidence of the Invasion from Outer Space". Coral E. Lorenzen. Signet Books. New York. 1966.

"Fying Saucer Occupants" Coral and Jim Lorenzen. Signet Books New York. 1967.

"UFOs: the Whole Story" Coral and Jim Lorenzen. Signet Books New York. 1969.

"Man and the Stars" Duncan Lunan. Corgi Books London. 1978.

"Abduction: human Encounters with Aliens" John E. Mack. Simon and Schuster Great Britain. 1994.

"Alien Agenda" Jim Marrs. Harper Collins London 1998.

"The Gosford Files" Moira McGhee and Bryan Dickeson. INUFOR Australia. 1996.

"From Outer Space" Howard Menger. Pyramid Books New York. 1967.

"Sightings: UFOs" Susan Michaels. Fireside Books New York. 1997.

"The Truth About Flying Saucers" Aime Michel. Pyramid Books New York. 1967.

"Living Wonders: Mysteries and Curiosities of the Animal World" John Michell and Robert J. M. Rickard. Thames and Hudson London. 1982.

"Phenomena: a Book of Wonders" John Michell and Robert J. M. Rickard. Thames and Hudson London. 1977.

"Bigfoot: the Yeti and Sasquatch in Myth and Reality" John Napier. Abacus Books London. 1972.

http://www.nicap.org/chronos/

"Strange Stories of UFOs" Len Ortzen. Coronet Books Great Britain. 1980.

"The Welsh Triangle" Peter Paget. Panther Books London. 1979.

"Impossible Possibilities" Louis Pauwels and Jacques Bergier. Mayflower Books London. 1974.

"The End of Eden- The Comet That Changed Civilization" Graham Phillips. Bear and Company. Rochester. Vermont. 2007

"Alien Honeycomb"John Pinkney and Leonard Ryzman. Pan Books Sydney Australia. 1980.

"Greatest Mysteries of the Modern World". John Pinkney. The Five Mile Press. Rowville. Victoria. Australia. 2004.

"Unexplained". John Pinkney. The Five Mile Press. Rowville. Victoria. Australia. 2006.

"Alien Airships Over Old America". John Pinkney. Inkypen Editions. Johnpinkneybooks. 2011.

"The Cycles of Heaven" Guy Lyon Playfair and Scott Hill. Souvenir Press London. 1978.

"Abduction" Jenny Randles. Robert Hale London. 1988.

"Alien Contacts and Abductions" Jenny Randles. Sterling Publishing New York.1994.

"Strange but True? Casebook" Jenny Randles. Judy Piatkus London.1996.

"The Paranormal Source Book" Jenny Randles. Judy Piatkus London.1996.

"UFO Retrievals: the Recovery of Alien Spacecraft" Jenny Randles. Blandford Books London. 1995.

"Spontaneous human Combustion" Jenny Randles and Peter Hough. Bantam Books London. 1992.

"Crash: When UFOs Fall From the Sky". Kevin D. Randle, PhD. New Page Books. Franklin Lakes. New Jersey. 2010.

"The Truth About the UFO Crash at Roswell" Kevin D. Randle & Donald R. Schmitt. Avon Books. New York. 1994.

"Faces of theVisitors" Kevin Randle and Russ Estes. Fireside Books. New York. 1997.

"The Abduction Enigma" Kevin D. Randle, Russ Estes and William Cone, Ph.D. Tom Doherty Associates New York. 2000.

"The UFO Dossier". Kevin D Randle. Visible Ink Press. Canton. MI. 2016.

"The Evidence for Alien Abductions" John Rimmer. Aquarian Press Wellingborough. 1984.

"Humanoid Encounters THE OTHERS AMONGST US 1 AD-1899" Albert S. Rosales Triangulum Publishing. Copyright © 2017 Albert S. Rosales

Rosales, Albert S. Humanoid Encounters: 1 AD-1899: The Others amongst Us Triangulum publishing. Kindle Edition.

Rosales, Albert S. Humanoid Encounters: 1900-1929: The Others amongst Us. Triangulum publishing. Kindle Edition.

Rosales, Albert S. Humanoid Encounters: 1930-1949: The Others amongst Us. Triangulum publishing. Kindle Edition.

Rosales, Albert S. Humanoid Encounters: 1950-1954: The Others amongst Us. Triangulum publishing. Kindle Edition.

Rosales, Albert S. Humanoid Encounters: 1955-1959: The Others amongst Us. Triangulum publishing. Kindle Edition.

Rosales, Albert S. Humanoid Encounters 1960-1964: The Others amongst Us. Triangulum publishing. Kindle Edition.

Rosales, Albert S. Humanoid Encounters 1965-1969: The Others amongst Us. Triangulum publishing. Kindle Edition.

Rosales, Albert S. Humanoid Encounters: 1970-1974: The Others amongst Us. Triangulum publishing. Kindle Edition.

Rosales, Albert S. Humanoid Encounters: 1975-1979: The Others amongst Us. Triangulum Publishing. Kindle Edition.

Rosales, Albert S. Humanoid Encounters: 1980-1984: The Others amongst Us. Triangulum Publishing. Kindle Edition.

Rosales, Albert S. Humanoid Encounters: 1985-1989: The Others amongst Us. Triangulum Publishing. Kindle Edition.

Rosales, Albert S. Humanoid Encounters: 1990-1994: The Others amongst Us. Triangulum Publishing. Kindle Edition.

Rosales, Albert S. Humanoid Encounters: 1995-1999: The Others amongst Us. Triangulum Publishing. Kindle Edition.

New Mexico Area UFO Reports—June/July 1947. copywrite 2002 by David Rudiak. Mirrored from http://roswellproof.homestead.com/NM_UFO_Reports.html

"Celestial Passengers: UFOs and Space Travel" Margaret Sachs and Ernest Jahn. Penguin Books Great Britain. 1977.

"The UFO Encyclopedia" Margaret Sachs. Corgi Books Great Britain. 1981.

"Abominable Snowman: Legend Come to Life" Ivan T. Sanderson. Pyramid Books New York. 1968.

"Investigating the Unexplained". Ivan T. Sanderson. Prentice-Hall, Inc. Eaglewood Cliffs. New Jersey. 1972.

"Invisible Residents" Ivan T. Sanderson. Tandem Books London. 1974.

"Uninvited Visitors" Ivan T. Sanderson. Tandem Books London. 1974.

"Things" and "More Things". Ivan. T. Sanderson. Adventures Unlimited Press. Kempton. Illinois. 2007.

"UFOs: A Scientific Enigma" D. A. J. Seargent. Sphere Books London.1978

"Wildmen: Yeti, Sasquatch and the Neanderthal Enigma" Myra Shackley. Thames and Hudson London. 1983.

"More Strange Unsolved Mysteries" Emile Schurmacher. Paperback Library New York. 1969.

"The Flying Saucerers" Arthur Shuttlewood. Sphere Books London.1977.

"The Warminutester Mystery" Arthur Shuttlewood. Tandem Books London. 1976.

"The Coming of the Gods" Jean Sendy. Berkely Medallion Books New York 1973.

"UFO: A deadly concealment." Derek Sheffield. Blandford Books. London. 1996.

"Bigfoot" B. Ann Slate and Alan Berry. Bantam Books New York. 1976.

"Supernatural two : More Australian Encounters. Keith Smith. Pan Macmillan Publishers. Sydney. 1991.

"This Hollow Earth" Warren Smith. Sphere Books London. 1977.

"UFO USA". The Society for the Preservation of Alien Contact Evidence and Geographic Exploration. Hyperion Books. New York. 1999.

"UFO Trek" Warren Smith. Sphere Books London. 1977.

"No Earthly Explanation" John Wallace Spencer. Bantam Books New York. 1975.

"Limbo of the Lost" John Wallace Spencer. Bantam Books New York. 1973.

"Phenomenon: Forty Years of Flying Saucers" John Spencer and Hilary Evans. Avon Books New York. 1989.

"The UFO Encyclopedia" John Spencer. Headline Books London. 1991.

"Socorro Saucer" Ray Stanford. Fontana Books Glasgow. 1978.

"Flying Saucers are Hostile" Brad Steiger and Joan Whritenour. Tandem Books London. 1975.

"Flying Saucer Invasion: Target Earth" Brad Steiger and Joan Whritenour. Award Books New York. 1969.

"The New UFO Breakthrough" Brad Steiger and Joan Whritenour. Tandem Books London. 1975.

"Project Blue Book" Brad Steiger. Ballantine Books New York. 1976.

"Gods of Aquarius" Brad Steiger. Granada Books London. 1980.

"Monsters Among Us" Brad Steiger. Berkley Books. 1989.

"Strange Disappearances" Brad Steiger. Lancer Books New York. 1972.

"Strangers from the Sky" Brad Steiger. Award Books New York. 1966.

"The Soviet UFO Files" Paul Stonehill. Quadrillion Publishing Godalming. 1998

"Is Anyone Out There?" Jack Stonely. Star Books London. 1975.

"Tunguska: Cauldron of Hell" Jack Stonely. Star Books London. 1977.

"Aliens Over Antipodes". Murray Stott. Space-Time Press. Sydney. 1984.

"Fate presents Strange Encounters". Curt Sutherly. Llewellyn Publications. St Paul, Minnesota. 1996.

"Forbidden Universe" Leo Talamonti. Futura Books London. 1976.

"Flying Saucers: Where do They Come From?" Richard Tambling. Horwitz Books Hong Kong. 1978.

http://www.thinkaboutitdocs.com/

"Flying Saucers Through the Ages" Paul Thomas. Tandem Books London. 1973.

"Alien Identities". Richard L. Thompson. Govardhan Hill Publishing. Alachua, Florida. 1995.

"Haunted and Mysterious Australia" Tim the Yowie Man. New Holland Pubishers (Australia) Sydney New South Wales Australia. 2006

"Wings of Mystery" Dale M. Titler. Tower Books New York. 1966.

"Challenge to Science: the UFO Enigma" Jacques and Janine Vallee. Tandem Books London. 1974.

"Anatomy of a Phenomenon: UFOs in Space" Jacques Vallee. Tandem Books London. 1974.

"Passport to Magonia: From Folkore to Flying Saucers" Jacques Vallee. Tandem Books London. 1975.

"UFO's: the Psychic Solution" Jacques Vallee. Panther Books London. 1977.

"Dimension : A Casebook of Alien Contact". Jacques Vallee. Ballantine Books. New York. 1988.

"Wonders in the Sky". Jacques Vallee and Chris Aubeck. Jermey P. Tarcher/Penguin Group. 2009. New York.

"The Alien Files" Gregory Van Dyk. Element Books Boston.1997.

"Impact: the Threat of Comets and Asteroids" Gerrit L. Verschuur. Oxford University Press Oxford. 1996.

"Journey to Infinity" Johannes von Buttlar. Fontana Books Glasgow. 1976.

"The UFO Phenomenon" Johannes von Buttlar. Star Books London. 1979.

"UFO Quest: In Search of the Mystery Machines" Alan Watts. Blandford Books London. 1994.

"UFOs: What on Earth is Happening?" John Weldon and Zola Levitt. Bantam Books London. 1976.

"Arthur C. Clarke's Mysterious World" Simon Welfare and John Fairley. Fontana Books London. 1982.

"Alien Dawn: An Investigation into the Contact Experience" Colin Wilson Virgin Publishing Limited. London. 1998.

"World Famous : Strange but True" Colin Wilson, Damon Wilson and Rowan Wilson. The Book Company International. Sydney, Australia. 1995.

"Strange Vanishings-Unexplained Disappearances". Colin Wilson. The Book Company International. Sydney, New South Wales, Australia. 1997.

"Our Mysterious Spaceship Moon" Don Wilson. Sphere Books London. 1976.

"Monsters of Pennsylvania". Patty A. Wilson. Stackpole Books. Mechanicsburg. Pennsylvania. 2010.

"Strange but True: UFOs Amazing Stories of the Unexplained" Rowan Wilson. The Book Company. Sydney, New South Wales, Australia. 1997.

"From the Devil's Triangle to the Devil's Jaw" Richard Winer. Bantam Books New York. 1977.